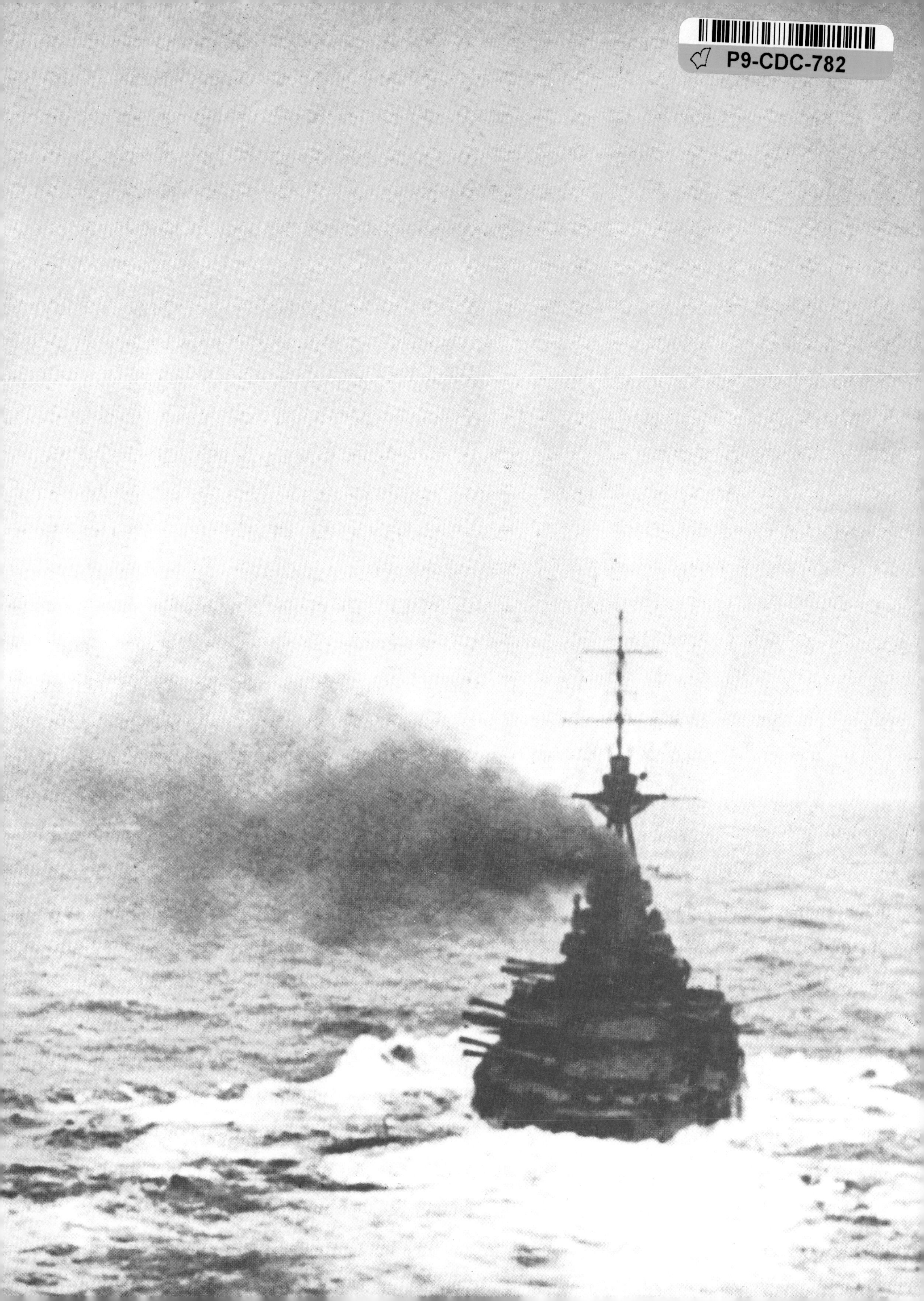

FIGHTING SHIPS
OF WORLD WARS ONE AND TWO

PEERAGE BOOKS

Illustrated by John Batchelor
Compiled by Anne Maclean and Suzanne Poole

First published in this form in Great Britain in
1976 by Phoebus Publishing Company/BPC Publishing Limited
(A division of Macdonald & Co (Publishers) Ltd)

This edition published in 1986 by
Peerage Books
59 Grosvenor Street
London W1

ISBN 1 85052 022 4

This material first appeared in Purnell's Histories
of the World Wars © 1966/72 BPC Publishing Limited,
History of the 20th Century © 1968/70 BPC Publishing
Limited and Purnell's History of the World Wars Specials
© 1974/5 Phoebus Publishing Company/BPC Publishing Limited.

Printed in Czechoslovakia
50588

ABOUT THIS BOOK

At the outbreak of World War I, the British and German navies, two of the mightiest fleets ever assembled, faced each other across the North Sea. Their admirals looked forward to the decisive battles they saw as the natural climax to the maritime race between the two countries.

And yet, apart from the abortive confrontation at Jutland, no full-scale engagement between the two fleets took place. The great dreadnoughts and battlecruisers lay at anchor while the war at sea was fought with the newer naval weapons – mines, torpedoes and submarines – giving the Germans a marked technical advantage. Also, the effectiveness of naval blockade in limiting an industrial nation's capacity to wage total war was made abundantly clear.

In 1939 both sides were largely unprepared when war was declared, but new developments in naval strategy soon became apparent. Not only could aircraft and submarines now operate independently, usurping the traditional role of the battleship, but they removed naval warfare from the realms of direct combat into a continual battle of wits, relying on intelligence and radar reports to direct ships which only rarely saw their enemy above the horizon.

In this book we examine the balance of naval power of the nations involved in both wars, show the technical advances that took place, look at some of the more significant naval exploits and great fleet encounters, and discuss changes in basic concept of naval strategy.

The text is written by acknowledged experts and is fully illustrated with action photographs and John Batchelor's detailed colour drawings of the ships that fought in the two world wars.

CONTENTS

1914: The Navies Weigh-in 7
The Admirals 18
Battle of Heligoland Bight 20
Blockade 28
Sinking of the *Aboukir, Hogue* and *Cressy* 34
The Raiders 39
The Battle of Coronel 45
Battle of the Falklands 52
The Clash at Dogger Bank 62
Naval War in the Mediterranean – Summer 1915 68
The Battle of Jutland 74
The U-Boats Overcome 88

The End of the High Seas Fleet 95
The Warships 104
Battle for the Atlantic 106
Battle of the River Plate 122
Operation Dynamo 131
The Mediterranean – September 1940/
    March 1941 135
The Last Hours of the *Bismarck* 143
The·Struggle for Crete 147
Naval Balance Before Pearl Harbor 152
Pearl Harbor: A Blow for Empire 154
The Battle of the Coral Sea 158

The Battle of Midway – Turning Point of WW2 166
The First Arctic Convoys 176
Ten Got Through 178
Malta: The Siege is Raised 182
Battle of the Barents Sea 186
Battle for the Atlantic: The Second Phase 195
The Life and Death of the *Tirpitz* 208
Carrier Warfare 214
Guadalcanal: The Sea Battles 223
Battle of Leyte 230
Death of a Behemoth 246
Behind the Allied Victory 250

If Germany began World War I with the most powerful army in the world there could be no doubt that the British Navy dominated the seas. Since the Battle of Trafalgar, a century earlier, no serious challenge had been made to the supremacy of the British fleet. Only the emergent Germany, flexing her naval muscles in the early 1900s, seemed to pose a long-term threat as she began to develop a huge naval building programme. And, as this programme gained momentum, the first tremors of doubt began to disturb the massive confidence of the British Admiralty.

So long as Britain reigned supreme as a naval power, the increasingly tense political and diplomatic situation in Europe between 1900 and 1914 could be viewed with equanimity. But, if that supremacy was put at risk, then the British Empire was at risk. Germany set out to create such a risk. The main instrument for this purpose was the new class of battleship to be designed in the early years of the century – the *Dreadnought*.

The *Dreadnought* was of 20,000-tons displacement, had a speed of more than 21 knots and was armed with ten 12-inch guns. She was the fastest, best-armed and most powerful battleship the world had ever seen. This revolutionary warship, which made all other battleships obsolete, was developed from the ideas of the Italian naval designer Vittorio Cuniberti and the driving genius of Admiral Sir John Fisher, who, in 1904, became Britain's First Sea Lord. The race between Britain and Germany to equip themselves with dreadnought fleets continued right up to the outbreak of hostilities in August 1914.

But if there was a revolution in the design and type of battleship in the run-up to 1914, no less a revolution was caused by the development of the submarine, which began to figure prominently in the naval building programmes of both Britain and Germany as the dreadnought race got under way.

Although Admiral Fisher had realised the seriousness of the submarine menace, he had not been able to fully convince his colleagues at the Admiralty or in the Government. It took the disastrous shipping losses of 1917, when the Germans declared unrestricted submarine warfare, to demonstrate just how unprepared Britain was to combat this threat.

However, when war came in 1914 Britain could feel secure within the protection of her naval might. She was able to deploy 65 battleships to Germany's 38. The Grand Fleet was able to maintain a stranglehold on Germany throughout the war. Only once was there a major clash between the British and German navies – the Battle of Jutland in 1916.

This engagement – the last between opposing fleets of such enormous proportions – resulted in a disappointing display of tactics and gunnery by the British. Three battlecruisers, three cruisers and eight destroyers were lost, compared with German losses of one battleship, one battlecruiser, four cruisers and five destroyers, and the British suffered 6,097 fatal casualties compared with 2,551 German. Nevertheless, the ultimate effect of this fierce but unsatisfactory encounter was to convince the German Commander-in-Chief, Admiral Scheer, that the risk of a further full-scale battle was too great. Germany's much-vaunted High Seas Fleet, therefore, remained blockaded until the end of the war when it was surrendered to the British. The end came on 21 June 1919, when all but one of the capital ships were scuttled by their crews at Scapa Flow.

A decisive battle was never fought, yet it was this very balance of naval strength that determined the fortunes of the great powers in the 1914-18 war. Britain's life-lines – her trading routes and her military shipments – were maintained, despite severe losses from submarine attack, throughout the war. Germany, on the other hand, came under constantly increasing economic pressure from the naval blockade. The result was the ultimate collapse of Germany in 1918.

1914 THE NAVIES WEIGH-IN

The British, with very few exceptions, believed they had the best navy in the world in 1914. Their superiority over Germany in numbers and tradition was obvious, but their inferiority in certain technical fields, especially mines and torpedoes, was not generally realised. *Below*: British dreadnoughts in 1911

Britain, in August 1914, had retained her immense lead in battleships and battle-cruisers over all other European nations. In spite of the periodical scares over the rate of German building during the immediate pre-war years, her own building rate had been just more than enough to maintain the declared 60% numerical superiority over Germany. These were her own ships, built for her own navy, but an immediate bonus was available on the outbreak of war in the shape of three dreadnought battleships being built (and virtually completed) in Britain for foreign navies. The *Almirante Latorre,* ordered by Chile, was taken over in September 1914 and commissioned as HMS *Canada,* and two battleships built for Turkey, the *Osman I* and *Rashadieh,* were requisitioned in August and added to the Grand Fleet as HMS *Agincourt* and HMS *Erin.* The two Turkish ships raised the British total of dreadnoughts at the outbreak of war to 24, to which Germany could reply with only 13. And looking ahead, the comparison was brighter still, with 13 British dreadnoughts on the stocks in various stages of construction (with two due to join the fleet later in 1914) and only ten laid down by Germany (of which two were also due later in 1914). Among the 13 British ships were five of the new *Queen Elizabeth* class, faster and more powerfully armed than any others in the world.

The battle-cruiser comparison was almost equally favourable in numbers. Counting HMS *Tiger,* to which only the finishing touches in the dockyard were required, there were ten British battle-cruisers, although one of these, HMS *Australia,* was in the service of the Australian government. And on the German side, counting SMS *Derfflinger* which was in the same state of completion as the *Tiger,* there were six such ships in commission. But they included the *Blücher,* a 15,800-ton armoured cruiser which carried only 8.2-inch guns compared with the 11-inch and 12-inch of the later German battle-cruisers and the 12-inch and 13.5-inch of the British battle-cruisers.

Of the other nations concerned, France and Russia were slightly ahead of Austria-Hungary and Italy. France had four battleships of the *Courbet* class, all launched in 1913 and 1914, of 23,500 tons and armed with twelve 12-inch guns,

whilst almost complete at the outbreak of war were three larger battleships of the *Bretagne* class, carrying ten 13.4-inch guns. And in addition she had six *Danton* class battleships, technically pre-dreadnoughts because of their mixed armament of 12-inch and 9.4-inch guns but, like the two British *Lord Nelsons,* being counted as dreadnoughts because of their recent construction and ability to maintain the speed of the dreadnought fleet.

The Russian fleet was divided into two, one part in the Baltic and the other in the Black Sea. There were four dreadnought battleships of the *Gangoot* class in the Baltic—each carrying twelve 12-inch guns in four triple turrets—and four more on the stocks, big ships of the *Borodino* class, 28,000 tons with nine 14-inch guns in triple turrets and a designed speed of 26½ knots. Also in the Baltic was the armoured

A huge disparity in overall strength . . .

cruiser *Rurik,* which compared roughly with the German *Blücher.*

There were no dreadnoughts in the Black Sea though there were three in process of completion which were just about equal in displacement and gunpower to those owned by Austria-Hungary. But as far as the Entente Powers were concerned, the Russian Black Sea fleet could count for little unless Turkey could be brought into the war on the side of Britain, France and Russia, and any prospect of this, remote at the best of times, was made even more unlikely in August 1914 by the British requisitioning of two Turkish battleships which had just been completed in Britain.

Austria-Hungary, whose only access to the sea was in the northern Adriatic, had three new dreadnoughts launched in 1914, with a fourth due to be launched in 1915. These were the *Viribus Unitis* class, ships of 22,000 tons with twelve 12-inch guns. She also had three *Franz Ferdinands,* small pre-dreadnoughts of 14,500 tons with a mixed armament of 12-inch and 9.4-inch guns, and thus ships of little value in terms of naval warfare in 1914. Like Russia in the Black Sea, the fleet's only

exit into the Mediterranean was through the Straits of Otranto, a comparatively narrow stretch of sea which the navies of Britain and France would have little difficulty in blocking.

An uneasy partner

The third member of the Triple Alliance was Italy, and it was no secret in London or Paris that she was an uneasy partner in the arms of Germany and Austria-Hungary. It was not expected that she would follow them into a European war, but in terms of the European political grouping her navy had to be counted. She had one dreadnought, the *Alighieri,* completed in 1912, and three more on the verge of completion. These, on paper, were powerful ships, carrying thirteen 12-inch guns in three triple and two twin turrets, but their displacement of 22,000 tons argued that they were either over-gunned or under-armoured.

A crude addition of dreadnought-type ships on both sides gave a superiority to the Entente Powers over those of the Alliance of 49 to 33. Such a comparison was virtually meaningless, if only because Britain's naval commitments were worldwide while those of Germany, apart from a tiny sprinkling of colonial possessions which were indefensible in war, were confined only to the North Sea and the Baltic. There were many other considerations which went a long way further to reduce the apparent disparity in overall dreadnought strength, which will be discussed later.

In smaller ships, the overall ratios were much the same as with the capital ships. Neither Britain nor Germany had built heavy cruisers after the step-up to battle-cruisers, but in what were known as light cruisers, Britain had 18, with eight being built, and Germany eight, and eight more projected. Only France, and to a lesser extent Russia, had continued to build heavy cruisers. France had four, headed by the *Quinet* and *Rousseau* of 14,000 tons and carrying fourteen 7.6-inch guns, while the Russian Baltic fleet had two *Bayan* class cruisers of 7,750 tons with a mixed armament of 8-inch and 6-inch guns.

In Britain's Royal Navy were 225 destroyers, of which 127 were fast, modern boats and the remainder, though mostly more than ten years old, still valuable in terms of the many naval duties which fell to the lot of destroyers in war. The comparable German figures were 152 overall, 108 fast and modern, and 44 more elderly though still useful. British submarines outnumbered German U-boats by 75 to 30, but most of the British boats were small and of use only in coastal operations. Germany, at the outbreak of war, had more submarines capable of overseas operations than Britain, and also more being built and projected.

Of the other nations concerned in the European line-up in 1914, France could muster 81 destroyers and 67 submarines, Russia, in the Baltic and Black Sea combined, 106 destroyers and 36 submarines, Austria-Hungary, 18 destroyers and 11 submarines, while Italy had 33 destroyers and 14 submarines.

Outside Europe there was one other navy to be taken into account, that of Japan. Under the Anglo-Japanese alliance of 1902 there was no obligation for Japan to enter the war, since the actual declaration on August 4, was a British initiative, but it was very obvious that, in her expansionist mood, she would do so. Her acquisitive eyes had long been focused on the well-equipped German base at Tsingtao in China, and there were German colonial islands in the Pacific which might come her way at the final peace discussions were she involved in a successful war. From the British point of view, the Japanese fleet had a potential value in war to cover and track down the powerful German East Asiatic Squadron and thereby release British ships for other operations nearer home. Japan had a useful fleet of four dreadnought-type capital ships, of which her two *Kongo* class battle-cruisers were as large, as powerfully armed (eight 14-inch, sixteen 6-inch), and as fast (27 knots) as any others in the world. The battleship *Asi* was a mixed armament ship which, however, ranked as a dreadnought, and her capital ship fleet was supported by two first-class *Nisshin* type cruisers and three second-class *Hirato* type, together with the older *Tone*. Of her 54 destroyers, all were of British design and most of them built in Britain.

Counting up their ships, the three Entente powers appeared overwhelmingly strong. Moreover, with Britain lying across the German exits from the North Sea into the world's oceans, the High Seas Fleet

was pinned into its home waters and unable to intervene in operations in other parts of the world. This geographical advantage had been rammed home in the naval staff talks between Britain and France in 1912 in which the French had agreed to withdraw their Atlantic and Channel squadrons, together with their Far East and Pacific squadrons, and concentrate them all in the Mediterranean, accepting naval responsibility for the whole of that sea. This decision, it is true, owed something to the effect of the Balkan War of 1912/13, as well as to the naval staff talks in London and Paris, but it effectively released the battleships of the British Mediterranean Fleet to swell the number of those in home waters.

Numbers, however, counted for little. It was quality which mattered more than quantity when it came to the actual test

...but quality not quantity when it came to the test

of battle. In pure design, there was little to choose between the British and German dreadnoughts, and although there were some naval experts, even in 1914 and before the results in action had pointed to deficiencies in the British ships, who thought the German design superior. They were eventually proved wrong when the battleship *Bayern* was raised after the holocaust in Scapa Flow at the end of the war. A minute examination of her construction proved that British naval architects in 1914 had nothing to learn from their German counterparts.

One of the considerable disabilities from which the British capital ships suffered in comparison with the German was their lack of beam. Successive Liberal governments in Britain, voted into power on promises of social benefits to all, had refused to spend money on new docks so that all British ships had to be built to fit the existing docks instead of the other way round. This meant that no British dreadnought could be built with a beam of more than 90 feet. At Wilhelmshaven there were two docks to take ships up to a beam of 102 feet; at Kiel there was a floating

dock with an available beam of 131 feet: while between the two new locks on the Kiel Canal at Holtenau was a huge space large enough to accommodate anything. In this respect Germany had a great advantage.

Ship for ship, all the German battleships and battle-cruisers had about 10 feet more on the beam than the British. This gave them an immediate advantage in that they were less susceptible to damage by mine or torpedo. It also enabled them to carry thicker armour on sides and gun turrets, a possibility which was enhanced by a considerable saving in weight which arose from the different functions of British and German ships. British ships were designed for a world-wide rôle. Their crews lived permanently on board, and they carried enough coal to give them a steaming radius of 4,000-5,000 miles. German capital ships were designed purely for North Sea or Baltic operations. Their crews lived ashore in barracks when the ships were in harbour, and the fuel they carried gave them a steaming radius of under 2,000 miles. Their great beam, allied to the saving in weight in fuel alone, and combined with the fact that crew habitability was not of primary importance in view of their short endurance and the living accommodation ashore, enabled a much more complete watertight subdivision below decks to be built into their hulls. As a result, the German capital ships were more nearly unsinkable than any of the British.

It all came down to the size of the available docks. When Admiral Jellicoe visited Kiel in 1910, the Kaiser told him that in Germany they built docks to take the ships, and not ships to fit the docks. Writing after the war, Sir Eustace Tennyson-d'Eyncourt, the Director of Naval Construction, had this to say: 'Had wider docks been available, and had it been possible to go to a greater beam, the designs on the same length and draught could have embodied more fighting qualities, such as armour, armament, greater stability in case of damage, and improved underwater protection.' With their greater beam, and therefore greater displacement, the German ships could have a considerably thicker armour belt built into them. In the first dreadnoughts, the British armour belt was 10 to 11 inches up to the main deck only, while the comparable German

Ullstein

dreadnoughts carried 12 inches. In the *Orion* to *Iron Duke* classes, British armour was 12 inches thick, but in the comparable *Kaiser* and *König* class, German side armour was 13¾ inches thick.

There was something of the same story in a comparison of the big guns of the two fleets. A considerable amount of capital had been invested by the main British gun manufacturers in wire-wound guns, and therefore all British big naval guns were wire-wound. The German navy had gone for the built-up gun, which had proved itself not only more robust but with a longer life. There was a tendency for the muzzles of big wire-wound guns to droop fractionally after firing a few rounds, with consequent inaccuracy in range keeping, while their life was estimated (by the Germans, it is true) as 80-100 rounds. The life of the built-up gun was estimated (again by the Germans) at 220 rounds. They fired their shells with a considerably greater muzzle velocity, and the muzzles did not droop.

Gun for gun, the German was smaller than the British. Taking ships comparable in size and date of completion, where the British fitted 12-inch guns, the Germans fitted 11-inch; when the British went up to 13.5 inches, the Germans replied with 12-inch. Allowing for the higher muzzle velocity of the German guns, there was nothing in the disparity of size so far as range was concerned, though the British ships held a substantial advantage in weight of broadside. Given equal accuracy in ranging and in shell and fuse design, this advantage could have been considerable since heavier shells are more accurate at long ranges than lighter ones.

In the ten years ending in 1914, the Royal Navy had made a striking advance in the range and accuracy of its gunnery. Whereas in 1904, battle practice ranges had been 3,000-4,000 yards and often with a stationary target, by 1914 the range had grown to 16,000 yards at towed targets. Accuracy was very good, but the individual gunlayers in the turrets were always handicapped by the smoke of burnt cordite, funnel smoke, shell splashes, and the difficulty of identification of the target. In 1911 Admiral Sir Percy Scott, who had been recognised as the greatest expert in gunnery in the Royal Navy, brought out his director system, by which all guns were trained, laid, and fired by a master sight in the foretop, well above the smoke. In addition to obtaining a clear view, the director sight made certain that all turrets were trained onto the same enemy ship, for the individual gunlayers in the turrets had merely to follow the electrically repeated elevation and bearing of the master sight.

Scott's director system, enthusiastically endorsed by Admiral Jellicoe, also a gunnery expert, ran into opposition from the Navy's Inspector of Target Practice, who argued strongly for the retention of individual gunlaying. This battle of opinions continued until the end of 1912 when a test between HMS *Thunderer*, fitted with Scott's director system, and her sister ship HMS *Orion*, using individual gunlayers, clinched the argument. In three minutes of firing at a range of 9,000 yards, with the ships steaming at 12 knots, the *Thunderer* scored six times as many hits as the *Orion*. But by now time was running short, and with opposition still being expressed by the diehards, only eight battleships in the Grand Fleet had been fitted with director firing by August 1914.

The Germans had a system of director firing, known as *Richtungsweiser*, which had much in common with Scott's director except that it was mounted in the ship's conningtower and not in the foretop. If there were any diehards in the German navy they were never permitted to interfere with technological development, and the *Richtungsweiser* system had been introduced throughout the High Seas Fleet by 1914. German gunnery was always excellent, their salvoes compact with very little spread, and always remarkably accurate for range.

This accuracy was based on the stereoscopic rangefinder, which had a telling advantage over the British type in that it absorbed very little light. This was particularly valuable in the North Sea, where in the frequent mist and bad light, little could be seen through the British type because of the high absorption of light through the lenses and prisms.

It was a similar story in shells, mines and torpedoes. When Jellicoe had been Third Sea Lord and Controller in 1910 he had sent a memorandum to the Ordnance Board asking them to produce an armour-piercing shell that would penetrate armour at oblique impact and burst inside. At the end of the year Jellicoe went to sea, and the responsibility to see this development through to its conclusion fell to his successor, Admiral Sir John Briggs, who was anything but energetic. Nothing had been done by 1914 on this requirement, and this sorry tale of incompetence had its result in the war when the British armour-piercing shell broke up on oblique impact against the German armour instead of penetrating and bursting inside.

German superiority

The German superiority in torpedoes and mines lay as much in better and more sophisticated workmanship as in a fatal British tendency to regard these as the weapons of a weaker power. In 1914, and indeed throughout all British naval history up to that year, the gun was always the dominant weapon. Officers who had specialised in gunnery had always enjoyed a better record for promotion to the higher ranks than officers of other specialities, and in this veneration of the gun as the queen of the naval battlefield, other weapons had had less drive put behind them in the race towards perfection. British torpedoes were unreliable in their running, and not infrequently ran deep or sank to the bottom after being fired; a somewhat strange state of affairs when it is remembered that the Royal Navy had pioneered the torpedo from its very birth. By 1914 the 21-inch torpedo had largely replaced the earlier 18-inch, and all the dreadnought battleships and all modern destroyers carried the larger version. The German navy had also two sizes of torpedo, 450-mm (17.7-inch) and 500-mm (19.7-inch), with a larger 600-mm (23.6-inch) torpedo under development. The four earliest German dreadnoughts *(Nassau* class) had the 450-mm, as also did the *Blücher* and *Von der Tann* among the battle-cruisers. All other dreadnoughts and all destroyers and U-boats from *G.174* and *U.19* onwards had the 500-mm torpedo. Any older boats which were still operational had the old 17.7-inch torpedo. But although slightly smaller, size for size, the German torpedo was a more reliable weapon in range, running, and depth-keeping than the British.

Negligence and inefficiency

If the performance of British torpedoes left much to be desired, that of British mines was shocking. No one at the Admiralty had been given responsibility to think out the use or value of mines in terms of naval strategy or tactics; no one had been charged with the technical development of mines. Those with which Britain went to war in 1914 were thoroughly inefficient, either breaking away from their moorings when laid or else frequently failing to explode when hit by an enemy ship. In the German navy as much attention was paid to the development of the mine as to every other weapon, and the sinking of the new dreadnought battleship *Audacious* by a single mine within a very few weeks of the declaration of war told the story.

In smaller ships of war, the Germans were in every way as good as the British. All their destroyers, to which they still gave the older name of torpedoboats, were excellent seaboats and very strongly constructed. Unlike British practice, they were in every case tested by running their acceptance trials in really bad weather to guarantee against leaking and straining. Their U-boats, too, were as well con-

Although in 1914 Italy had only one dreadnought, her commanding position in the Mediterranean made her navy a factor to be reckoned with

Imperial War Museum

structed as British submarines throughout, not even excluding the new British E-class boats which were one of the most successful classes of submarines ever built in Britain at least up to 1925, and they had turned their attention to the long endurance submarine for ocean warfare some years before Britain had faced this challenge.

One reason for this German superiority in *materiel* was that in Germany, technology in the metallurgy, engineering, shipbuilding, and chemical industries was in a very advanced state. This stemmed, at least in part, from the different educational backgrounds of the two countries. In England, most higher education was devoted to training for the professions, but in Germany its main emphasis was on training for trade purposes. All through the naval *materiel* picture in Germany was an emphasis on attention to detail which extended right through from top to bottom. It was not only in shells and fuses, rangefinders, mines, and torpedoes that they were far ahead. Their attention to detail even reached down as far as saving life after ships had been sunk in action. While the British navy still relied on the boats carried on board to save life after action, the German ships were issued with sufficient special lifejackets for the whole crew designed to hold men upright while floating in the water.

This was a product of the basic German mentality and planning, meticulous in every detail and allied to an urge to be prepared for any and every emergency. The British mentality was not geared in that age to so deep a regard for perfection in

The crucial ratio – the balance of dreadnoughts

Below: **SMS Rheinland**, of the *Westfalen* class, the first German dreadnoughts. *Displacement:* 18,900 tons. *Length:* 472 feet. *Beam:* 89 feet. *Armament:* Twelve 11-inch, twelve 5·9-inch and sixteen 3·4-inch plus six 17·7-inch torpedo tubes. *Power/speed:* 26,100 hp/20 knots. *Armour:* Belt 11½ inches, turrets 11 inches. *Crew:* 963

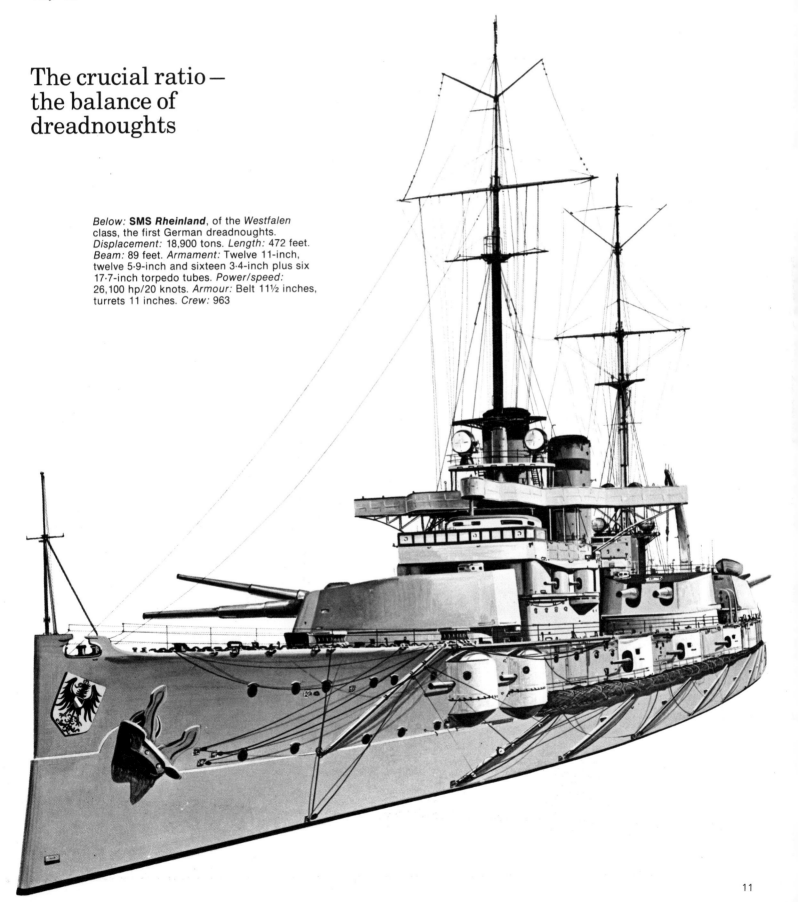

such detail. Britain had its engineers and shipbuilders who were in every way as brilliant as any in Germany, but their attitude was more that of the gentlemanly amateur than that of the dedicated technologist. There was a complacency in Britain, founded upon its broad industrial base which could guarantee a faster rate of naval building than Germany could ever achieve, which perhaps militated against such a perfectionist doctrine. Every argument which was produced to sustain the naval race against Germany in the decade leading up to 1914 was based entirely on quantitative rather than qualitative superiority. What was perhaps perplexing was the sincere belief in Britain, and particularly in the British Admiralty, that ship for ship, those built in Britain were undoubtedly superior to those built in Germany. There had been no lack of reports from the British Naval Attaché in Berlin stressing the excellence of German ships, as well as of their guns, their gunnery results, their shells and fuses and their torpedoes. Yet the belief in British superiority was quite genuinely held and believed. One man only seemed to have doubts, but this one man was Admiral Jellicoe, the Commander-in-Chief designate of the Grand Fleet in the event of a war against Germany. Three weeks before the outbreak of the war, in a memorandum addressed to Churchill, the First Lord of the Admiralty, he drew attention to the 'very striking inferiority' of the armour

and underwater protection of British battleships and battle-cruisers as compared with German. He concluded with a statement that it was 'highly dangerous to consider that our ships as a whole are superior or even equal fighting machines'.

This memorandum by Jellicoe followed a speech a few days earlier by Churchill in which he spoke of 'the undoubted superiority of our ships unit for unit'. Churchill was quite sincere when he said that, and was in fact only echoing the genuine beliefs of the Admiralty as a whole.

This German thoroughness and attention to detail extended to dockyards as well as to ships. Theirs were not only magnificently organised for the building, equip-

ping, and repairing of warships but were also tied into the German system of mobilisation, the whole operation being brought together under a single directing staff. The German dockyards had benefitted, of course, not only from the fact that they were relatively new and had thus been initially planned and laid out to cope with modern methods of warship design and construction, but also from ungrudging investment of public money in the needs and growth of the new navy. Britain's dockyards, on the other hand, had been developed through the centuries, originally planned and laid out for a sailing navy, and adapted time after time to try to keep pace with the technological changes of

'Undoubted superiority' or 'Striking inferiority'?

The dreadnought battleship — Queen of the seas. Before the war it had been assumed that the British and German fleets would immediately fight it out to a finish in a fleet action similar to Trafalgar. But until 1916 at Jutland, no such confrontation took place. For the greater period of the war, the Grand Fleet waited at Scapa Flow and exerted a tacit authority over the Germans. HMS *Dreadnought. Displacement:* 17,900/20,700 tons. *Length:* 526 feet. *Beam:* 82 feet. *Power/speed:* 22,000 hp/22 knots. *Armament:* Ten 12-inch and 24 12-pounder guns. *Armour:* Belt 11 inches, turrets 8 inches. *Crew:* 862 men

naval warfare. Not that they were in-efficient—the *Dreadnought* had been built in Portsmouth Dockyard in the incredibly short space of 11 months—but many of their facilities suffered from a lack of modern layout and from the legacy of the more unhurried days of sail.

Obsolete dockyards

Of more immediate importance in the context of a war against Germany was the actual situation of the three major British dockyards at Chatham, Portsmouth and Devonport. Their position had largely been dictated by the wars of the 16th, 17th and 18th Centuries when the traditional enemies of Britain had been Spain, Hol-land, and France. The western approaches to Britain, the English Channel, and the southern North Sea had been the naval battlegrounds of those years, and the English dockyards had been developed on the strategic realities of war against the traditional foes. But with the emergence of Germany as the only obvious enemy, the focus of naval warfare had shifted from the Channel to the northern half of the North Sea, and Chatham, the only major dock-yard on the east coast of Britain, was too far south to provide immediate support to a Grand Fleet which would necessarily have to be stationed in the north of Britain.

The need for a fully equipped base in the north had been recognised by the British Admiralty as far back as 1903 when it was decided to develop Rosyth, on the northern side of the Firth of Forth, as a first-class naval base. When Sir John Fisher came to the Admiralty in 1904 as First Sea Lord he did his best to hold back the work at Rosyth partly because he had doubts about the safety of Rosyth as a fleet anchor-age and partly because he preferred the Cromarty Firth on the grounds that it was farther north than Rosyth and thus a better base from which to command the northern exit from the North Sea into the Atlantic.

Farther north still, in the Orkney Islands,

was the immense anchorage of Scapa Flow. Having decided on the development of Rosyth as a first-class dockyard against Fisher's opposition—first-class being de-fined as a port where the dockyard was capable of building, equipping, and re-pairing warships of any size in every respect, where permanent depots of men and stores of all descriptions were main-tained, and where the scale of defence was heavy enough to deter attacks by battle-ships, the Admiralty next considered the possibility of developing a second-class base in the north to back up Rosyth—second-class being defined as a base where smaller repairs could be undertaken and only stocks of the more immediate stores were maintained. The choice lay between Cromarty and Scapa Flow, and after much discussion Cromarty was chosen. Scapa Flow was designated as a fleet anchorage in war, but the Committee of Imperial Defence, to whom the whole question of east coast bases was referred, recom-mended that no defences should be erected there. The Admiralty protested, but when it was discovered that the cost of setting up fixed defences would come to £379,000 and that the annual cost of upkeep would amount to £55,000, even the Admiralty agreed that it was time the financial horns were pulled in.

When war came in August 1914, the plight of the Grand Fleet in respect of bases was frightening. The strategic re-quirements of the policy of distant blockade dictated the stationing of the Grand Fleet as far to the northward as possible in order to command the northern North Sea be-tween the Orkneys and the Norwegian coast, and Scapa Flow was the only answer. It was completely undefended, with no nets or booms to prevent entry by U-boat, and no searchlights to detect enemy marau-ders by night. Both Cromarty and Rosyth had by 1914 been given a sketchy coastal artillery defence designed to keep surface ships at bay, but both were wide open to U-boat attack and their approaches were easy to mine. The dockyard at Rosyth, which had been subject to interminable delays on the grounds of economy, had only just been begun to be constructed and would not be operational for some years later. Only Chatham still remained as a first-class east coast base, but was much too far away adequately to nourish a Grand Fleet with Scapa Flow as its main operational base. There was, it is true, a second-class base at Harwich, but that again was too far south for the Grand Fleet and was in any case earmarked as a base for light craft.

The situation in Germany was exactly the opposite. On the German North Sea coast, protected by the island of Heligo-land, were two of the three main fleet bases, Cuxhaven and Wilhelmshaven. In the Baltic, but readily accessible to those in the North Sea through the Kiel Canal which had been widened and dredged to take dreadnoughts, was the third great naval base at Kiel. Subsidiary bases at Hamburg, Bremen, and Emden were inter-connected through the rivers Elbe and Weser, and the Ems-Jade Canal. The islands of Heligoland, which protected the mouths of the Elbe and Weser rivers, and Borkum, which provided the same service for the Ems, were both heavily fortified, and at strategic points along the coast, powerful forts and gun emplacements gave

additional security. Nature, too, had been kind to Germany by providing shoals and sandbanks off the coast which restricted approach by heavy ships to narrow chan-nels which were easily defensible.

One final area of comparison on the *materiel* side lay in the air. Both Britain and Germany had recognised the possible importance of aircraft in sea warfare at roughly the same time, mainly for use as advanced scouts. Whereas Germany had fixed her eyes firmly on the rigid airship as the most desirable means of long-distance scouting, Britain had vacillated between airships and aeroplanes. Her air-ship policy had been a sorry tale of in-decision throughout. Money for a rigid airship had been voted in the 1909 Naval Estimates, but the resultant *Mayfly* had had her back broken during her trials when a gust of wind caught her when she was halfway out of her hanger. This was in 1911, the same year in which Jellicoe, during a visit to Germany, had been taken for a flight in a Zeppelin, and returned to London with glowing accounts of their value to a fleet at sea. However Jellicoe's enthusiasm carried less weight with the Board of Admiralty than the disaster to the *Mayfly,* and in 1912 the Committee of Imperial Defence agreed with the Ad-miralty that airships were useless. This odd decision, which went in the face of all German experience, was largely influenced by Admiral of the Fleet Sir Arthur K. Wilson, First Sea Lord until December 1911, who argued that airships presented as large a target as battleships and could be brought down by naval guns. He did not explain, and nobody seems to have asked him, how the guns were to be sufficiently elevated to engage a Zeppelin and how the fall of shot was to be spotted. Nevertheless, in 1914 the Royal Navy ordered eight rigid airships, none of which were ready by the outbreak of war. There were already seven small non-rigid air-ships, of which four were too unreliable for operations at sea and one was used for training.

The first aircraft-carrier

Such enthusiasm as the Admiralty could muster for naval flying was directed mainly into heavier-than-air machines. In 1912 an aircraft had been successfully launched from the deck of HMS *Africa* while the ship was at anchor. In 1912, during the course of the naval review at Weymouth, an aircraft was successfully flown off from the fore-castle of HMS *Hibernia* while she was under way. In 1913 the old cruiser HMS *Hermes* was commissioned as the first air-craft-carrier in any of the world's navies, accommodating three seaplanes. When war came in 1914, the Royal Naval Air Service could boast a strength of 52 seaplanes (though only 26 of them were airworthy) and 39 land-based aeroplanes.

In Germany there had been no deviation from the Zeppelin programme. They were based mainly at Cuxhaven and, while their primary rôle was for scouting purposes over the North Sea, they had a subsidiary rôle as potential bombers against land targets. In 1914 there were some 28 avail-able for fleet work, though some of these could be withdrawn temporarily for other purposes. In addition, seaplanes and land-based aircraft for naval purposes were stationed at air bases around the German North Sea coast.

Above: 'Kaiser-class' dreadnought SMS *Kaiserin. Left:* Admiral Reinhard Scheer, Commander-in-Chief of the High Seas Fleet. *Below:* SMS *Prinzregent Luitpold,* a 'Kaiser-class' dreadnought. The five 'Kaiser-class' dreadnoughts—SMS *Kaiser, Friedrich der Grösse, Kaiserin, Prinzregent Luitpold, König Albert*—were completed between October 1912 and August 1913. In 1914 *Friedrich der Grösse* became the flagship of the C-in-C, the others formed the *3rd Battle Squadron.* All except *König Albert* were at Jutland. *Displacement:* 24,380 tons. *Length:* 564 feet. *Beam:* 95¼ feet. *Power/speed:* 30-35,000 hp/21-23 knots. *Armament:* Ten 12-inch, 14 5.9-inch, eight 3.4-inch, four 3.4-inch anti-aircraft guns and five 19.7-inch torpedo tubes. *Armour:* Belt 13¾ inches, turrets 11¾ inches. *Crew:* 1,088-1,178 men

The evolution of strategic thought in the two major naval powers, Britain and Germany, during the years leading to the outbreak of war is interesting. Both navies had been obsessed more by the development in material than by its relation to strategy and tactics, and little thought was given to the best way in which these magnificent new fighting ships should be used. It was not the day of the naval thinker but the day of the naval specialist. Almost the whole of naval education in both countries was directed towards the technical aspects of a naval life, and virtually none to its more philosophical aspects of the strategical and tactical uses of a fleet. In Britain, with her long heritage and expertise in the use of sea power on a world scale, this was inexcusable. In Germany it was, if not wise, at least understandable for her experience of sea power extended back less than 20 years.

A second Trafalgar?

Most British naval officers were at least aware of the fact that in most of the wars of the past the principle of close blockade of an enemy in his ports had led to satisfactory conclusions in the end. When, in about 1904, it became apparent that the next enemy upon the seas would be Germany, it was accepted that the general war strategy would consist of a close blockade of the German North Sea coast. Its total length was no more than 150 miles in the form roughly of a right angle, so that a blockade would lie roughly along the hypotenuse. A corollary of this close blockade was the capture of one or more of the German islands—Sylt and Heligoland were those most frequently mentioned—for development as a forward British base for light craft charged with the blockade. Behind the advanced light forces would lie the main fleet of Britain, ready to engage the High Seas Fleet as it came out and inflict upon it a second battle of Trafalgar.

It took a long time for the realities of modern naval warfare to impinge upon this strongly held British belief. It was, of course, unrealistic even in 1904, for the mine and the torpedo, the submarine and the torpedo-boat, and the long-range coastal gun were all realities before that date. At least as late as 1907, in a series of war plans drawn up in that year, and later still in the minds of many senior admirals whose task it was to decide British naval strategy, the doctrine of close blockade held sway. Even when at last the facts did percolate through naval thinking, the plan was modified to a close blockade in daylight hours by light craft with fleet support and a withdrawal of the supporting fleet at night to a distance beyond which German light forces could not reach if they sailed at sunset and were back in their harbours by sunrise the next morning. This distance was worked out as 170 miles, and the scheme incorporated in the war plans.

By as late as August 1911 close blockade was still in fashion. In a memorandum issued during that month by the Commander-in-Chief Home Fleet, the agreed strategy was indicated in some detail: *The present War Plans provide for a blockade of the Heligoland Bight by the 1st and 2nd Destroyer Flotillas, supported by the 1st, 2nd and 3rd Cruiser Squadrons, with the principal objects of*

● *preventing raiding expeditions leaving German ports in the earlier stages of hostilities;*

● *preventing the German Fleet putting to sea without the British Commander-in-Chief knowing it and, when it is known to be at sea, conveying him such information as to its movements as will enable it to be brought to action by the British Main Fleet.* Here we were, back to the days of Hawke, Cornwallis and Nelson!

By 1912, at long last, even the naval diehards had come to the conclusion that close blockade was too risky an operation to consider. The German islands, on the capture of which the original scheme had depended, were now heavily fortified. German submarines and torpedo boats, it was at last agreed, could carry out a war of attrition against British advanced forces that could, in a reasonably short time, whittle away the numerical advantage on which the ultimate safety of the nation depended. Some other scheme was needed.

It took the form of a proposed 'observational blockade', to consist of a line of cruisers and destroyers stretching from the south-westerly tip of Norway to a point in the centre of the North Sea, and then southward to the coast of Holland. The main battle fleets would be at sea to the westward of this line. As the 1912 War Plans stated: 'The general idea of these plans is to exercise pressure upon Germany by shutting off German shipping from oceanic trade through the action of patrolling cruisers on lines drawn across the approaches to the North Sea, and supporting these cruisers and covering the British coasts by two battle fleets stationed so as to be in a position to bring the enemy's fleet to action should it proceed to sea with the object of driving the cruisers off or undertaking other offensive action.'

'Observational blockade'

For the next two years, almost to the brink of war, the 'observational blockade' remained the official strategy of the Royal Navy, in spite of the obvious impossibility of maintaining a blockade line of 300 miles in length with its invitation to the enemy to attack the blockading ships one by one in a series of concentrated raids. But right at the end, in the war plans issued to the fleet in July 1914, the overall strategy was changed finally to that which in the final reckoning would bring victory to Britain. The observational blockade was abandoned and the policy of distant blockade adopted, closing the two exits from the North Sea, first, by the Channel Fleet in the Dover Straits, and second, by the Grand Fleet stationed in the north of Scotland to guard a line from the Orkney Islands to the Norwegian coast. *The maritime domination of the North Sea,* ran the new War Plan, *upon which our whole policy must be based, will be established as far as practicable by occasional driving or sweeping movements carried out by the Grand Fleet traversing in superior force the area between the 54th and 58th parallels [roughly the latitudes of Heligoland and the southern tip of Norway]. The movements should be sufficiently frequent and sufficiently advanced to impress upon the enemy that he cannot at any time venture far from his home ports without such serious risk of encountering an overwhelming force that no enterprise is likely to reach its destination.*

German basic strategy had gone through changes almost as radical as those in Britain. It had begun with the *Riskflotte* theory, with the building of a fleet strong enough to dissuade a British encounter with it because of the resultant British inferiority with the navies of France and Russia. After 1904, with the entente with France, and especially after 1907, when Russia, too, joined hands with Britain, a new strategy had to be worked out, and a satisfactory one was found based on the known British policy of a close blockade of the German North Sea coast. During such a blockade, the German Admiralty expected, there would be countless opportunities for bringing to action detached squadrons of the British fleet whose duty it would be to support the blockade. This attritional warfare, in which by reason of the proximity of their bases the German fleet could ensure local superiority, would in the end produce the situation where the numerical superiority of the Royal Navy had been whittled away, and in which the High Seas Fleet could risk the full-scale battle.

The British change from close blockade to observational blockade, and from that to distant blockade, was unknown in Germany. It was realised in naval circles in Berlin that close blockade was no longer a feasible operation of war in the face of modern weapons, and that Britain was bound to modify her plans to a distant blockade. They confidently expected the Royal Navy to use both forms of blockade, which would 'alternate frequently or merge into one another as the situation changes. It is very probable that during the first days of the war, when attacks on our part may be expected, our waters will be closely blockaded, also when it is intended to transport the Expeditionary Force to France'. These were the occasions, it was thought, when a sudden *sortie* of the High Seas Fleet could make a killing of a detached squadron of British ships.

From the very start, the High Seas Fleet had no intention of coming out into the North Sea to try conclusions with the Grand Fleet. That was never a part of their basic strategy. It remained, even after it became clear that there was to be no close British blockade, based on the hope of meeting, in superior force, detached British squadrons and destroying them until parity with the Grand Fleet had been reached. Britain, on the other hand, so misread the German strategy that she was convinced that the High Seas Fleet would steam out into the North Sea within a few days of the declaration of war to do battle with the Grand Fleet. It would have suited her book admirably, but the Germans were much too wise to risk everything on one such desperate fling.

If Britain had somehow stumbled, so far as the Navy was concerned, into a correct strategical posture for a war against Germany, the evolution of the tactical art had taken a long step backwards.

The line of battle
The line of battle, hallowed for centuries in the *Fighting Instructions* of the sailing navy, had always been a producer of sterile battles at sea, and it had only been when admirals like Hawke or Boscawen in the Seven Years' War, or Rodney in the War of American Independence, or Nelson in the Napoleonic War, had risked their reputations and disregarded the rules of the *Fighting Instructions* that decisive actions had resulted. Now, in the age of steam

when the wind no longer dictated the course a ship could steer, there was a fine chance to break clear from the straight-jacket of the rigid line of battle. All it needed was men of vision, admirals who were prepared to trust their subordinate commanders of squadrons and divisions to do the right thing in the stress of battle. But in the Royal Navy, and very largely in the German navy too, there were few such admirals. Command at sea was centralised in the Commander-in-Chief, and for a junior admiral to act on his own initiative was to court relegation to an operational backwater. All tactical training in the past 50 years had consisted of intricate manoeuvres executed by signal from the flagship, not unlike an old-fashioned courtly dance by mastodons on the surface of the sea. Even when the manoeuvres ordered involved ships in danger of collision, there was no questioning an admiral's instructions, and in 1893 the battleship *Victoria* had been rammed and sunk by the battleship *Camperdown* because the Commander-in-Chief had ordered a particular manoeuvre with too little sea room in which to perform it. No one questioned him. The manoeuvre was carried out and the *Victoria* was sunk.

In battle, with smoke from funnels and guns reducing visibility and with a line of ships which might stretch as far as five miles, tactical manoeuvring by signal from the flagship was fraught with hazard. It took time to pass the signal by visual means up and down the line (Jellicoe, for example, distrusted wireless), and often the flagship was obscured from the view of cruiser squadrons and destroyer flotillas in attendance on the fleet, when signals never got through at all. Although in the various fleet battle orders there was a certain amount of lip service paid to decentralisation and individual initiative, it never worked out in practice. The fleet battle orders were themselves too rigid and too mandatory to allow any individual leeway.

It was not very different in the High Seas Fleet, though admirals commanding squadrons were allowed some discretion in the tactical handling of their ships. But in general, like the British, once the line of battle had been formed it was subject to centralised control. The only real difference between the two fleets lay in their night-fighting capabilities. One or two British attempts to introduce night encounters in the pre-war fleet manoeuvres had ended in uncertainty and muddle, and Jellicoe in particular would have none of it. 'The difficulty of distinguishing friend from foe,' he wrote, 'and the exceeding uncertainty of the result, confirmed the opinion I had long held that a night action between fleets was a pure lottery.' The German fleet, on the other hand, had practised night action in a big way, and had made itself very proficient in the art.

For all the German advantages, and they were many in such things as broad-beamed ships, better guns and shells, better rangefinders and searchlights, and a more meticulous attention to every detail of naval warfare, there was one sphere in which the Royal Navy excelled. It was a long-service fleet, manned by officers and men who were volunteers and who were making service in the Royal Navy their career. German sailors were enrolled on a short-service basis, and their training was

neither as long nor as thorough as that of the British seamen. There were other weaknesses as well, and one over-riding handicap was the incredibly chaotic arrangement whereby naval policy was placed under the control of the General Staff of the army. But it was the short-service basis of German enrolment which was the telling factor. Three years was the service spell of the German seaman, compared with 12 years, and a chance of re-enlistment for a further ten to qualify for a pension, which was the British system. Compared with the German, British ships spent far more time exercising at sea, and the innate sense of seamanship which this developed amongst officers and men stood them in good stead in the war which was coming.

Of the qualities of leadership, there was not much to choose between British and German. If Jellicoe's weakness was an excess of caution allied to an inability to decentralise in the control of an immense fleet, his opposite numbers in the High Seas Fleet, first Ingenohl and later his successor, Pohl, were no better, if in fact as good. Lower down the scale, in the vice- and rear-admirals and captains, there was about an equal proportion of good and bad on both sides, if one counts ship handling, tactical skill, and professional knowledge as the criteria of judgment.

One priceless intangible
Above this, however, there remained for the Royal Navy one priceless intangible. The officers and the men they led had no knowledge of the *materiel* advantages of the German fleet, of more robust ships and more efficient weapons, nor would they have believed it if they had. They had complete confidence in the ships and weapons they manned, complete confidence in their leaders, and complete confidence that in their own skills and training they held the key to invincibility. This supreme confidence, as clearly recognised in Germany as in Britain, bred in its turn an inferiority complex which pervaded so much of German naval thought and action. Perhaps one can allow the last words to the German Admiral Scheer, writing of the Royal Navy as he saw it in 1914. 'The English fleet had the advantage of looking back on a hundred years of proud tradition which must have given every man a sense of superiority based on the great deeds of the past. This could only be strengthened by the sight of their huge fleet, each unit of which in every class was supposed to represent the last word in the art of marine construction. The feeling was also supported by the British sailor's perfect familiarity with the sea and with conditions of life on board ship.' How, indeed, could a new and untried navy hope to win in battle against men such as these?

Right: The Russian armoured cruiser *Rurik*, a rough equivalent of the German *Blücher*, was stationed in the Baltic at the outbreak of the war. She went aground in a heavy snowstorm but miraculously escaped detection by the German ships. *Displacement:* 15,000 tons. *Length:* 529 feet. *Armament:* Four 10-inch, eight 8-inch, and 20 4.7-inch guns. *Armour:* Belt 6 inches, turret 8 inches. *Crew:* 899

THE ADMIRALS

In 1914 many of these men were over 50 years old and several had joined the navy while still in their teens. Almost all of them had seen colonial service and some had been involved in local fighting there – but none had any experience of a major naval conflict

JELLICOE, John Rushworth (1859-1935), entered the Royal Navy in 1872. As a lieutenant he showed great courage during the Arabi Pasha rebellion of 1882 in Egypt when he adopted native disguise to carry secret despatches to Sir Garnet Wolseley through a hostile horde. He specialised in gunnery, and the brilliance with which he passed all examinations was a measure of his exceptional intellect, so much so that as a young officer he was brought to the Admiralty to assist the director of naval ordnance, then Captain J. A. Fisher, with the implementation of the Naval Defence Act of 1889.

He was promoted commander in 1891 and appointed as executive officer of HMS *Victoria*, flagship of the Mediterranean Fleet, being on board at the time of the accident during manoeuvres when she was rammed and sunk by HMS *Camperdown*. Though ill with Malta Fever, he survived the disaster and was picked up clinging to a sea chest. In 1897 he was promoted captain and narrowly escaped death in the Boxer rebellion in China in 1900 after a bullet passed through his lung during the abortive attempt by Admiral Seymour to lead an international naval brigade to the relief of the legations in Peking. When Sir John Fisher became First Sea Lord in 1904, he brought Jellicoe with him to the Admiralty to be his director of naval ordnance.

Promoted to rear-admiral in 1907, Jellicoe served a year as second-in-command of the Atlantic Fleet and then returned to the Admiralty as Third Sea Lord and Controller, where his exceptional talent proved of immense value in helping to maintain Britain's lead in dreadnought design and construction over Germany. During this period he was selected by Fisher as the eventual commander-in-chief of the British fleet in the event of a future war with Germany. All his future appointments were chosen with a view to giving him experience for this task, and as, successively, commander-in-chief of the Atlantic Fleet, the Second Division of the Home Fleet, and Second Sea Lord, his tactical skill and undoubted talent for leadership were developed to the full. His appointment as Second Sea Lord was cut short by the murder at Sarajevo of the Austrian Archduke Franz Ferdinand, and at the end of July 1914 he was ordered north to Scapa Flow to hoist his flag as commander-in-chief of the Grand Fleet in the super-dreadnought HMS *Iron Duke*.

Jellicoe – tactical skill and an undoubted talent for leadership

BEATTY, David, (1871-1936) joined the Royal Navy at the normal age of 13. His first opportunity to distinguish himself came during Kitchener's reconquest of the Sudan in 1896-8 after the murder of General Gordon, when he was given command of a gunboat on the Nile. His dash and courage, coupled with a strong personality, gained him the DSO and promotion to commander at the early age of 27. Two years later, when he was executive officer of the battleship HMS *Barfleur* on the China Station, he led a naval detachment to Hsiku to free Admiral Seymour who was held there by the Boxer rebels although at the time he was suffering from a wound received while serving with the besieged Tientsin garrison.

He was specially rewarded by promotion to captain at the age of 29. The average age at which commanders were promoted to captain was 43.

Beatty's marriage to a wealthy American lady and his passion for fox-hunting made it seem for a time as though a career in the navy had no great attraction for him, for his length of service in command of cruisers and the battleship HMS *Queen* was insufficient to qualify him for promotion to flag rank. His outstanding record however, could not be overlooked, and in 1910 the Admiralty promoted him to rear-admiral by a special Order in Council. He was 38 at the time, an unprecedently early age at which to reach flag rank.

He was offered the appointment of second-in-command of the Atlantic Fleet, but once again jeopardised his career by refusing it. He was offered no other appointment until 1912, after a chance meeting, Winston Churchill, First Lord of the Admiralty, asked him to come as his Naval Secretary. Beatty agreed, and his wide understanding of the art and technique of naval warfare so impressed Churchill that in 1914 he chose him to command the battle-cruiser force with the rank of vice-admiral. At the outbreak of war the battle-cruisers, with Beatty in command, were concentrated at Rosyth.

Beatty – his outstanding record could not be overlooked

BATTENBERG, Prince Louis Alexander of, (1854-1921) was the eldest son of Prince Alexander of Hesse and the Rhine. He came to England as a boy, was naturalised, and joined the Royal Navy in 1868. His early career was one of distinction and his promotion was rapid. As a captain in 1894 he became secretary of the naval and military committee on defence, which developed later into the Committee of Imperial Defence. He was assistant director of naval intelligence in 1900, and after a year's service in the Mediterranean, returned to the Admiralty in 1902 as director. On promotion to flag rank he was appointed to the command of a cruiser squadron and in 1907 became second-in-command of the Mediterranean Fleet. A year later he was selected as commander-in-chief of the Atlantic Fleet and in 1911 joined the Board of Admiralty as Second Sea Lord.

On the retirement of Admiral Sir Francis Bridgeman, Battenberg stepped up to the post of First Sea Lord, and it was in this appointment that, in July 1914, he was faced with the decision whether or not to keep the reserve fleet in being on completion of a test mobilisation in view of the threatening European situation. It was due to his initiative and understanding that when the declaration of war came on August 4, the reserve ships and their crews were not dispersed.

Shortly after the outbreak of war a scurrilous press campaign was started, concentrating on Battenberg's German origin. His great patriotism and love for England led him to resign his position as First Sea Lord. It was the final great act of a most distinguished naval career.

Battenberg – forced to resign by a scurrilous press campaign

TIRPITZ, Alfred von (1849-1930), entered the Prussian navy in 1865, and after specialising in torpedoes, commanded the Far Eastern Cruiser Division, setting up Tsingtao, in China, as a future German naval base. In 1897 he was selected as secretary of state for the navy, and as such was responsible for the drafting and passing of the two Navy Laws of 1898 and 1900, setting out a programme of naval building which was designed to lift Germany to the position of a great naval power. In this task he was able to interest the German Emperor and to foster his naval mania to an extent where the two in alliance were strong enough to override all political opposition to rapid naval growth.

The great achievement for which Tirpitz will always be remembered is his transformation, within the space of 20 years, of a naval coastal defence force into a high seas battle fleet. Although he realised that Germany could never match the naval strength of Britain, and that German rearmament on such a scale was certain to sour relations between the two countries, he took comfort in the belief that Britain, faced with the reality of a strong German navy, could not contemplate war against it because of the risk of losing her superiority at sea. It was this aspect of German naval rearmament which was in large degree responsible for the British entente with France in 1904 and with Russia in 1907, which effectively countered Tirpitz's *Riskflotte* theory.

Tirpitz was promoted to admiral in 1903, and *Grossadmiral* in 1911. On the outbreak of war he attempted to obtain effective command of the High Seas Fleet either by himself becoming its commander-in-chief or through the creation of a supreme navy command structure which he would dominate. Both these moves were rejected, and he remained as secretary of state for the navy unable to exercise any strategic or operational control over the navy which he had so largely brought into being himself.

Popperfoto

Tirpitz – transformed a coastal defence force into a high seas battle fleet in 20 years

SCHEER, Reinhart (1863-1928) was born at Obernkirchen, Hesse-Nassau, and his early service in the German navy was connected with the colonial expansion of Germany in the Cameroons and East Africa. In 1903 he commanded the First Torpedo Division, and seven years later was appointed Chief-of-Staff to Admiral Henning von Holtzendorf, Commander-in-Chief of the High Seas Fleet. On promotion to flag rank he was given command of a battle squadron of the fleet, and was stationed at Kiel at the outbreak of the First World War. He had been, throughout his naval career, interested in the development of submarines, and with the early operational use of these craft in the war he was able to develop and introduce new ideas for their tactical use in action. Many of his ideas in this field proved of extreme value, and with the startling successes of the U-boats in the early months of the war, he was marked out for rapid promotion, particularly as he had shown a distinct tactical flair in the handling of his battle squadron and in the use of smaller craft in action. In 1916 he was Commander-in-Chief of the High Seas Fleet.

Bundesarchiv

Scheer – valuable work in the development of U-boats and their tactical use

HIPPER, Franz von (1863-1932), entered the German navy in 1881 and as a midshipman in the *Leipzig* was engaged in colonial adventures which added Togoland to the German empire. He specialised in torpedoes and in 1895 was appointed to the Second Torpedo Division at Wilhelmshaven as an instructor. This was followed by three years as navigation officer of the imperial yacht *Hohenzollern,* from which he was appointed to command the Second Destroyer Division. He was selected for a staff course in 1905, and on promotion to commander took charge of the trials of the new cruiser *Leipzig* in 1906. On promotion to captain in 1907, he commanded the armoured cruiser *Gneisenau.* After another short spell as captain of a destroyer flotilla, Hipper was promoted commodore in 1911 and appointed Chief-of-Staff to the second-in-command of the cruiser force of the High Seas Fleet. He reached flag rank in 1912, and with a change in the organisation of the cruiser force, was placed in command of the High Seas Fleet destroyer forces. On October 1, 1913, he became Flag Officer Commanding Scouting Force, High Seas Fleet. He was still holding this appointment at the outbreak of the First World War, flying his flag in the battle-cruiser *Seydlitz.*

Bundesarchiv

Hipper – a torpedo specialist, a field in which the German navy excelled

HENRY, Prince Albert William of Prussia (1862-1929) was the younger brother of Kaiser Wilhelm II of Germany. His father decided that he should be trained as a naval officer and his first experience of the sea was in the sail-training ship *Niobe* in 1877. Prince Henry's promotion, due to his royal connections, was rapid and in 1890 he was made captain of the cruiser *Irene.* As a commanding officer he was always imperious, but in spite of his strictness he was never less than just. On one occasion, having ordered his ship's company to bathe on an icy day and on receiving his first lieutenant's protests, he went below to his cabin, came up on deck naked, and dived over the side into the sea.

He was promoted rear-admiral in 1895 and in 1897 commanded the Second Cruiser Squadron in the Far East, bearing with him his brother's famous directive 'If anyone dare to interfere with our good right, ride in with the mailed fist'. It was under Prince Henry that much of the German colonisation in this area was carried out. He was appointed Commander-in-Chief of the Baltic Fleet in 1903, and almost immediately on completion of this appointment was made Commander-in-Chief of the High Seas Fleet, holding this appointment until 1909.

On the outbreak of the First World War he was made Commander-in-Chief of the Baltic Station, flying his flag in Kiel. The active operations in this area, however, were carried out by other officers, and Prince Henry was little more than a figurehead. He had by this time been promoted to the rank of *Grossadmiral,* senior to all other German naval officers, and it is recorded that his conservatism and lack of drive did much to hamper German naval operations during the early years of the First World War, for he still wielded considerable influence with the Kaiser.

Ullstein

Prince Henry – his conservatism and lack of drive did much to hamper the German navy

BATTLE OF HELIGOLAND BIGHT

The first British shot of the war was fired by the destroyer HMS *Lance* during a sweep of the North Sea as part of the British policy of distant blockade. Another sweep on August 28 resulted in the battle of Heligoland Bight—the first full scale naval fight of the war

No one knows who fired the first British shot in the First World War. The gun, from the forecastle of HM Destroyer *Lance* is at the Imperial War Museum in London, but the name of the gunlayer has vanished both from the records of the Admiralty and from the memories of the few men who still survive the events of the morning of August 5, 1914.

The war had started officially at 2300 hours on August 4. By that time the German auxiliary minelayer *Königin Luise* was already making her way down the North Sea from her base at Emden to lay mines at the entry to the Thames.

The *Königin Luise* was a former excursion steamer that, in peacetime, ran from Hamburg to Heligoland with holiday-makers. She had been converted into a minelayer in the space of 12 hours, so hastily that the main armament planned for her, a pair of 3.4-inch guns, had not been mounted. In addition, the windows had been left in her glass-enclosed promenade deck. With her two raked masts and two raked funnels the German ship looked very like one of the Great Eastern Railway steamers running between Harwich and the Hook, and in keeping with this impression she had been specially painted with black hull, buff upper-works and yellow funnels with black tops, the standard Great Eastern Railway colour scheme for its ships.

When minelaying began it was under the cover of a rain squall, out of which loomed long, low, dark shapes. Two of these changed suddenly into small, squat lumps as two destroyers changed course and headed for the German ship. They came out of the mist and opened fire at once.

An unknown steamer

The ships were HMS *Lance* and HMS *Landrail*, part of the British 2nd Destroyer Flotilla which, with 20 other destroyers of the 1st Flotilla, had left Harwich at dawn on the first day of the war to sweep northward towards German waters. The 1st Flotilla followed the Dutch coast and the 2nd Flotilla, led by the light cruiser HMS *Amphion*, steamed up the middle of the North Sea. A few hours after leaving port they met a British fishing vessel which reported that she had seen an unknown steamer 'throwing things overboard' about 20 miles north-east of the Outer Gabbard. When the destroyers came up with the *Königin Luise* through the mist she was still throwing things overboard, but she turned to run for home. The only guns which there had been time to mount were a pair of pom-poms and to reinforce these, as the British drew close, the Germans opened fire with rifles and revolvers. Once her mines had been laid there was nothing for the *Königin Luise* to do except scuttle herself, for her tiny armament was too weak to harm the enemy. Within a few minutes the German ship lay over to port with steam and smoke trailing from her funnels.

The British ships stopped and picked up survivors who were, according to the German Official History, 'chivalrously treated'. The destroyers then continued their sweep and very soon sighted another ship resembling the *Königin Luise,* at which they steamed full speed to attack. Fortunately, although the ship was flying a huge German flag, Captain Cecil H. Fox of the *Amphion* recognised her as a genuine Great Eastern Railway steamer, the *St. Petersburgh,* carrying the German ambassador to Britain back to Germany—hence the huge German flag.

At first the excitement of the chase was too much for the British destroyers and, failing to heed the signals, they pressed home their attack until Fox took the *Amphion* between the destroyers and the *St. Petersburgh,* deliberately fouling the range. The British ships withdrew but, next morning, on her way back to Harwich the *Amphion* struck one of the *Königin Luise's* mines. The first explosion broke her back forward, killing members of the British crew and their German prisoners, and then, a little later, there was another explosion of a ghastly lemon colour and the ship sank. The total number killed was one British officer and 150 ratings, together with 18 Germans.

On the same day, August 6, the Cabinet in London authorised the despatch of four divisions of the British Expeditionary Force (BEF) to France. They were to sail from United Kingdom ports, covered by the Channel Fleet, a force of elderly battleships commanded by Vice-Admiral Sir Cecil

HMS *Arethusa*, the British light cruiser commanded by Commodore Tyrwhitt. *Length* 450 feet. *Beam:* 39 feet. *Displacement:* 3,520 tons. *Main armament as built:* Two 6-in., six 4-in. *Armour:* Belt 3-in., Deck 1-in. *Speed:* 30 knots

The *Königin Luise* in her peacetime garb. She was sunk while minelaying off the Thames.

Staatsbibliothek/Berlin

Burney. This fleet was judged strong enough to deal with any German surface ships which might be risked so far from home as the English Channel, while the British main force, the Grand Fleet under the command of Vice-Admiral Sir John Jellicoe, was to cruise in the North Sea, in case the High Seas Fleet intervened.

The old battleships of the Channel Fleet faded away as it became clear that the German surface ships would present no real threat to the movements of the BEF, but two forces of British light craft were formed at the time of mobilisation which were to serve throughout the war and to become famous. One was the 'Harwich force' of light cruisers, destroyers and submarines, and the other was the 'Dover Patrol' consisting of destroyers and small craft.

There were many surprises on both sides during the early weeks of the war, and one of the first was the failure of the German navy to interfere with the movement to France of the BEF. No one seems to have expected a fleet action but it did seem possible, even probable, that German light surface craft and U-boats would make an attempt on the troop convoys which had consequently been routed across the central and western part of the English Channel, the principal route being that from South-ampton to Le Havre. The main reason why the Germans did not attack, according to the German Official Naval History, was that the German army was completely confident of victory over the Allied armies on

the Western Front, so that it did not matter to them whether the BEF was attacked on its way to France or defeated in battle after it had arrived there.

The first submarine operations

With the exception of a few fruitless cruises by a pair of Greek submarines off the Dardanelles during the First Balkan War in 1912, the operations of August 1914 were the first occasion in which submarines, as we know them, were used in warfare. The submarine was an untried weapon and, compared with the submarines of today, they were very primitive. When submerged their speed and radius of action were very small, so that their passage to the positions where they hoped to meet the enemy was made on the surface. Until the anti-submarine measures of their opponents were much better developed they preferred to wait on the surface in daylight, diving only when a possible enemy came in sight. The early U-boats had a great capacity for attracting attention to themselves, during daylight by the smoke from the exhausts of their Körting petrol engines, while at night these same exhausts gave forth brilliant flames, and at all times the noise of the engines served as a warning to any foe for miles around. In addition, at the beginning of the war these boats were without the chronometers essential for accurate navigation.

From the very beginning of the war it was clear that submarines were first rate scouting craft although British submarines

were hampered for a long time by the very short range of their wireless sets. Within two days of the outbreak of the war both the British and the Germans had submarines in enemy waters seeking information.

On August 5 two British submarines, *E6* and *E8*, left Harwich for the Heligoland Bight. Their captains were, respectively, Lieutenant-Commander C. P. Talbot and Lieutenant-Commander F. H. H. Goodhart. On the first day of their patrol the area seemed full of small craft, but orders to remain submerged throughout the day and watch shipping through their periscopes, restricted them to a very small area of the Bight. On the next day, therefore, they decided to surface but by that time the German ships had withdrawn and the British submarines returned to port. In those days a patrol lasting between five and seven days was considered the maximum that could be carried out.

The German submarines were soon engaged on a similar enterprise. From July 30, when a state of 'War imminent *(drohende Kriegsgefahr)*' had been proclaimed in Berlin, they had been disposed as a reconnaissance screen across the Heligoland Bight, escorted out to sea every morning by the light cruiser *Hamburg* which, rather like an anxious mother taking a large family out to play, saw them to their stations and then watched them submerge – a lengthy process which took between five and seven minutes.

On August 6, the 1st U-boat Flotilla of

ten boats, strung out in line abreast over 70 miles, headed in a north-westerly direction up the North Sea, hoping to find the British Grand Fleet, whose location was unknown at that time. One boat broke down and returned to port, one disappeared apparently as the result of an accident (U13), and a third (U15) was sunk. She alone found the Grand Fleet and, early on the morning of August 9, was spotted on the surface in hazy weather by the British light cruiser HMS *Birmingham* and sunk by ramming.

This was the first encounter between ships of the Grand Fleet and a U-boat. From the beginning of the war the Grand Fleet was very U-boat conscious. The Fleet's base at Scapa Flow in the Orkneys was almost ideally placed for the first tasks of the British navy, to blockade Germany and cut off her warships from the Atlantic. But, at the beginning of the war, Scapa Flow possessed no anti-submarine defences of any sort and at any moment a U-boat could have entered the Flow and carried out an attack. Under these circumstances, there were many false alarms that caused picket boats, destroyers and trawlers to be sent to search a suspected area in all weathers, while the entire fleet raised steam and gun crews were called to action stations. In August 1914 U-boats continued to be one of Jellicoe's greatest worries. On an early occasion he felt obliged to move the Grand Fleet out of the North Sea to Loch Ewe on the west coast of Scotland, only to bring it back almost immediately as there was a false alarm of a German invasion attempt.

Since the Grand Fleet was in northern waters, and the High Seas Fleet lay in the estuaries of the Elbe, the Jade and the Ems, the southern part of the North Sea became a non-man's land, though the British were able to protect ships trading between the United Kingdom and Holland and those conveying the BEF.

'A certain liveliness'
In search of this traffic there were U-boat reconnaissances as far south as the line from Harwich to Rotterdam, and on August 17 two German light cruisers, *Stralsund* and *Strassburg,* with two more U-boats, were sent south to try to get a clearer idea of what was going on. There was a brief

Above: U35, a German ocean-going submarine
Below: **SMS Stettin**, a German light cruiser.
Length: 385 feet. *Beam:* 44 feet. *Displacement:* 3,550 tons. *Main armament:* Ten 4.1-in guns. *Speed:* 23 knots

A German light cruiser had put 16 destroyers and *Fearless* to flight

exchange between the German light cruisers and the British light cruiser *Fearless* with accompanying destroyers. These operations were described in an Admiralty communique as representing 'a certain liveliness'.

To Commodore Keyes, however, the action was not to be dismissed with a phrase. He wrote to the Director of the Operations Division of the Admiralty a private and nearly insubordinate letter: 'I feel sore and sick. Owing to our scattered destroyer disposition a German light cruiser, equal in offensive power to the *Fearless,* had put 16 destroyers and the *Fearless* to flight. It is not by such incidents we shall get the right atmosphere.'

Two days later Keyes followed up this letter with a plan of his own for creating the 'right atmosphere'. Reconnaissance by Keyes' submarines since the beginning of the war had made clear the routine of the German patrols by day and by night around Heligoland. On this knowledge Keyes proposed that a force of British destroyers should infiltrate the German positions, just as the night patrols were relieved by the day patrols, slip in behind the latter and, turning back westward, get between them and their base. As a bait to lure the Germans farther out to sea three British submarines were to show themselves on the edge of the German patrol area.

The plan was adopted, although Keyes' proposal that the battle-cruisers under Vice-Admiral Sir David Beatty should take part was rejected. Commodores Tyrwhitt and Keyes accordingly sailed from Harwich in the light cruiser HMS *Arethusa* and the destroyer HMS *Lurcher* respectively, convinced that any big ships they met would be German. After they had sailed, however, the Admiralty changed its mind.

The BEF and the French armies were being forced out of Belgium by the advancing Germans and the Belgian coast would soon be open to attack by German forces from the direction of Brussels. Accordingly it was decided to send some 3,000 Royal Marines to Ostend.

To protect the ships carrying them the Admiralty now decided that Beatty's battle-cruisers should, after all, take part in the Heligoland operation but, because of the need for wireless silence, Keyes and

Tyrwhitt were left in ignorance of this change of plan. Accordingly when they met Beatty's ships early on the morning of August 28 there were a few tense moments, during which fatal mistakes might have been made.

As the sun rose on that day there were patches of white mist scattered all over the sea. On occasion, visibility from the decks of the ships was reasonably good, while the lookouts at the mastheads could see little or nothing. At other times, ships' masts could be seen sticking out of banks of mist, while their hulls were invisible below.

Meanwhile, the Germans guessed that the British attack was about to develop, although they did not expect that heavy British ships would be involved. Their own heavy ships were in harbour, for the most part behind the sand bar at the mouth of the river Jade, which could only be crossed near high tide. The British striking force, made up of the two light cruisers *Arethusa* and *Fearless* and 31 destroyers of the 1st and 3rd Flotillas arrived at first light in the area from which it was to begin its raid into the Bight. Here they were joined by six vessels of Commodore Goodenough's command which were to follow Tyrwhitt into the Bight.

The raid began: Tyrwhitt's force was to steam south until Heligoland lay 12 miles on its port beam, then turn westward between the German outpost vessels and their bases and roll up the line. There was an excessive amount of wireless traffic between the British ships so the Germans were soon on their guard and they despatched light cruisers and torpedo craft to investigate.

At 0650 hours Greenwich Mean Time Tyrwhitt's force sighted one group of German destroyers on the port bow and, shortly afterwards, another to starboard. Both groups turned for home, with the British in chase. The first serious opposition encountered was from the light cruiser *Stettin,* which had been lying at anchor off Heligoland. Today it may seem almost unbelievable that a light cruiser on patrol duty expecting an enemy attack and exposed to submarines, should have been at anchor in the open sea.

The action between the *Arethusa* and the *Stettin* lasted about 25 minutes. The two ships steamed south at full speed. The

Commodore Sir Reginald Tyrwhitt *(right)* with Flag-Lieutenant Floyer

Stettin was a coal-burning ship and sent up great rolling clouds of smoke, while the three funnels of the oil-fired *Arethusa* was crowned by a slight heat haze and nothing more. Both ships had great waves of spray like a pair of glistening wings at their bows and tumbling white wakes behind. The *Stettin* was joined by another light cruiser, the *Frauenlob,* and the *Arethusa* soon began to suffer. The range fell from 9,000 yards to 3,400 yards and the British and German ships settled down on a severe and parallel course. The brand new guns of the *Arethusa* gave trouble. Three jammed and a fourth was put out of action when its ammunition was hit and the cordite began to blaze. Soon she had only one gun in action, the forecastle 6-inch. On her bridge the signals officer was killed by Tyrwhitt's side. With her single gun the *Arethusa* in turn got a hit on the *Frauenlob's* bridge and both Ger-

man ships hauled away. It was high time, as far as the *Arethusa* was concerned. Her forward engine room was flooded to a depth of three feet, her speed dropped, her wireless was out of action and her signal halliards shot away.

After the Germans had disappeared into the mist, the *Arethusa* and *Fearless* came up from astern, lay stopped side by side while they communicated by semaphore and Tyrwhitt tried to reassemble his scattered destroyers. Within a short time this was done, the *Arethusa* managed to raise steam again, and with *Fearless* and the combined destroyer force Tyrwhitt started westward to roll up the German patrol line. A new and much bigger destroyer, *V 187,* was now sighted. Dodging the British destroyers she ran into two of Goodenough's light cruisers which, after following the *Arethusa* and *Fearless* into the Bight, had now come up with them. *V 187* altered course violently once again, only to run into more British destroyers. She had got to within 2,000 yards of a division of four boats before their 4-inch shells stopped her, set her on fire, killed most of her crew and tore her hull to pieces. She slowly sank, in clouds of black smoke and escaping white steam.

The spirit with which men had gone to war in August 1914 then showed itself, for some of the British destroyers stopped and lowered boats to pick up survivors. While they were doing this the *Stettin* reappeared and opened fire, so the destroyers, collecting their boats as best they could, made off, leaving two belonging to HMS *Defender* behind for rescue later in the morning by the British submarine *E4*. This took the British officer and seamen from the boats, together with a few German prisoners— 'as a sample' said the submarine's commanding officer later—and gave the remaining Germans water, biscuits, a compass and the course to steer for Heligoland.

During this time the British steamed westward, departing from their course from time to time to chase reported enemy ships, or to attack those actually sighted. Much confusion and, to quote an official report 'a distinct element of excitement' was added to the operations by the signals of Keyes, who had sighted Goodenough's light cruisers, taken them to be enemy and reported them as such.

The British submarine *E4*, which was completed in 1913, rescued survivors after the German destroyer *V187* sank at Heligoland

Meanwhile, Goodenough realised that there was great danger of British light cruisers and submarines attacking each other and accordingly withdrew his light cruisers from the scene and waited in the hope that the situation would soon clear itself up.

Mistaken identity

There were other cases of mistaken identity as the British ships, seeing brief and shadowy manifestations of ships appearing and disappearing in the mist, reported them as enemy and then proceeded to chase. These chases sometimes ended with the recognition of each other as British, but sometimes the chaser lost the chased in the mist without realising that he had been chasing a friend.

However, by about 1010 hours the situation, so far as the British destroyers were concerned, was much clearer, and Tyrwhitt's force, more or less reconcentrated, started westward again. The *Fearless* and *Arethusa* were in company and steaming at 10 knots, which was now the latter's maximum speed.

The morning had not been as successful as the British had hoped. True, they had sunk one destroyer, but, on the other hand,

it was by no means certain that the *Arethusa* would be able to get home. The Germans were recovering from the surprise of the British attack, and their light cruisers, which had been on guard duty close under the coast, were now putting to sea, although the battle-cruisers were still penned up behind the bar at the mouth of the Jade.

The first of the German light cruisers on the scene was the *Strassburg*; the British destroyers, on their way westward and homeward, turned back to engage her and at this providential moment Commodore Goodenough's light cruisers came down from their waiting position to the north, in answer to a call for help from the *Fearless*. The *Strassburg* was driven off, but almost at once another light cruiser, the *Mainz,* appeared, having hurried up from the Ems where she had been lying.

Tricks of light and fog had greatly magnified the size of the *Strassburg,* so that she appeared to be a cruiser of the *Roon* class of about twice her displacement. It seemed likely that a ship of that size would be scouting in front of the big ships of the High Seas Fleet so that when the message reporting her supposed presence was received by Beatty, who had been steaming backwards and forwards some 40 miles

away waiting for his chance, it seemed to him that the time had now come for the battle-cruisers to be committed. Tyrwhitt signalled 'Respectfully request that I may be supported. Am hard pressed.' The *Arethusa* and the other British light craft would stand no chance if, by themselves, they were to encounter the big ships of the High Seas Fleet, and Beatty took his ships into the Bight. At least one of the dangers which confronted them, that of submarine attack, was much reduced by the still calm which kept the sea in a state of glassy calm, thus making it comparatively easy to spot an attacking submarine and avoid it.

By now the destroyers, which had started out at dawn into the Bight with *Arethusa* and *Fearless,* had begun to head for home, but they were ordered to return to the battlefield. Captain Blunt in the *Fearless* signalled those short of ammunition to return home at once; no one did so and the destroyers were soon in action against the *Mainz.* For 15 minutes, from 1135 to 1150, they engaged the German ship without hits by either side. Then, when the destroyers closed it could be seen what was implied when unarmoured ships were engaged at ultra short range. The destroyer HMS *Laurel* was hit amidships; the ready-

The British light cruiser *Fearless,* leader of the 1st Destroyer Flotilla during the battle at Heligoland

use ammunition of No. 2 gun exploded and put the gun and its crew out of action, blowing away half the after funnel. Beams in the engine room were twisted and the captain seriously wounded. Another shell from the *Mainz* hit the forward funnel and exploded inside, causing a back draught in the boiler which set fire to the oil fuel. This fire was soon put out with sand, but a third shell cut the main steam pipe, the fire main and the electric wires taking light to the stokeholds which were thus suddenly plunged into total darkness. A fourth shell passed straight through the ship, exploding outboard. *Laurel's* crew then rigged emergency oil lighting in the stokeholds, only to find that forced draught blew out the lamps.

Nevertheless, the ship managed to steam slowly away, amid great clouds of smoke that partially hid her from the enemy. *Laurel's* sister ship, HMS *Liberty,* was hit in a number of places, her mast and bridge shot away and her captain killed. At 4,000 yards a single salvo of four shells hit HMS *Laertes* in the bows, in No. 2 boiler room, at the base of her centre funnel and also aft. There was no water left in her boilers and she stopped dead.

The *Mainz* was now attacked by Goodenough's light cruisers, only half visible through the mist until they fired their broadsides, when the gun flashes glowed bright. The first salvos fell close to the German ship and the yellow smoke and fumes of the British shells drifted across her deck, mixed with white steam from a broken steam pipe. A hit aft killed or wounded the crews of the two quarter-deck 4.1-inch guns and their places were taken by others.

Another hit aft damaged the *Mainz's* rudder and she began to circle round to starboard, a circle interrupted by a crash heavier and louder than that of her 4.1-inch guns. A huge column of dirty grey water leaped out of the water alongside, the ship rocked and then settled down on an even keel, torpedoed and rapidly losing speed.

Firing by clockwork

Mainz was now surrounded by British light cruisers and destroyers. A German survivor afterwards described the light cruisers as firing as if by clockwork. Her main mast came down with a run and the midships and after funnels crashed down on the deck. Smoke and flames drifted across the ship, and all the time shells were whistling overhead or exploding in the ship or in the water and huge splashes of water were leaping up in the air and slowly falling back again.

There was a sudden silence; only one of the German's twelve 4.1-inch guns was still in action. *Kapitän* Paschen, the commanding officer of the *Mainz,* gave the order to sink his ship then but the order miscarried. The pause in the action ended as the British opened fire once more, and it was at once clear that these shells were much heavier than the 6-inch guns of the 'Town' class cruisers which had done the damage so far. Close at hand, through the mist and smoke came Beatty's battle-cruisers, HMSs *Lion, Princess Royal, Queen Mary, New Zealand* and *Invincible,* five times the size of the *Mainz* and looking even more impressive because they were neat and tidy, in order, undamaged, steaming fast and firing as if at exercise.

The *Mainz* was in her great and final agony, but she managed to get out a signal telling the High Seas Fleet and Hipper's battle-cruisers that the British heavy ships were actually in the Bight.

The last gun of the *Mainz* was now still: the order to sink the ship was given once more and the necessary preparations were made. Members of the crew began to jump

The German cruiser *Mainz* was attacked by British destroyers, light cruisers and battle-cruisers and sunk at Heligoland

SMS *Seydlitz*, one of the three German battle-cruisers penned up behind the Jade Bar during the action of the Heligoland Bight

The German light cruiser *Köln* — badly damaged by two salvoes from HMS *Lion* and then shot to pieces by the British battle-cruisers

into the sea and were picked up by the British. But this rescue work took time so Keyes brought the *Lurcher* alongside the quarter-deck of the German ship so that many of the Germans were able to climb on board and save their lives. Other destroyers helped and every living person was brought to safety except for one young officer who stood apart and watched the proceedings. Keyes shouted to him that everything possible had been done and urged him to come over to the *Lurcher*. The young man stood to attention, saluted and refused. The *Lurcher* backed away, her upper deck crowded with survivors, and the *Mainz* sank. One of those rescued was Lieutenant von Tirpitz, son of the German Minister of Marine. He was brought to England as a prisoner of war. Churchill, on learning of this, at once sent a personal message through the International Red Cross to young Tirpitz's father, reassuring

him as to the fate of his son.

The *Mainz* sank at 1310. The German officer who had refused Keyes' offer of rescue, and another officer who had also stayed with the ship until she sank, were both picked up by the Germans. The last act of the crew of the *Mainz* had been to throw overboard the confidential books in a bag weighted with a 4.1-inch shell. When the bag was thrown the shell fell out and the bag floated away, spreading secret papers on the waters of the Bight. Horrified, even in those moments which might have been their last, the Germans threw used cartridge cases at the contents of the bag as they drifted by and succeeded in sinking them. Their work was in vain, for two days previously the Russians had recovered from the wreck of the light cruiser *Magdeburg*, at the entrance to the Gulf of Finland, the vital German cyphers which were handed over to the British. For months the

Admiralty in London was able to read the secret German messages.

By the time that the *Mainz* had sunk, Beatty's battle-cruisers had been in action with two other German light cruisers, both of which sank as the result of the damage they had received during a brief blasting from the heavy guns of the British ships.

Fog and confusion

The *Köln* was making her way through the confusion of the misty sea when suddenly from out of the mist there emerged, vast and terrific, the form of a great cruiser steaming at full speed. This was the *Lion* and two salvoes from her settled the fate of the *Köln*. Yet another of the German light cruisers, the *Ariadne,* then appeared. Engaged, she at once caught fire. She was an old ship, painted and repainted time and again, so that the paint on her hull was at least a quarter of an inch thick. This

HMS *Lurcher (left)* backing away from the sinking German cruiser *Mainz* after picking up survivors

HMS *New Zealand*, the dominion's contribution to British naval power, steams into action at Heligoland

caught fire and blazed away, so that the very steel plates of the ship's hull seemed to have burst into flames. She staggered back into the mist from which she had come and, some two hours later, sank.

Meanwhile the British battle-cruisers, steaming very slowly, undertook the destruction of the *Köln*. She was the flagship of *Konteradmiral* Leberecht Maass commanding the destroyers and torpedo boats in the Bight, and of her company of 380 men only one survived that afternoon. He was a leading stoker, stationed as a messenger on the 'tween decks', where he was protected from the worst effects of the enemy fire until smoke and flames drove him into the open. Here he saw *Lion* and the other British battle-cruisers steaming slowly by and deliberately shooting the *Köln* to pieces. Maass had been killed, presumably when the bridge was shot away. The *Köln*'s funnels were full of holes, the deck was littered with half-burnt bits of boats, woodwork, life-jackets and tangled bits of aerials and signal halliards which had been shot away. The whole of the deck seemed to be glazed with green and yellow stuff from the incomplete explosion of the British lyddite shells that gave out a suffocating smell.

The ship lay for a while sinking on an even keel. When the order came to abandon ship the leading stoker and a handful of men clung to the remains of a lifeboat, but 76 hours later he was the only man left alive of the entire ship's company.

At about 1310 hours, having sunk the *Mainz* and the *Köln* and with the *Ariadne* sinking, Beatty considered his position.

There were still a number of German light craft scattered around in the mist patches of the Bight—in fact there were now no fewer than seven light cruisers in the area, *Stralsund*, *Strassburg*, *Stettin*, *Frauenlob*, *Kolberg*, *Danzig* and *Hela*. Beatty's force was scattered, the *Arethusa* was still in a critical condition and, most important of all, at 1200 hours it would have been possible for the German battle-cruisers to begin to cross the Jade Bar. In fact orders for them to do so had been given at 1207 hours, which meant that all three, *Seydlitz*, *Moltke* and *Von der Tann* would be on the scene of the battle at about 1500 hours to snap up detached British light cruisers and destroyers. Accordingly Beatty ordered the recall to be sent out. Just then the *Arethusa's* hard-pressed engines finally broke down and she had to be taken in tow by the armoured cruiser *Hogue*. Altogether she had lost one officer and ten men killed, and one officer and 16 men wounded. The total British losses were 35 killed and about 40 wounded. The Germans had lost three light cruisers and a destroyer, together with over 1,000 men killed, wounded or taken prisoner.

It had been a notable British success—perhaps too well celebrated since in the excitement and pleasure of the moment nobody seems to have considered how poor communications between the various groups of British ships had been and how disastrous that might have proved. Poor communications were to dog the British navy throughout the war, but the Germans too suffered from a notable failure of communications. During this battle the

weather in the Jade was fine and clear; no one reported mist around the sea of battle so the German command imagined that the cruisers reporting from around Heligoland could see everything which was going on, and that when they reported sighting individual enemy units these units were all there were to see. Nobody mentioned the mist which was concealing powerful enemy forces.

The effect of the battle on the Germans was immediate and conclusive. The success of the British attack was a tremendous shock and made the Kaiser even more determined than before to protect the High Seas Fleet from damage, for he considered that an undamaged German fleet would be a card of first-class importance for him to play when the time came to discuss peace terms. At the end of August 1914 it seemed to the Germans this time was close at hand, for the Russian invasion of Germany had been repelled, and the success of the German invasion of France and Belgium looked as though it would bring the Germans to Paris very shortly.

In the meantime, the Germans decided to lay mines in the Bight to keep British ships out instead of risking precious warships.

For the British, the first month of the war at sea had ended well. German merchant shipping had disappeared from the sea, Allied merchant shipping was moving almost unchecked all over the world, and so were Allied troops on their way to the various battlefields of the war. Only in the Baltic was the British navy unable to support the armies of its Allies.

BLOCKADE

The outcome of the war was at stake in this struggle—for each nation could have been strangled by a successful blockade. On her side Great Britain had the vigilance and numerical superiority of the Royal Navy. Germany had the devastating effectiveness of her U-boats

By the early years of the 20th century technical progress, and especially the development of the mine, the submarine, the torpedo, and aircraft had obviously made the old concept of close blockade on the Napoleonic War model totally obsolete. Nonetheless, there was in British naval circles a good deal of hesitation about abandoning what was regarded as a well-tried and provenly effective strategy. Not until the middle of 1912 was close blockade replaced by what was called an 'observational blockade' of the Heligoland Bight. This was to be enforced by a line of cruisers and destroyers patrolling the North Sea from the south-west coast of Norway to the Dutch coast, with heavy squadrons from the main fleet in support to the north and west. But this idea proved short-lived, since it was plainly impossible to patrol a 300-mile-long line effectively, by night and day, in winter and summer.

The blockade plan laid down

A month before the outbreak of war the observational blockade was therefore abandoned in favour of a 'distant blockade' designed to control the exits from the North Sea. This was made possible by the geographical chance which has placed the British Isles like a breakwater across the passages leading from the outer oceans to the German seaports and naval bases on their North Sea and Baltic coasts. The British plan was that the Channel Fleet, based chiefly on the Thames estuary ports, Dover, and Portsmouth, would close the Straits of Dover, while the much more powerful Grand Fleet would be based on Scapa Flow in the Orkneys and would throw out a line of cruisers or armed merchant cruisers (called the Northern Patrol) to watch the remote and stormy waters between the Shetland Islands, Norway, and Iceland. Such was, in brief outline, the final naval blockade plan which was brought into force in August 1914.

But recent technical developments had a much wider influence than merely to render the concept of close blockade obsolete. They all, but especially the mine, proved potent instruments of blockade in their own right, and both sides laid large numbers of mines, and disposed submarines in the approaches to the other side's ports and bases for this purpose. Unfortunately, the early British mines, like their torpedoes, were extremely inefficient, and it was not until 1917, when an exact copy of the German mine was produced in quantity, that the Royal Navy was provided with an efficient mine.

The Admiralty always expected that the enemy's reply to the British blockade would, as in all earlier wars, take the form of an attack on commerce by cruisers and armed merchantmen. This was a perfectly legal form of warfare, subject to the regulations incorporated in the Hague Conventions regarding the safety of the crews of captured merchant ships; and the German surface raiders in fact showed humanity in their observance of those regulations. Before the war the CID reviewed the measures necessary to keep shipping moving despite the possibility of capture, and recommended that the State should receive eighty per cent of the insurance premiums required to cover war risks on merchant ships and stand eighty per cent of the losses. The Treasury, however, was not at first willing to accept such an intrusion into the field of private enterprise, and the War Risks Insurance scheme did not actually come into force until the outbreak of war.

By July 1915 all the German raiders which had been at sea during the early part of the war had been destroyed. Allied (mainly British) seapower so dominated the outer seas and oceans that German trade had been brought to an almost complete halt immediately war broke out—except in the Baltic. Many German merchant ships sought refuge in neutral ports, and the transfer of cargoes destined for Germany to neutral ships began at once. Freight rates rose very sharply, and the neutral nations began to reap enormous profits. These developments stimulated British concern over the emasculation of Belligerent Rights by the Declarations of Paris and London. The first step taken to restore the earlier state of affairs was to issue Orders in Council transferring various commodities from the 'free goods' to the contraband list, and in 1915 the distinction between conditional and absolute contraband was all but wiped out.

On 20th November 1914 a small British merchant ship was sunk by a German submarine in the North Sea and the crew left in the boats—contrary to the Hague Conventions. Other sinkings by submarines soon followed, and thus was ushered in an entirely new element in the German attack on trade—and one for which the Royal Navy was almost totally unprepared. Plainly the implications were very serious. On 11th March 1915 the British government issued an Order in Council, generally referred to as the 'Reprisals Order', since it was made in

reprisal for the illegal use of submarines. It declared that goods which could be shown to be destined for Germany were liable to seizure, even though the vessel carrying them was bound for a neutral port.

This led to strong protests from the neutrals, and especially from the USA, regarding interference with what they regarded as legitimate—and of course highly profitable—trade. The USA never moved from the position that the Reprisals Order was illegal—until they themselves were at war. But the real reason for the issue of the order was that the British government was aware that the Scandinavian countries and Holland were importing vastly greater quantities of goods which were on the British contraband list than they had taken before the war. Obviously the surplus was being passed direct to Germany, and the shipping services of the neutral nations were thus replacing the immobilized German merchant fleet. The leak through the blockade via Italy was never serious, and when she entered the war on the Allied side in May 1915 it stopped altogether. But with the Scandinavian countries and Holland the leak was very large indeed, and it did not prove easy to stop it.

In home waters the British blockade was operated through contraband control stations in the Orkneys and the Downs (the anchorage in the Channel between the Goodwin Sands and the coast), and ships intercepted were sent into one or other unless their cargoes were above suspicion. In 1915 the Northern Patrol cruisers intercepted 3,098 ships, and in the following year 3,388. Those sent in for examination totalled 743 and 889 respectively. Many neutral ships called voluntarily at the examination stations, and they were given priority for clearance; but there were always some to whom the prospect of high profits outweighed the risks involved in not conforming with the British regulations. When flagrant cases came to light a series of seizures in prize would probably be organized. For example the very high shipments of lard from USA to Scandinavia were stopped by the seizure of four cargoes in rapid succession in October and November 1914.

Ruffled neutral feathers

On the outbreak of war the CID set up a 'Trading with the Enemy Committee' to control imports through neutral countries; but its procedure proved too slow and cumbrous, and its functions were therefore taken over in March 1915 by the War Trade Intelligence Department, which collected evidence regarding consignees, studied the scale of neutral imports of all commodities and generally 'acted as a clearing house for the collection, analysis, and dissemination of economic data relating to enemy and neutral trade'. The Exports Control Committee under the Intelligence Department was responsible for issuing import and export licences to shippers, and ruffled neutral feathers were often smoothed by purchasing detained cargoes instead of seizing them in prize.

Nonetheless, difficulties with neutral nations sometimes became acute. Intercepted ships were often subject to long delays, and sometimes they were sunk while being taken into port under British armed guard. After the war the British government paid full value plus five percent accrued interest on all ships sunk in such circumstances. Because of neutral susceptibilities the British government had to move with caution and moderation, especially in dealings with the USA, where the anti-British lobby was powerful and vociferous. The process of keeping American public opinion sweet was, however, greatly helped by German ruthlessness — notably over the sinking of the great Cunard liner *Lusitania* on 7th May 1915 with a heavy loss

Imperial War Museum

Bibliothek für Zeitgeschichte, Stuttgart

Top right: British Q ship B2. Posing as unarmed merchantmen, Q ships sailed in submarine-infested waters shelling unwary German submarines with their concealed guns.
Right: German raider *Möwe*. A disguised merchantman, it made two cruises and sank 122,000 tons of shipping

Dazzle-painted Anti-submarine escorts. The sloops *Polyanthus*, shown here in her official dazzle-painted scheme, and *Gardenia*, were converted during construction from conventional escorts. They were armed with a variety of 4-in and 3-in guns, depth-charges and bomb-throwers, and differed from the 'Q-Ship' decoys in that they were warships pure and simple

of civilian lives including 128 Americans.

The German reply to the tightening British blockade was to declare on 4th February 1915 the whole of the waters around the British Isles a 'War Zone' in which any ship might be sunk without warning. Thus began the first unrestricted submarine campaign. It lasted until August, when the rising tide of neutral protests caused the German government to order a return to less flagrantly illegal methods. However, the substantial tonnage sunk by submarines in that phase caused anxiety in Allied circles, and should have provided an opportunity to find the proper antidote—namely convoy. Such, however, was not the case, since the Admiralty remained stubbornly opposed to convoy.

The winter of 1915-16 saw a revival of German surface ship raiders; but this time disguised merchantmen instead of war-ships were employed. Altogether five such ships were sent out, and one of them (the *Möwe*) made two cruises and sank 122,000 tons of shipping. Two were caught right at the beginning of their careers, but the others proved skilful and elusive enemies. Like their predecessors of the cruiser period they caused considerable delay and dislocation to shipping, and the last of them was not eliminated until early in 1918.

Despite the success achieved by the first unrestricted submarine campaign, the situation as regards the blockade and counterblockade at the end of 1915 was

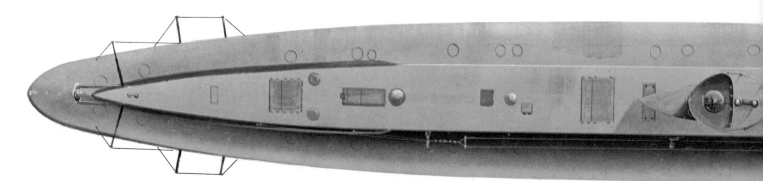

not unfavourable to the Allies. This was the more fortunate because in all theatres of military operations that year was one of unmitigated defeat and disaster for the Allied cause. True, there was a shortage of shipping, caused partly by excessive requisitioning by the service departments; but the flow of supplies of all kinds had been kept up, and losses of merchant ships, which had totalled 855,721 tons during the year, had been replaced by newly built and captured vessels.

With complete deadlock prevailing on the Western Front, the commercial blockade of Germany had obviously gained in importance. Accordingly in February 1916 the British government set up a new Ministry of Blockade under Lord Robert Cecil to co-ordinate the political and administrative measures necessary to cripple the Central powers' resources. The new ministry, working closely with the War Trade Intelligence Department, gradually built up world-wide control over the movement of all merchant ships and the shipment of cargoes. Consular shipping control officers were installed in all important ports, and they transmitted to London a stream of information regarding the true shippers and consignees of cargoes. With this knowledge in hand the ministry was able to compile a list of firms known to be trading with the enemy, and great ingenuity was shown in exerting pressure to curb their activities. Because bunkering facilities in many overseas ports were British-controlled it was possible to deprive ships of coal and other essential supplies when they called. The location of the greater part of the world's banking and insurance business in London enabled credit and insurance cover to be refused to firms whose activities were not

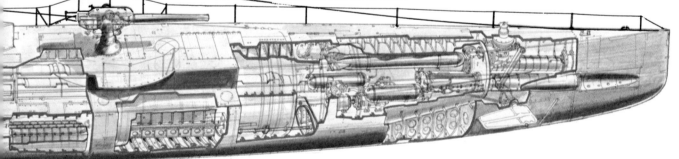

German *U31*

U31 was a typical U-Boat of pre-1914 design, ordered in 1912 but not completed until late 1914. She was lost in the North Sea in January 1915 from unknown causes (probably a mine). She was armed with two torpedo-tubes in the bow and two in the stern, and carried a 10.5-cm deck gun. On the surface her two-shaft diesels gave her an endurance of 4,440 miles at 8 knots, but when submerged this fell to 80 miles at 5 knots. Length: 212 ft 6 in. Beam: 20 ft 9 in. Crew: 35 officers and men

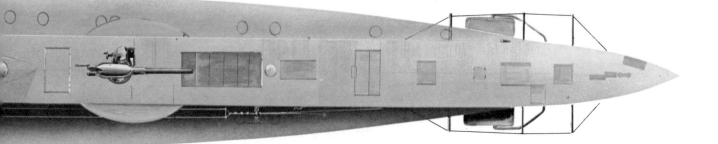

above suspicion. And British control over most of the world's wireless and cable communications made it improbable that such activities would long remain uncovered. Finally, if a ship did sail with an illicit cargo, the Admiralty would be asked to take special steps to intercept it; and if that succeeded condemnation in prize was virtually certain.

But the Ministry of Blockade did not only work to prevent shipment of contraband cargoes. Neutral nations' imports were rationed with increasing stringency at a figure no greater than they had taken before the war; and goods which were particularly vital to the enemy war effort, such as the special minerals (wolfram and tungsten, for example) used in weapon and armour plate manufacture, were con-trolled by the pre-emptive purchase of the whole available supply.

One of the first actions of the Ministry of Blockade was to issue (29th February 1916) a 'Statutory Black List' of firms in neutral countries with whom all transactions were forbidden. This aroused strong American protests—since a number of the firms were American. In the following month a system known as 'Letters of Assurance' for approved shippers was introduced. These were always referred to as 'Navicerts' (from the code word used in cables referring to them), and possession of such a letter ensured a ship unhindered passage through the blockade. Encouragement was given to shippers to arrange with London for advance booking of cargoes, which would then be approved or dis-approved by the Contraband Committee.

Neutral shipowners were also given every encouragement to order their ships to call in voluntarily for examination at Scapa Flow and the Downs or at Halifax, Alexandria, and Gibraltar where additional stations were set up. In 1916 no less than 1,878 neutral vessels called in voluntarily, 950 were intercepted and sent in, and only 155 (some five per cent of the total) successfully ran the blockade. New Orders in Council were issued to increase the stringency of the blockade—notably that of 7th July 1916 which repealed the Declaration of London Order in Council of August 1914. Throughout 1916 the effectiveness of the Allied machinery of commercial blockade steadily increased.

The Germans did not, of course, take this

British R12
The British 'R' Class are outstanding as the first attempt to produce an anti-submarine submarine, or 'hunter-killer' as they are known today. They were also a quarter of a century before their time in having a streamlined hull designed for higher speed under water than on the surface. The bulbous bow contained listening gear, and the armament of six 18-in torpedoes was designed for maximum effect against submarines. Speed: 9 knots (surfaced) 14 knots (submerged)

'UK' (U-cruiser) type specifications			
	U135	U139	U142
Length (ft)	275.5	302.5	320
Beam (ft)	25	29.5	31.5
Draught	14.5	15.1	17.5
Displacement (tons) surface/submerged	1190/1560	1950/2500	2160/2760
Machinery (hp) surface/submerged	3500/1940	3500/1760	6000/2600
Fuel (tons)	66	102	
Torpedo tubes (19.7 in)	4 Bow; 2 Stern	4 Bow; 2 Stern	4 Bow; 2 Stern
Guns	1 × 5.9-in	2 × 5.9-in	2 × 5.9-in
Crew	46	62	83

escalation of Allied blockade measures lying down. In March 1916 they renewed the unrestricted submarine campaign, and again quickly achieved a fairly high rate of sinkings – 126,000 tons in April. However, they once again caused the loss of American lives, and the resultant protests produced a temporary lull. In September they tried again, and despite the wide variety of measures introduced by the Admiralty to combat the submarine menace – minefields, nets, surface patrols, and the much advertised 'mystery' or 'Q-ships' – German submarines sank nearly 147,000 tons of shipping in October. The implications were plainly very serious, since if the upward trend continued the loss to be anticipated in 1917 would exceed 2,000,000 tons. Furthermore the total Allied shipping losses in 1916 amounted to 1,237,634 tons, which was nearly fifty per cent higher than in the previous year; and, finally, the rate of sinking of U-boats had not been satisfactory in relation to the speed at which new ones were built. From the beginning of the war to the end of 1916 only forty-six had been sunk.

But if the closing months of 1916 brought little comfort to those responsible for maintaining the flow of Allied supplies, to the German people the implication of that year's developments were far more threatening. Though their armed forces had not yet suffered appreciably, since they were given priority for all available supplies, the condition of the civilian population was beginning to deteriorate seriously. The 1915 and 1916 harvests had been bad, due chiefly to lack of imported fertilizers, the conquered territories in eastern Europe had failed to replace supplies from overseas, home producers of foodstuffs were withholding their produce or selling it on the extensive black market, the calorific value of the civilian ration was falling steadily, and the shortage of clothing was becoming increasingly acute. With the winter of 1916-17 approaching – it was to be remembered in Germany as the 'Turnip Winter' – the outlook was grim indeed.

Such was the state of affairs that led the German government to adopt the desperate expedient of renewed submarine warfare on merchant shipping in February 1917; and that led to the entry of the USA into the war, and so to the utter defeat of the Central powers.

British *L52*

The British *L52* represents the final evolution of the standard submarine in the Royal Navy. Basically an improved 'E' Class, they had a heavy torpedo- and gun-armament, and were highly successful in service. Three survived until the Second World War. They were armed with six 21-in torpedo-tubes and two 4-in guns

German U-boat losses

	'U' Type	'UB' Type	'UC' Type	Total
1914	5	–	–	5
1915	14	2	3	19
1916	7	8	7	22
1917	19	12	32	63
1918	17	42	10	69
Total	62	64	52	178

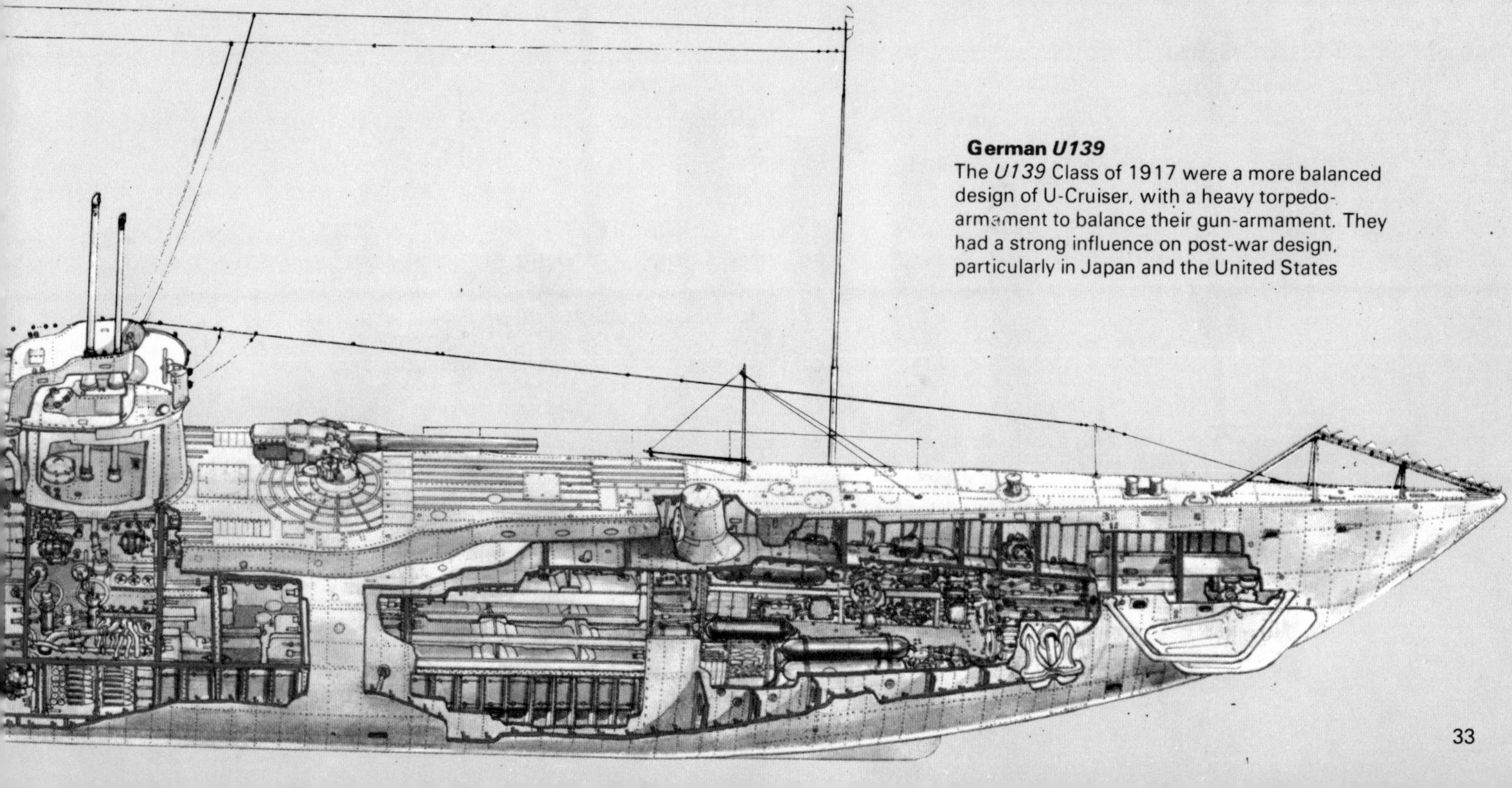

German *U139*

The *U139* Class of 1917 were a more balanced design of U-Cruiser, with a heavy torpedo-armament to balance their gun-armament. They had a strong influence on post-war design, particularly in Japan and the United States

SINKING OF THE ABOUKIR HOGUE AND CRESSY

Less than two months after the beginning of the war, Britain's confidence in her mighty navy was rudely disturbed. Three armoured cruisers were sunk by a single German submarine — a weapon whose potential had been guessed at and which now seemed about to be realised. The loss of life was considerable, though the sinking of the three ships was of little consequence to overall British naval supremacy. *Below:* HMS *Aboukir,* first of the *U 9*'s victims.

HMS *Hogue*, the U9's second victim, was hit by both the submarine's bow torpedoes and within 3 minutes she was listing at 40 degrees

In late September 1914, the Royal Navy experienced its first contact with a new form of naval warfare. It was a shock which brought home the vulnerability of surface warships to an invisible underwater enemy. On September 22, three armoured cruisers, HMS *Hogue, Aboukir* and *Cressy,* were sunk in the North Sea by a solitary German submarine in an action which lasted scarcely an hour. For the first time, many naval chiefs and commanders of some of the world's largest and most powerful fighting ships were brought face to face with the practical possibility of destruction by a craft inferior in armament and size, operating secretly in the enemy's home waters. The unhurried but inexorable progress of technology since Nelson's victories 100 years before, had at last come to fruition.

Hogue, Aboukir and *Cressy* were pre-dreadnought ships whose design and construction dated from 1898 to 1902. They were three of the four *Cressy* or *Bacchante* class ships which made up 7th Cruiser Squadron, stationed at the Nore under Rear-Admiral Henry Campbell. The fourth ship was HMS *Bacchante,* Campbell's flagship. This squadron, together with the 1st and 3rd Destroyer Flotillas at Harwich and ten submarines of the 8th Flotilla, formed the 'Southern Force' under the overall command of Rear-Admiral Arthur Christian, whose flagship was HMS *Eur-*

yalus—yet another *Bacchante* class cruiser.

The task of the Harwich flotillas was to keep the area of the North Sea below the 54th parallel free of German minelayers and torpedo craft, and one of the 7th Cruiser Squadron's duties was to support the destroyers in these sweeps. Two areas of the North Sea were earmarked for patrols by Southern Force—the Dogger Bank, and an area off the Hook of Holland known as the 'Broad Fourteens'.

The Broad Fourteens was an area of concern to the Admiralty both from a tactical point of view and for political reasons. Firstly, it was an ideal position from which to get early warning of any attempt by German ships to attack the transports taking the BEF, and later its supplies, across the Channel to France. It was also a good station from which to intercept enemy minelayers making for British coastal waters. Apart from its purely tactical importance, however, dominance of the Broad Fourteens was necessary politically in order to honour a pledge given to Belgium at the beginning of the war.

Part of Britain's guarantee to Belgium —the ostensible cause of Britain's entry into the war—was to ensure that the river Scheldt, Belgium's chief exit to the sea, remained clear for shipping. In order to fulfil the guarantee the Admiralty was anxious to maintain a British presence in the area and accordingly ordered patrols.

The four cruisers of the 7th Squadron and *Euryalus,* which had to undertake patrol duties as a result of the general shortage of cruisers, were usually split between the patrol areas. On September 17, bad weather conditions forced both destroyer flotillas to return to Harwich, leaving Rear-Admiral Campbell patrolling the Dogger Bank area with the four cruisers alone (*Bacchante* was in harbour for repairs at the time.)

At this time, Churchill, First Lord of the Admiralty, was visiting the Grand Fleet at Scapa Flow, and on the same day as the destroyers were forced back to port a conference was held on board Jellicoe's flagship, HMS *Iron Duke.* The conference was attended by Churchill, Sturdee, Chief of the War Staff, Keyes, in charge of the Submarine Service, and Tyrwhitt, commander of the Harwich Force. During his visit to the Grand Fleet, Churchill had been infuriated to overhear the expression 'live-bait squadron' and on enquiry discovered it was the fleet's nickname for the 7th Cruiser Squadron. When Churchill raised the matter of the *Bacchantes,* Keyes and Tyrwhitt took the opportunity to point out the danger of exposing the cruisers to such an advanced position, especially without a destroyer screen and in an area where numerous fishing boats could report their movements.

Churchill recognised the danger in which

HMS *Cressy* which spotted the U9's periscope but could not manoeuvre fast enough to avoid the torpedoes

the cruisers were, and the following day, on his return to London, he recommended to the First Sea Lord, Lord Louis Battenberg, that they should be removed. His minute read: 'The *Bacchantes* ought not to continue on this beat. The risk is not justified by any service they can render. The narrow seas, being the nearest point to the enemy, should be kept by a small number of good modern ships. The *Bacchantes* should go to the western entrance of the Channel and set Bethell's battleships—and later Wemyss' cruisers—free for convoy and other duties. The first four *Arethusas* (light cruisers of 1914 vintage) should join the flotillas of the narrow seas.

A major blunder

Battenberg concurred with Churchill's recommendations, especially since he had never been very enthusiastic about the *Bacchantes* steaming up and down alone in the North Sea. He was willing therefore to adopt Churchill's plan. But two days later, on September 19, Sturdee persuaded the First Sea Lord to approve an order moving the cruisers not to the western approaches, but to the southern patrol area.

Meanwhile, Admiral Christian was patrolling off the Dogger Bank with the *Bacchantes*, still unescorted. He signalled to the Admiralty that he intended to maintain his position, but before this was received, the Admiralty sent him this message: 'The Dogger Bank patrol need not be continued. Weather too bad for destroyers to go to sea. Arrange for cruisers to watch Broad Fourteens.' Churchill did not see the signal, which was described as 'routine'. Admiral Christian duly moved his patrol south, and by dawn on September 20 had reached the Maas Light Vessel, where it was found that his flagship *Euryalus* needed coal and repairs to her wireless. But as the weather was too bad for him to transfer his flag to another ship, Christian returned to port leaving in command the Senior Officer, Captain John Drummond of the *Aboukir*.

At last, on the night of September 21-22, the weather moderated, and the cruiser *Lowestoft* and eight destroyers, under Admiral Tyrwhitt, left Harwich late on September 21. This force had not, however, joined up with the three cruisers by dawn on the 22nd.

At dawn on September 22, the stage was thus set. The three elderly cruisers were deployed in a regular order, steaming at a dangerously low constant speed of under ten knots, in an area sandwiched between the Dutch coast and a German minefield, without escort and almost on the enemy's doorstep. Only the other principal in the drama, the *U 9*, had yet to appear.

In common with the adversaries she was soon to meet, the *U 9* was not a modern craft. Her surface propulsion was by Kort-ing diesel engines, underwater propulsion being by electric motors whose batteries needed frequent recharging. For armament, she had four torpedo tubes of 17·7-inches, two bow and two stern, and one 2-inch gun. The bow tubes had reloads, giving the *U 9* a total of six torpedoes.

Under the command of Leutnant Otto Weddigen, the *U 9* sailed from Kiel on September 20, the same day as the *Bacchantes* were moving to their southern patrol area. Her destination was the Flanders Bight, where she was to try to prevent landings by British troops on the Belgian coast during the battle of the Marne. On the voyage south, her gyro compass proved to be faulty and, unable to navigate precisely, Weddigen found himself off the Dutch coast, some 50 miles from his destination, on the night of September 21. Here the *U 9* encountered the tail-end of the heavy weather that had forced the Harwich destroyers to return to port, and was obliged herself to remain submerged at a depth of 50 feet all night.

A single torpedo

At dawn on September 22 the weather moderated and Leutnant Weddigen surfaced the *U 9* in order to recharge her batteries. Visibility was good and Weddigen soon saw the masts of the three cruisers to the south of him. The U-boat's heavy-oil engines were making a lot of smoke, but as

Out of date by contemporary standards, the *U 9* was nevertheless able to send three British warships to the bottom of the North Sea

Otto Weddigen, a daring commander after luck put prey in his way

German submarine *U 9*
Displacement: 493/611 tons. *Length:* 188 feet. *Beam:* 19¾ feet. *Power/speed:* 1,050/1,160 hp and 14/8 knots. *Armament:* four 17.7-inch torpedo tubes and one 2-inch gun. *Crew:* 28

The southern patrol area of the Royal Navy in the North Sea. Here a series of coincidences, bad management and the weather brought together four old vessels and led to the loss of three British ships and 1,459 men

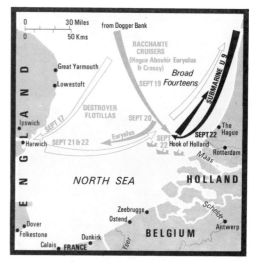

for action it was better to operate submerged, Weddigen dived immediately without completing the recharging of the batteries. Once submerged, the U-boat commander could see that the cruisers were without a destroyer screen and were approaching on a steady course of about nine knots in line abreast, two miles apart. Weddigen at first took the ships to be light cruisers, possibly of the *Birmingham* class. At 0620 hours he fired only a single bow torpedo at the *Aboukir* from a range of 500 yards. The torpedo struck the *Aboukir* on the starboard side and she began to sink.

Captain Drummond apparently believed that he had struck a mine and signalled to the *Hogue* and *Cressy* to close in, but to keep ahead of him. The captains of the other cruisers complied with Drummond's signal and stopped their ships to pick up survivors.

The *U 9* had dived deep after her first shot to reload the torpedo tube and now returned to periscope depth. The sea was still choppy following the bad weather and four-to-five foot whitecaps helped obscure the periscope. The U-boat commander saw the *Aboukir* going down and the other two ships standing by. Now he correctly identified the targets as armoured cruisers, and at 0655 hours he fired both bow torpedoes at the stationary *Hogue,* from a range of only 300 yards. Both torpedoes hit and the *U 9* was so close to her target that she had to manoeuvre to avoid a collision.

The *Hogue* was doomed, however, as she began to heel over a moment after being struck for the second time. One of her officers recalls: *Within three minutes of the first torpedo hitting, the list had increased to about 40 degrees, and realising that her end was very near all hands began to tear off their clothes and crawl down the high side or jump overboard to leeward. To add to the general confusion the stokehold crowd suddenly poured up on deck, their blackened faces dripping sweat and tense with apprehension. It was now a case of every man for himself, and tearing off my boots and clothing and then fastening to my wrist by its chain my gold watch, which I greatly prized, I walked down the sloping deck into the water and struck out for dear life.*

Undeterred by any thought of a British counterattack, Weddigen recklessly surfaced to ascertain whether the *Cressy* was stationary or still moving, and found her stopped with her boats away picking up survivors from her two sister ships.

The U-boat's batteries were almost completely exhausted by now, but she still had two stern torpedoes and a single reload left for a bow tube. The *U 9* submerged and manoeuvred for a stern shot but her periscope was spotted by the *Cressy* just before she fired. The *Cressy's* captain ordered full speed ahead, but one of the two torpedoes hit and stopped her. The *U 9* turned again for a bow shot and with her last torpedo sank the remaining cruiser. The U-boat then disengaged and surfaced north of the scene of the action to recharge her batteries.

In the distance the victims were struggling for survival, seen by one of their number as: 'Two thousand swimming or drowning men all herded together, hardly with elbow room. Strong swimmers were dragged under in the frenzied clutches of weak swimmers or men who could not swim at all. The cries for help were loud and full-throated at first, but they gradually subsided into a low wailing chant and fell like surf on a distant shore.'

As we have seen, the Harwich destroyers had eventually set sail to rejoin the cruisers, but they arrived too late to participate in the action. Now they were redirected to Terschelling at the mouth of the Zuider Zee in order to try to cut off the *U 9*. But the submarine steered a northerly course close in along the Dutch coast to make Kiel without further contact with the British and to receive a jubilant welcome. Leutnant Weddigen was awarded the Iron Cross for his exploit by a Kaiser reported to be 'in seventh heaven'.

First real defeat
In Britain the news was a bombshell. At first it was widely believed that the sinkings were the work of a 'pack' of submarines ravaging unescorted ships. When it became known that only a single U-boat was responsible, both the public and naval chiefs were shocked. The total complement of the three ships was about 2,200. Of these,

62 officers and 1,397 men had been lost in the action. The public was appalled both at the loss of life and at the loss of three cruisers, not realising that the ships were virtually obsolete, and that their loss did not materially diminish the superiority of the British navy over the Germans. But Britain was also smarting under her first real defeat, and outraged public opinion demanded that culprits be found.

As was often the case in the war years, Churchill came under fire. He was blamed for taking on himself the responsibility for the positioning of the cruisers, against the advice of the Sea Lords. Few of his critics knew that the disposition of the ships was the result of the signal of September 19 from the First Sea Lord and the Chief-of-Staff.

A court of enquiry sat to ascertain who was to blame for the disaster and interviewed the principals involved. In judgement, the court blamed the captains of the cruisers and also criticised in strong terms the Admiralty's decision to place them on the Broad Fourteens. The report of the court blamed Captain Drummond for failing to 'zigzag' the formation when the weather moderated and also for ordering the other two ships to close when the *Aboukir* was hit. The captains of the *Hogue* and *Cressy* were blamed for stopping their ships to pick up survivors, and all three were blamed by the court for failing to anticipate the possibility of submarine attack and failing to post sufficient lookouts. The court criticised the Admiralty for placing the cruisers in a hazardous position, but made it clear that it was unable to evaluate properly the reasons for so positioning the ships.

What the enquiry showed was that the object of the patrol was not clearly understood and that the command arrangements were not clearly laid down, especially regarding the responsibility for ordering the Harwich destroyers to sea again. There was also the question of why both admirals were in port at the time of the incident, with the knowledge and consent of the Admiralty. The court was not given an explanation as to why Admiral Campbell had not transferred his flag when the *Bacchante* had to put in for repairs. In the case of Admiral Christian, the bad weather had prevented him from shifting his flag to one of the other cruisers when the *Euryalus* left the patrol.

Perhaps in looking for the culprit, in a more objective mood, the whole of 19th-Century naval thinking should not be overlooked. The submarine was still a relatively unknown quantity (although great strides had been made in improving it since 1900), but it would not be fair to say that the Admiralty ignored the threat posed by the submarine. Indeed, extensive memoranda had been written on its importance by Fisher, Jellicoe, Bacon and Keyes. The point is, though, that although the naval high command realised the danger represented by the submarine, the same was not true throughout the navy.

Before September 1914 no one had experienced the full potential of the submarine in action. Thus as no one really knew what to expect of the submarine in war, no extensive precautions had been taken against them in the planning of evasive manoeuvres and what to do in the event of any ships coming under submarine attack.

Left: The German view of British naval power – formidable on top but vulnerable below. Right: Germany nursing her latest offspring, a submarine. The Kaiser and Admiral Tirpitz smile down from their portraits

THE RAIDERS

The Royal Navy might be the most powerful in the world, but it could not—to the dismay of the British empire—guarantee the safety of Great Britain's world-wide shipping against a small number of daringly led German cruisers. To German soldiers in western Europe and in the snowbound trenches of the Russian front the names of *Emden*, *Karlsruhe*, *Dresden* and *Königsberg* brought pride—and hope for the future

Above: The German admiral, von Spee: a highly respected opponent

The exploits of the raiders, 1914-15.
Below: *Karlsruhe* and *Dresden* terrorized the coast of Brazil. When Spee summoned *Dresden* to meet him in the Pacific, *Karlsruhe* turned north. She was making for the rich British colony of Barbados when, unaccountably, she blew up

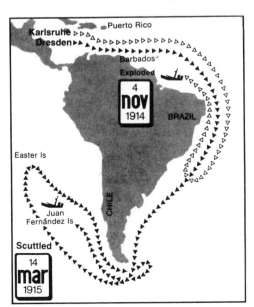

Until at least the 1890's, as an Englishman once said to Grand Admiral von Tirpitz, Germany 'was not a sea-going nation'. Plans for a navy, inspired as much by nationalism as by strategic needs, stagnated in disputes between the competing authorities, the admiralty, executive command, and the naval cabinet, between the Kaiser and the general staff. Even after Tirpitz gained the Kaiser's favour in 1892 and began to create the nucleus of the German navy, there remained the dilemma of what sort of force it should be. Was there to be a High Seas Fleet to wear down Great Britain (because there was never any doubt of the ultimate naval enemy) from a strong centralized position as Great Britain herself had done in the Napoleonic Wars? Or should they build fast cruisers, like 18th-century privateers, to destroy the enemy's trade and distract their main fleet as well?

German naval authorities argued about this crucial decision for ten years after 1895 —the year in which Tirpitz resigned because his battle fleet was being subordinated to the political arguments for cruiser warfare. Colonial ambition was proving a strong argument in favour of a far seas strategy. Not only were the new fast cruisers to fly the German flag in every port of the world, reinforcing pro-German sympathies in South America, Africa, and Asia, but they provided the defence of the scattered islands and territories proudly called the German 'empire'. Frequently they were the reason for acquiring them: Tirpitz himself negotiated the acquisition of the last of the treaty ports in China, Tsingtao, as a base for the East Asia Squadron.

The primacy given to cruiser warfare faded after Tirpitz returned. The second Navy Bill of 1900 outlined the need for a strong home fleet. But as a *quid pro quo* to the cruiser strategists, it also attempted to define an important role for the warships in the far seas: 'to represent the German navy abroad . . . and to gather fruits which have ripened as a result of the naval strength of the Reich embodied in the Home Battle Fleet'.

Until 1910 this policy backed a programme of building fast, well-armed cruisers and light cruisers, capable of from 24 to 27 knots and fitted with 4·1-inch and 6-inch guns which were, at that date, the most accurate for their size in the world. When, under the pressure of the race to build larger and larger capital ships, the emphasis changed, and all new cruisers

were kept for the battle fleet, it was the cruisers of the period 1905-10 which were assigned to foreign stations. They were superior both in speed and gunnery to the equivalent British ships, although this was not obvious to either side before hostilities began. They were intended, however, not for direct action against warships, but to draw away vital units from the British Grand Fleet and leave the North Sea open to a blow from the German North Sea Fleet.

British strategy did not rely on a counterpart to the German cruisers. It was hard enough to get money to build battleships— even the dreadnoughts—and only enough new cruisers were laid down for home waters. This left a fair number of County Class cruisers, built in a period of bad naval design between 1895 and 1905, too costly to scrap, whose failings in speed and armaments were not shown until they were actually under fire. To make up these deficiencies, and to guard her immensely long trade routes and communications, Great Britain relied on the alliance with Japan— whose fleet could blockade Tsingtao, Germany's only effective Asiatic port—and on the combined forces of Australia and New Zealand, which were to neutralize Germany's Pacific colonies. No specific defences were provided for the Indian Ocean, which was felt to be a British preserve.

When war was declared, the main German strength lay in the East Asia Squadron, commanded by Vice-Admiral von Spee, which consisted of the heavy cruisers *Scharnhorst* and *Gneisenau* and three light cruisers *Emden*, *Leipzig*, and *Nürnberg*. In the Caribbean were two of the fastest light cruisers, *Karlsruhe* and *Dresden*, and in the Indian Ocean, based on German East Africa, *Königsberg*. In the Mediterranean there was *Goeben*, one of the finest battle-cruisers in the German navy, and *Breslau*. Finally, mainly in American or German ports, there were the great liners of the passenger fleet, ships of over 20,000 tons, capable of 25 knots, fitted with gun mountings, waiting for the signal to rendezvous with warships and collect their armaments.

The Allied defences appeared far greater on paper than they were in practice because of the immense distances to be covered. Eastern command was based in Hong Kong and Singapore and combined with the small, but modern, Australian fleet. The North Pacific was left to the Japanese; three cruiser squadrons and one French squadron defended the Atlantic; two obsolete squadrons in the Indian Ocean completed the preparations in the far seas. Churchill, the first lord of the Admiralty, and his staff were aware that the line was thin – they did not realize how severely it was to be tested.

Impressive initial successes

Immediately after the declaration of war, Germany chalked up an impressive list of successes. *Goeben* bombarded the French bases of Bône and Philippeville in North Africa and, with bewildering speed, evaded the French and British fleets in the Mediterranean. She then escaped to Constantinople where she was sold to the ostensibly neutral Turkish government. The persuasive force of her presence in Constantinople and, even more, the intrigues of her powerful commander Admiral Souchon, helped materially to bring Turkey into the war on the side of Germany in the autumn of 1914. Meanwhile, in early August, *Königsberg* sank the *City of Winchester* with most of the Ceylon tea crop on board, off the coast of Aden, and threatened the safety of the Suez route to India. Two armed liners escaped through the North Sea and another, *Kronprinz Wilhelm,* ran the blockade of the American ports, while *Karlsruhe* sank her first merchant ship in the Caribbean.

Before the British Admiralty had time to react to these threats, the necessities of the war on the Western Front made the job more difficult. After the retreat from Mons the demand for more power rose dramatically. As the front extended itself from the Channel to Verdun, Kitchener, the secretary of state for war, summoned the reserves, subordinating the Admiralty's other plans in order to escort home the vital battalions of the British army in India. Added to this were the divisions from Australia and New Zealand which, with *Königsberg* at large, would need to be escorted at least through the Red Sea. For weeks half the far seas squadrons were diverted from chasing the German cruisers.

But what might have been a great opportunity for the raiders was lost. One of the decisive battles of the war, the minor engagement in the North Sea off Heligoland on 28th August, in which the Germans lost three light cruisers, so disturbed the Kaiser that he shrank from endangering his cherished fleet again. A defensive strategy took the place of that worked out before 1914; a defective one as far as cruiser warfare was concerned. Instead of ordering immediate strikes at vulnerable points, German planning took account of the imminent loss of her Pacific bases, Samoa, Nauru, New Guinea, and Tsingtao, and the difficulties of supplying and coaling the raiders, rather than of their immense potential. Tirpitz wanted to order Spee home, but such was the atmosphere in Berlin that no orders were sent at all: Pohl, the chief of naval staff, said: 'it is impossible to tell from here whether the squadron will be able to choose against whom it will deal its dying blows'. Within a month of hostilities, the German admiralty had entirely abandoned the preparation of years, the network of colliers and supply ships, communications, and neutral sympathizers. The successes of the raiders in the autumn were obtained without even moral support from home.

The raiders harried two main areas, both vital to the British war effort: the mid-Atlantic and the Indian Ocean. The most vital British interests in August were the troop convoys from India through the Suez Canal. None of these were safe until the whereabouts of *Königsberg* were known. But Captain Looff and his ship had disappeared; he had gone back to German East Africa and did not emerge until 20th September when at dawn he attacked the quiet harbour of Zanzibar, shelled the port, and sank the British light cruiser *Pegasus*. In these anxious months, the calm of the waters between Australia and India, so long a British preserve, was shattered by the foremost raider of all, *Emden*.

The *Königsberg,* which was to prove her superior speed and guns in the Indian Ocean

'There are great prizes to be won'

Admiral von Spee had left Tsingtao on manoeuvres before war broke out and he was soon deprived of his base by the Japanese blockade. He foresaw the dilemma of his squadron: that if he stayed in the Pacific he must ultimately run out of coal or be destroyed by the Singapore and Japanese squadrons. Instead, he chose to sail round Cape Horn, break through the Atlantic defences, and run for home through the North Sea. But Karl von Müller, captain of *Emden,* asked permission to raid in the Indian Ocean. Spee wrote: 'A single light cruiser can coal from captured vessels and maintain herself for longer . . . as there are great prizes to be won there, I despatched the fastest light cruiser.'

Heavily disguised, with a false funnel, *Emden* crept through the Sumatra channel and began her raiding career on 7th September by sinking nine ships in a week. When the news reached London it produced consternation and a steep rise in insurance rates; and Australia and New Zealand demanded a strong escort for the Anzac troop convoy. Nothing could be given because of the war office priority for the Indian convoys endangered by *Königsberg.* On 21st September Müller carried the war on to enemy territory and bombarded the city of Madras by night, setting fire to the great oil tanks and, by the light of the blaze, destroying the harbour installations. He then turned south and in the seas around Ceylon, impudently within range of the defences of Colombo, captured or sunk another ten merchant ships. Loss of confidence and prestige caused bitter questions – what was the Admiralty doing? Australia and New Zealand bluntly postponed the convoy for three weeks.

Emden did not strike again until mid-October – just when the convoy, with an escort, was ready, and at a time when the war in South Africa against the German-backed rebels under Christian de Wet was at its most dangerous. Several more sinkings preceded one of the boldest strokes of the war: Müller sailed into the harbour of Penang on the Malay peninsula and sank the Russian light cruiser *Zhemchug* and a French destroyer. Combined with the steady toll taken in the Atlantic by *Karlsruhe* and the armed liners, and Spee's attack on the French colony of Tahiti, the raiders were achieving their object of distracting the enemy. By the end of October they had captured or sunk more than forty Allied ships.

Karlsruhe alone had accounted for nearly 100,000 tons of shipping. She had nearly been caught by Admiral Cradock's squadron in the Caribbean in early August, but she refuelled from the armed liner *Kronprinz Wilhelm* and escaped to Puerto Rico with almost empty bunkers. But thereafter Captain Köhler could easily evade pursuit in his 27½-knot ship, as Cradock wearily traversed the mid-Atlantic. In concert with *Dresden* during August and September, the two raiders terrorized the waters off the coast of Brazil where all the trade routes to South America converged. They held up cargoes of frozen meat in Argentine ports and gave a strong stimulus to pro-German feeling among neutral Latin American countries.

Then Spee summoned *Dresden* to meet him in the Pacific, luring Cradock south and leaving the West Indies open to *Karlsruhe* – a chance which Köhler did not miss. He drew his information about the sailings of merchant vessels from German intelligence in Brazil, the Argentine, and Chile, and waited for them to arrive. Working with *Kronprinz Wilhelm* he sank twenty ships in late September, taking what he needed from their cargoes and coaling at sea.

The extent of this damage was only realized when he landed 400 prisoners, and the pursuit was not fully organized until 14th October, when Admiral Stoddart was given overall command of the mid- and North Atlantic and the modern cruiser *Defence.* But Köhler was warned in advance; he sank two more rich cargoes and turned north, planning a spectacular blow to Allied morale in the heart of the West Indies, by destroying Barbados and Forte de France in Martinique.

So far, the only British successes had been the sinking of two armed liners, *Kaiser Wilhelm der Grosse* on the African coast, and *Cap Trafalgar* (by another armed liner, the Cunard *Carmania*) which disrupted supplies of coal to *Karlsruhe.* In the Pacific, all the German bases had been captured by combined operations with the dominions and Japanese. But the main danger was the unknown, powerful squadron of Spee, of which Admiral Cradock, now commanding the South Atlantic, was more aware than the British Admiralty. No one could know that Spee had decided to bring his ships home, if possible, intact. If he passed Cape Horn, Cradock reasoned, he could attack Capetown or even cross to head off the Anzac convoy. It was this which led him, at loggerheads with the Admiralty, to seek out Spee on the Pacific coast – and to the disastrous battle of Coronel. The first British naval engagement for a century ended on 1st November in almost total disaster.

At once the strategic picture changed. Spee must be destroyed. Two battle-cruisers were withdrawn from Jellicoe's Grand Fleet and despatched with such urgency that the fitters were left on board. A great concentration took place off the Brazilian coast and a net of steel was stretched on either side of Cape Horn. The Japanese and Australian fleets cut off the retreat to the Pacific. The urgency of the war in Europe was at last transferred to the far seas and finally ended the careers of the raiders: only as a result of a major humiliation was Pohl's gloomy prophecy fulfilled.

End of the 'Swan of the East'

After two months of unparalleled havoc in the Indian Ocean, pursued by the game but ineffective Captain Grant in *Yarmouth,* *Emden*'s luck changed. Müller decided to attack the wireless station in the Cocos Islands to cut the trunk cables to Australia and South Africa, and ran straight into the path of the Anzac convoy which, heavily escorted, had at last left Perth. HMAS *Sydney,* under Captain Glossop, was detached in pursuit, and after a long running battle, Müller ran the ruined shell of *Emden,* the 'Swan of the East', on the coral

Karlsruhe – a daring and dangerous raider

Dresden, tracked down, shows the white flag

Survivors from the scuttled *Dresden,* with the Chilean sailors who picked them up

reefs of the Cocos Islands. He was taken prisoner and, in unusual recognition, allowed to keep his sword.

Captain Köhler was meanwhile steaming towards Barbados. With all the Atlantic warships to the south, nothing could have saved the unsuspecting colony, but on a clear day, for no known reason, *Karlsruhe* suddenly exploded and was torn in two, sinking at once with the loss of her captain and most of the crew. It was ironic that, on the same day, the German admiralty cabled: 'Return home, your work is done.'

The danger of armed liners was also largely over. They had been, at best, an extravagant form of raider, fast but requiring immense quantities of coal. An organization for supplying them existed, run by Captain Boy-Ed of the German embassy in Washington, but the British warships waiting outside US territorial waters were too great a deterrent and the majority were interned. Only *Kronprinz Wilhelm* had a successful raiding career, sinking in six months some 60,000 tons of shipping. But although her speed was 25 knots she had to spend valuable weeks coaling at sea from captured colliers and, after November, was largely disregarded by the British forces concentrating on the threat at Cape Horn.

On 9th December came the news of the battle of the Falkland Islands in which

H.M.A.S. "Sydney",
at sea,
9th November 1914.

Sir,

I have the honour to request that in the name of humanity you now surrender your ship to me. In order to show how much I appreciate your gallantry, I will recapitulate the position.

(1) You are ashore, 3 funnels and 1 mast down and most guns disabled.

(2) You cannot leave this island, and my ship is intact.

In the event of your surrendering in which I venture to remind you is no disgrace but rather your misfortune I will endeavour to do all I can for your sick and wounded and take them to a hospital.

I have the honour to be,
Sir,
Your obedient Servant,

John C.T. Glossop
Captain.

The Captain,
H.I.G.M.S. "Emden".

'Müller and *Emden* seemed romantic survivals in a world sliding rapidly into the ruthless realities of total war'

Top, left to right: The *Emden's* captain, Karl von Müller – 'quiet, withdrawn, lonely and conscientious', his chivalry and daring caught the imagination of the world; the letter from Captain Glossop requesting Müller to surrender his ship – sporting and polite, it reads rather like the winning captain's speech after a game of cricket; Captain John Glossop of HMAS *Sydney*; the *Sydney* immediately after action against the *Emden* – the latter's fourth salvo knocked out the *Sydney's* fire direction system, causing her to withdraw out of the *Emden's* range.
Below: The wreck of the *Emden* aground on a coral reef south of North Keeling Island – placed at a disadvantage by *Sydney's* greater range, her guns and torpedoes no longer operable, Müller decided that he should run her aground

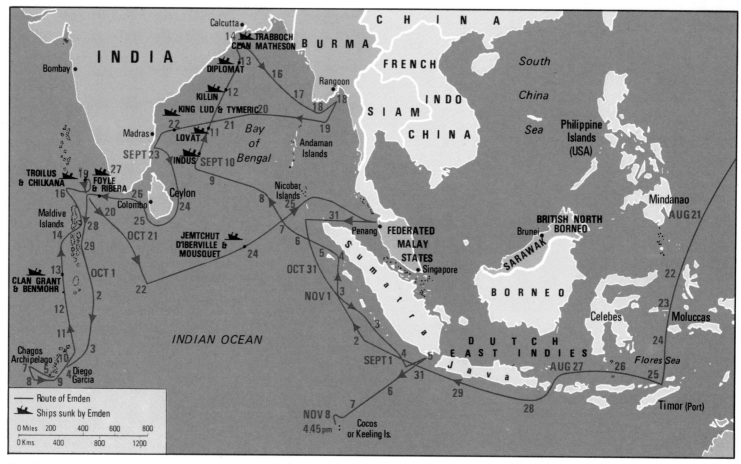

The map shows labels including:

Calcutta, TRABBOCH, CLAN MATHESON, CHINA, BURMA, INDIA, DIPLOMAT, Bombay, KILLIN, Rangoon, FRENCH, INDO, KING LUD & TYMERIC, SIAM, CHINA, South China Sea, Philippine Islands (USA), Madras, LOVAT, Bay of Bengal, SEPT 23, INDUS, SEPT 10, Andaman Islands, TROILUS & CHILKANA, FOYLE & RIBERA, Nicobar Islands, Mindanao, AUG 21, Maldive Islands, Colombo, Ceylon, OCT 21, JEMTCHUT D'IBERVILLE & MOUSQUET, Penang, FEDERATED MALAY STATES, BRITISH NORTH BORNEO, Brunei, SARAWAK, Singapore, BORNEO, CLAN GRANT & BENMOHR, OCT 1, INDIAN OCEAN, OCT 31, NOV 1, Celebes, Moluccas, Chagos Archipelago, Diego Garcia, DUTCH EAST INDIES, Java, Flores Sea, SEPT 1, AUG 27, Timor (Port), NOV 8 4.45pm, Cocos or Keeling Is.

Route of Emden
Ships sunk by Emden
0 Miles 200 400 600 800
0 Kms. 400 800 1200

The *Emden's* daring 30,000-mile cruise

The end of a glorious career – Emden, the 'Swan of the East', now a battered shell, on the coral reefs off the Cocos Islands

Admiral Sturdee destroyed the whole of Spee's squadron except the raider *Dresden*. This was, practically speaking, the end of the war in the far seas. *Dresden* escaped along the myriad inlets of the Chilean coast but remained a hunted vagrant, finally tracked down and scuttled at Juan Fernández. The German colliers still slipped out from Brazilian ports to supply *Kronprinz Wilhelm* and another armed liner, *Prinz Eitel Friedrich,* which had escaped before the battle of the Falklands. Between them they took eighteen merchant ships during the winter but in March, for lack of coal, unable to undertake the long voyage home, they both ran in to Newport harbour in the United States and were interned. Six months later the recall of Captain Boy-Ed was demanded by the American government. His activities probably did more to swing American opinion against Germany than to create any lasting advantage for German seapower.

Königsberg alone remained. After the successful raid on Zanzibar Captain Looff had returned to his secret base, charted before the war, in the intricate muddy channels of the Rufiji river in German East Africa where he was tracked down and bottled in by a strong British squadron commanded by Captain Drury-Lowe. But *Königsberg* was out of range and hidden behind the forests and mangrove swamps, while her men were entrenched in efficient land defences. Supplies reached them from the interior. One of the channels was blocked by sinking an old collier, but others were open: *Königsberg* posed a unique problem and tied down three modern cruisers.

Primitive aircraft brought by ship from Capetown were able to locate her, but tropical rain and heat made them unusable. Both sides settled down to stalemate and nothing happened until March, when the German admiralty sent the collier *Rubens* to refuel the raider and give Looff the chance to break for the open sea and return home. After circling the north of Scotland and running down past the Cape, *Rubens* was sunk within a day's sail of the Rufiji. Looff sent half his men inland to help General von Lettow-Vorbeck in the war on Lake Tanganyika and abandoned hope of escaping. But *Königsberg* was still indestructible. More aircraft were sent out, and finally two monitors – flat gun emplacements, drawing only five feet of water. In the first air-sea operation ever mounted they steamed up river, firing indirectly at *Königsberg*, the fall of shot spotted from the air. At the first attack they were withdrawn, severely damaged. But the Germans were short of ammunition and the next assault, a week later, succeeded. The last of the German raiders was left, a riddled hulk on a mosquito-plagued shore, nearly a year after the start of the war.

The daring of the privateers

The raiders inherited the tradition of 18th-century privateers. Their orders debarred them from attacking warships except in emergency. German planning of bases, supplies of coal, and repairs was as efficient as the scattered nature of her colonies and the benevolence of neutrals would allow. But because of reverses in Europe, there was no subsequent strategy except, at the end, the order for recall. Yet, in the North Sea, few of the raiders would have had a use comparable to their value abroad. Events called in question the whole conception of far seas strategy. The German cruisers were superior in speed and gunnery to their British counterparts. *Karlsruhe* could have taken on Cradock's whole squadron and escaped – and if Spee, instead of turning away to preserve his ships had sailed straight into Port Stanley itself, he would have caught a fleet half at anchor, and sunk or severely damaged some of the best units in the British fleet, 6,000 miles from a British port. The German admiralty seems to have been dominated by calculations of sheer number. If the staff really believed the cruisers were doomed, they could have sent them down in crippling attacks on troop convoys or even harbours like Hong Kong. **The courage and dash came from the raiders themselves not from Berlin.**

The war of movement took both sides by surprise. The effectiveness of the raiders, the daring of *Emden* and *Karlsruhe,* had not been foreseen. The needs of the army in Flanders overrode naval advice and it took Coronel to galvanize the British defences. Then the truth became clear: surface raiders had only a limited life. Submarines, two years later, were needed to bring Great Britain to the edge of starvation.

But the raiders meant something more. They pointed the contrast between war in the far seas and the struggles on the Western Front and the stagnation of embittered fleets facing each other across the North Sea. The raiders hit the headlines and the imagination. The gamekeeper's pursuit of the poacher did not. To German soldiers in Europe and in the snowbound trenches of the Russian Front the names of *Emden, Karlsruhe, Dresden,* and *Königsberg* brought pride and, above all, hope for the future.

THE BATTLE OF CORONEL

With the realisation in Whitehall that the German East Asiatic Squadron was heading for South America came a desperate concern for England's trade link with Argentina. At whatever cost, the East Asiatic Squadron must be prevented from destroying so vital a communication. *Below:* The German East Asiatic Squadron heads through the Pacific in stormy seas

At the outbreak of war German possessions in the Pacific were many and far-flung. They included the Marianas, the Carolines, the Marshall Islands, Bougainville in the Solomons, German New Guinea and the islands now known as New Ireland and New Britain which lie off that coast, and Samoa. Perhaps most important of all, there was the young and vigorous German colony in the Kiao-chow territory up in the Yellow Sea, grouped about its capital, the naval base of Tsingtao. From this base operated the ships of the German East Asiatic Squadron.

The composition of this squadron was well-known, and so was its reputation. In Whitehall it was recognised as a naval unit of compact strength, excellent morale and high efficiency, officered and led by sailors of character and experience. The information about it which Whitehall lacked, however, was in some ways the most important—the location of its principal ships and the intentions of the officer who commanded them all—and these vital facts were to remain largely matters of constant and rather harassed speculation in the minds of a number of important people, for the best part of three months.

One of the light cruisers of the squadron—SMS Emden—did in fact reveal her position much earlier than did the others, for she suddenly appeared in the Bay of Bengal upon a commerce-raiding cruise which paralysed trade in the area, thoroughly frightened business interests from Singapore to Ceylon, and compelled the admiration of all whose pockets, lives or sentiments were not immediately threatened by her activities.

But it was quickly evident that she was operating alone. The other ships of the squadron—SMS Scharnhorst, Gneisenau, Nürnberg and Leipzig—vanished into the limitless expanse of the Pacific, and although at intervals news would arrive of their sudden appearance at such places as Fanning and Christmas Islands, at Samoa and later off the French port of Papeete at

Tahiti, they vanished again long before British or Allied naval forces in the area could concentrate and bring them to action.

Then in the middle of October they arrived at Easter Island, and when the reports reached Whitehall the conclusion hardened that they were heading for South America and the co-operation of the German interests in Chile. This could hardly have come as much of a surprise to the Admiralty, for the alternative courses of action which faced the Commander-in-Chief of the East Asiatic Squadron, once Japan had entered the war on the Allied side, were not very attractive.

Whether it was a surprise or not, the fact remained that by the beginning of November a German force of considerable strength would be off the west coast of South America, and might shortly afterwards come around the Horn to the east coast. The damage it could then cause among the trade lanes bearing vital supplies of foodstuffs and war materials from the Plate might be so serious as to be fatal, for it was realised that England could be brought to the point of starvation and collapse in six weeks if her overseas trade was brought to a standstill. All the might of the Grand Fleet would be unable to save her in these circumstances.

At all costs, the ships of the German East Asiatic Squadron must be found and annihilated before they could bring about such a perilous situation.

But how—and by whom? For British forces in the area were very inadequate.

A single British cruiser
As the harsh afternoon glare softened into twilight on Saturday October 31, 1914, the slim, low-built shape of a British light cruiser slipped into Coronel Bay and anchored. Her sides were streaked with salt and rust; her boats, though seaworthy, showed signs of rough handling, and the bareness of her upperworks was not entirely due to war conditions. HMS Glasgow had come round the Horn from the Falk-

lands in weather which lived well up to its reputation, and had since been battling up and down the Chilean coast in gales which tossed her about like a piece of cork and swept away all fittings not voluntarily removed three months before. She had been hard worked since summer, and now she was battered—but her engines were still sound and her crew alert.

A boat sped away from her side and from the bridge Captain John Luce watched her go, reckoned the odds against them all once again and hoped that Lieutenant Hirst, the Fleet Intelligence Officer, who sat in the boat's sternsheets, would quickly send and collect his telegrams and return on board. Down in the wireless room, as Captain Luce well knew, his telegraphists were listening to the almost continuous, high-singing Telefunken signals which indicated the presence in the immediate vicinity of enemy ships, one call-sign in particular so dominant that he almost expected to see its user, SMS Leipzig, sliding into the bay alongside him.

And if the situation to seaward was ominous, it was not improved by conditions ashore. The strong German and pro-German element along the Chilean coast had already proved actively hostile and there was little doubt that someone in Coronel was at that very moment sending out the news that the Glasgow was in the bay. Thus if the efforts of Vice-Admiral Graf von Spee, Commander-in-Chief of the German East Asiatic Squadron, were directed towards cutting off the Glasgow from the other ships of her squadron, then his task was being greatly facilitated.

Altogether, Glasgow was in a tricky situation and Captain Luce was not the only one on board to appreciate it. In the wardroom there was speculation on the chances of getting to sea before the trap was sprung and—less immediately—cool consideration of the chances of battle even if they did manage to regain the Flag and join company with the armoured cruisers Monmouth and Good Hope and the armed mer-

chant cruiser *Otranto* which together formed the command of Rear-Admiral Sir Christopher Cradock.

Given half a chance, Cradock would fight —that was the general opinion, and despite the almost overwhelming power and efficiency of the enemy squadron, no one doubted that Cradock's course would be the correct one. From a purely practical point of view one telling hit on one of Spee's ships could wreck the squadron. There was no German base available for repairs, and a neutral port could only offer shelter for 24 hours, after which internment for ship and crew were automatic—leaving the rest of the squadron weak and unbalanced to run the gauntlet home.

About the ship the *Glasgow's* men worked steadily, making good gale damage, cleaning and re-oiling the guns, checking ammunition and trimming the coal bunkers, while all the time the Telefunken signals whined in the ears of the wireless telegraphists. Ashore Lieutenant Hirst talked long and urgently to official and unofficial members of the British service, and it was daylight before he completed his business and returned to the *Glasgow*, still with hours of work ahead of him. As he reached his cabin the anchor cable was already coming in, the little cruiser swinging free.

As they cleared the bay there was as yet no immediate sign of the enemy—not that the men aboard *Glasgow* need be unduly worried if it was to be a meeting with the *Leipzig* only, for, on paper at least, there was an exciting equality of strength between them. The *Glasgow* and *Leipzig* were light cruisers manned by long-service officers and men; they had been in commission for over two years and were thus presumably efficient in seamanship and gunnery, and both were armed with ten 4-inch guns. The German guns were in fact 4·1-inch, and some on board *Glasgow* were aware of the fact that these guns compared very favourably with the older British 6-inch guns. However, to offset this, *Glasgow* herself mounted two more

modern 6-inch guns which were reputed to have the range of the old 9-inch batteries.

Should the *Glasgow* and *Leipzig* meet then, there appeared the possibility of a single-ship action—but reflection revealed the possibility as slight. Unless the *Leipzig* actually forced an action, the *Glasgow* must first attend to other work and responsibilities—for her primary duty was to return to the Flag and deliver the telegrams and information. Quite possibly, in company with the armoured cruisers and the *Otranto,* a search might then be made for the *Leipzig* which, if successful, would undoubtedly be of fundamental importance, for every chance must be taken to reduce the strength of Admiral von Spee's command before the British and German squadrons met.

The *Glasgow* and *Leipzig* might be reckoned as equals, but the combined British ships in the locality were certainly no match for the crack squadron of the Imperial German Navy. The two German armoured cruisers *Scharnhorst* and *Gneisenau* by themselves would constitute an enormous menace to the heterogeneous collection of ships which composed the British squadron, for the German ships held superiority in speed and also in broadside weight and range. Add to them the light cruiser *Leipzig* and her two sister ships, the *Nürnberg* and *Dresden,* and the squadron under Admiral Graf von Spee's command became an admirably balanced— and modern—fighting force.

Only one hope

Against this force, the British had two elderly armoured cruisers (one of which had already been condemned as unfit for further service), one fairly modern light cruiser, and a converted merchantman.

One hope—and one hope only—seemed to exist for even an avoidance of overwhelming defeat, should the ships of the Royal Navy meet the East Asiatic Squadron in force. Somewhere to the south was the old battleship HMS *Canopus*—her

exact position was by no means certain— and perhaps with the help of her 12-inch guns the German cruisers could be fought off. But even this was a slim chance, for the guns aboard *Canopus* were as old as herself, and although she had now been for some weeks under Admiral Cradock's command, he had been able to hold only one hurried conference with her commander, for the *Canopus* had arrived at the Falklands on the morning of the day the rest of the squadron must leave. That conference, however, had been enough to convince Cradock that the *Canopus's* engines were in such a state of disrepair that the voyage down from the Mediterranean had practically crippled them, and that a hasty overhaul at Port Stanley would be essential in order to get the battleship around the Horn.

But if Cradock couldn't wait for the *Canopus* perhaps the battle would—should Fate prove kind. It was at least arguable that Spee would keep his distance if her four 12-inch guns were present in the British battle-line.

However, if the *Glasgow, Monmouth* and *Good Hope* could catch isolated units of Spee's command and thus deal with it piecemeal, then the whole strategic situation in the Southern Seas might be successfully dealt with.

But it seemed rather a lot to hope for.

At sea again, the *Glasgow* steered first north and then Captain Luce took his ship around to the south-west, plunging ahead into wind and a rising sea as fast as the engines would take her, in order to deliver the telegrams and naval intelligence into Cradock's hands without breaking wireless silence. Seas swept the foredeck and the wind sang in the signal halliards.

Four hours later the *Glasgow* rejoined the Flag some 40 miles west of Coronel Bay. The *Good Hope* and *Monmouth* were there, rolling like barrels in the heavy seas, and the *Otranto* developed a list whenever she came broadside to the wind. There was no sign of the *Canopus*.

Below: The German light cruiser, SMS *Nürnberg.* In a state of sad disrepair, she nevertheless played an important part in the battle

The seas were far too heavy for boatwork, so the *Glasgow* towed a cask containing the vital papers across the *Good Hope's* bows—and in the ruling weather conditions she was both extremely lucky and extremely adept, for the manoeuvre was immediately successful. It was also to some effect, for by two o'clock a string of signals was fluttering from the *Good Hope's* halliards and Captain Luce's appreciation of the situation was confirmed.

The squadron were to form line abreast, about 15 miles apart, with the *Good Hope* to the west and the *Glasgow* to the east of the line, and sweep north-west by north at ten knots. The signals preceded by the *Leipzig's* call-sign bleated loud through the dull-grey afternoon, and Cradock had decided that she was to be found and annihilated before the heavy might of the German armoured cruisers could come to her protection. For this task the guns of the *Canopus* would not be necessary.

The squadron spread out—cold, wet, and pitching now on the steep following sea. The *Good Hope,* carrying the Admiral aboard, treasuring the honour and reputation of the Royal Navy above all else; the *Monmouth,* with her crew of Scottish fishermen and coastguards, her 12 young naval cadets fresh from Dartmouth, and her outdated engines kept going only by the superhuman efforts of Engineer-Commander Wilshin and his staff; the *Otranto* looming out of the tumbled seas; the *Glasgow* plunging on, grim and hardbitten. Officers and men with enough experience to cause

them misgivings kept them to themselves.

It was part of the pattern of that day that the *Glasgow* should see the smoke first. She reported it to the Flag and moved off to starboard to investigate, with the *Otranto* still in company (for the sweep line had not yet formed) and the *Monmouth* only four miles astern. The cloud grew wider as it came up over the horizon, and as the *Glasgow* approached it, it was seen to have three stems. By 1625 hours the *Scharnhorst* and *Gneisenau* were recognisable, and astern of the armoured cruisers came the *Leipzig* whose signals had baited the trap. The *Glasgow* steamed nearer to establish the course, while, incredibly, the enemy squadron remained apparently unaware of her presence.

Then at 1630 hours black smoke belched from the German funnels as Spee ordered full steam for a chase, and the *Glasgow* turned to race back towards the Flag. Immediately she turned, her telegraphists were deafened by the scream in their earphones as German keyboards jammed her signals—but by 1645 hours Cradock knew that the meeting he had long anticipated was at hand, and he also knew the strength of the enemy force in sight and their course. He ordered concentration on the *Glasgow* and formation of the battle-line, and at 1710 hours on that grey, squall-swept Sunday afternoon the British ships were together and turning.

At this moment the armoured strength of the opposing force was nearly 15 miles away, and the German squadron had yet

more units detached. For the British ships —even against such preponderant strength —it might still be possible to attain some success if conditions of wind and sea could be used to advantage, and with this in mind the British line was formed by 1730 hours and was driving south-east across the rising sea—the *Good Hope* leading, then the *Monmouth, Glasgow* and the huge, lumbering, thin-skinned *Otranto*—in an effort to secure the inshore position. Once there the wind would blow the British smoke clear of the guns while at the same time it would blanket the *Scharnhorst's* black pall across the German gun-sights.

The race is lost
There was even a chance that if the British could win through to this position, they might, whilst doing so, execute the classic naval manoeuvre of crossing the enemy's 'T', and at the moment of passing thus bring their whole broadside weight to bear upon the *Scharnhorst* at a time when she could only reply with her foredeck guns and be masking those of her consort. But by 1745 hours the hopes were falling. The gap between the squadrons had narrowed— and Spee's ships were working up to 20 knots whilst *Otranto* was holding the British back to 15; she was almost as much of a drag as the *Canopus* would have been, without the possible compensation of 12-inch guns.

By 1750 hours it was evident that the race was lost.

At 1800 hours Admiral Cradock ordered

Below: SMS *Gneisenau* and SMS *Scharnhorst* (four funnels), SMS *Nürnberg* (right, in background) and SMS *Dresden* (three funnels) with vessels of the Chilean Navy at Valparaiso after their action at Coronel

a turn away to the south—they were then four points to starboard of an enemy who obviously had both the intention and speed to keep them there; for the Germans a battle in line, broadside pounding against broadside, held every advantage.

But there were still some benefits to be obtained from factors of light and wind. The clouds were broken and the sun was sinking. If the British could close the range with the setting sun behind them, it would serve to blind the German gun-layers whilst at the same time lighting up the German ships into perfect targets. Somehow Cradock must close until the *Monmouth's* old 6-inch guns—and perhaps even *Glasgow's* puny 4-inch armament—could inflict damage, for at long range there were only the *Good Hope's* two 9·2-inch guns to battle it out with twelve 8·2-inch guns which the *Scharnhorst* and *Gneisenau* could bring to bear—although possibly the *Glasgow's* modern 6-inch guns might be able to play some part.

At 1804 hours then, the admiral ordered each of his ships to turn four points towards the enemy, and in line abreast they steamed towards them.

Spee turned his squadron away and kept his distance. He was not ready to come to action yet.

Thwarted, and to ease the labours of his battling squadron, Cradock turned back to a southerly course, reformed his battle-line and grimly watched the strength arraying itself against him. The *Leipzig* had closed up and the *Dresden* was now

racing in over the horizon only a mile astern of her; doubtless the *Nürnberg* would soon arrive. The two lines were separated by 18,000 yards of water.

To the west the British line still rolled until their maindeck guns were awash and spray drenched telescopes and gunsights, encrusting them with salt: the *Good Hope, Monmouth, Glasgow, Otranto*—for what use a merchantman would be in a naval battle.

To the east steamed the Germans: the *Scharnhorst, Gneisenau, Leipzig, Dresden.* Their guns were high above the waterline, their equipment was dry.

The scene was set, but hardly for a battle. Only a miracle could avert a massacre. Two old armoured cruisers, one light cruiser and one armed merchantman were pitted against two modern armoured cruisers with two, and perhaps three, light cruisers. Two British 9·2-inch guns and two 6-inch guns had to answer at long range twelve 8·2-inch guns. Even at short range the odds were not appreciably less, for the Germans fired a broadside of 3,812 pounds against the British 2,815.

Most significant of all—and most tragic—against some 2,200 fully trained, long-service German sailors who were reckoned among the most efficient in the Imperial German Navy, were to fight a similar number of Britons the vast majority of whom had been happily pursuing civilian vocations less than six months before, and who now had little more than their pride and their courage to give them confidence.

But they had their admiral—and whether

he was brave or quixotic, resolute or reck-less, impelled by honourable motives or by incredible stupidity, it seems that Sir Christopher Cradock had their hearts. When at 1818 hours he wirelessed to the *Canopus*, still trudging up through the seas over two hundred and fifty miles away to the south 'I am going to attack the enemy now!' they cheered him as their fore-fathers at Trafalgar had cheered 109 years before, drifting down on to the Franco-Spanish crescent.

From the *Good Hope's* masthead flut-tered the battle-ensign, and from her halliards the signal 'Follow in the admiral's wake'. Carefully, imperceptibly, the British line edged in towards the enemy, striving for a converging course, hoping to close the range.

Five minutes later, the *Scharnhorst* led the German line away one point to the eastward and the lines were parallel again. From the British decks men watched across the grey waste in silence and grim resolve.

The scene was now one of ominous clarity. The *Scharnhorst* and *Gneisenau* rode powerfully over the seas, the details of their heavy armament picked out by the sun, the seas racing along the towering sides and occasionally sweeping the fore-decks. Behind the armoured ships came the light cruisers, crashing through the seas with only their upper-deck guns workable: it was some slight consolation to the British to know that at least the weaker units of the enemy force suffered the same discomforts as themselves.

Right: Rear-Admiral Sir Christopher Cradock, who was responsible for keeping the North and South Atlantic sea lanes open for British trading. He was defeated at the Battle of Coronel by a squadron headed by Admiral von Spee and went down with his flagship, the *Good Hope* (shown above). The *Good Hope* was finally brought to a halt when both the *Scharnhorst* and *Gneisenau* opened fire upon her with full broadsides. The explosion which followed almost an hour later lived for years in the memories of those who witnessed it

For another half-hour the two battle-lines plunged southwards in parallel lines at about 16 knots – the highest speed of which the *Otranto* was capable. Then, behind the British, the sun's rim touched the horizon, and as it slid down to become first a semi-circle and then a gradually diminishing segment the light conditions began to change.

Evening crept over the sea from the east and touched the German battle-line, greying it into the sea and the sky beyond. As twilight thickened, the moon came up behind heavy clouds to show fleetingly through them, briefly outlining the German ships – and now it seemed that the *Scharnhorst* and *Gneisenau* were closing in. Spee was edging forward. To the west, the afterglow of the sun made a fiery, yellow-shot tapestry of the windswept sky against which the British ships stood out in black, hard-edged relief; nothing would help them tonight but their courage and their pride in the long tradition of the Royal Navy.

Outranged and outgunned
At 1902 hours on Sunday November 1, the 8·2-inch guns of the German East Asiatic Squadron at last opened fire upon the British ships, at a range of 12,000 yards.

From the bridge of the *Glasgow* were seen two orange flashes from the *Scharnhorst* and *Gneisenau*, and as the thunder of *Good Hope's* 9·2s answered, grey-white mushrooms blossomed from the sea five hundred yards short of the British flagship, beautifully aimed, beautifully grouped.

The *Glasgow's* pair of modern 6-inch guns fired experimentally into the darkness, but even while the gunnery-control officer was vainly searching the east for some sign of fall of shot, the orange lines sparkled again and then again – and the lines were lengthened now as the *Leipzig* and *Dresden* also opened fire. For a few more brief seconds, only the crash of the seas and the sounds of their own movements were heard by the *Glasgow's* crew – then shell splinters whined shrilly overhead, the seas erupted around them, the *Monmouth* ahead steamed through a forest of water, and the *Good Hope's* foredeck exploded in a sheet of flame, which twisted

the fore 9·2-inch gun into a hopeless, useless knot of steel protruding from a turret like a blazing cauldron.

Before the mind could react, the next salvo arrived.

The *Monmouth's* foredeck flared up in hard-edged flame and black smoke billowed from sudden, sharp fires along her port side. As she rolled, her gun-crews fought with their guns – still hopelessly outranged by the German guns which now straddled the British line along its length, filling the night with screaming shells and the vicious irritating whine of splinters. The *Good Hope's* deck amidships threw up a fan of sparks, her upper bridge, masthead and foretop glowed redly as high-explosive shell from the *Scharnhorst* burst against them, then the glow died as cordite flared on the deck below, and ammunition exploded whitely along the gun-deck.

Alongside the looming *Otranto*, water spouted up to reach her deck level. She drew out of line on the *Glasgow's* port quarter, and as her huge bulk made an excellent ranging device for the enemy her captain took her away to the westward – though not before she had been neatly straddled by three shells from the *Gneisenau*, whose marksmanship was upholding her claim to the Kaiser's Gold Cup for gunnery. One of the minor miracles of the day was the *Otranto's* unscathed departure from the line.

Now the action was at its thickest. With the early loss of the *Good Hope's* fore 9·2-inch gun the British chances of harming the enemy at anything but short range had been halved – and with no alternative, Cradock led across the shell-torn seas to bring the 6-inch guns of the flagship and *Monmouth* into action. The after 9·2-inch still fired – once a minute – but its noise and flame were lost amid the holocaust which raged around it, for ammunition blazed fiercely and fire was already spreading through the flagship's decks below.

Still they plunged across towards the German line, still the shells crashed into them and still flame scoured the decks. Then both the *Good Hope* and *Monmouth* turned broadside to their antagonists and the port 6-inch batteries burst into action. Hope and feverish activity galvanized the

gun-crews; salvo after salvo thundered from the gun-decks.

Abruptly, the *Gneisenau's* guns shortened range, one of her high-explosive shells hit the *Monmouth's* fore-turret, blew off the roof and burnt out the housing. As flames licked up out of the steel shell, a violent explosion shattered the forecastle and when its anger died no sign of gun or turret remained.

Then, ominously, the *Monmouth's* ports glowed redly in the gathering darkness as burning cordite turned the narrow confines of her mess decks into a choking hell. Still the *Gneisenau's* shells crashed through her decks and exploded with sickening violence amid the shambles below. An armour-piercing shell came through the body of the ship and exploded among ammunition stacked for the starboard battery, a curtain of flame spread upwards along the starboard side, outlining the upperworks in black, and twisting, tortured debris cartwheeled away into the night.

As though beaten out of line by sheer weight of metal, the *Monmouth* began to sag away to starboard, losing speed as she did so until the *Glasgow*, still punching up through the seas astern of her, had to drop away in order to avoid masking her still-defiant, though now sporadic fire; in order, too, to avoid entering the zone of fire still laid down by the indefatigable German gunners. Again the shells found the *Monmouth*. Flames burst out on her quarter-deck, she listed heavily to port, her head was lower and her fire slackened. Heavy seas flooded through gaping bows and dragged her away from the line – but she was not yet beaten, and to those on board the *Glasgow* who could spare her a glance it looked at this time as though she was having some success in overcoming the fires within, which now sulked dully.

But she never rejoined the line, and as time passed her guns lapsed into silence.

All that could now be seen of the enemy were the flashes from the batteries.

Not so the *Good Hope*. She flared like a beacon. Since action had commenced the British flagship had received the undivided attention of the gunners aboard *Scharnhorst* who had first hit her with their third salvo, and who since then had been firing at her, coolly and extremely competently, at a rate of nearly four salvoes every minute. By 1923 hours the range was down to 6,600 yards.

Burning but defiant
On through the raging and shell-torn sea, Cradock held the converging course – so steadily, in fact, that Spee began to suspect a torpedo attack and edged off another point to eastward. Still the shells crashed into the *Good Hope*, ripping away her decks and bulkheads, bursting in the crowded flats, spreading fire and chaos through her riven hull: still, stubbornly, she pushed on through the waves, her port 6-inch battery defiant, but firing slowly and spasmodically now as gun-crews perished in the consuming flames or were cut down by flying steel. At 1940 hours she seemed to slow and the clouds of steam and smoke which billowed around her glowed sullenly – but she still was moving towards the enemy.

A sheet of flame played continuously along her sides upon which the seas had no effect. She might roll until her casemates were awash but as she heaved herself up again the flames flickered weirdly between the waterline and the deckrail.

At 1942 hours the *Good Hope* seemed to gather up all her remaining strength, turn directly towards her tormentors and charge them. Firing as she went, she heaved her stricken weight over the mounting seas trailing flame and wreathing clouds behind her—and as Spee ordered his ships out of her course there was for a few brief moments a pause in her agony. Then abruptly both the *Scharnhorst* and *Gneisenau* opened fire upon her with full broadsides. Blanketed under a dreadful fire, she was at last brought to a halt with her upper deck a sea of flame, and her last desperate throw defeated.

As though stunned, she drifted down silently between the lines.

Then the fires reached a main magazine and at 1953 hours—50 minutes after the first salvo had been fired at her—the *Good Hope* was shattered by an explosion which lived for years in the memories of those who witnessed it. A broad column of flame rose upwards from between her main and aftermost funnel until it towered two hundred feet above her decks, and in its awful light jagged and incongruous shapes soared up and away into the darkness, twisting and weaving in the blast, tumbling in the sudden vacuums.

Then the column of fire broke, flooding outwards at its base to wash along the decks and fill the gutted hull with lazy waves of fire. Debris crashed down into the sea, the whole mass of the forepart of the ship silently detached itself and slid down into oblivion, and, incredibly, two 6-inch guns of the port aft battery each fired twice into the darkness.

Then the waves took the blazing hulk further off into the darkness, the flames sulked, the pall above glowed luridly, and all that remained of Admiral Sir Christopher Cradock and his men drifted out of the battle.

And, for the moment, the battle was done.

The *Glasgow* had borne a charmed life. Circumstances had also added a most bizarre note to the atmosphere in which she played her part in the battle, for at the outbreak of war her commission on the South American station had been almost complete and many of her complement had acquired parrots to take home to England. When action became inevitable, these birds—some 60 of them—were released from their cages and given a chance to escape to the mainland. They rose in a cloud of brilliant blues and greens and oranges, then, unwilling to risk the rising power of the gale, they all settled back on the *Glasgow's* upperworks and remained there despite all attempts to scare them away.

When the first salvoes thundered out, they rose again, cawing and screaming, but as the battle wore on they gradually ceased their protests and returned to the ship, clinging drunkenly to stays and yards until either violent movement or their own failing strength loosened their hold. As the action progressed so their numbers fell, and only ten were eventually recovered.

Incredibly, this loss of the parrots was almost the heaviest casualty sustained by the cruiser. It was afterwards estimated that some 600 shells were fired at the *Glasgow,* but some protecting fate guarded her from all except five, of which three lodged harmlessly in her coal bunkers, one entered and broke up against a conning-tower support without exploding (though it wrecked the captain's pantry), and another burst aft, just above the port outer propeller, and tore an irregular hole in the ship's side just as though she had been rammed. It flooded one compartment but did nothing to affect the *Glasgow's* steaming abilities.

Fury and desperation

In return, the *Glasgow* had engaged both the *Leipzig* and the *Dresden* for the major part of the battle and at the end, in fury and desperation, she had taken on the *Gneisenau* and *Scharnhorst* and even hit the latter ship with one of her puny 4-inch shells, which, however, apparently exhausted itself on the journey and failed to explode on arrival. But with the *Good Hope* and *Monmouth* out of the fight, every time the *Glasgow* fired the whole enemy line answered and she steamed through chaos.

At 2030 hours, with the *Good Hope* gone and the enemy invisible, Captain Luce ordered cease fire, and then took his ship around to the west to find, and offer succour to, the *Monmouth.* When he found her, the badly battered cruiser was listing and her head was still down, but her upper decks were no longer aflame and only the portholes below the quarterdeck still glowed.

The tragedy, however, was not yet ended.

As the *Glasgow* bore up to render what assistance she could, the moon made one of its rare appearances to light up a tumultuous sea, the two ships—and four enemy ships sweeping in search of them. If the *Monmouth* could turn her stern to sea she might last, and if she could hold the northwest course she might, by the grace of God, keep clear of the German line—and perhaps even limp as far as the Chilean coast; but the *Glasgow* must leave her or perish.

She signalled to the *Monmouth* twice, passed close under her stern, and, with misery aboard at the thought of the compulsory desertion, steamed west and away into the darkness. The *Glasgow,* alone among the British squadron, had speed, and it was soon evident that she must have shaken off any pursuit and was free to turn south to race after the *Otranto* for the Magellan Straits, her wireless at last clear of the enemy attempts to jam it and able to tell the dreadful story to the *Canopus,* still labouring up miles to the south.

A column of smoke

For a time there was hope that the *Monmouth* had eluded the enemy and was limping towards some sort of safety. But at 2100 hours firing broke out again to the north, and with ice in their hearts the men aboard *Glasgow* counted the gun-flashes and watched a searchlight stretch its pallid fingers over the horizon. The *Nürnberg* had found her.

Captain von Schönberg had known from the moment he received the first signal ordering formation of the battle-line that his chances of getting *Nürnberg* into position were extremely remote. Her boilers were in sad need of repair, her engines of replacement, and her port propeller of two new blades—so, despite the eagerness with which he and his officers might stare into the torn, growling darkness ahead, he knew that their hopes of adding to the tumult were small. The wind from the south howled through the stays, the seas swept the forecastle and flooded the conning-tower—and the *Nürnberg* pile-drove through them in an effort to reach the battle.

Then came the explosion—and apparently the end—and although much relief was felt when wireless signals indicated the highly satisfactory result, there was some disappointment and dissatisfaction at the rôle of spectator which the *Nürnberg* had played.

Then at 2035 hours the look-out reported a column of smoke on the starboard bow, for which Schönberg at once steered. Apparently the smoke must have been made by the *Glasgow,* for although no mention is made of the *Nürnberg* in Captain Luce's report, Schönberg chased the British ship until she disappeared from sight, her speed taking her rapidly over the horizon.

As the *Nürnberg* turned back towards the ships of her squadron, Schönberg saw the *Monmouth* against the light of the moon. The armoured cruiser was listing, but she was undoubtedly under way.

At first Schönberg thought that he had come across one of the ships of his own squadron, so he bore down on her from the south-west, making the agreed recognition signal and passing close to port. There was no reply, but not wishing to harm a friend, he closed in and switched on his searchlight. It picked out first the white ensign—still flying—then the details of the torn and shattered hull, then the working-parties scurrying about the decks. Foam threshed under her stern; the *Monmouth* was making progress.

In fairness to Schönberg it must be stated that he gave the *Monmouth* every chance to haul down her flag. He waited some minutes before opening fire, his searchlight still pointedly illuminating the white ensign from some 600 yards away. His first salvoes were from 4-inch guns aimed high, and although, when this brought about no lowering of the flag, he fired a torpedo at the *Monmouth,* he was not upset when it failed to explode on the hull, having possibly passed underneath the rolling ship.

He then ceased fire and waited for *Monmouth's* next move. It was not long in coming. She seemed to gather speed and begin to turn—and two of Schönberg's officers on deck heard instructions shouted from the *Monmouth's* bridge ordering the men back to the guns from their tasks about the ship. Either the intention was to ram *Nürnberg,* or turn to bring the starboard guns to bear on her.

There is no need to doubt the regret with which Schönberg states he then acted, but unless the *Monmouth* hauled down her flag, his course—his duty—was obvious. As the *Monmouth* circled, so did the *Nürnberg* —at twice the speed—and as the German light cruiser came round close under the *Monmouth's* stern, she opened fire on the unprotected part of her hull, tearing it open and ripping the decks apart. Under the onslaught, the *Monmouth* shuddered and listed over further and further. The seas washed up to the port deck-rail, then across to flood around the funnels.

Slowly, still under a hail of shell, *Monmouth* leaned completely over and capsized. At 2158 hours the waters closed above her stern—from which her flag had flown until the end.

BATTLE OF TH

With the arrival of the British squadron in Port Stanley, the strategic situation in the South Atlantic was reversed. But the British Commander-in-Chief, Sir Frederick Doveton Sturdee, still faced a difficult problem: where was Admiral von Spee? At dawn on December 8 he was informed by a lookout

It was 0735 hours on the morning of Tuesday December 8, 1914, when the lookout on Sapper Hill, the best vantage point in the Falkland Islands, first noticed the smudge of smoke on the horizon which heralded the approach of German warships.

No doubt he was desperately pleased that after the fear of waiting through the previous three weeks, during which the islands' population had been defended only by the old battleship *Canopus,* there now lay at anchor in the two harbours behind him a force of British ships big enough, fast enough and sufficiently powerfully gunned to take on all the naval might that the Imperial German Navy could conceivably send against them in those waters. Although a Scandinavian, and therefore strictly an impartial neutral, the lookout must surely have felt a certain inner satis-

faction as he picked up the telephone to set into action the defence of his temporary homeland, by reporting to the *Canopus:* 'A four funnel and a two funnel man-of-war in sight steering northwards.'

But as far as the British squadron was concerned the Germans could hardly have arrived at a more inconvenient time. Having sailed his ships into the harbour on only the previous day, Vice-Admiral Sir Frederick Doveton Sturdee was not planning to put to sea again until that evening, and his ships were in various stages of preparation for what he thought would be an extended chase. The only vessel under way was the tiny armed merchantman *Macedonia,* patrolling off the islands in course of relief by the cruiser *Kent.* Of the others, the two battle-cruisers, *Invincible* and *Inflexible,* were in

the early stages of coaling, and in addition to having taken on only 400 tons each: both would take some two hours to cast off the colliers and work up steam to leave the harbour. The light cruiser *Glasgow* had in fact finished coaling, but as she was in the middle of repairing machinery, she also would require at least two hours to raise steam. The month-long voyage from Europe had also impaired the efficiency of the light cruiser *Bristol,* and to give the engineers ample opportunity to effect repairs, she had both her engines opened up and would not be fit to sail for some three and a half hours. Of the three armoured cruisers, *Cornwall* and *Kent* had not even begun coaling, whereas the *Carnarvon,* ironically enough, was if anything over-ready. Having finished the necessary fuelling, her decks were covered in stacked coal for an

Below: The battle-cruiser HMS *Invincible* flying Admiral Sturdee's flag off the Falkland Islands

that two German warships had been sighted. Luck as well as careful planning had brought the two great forces together. Admiral Sturdee received the message calmly and only after he had made sure that his men had breakfasted gave the order for 'Action'

extended cruise, and this, in the event of enemy action, could prove extremely dangerous to the ship's personnel.

Nor was the mechanical condition of the ships the only indication of their state of preparedness. From where the *Canopus* lay in her mud berth, it was impossible to communicate directly with the flagship *Invincible,* coaling in the outer Port William harbour, and the officers on the *Canopus* therefore passed the message on to the *Glasgow,* which was conveniently placed in visual contact with both the *Invincible* and the *Canopus.* But the *Glasgow's* signalling lamp was either not noticed or not read through the cloud of coal dust rising from the *Invincible,* and for five minutes there was no acknowledgement. Five minutes was long enough for the German ships, sailing at their best

speed, to be two miles closer to the base than when first spotted. Finally it was the captain of the *Glasgow,* John Luce, who applied his wits to the problem and ordered a gun to be fired. The report of the *Glasgow's* 3-pounder attracted attention on the *Invincible* and the flag lieutenant raced down to the admiral's cabin. It was already 0800 hours.

Various minor legends have grown up around the situation in that cabin—that Sturdee was in his bath; or shaving; or still in his pyjamas; that he remarked with a calm imperturbability in the true Drake tradition 'Then send the men to breakfast'. In fact, this order carried less of the aristocratic disdain of imminent danger than is at first apparent. For excepting the stokers and engineers, who were concerned in raising steam, the crew were

better employed in filling their stomachs than in getting to battle stations too early and sitting around becoming progressively more tense while waiting for the action to start. At any rate, all ships were ordered to prepare to weigh anchor, and at 0830 hours the order 'Action' was at last given.

Inevitable confusion

It was a pity, for the Germans that they could not know, or did not guess, the true state of readiness of the British squadron. With gunnery of the high standard displayed at the Battle of Coronel, and with a measure of determination, Spee's best course might well have been to attack before the enemy ships could gain room to manoeuvre on the open sea, cause as much damage as he could in the shortest possible time, and make off,

leaving the British to sort out the inevitable confusion before they could give chase.

But that would be presuming clairvoyancy on the part of the Germans. The course they in fact adopted was the natural reaction to the situation as they saw it.

Shortly after 0800 hours the two ships concerned in the first phase of the attack on the Falklands, the *Gneisenau* and the *Nürnberg*, came within sight of land. In the far distance, and well out of gunnery range, the crews could see the tall masts of the wireless station. It was a clear, calm morning, with exceptional visibility, and only the slightest rustle of a breeze on the surface of the sea. Soon the long, low promontory of land came into view, stretching out to the east and masking the harbour. Then other, unexpected features appeared. First, from the end of that promontory, near the Cape Pembroke lighthouse, a tall column of smoke rose up, moving from right to left as they approached it, that is from east to west, and in the direction of the harbour. It was 0840 hours. Then from the control top of the *Gneisenau's* foremast the gunnery officer, Lieutenant-Commander Johann Busche, fancied he saw through his binoculars the large tripod masts of a battle-cruiser. A battle-cruiser! It must have been a devastating moment. As he peered for confirmation, the masts were obscured by a vast cloud of smoke. Was it the English burning their coal stocks? Or was it, perhaps, the smoke from a ship using oil fuel to work up a head of steam in a hurry? Shortly, the masts became visible again. At ten miles, it was difficult to tell what they were, but as the moments progressed the evidence began to accumulate, and in Busche's mind the truth gradually began to dawn. First there were two masts, then six, then another two. And the biggest of them were very big, tall tripod masts, four of them, and that could only mean two battleships or battle-cruisers, either of which would be an insuperable foe for the German squadron. When Busche transmitted the news down to the bridge, he was told rather impatiently by his commander, Captain Maerker, that there were no battle-cruisers nearer than the Mediterranean. Even so, as the *Gneisenau* and the *Nürnberg* steamed steadily towards Cape Pembroke, the news that there were warships in the harbour, as yet unidentified, was tapped out by wireless to Spee in the *Scharnhorst*, lurking over the horizon. For the moment, Spee did nothing, and for a few still, almost ephemeral minutes the *status quo* was maintained. It changed suddenly at 0920 hours when the *Gneisenau* was subjected to the first shot of the day. It landed short, but Maerker wasted no time in turning through 90 degrees to evade the next salvo, and making off to the south-east. In fact the old battleship *Canopus* had enjoyed the distinction of firing the first shells. Two of its initial salvo of four were practice shells, loaded the night before by a keen gun-crew for a practice shoot planned for 0900 hours that morning, and it was one of these which ricocheted off the water and hit the base of the *Gneisenau's* funnel, causing Maerker to change his mind about the attack. After ten minutes of flight to the south-east, Maerker turned his two ships again on to a north-easterly course, but after steaming for seven minutes in that direction he received orders from Spee at 0937 hours

to close with the rest of the fleet, and turned once more to the south-east, away from Cape Pembroke. The Germans were on the run.

Brisk and efficient
Within a few more minutes, at 0940 hours, the British ships began to move out of the harbour. The armoured cruiser *Kent* had already been ordered out to replace the armed merchantman *Macedonia*, which was in fact the vessel whose smoke the Germans had first noted. The *Glasgow*, a brisk and efficient light cruiser, was next to leave, and set off in pursuit of Spee's squadron right away, with the task of keeping in touch and reporting back enemy movements, until the more powerful ships had caught up. At 0950 hours the big ships began to leave the harbour, first the *Carnarvon,* followed by the *Inflexible, Invincible* and *Cornwall* in that order. The *Macedonia* was to remain behind. By 1030

Above: Vice-Admiral Sir Frederick Doveton Sturdee. Fisher was his foremost critic

hours the last of the line had threaded its way through the mines laid down by *Canopus,* and all were straining to comply with the exciting signal flown from the *Invincible* – 'General Chase'.

The pursuit was on.

Among the most disappointed men that morning were surely the stokers of the *Canopus* herself. When the enemy appeared, they had climbed into the rigging of their ship, anticipating a spectacular view of their colleagues annihilating the enemy. And what a sight they were promised. As Englishmen, they surely revelled in the prospect of a quick and convincing victory, before going down to lunch secure in the knowledge that those southern seas were rid for ever of the threat from the East Asiatic Squadron. On paper, their original optimism was fully justified, as an examination of the number, size and strength of ships shows.

It is evident that not only were all the British ships able to outpace the German ships so long as the latter stayed together but even if the slower *Leipzig* were detached the British could still catch and fight the two German armoured cruisers with at least their two battle-cruisers and the light cruiser *Glasgow,* while the re-

mainder dealt with the *Leipzig*. In whatever permutation Spee combined or detached his ships, the British still had ample strength and speed to overwhelm him. Most important, the power of the gunnery was tipped heavily in the Royal Navy's favour.

It was perhaps this overwhelming superiority of numbers and armament that dissuaded Sturdee from being hasty. For a time, he pressed on at 26 knots, and rapidly gained on the Germans, who had by this time joined forces again and were steaming due east, but between 1048 and 1115 hours he ordered two reductions of speed, to give his slower ships time to catch up and to clear the cloud of smoke that hampered his gunnery controller's vision. By now the Germans had been able to evaluate the strength of their pursuers, and see and confirm that these were battle-cruisers, stronger and faster by far than their own vessels. If they were to have any chance of escape that day, it would be into the mists and fogs and storm haze that appear so frequently and with so little warning in that corner of the South Atlantic. Already nearly three hours had passed since they first realised that they were opposed. At the moment the skies were still clear and visibility was good – damnably good: but how long would that last? If the normal course of a day's weather were a true guide, their chances of escaping to safety increased with every minute in which the British stayed out of gunnery range. At 1122 hours Spee decided that he had gone for long enough to the east, turned a few points to starboard, and steamed off to the south-east. The British followed suit, and both squadrons were again on parallel course. Another hour passed, during which Sturdee, held back to 18 knots by the speed of his slower ships, failed to gain on the Germans. At last, however, with half the day gone, and half a day gained by the Germans in their effort to play for time, Sturdee reverted to his former policy, to the relief of his fellow officers, and ordered the two battle-cruisers to put on speed to 26 knots. For the time being, they would have to work without the armoured cruisers *Carnarvon, Kent* and *Cornwall,* but they still had the little light cruiser *Glasgow* three miles ahead.

A tactical advantage
Shortly after 1230 hours Spee made another turn slightly to starboard, and further to the south, and as the two fleets veered more and more in the direction of the wind, it became more and more depressingly apparent to the British that Spee was building up a tactical advantage, as the breeze blew the smoke from the British vessels downwind directly in front of their bows, and promised to obscure their vision for sighting and spotting when the gunnery duel eventually began. Was Sturdee being outwitted, despite his overwhelming superiority of strength and speed?

The gunnery duel in fact began at 1250 hours, when Sturdee ordered his ships to engage the enemy and the *Inflexible* fired off her first pair of shots. The distance was still some 16,000 to 16,500 yards, or over nine miles, and within range of 12-inch guns of the mighty battle-cruisers, although they had never before fired at more than 12,000 yards. The shells fell short. The *Invincible* then joined in but her shots also fell short, at least of the

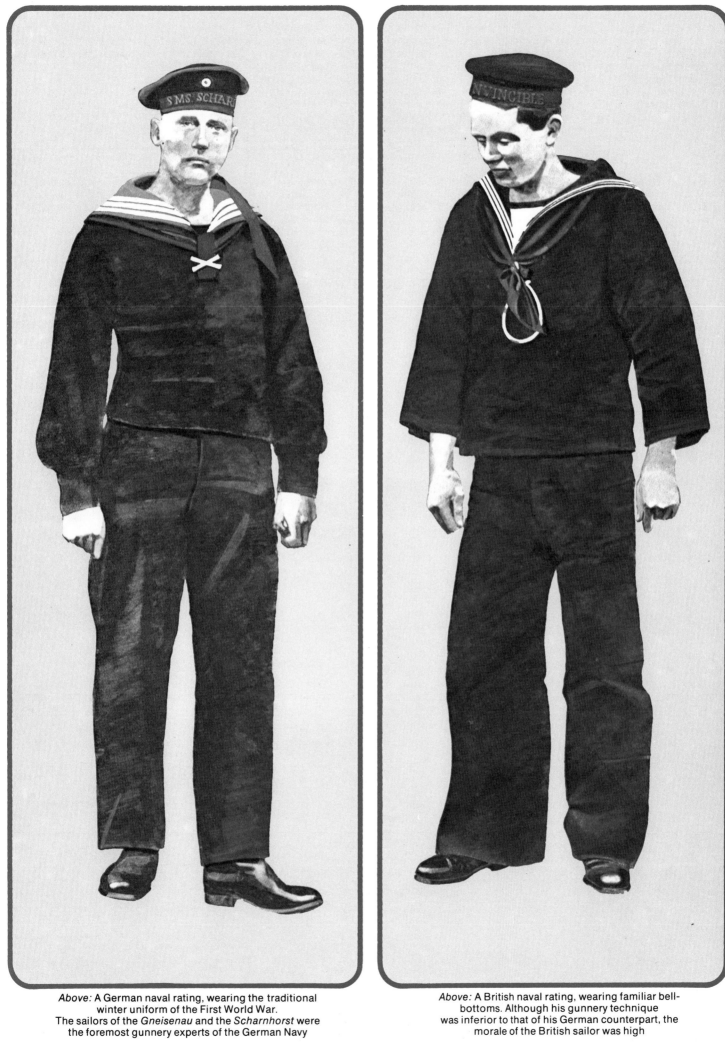

Above: A German naval rating, wearing the traditional winter uniform of the First World War.
The sailors of the *Gneisenau* and the *Scharnhorst* were the foremost gunnery experts of the German Navy

Above: A British naval rating, wearing familiar bell-bottoms. Although his gunnery technique was inferior to that of his German counterpart, the morale of the British sailor was high

Julian Allen

cruisers. The only vessel endangered by this expenditure of ammunition was the light cruiser *Leipzig,* limping along at the back of the German squadron, but she escaped with no more than a splashing. By 1315 hours the shots were beginning to fall more accurately, though still so wide that the crew of the *Glasgow,* which still had the best view ahead of the battle-cruisers, were thrown into despair over the lamentable inaccuracy of the British gunnery. At 1320 hours Spee took the inevitable decision. Already the light cruisers *Dresden, Nürnberg* and *Leipzig* were falling behind, and he faced the choice of either having his squadron attacked by the main part of the British squadron, or of splitting up his ships and allowing them to run on their own. He therefore gave the signal 'Part company. Try to escape', and as the three light cruisers turned away to starboard the two armoured cruisers turned to port, to close with the approaching enemy on a north-easterly course.

The battle thus divided into two distinct engagements, both weighted heavily in the Royal Navy's favour—the action between the two pairs of battle and armoured cruisers; and the chase of the light cruisers, with *Glasgow, Kent* and *Cornwall* chasing the *Dresden, Leipzig* and *Nürnberg. Carnarvon* was still some ten miles astern and trying to catch up with the battle-cruisers.

When the *Scharnhorst* and *Gneisenau* turned to port, the *Inflexible* and *Invincible* made a similar turn and, from being in line behind the German ships, came on to an almost parallel course. It was the ideal situation for a broadside action, and at about 1330 hours both sides opened up. The range was down to 14,500 yards, the wind blowing almost directly from the British ships to the German ships and the weight of the British broadside almost three times that of the German.

Because of their respective positions in the line, when the firing began in earnest, the *Invincible* was matched against the *Gneisenau,* the *Inflexible* against the *Scharnhorst.* And it soon became obvious whose gunnery was the better. It was Fisher himself who told the Royal Navy in unforgettable words that 'Gunnery! Gunnery! Gunnery!' would win battles at sea. But it seemed that the Germans had taken the better note of his dictum. Their broadsides were most impressive. With perfect timing, tidy ripples of fire ran along the side of both ships, with brown puffs of cordite smoke circling vivid flashes of flame as each gun fired. Moreover, the aim of the Germans was accurate, and within 15 minutes the *Scharnhorst,* which had overtaken its sister ship, hit the *Invincible.* Sturdee's reaction was to turn a couple of points to port, to move to the advantageous position where he was outside the range of the German ships, but still had them in his own range. From here he managed three hits, one on the *Scharnhorst* and two on the *Gneisenau,* but no serious damage was done. However, the smoke from his own

Below: Survivors of the *Gneisenau* flounder in icy waters off the Falkland Islands. Some were picked up by the *Inflexible* (in background) and the *Carnarvon,* but many drowned

guns blinded his view of the enemy, and he was forced, soon after 1400 hours, to turn four points towards the enemy to clear his vision. Nevertheless, when the smoke finally drifted away on the breeze, it was seen that the German ships had abruptly turned off to the south again, and the range had lengthened to 17,000 yards. Sturdee had been outwitted and had to make another cumbersome turn in pursuit.

But again, through superior material rather than superior skill, he began to regain the advantage. His margin of speed brought the range down to 15,000 yards, and at 1448 hours the British were able to fire on the Germans again, without themselves being fired on.

It was a situation which Spee could not allow to continue. Rather than prolong the agony, he decided on direct action, and at 1455 hours, as the near misses from the British ships grew ever nearer and began to strike home, he turned hard to port in an attempt to cross his enemy's line so

that his full battery and secondary armament, 5·9-inch guns, could be brought into action while the British were only able to bring their forward turrets to bear. Both sides were scoring hits, and the flash of explosive shell on the British armour punctuated the fountains of spray as other shells fell short, wide of, or over the target. Sturdee responded to Spee's move by turning his own ships to port, which brought the adversaries back on to almost parallel courses, and allowed both to bring their broadsides again into play. Now it was no longer a question of manoeuvre or tactics. By 1500 hours all considerations of escape or chase had been banished. It was a matter entirely of gunnery and, at the range of only 12,500 yards, strength of armour.

Salvo after salvo

For a seemingly endless time, the two pairs of ships fired off salvo after salvo at each other. For almost all the British sailors this was their first experience of battle,

and the continuous thunder of the guns, the scream of the shells, the hiss of water from missed shots, and the fury and blast of explosions around them made the sight a stunning experience. Even for the Germans, who had fought at Coronel, this was their first experience of gunfire of this magnitude. For minutes on end the crews raced to wheel the ammunition on the noisy trolleys from magazine to gun position, load the gun, wait while the gunnery officers gave out details of range, elevation and aim, and then the order to fire, then begin the whole racing drill again, exactly as in the 1,000 practice shoots they had carried out, only different, vastly different, this time. This time they were firing for their lives.

Then, at the very height of battle, a beautiful, full-rigged sailing ship came into sight on the eastern horizon, and sailed towards the thunder and fire and smoke of the battle. It later transpired that she was a French vessel, which, having

Above: After the battle: members of *Kent's* crew pose on her damaged upper deck

left Europe four months earlier, remained in blissful ignorance of the outbreak of war. She was soon gone, as the captain hoisted his colours and fled.

The battle went on, with hits being scored on all ships, and with the Germans, despite excellent gunnery, suffering far the worse damage. Their own shells failed to penetrate the British ships' armour, and although they exploded against the superstructure, they did little to impair British gunnery or injure British sailors. The British, by contrast, were using new shells filled with lyddite, an explosive based on picric acid and named after the town of Lydd in Kent where they were first tested some twenty-five years before this battle. With their terrible explosive effects they penetrated the armour of the German ships and burst in fragments. Splinters of jagged steel wrecked the ships' machinery, and tore into the gentle flesh and brittle bone of the men. There were many that day who learned that although serving one's country had a great appeal in those patriotic days, there was nothing glamorous about the naval battle itself. Quite simply, in the German ships men were dying. Below decks, fires raged and water flooded in, and those who had not been killed outright in the explosions were being burned or drowned. Everywhere lay bodies without limbs, limbs without bodies. All were thrust aside by those who still survived, to be accorded later the dignity of being covered with a flag.

In the *Scharnhorst,* soon after 1500 hours, the fires were gaining an unbreakable hold. Her upperworks, a mangled web of twisted steel, bore no resemblance to the designer's intentions; her three funnels were all blown away, and she was developing a list. The *Gneisenau* was also listing, from the flooding of water through a hole in her side made by an underwater hit. Other hits, from the increasingly accurate British gunnery, caused devastation in the starboard engine room, and smashed one of the boilers, which caused her speed to fall. At about 1510 hours, Sturdee turned the British ships away from the Germans to port, to clear their smoke, and as they came round on to the opposite course 'Spee ordered his ships correspondingly to turn to starboard, to prevent the British gaining the leeward position. By 1527 hours this manoeuvring had put the ships on approximately southwesterly courses, again parallel, but now with their opposite broadsides firing, and they had again changed targets, with the *Inflexible* exchanging fire with the *Scharnhorst.* Then the *Gneisenau* became veiled from the British ships by the smoke from the *Scharnhorst,* and this latter ship had the fire of both battle-cruisers turned on her. Despite this, her crew for long minutes managed to maintain their rate of firing, until at last, at 1537 hours, they could do no more. It was astonishing that she had been able to keep up the fight for so long. Her upper decks were wrecked, her lower decks an inferno of roaring flame and billowing smoke.

Decks awash

Spee clearly knew that his ship was near its end, and signalled to the *Gneisenau* 'Try to escape if your engines are intact.' He then made his last gallant, defiant gesture, turning to starboard to close with the two British ships and attack with torpedoes and to give the *Gneisenau* a chance to get clear. But he never got within range. With his decks awash, his speed slackening, and his ship listing heavily, Spee bowed out of the battle. The *Scharnhorst* turned over on her side, her propellers churning helplessly out of the water, and after seven minutes sank with the admiral on board.

The *Gneisenau* now came under fire from both British ships, and with her speed reduced to 16 knots had no chance of obeying the admiral's order to escape. Maerker, like his admiral, prepared for a fighting end, and ordered several of his engine-room personnel to help man the guns. They would certainly not be needed at their usual posts, since the starboard engine room, one boiler room and one dynamo room were wrecked and filling with water. British gunnery was improving all the time, and the situation below deck on the *Gneisenau* deteriorating as it did so. As shell after shell struck home, fires broke out, raged, were extinguished, only to start again when the job became too enormous for the fire parties to tackle. The starboard forced draught intake fans were smashed and the pressure cut. The foremost funnel was finally blown away, and a shot fell into the dressing station, where men, who had already been badly wounded and waited for medical attention, were put out of their agony. The guns themselves received hits, and one by one the 8·2-inch turrets, and then the 5·9-inch casemates, were blown away and their crews killed. This loss of so many guns coincided with a failure in the ammunition service, and the *Gneisenau's* fire ceased for some minutes. Since she could no longer fly any colours from her twisted masts, the British believed she had surrendered, and held their fire. But the Germans, like the British at Coronel, had no such thoughts. For them proverbial discretion held no appeal over sacrificial valour, and when the ammunition service was restored by the repair of a hoist, the *Gneisenau* fired off one single, futile shot, and promptly brought down on herself once again a deluge of devastating fire not only from the battle-cruisers, but also from Admiral Stoddart's ship *Carnarvon*, which had by now caught up with the fighting. The three British ships ceased fire once again when the *Gneisenau* failed to reply further. *Gneisenau's* reaction was the same — another valiant and futile effort, but this time it became possible to fire when the steering gear jammed and the ship involuntarily turned to starboard, bringing the port guns into operation. Again the British loaded and fired in reply, and within five minutes, at 1720 hours, *Gneisenau* had come to a complete halt, listing badly, and obviously on the point of sinking. Then astonishingly, as the British crews ceased fire and relaxed to await the end of their enemy, another single shell was found in the *Gneisenau*, loaded into the still-functioning fore turret, and incredibly, suicidally, fired off. It missed the *Inflexible*, and the crews of all three British ships prepared to open fire again.

It was a tribute to the skill of her builders that the *Gneisenau* still failed to sink, and Captain Maerker refused to allow her to fall into enemy hands. Everybody now prepared to abandon ship, grabbing hammocks, planks of wood, anything that would float. The boats were no use — they had been reduced to a splintered shambles in the explosions. Then two officers went below, and put into effect plans for just such a contingency which had been built into the ship by her designers. Explosive charges were carried between the twin skins of the *Gneisenau's* hull, and the ship seemed to shudder as they were fired. At 1802 hours the *Gneisenau* sank, with the sound of three cheers for the Kaiser to mark her end, and with the crew's patriotic singing growing ever fainter as men drowned or perished in the freezing water.

From this ship, unlike the *Scharnhorst*, several survivors were picked up, including one who shivered in the *Carnarvon*, sipped hot cocoa, and announced cheerily: 'I believe I have a cousin in one of the British ships. His name is Stoddart.'

Among those who did not survive was one of Admiral von Spee's sons, Heinrich.

The chase begins

During the four hours in which the *Scharnhorst* and *Gneisenau* had fought the British ships on their own, the three German light cruisers had been trying to make their escape, with two British armoured cruisers and a light cruiser in pursuit.

When the chase began, the two small squadrons each formed a triangle. The *Dresden* led the fleeing Germans, followed by the *Nürnberg* to port and the *Leipzig* to starboard. Behind them came the *Glasgow*, with the *Kent* and *Cornwall* working

up astern of her. From the first it was obvious that the *Dresden*, which had only recently joined the squadron, was in excellent mechanical condition and might well outrun the British fleet. At first the best-placed British ship, the *Glasgow*, set off in hot pursuit, and it seemed that the other two pairs would ultimately come to battle. But the two slower German ships were masking the *Dresden*, and Captain Luce in the *Glasgow* had to choose his best course. Since he would have to detour widely round the other two to come up with the *Dresden*, and since it would be well past 1700 hours before he could possibly close, he elected to let her go, and the *Dresden* sped off towards the southern Antarctic mists.

This left the *Glasgow* in close contact with the German ships. Soon after 1500 hours Luce opened fire on the *Leipzig* to make her alter course to starboard in order to return the fire and thus lose some of her lead. When the *Leipzig* found the range, Luce turned away and the *Leipzig* resumed her southerly course, having lost about one and a half miles. Luce at once closed the range again to repeat the tactic and the *Leipzig* lost another one and a half miles of her lead. It was these tactics which allowed the *Cornwall* to catch up and get within range. Meanwhile, although the *Glasgow* was not damaged, one hit was scored on the *Leipzig*. It started a fire in the clothes store. At first this had little effect and it was not noticed until it had spread through the compartments below deck and gained an unbreakable hold. While this fire raged, the two other British ships were gradually catching the *Leipzig* and *Nürnberg*.

It would have seemed that the weak link in the British chain was the *Kent*, an old ship of long service which on paper had not the speed to keep up with the 23 to 24 knots of the German ships. But the crew of the *Kent* were equal to the unprecedented situation. They had the advantage of a light ship, not having had a chance to coal at the Falkland Islands, and to compensate for their lack of fuel every available piece of wood, from the chaplain's lectern to the decks themselves, was broken up and thrown into the furnaces to keep up the pressure. The result was a strain on the boilers which it seemed impossible for the old machinery to bear, but it did so. By 1617 hours the *Kent* and *Cornwall* were within range of the *Leipzig* and opened fire. The *Leipzig* was now faced with three separate opponents, but she gained some temporary respite when the *Nürnberg* turned off to eastwards, and the *Kent* swung away to follow, while at almost the same time the *Glasgow* fell away in pursuit of her original tactics.

It was obvious now that the fate of the *Leipzig* would depend on the *Cornwall*. But the *Cornwall's* 6-inch guns were outranged by the *Leipzig's* 4·1-inch guns, and the *Cornwall* therefore took the only course open, and moved up to close range, through the hail of accurate rapid fire which the *Leipzig* could still produce. Ten shells hit the *Cornwall*, but did no significant damage. Meanwhile, 50 shells had hit the *Leipzig* and by about 1830 hours the fire had become so strong that the ship became almost unworkable and began to slow down. Almost all her ammunition had gone. Ellerton in the *Cornwall* kept closing on the *Leipzig*, firing with his forward guns and then turning away to bring his broad-

side to bear, but thus opening the range — a manoeuvre he repeated over and over again, while *Glasgow* hammered away all the time. With these tactics Ellerton kept the range between 7,000 and 10,000 yards. At last the German vessel ceased fire altogether, and the *Cornwall* flew out the signal 'Am anxious to save life. Do you surrender?' The reply was a final broadside from the *Leipzig*, whose captain took the same view of surrender as the captain of the *Gneisenau* had done, and as Cradock had done at Coronel, and as no doubt most other captains would do of those two seafaring nations.

Cornwall and *Glasgow* both therefore opened fire once again, using the devastating lyddite shell, and at such range, with no reply from the *Leipzig*, the effect was as might be expected. It was summed up by a survivor, who told an officer of the *Glasgow*, Lloyd Hirst: 'The lyddite would burst in the middle of a group and strip them of arms and legs — men would rush about with exposed bones, crazy from the effects of the shell — each explosion would account for about 40 men.'

But the captain still refused the offer of surrender, and instead, like the *Gneisenau's* captain, scuttled his ship. The underwater torpedo tubes and seacocks were opened, and as the fire continued to ravage the upperworks, and the men began leaping into the sea, the commander, Captain Haun, at last told his crew that anybody who could reach the flag could haul it down. The fire was such that nobody could do so, and because it still flew, the *Glasgow* and *Cornwall* opened fire again with lyddite, and killed many of the men waiting on deck to go into the sea. The fire, the explosive lyddite, and the shock of the icy water killed almost all the *Leipzig's* crew. The ship was still floating on her port side when the British boats picked up the last of only 18 survivors, and she eventually sank at 2123 hours.

Luck runs out

When the *Kent* turned away in pursuit of the *Nürnberg*, at 1615 hours, the weather was still clear and visibility good. By 1700 hours a mist had appeared, there was drizzle in the air and it seemed that the ill weather and obscure conditions that the Germans had prayed for might save them yet. The *Kent* was still out of range, so far as her officers could tell without the benefit of accuracy in their range-finding gear, rattling and shaking as the ship bore on at her unaccustomed pace. The Germans had no such disability, and at 1700 hours they opened fire with their stern 4·1-inch guns, which continued to pour shells, mostly near misses, at the British. The British replied but their shots fell short and wide, and for a time it looked as if the *Nürnberg* would hold them off until the mist, thickening by the minute, saved them altogether. But her luck ran out. At 1735 hours two boilers burst almost simultaneously, and her speed dropped to only 19 knots. Her captain, Schönberg, had no alternative but to turn and fight, and as the *Kent* raced up, closing the range to only 6,000 yards and firing her starboard batteries, the *Nürnberg* replied with all her port guns. For a few minutes, the fire was about even, and the *Nürnberg* almost destroyed the *Kent* with a single shot. It happened when the *Nürnberg* scored a hit on a casemate on the *Kent*, killed several men and sent a flash of flame down the ammunition passage, and ignited some empty shell bags. It could easily have reached the shell room, in which case the greatest danger to the *Nürnberg* would have been the fall of debris from what remained of the *Kent*. But a Royal Marine sergeant with great presence of mind slammed shut the access door in the hoist to isolate the shell room, and smothered the burning charge with shell bags until a fire party arrived with hoses to extinguish the fire and flood the compartment. Thus the action of one man saved the *Kent*, but sealed the fate of the *Nürnberg*. Shortly after this incident the *Kent* changed from orthodox shells to lyddite, again with the dreadful results that had decimated the *Leipzig*. *Nürnberg's* top mast, funnels, guns were shot away in turn, and although she poured incessant fire into the *Kent* for some 20 minutes, at 1802 hours some other course of action was vital if she were to avoid simply being pounded to destruction. The course her captain chose was to turn in towards the enemy to fire his starboard battery—and it was fatal. The result was that the *Kent* 'crossed the T' of the *Nürnberg,* and was able to give the ship a full lyddite broadside while the *Nürnberg* could fire only from its two forward guns which were immediately shot away.

A short, macabre ceremony

By 1825 hours the *Nürnberg* had slowed almost to a halt, and the rest of the battle was startlingly similar to the others that day. At 1836 hours the *Nürnberg* could fire no more, and the *Kent* withdrew to await a surrender. None came, so the *Kent,* after 15 minutes, opened fire again, and this time at last a German ship hauled down its colours. There was the short, macabre, but almost traditional ceremony as the captain fell in with his few remaining men, thanked them for fighting the ship so bravely, and ordered the one serviceable boat to be lowered. It was not serviceable after all, and in fact sank on reaching the water. The captain remained with his ship, and at 1927 hours the *Nürnberg* turned on to her starboard side and quietly sank. At this moment the *Kent* lowered two boats, which searched for survivors until darkness fell at 2100 hours. Perhaps the most bizarre aspect of all the day's fighting came during the search for survivors. With men wallowing about in the water, clinging to spars and hammocks, and any other piece of wood that might offer support in the increasingly choppy and freezing sea, large numbers of albatrosses appeared and swooped down in savage attacks on the survivors. Several men met their end pecked by the bills of these gigantic southern birds of prey. Only 12 men were picked up by the *Kent,* and of these only seven survived. Spee's elder son, Otto, was one of those killed.

The *Dresden* had escaped: the other four ships concerned in the battle were sunk: there remained only the small supply ships, the *Seydlitz, Santa Isabel* and *Baden.* When the time came for the attack on Port Stanley, these three ships were ordered to wait off Port Pleasant, some 30 miles to the south, and they would have been entirely safe there but for the determination and courage of the only inhabitant within sight, a Mrs Felton. In true adventure story tradition, she went to the nearest high ground, and organised her

maid and a small boy into a miniature Intelligence network. She observed the movements of the ships, and sent the boy off as runner to the maid, who stayed by the telephone and reported Mrs Felton's messages to Port Stanley. When the first message was transmitted to Sturdee, at 1127 hours, he directed the *Bristol* and the *Macedonia* to 'destroy the transports'. By the time the order was received, the *Bristol* had worked up steam and was racing to join the big ships, but she immediately turned back to assist the *Macedonia.*

The *Seydlitz,* by far the fastest of the three auxiliaries, made off at the first sign of trouble, but the *Baden* and *Santa Isabel,* still observed by Mrs Felton, were too slow to escape and the *Bristol* was quickly up with them. The *Bristol's* captain ordered a shot fired across their bows, and both ships surrendered, whereupon the two English ships took off their crews and sank the ships by gunfire, rather stupidly, as it turned out, since they also sank valuable tons of coal and supplies. In mitigation it must be pointed out, however, that the naval battle was still undecided, and the transports were thought to be an invasion force—so Captain Fanshawe, acting on Sturdee's orders, had little option. The *Seydlitz* raced off eastwards, but found herself running into the battle area of the bigger ships. She changed course several times, and, sailing in wide evading sweeps, managed to get away. She eventually arrived at San Antonio on December 18, and was interned there. For the British, there was one redeeming feature of her escape; she carried the crew of the captured British supply vessel *Drummuir,* who were thus spared a possible death by gunfire from their own countrymen.

On December 16 Sturdee had sailed in the *Invincible* for home waters. Three days later *Inflexible* followed, and Admiral Stoddart resumed command of the area.

From the moment news arrived in London giving the details of the battle, arguments began to rage as to the merits of his victory. Lord Fisher himself was one of his greatest detractors, and on December 11 he announced that Sturdee would have to transfer his flag to the old armoured cruiser *Carnarvon,* send the battle-cruisers home, and stay down there until the *Dresden* had been tracked down. Churchill refused to countenance the idea. On December 10 Fisher had already warned Churchill against over-enthusiasm: 'let us be self-restrained—not too exultant!—till we know details! Perhaps their guns never reached us! It may have been like shooting pheasants: the pheasants not shooting back! Not too much glory for us, only great satisfaction.' When he did hear that the *Dresden* had got away, Fisher sent a string of telegrams to Sturdee demanding an explanation: 'Report fully reason for the course which you have followed since the action.' Sturdee ultimately replied: 'I submit that my being called upon in three separate telegrams to give reasons for my subsequent action was unexpected.'

However, the *Dresden* did not escape for long. She reached Punta Arenas three days after the battle, passed through the Magellan Straits and played hide and seek with the British pursuers until the morning of March 14 1915, when she was found by *Glasgow* and *Kent* sheltering in Cumberland Bay on Juan Fernández Island.

But there was no battle. Tamely, her

captain ran up a white flag, evacuated the crew ashore and then blew up the main magazine—and *Dresden's* wreck still lies in the bay. After the fire and fury of the two battles, this was something of an anti-climax, but it should be remembered that *Dresden* was not an original member of the East Asia Squadron.

But not even Fisher could prevent Sturdee receiving a hero's welcome in London when he arrived home, and King George followed this with the award of a baronetcy, a grant of £10,000, and, after Fisher's death, the rank of Admiral of the Fleet.

How well had Sturdee fought in the Battle of the Falkland Islands? To his credit, he had sunk four of the five main ships he was sent against, and the German admiral and 2,200 of his men had been killed. It was a severe blow to the German navy, and it cleared for good the threat to British trade in remote waters. Winston Churchill later expounded the implications of Sturdee's victory: 'Within twenty-four hours orders were sent to a score of British ships to return to Home Waters. For the first time we saw ourselves possessed of immense surpluses of ships of certain classes, of trained men and of naval supplies of all kinds, and were in a position to use them to the best advantage.'

Sturdee had also achieved his victory with only minimal damage to his ships, and with few losses (six killed, 19 wounded) among his men. The *Invincible* received 23 hits, but damage was confined to two flooded bunkers, a wrecked piano, and a burst money chest which spread gold sovereigns over a wide area. The *Inflexible* was hardly touched and the *Carnarvon* not at all. The *Cornwall* was hit 18 times, the *Glasgow* six, and the *Kent* 37, but no serious damage was done. There was a good reason for this, and one which perhaps mitigated all criticism of Sturdee. The principal charge against him was that he took all day to finish off 80% of a vastly inferior force, and expended nearly 1,000,000 pounds of ammunition, almost emptying his magazines. But he had fought the battle at long range, and had thereby saved casualties. Had he raced in to close quarters he would perhaps have finished the task far more quickly, but the *Scharnhorst* and the *Gneisenau* would also have been able to fire more effectively. As it was, their shells were fired off at full range and high trajectory, and those that were on target came down on the British ships from a high angle and failed to pierce the armour plating. The upperworks were damaged, but this was not too serious.

Where Sturdee can validly be criticised is in failing to secure a better position. Spee constantly succeeded in keeping him to windward, and had the benefit of a clear target, while Sturdee's gun-layers were continually hampered by smoke from their own guns. Sturdee also had two enormous slices of luck on the first morning, when the Germans sailed right into his hands. The first was in being there at all, and had it not been for Fisher's and Churchill's decisiveness the Falkland Islands base would have been destroyed while Sturdee was still cruising southwards at his own comfortable pace. The second was that Spee turned away on sighting the British ships in harbour. Sturdee was at that hour of the morning ill-prepared for action, and had Spee pressed home his attack, he might have done inestimable damage.

A family affair

We lowered what boats we had (two small cutters and one whaler) as fast as we could. I went away in one of the cutters. It was slightly rough and very cold. It was an hour before the ship had got to the scene of the sinking and had lowered her boats. We saved about a hundred and fifty. It was horrible, so I will say no more. I got one officer and about sixteen men into my boat. There were none left struggling in the water when we returned. All the *Scharnhorst*'s were killed or went down with their ship. One of the officers saved was a first cousin of our admiral's (Stoddart). He is a strong chap and quite a good fellow. He had an extraordinary experience. Half the *Gneisenau's* men were killed by shell fire alone. He was in an 8.2 turret as second torpedo officer. The turret was knocked out and he

was the sole survivor. He then went to a casemate gun, which was also knocked out and practically all the crew killed. He went to a third (another casemate), which was also knocked out, and he was again practically the sole survivor. He went to another gun and the ship was then sunk. He remained in icy water for nearly one and a quarter hours, and was picked up by one of our cutters. He was rather dazed, but cool and collected in the boat. After lying shivering in the bottom of a cutter for half an hour he was hauled up by a bowline into one of his enemy's ships. When he got on board he said, 'I believe I have a first cousin in one of your ships. His name is Stoddart.' Then to find him as admiral in the ship that picked him up!

Lieutenant Commander A.C. Iff (then a Midshipman)

THE CLASH AT DOGGER BANK

Shortly before noon on January 23, 1915, Winston Churchill returned to his room at the Admiralty after a long talk with Admiral Fisher, who was laid up in bed with a cold. Hardly had he sat down, Churchill recounts, when Admiral Sir Arthur Wilson strode hurriedly into the room with a 'glow in his eye' and baldly announced: 'First Lord, those fellows are coming out again.' The fellows referred to were of course the Germans, and the decisions and orders which followed from this announcement were to lead to the greatest clash in the North Sea since the war began.

The movements had begun only a short while earlier at 1025 hours that same morning when Rear-Admiral Hipper, resting with his battle-cruisers off Wilhelmshaven, received orders to take them, together with some cruisers and destroyers, and to sweep into the Dogger Bank area that night. The German intentions were not very clear but it was hoped to disrupt the British fishing fleet there and to sink a few of their escorts. Moreover, the report of British scouting operations in that area, brought in by a German seaplane on the 19th, had aroused curiosity at the German admiralty and also the anticipation that some light forces of the the British might be caught unawares by a swift one-day reconnaissance mission from Wilhelmshaven. Such a sweep was in any case well in line with the Kaiser's recent decision that the battle-cruisers could sortie to harass the British, although a major fleet action was still considered to be undesirable.

It was the efficiency of its Intelligence services which enabled the Royal Navy to learn so very quickly about the planned German operation and to take steps to meet it. The chance recovery by the Russians in August 1914 of the German navy's cipher signal books and squared reference charts from the wrecked cruiser *Magdeburg* had been a boon to the British deciphering team, who, from then on, were able to decode the Germans' intercepted wireless messages. In addition, the establishment of radio direction-finder stations along the east coast of England enabled the Admiralty to pinpoint the position of German vessels when they used their radios. Thus Churchill had news of the German plans and the probable size of their forces only one hour and a half after Hipper had received his instructions.

Shortly after Hipper's ships slid out of the Jade estuary on the evening of January 23, a variety of British squadrons emerged from harbour and also proceeded towards the Dogger Bank. Rear-Admiral Hipper's force consisted of the 1st and 2nd Scout-

ing Groups and two flotillas of destroyers. The 1st Scouting Group had to sail without the *Von der Tann*, which was in dockyard hands, and therefore was composed of four battle-cruisers, *Seydlitz*, Hipper's flagship, *Moltke*, *Derfflinger* and *Blücher*. The first three vessels were similar, each carrying ten 11-inch guns, (the *Derfflinger* had eight 12-inch guns), adequately armoured and able to steam at about 25/26 knots. The *Blücher* however was an older, large armoured cruiser rather than a battle-cruiser. Her armour, main armament and displacement were consequently all much smaller than that of the rest of her squadron. Most important of all, her maximum speed was some 2/3 knots less than theirs and this tended either to slow down the whole squadron when in action or to cause the *Blücher* to gradually fall behind. Tactically she was a liability to the squadron.

The 2nd Scouting Group consisted of the four light cruisers *Stralsund*, *Rostock*, *Kolberg*, and *Graudenz*, all of which carried twelve 4.1-inch guns. These were accompanied by 18 destroyers.

In numbers the balance of strength clearly lay with the British, but in gun-power there was less of a discrepancy since the German 11-inch gun was superior to the British 12-inch gun. Hipper's main opponents were to be Vice-Admiral Beatty's powerful battle-cruisers *Lion*, *Tiger*, *Princess Royal*, *New Zealand* and *Indomitable*, all based on Rosyth. Although the last two ships were smaller and not as well armoured as their German opposite numbers and the *Indomitable*, constructed in 1908, was slightly slower, they both carried eight 12-inch guns as main armament. Moreover the *Lion*, *Tiger* and *Princess Royal* were faster than Hipper's squadron and each carried the powerful 13.5-inch guns, although the British battle-cruisers carried less armour than Hipper's three big ships.

Administrative and tactical reasons had caused the British battle-cruisers to be divided into a fast and a slow division. Thus Beatty directly controlled the 1st Battle-Cruiser Squadron which included the *Lion* (his flagship), *Tiger* and *Princess Royal*, while Rear-Admiral Moore, his Second-in-Command, directed the newly-formed 2nd Battle-Cruiser Squadron, which consisted of the *New Zealand* (Moore's flagship) and the *Indomitable*—though remaining under Beatty's control throughout. These ships were accompanied from Rosyth by Commodore Goodenough's 1st Light Cruiser Squadron, consisting of *Southampton*, *Birmingham*, *Nottingham* and *Lowestoft*, all carrying eight or nine 6-inch guns.

January 24, 1915 saw the largest naval clash of the war up to that date: four German battle-cruisers pitted against five British ones. The conflict was confused, and poor British signalling was mainly responsible for the major elements of the German squadron slipping away, leaving only the hybrid battle-cruiser *Blücher* to be finally crushed by the storm of British fire. In the battle, however, points of enormous importance for future naval operations had become apparent. Signalling had to be improved, gunnery, in the British vessels particularly, needed drastic attention, armour protection for the ships' vitals needed strengthening and a way of stopping flash travelling down to the magazines needed devising. These lessons were apparent to both admiralties, but whether or not the lessons had been learnt fully would have to wait till the next clash. Here the course and lessons of this vital battle are analysed. *Below:* White plumes of spray mark the fall of British shells among the German battle-cruisers. In the foreground, emitting a cloud of black smoke, is the *Blücher*, already hit and damaged by British fire. Throughout the action she was a hindrance to the German force, and by abandoning her the rest of the German squadron made their own escape easier

Other British forces were also on the move on the evening of the 23rd. As soon as the Admiralty had received the news of an imminent German sweep, Wilson and Vice-Admiral Oliver (the Chief of Admiralty War Staff) had worked out in Churchill's office the most likely position for an interception. With professional expertise they ordered Beatty to be at a point about 30 miles north of the Dogger Bank at 0700 hours on the 24th and also ordered Commodore Tyrwhitt with his three light cruisers *Arethusa* (his flagship), *Aurora* and *Undaunted,* together with 35 destroyers, out of Harwich, to join Beatty there and provide the escort for the battle-cruisers.

Strict radio silence

Although the Admiralty was almost certain that only the German battle-cruisers would come out and that their cartographical calculations were correct, they were still not inclined to take chances. The seven pre-dreadnought battleships of Vice-Admiral Bradford's 3rd Battle Squadron, also based on Rosyth, accompanied by Rear-Admiral Pakenham's 3rd Cruiser Squadron, were ordered to a position about 40 miles north-west of Beatty, to intercept Hipper if he came by a more northerly route or to support the British battle-cruisers if they got into trouble. Much further south, Commodore Keyes was moving from Harwich to the Heligoland Bight in the hope of intercepting and torpedoing any German vessels with his 'Overseas' squadron of *Firedrake, Lurcher* and four submarines.

Finally, Admiral Jellicoe, resting at Scapa Flow with the main battleship force of the Grand Fleet, cleared harbour at 2100 hours on the 23rd with three battleship squadrons, covered by three cruiser squadrons and 28 destroyers. Further ahead of him ranged Rear-Admiral Napier's 2nd Light Cruiser Squadron. These forces, while covering the Scottish coast in the early stages of their cruise, were to sweep down to the rendezvous with Bradford's vessels by mid-morning.

During the night the various squadrons picked their way between the minefields (Beatty's force actually dashing through an area which was reportedly mined) and approached the Dogger Bank from different directions. The British ships kept a strict radio silence while the occasional German wireless traffic intercepted by the D/F stations continued to confirm the Admiralty's belief that something was afoot on the German side. The weather

was calm and the sea still. Apart from Tyrwhitt's forces, which were a little delayed by fog at Harwich, all the British ships appeared to be moving according to schedule and Churchill was thrilled with the idea of 'a beast of prey moving stealthily forward hour by hour into the trap'.

At 0700 hours on the 24th Beatty, with Goodenough's cruisers steaming parallel on his port beam, reached the rendezvous area. Ten minutes later, with the dawn breaking to give almost perfect visibility, the *Arethusa* with seven new 'M' class destroyers of the Harwich force were sighted straight ahead. The *Aurora, Undaunted* and the rest of the destroyers were then some 13 miles astern, delayed because of the early fog.

It was this latter group, still south of the rendezvous point, which first clashed with Hipper's forces. The *Aurora,* leading the 1st Destroyer Flotilla, sighted a three-funnelled cruiser and four destroyers on her starboard bow shortly after 0700 hours and moved closer to challenge, expecting to meet up with Tyrwhitt's flotilla again. The cruiser was, in fact, the *Kolberg,* which was guarding the port flank of Hipper's battle-cruisers, then steaming around the north side of the Dogger Bank. Opening fire on the *Aurora* at 0715 hours the *Kolberg* managed to get in three quick hits although they did little damage. Recovering from this surprise, the *Aurora* began to return the fire and soon scored a hit on the *Kolberg's* forebridge, which killed two men and forced her to turn away. The *Aurora,* proceeding north-eastwards again and joined by *Undaunted's* flotilla, soon sighted more German warships to starboard and then, at about 0730 hours, saw the *Southampton's* shape at the head of Goodenough's squadron, looming out of the dusk to the north. Some five miles behind the *Southampton* steamed Beatty's five battle-cruisers.

Confident that he was about to surprise a weaker enemy, Beatty had ordered his battle-cruisers to steer SSE towards the sounds and flashes of the guns and to increase speed to 22 knots, while sending the cruisers on ahead. Hipper, on the other hand, had not expected an immediate encounter and therefore had to act warily in case he came up against the Grand Fleet or a part of it. The engagement with the *Aurora* to the westward was soon followed by sightings of more destroyers and Goodenough's squadron, and then by the sight of heavy smoke further north. Although not greatly increasing his speed, Hipper therefore ordered an almost complete turn so that his forces were steaming south-eastwards by

Südd Verlag

Squadron, was ordered to steer eastwards to cut off Hipper if he fled to the north-east. The German admiralty, which first received the news of *Seydlitz's* sighting at about 0750 hours, ordered all ships at Wilhelmshaven to get up steam and to assemble in the Schillig Roads, but having left it so late it would be many hours before they could join in the battle.

Closing at 28 knots

Settling down to a steady pursuit and increasing speed, Beatty sent the fast 'M' class destroyers ahead to report on the exact strength of his opponent. By 0845 hours, despite the shelling which the destroyers encountered as they closed to within 9,000 yards of the *Blücher,* the composition of the German force was clear. It was also clear by then that Beatty's ships had the edge as regards speed and were gradually closing up to the German battle-cruisers. The British ships reached 25 knots, increased to 26 and then met Beatty's demand for 27 knots, although the *Indomitable* slowly began to be outpaced. Beatty afterwards stated that at one point his ships had reached the almost incredible speed of 28.5 knots, and indeed even the 'M' class destroyers found it hard work later to move ahead of the battle-cruisers.

As a result of these high speeds the *Lion* drew to within 20,000 yards of the *Blücher* shortly after 0900 hours and then commenced firing at a range hitherto had been considered impossible; (the experimental maximum in 1914 had been 16,000 yards). Shortly afterwards the *Tiger* and *Princess Royal* were also able to open fire on the *Blücher,* which began to suffer from this concentrated fire. Soon the German battle-cruisers, echeloned to enable all four of them to return the fire from their starboard side, were answering vigorously although greatly inconvenienced by the smoke from the English destroyers to the north-east.

Naturally enough the rearmost German and the foremost English vessels attracted the most attention and suffered as a consequence. The *Lion, Tiger* and *Princess Royal,* swinging slightly to starboard, brought their after turrets into action and began to damage the *Blücher* seriously with regular salvoes. At the third salvo the German vessel was hit on the water-line and had her speed reduced; and at the fourth, explosions shattered the after superstructure and two turrets, killing or injuring over 200 sailors. The *Lion,* being the nearest English ship and the one surrounded by least smoke, also took punishment. At 0928 hours she received a hit on her water-line, which penetrated the bunkers. Hammocks, mess-stools and anything else available were quickly used to make good the damage and the *Lion* steamed ahead unhindered, but Beatty was getting worried about the Germans' concentration on his ship. At 0935 hours therefore, seeing that the *New Zealand* had come within range of the *Blücher* and was

Süd Verlag

0740 hours. By that time the heavy smoke to the north-west had resolved itself into the five British battle-cruisers, which were steadily working themselves up to full speed.

Hipper, suddenly aware of his critical position 170 miles from Heligoland without any hope of support from the High Seas Fleet, ordered his destroyers to push on ahead and his main force to increase speed to 23 knots, which was *Blücher's* maximum. The German battle-cruiser squadron then steered south-easterly in line ahead formation, led by *Seydlitz* with *Moltke, Derfflinger* and *Blücher* following in that order. Beatty, who had originally hoped to get to the Germans' leeward (the port side, in this instance) before engaging and thus avoid his own smoke as well as eventually cutting off the Germans from their base, was forced by Hipper's manoeuvre to follow on the starboard and fear of mines being dropped from the enemy's stern, and of loss of time, now prevented his battle-cruisers from switching over to port.

As the chase developed, the respective admiralties were being acquainted with the situation. Churchill, Fisher, Wilson and Oliver, gathered together in the War Room of the Admiralty, could do nothing but wait and hope as confused messages came flooding in. In the middle of the North Sea and about 140 miles NNW of the action, Jellicoe's great fleet of ships swung slightly more to starboard to intercept if the German battle-cruisers turned north. Further south, Vice-Admiral Bradford's force, cruising north of the Dogger Bank and joined by the 2nd Light Cruiser

Above: The *Blücher* steams into her last action. *Above right:* Mortally hit, *Blücher* burns and begins to list to port. *Below:* The end for Germany's first 'battle-cruiser'. The crew scurries over *Blücher's* revolving hull as she capsizes prior to sinking, abandoned by her fellows

engaging her, Beatty gave the order to fire at opposite numbers.

Consequently, while the *New Zealand* continued to pound away at the *Blücher*, the *Lion* shifted her fire to Hipper's flagship *Seydlitz* and the third English vessel, *Princess Royal*, turned upon the third German battle-cruiser, the *Derfflinger*. However, the commander of the *Tiger*, Captain Pelly, who had begun to direct his ship's fire upon the *Seydlitz* a few minutes earlier, continued to shoot at this target in the belief that *Indomitable* was by then engaging *Blücher*. Thinking that the rear three ships of the opposing battle-lines were respectively firing at each other, Pelly felt that his task was to assist the *Lion* in crippling the German flagship. Though sound enough in theory this idea failed in practice because the *Indomitable* was still not within reach of the *Blücher*. This meant that with the existing dispositions the second German battle-cruiser, *Moltke*, was able to lob salvo after salvo undisturbed at *Lion*.

Beatty had therefore failed to divert any of the German fire from himself and all three battle-cruisers continued to shoot at his flagship. At first this did not appear to be so serious a matter since it was the English ships who were handing out the punishment. The *Lion's* salvoes had found *Seydlitz* almost at once, from a range of some 17,500 yards, and a 13.5-inch shell penetrated the working chamber of the rearmost turret. The flames roared downwards threatening the turret magazine and then along towards the magazine of the adjacent turret. The ammunition in transit exploded and killed 159 men, put both after turrets out of action and sent flames shooting up high above the ship. Only the action of the executive officer, who promptly flooded both magazines, avoided the explosion of the stored ammunition and the probable destruction of the battle-cruiser. Moreover, far at the rear of the German line, *Blücher* was also taking a battering and slowly dropping further back.

British gunnery hampered

Nevertheless, the British gunnery was greatly hampered by smoke drifting from Tyrwhitt's squadron which had moved to the north-east. The *Tiger*, a newly commissioned ship with an inefficient gunnery officer, spotted *Lion's* shells as her own in consequence of the smoke and did not realise that she was in fact firing 3,000 yards over *Seydlitz*. On the other side, however, the more efficient German gunners were making themselves felt on board the *Lion*. Shortly before 1000 hours she was hit on the roof of her foremost turret and one of the guns was disabled. A few minutes later an 11-inch shell from the *Seydlitz* pierced the *Lion's* armour, flooding the engineer's workshop and putting two dynamos, the after fire control and the secondary armament circuits out of action.

At 1018 hours the *Derfflinger*, which was on fire herself from one of *Princess Royal's* shells, managed to land two 12-inch shells on Beatty's flagship. One of these flooded the port bunkers, the other flooded the torpedo flat and adjacent compartment. The *Lion*, with speed gradually falling, was by then zig-zagging desperately while Beatty still stood on the open bridge with his staff, all drenched by the 'near-misses'.

As the German battle-cruisers continued to pour shells at the *Lion*, the battered *Blücher* was burning fiercely and dropping even further behind. At 1048 hours she sheered off to port, apparently out of control, and came under a concentrated fire from the Harwich flotillas and the *Indomitable*, which had at last caught up with the action. The *Blücher*, to all eyes, was obviously finished.

Beatty's overriding concern, however, was to catch the rest of Hipper's squadron. The prospects for this looked bright with the slower German battle-cruisers still over 100 miles from Heligoland and many hours of daylight left, but a whole series of incidents altered the course of the battle. The *Lion*, still under an intense bombardment, was hit at about 1052 hours by a shell which penetrated the boiler-rooms and flooded the feed tank, stopped the port engine and reduced speed to 15 knots. Moreover, as the ship listed 10 degrees to port, the remaining dynamo suddenly failed and cut off lighting and power. Most important of all was the fact that Beatty could henceforward only signal with flags, since the wireless and signal lights were also put out of order. Falling out

of line, Beatty was forced to watch as the *Tiger, Princess Royal* and *New Zealand* rushed past and Rear-Admiral Moore was left with the command.

It was at this point that Beatty and others on board the *Lion* thought they saw submarines on the starboard bow. In fact the nearest German submarines were many miles away, but Beatty was not to know that and anticipated a submarine trap. He therefore signalled for a sharp turn to port, which would take Moore's vessels away from the danger – a manoeuvre which enabled the *Indomitable,* by cutting the corner, to catch up with the squadron again. Since this new course also took the British battle-cruisers away from Hipper's at almost right angles it meant that they would later have to cross the enemy's wake and run the risk of mines. As it happened the German ships carried no mines on this occasion, but nevertheless Beatty soon changed his mind and modified his ships' course to the north-east.

This was not a great modification, however, and it carried Moore's vessels more towards the battered *Blücher* than towards the rest of Hipper's battle-cruisers just when they were beginning to turn back in a gesture to help the *Blücher*, and their destroyers were rushing ahead to launch torpedo attacks against the British squadron as it made its swing to the north-east. With the distance between the two forces rapidly widening, Hipper seized this chance to extricate the rest of his force and ordered a resumption of the south-easterly course. Since *Seydlitz's* after turrets were out of action and her ammunition supplies were running short, it would have been an expensive gesture in any case to have tried to recover the shattered wreck of the *Blücher.*

This temporary breathing-space afforded to the German squadron was now prolonged by confused communications on the British side. Beatty, breathing fire at his ship's disablement, was determined to make it quite clear to Moore that Hipper's main force was to be destroyed and ordered the flag signal 'Attack the rear of the enemy'. In confused circumstances such as these this message was not the clearest expression of the Admiral's intentions, but it was made even less clear when the flags for this signal were hauled down together with those for the previous signal 'Course NE' thus combining two separate messages with one executive order. As a result, the British battle-cruisers read the message as 'Attack the rear of the enemy, bearing NE', which was where the crippled *Blücher* lay. Moore, who was unaware of the reported submarine threat and thought that the earlier turns to port had been to get nearer to the *Blücher,* became convinced that this was Beatty's intention when he saw the German vessel bearing to the north-east. With no thoughts of questioning such orders, the four battle-cruisers gave up the pursuit of Hipper's force and turned towards the *Blücher.*

Beatty had indeed tried to make his intentions clearer by later hoisting Nelson's famous signal 'Engage the enemy more closely' and incidentally but perhaps symbolically found that this had been replaced in the signal book by the less inspiring phrase 'Keep nearer to the enemy'. In any case the fast-disappearing British battle-cruisers could no longer read the *Lion's* signals. Shortly afterwards, being eager to discover what was really happening and having ascertained that immediate repairs to his ship were impossible, Beatty transferred to the nearest destroyer, the *Attack,* and set off in pursuit. The *Lion* meanwhile limped slowly away towards the north-west.

Over the horizon to the south-east the *Blücher* was suffering in isolation as more and more British ships closed in upon her and as the rest of Hipper's force steamed hurriedly towards Wilhelms-haven. *Blücher* continued to fight stubbornly against the overwhelming odds. By this time she was on fire in many places and only two of her main guns were in action, trying to keep her enemies at bay. By 1120 hours the *Arethusa* and her 'M' class destroyers were also in the fray and the *Meteor* went in close to launch torpedoes. She was then suddenly hit by an 8.2-inch shell, which burst in the front boiler-room and put her out of action. *Blücher* was still a danger to those impetuous enough to get too close to her.

The other three 'M' class destroyers and the *Arethusa* were by now closing in and firing torpedoes. Tyrwhitt steered his cruiser to within 2,500 yards of the *Blücher,* blasting away at her continuously with *Arethusa's* 6-inch guns and finally let fly with two torpedoes, both of which hit. Even now the *Blücher* was not only firing her guns at the *Arethusa* but also launching torpedoes at the British battle-cruisers, which were contributing to the destruction. Overhead the whole scene was being watched by the helpless crew of a Zeppelin, who could do nothing other than chronicle *Blücher's* end.

This came shortly after noon, at about 1210 hours. Hit by seven torpedoes and over 70 shells, *Blücher* had been a blazing wreck

long before that and had her last gun put out of order about 1145 hours. Tyrwhitt again ordered the *Arethusa* to close the German ship but this time only to rescue the survivors, who cheered at her coming. Turning over completely, *Blücher* lay bottom upwards for a few minutes while *Arethusa's* small boats picked up the German seamen and then suddenly she disappeared. The *Arethusa* and her destroyers managed to rescue 260 of these gallant men, who had been under more or less continuous fire for three hours, before a German seaplane arrived and unfortunately forced an end to this rescue operation by bombing the small boats. In fact the pilot, an inexperienced flyer, was trying to attack the destroyers, but his action was later criticised by the German admiralty.

Moore's battle-cruisers had turned north a short while before. The Rear-Admiral knew that his squadron would probably be in sight of Heligoland before they could catch up with Hipper again and that the risks were therefore too great. Already Keyes had reported that the High Seas Fleet was on the move. Moreover Moore knew nothing about the condition of the *Lion* after seeing her limp away to the north-west and greatly feared for her safety.

At 1220 hours they met the destroyer *Attack* coming southwards with Beatty on board. Hastily transferring his flag to the *Princess Royal,* the Admiral rushed aboard the battle-cruiser and learnt for himself the sad news. Bitterly disappointed, he impetuously signalled for an immediate about-turn and set off after Hipper. After further enquiry, however, he also realised that their task was by then impossible. Hipper had slipped out of his net for the second time within six weeks and could not be caught. It was, as his Flag Lieutenant Seymour put it, 'like trying to win the Derby after falling at Tattenham Corner'. The British battle-cruisers therefore turned to find the *Lion* and to escort her home.

The *Lion* had in fact to be towed to Rosyth. By 1530 hours with her speed below 8 knots, she was forced to take a towline from the *Indomitable.* Surrounded by a large force of destroyers and cruisers, with the battle-cruisers and the Grand Fleet battleships providing a more distant cover in case of a surprise German attack, these two exposed vessels slowly edged their way home all that day and the next. Early on January 26 the *Lion,* whose engines had by then completely failed, was anchored in the Forth. On the other side of the North Sea, with ideas of surprise attacks on the Grand Fleet very far from their minds, Hipper's very relieved squadron had been met at about 1430 hours on the 24th and escorted back to the Jade estuary.

On the face of it, the battle of the Dogger Bank was a clear-cut British victory. They had chased Hipper's squadron from the seas and destroyed one of his larger vessels without losing so much as a destroyer themselves. The *Seydlitz* had also been seriously damaged, while both the *Derfflinger* and the *Kolberg* suffered to some extent. Against this, the *Lion* was to stay out of action for four months while the *Tiger* had trifling damages. The destroyer *Meteor* had been damaged by the *Blücher,* and the *Aurora* only scratched by the *Kolberg.* The Germans lost almost 1,000 men killed, but fatal casualties on the British side totalled only 15.

Misunderstanding or tragedy?

But if this victory appeared decisive to the British press, it was not so obvious to the professional critics. Beatty was unanimously praised for his part and Fisher's only quibble with that the battle-cruisers had carried enough fuel for 3,000 miles instead of the probable 500 miles, and therefore reduced their speed by a knot or two. The actions of the other officers, however, were not so well received, and with some reason. Keyes was later to admit that 'the spectacle of Moore and Co yapping around the poor tortured *Blücher,* with beaten ships in sight to be sunk, is one of the most distressing episodes of the war'. Like everyone else, he saw the lucky escape of the German battle-cruisers, due to a simple misunderstanding, as a tragedy for the Royal Navy.

Fisher criticised Moore's decision to give up the chase, calling it 'despicable' and 'absolutely incomprehensible'. While sympathising with Moore's confusion and bewilderment at Beatty's signals from the crippled *Lion,* one is forced to conclude that he did not show any of the initiative necessary in such tense encounters. Before the *Lion* was knocked out of the battle, Beatty had clearly shown that his primary concern was to catch the main body of Hipper's force and not just to finish off the already doomed *Blücher.* With the advantage in numbers, armament and speed the British had a unique chance to destroy all of the German battle-cruisers, but Moore had let the opportunity slip. Churchill and Fisher shortly sent him away to command a cruiser squadron in the Canary Islands region.

Moore's attitude was symptomatic of the rigid adherence to orders which characterised the Royal Navy's outlook at that time. Initiative and independent judgement were not encouraged. Fisher might fume that 'in war the first principle is to disobey orders. Any fool can obey orders!', but he was hardly renowned for his tolerance when subordinates ventured to cross his opinions and commands.

There was also a failure on board the *Lion* to communicate Beatty's wishes exactly. The order to engage the enemy's rear was both unnecessary and confusing, and was in any case mixed up with the flags of his previous direction. Without this ambiguous signal Moore would have continued to fire away at the *Seydlitz* and *Derfflinger,* and perhaps this was the reason why Beatty was not very eager to chastise his Second-in-Command afterwards. But it is worth remembering that Seymour, Beatty's Flag Lieutenant, had had no specialist training in signals, and had sent unclear messages during the Scarborough Raid action.

Probably Captain Pelly of the *Tiger* was the person who came in for most criticism, especially from Fisher, who thought that his failure to engage the *Moltke* was 'inexcusable', and that he was a 'poltroon' for not charging after the enemy when the *Lion* sheered out of line. The first point is worth examining. The official naval historian is to some extent correct in following Fisher and pointing out that 'the master principle was that no ship should be left unfired upon', but there is another side to the matter. Pelly's information regarding the position of the *Indomitable* was in fact incorrect but his tactics were right. After all, the leading three German battle-cruisers continued to concentrate upon the *Lion* (though the *Tiger* was also engaged and suffered six hits) and achieved great effect. Crippling the enemy's leading ship had been, and still remained, a major stepping-stone on the path to winning the battle, and the official historian was forced to admit that the German firing policy 'was all that the advocates

The battle orders were reworded so that Pelly's mistake regarding fire concentration could be avoided in the future and the signalling system was improved by the installation on each ship of an auxiliary wireless set and by further additions to the signal book which would clarify the sort of instructions which Beatty had so desperately wished to send when his flagship fell out of line.

The other innovation which Churchill and Fisher pressed for, the transfer of the battle-cruisers to the Humber and the Grand Fleet battleships to Rosyth, was abandoned after vigorous protests from both Jellicoe and Beatty. For although this move would put both forces in a better intercepting position, these two bases did not compare with Scapa as an anchorage or a practice area, were navigationally unsuitable and could easily be mined. In the field of tactics the British did not seek for, or perhaps did not think of, any answers to the threat posed by German mines and submarines during the action. Yet without such answers and in view of the Grand Fleet's super-sensitiveness to such attacks, their only reply remained that of swinging away, disengaging, temporarily at least, from the battle. Temporary disengagements, however, could swiftly develop into more permanent ones if great care were not taken.

Finally, the Dogger Bank action tended to confirm the opinion of Fisher, Beatty and perhaps others that the battle-cruisers themselves 'will finish the job'. This was a rather natural thing to say in view of their performance here and earlier at the Falklands, but in both battles the British warships had possessed a large numerical superiority and the enemy had retreated without engaging in a 'toe-to-toe' boxing match. In other words, although the *Lion* indeed took some heavy punishment, the British battle-cruisers were not yet proven in full battle, especially in their defence capabilities. In particular the weaknesses of Beatty's ships to plunging shells and to the possibility of the magazines

Survivors from the *Blücher* dot the surface of the cold North Sea as they wait to be picked up by British destroyers

of concentration on the van could wish'.

Finally, and perhaps more important still, the fuss over Pelly's decision tended to obscure the much more vital fact that the British standards of shooting were rather poor. Here indeed could the *Tiger* feel somewhat ashamed, for despite being the only British battle-cruiser equipped with a director fire-control system she had not registered a single hit. The *Southampton*, had seen her shots regularly land some 3,000 yards over the German ships. The *Tiger* was in fact a special case, with a gunnery lieutenant who was 'villainously bad' (Fisher) and a large number of recovered deserters among the crew. Moreover, being a relatively new ship, she had not fired at a moving target!

Nevertheless she serves as a symbol for the gunnery standards of the British battle-cruisers, which, even allowing for the vast clouds of smoke often obscuring the view, was very poor when compared with that of their opponents. Apart from the *Blücher* and the *Kolberg,* which suffered at the hands of *Aurora* in the first encounter, the only hits made upon the German ships during the entire battle were the two on *Seydlitz* and the one on the *Derfflinger.* In contrast the *Lion* received 16 hits while the *Tiger*

was hit six times. Had the German shells been more effective, the battle of the Dogger Bank might have had a different ending, but the British also lacked a really good armour-piercing shell.

Correcting the failures
Some, but not all, of the failures on the British side were recognised and attempts were made to correct them. The *Tiger* and the other battle-cruisers were urged to improve their gunnery, which to Jellicoe had always been suspect, and the Admiralty accelerated its programme of installing director firing systems in all ships. being ignited by flashes in the turrets had not shown itself, as it had done in the case of the *Seydlitz,* where the Germans took the necessary corrective action.

The battle of the Dogger Bank had seen the British and German battle-cruisers engage each other and the weaker force once again evade the stronger. In that it revealed where command of the sea lay, the action justified the eulogising of the British press. But it also produced evidence of serious weaknesses on both sides. Whether this would be enough to tilt the balance of power in the North Sea in the future was another question.

NAVAL WAR IN THE MEDITERRANEAN
—SUMMER 1915

The blockade of the Austrian fleet in the Adriatic countered one of the threats to the Gallipoli supply route, even if it did make the Italian coast the target of Austrian wrath. Another threat, that of German submarines operating from Adriatic ports, was not solved by the blockade, and the U-Boats continued to prey on Allied shipping.
Below: The Italian cruiser *Giuseppe Garibaldi* sinking after she had been torpedoed by a German U-Boat, July 1915

The naval war in the Mediterranean in 1915 was one of vast complexity. At the far end of this huge inland sea was being waged the campaign in the Dardanelles under entirely British control and command. Over the rest of the Mediterranean the war at sea followed a somewhat spasmodic course dictated partly by the moves of the enemy and partly by the difficulty of bringing together the operations of three separate allies each with different anxieties which dictated the movements of their ships and squadrons.

The immensity of the task can perhaps best be realised by the recollection that the Mediterranean Sea covers an area of more than 1,000,000 square miles. Across this vast expanse of sea had to be carried all the supplies and logistic support for the army engaged in Gallipoli, for considerable British forces stationed in Egypt and the Suez Canal zone, and for the struggling Serbian army trying to hold at bay, on the line of the River Danube, the attacking troops of Germany and Austria. Grand Admiral von Tirpitz, Minister of Marine in Germany, had been quick to appreciate the length and vulnerability of these lines of supply, and on April 25, 1915 had ordered the first German U-Boat to proceed into the Mediterranean. It was no coincidence that this was *U21,* commanded by Korvettenkapitän Hersing. Tirpitz chose his best submarine commanders for the Mediterranean, and at this period Hersing was outstanding. He was followed by five others—Forstmann, Valentiner, Rücker, Gansser, and Kophamel —the pick of the German U-Boat arm, and between them they were to create havoc in the Mediterranean. In addition to the U-Boats which came by sea from Germany, ten smaller U-Boats were sent overland in parts to Pola (Pula), where they were assembled in the naval dockyard. Of these, one was lost with all hands in the summer of 1915 and five were sent to Constantinople to operate from there.

French and British problems in the Mediterranean were not eased by the oddity of the Italian entry into the war. She remained neutral until April 26, 1915 when she denounced her adherence to the prewar Triple Alliance of Germany, Austria, and herself, but without as yet declaring war on any of the Central Powers. This anomalous situation was eased when a declaration of war against Austria followed a month later. Turkey was included amongst her enemies on August 21, 1915, but war against Germany was not finally declared until August 1916. As the majority of the German U-Boats operating in the Mediterranean made their base in Austrian ports in the Adriatic, and as Italy was not officially at war with Germany during 1915, allied operations against them were thereby fraught with difficulties.

It was the influence of these German U-Boats and the realisation of the profound effect they could have on the Gallipoli campaign that determined the British Admiralty to order Admiral Pierse, whose command stretched from the East Indies to the Suez Canal and the coast of Syria, to neutralise the port of Smyrna (Izmir) in case it should be developed as a U-Boat base on the flank of the Gallipoli operations. With his flag in the *Euryalus,* and with the *Triumph* and *Swiftsure* temporarily borrowed from Admiral Carden's Dardanelles force, Admiral Pierse arrived off the port and proceeded to bombard the forts at the entrance.

For five days the three battleships poured shells into the Turkish forts and gun batteries while minesweepers cleared a channel up to the narrow entrance of the harbour, in which the Turks promptly sank two blockships. After the long bombardment, Admiral Pierse sent an ultimatum ashore demanding the unconditional surrender and destruction of all forts and batteries. The local governor refused the British demands. There was nothing left for Admiral Pierse but to withdraw, for a continuation of the bombardment without decisive result could only incur a loss of prestige and it would need an overwhelming force of battleships to make Smyrna surrender. On the eve of the Gallipoli landings, such battleships were just not available. Nor, in fact, was Smyrna ever developed as a U-Boat base.

French blockade Adriatic

It was, however, in the Adriatic that the main activity of the naval war in the Mediterranean, apart from the Dardanelles, was taking place during 1915. The problem there was the presence of the considerable Austrian fleet. The whole of the eastern coast of the Adriatic, with its magnificent deep-water harbours, was a part of the Austrian Empire, extending from Trieste in the north to as far south as Cattaro (Kotor). The main naval base was at Pola (Pula) while at Trieste and Fiume (Rijeka) were subsidiary bases with useful repair and docking facilities. Further to the south were fleet anchorages at Spalato (Split), Zara (Zadar), Sebenico (Sibenica), and Ragusa (Dubrovnik), while right in the south was the finest anchorage of them all at Cattaro (Kotor).

△ Italian Dreadnoughts (with a torpedo boat in the foreground) in the Adriatic. The Italian C-in-C, the Duke of the Abruzzi, commanded the Allied naval forces in this area when Italy entered the war
▷ Part of the considerable Austrian fleet at sea in the Adriatic. The magnificent harbours of the eastern Adriatic belonged to Austria, while the Allies' nearest base, until Italy entered the war, was Malta

Until Italy entered the war, the nearest naval base available for the Allies was Malta, with Durazzo (Durrës) and Valona (Vlonë), on the Albanian coast and under Serbian control, useful as anchorages but with no base facilities. Italy's entry into the war provided the Allies with Brindisi and Taranto as main fleet bases, and with Venice in the far north as a subsidiary naval station but with limited maintenance facilities.

Because of the length and vulnerability of the supply routes through the Mediterranean, the first consideration for the Allies was to prevent units or squadrons of the Austrian fleet from emerging from the Adriatic. It was here that geography took a useful hand on the side of the Allies, for the Straits of Otranto, the only exit from the Adriatic into the Mediterranean, had a width of no more than 45 miles. With the British Mediterranean fleet so actively engaged in the Dardanelles operations, naval responsibility for the central and western Mediterranean fell upon the shoulders of the French Commander-in-Chief, Admiral Boué de Lapeyrère, and one of his first actions was the institution of a blockade of the Straits of Otranto.

The overwhelming superiority of the French naval force was sufficient to deter the Austrian surface ships from any offensive movements, but it was no deterrent to the activities of submarines. A foretaste of the trouble they were to cause came on the night of April 26/27 when the armoured cruiser *Leon Gambetta,* flagship of the 2nd Cruiser Division, was torpedoed by *U5,* commanded by Lieutenant Georg Ritter von Trapp, and sank with very heavy loss of life.

The loss of the *Leon Gambetta* underlined the fundamental weakness of the French blockade of the Otranto Straits, which was the lack of fast light cruisers. This lack was forcefully exposed on May 6 when the Austrian light cruiser *Admiral Spaun* made a rare sortie into the Mediterranean. She was sighted east of the toe of Italy by the armoured cruiser *Jules Ferry* and the destroyer *Bisson,* but had no difficulty in escaping from the slow French

ships. But by now Italy had denounced the Triple Alliance and was on the verge of signing a Naval Convention with Britain and France, in which the command in the Adriatic would devolve on the Italian Commander-in-Chief, Admiral H. R. H. Luigi di Savoia, Duke of the Abruzzi. Under the terms of the convention the Italian fleet in the Adriatic was to be reinforced by 12 French destroyers and as many French torpedo boats, submarines (minimum six), and minesweepers as the French could spare, six French seaplanes and a seaplane carrier. In addition, four British light cruisers and four British battleships, as soon as they could be relieved from the Dardanelles, were also to be placed under Italian command. This was to be known as the First Allied Fleet, based at Brindisi. A Second Allied Fleet was to be constituted from French, British, and Italian ships not included in the First Fleet, to be under the command of Admiral de Lapeyrère but to be available to the Duke of the Abruzzi on call for any major operations. The British contingent in the Adriatic, which was to consist of the battleships *Queen, Prince of Wales, London,* and *Implacable,* and the light cruisers *Dublin, Dartmouth, Sapphire,* and *Amethyst,* were under the command of Rear-Admiral Cecil Thursby, who took his orders from the Italian Commander-in-Chief.

With the coast on both sides of the Straits of Otranto now in Allied hands resulting from Italian ownership of Brindisi on the western side and the use of Valona on the eastern, the blockade was rendered easier. The Italian admiral set up three patrol areas which effectively covered the Straits, together with a covering force of destroyers. Three Italian light cruisers, with the four allocated from British sources, were not detailed for blockade duties but now were held available for additional support if required, for operations against the Austrian coast line, and for fleet scouting.

Austrians dominate Adriatic

The Austrians opened their naval war against Italy by bombarding the towns of Ancona, Rimini, and other small ports on the night of the declaration of war, catching Italian ships still unprepared for hostilities. Italian submarines at Ancona, instead of being at sea, were still in harbour. On the whole, not a great deal of damage was done, though the Italian destroyer *Turbine,* caught unsupported by a force of two Austrian light cruisers and three destroyers, was annihilated. Various small-scale operations against the Austrian coast were carried out in retaliation, though none of them really amounted to more than the destruction of a few lighthouses and signal stations.

This early phase of Adriatic operations came to an end on June 9 when the British light cruiser *Dublin* was torpedoed by an Austrian submarine and other losses were suffered by the Italians. On this same day the Italians suffered two losses. One was the submarine *Medusa,* returning on the surface to Venice from

patrol, which was torpedoed by one of the small German U-Boats which had been brought overland in parts and assembled at Pola. The other was the rigid airship M2, which had been bombing the dockyard at Fiume (Rijeka) but had run out of fuel, coming down in the sea. She was burnt by the Austrians and her crew captured.

A series of minor coastal bombardments by the Austrians, including one at Bari, which was the home and the parliamentary constituency of the Italian Prime Minister, raised so much outcry that the Italian Admiralty decided to station a division of armoured cruisers at Venice. This, to say the least, was an odd decision as the armoured cruisers were fast enough neither to prevent Austrian ships bombarding Ancona nor to cut them off on their return home. This mistaken policy had its inevitable result on July 7 when the *Amalfi* was torpedoed and sunk, a painful demonstration of the danger to which heavy ships were exposed in those waters. Her loss resulted in the even odder decision not to withdraw the armoured cruisers from Venice, in spite of their obvious uselessness there, but to forbid them to go to sea. What purpose they were meant to serve was never made clear.

Another Italian cruiser, the *Guiseppe Garibaldi,* was lost on July 18. She, with others of her division based on Brindisi, had been sent out to destroy the railway bridge at Ragusa (Dubrovnik), which had been repaired after an earlier bombardment. The cruisers were sighted by an Austrian aircraft on their way across the Adriatic and a submarine from Cattaro was sent to cut them off. One torpedo hit the *Garibaldi* as she was returning from Ragusa and the ship capsized and sank shortly afterwards.

This last loss resulted in a yet further pulling in of Italian horns in the Adriatic. For some months now these waters had been considered too dangerous for battleships and for heavy cruisers, and the ridiculous situation had arisen in which the two major Mediterranean battlefleets, those of France and Italy, were being employed as no more than a distant covering force for the Dardanelles operations while a third and much smaller Mediterranean battlefleet (Austrian) dominated the Adriatic unchallenged. All British attempts to secure a more rational co-operation of the French and Italian forces under the command of one admiral, whether French or Italian, foundered against the rock of national pride. The results of the Adriatic campaign during the four months since Italy had entered the war had been profoundly discouraging. Italian losses had been two armoured cruisers, one destroyer, two torpedo boats, three submarines, and two rigid airships. In addition the *Dublin,* torpedoed in June, was still out of action and under repair at Malta. Against these, the Austrians had lost two submarines and three naval aircraft.

Public discontent was profound, and made yet more apprehensive by the frequency with which Austrian ships appeared off the Italian coast and bombarded towns and villages. On no occasion had the Italians succeeded in bringing the raiders to action. 'In four months,' wrote the British Naval Attaché in Rome,

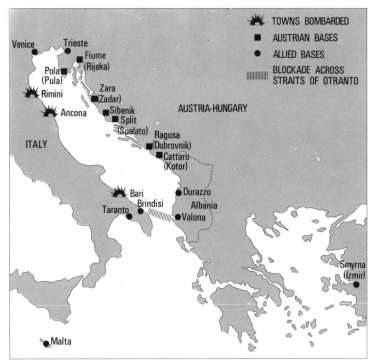

TOWNS BOMBARDED
AUSTRIAN BASES
ALLIED BASES
BLOCKADE ACROSS STRAITS OF OTRANTO

The blockade of the Adriatic: it cleared the Mediterranean of Austrian warships, but could not prevent the Adriatic becoming an Austrian lake

'the Austrian fleet has established a moral ascendency in the Adriatic and has played the part of a weaker force with conspicuous success. Not only has it succeeded in weakening the Italian fleet, but it has immobilised a force very considerably superior to itself.'

The Italian Minister of Marine bowed to the public distrust and resigned on September 25. The serious deficiencies in light craft, and particularly in submarines, were laid at his door. In order to mitigate the shortage of submarines Britain offered to send six of her B-class boats to the northern Adriatic. Their small radius of action limited their use in the wide waters of the Mediterranean, but in the narrow waters of the Adriatic there were possibilities of a more advantageous employment. By the end of October five of them had reached Venice, the sixth was still in dockyard hands in Malta and could not be sent until she had completed her refit. Although the submarines had little actual operational success, their presence considerably restricted Austrian fleet movements, and the almost daily bombardment of towns on the Italian coast became a thing of the past.

△ Admiral Sir Richard Pierse; he tried unsuccessfully to neutralise the port of Smyrna in case it should be used as a U-Boat base on the flank of the Gallipoli operations
◁ The sinking of HMS *Triumph* off Gaba Tepe (Gallipoli), May 25, 1915. Small naval steamboats rush to aid the *Triumph* which had been torpedoed by the *U21*. The *Triumph* is a smudge on the horizon
▷ The sailors of the rival Austrian and Italian navies. Here both the Austrian *(left)* and Italian *(right)* are shown wearing the dark-blue winter uniform
▽ Admiral de Lapeyrère, commander of the Second Allied Fleet. British attempts to secure a rational co-operation between French and Italian naval forces foundered against the rock of national pride

Julian Allen

BATTLE OF JUTLAND

Here at last was the 20th-century Trafalgar: the long-awaited clash of the mighty dreadnoughts. As the two fleets collided in the North Sea and turned the full fury of their huge guns upon each other, the unexpected happened, suddenly, in many quarters. The story of this most controversial battle is told both by a British and a German Naval historian

British View

With the arrival of spring 1916, the First World War was eighteen months old. On land a decision had eluded the opposing armies; they had settled into a war of attrition bleeding both sides white. At sea the two most powerful fleets the world had ever seen faced each other across the North Sea, each eager to engage the other, but neither able to bring about an encounter on terms favourable to itself.

The British Grand Fleet, under Admiral Sir John Jellicoe, was concentrated at Scapa Flow, in the Orkneys, whence, it was calculated, the northern exit from the North Sea could be closed to the enemy, while the German fleet could still be intercepted and brought to battle should it threaten the British coasts. The British ability to read German coded radio messages enabled them to obtain warning of any impending moves.

The German High Seas Fleet, numerically much inferior to its opponent, could contemplate battle with only a portion of the British Grand Fleet. From almost the beginning of the war its strategy had been aimed at forcing the British to divide their strength so that this might be brought about. Raids by the German battle-cruiser force, commanded by Rear-Admiral Hipper, on English east coast towns had been mounted. The failure of the Grand Fleet to intercept these had resulted in the Grand Fleet's battle-cruiser force, under Vice-

Admiral Sir David Beatty, being based at Rosyth; and when Hipper again sortied in January 1915 he had been intercepted. In the battle of Dogger Bank which had followed, the German armoured cruiser *Blücher* had been sunk and the battle-cruiser *Seydlitz* had narrowly escaped destruction when a shell penetrated her after turret, starting a conflagration among the ammunition. Only flooding the magazine had saved her.

Further adventures by the High Seas Fleet had been forbidden by the Kaiser and the Germans had launched their first unrestricted U-boat campaign against Allied merchant shipping. For the rest of 1915 the High Seas Fleet had languished in port, chafing against its inaction.

But in January 1916, its command had been taken over by Admiral Reinhard Scheer who had at once set about reanimating it. Raids on the English coast were resumed. As before, the Grand Fleet, in spite of the warnings received through radio interception, had been unable to reach the scene from Scapa Flow in time to interfere. Jellicoe was forced to agree to his 5th Battle Squadron — the fast and powerful Queen Elizabeth-class ships — joining Beatty's Battle-cruiser Fleet at Rosyth.

When in May 1916, the U-boat campaign was called off at the threat of American intervention on the Allied side and the submarines recalled, Scheer had the conditions necessary for his ambition to bring

about a fleet action on favourable terms by bringing the three arms of the fleet simultaneously into play. His surface forces were to sortie for a bombardment of Sunderland and lure the enemy to sea where his U-boats could ambush them, while his Zeppelin airships would scout far afield and so enable him to avoid any confrontation with a superior enemy concentration.

Plans were drawn up for the latter part of May; the actual date, to be decided at the last moment, would depend upon when the fleet was brought up to full strength by the return of the battle-cruiser *Seydlitz* from repairs caused by mine damage during a previous sortie, and upon suitable weather for the airships to reconnoitre efficiently. Meanwhile the U-boats, sixteen in number, sailed on 17th May for their stations off Scapa, Cromarty, and the Firth of Forth. Their endurance made the 30th the latest possible date. The *Seydlitz* did not rejoin until the 28th, however, and then a period of hazy weather set in, unsuitable for air reconnaissance.

Against such a development, an alternative plan had been prepared. Hipper's battle-cruiser force was to go north from the Heligoland Bight and 'trail its shirt' off the Norwegian coast where it would be duly reported to the British. Beatty's battle-cruiser fleet from Rosyth would come racing eastwards to fall into the trap of the High Seas Fleet battle squadrons, waiting some forty miles to the southward of

Right: The context of the first phase of the battle: the battle-cruisers' run to the south. Realising that he cannot hope to deal with Beatty on his own, Hipper decides to turn and lure Beatty's battle-cruisers down onto Scheer's main part of the High Seas Fleet to the south. As a result of signalling faults, the most powerful element of Beatty's force, the 5th Battle Squadron, is left behind at first, giving Hipper a slight superiority of numbers. Combined with their initial better shooting, and the poor protection for the vitals of the British ships, this enables the German battle-cruisers to despatch two of their opponents. And then over the horizon appears Scheer. *Above:* Phase One of the engagement in detail

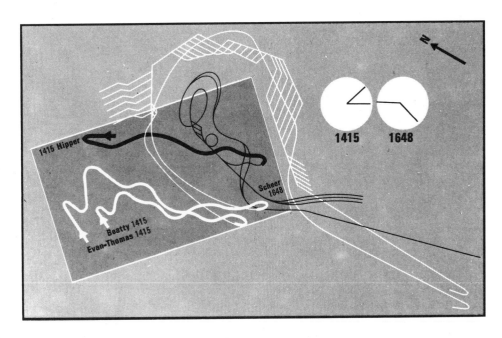

Hipper, before the Grand Fleet from Scapa could intervene.

The trap is set

Such a plan – assuming an unlikely credulity on the part of the British – was naïve, to say the least, even allowing for the fact that the British ability to read German wireless signals was not realized. Nevertheless, when the thick weather persisted throughout the 28th and 29th, it was decided to employ it. On the afternoon of 30th May, the brief signal went out to the High Seas Fleet assembled in the Schillig Roads – 31GG2490, which signified 'Carry out Secret Instruction 2490 on 31st May'.

This was duly picked up by the Admiralty's monitoring stations and though its meaning was not known, it was clear from various indications that some major operation by the German fleet was impending. At once the organization for getting the Grand Fleet to sea swung into action; the main body under the commander-in-chief, with his flag in the *Iron Duke*, including the three battle-cruisers of the 3rd Battle-Cruiser Squadron, who had been detached there from Rosyth for gunnery practice, sailed from Scapa Flow; from the Cromarty Firth sailed the 2nd Battle Squadron, the 1st Cruiser Squadron, and a flotilla of destroyers. These two forces were to rendezvous the following morning (31st) in a position some ninety miles west of Norway's southerly point. When joined,

they would comprise a force of no less than 24 dreadnought battleships, 3 battle-cruisers, 8 armoured cruisers, 12 light cruisers, and 51 destroyers. Beatty's Battle-Cruiser Fleet – 6 battle-cruisers, the four 15-inch-gun, fast Queen Elizabeth-class battleships, 12 light cruisers, 28 destroyers, and a seaplane carrier – was to steer from the Firth of Forth directly to reach a position some 120 miles west of the Jutland Bank at 1400 on the 31st, which would place him sixty-nine miles ahead of the Grand Fleet as it steered towards the Heligoland Bight. If Beatty's fleet had sighted no enemy by that time, it was to turn north to meet Jellicoe.

Thus, long before the first moves of Scheer's plan to lure Beatty out had been made, the whole vast strength of the British fleet was at sea. The schemer was liable to have the tables turned on him. The first aim of Scheer's project had already been missed. His U-boats had failed to deliver any successful attacks on the British

squadrons as they sortied; furthermore their reports of what they had seen added up only to various isolated squadrons at sea and gave no warning that the Grand Fleet was at sea in strength.

At 0100 on 31st May, therefore, the first ships of Hipper's force – five battle-cruisers of the 1st Scouting Group *(Lützow* (flag-ship), *Derfflinger, Seydlitz, Moltke, Von der Tann),* four light cruisers of the 2nd Scouting Group, and 33 destroyers led by another light cruiser – weighed anchor and steered north past Heligoland and through the swept channels, leaving the Horn Reef light vessel to the eastward of them. They were followed, fifty miles astern, by Scheer, his flag in the *Friedrich der Grosse,* leading 16 dreadnought battleships, 6 pre-dreadnoughts, and accompanied by 5 light cruisers of the 4th Scouting Group and 39 destroyers led by a light cruiser.

By 1400 Hipper was abreast the Jutland Bank off the Danish coast – his scouting light cruisers spread on an arc extending

HMS *Agincourt* (foreground) with HMS *Erin* beyond her. The *Agincourt* carried the largest number of heavy guns mounted on any one capital ship: 14 12-inch guns in seven centreline turrets. The *Erin* was armed with ten 13.5-inch guns in five turrets. Both ships were originally ordered by foreign buyers (the *Erin* by Turkey and the *Agincourt* by Brazil) but taken over by Britain at the beginning of the war

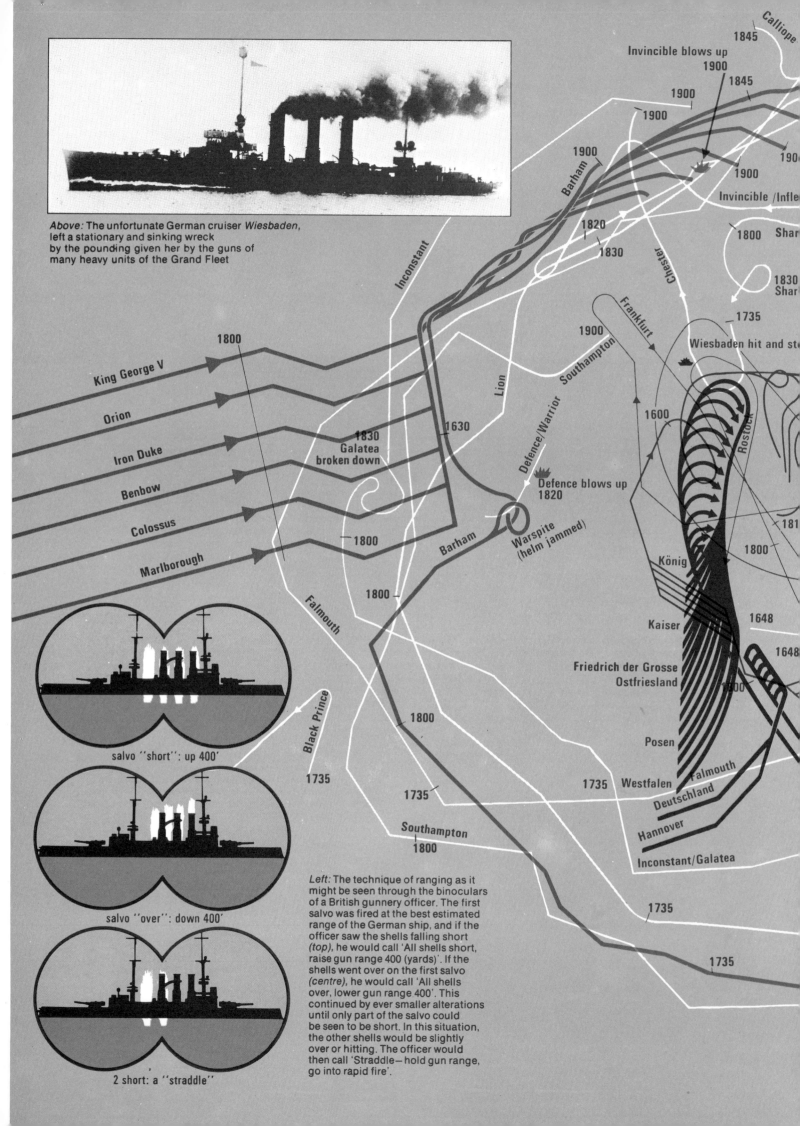

Above: The unfortunate German cruiser *Wiesbaden*, left a stationary and sinking wreck by the pounding given her by the guns of many heavy units of the Grand Fleet

salvo "short": up 400'

salvo "over": down 400'

2 short: a "straddle"

Left: The technique of ranging as it might be seen through the binoculars of a British gunnery officer. The first salvo was fired at the best estimated range of the German ship, and if the officer saw the shells falling short *(top)*, he would call 'All shells short, raise gun range 400 (yards)'. If the shells went over on the first salvo *(centre)*, he would call 'All shells over, lower gun range 400'. This continued by ever smaller alterations until only part of the salvo could be seen to be short. In this situation, the other shells would be slightly over or hitting. The officer would then call 'Straddle—hold gun range, go into rapid fire'.

Calliope

Invincible blows up
1900
1900
1845
1900
1900
1900

Barham

1900

Invincible /Infle

1820

1800   Shar

1830

1830
Shar

Chester

1735

Frankfurt

Wiesbaden hit and ste

1900

Southampton

1600

1735

Rostock

King George V   1800

Inconstant

Lion

Defence/Warrior

Orion

Iron Duke

1630

1810

Benbow

1830
Galatea
broken down

Defence blows up
1820

1800

Colossus

König

1800

Marlborough

Warspite
(helm jammed)

1800

Kaiser

1648

Barham

1648

Friedrich der Grosse
Ostfriesland

Falmouth

1800

1800

1800

Posen

Black Prince

Falmouth

1735

1735   Westfalen

Deutschland

1735

1800

Southampton
1800

Hannover

Inconstant/Galatea

1735

1735

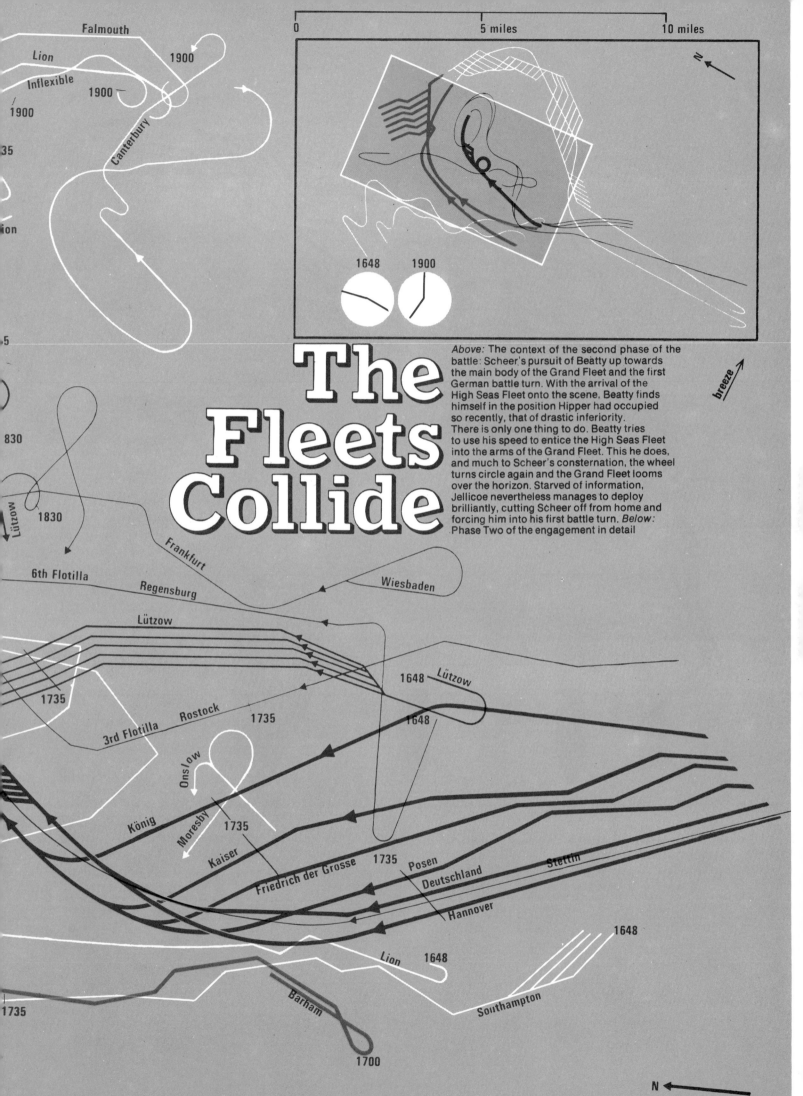

The Fleets Collide

Above: The context of the second phase of the battle: Scheer's pursuit of Beatty up towards the main body of the Grand Fleet and the first German battle turn. With the arrival of the High Seas Fleet onto the scene, Beatty finds himself in the position Hipper had occupied so recently, that of drastic inferiority. There is only one thing to do. Beatty tries to use his speed to entice the High Seas Fleet into the arms of the Grand Fleet. This he does, and much to Scheer's consternation, the wheel turns circle again and the Grand Fleet looms over the horizon. Starved of information, Jellicoe nevertheless manages to deploy brilliantly, cutting Scheer off from home and forcing him into his first battle turn. *Below:* Phase Two of the engagement in detail

Falmouth
Lion
Inflexible
1900
1900
1900
1900
Canterbury
35
ion
5

0   5 miles   10 miles
1648   1900

breeze

830
Lützow
1830

Frankfurt
6th Flotilla
Regensburg
Wiesbaden
Lützow
1735
1648 — Lützow
Rostock   1735
3rd Flotilla   1648
Onslow
König
Moresby   1735
Kaiser
Friedrich der Grosse   1735   Posen
Deutschland   Stettin
Hannover
1648
Lion   1648
Barham
Southampton
1735
1700

N

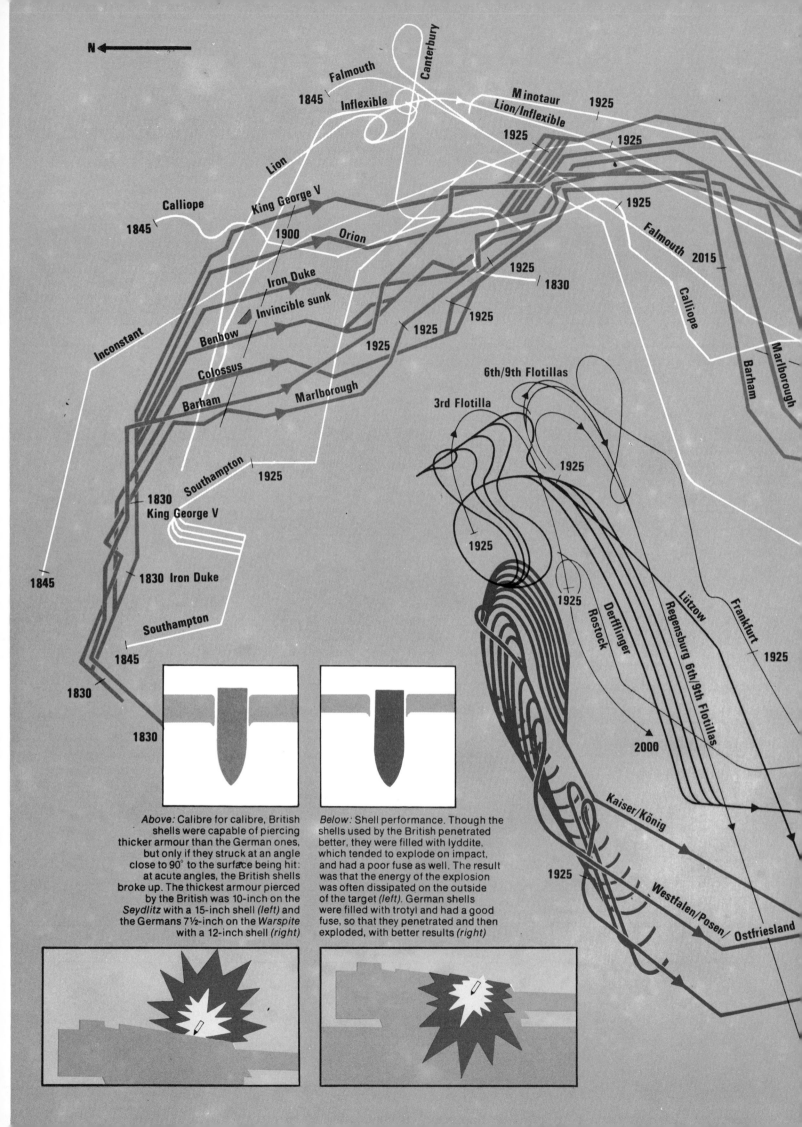

Above: Calibre for calibre, British shells were capable of piercing thicker armour than the German ones, but only if they struck at an angle close to 90° to the surface being hit: at acute angles, the British shells broke up. The thickest armour pierced by the British was 10-inch on the *Seydlitz* with a 15-inch shell *(left)* and the Germans 7½-inch on the *Warspite* with a 12-inch shell *(right)*

Below: Shell performance. Though the shells used by the British penetrated better, they were filled with lyddite, which tended to explode on impact, and had a poor fuse as well. The result was that the energy of the explosion was often dissipated on the outside of the target *(left)*. German shells were filled with trotyl and had a good fuse, so that they penetrated and then exploded, with better results *(right)*

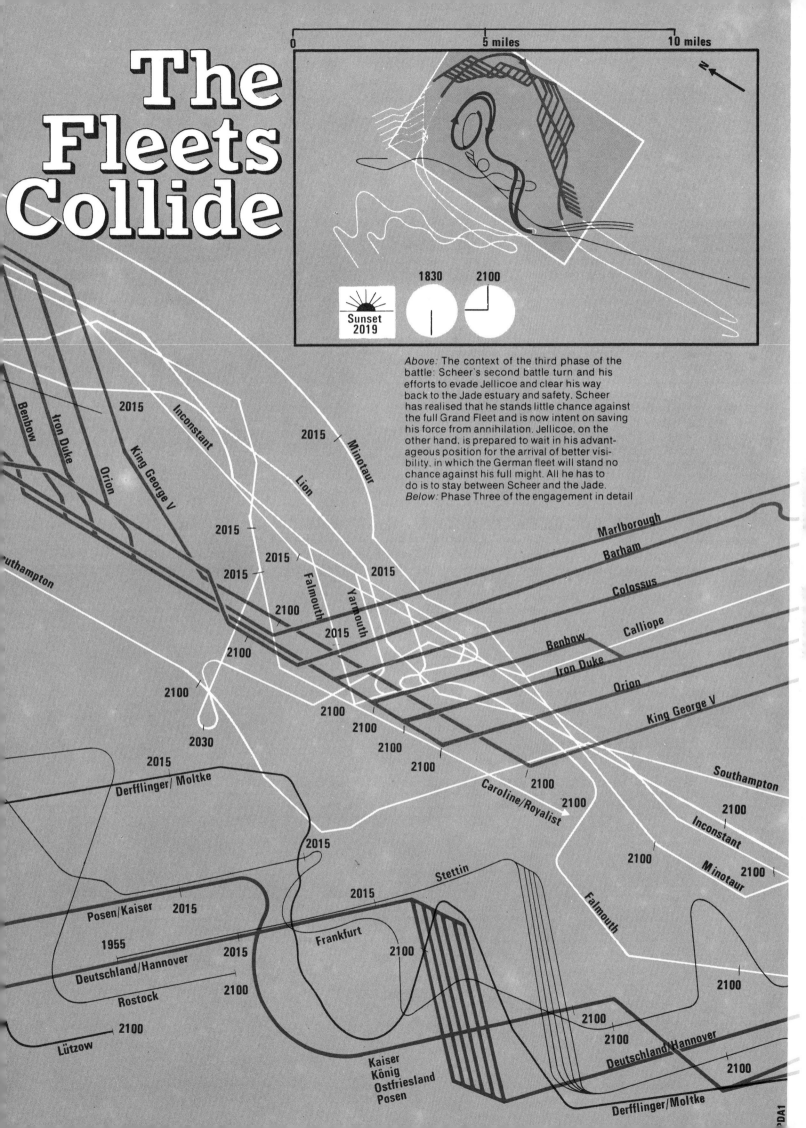

The Fleets Collide

0   **5 miles**   **10 miles**

1830   **2100**

Sunset 2019

Above: The context of the third phase of the battle: Scheer's second battle turn and his efforts to evade Jellicoe and clear his way back to the Jade estuary and safety. Scheer has realised that he stands little chance against the full Grand Fleet and is now intent on saving his force from annihilation. Jellicoe, on the other hand, is prepared to wait in his advantageous position for the arrival of better visibility, in which the German fleet will stand no chance against his full might. All he has to do is to stay between Scheer and the Jade.
Below: Phase Three of the engagement in detail

Benbow

Iron Duke

Orion

King George V

Inconstant

2015

2015

Lion

Minotaur

Southampton

2015

2015

2015

2015

Falmouth

Yarmouth

2015

2015

2100

2100

2100

2100

2030

2015

Marlborough

Barham

Colossus

Calliope

Benbow

Iron Duke

Orion

King George V

2100

2100

2100

2100

Caroline/Royalist

2100

Southampton

2100

Inconstant

Minotaur

2100

2100

Derfflinger/Moltke

2015

2015

Stettin

Falmouth

Posen/Kaiser

2015

2015

Frankfurt

2100

1955

2015

Deutschland/Hannover

Rostock

2100

2100

Lützow

2100

Kaiser
König
Ostfriesland
Posen

2100

2100

Deutschland/Hannover

2100

Derfflinger/Moltke

from ahead to either beam, some seven to ten miles from the battle-cruisers. It was a clear, calm, summer day with visibility extreme but likely to become hazy as the afternoon wore on. Unknown to Hipper and equally ignorant of his presence, Beatty was fifty miles to the north-westward, zig-zagging at 19 knots on a mean course of east and approaching the eastward limit set for his advance, with his light cruisers scouting ahead in pairs. The signal to turn north was made at 1415 and was obeyed by all except the light cruiser *Galatea* which held on to investigate smoke on the eastern horizon. This came from a Danish merchantman and was simultaneously being investigated by the western-most of Hipper's light cruisers, the *Elbing*. The two warships thus came in sight of one another, reported, and fired the opening shots of the battle of Jutland.

The two battle-cruiser admirals turned at once towards the sound of the guns which soon brought them in sight of one another on opposite courses, when Hipper altered course to the southward to lead his opponents towards the advancing German battle squadrons. That these were at sea was still unknown to either Beatty or Jellicoe. The British radio monitoring stations had been led to believe that the High Seas Fleet was still in harbour, misled by an arrangement on the part of

Beatty's flagship, HMS *Lion*, in action at Jutland after her 'Q' turret had been destroyed by cordite flash after a hit by a heavy shell fired by the *Lutzow*

Scheer's staff which transferred the flag-ship's call-sign to a shore station so that the commander-in-chief would not be distracted by administrative matters.

The battle-cruisers open fire
The *Lion*, leading *Princess Royal, Queen Mary, Tiger, New Zealand* and *Indefatigable* (in that order), turned on a parallel course and at 1548 each side opened fire. Hipper was outnumbered, six ships to five. He would have been even more, perhaps disastrously, inferior, but for Beatty's impetuosity in racing at full speed into action without waiting for the 5th Battle Squadron, which was not only initially six miles farther from the enemy but, owing to signal confusion, failed to conform at once to Beatty's movements. By the time it did so, it was ten miles astern, and it was not until twenty-seven minutes after action had been joined that the 15-inch guns of the British battleships could open fire.

In the interval much had happened. Hipper's ships had quickly displayed a gunnery superiority over their opponents who were very slow to find the range. The *Lion, Princess Royal,* and *Tiger* had all been heavily hit before a single German ship had suffered; though the *Seydlitz, Derfflinger,* and *Lützow* were then each hit hard, the advantage had continued to lie with Hipper's ships and at 1600 Beatty's rear ship, *Indefatigable,* had blown up and sunk as shells plunged through into her magazines. Almost simultaneously the *Lion* had been only saved from a similar fate by flooding the magazine of her mid-ship

turret when it was penetrated by a shell from the *Lützow*.

But now, at last, the 5th Battle Squadron (*Barham, Valiant, Warspite, Malaya,* lying in that order) was able to get into action. Their gunnery was magnificent. The two rear ships of Hipper's line were quickly hit. Disaster must have overwhelmed him but for a defect of the British shells, some of which broke up on impact instead of penetrating the armour. Nevertheless, it seemed impossible Hipper could survive long enough for Scheer's battle-squadrons, still over the horizon, to come to his rescue. In spite of this the German battle-cruisers continued to shoot with deadly accuracy and at 1626 the *Queen Mary,* betrayed, like the *Indefatigable,* by her inadequate armour, blew up.

Meanwhile, a destroyer battle had been raging between the lines, the flotillas on each side moving out to attack with torpedoes and meeting to fight it out with guns. Of all the torpedoes fired, one only, from the British *Petard,* found a billet in the *Seydlitz,* but did not damage her enough to put her out of action. Two British destroyers were sunk.

The fast-moving battle had left the majority of Beatty's scouting cruisers behind, except for Commodore Goodenough's 2nd Light Cruiser Squadron which by 1633 had succeeded in getting two miles ahead of the *Lion*. At that moment to Goodenough's astonished gaze the top masts of a long line of battleships hove in sight. In the radio rooms of the ships of the British fleet, the message, which all had

almost despaired of ever hearing, was taken in: 'Have sighted enemy battle fleet, bearing SE. Enemy's course North.'

Hipper had been saved in the nick of time, and his task of luring Beatty brilliantly achieved. Goodenough's timely warning, however, enabled the latter to escape the trap. Before the enemy battle fleet came within range, Beatty reversed course to the northward. The 5th Battle Squadron held on for a while to cover the damaged battle-cruisers' retreat. By the time they turned back themselves they came under heavy fire from the German battle squadrons and *Malaya*, in particular, received damaging hits. In reply they did heavy damage to the *Lützow*, *Derfflinger*, and *Seydlitz*, as well as hitting the leading German battleships.

The situation had now been reversed, with Beatty drawing the enemy after him towards a superior force the latter knew nothing of—the Grand Fleet, pressing southwards at its best speed of 20 knots. Jellicoe's twenty-four battleships were in the compact cruising formation of six columns abeam of each other, with the fleet flagship leading the more easterly of the two centre columns. Before encountering the enemy they would have to be deployed into a single battle line to allow all ships to bring their guns to bear. If deployment was delayed too long, the consequences could be disastrous. To make a deployment by the right method, it was essential that the admiral should know the bearing on which the approaching enemy would appear.

For various reasons—discrepancy between the calculated positions of the two portions of the fleet and communication failures—this was just what Jellicoe did not know. And, meanwhile, the two fleets were racing towards each other at a combined speed of nearly 40 knots. Even though Beatty's light cruisers had made visual contact with Jellicoe's advanced screen of armoured cruisers at 1630, though the thunder of distant gun-fire had been audible for some time before the *Marlborough*, leading the starboard column of the Grand Fleet battleships, sighted gun-flashes through the gathering haze and funnel smoke ahead at 1750, and six minutes later Beatty's battle-cruisers were sighted from the *Iron Duke* racing across the line of Jellicoe's advance—and incidentally spreading a further pall of black smoke—it was not until nearly 1815 that at last, in the nick of time, the vital piece of information reached the commander-in-chief from the *Lion:* 'Enemy battle fleet bearing south-west.'

Jellicoe's vital decision

During the next minute or so, through the mind of Jellicoe as he stood gazing at the compass in its binnacle on the bridge of the *Iron Duke,* sped the many considerations on the accurate interpretation of which, at this moment of supreme crisis, the correct deployment and all chances of victory depended. The decision Jellicoe made—to deploy on his port wing column on a course south-east by east—has been damned and lauded by opposing critics in

the controversy that was later to develop.

To the appalled Scheer, as out of the smoke and haze ahead of him, between him and retreat to his base, loomed an interminable line of dim grey shapes from which rippled the flash of heavy gunfire, and a storm of shell splashes began to fall round the leading ships of his line, there was no doubt. His 'T' had been crossed—the worst situation possible in a fleet action. Fortunately for him a counter to such a calamity, a simultaneous 'about turn' by every ship of the battle columns—a manoeuvre not lightly undertaken by a mass of the unwieldy battleships of the day—had been practised and perfected by the High Seas Fleet. He ordered it now, and so, behind a smoke screen laid by his destroyers extricated himself from the trap so brilliantly sprung by Jellicoe.

His escape was only temporary, nevertheless. Between him and his base was a force whose full strength he had been unable as yet to determine, which he must either fight or somehow evade.

While the trap was thus being sprung on Scheer, some final spectacular successes had been achieved by the Germans. Of the 5th Battle Squadron, the *Warspite,* with her helm jammed, had charged towards Scheer's battle line and before she could be got under control again, had been severely damaged and forced out of action. Jellicoe's advanced screen of armoured cruisers had been caught at short range by Hipper's battle-cruisers and the leading German battleships as they emerged from the smoke haze. The *Defence* had been

overwhelmed and blown up, the *Warrior* so heavily damaged that she staggered out of action to sink on her way back to harbour. Then the German battle-cruisers had encountered the three battle-cruisers attached to the Grand Fleet. In a brief gun duel at short range, the Germans had suffered many hits and further damage; but in reply had sunk the *Invincible* whose magazine was penetrated in the same way as in the *Indefatigable* and *Queen Mary*.

This was the last major success for the Germans, however. They had fought magnificently and, with the aid of superior ship design and ammunition, had had much the better of the exchanges, though the *Lützow* was by now fatally crippled, limping painfully off the scene, and only the stout construction and well-designed compartmentation of the other battle-cruisers was saving them from a similar state. But Scheer was now desperately on the defensive, though he had not yet realized that it was the whole Grand Fleet he had encountered. As soon as his initial retreat brought relief from the concentration of fire on his van, he reversed course once again in the hope of being able to cut through astern of the enemy to gain a clear escape route to the Horn Reef lightship and safety behind his own minefields. Once again he ran up against the immense line of dreadnoughts of which all he could see in the poor visibility to the eastward was the flickering orange light of their broadsides. Once again he had hastily to retire or be annihilated.

While he was extricating himself he launched his much-tried battle-cruisers on a rearguard thrust and his destroyer flotillas to deliver a massed torpedo attack. The former miraculously survived a further hammering before being recalled. The latter launched a total of twenty-eight torpedoes at the British line. More than any

SMS *König*, one of the German dreadnoughts, opens fire. Her broad beam, which all the newer German ships possessed, gave her a much steadier firing platform than the narrower British ships

other single factor they were to save the High Seas Fleet from disaster, robbing Jellicoe of the fruits of the strategic masterpiece he had brought about.

The counter to the massed torpedo attack by destroyers, which could be backed by long-range torpedo fire from retreating battleships, had been carefully studied. There were several alternatives; the only one sufficiently effective in Jellicoe's opinion, was a simultaneous turn away by his own battle line. This was promptly carried out—a turn of 45 degrees.

Contact lost

The two battle fleets were now on widely diverging courses and rapidly ran out of range and sight of one another. By the time the twenty-eight torpedoes had been avoided—not one scored a hit—and the British battle line turned back to regain contact, more than fifteen miles separated Jellicoe and Scheer. Sunset was barely half an hour away. Yet there was time in the long summer twilight ahead for the battle to be renewed on greatly advantageous terms for Jellicoe if he turned at once to an interception course. That he did not do so until too late for various reasons, not the least of which was the failure of his scouting forces to keep him informed of the enemy's position and movements, was to be the central feature of much criticism.

The van of the German battle fleet came, in fact, briefly into view from the nearest British battleship division at the moment that Jellicoe, who was not willing to accept the uncertain fortunes of a night action, ordered a turn away and the adoption of a compact night cruising disposition. The opportunity was let slip, never to return.

Nevertheless, at this stage, as night settled down over a calm sea, the outlook for Scheer was bleak, indeed. Between him and his base was an overwhelming enemy force. Unless he could get past it during the night, the battle must be resumed at daybreak and, with a long summer day ahead, it could only spell annihilation for him. He decided his only hope was to try

to bludgeon his way through, regardless of consequences. To his fleet he signalled the course for the Horn Reef Light at a speed of 16 knots, adding the instruction that this course was to be maintained at all costs.

Jellicoe, having formed his night disposition and ordered his flotillas (many of whom had not yet been in action) to the rear, was steering a course slightly converging with that of Scheer but at a knot faster. From Jellicoe's point of view, Scheer had the choice of two routes—to the entrance of the channels which began at the Horn Reef Light or southward into the German Bight before turning eastward round the mined areas. The extra knot would keep the Grand Fleet between Scheer and the latter. If he chose the former he must pass astern of Jellicoe's battle squadrons, where he would encounter the massed British flotillas which could be counted on to inflict severe losses and to keep Jellicoe informed.

In the event the British flotillas failed to do either of these things. The pre-dreadnought battleship *Pommern* and a light cruiser were their sole victims in a series of night encounters, and they passed no information of the position and course of the enemy. On the other hand Scheer's message to his fleet was intercepted by the Admiralty and was passed to Jellicoe, though a further message in which Scheer asked for airship reconnaissance of the Horn Reef area at dawn which would have clinched the matter, was withheld.

In the absence of certain knowledge of the enemy's movements, Jellicoe held on through the night. Scheer crossed astern of him and by daylight was safe, a development which seemed little short of miraculous to the German admiral.

The battle of Jutland was over. Controversy as to its outcome was to rage for decades. The bald facts, of which German publicity made the most in claiming a great victory, while the British Admiralty's communiqué did nothing to explain or qualify them, showed that a superior British force had lost three capital ships,

three cruisers, and a number of destroyers against one battle-cruiser, a pre-dreadnought battleship, four cruisers, and some destroyers sunk on the German side.

Even to-day more than fifty years since the battle, it is not easy to strike a balance sheet of victory and defeat. British losses were largely the result of inferior armour protection in their battle-cruisers, which had been accepted in favour of mounting bigger guns, the advantage of which had been lost through faulty design of armour-piercing shells. Even so, one of the surviving German battle-cruisers only reached harbour in a sinking condition, another was a hideous shambles with 200 casualties, bearing witness to the pounding they had received even from defective shells.

The High Seas Fleet was no longer fit for battle on the morning of the 1st June 1916 and could only make for harbour and repairs, fortunately close at hand. The Grand Fleet was largely intact and ready to renew the fight. Jellicoe may be said, perhaps, to have lost the battle of Jutland. Scheer can hardly be judged to have won anything but an escape from annihilation.

So much for the immediate results of the encounter. They do not add up to a victory for either side. In the larger context of the war at sea as a whole, it is no easier to weigh the results. When Scheer led the High Seas Fleet out once again in August 1916 (except for *Seydlitz* and *Derfflinger*, still under repair), he narrowly escaped being caught in a second Jutland trap, with no safe base under his lee this time, in spite of Zeppelin reconnaissance aloft. Both Scheer and the Kaiser's general headquarters were finally convinced that the risks to be faced in attempting to bring about a sea fight were unacceptable. The High Seas Fleet, built at such cost to challenge Great Britain's seapower, was ordered back on to the defensive. The fatal decision was taken to revert to the unrestricted submarine warfare which was to bring America into the war.

It is true, of course, that the High Seas Fleet kept 'in being', forced the continued maintenance of the huge Grand Fleet, absorbing many thousands of trained seamen and a hundred destroyers which could have been more profitably employed combating the U-boats. On the other hand, that same High Seas Fleet, its ships lying idle in harbour, the morale of its crews sinking, degenerated into a centre of discontent and revolution. In August 1917 Scheer had to quell an open mutiny. A year later, when ordered to sea by its new commander, Hipper, it flared into revolt and led the disintegration of the Kaiser's Germany. This, too, can be accounted one of the consequences of Jutland – perhaps the most important when reviewing the whole war.

German View

Jutland was the last of many naval battles fought by long lines of closely spaced big ships with heavy guns. Its tactical details are well-known, for each ship kept a log. Its results were inconclusive. It was the climax of the Anglo-German naval rivalry, with the scuttling of the German fleet at Scapa Flow three years later as the anti-climax.

This rivalry, which cost both nations dearly, was at least partly caused by the fact that the Germans did not fully realize the implications of seapower. In their difficult position in central Europe they needed a navy of some strength to balance the fleets of the Franco-Russian alliance. But from their inferior strategic position in the south-eastern corner of the North Sea they could neither protect their overseas trade nor attack the sea routes vital to Great Britain. When war broke out in 1914 the Royal Navy was not compelled to attack the German bases but could content itself on the whole with a distant blockade from Scapa Flow.

In the first two years of the war there were a number of operations and clashes in the North Sea which did not change the situation, since neither side wanted to give battle too far from their own bases. In 1916 this changed to some extent. Admiral Reinhard Scheer, the new commander-in-chief of the German High Seas Fleet, was more aggressive than his predecessors. On the Allied side, the Russians felt the blockade heavily and clamoured for the British to force the Baltic so that they might receive ammunition and raw materials which they needed desperately. An operation of that kind had no prospects of success, however, as long as the High Seas Fleet was intact. Therefore it was decided that stronger efforts should be made to bring it to battle. The Grand Fleet under Admiral Sir John Jellicoe had been considerably reinforced by new ships. In spring 1916 it was almost twice as strong as the German fleet.

Early in March, the German fleet made a sortie into the southern North Sea and came within sixty miles of Lowestoft. On 25th March British light forces operated south of Horn Reef, and aircraft from a seaplane-carrier tried to bombard airship sheds. Bad weather prevented contact of the heavy ships. On 25th April German battle-cruisers bombarded Lowestoft. Early in May the British repeated the attempt to attack airship sheds. Both fleets were at sea, but no contact was established.

For the second half of May, Admiral Scheer planned an operation with all his forces. The battle-cruisers were to bombard Sunderland, and twelve submarines were stationed off the British bases to attack the squadrons of the Grand Fleet when they put to sea. Scouting by airships was necessary for the German fleet to avoid being cut off by superior forces. When the time ran out for his submarines after two weeks at sea and the weather remained unfavourable, Scheer compromised on a sweep of his light forces through the Skagerrak backed up by the battle fleet. Shortly after midnight of 30th to 31st May 1916 the German scouting forces (5 battle-cruisers, 5 light cruisers, and 30 destroyers under Rear-Admiral Hipper) left Schillig Roads near Wilhelmshaven, soon followed by the battle fleet (16 new and 6 old battleships, 6 light cruisers, and 33 destroyers).

The Grand Fleet at sea

At that time the Grand Fleet was already at sea, course set for the Skagerrak, too. The bombardment of Lowestoft had roused public opinion, the situation of the Russians had deteriorated, and Jellicoe now planned to set a trap for the German fleet. Light cruisers were to sweep through the Skagerrak deep into the Kattegat; in the meantime the main forces would take up position near Horn Reef to meet the Germans who were sure to come out in order to intercept the British cruisers operating in the Kattegat.

In the early afternoon of 31st May occurred the first of the incidents which greatly changed the course of the events. The British battle-cruiser fleet, under Vice-Admiral Sir David Beatty in *Lion*, changed course from east to north to rendezvous with the battle fleet under Admiral Jellicoe in *Iron Duke*. At 1430 *Lützow*, flying Admiral Hipper's flag, was only forty-five miles east of *Lion* steering a slightly converging course. Contact would have been made considerably later but for a small Danish steamer plodding along between the two forces. Two German destroyers and a British light cruiser were dispatched to examine her. Soon the first salvoes were fired; the first hit (a dud) was made by *Elbing* on *Galatea*.

Within minutes wireless messages informed the admirals of the situation. Signals went up, Hipper swung his force round, and Beatty soon followed suit. The crews were alerted by bugles sounding action stations, guns and powder rooms were manned, steam was raised in reserve boilers, and damage parties assembled deep down in the ships. The gunnery officers climbed to their elevated positions, received ready reports from turrets, range-finders, and fire-control-stations, and then reported their batteries ready for action to their captains. Now a hush of expectancy fell over the great ships while the distance decreased by nearly a mile a minute.

At first, sight was obscured by the smoke of the cruisers. Then these fell back on their battle-cruisers, and the huge shapes of the adversaries came into each other's sight, but only for the few men whose duty was to watch the enemy. Almost all the technical personnel and most of the sailors fought without seeing an enemy ship.

Hipper faced heavy odds, ten ships with heavier guns against his five. His plan was simple: to draw the enemy to Scheer's battle fleet, which was following at a distance of fifty miles. His smaller calibres (11- and 12-inch as against 12-, 13-, and 15-inch in the British ships) made it imperative for him to get comparatively close before opening fire. He offered battle on a north-westerly course, reversed course when Beatty tried to cut his force off, and with a few terse signals coolly manoeuvred his fine ships through the danger zone. At 1548 they were at the right distance (16,500 yards) and in perfect order. The *Lützow* opened fire.

Beatty's ships started answering quickly but they were not yet in formation to use all their guns. Because of delays in signalling, the four powerful and fast battleships of the Queen Elizabeth-class had fallen astern and were out of range. Conditions for a gunnery duel were perfect: visibility was good, especially to the west, and there was hardly any seaway.

The Night Action

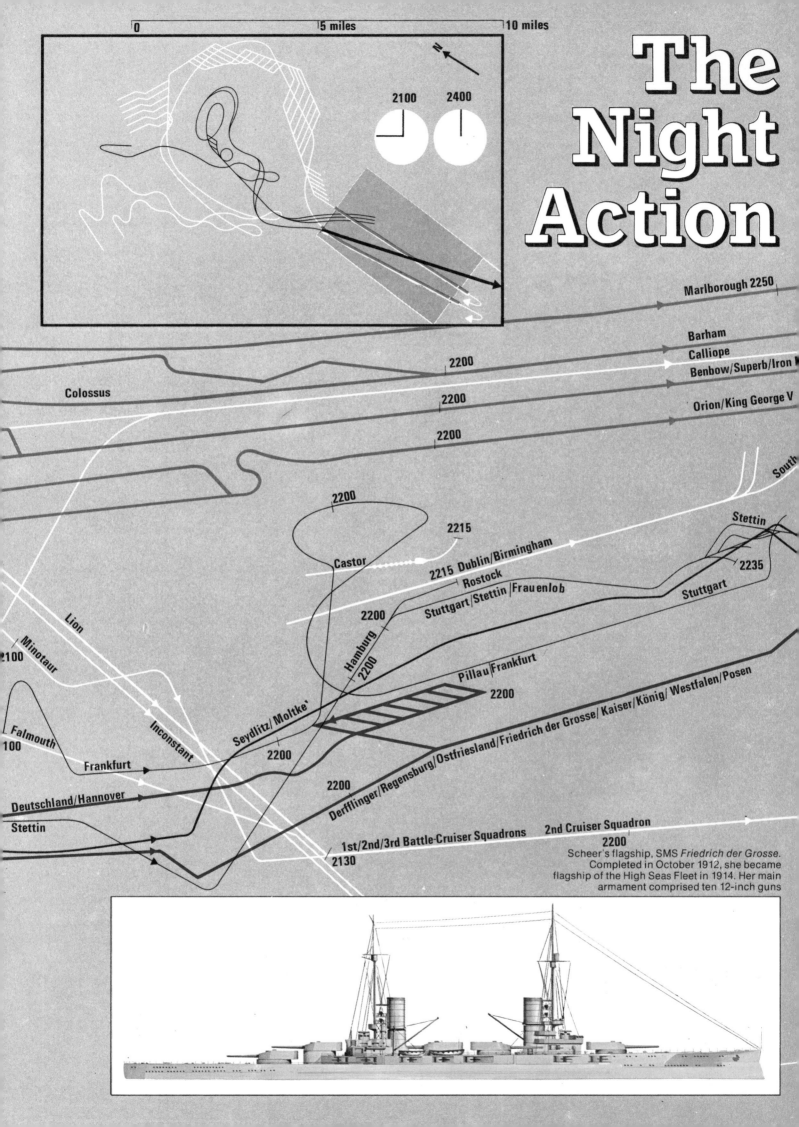

0   **5 miles**   **10 miles**

2100   2400

Marlborough 2250

Barham
Calliope
Benbow/Superb/Iron

Colossus

2200

Orion/King George V

2200

2200

South

2200

2215

Stettin

Castor

2215 Dublin/Birmingham

2235

Rostock

Stuttgart

Stuttgart/Stettin/Frauenlob

Lion

2200

Minotaur

Hamburg

2200

2100

Pillau/Frankfurt

2200

Falmouth

Inconstant

Seydlitz/Moltke

2200

100

Frankfurt

Derfflinger/Regensburg/Ostfriesland/Friedrich der Grosse/Kaiser/König/Westfalen/Posen

Deutschland/Hannover

2200

Stettin

1st/2nd/3rd Battle-Cruiser Squadrons

2nd Cruiser Squadron

2200

2130

Scheer's flagship, SMS *Friedrich der Grosse*.
Completed in October 1912, she became
flagship of the High Seas Fleet in 1914. Her main
armament comprised ten 12-inch guns

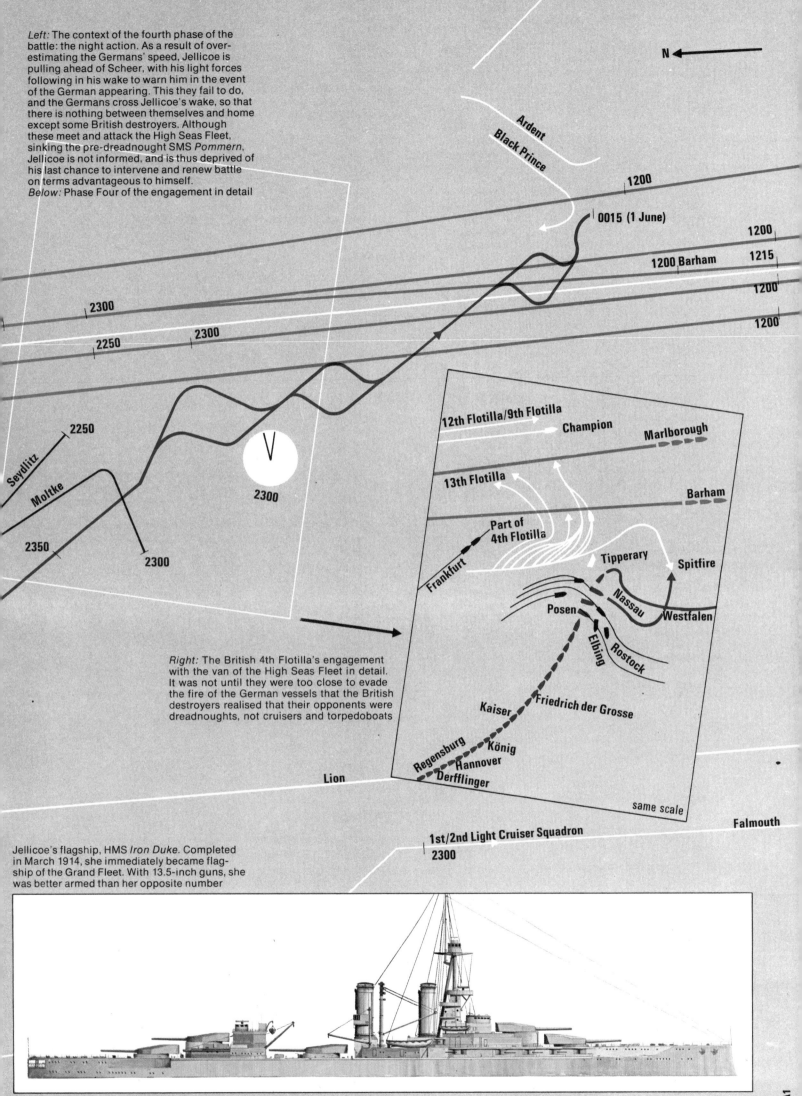

N

Left: The context of the fourth phase of the battle: the night action. As a result of over-estimating the Germans' speed, Jellicoe is pulling ahead of Scheer, with his light forces following in his wake to warn him in the event of the German appearing. This they fail to do, and the Germans cross Jellicoe's wake, so that there is nothing between themselves and home except some British destroyers. Although these meet and attack the High Seas Fleet, sinking the pre-dreadnought SMS *Pommern*, Jellicoe is not informed, and is thus deprived of his last chance to intervene and renew battle on terms advantageous to himself.
Below: Phase Four of the engagement in detail

Ardent

Black Prince

1200

0015 (1 June)

1200

1200 Barham 1215

1200

1200

2300

2250 2300

2250

Seydlitz

Moltke

2350

2300

2300

Right: The British 4th Flotilla's engagement with the van of the High Seas Fleet in detail. It was not until they were too close to evade the fire of the German vessels that the British destroyers realised that their opponents were dreadnoughts, not cruisers and torpedoboats

12th Flotilla/9th Flotilla Champion

Marlborough

13th Flotilla

Barham

Part of 4th Flotilla

Frankfurt

Tipperary

Spitfire

Nassau

Posen

Westfalen

Elbing

Rostock

Kaiser Friedrich der Grosse

Regensburg König

Hannover

Derfflinger

same scale

Lion

Falmouth

1st/2nd Light Cruiser Squadron

2300

Jellicoe's flagship, HMS *Iron Duke*. Completed in March 1914, she immediately became flagship of the Grand Fleet. With 13.5-inch guns, she was better armed than her opposite number

First blood to the Germans

The first salvoes all appear to have fallen wide, perhaps because the range-takers were more interested in the details of their foes than in measuring the distance exactly. After three minutes the Germans obtained hits on *Lion*, *Princess Royal*, and *Tiger*. Because the first target in sight had been light cruisers, the gunnery officer of *Lützow* had given orders to load shells detonating on impact. For reasons of ballistics he did not change over to armour-piercing shells. *Lion* was hit twelve times and suffered heavy casualties, but minor injuries only, except for one shell which penetrated the roof of a turret, killed the gun crews, and ignited powder-bags. The turret-commander, Major Harvey of the Royal Marines, was fatally wounded but before he died he ordered the magazines to be flooded and thus saved the ship.

Now disaster struck the rear of the British line. Here *Indefatigable* and *Von der Tann* fought an even match. At 1604, *Indefatigable*, hit by two salvoes in quick succession, erupted in a violent explosion, turned over to port and disappeared in the waves. *Von der Tann* had fired fifty-two 11-inch shells in all. Twenty minutes later a similar fate overtook *Queen Mary* who had come under the concentrated fire of *Derfflinger* and *Seydlitz*. After vehement detonations she capsized and went down with her propellers still turning. *Tiger*, the next astern, barely avoided crashing into the wreck.

In spite of these losses the situation now eased for the British. The magnificent 5th Battle Squadron, ably handled by Rear-Admiral Evan-Thomas, came up and took the rear ships of the German line under fire. When one of the projectiles, weighing almost a ton, struck *Von der Tann* far aft, the whole ship vibrated like a gigantic tuning-fork. Hipper increased speed and distance and sent his destroyers to the attack. They were met by British destroyers, and in the ensuing mêlée

Nomad and two Germans were sunk. At the same time 1630 the 2nd Light Cruiser Squadron under Commodore Goodenough sighted smoke to the south-east and, soon after, a seemingly endless column of heavy ships surrounded by light cruisers and destroyers.

Now the tables were turned. Under heavy fire Beatty reversed course and steered to the north to draw the High Seas Fleet to the British Battle Fleet. *Barham* and *Malaya* received several hits which did not, however, impair their speed, but, *Nestor*, attacking the German van with some other destroyers, was sunk. When her boatswain was rescued with other survivors he was mainly disgusted at the smallness and squalor of the coal-burning torpedo-boat which had picked him up.

All through these events the British Battle Fleet had been steadily drawing nearer, in cruising formation with its twenty-four battleships in six divisions, these in line abreast, screened by armoured and light cruisers and destroyers. The 3rd Battle-Cruiser Squadron, under Rear-Admiral Hood in *Invincible*, was twenty-five miles ahead and far to the east of its calculated position. Jellicoe, 'the only man who could lose the war in an afternoon', was now faced with the decision on which course to form his divisions into single line ahead. In all war games and exercises the rule had been 'towards Heligoland'. Yet the reports he received were incomplete and contradictory, it was impossible to get a clear picture of the situation. At the last moment, when Beatty's battle-cruisers came in sight, Jellicoe ordered his division to turn together to port to the north-east. In this way he gained a favourable position for crossing the enemy's T. He was unintentionally assisted by the 3rd Battle-Cruiser Squadron, which almost missed the Germans, but now closed in from the east and brought the German van between two fires. The light cruiser *Wiesbaden* soon lay dead in the water. For

hours the battle raged around her, she was fired upon by many British ships, but did not sink until 0200 on 1st June. Only one survivor was picked up.

The delay in forming the line of battle put part of the screen and the 5th Battle Squadron in a difficult situation at what was later called 'Windy Corner'. Making room for Beatty's battle-cruisers to go to the van of the line, some armoured cruisers came into range of the German battleships. *Defence* blew up in view of both fleets; *Warrior* was saved a similar fate by the chance intervention of *Warspite*. The 5th Battle Squadron was forced to counter-march and came under the fire of several battleships. After a hit *Warspite*'s rudder jammed; she turned towards the German line, thus masking *Warrior*, who was able to creep away, but sank on the next morning. *Warspite* almost collided with *Valiant* and made two full circles at high speed before her rudder was in working order again. Heavily damaged she was ordered home and reached Rosyth after evading the attack of a German submarine.

Visibility was now generally decreasing and greatly varying as a result of masses of funnel and artificial smoke. For the commanders-in-chief it was most difficult to gain a reliable picture of the actual situation from their own limited observations (radar was not yet invented) and the reports of their subordinates. For a few moments Scheer toyed with the idea of splitting his line to take Windy Corner under two fires. However, there was no battle signal for this promising but unusual procedure, his van was evidently hard pressed, and so he continued with his battleships in line ahead. With the loss of the destroyer *Shark* the 3rd Battle-Cruiser Squadron had inflicted heavy damage on the Germans and now took up station at the head of the British line followed by Beatty's battle-cruisers.

For more than half an hour the German ships could see no more than the flashes of

The might of the Royal Navy concentrated in the North Sea: seemingly interminable lines of dreadnoughts and super-dreadnoughts

the enemy guns. Then at 1830 visibility suddenly improved, *Lützow* and *Derfflinger* sighted *Invincible,* the leading ship, at a distance of 9,500 yards and sank her in a few minutes. There were only six survivors, among them the gunnery officer who, as he said, 'merely stepped from the foretop into the water'.

At that time Scheer ordered a battle turn reversing course to get his ships out of the overwhelming enemy fire. Beginning from the rear the heavy ships had to turn to starboard in quick succession until single line ahead was formed on the opposite course. Light cruiser squadrons and destroyer flotillas had to conform. This manoeuvre was all the more difficult because the fleet was now disposed almost in a semi-circle, but it was successful, supported by a destroyer attack on the centre of the British line. The fleets drew apart, and the fire slackened and then ceased altogether. A German destroyer was crippled and sank later, and the battleship *Marlborough* received a torpedo-hit which reduced her speed.

The German fleet now steamed to the west south-west, and the British fleet slowly hauled round to the south. With its higher speed it had a good chance of cutting off the Germans from their bases. Scheer sensed this even though contact had been lost completely. Therefore he ordered another battle turn to the old course with the express intention to deal the enemy a heavy blow, to surprise and confuse him, to bring the destroyers to the attack, to facilitate disengaging for the night, and, if possible, to rescue the crew of the *Wiesbaden*. The execution of this plan has been criticized but there is no doubt that Scheer succeeded in getting his fleet out of a difficult situation although his van suffered heavily.

The German thrust was directed against the British centre. The attacking ships soon came under heavy fire without being able to reply effectively because visibility was better to the west and favoured the British gunnery. Scheer saw his fleet rush into a wide arc of gun flashes and decided to support the destroyer attack by the battle-cruisers while the battle fleet executed its third battle turn. To the battle-cruisers he made the well-known signal, 'Ran' ('At them'), which meant charging regardless of consequences. *Lützow* could not take part because after twenty-three hits she was far down by the bow and could steam no more than 15 knots. So *Derfflinger* led that death ride. Her captain transmitted Scheer's signal to all battle stations and was answered by a thundering roar, gun crews shouting, stokers banging their shovels against bulkheads. The destroyers went in, fired torpedoes, and retreated, the battle-cruisers then turned after receiving numerous hits. Not a single torpedo reached a target, for Jellicoe turned away. Contact ceased again and a lull in the battle followed. Both fleets hauled round to the south until their courses converged. The Germans proceeded in inversed order and in several columns, the British in single line ahead, sixteen miles long.

At sunset (2020) the terribly mauled battle-cruisers again came under the fire of the leading British battleships, the old ships of the II Battle Squadron under that of the British battle-cruisers. The Germans were silhouetted against the western horizon, their opponents were hardly visible to them. As a British officer later wrote: 'I sighted an obsolete German battleship firing in a desultory way at apparently nothing.' All the German columns turned to the west; the British did not follow but took up night-cruising order, the battleships in divisions abreast, destroyer flotillas following in their wake, course south-east, speed 17 knots. Jellicoe intended to put himself between the Germans and their bases and to renew the battle at daylight. Scheer collected his units practically on the same course which took some time, and at 2300 headed south-east for Horn Reef, speed 16 knots. Because of the heavy odds against him, he wanted to fight a renewed battle nearer to his bases. It was another whim of fate that, as a consequence, the German main body crashed through the British flotillas which were not looking for the enemy but were waiting for the day battle. In contrast the German destroyers searched in vain for the heavy ships of the enemy.

The night actions

During the short northern summer night there were numerous clashes. They started with a furious fight between light cruisers at short distance. *Dublin* and *Southampton* suffered heavy damage and casualties; the obsolete *Frauenlob* was hit by a torpedo and sank with most of her crew. Next the 4th Destroyer Flotilla, led by *Tipperary*, converged upon the German van, came under the fire of half a dozen battleships, and turned away in disorder firing torpedoes and leaving *Tipperary*, burning fiercely, behind. When the battleships turned to starboard to avoid the torpedoes, the light cruiser *Elbing* was rammed and remained stopped with flooded engine-rooms. The battleship *Nassau* tried to ram the destroyer *Spitfire*: they collided on nearly opposite courses, and the destroyer bounced off the side armour of her robust opponent leaving part of her bridge behind. With her forecastle a shambles, *Spitfire* succeeded in limping home.

Both sides resumed course and soon met again. In the intense fire *Broke*, and immediately afterwards *Contest*, rammed *Sparrowhawk*, which kept afloat to the morning. This time a torpedo crippled the light cruiser *Rostock*. Half an hour later, shortly after midnight, the unlucky 4th Flotilla encountered the same ships for the third time and lost *Fortune* and *Ardent*. Most of the other destroyers were damaged, it was no more a fighting unit.

A short time later a large ship approached the centre of the German line from port. It was the armoured cruiser *Black Prince*. She had probably been damaged when *Defence* blew up, and had tried to follow the battle fleet. Too late she turned away, and in minutes was a blazing pyre. Without firing a single shot she disintegrated.

These clashes saved the 6th Battle Squadron from an encounter with German battleships. It lagged behind because torpedo damage prevented *Marlborough*, the flagship, from keeping up 17 knots. As it were the German van passed no more than three miles astern at around 0100. A little later it hit the rear of a line of thirteen destroyers belonging to four flotillas. *Turbulent* was sunk, others damaged, the Germans carried on. At early dawn, after a calm of an hour, they were sighted and attacked by the 12th Flotilla. The German ships succeeded in evading a great number of torpedoes but the old battleship *Pommern* was hit and broke in two after several detonations.

The great battle was over. At 0300 the Germans were approaching Horn Reef, the British battle fleet, thirty miles to the south-west, reversed course, neither commander-in-chief was inclined to renew the fight. Jellicoe went north to look for German stragglers. However, *Lützow*, *Elbing*, and *Rostock* had already been scuttled after German destroyers had taken their crews off. Both fleets steered for their bases. The *Ostfriesland* struck a mine in a field laid a few hours earlier by *Abdiel* but reached port without assistance.

The battle changed neither the ratio of strength between the two fleets nor the strategic situation. The British blockade continued, and Russia remained cut off from the supplies she needed urgently. The tactical advantage was with the Germans: they had inflicted about double their own losses on a greatly superior opponent. The fleet was proud of this achievement, and Scheer was willing to go on baiting the British. On 19th August 1916 both fleets were again in the North Sea but missed each other by thirty miles. However, it was evident—and Scheer said so in his reports—that the war could not be decided by this strategy. The situation on the fronts deteriorated after Allied offensives, and lack of food was painfully felt at home. Therefore the German government declared unrestricted submarine warfare two weeks before the Russian revolution broke out. The submarines did great havoc to Allied shipping, but brought the United States into the war.

As to the High Seas Fleet it did not

The losses in battle

	British	German
Battle-cruisers	3	1
Armoured cruisers	3	-
Old battleships	-	1
Light cruisers	-	4
Destroyers	8	5
	tons 112,000	tons 61,000
Killed	6.000	2.500

remain inactive in port as has been alleged. In April 1918 it made its last sweep to the latitude of Bergen/Shetlands. But its main duty was now to support the submarine war by protecting the minesweepers and by giving its best young officers and ratings to the submarine arm. Other reasons for the sudden break-up of this efficient fighting force in November 1918 were psychological mistakes, malnutrition, and subversion, aggravated by the hopeless political and military situation of Germany.

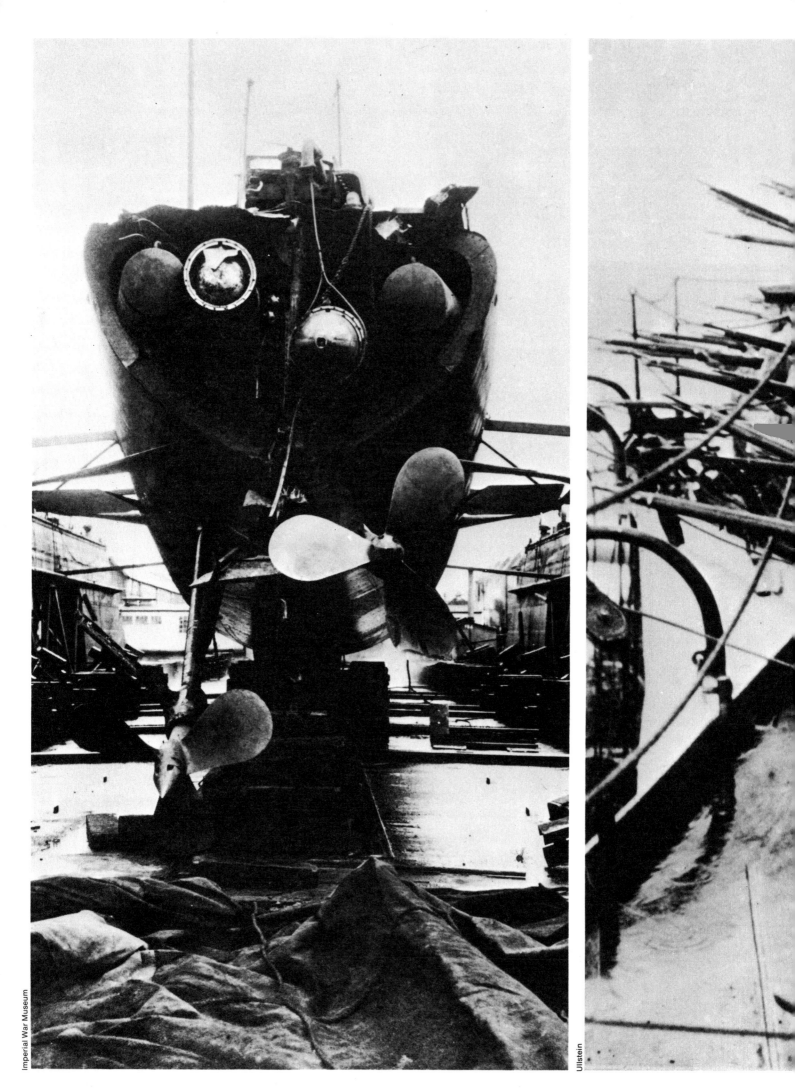

Imperial War Museum

Ullstein

THE U-BOATS OVERCOME

Many Germans were pessimistic when the war-leaders decided to stake everything on an all-out submarine campaign against Great Britain in the early months of 1917. And they proved to be right. Hope that the island could be brought to starvation in six months turned to dismay as the British flung every available ounce of energy into a deadly chain of mines, a shepherd-force of aggressive convoys, and a counter-blockade that blasted morale in civilian Germany

Far left: Victory at sea – a damaged U-boat, hit by a mine, in dry dock, 1917. Left: German sailors take aim for mines, the U-boats' most dangerous enemies

Whereas in 1915-16 the German naval and military 'Hawks' had been subdued by the political 'Doves' over the prosecution of unrestricted U-boat warfare, at the beginning of 1917 the renewed tussle in Berlin ended in success for the 'Hawks'. They guaranteed victory within six months—despite the likelihood of the USA entering the war on the Allied side. Accordingly, orders were issued to resume unrestricted warfare on 1st February; and three days later President Wilson broke off diplomatic relations. Meanwhile, on 16th January, the German foreign minister had sent via Washington to the ambassador in Mexico City the message still known as the 'Zimmermann Telegram'. It promised to Mexico that in return for alliance with Germany the 'former lost territory' of the southern states of the USA would be restored to her. This astonishing *gaucherie* was intercepted and deciphered in London, and was passed to the American ambassador, Walter Page, at a carefully chosen moment. The indignation it aroused in America made active intervention certain, and on 6th April the USA declared war on Germany.

In actual fact, the claims put forward by the German 'Hawks' were by no means as fantastic as they may now appear, and for the first four months it seemed quite likely that they would be fulfilled. In 1916 the U-boat fleet had more than doubled (from 54 to 133) and only twenty-two had been sunk. Allied and neutral shipping losses rocketed from 386,000 tons in January 1917 to the colossal total of 881,000 tons in April—a figure which, if maintained for a few more months, would have brought a German victory. The chief burden of countering the U-boat campaign naturally fell on the British navy, and as the many and varied antidotes adopted had failed to prove effective the dispute over whether convoy should be introduced grew hotter. The Admiralty, supported by a good deal of Merchant Navy opinion, considered that the disadvantages, such as lengthened 'turn-round' of ships, outweighed the possible advantages. But the Ministry of Shipping was confident that such arguments, which were in fact supported by wholly misleading Admiralty statistics regarding the relation between losses and safe arrivals of ships, were false. Lloyd George, the

prime minister, took the same view. At the end of April he forced the Admiralty to try convoy, and the recommendations of the Atlantic Convoy Committee, which was set up in May and produced a comprehensive scheme early in the following month, were at once adopted. Admiral W.S.Sims, commander of the US Naval Forces in Europe, was also a strong supporter of convoy, and with the help of the American destroyers, which soon began to operate from Queenstown (now Cobh) in southern Ireland, the experiment proved wholly successful. Not only did shipping losses decline sharply after April, but sinkings of U-boats increased from twenty in the first half of the year to forty-three in the second half. However, the confrontation between Lloyd George and the Admiralty caused a considerable loss of confidence in the Board on the part of the political leaders. In July therefore Lloyd George appointed Sir Eric Geddes first lord in place of Sir Edward Carson, who had consistently supported the sea lords' views on the convoy issue; and in December Geddes abruptly dismissed Admiral Sir John Jellicoe, the first sea lord.

A barrage of mines

Though the introduction of convoy was without doubt the most important factor in surmounting the crisis, it would be misleading to ascribe it entirely to that measure. The conflict between minelayer and minesweeper was now at its height, and in the autumn the British at last had available an efficient mine—copied from the Germans. The Straits of Dover were the crucial area, since unless both the long-range High Seas Fleet U-boats working from the German North Sea bases and the smaller boats based on Zeebrugge and Ostend could pass through the English Channel they would be forced to take the much longer route round the north of Scotland to reach their operational areas in the western approaches to the British Isles. In consequence the British concentrated a great effort on creating an impenetrable barrage of mines and nets, with surface vessels patrolling constantly overhead, in the Dover Straits. Though these measures gradually took effect, in 1917 U-boats made no less than 250 successful transits through the English Channel, mostly at night and on the surface. Not until the end of the year, by which time the barrage had been provided with night illumination, did it become really dan-

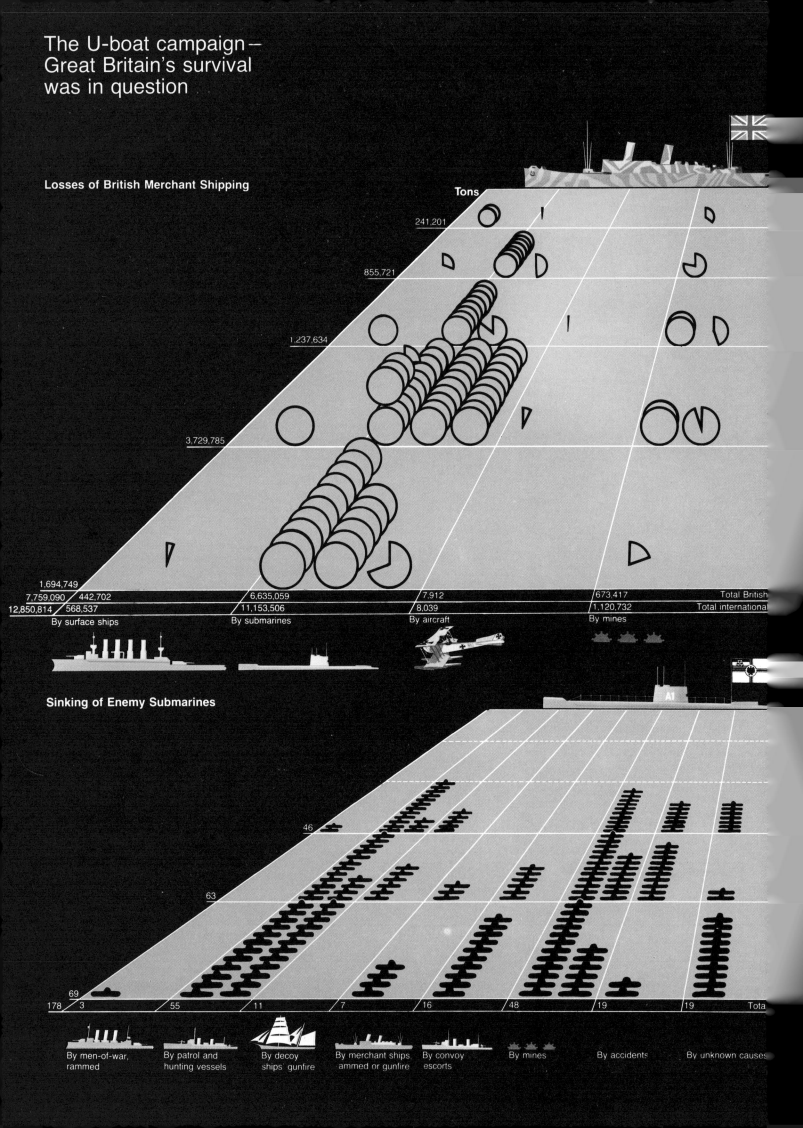

The U-boat campaign –
Great Britain's survival
was in question

Losses of British Merchant Shipping

Tons

	By surface ships		By submarines		By aircraft		By mines	
241,201								
855,721								
1,237,634								
3,729,785								
1,694,749								
Total British	7,759,090	442,702		6,635,059		7,912		673,417
Total international	12,850,814	568,537		11,153,506		8,039		1,120,732

Sinking of Enemy Submarines

By men-of-war, rammed	By patrol and hunting vessels	By decoy ships' gunfire	By merchant ships, rammed or gunfire	By convoy escorts	By mines	By accidents	By unknown causes	
46								
63								
69								
178	3	55	11	7	16	48	19	19

gerous for U-boats to attempt the short passage. Nor was minelaying confined to the narrow waters of the Channel. The British discovered, from deciphered messages, the routes used by the U-boats to pass in and out of the Heligoland Bight, and hundreds of mines were laid to catch them at the beginning or end of their patrols. The Germans did not, of course, take the strengthening of the Dover Barrage and the obstruction of the U-boat routes lying down. Their minesweeping service struggled hard to keep the channels to and from the North Sea bases clear, while their surface ships several times attacked the vessels patrolling the Dover minefields. But although the British patrols sometimes suffered quite heavy losses, the Germans could not reverse the current trend, which showed all too plainly that the passage of the Straits was becoming unacceptably hazardous.

Of all the many anti-submarine measures adopted in 1917 the mine, with twenty U-boats sunk, was by far the most successful U-boat killer. Surface ship or submarine patrols sank sixteen enemies, convoy escorts and Q-ships (decoys) each sank six, and about a dozen were lost through accidents of one sort or another. Yet although the total sinkings in 1917 (sixty-three) were nearly three times greater than in the previous year, new construction more than kept pace with losses. At the end of the year the U-boat fleet of 142 was actually greater by nine than it had been twelve months earlier; and many of the new boats were of improved types. Plainly, then, the battle was as yet far from won by the Allies.

Blocking the blockaders

To turn back to the German scene, the entry of the USA into the war enabled the Allied naval-economic blockade to be tightened to a stranglehold. German merchant ships which had long sheltered in American ports were seized; and—more important still—there was no longer any question of American firms trying to send contraband goods to Germany, or of American merchant ships running the British blockade to reach Scandinavia or Dutch ports with such cargoes. Almost overnight on 6th April 1917 Allied control of seaborne traffic became worldwide and complete. To make matters worse for Germany the 1917 harvest was again bad, largely because of the lack of imported fertilizers; and civilian food rations were cut to a level at which it was no longer possible to remain in good health. Furthermore, there was now an acute shortage of many metals, and in consequence the equipment of the armed forces began to suffer. The renowned discipline of the German people had not yet weakened seriously, but by the end of 1917 it was becoming plain that unless the shortages of every kind, and sheer hunger, were alleviated in the fairly near future a collapse was likely on the home front.

By the beginning of 1918 some 5,000 mines had been laid in the Dover Barrage, but U-boat transits none the less continued—in March there were twenty-nine. The British were especially anxious to put the Flanders U-boat bases out of action—if the army could not capture them. Indeed

the terribly costly prolongation of the 3rd battle of Ypres into the autumn of 1917 must be ascribed partly to Admiralty pressure to capture Ostend and Zeebrugge. When that offensive had plainly failed the earlier idea of a blocking operation was resurrected, and after several false starts it was carried out on the night of 22nd-23rd April. Although at the time the British believed that Zeebrugge had been effectively blocked, it is now clear that this was not so. Despite the great gallantry with which the attack was carried out (no less than eleven Victoria Crosses were awarded to participants) by early May the U-boats could work their way round the blockships. And the attack on Ostend, though repeated on 10th May, was a total failure on both occasions.

Germany feels the pinch

With the U-boats forced increasingly to use the long route round the north of Scotland the possibility of laying a gigantic minefield between the Orkneys and the Norwegian coast was raised. As the distance was some 250 miles, and the depth of water was in places far greater than the Straits of Dover, this was an undertaking of a very different order from the blocking of the twenty-mile-wide Straits. In July 1917 a new American mine was ready for mass production, and the decision was taken to go ahead. The US Navy carried out the lion's share of the laying, often in very bad weather. By the end of the war 56,000 American and 13,000 British mines had been laid in this Northern Barrage. Unfortunately, many of the American mines exploded prematurely, and there was always a gap at the eastern end in Norwegian territorial waters—which the U-boats were not slow to exploit. Though this barrage probably did make U-boat passages to their operational areas slower and more dangerous, the results achieved (three U-boats possibly sunk and another three damaged) were hardly commensurate with the effort involved.

The Mediterranean had until 1918 been a happy hunting ground for U-boats, which had sunk merchant ships with almost complete impunity. The Austrian submarine fleet totalled twenty-seven boats, most of them ex-German, and they were reinforced by German boats sent out periodically through the Straits of Gibraltar to work from Cattaro (now Kotor) or Pola. Hence arose the attempt to construct yet another barrage—across the Straits of Otranto—to block the routes to and from the Adriatic bases. Once again mines, nets, and surface and air patrols were all used; but with very little success. It was without doubt the introduction of convoy which defeated the Mediterranean U-boats. Of the ten sunk in those waters in 1918 at least half can be attributed to convoy escorts. One of the most interesting of these successes was the capture of Karl Dönitz from UB.68 on 4th October 1918, since he was to command Germany's U-boat fleet in the Second World War.

Right: A victim of the German blockade – a steamer torpedoed by a U-boat. In April 1917 the U-boats sunk 881,000 tons of Allied shipping

In July 1918 the Germans made a last desperate attempt to pass U-boats down-Channel to attack the troopships which were bringing an ever increasing flood of American soldiers to the Western Front. Of the six boats sent out only three returned home, and two of them were severely damaged. The last west-bound transit took place in August, and at the end of that month the Germans accepted that only the long northern route remained open to them. Meanwhile, a mine barrage had been laid off the east coast of England, where U-boats had previously achieved considerable successes; and more mines were laid in the Heligoland Bight. It was at this time that the British laid the first magnetic mines, off the Flanders bases, which were now virtually useless to the Germans. Also in August a heavy attack was made on the morale of the U-boat crews by publishing the names of 150 officers, most of them captains of boats,

Below: Survivors from the *Jacob Jones,* painted by Beal. It was impracticable for submarines to pick up survivors at sea. The underwater menace often spelt death to passengers and crew, who in earlier naval warfare had been warned to get into lifeboats, and then were picked up by the attacking vessel

known to have been killed or captured. Recent analysis of this list shows how well-informed were the Admiralty's anti-submarine and intelligence departments.

Submarine death toll
On 25th October Admiral Reinhard Scheer, commander of the High Seas Fleet, recalled all U-boats from the sea routes with a view to their taking part in a final sortie by his fleet. There were twenty-three at sea at the time. Nine days later all possibility of carrying out that desperate plan was eliminated by widespread mutinies among Scheer's major warships; but the U-boat crews remained loyal to the end. A condition of the armistice terms signed at Compiègne on 11th November was that all surviving U-boats should be surrendered.

There is no doubt at all that in 1918 Allied anti-submarine forces inflicted a heavy defeat on the U-boats. Though seventy new ones had been built, sixty-nine were sunk, and total strength declined from 142 to 134. The convoy escorts and surface ship patrols between them accounted for thirty-four enemies; but mines, with eighteen U-boats destroyed, again proved very effective. Air escorts and patrols sank few, if any, enemies; but they played an increasingly important part by reporting U-boats' positions and forcing them to re-

main submerged. Of all the varied weapons in the armoury of the Allied anti-submarine forces the mine was, taking the war as a whole, much the most effective, with forty-eight successes to its credit. The depth charge with thirty came second, the torpedo with twenty third, and the ram with nineteen fourth. But the sinkings achieved by the U-boats totalled the immense figure of 11,153,506 tons out of total losses by all nations from all causes of 12,850,814 tons. The British Merchant Navy was by far the heaviest sufferer, and the 7,759,090 tons lost was no less than thirty-seven per cent of its pre-war total tonnage. The loss of 178 U-boats was perhaps a small price to pay for the amount of shipping destroyed.

As to the Allied blockade of the Central powers, by August 1918 the civilian ration in Germany was reduced below 2,000 calories daily, resistance to disease had been much lowered by malnutrition, and the death rate was rising very sharply. Perhaps the best indication of the effect of the blockade on the German people is the fact that during the four years 1915-18 civilian deaths exceeded by 760,000 the number which pre-war statistics indicated as probable. Though the German armies were as thoroughly defeated on land as their U-boats were at sea, and the so-called 'stab in the back' by the civil

Above: H21 returning to Harwich with a broom tied to her periscope. This is an old naval joke dating back to the 17th century. Right: Postcards printed after the war of, respectively, the torpedo room, and the control room of U90

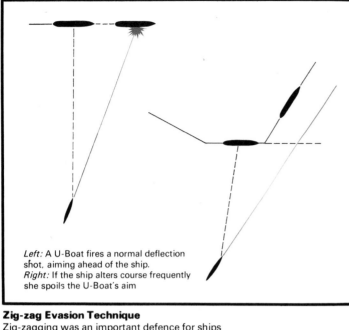

Left: A U-Boat fires a normal deflection shot, aiming ahead of the ship.
Right: If the ship alters course frequently she spoils the U-Boat's aim

Zig-zag Evasion Technique
Zig-zagging was an important defence for ships against U-Boats. One of the biggest problems was the co-ordination of zig-zagging in a convoy formation; to avoid collisions, it was done to a pre-arranged system

Explosive Sweep
The Explosive Sweep was an early device for towing behind destroyers. It was fitted with an electric indicator which registered an obstruction, and the explosive charge could then be fired from the destroyer

German 15-cm Submarine Gun
The German 15-cm/L 45 was mounted in the U-Cruisers of the *U151* and *U139* Classes

British Depth-charge
The 'D' Type depth-charge Mk III. This simple weapon proved to be the most successful method of sinking U-Boats, but it was not ready until 1916, and only available in quantity in 1917. The hydrostatic device was set to the estimated depth of the U-Boat by hand, and the depth-charge was then rolled off the stern of the escort. Known to the Germans as the 'Wasserbom' or 'Wabo' for short, it could destroy a U-Boat up to 25 ft away, and inflict damage as much as 50 ft away

population's collapse is a fiction of German militaristic imagination, it is nonetheless true that the blockade inflicted great suffering on the German and Austrian people. In Great Britain and France, though rationing of food was made increasingly stringent after 1916, there was no comparable degree of suffering; nor did the war industries of the Allied nations suffer difficulties such as the shortage of raw materials caused in Germany. Thus there is a good deal of truth in the saying that the Allied victory of 1918 was achieved through 'the triumph of unarmed forces', as well as by the successes of the fighting services on land, at sea, and in the air.

THE END OF THE HIGH SEAS FLEET

The nadir of dishonour and low cunning, or a noble action in the face of defeat? And was the demise of the German High Seas Fleet a blessing in disguise for the Allies? *Above:* The royal progress of the HMS *Queen Elizabeth*, Beatty's flagship, with the Grand Fleet on November 21, 1918

'The German fleet has assaulted its jailor, but it is still in jail', observed a New York newspaper immediately after the battle of Jutland. Through her geographical position, Britain dominated the exits from the North Sea; and this fact, together with the superiority of her Grand Fleet, meant that she could implement a policy of 'wide blockade' and wait until the High Seas Fleet ventured out to challenge this mastery, which was not likely to happen, given the disparity in numbers and the Kaiser's caution. Though not a very exciting policy, it was extremely effective.

While this was undoubtedly the correct strategy, the Royal Navy's unadventurous rôle attracted much criticism in later years

and even at the time was hard to justify in the face of the army's great exertions on the Western Front. Moreover, the prolonged periods of inaction led to acute frustration in the Grand Fleet, with Beatty confessing himself to be 'War-weary. Scapa-weary, weary of seeing the same old damned agony of grey grey grey, grey sky, grey sea, grey ships.' Nevertheless, morale was high compared with that of the High Seas Fleet, where the situation was very serious indeed. Aware of the superiority in size and numbers of the British warships, the German crews were deeply pessimistic about the outcome of any large-scale action. Confined to their cramped quarters on board ship, subject to fierce discipline without much sport or entertainment, given very poor food rations, and seeing all the best young officers taken away for U-Boat service, the sailors became daily more distrustful and bitter against the leaders. 'What a shame that we cannot lay down our arms for at least a day and allow the Indians and the New Zealanders to run amok upon the estates of the Junkers,' wrote one of them, Seaman Richard Stumpf, in his diary.

This gloom and frustration was merely deepened by the news that Germany's allies were collapsing on all sides and that the government had asked for an armistice on October 4, 1918. Two weeks later, with the bases at Ostend and Zeebrugge abandoned, and Scheer forced to agree to Wilson's demand that all U-Boats should be recalled, it seemed that the war at sea was at last over for Germany. In fact, Scheer and Hipper (now Chief of Admiralty Staff and C-in-C, High Seas Fleet, respectively) were planning upon one final sortie, which was to redeem the navy's reputation and perhaps affect the Armistice terms. This scheme was quickly abandoned after the Wilhelmshaven mutinies on October 29. The German challenge to the Royal Navy's supremacy had ended, as no-one would have dared to forecast even a few months previously, with a whimper rather than a bang.

A more humiliating event was to follow, however. Throughout October, the Allies had been discussing the demands they would present to the Central Powers as conditions for granting an armistice. Beatty and the Admiralty, naturally crestfallen at the receding chances of a great naval battle, pressed for the complete surrender of the German navy; but Lloyd George, influenced by the army and by the French and American governments, refused this demand out of fear that it might provoke Berlin into continuing the war to gain better terms. Eventually, the Supreme War Council decided that the enemy vessels should be interned in a neutral harbour until the peace terms were settled, and during the Armistice negotiations with Germany between November 8 and 11 it was agreed that this force should include ten battleships, six battle cruisers, eight light cruisers, 50 destroyers and all the U-Boats. While this decision appalled the British admirals, it was even more shocking to the Germans themselves; even the revolutionary sailors at Wilhelmshaven were chilled by the terms. By this stage, though, peace was essential for Germany and the government was determined to accept the conditions.

Neutral countries, perhaps understandably, declined to allow the High Seas Fleet to be interned in their harbours and thus the Allies decided on November 13 that, while the U-Boats would be directed to English ports, the surface ships should be interned in Scapa Flow. Two days later, the cruiser *Königsberg* brought Rear-Admiral Meurer to the Firth of Forth, where the final details were worked out with Beatty and his staff; the U-Boats would surrender to Tyrwhitt at Harwich and the High Seas Fleet would come to the Forth before sailing north to Scapa.

'Der Tag'

November 21, 1918 was *Der Tag*, as the Germans called it. Despite the activities of the rebel sailors and the uncertain political situation, those ships which were to be interned were prepared for the journey. Only the minimum crews necessary to run these vessels were to be used, which meant about 400 men in the capital ships and the rest in proportion. Gloomily, Seaman Stumpf described the scene at Wilhelmshaven a few days earlier and uttered the feelings of many: 'At this moment *Friedrich der Grosse* and *König Albert* are in the locks and the other ships are ready

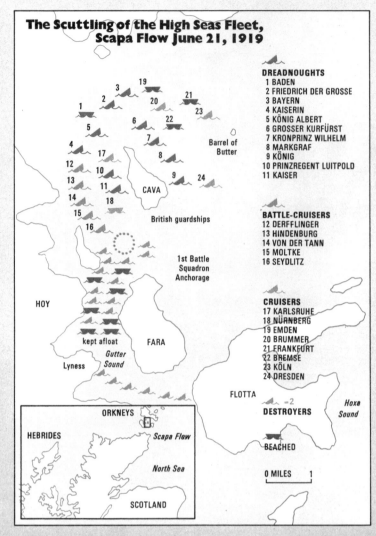

The Scuttling of the High Seas Fleet, Scapa Flow June 21, 1919

Barrel of Butter

CAVA

British guardships

1st Battle Squadron Anchorage

HOY

kept afloat FARA

Gutter Sound

Lyness

FLOTTA

ORKNEYS

HEBRIDES

Scapa Flow

North Sea

SCOTLAND

Hoxa Sound

BEACHED

0 MILES 1

DREADNOUGHTS
1 BADEN
2 FRIEDRICH DER GROSSE
3 BAYERN
4 KAISERIN
5 KÖNIG ALBERT
6 GROSSER KURFÜRST
7 KRONPRINZ WILHELM
8 MARKGRAF
9 KÖNIG
10 PRINZREGENT LUITPOLD
11 KAISER

BATTLE-CRUISERS
12 DERFFLINGER
13 HINDENBURG
14 VON DER TANN
15 MOLTKE
16 SEYDLITZ

CRUISERS
17 KARLSRUHE
18 NÜRNBERG
19 EMDEN
20 BRUMMER
21 FRANKFURT
22 BREMSE
23 KÖLN
24 DRESDEN

= 2
DESTROYERS

Below: German battleships in line on their way to be interned, SMS *Bayern* nearest the camera. *Inset above right:* German submarine *U 126*. One of the U 117 class built for general service and minelaying off the coast of the United States. U-Boats were not interned at Scapa, but surrendered at Harwich. *Right:* The dreadnought SMS *König*. One of a class of four completed in 1914, the first German battleships to have all main armaments on the centre-line and the last with 12-inch guns. They were all scuttled at Scapa Flow and never raised

to follow. They are assembling at Schillig Roads for their final difficult voyage. The submarines will also go along. It is like a funeral. We shall not see them again. Impassively holding their sea-bags, the men who are being left behind stand at the pier. At the last minute they feared for their lives and threw down their weapons. I, too, feel too disgusted to remain here any longer. I wish I had not been born a German.'

On the other side of the North Sea, the greatest naval force in the world had sailed from Rosyth early on the morning of the 21st. Two days earlier, the U-Boats had begun to surrender at Harwich without much of a reception, but now the British were determined to put on as spectacular a display of might as possible. Apart from the Grand Fleet itself, there were detachments from the Channel and other stations: 90,000 men in 370 warships, flying as many white ensigns as they could, as if they were going into action. The Americans were represented by the 6th Battle Squadron and the French had sent an armoured cruiser and two destroyers. In one immense line, they had steamed in single file to the rendezvous 40 miles east of May Island, where they divided into two long columns, about six miles apart, and waited for the German fleet. The light cruiser *Cardiff* and the destroyer flotillas were sent forward to make contact and to lead in the German ships. At 0930 hours these could be spotted in single line ahead. Admiral von Reuter in the *Friedrich der Grosse* was followed by the other eight battleships, five battle cruisers and the smaller warships. (One destroyer had been sunk by a mine on the way; the battleship *König* and a light cruiser were in dock and came over later; while the battle cruiser *Mackensen* was still in the builder's yard.)

Silently, almost eerily, the *Cardiff* led the German fleet down the line formed by Beatty's two columns, which promptly reversed course and shepherded their enemies towards the Forth. Fearing a desperate last-minute, blow, all the British ships were at action stations but, as the minutes ticked by and nothing untoward occurred, the tension diminished. Nevertheless, there was no cheering, no jubilation, until this vast assembly of warships had anchored, Reuter's vessels and their escorts halting at Inchkeith, while the Grand Fleet proceeded to its customary berths higher up above the Forth Bridge. By this stage, the Forth was full of small boats, packed with journalists and sightseers, and the atmosphere was far more relaxed. Beatty himself was repeatedly cheered by the crews of the Grand Fleet, and he announced his intention of holding a service of thanksgiving on the *Queen Elizabeth* 'for the victory which Almighty God has vouchsafed to his Majesty's arms'.

Despite all this, an air of unnaturalness persisted on board the ships throughout that historic day. That there had been no great Trafalgar-style battle, no real chance to re-fight Jutland, was due, as everyone realised, to the immense superiority of the Royal Navy; that the Kaiser's navy had not dared to challenge Britain's control of the North Sea was an acknowledgement of defeat; that the German fleet had voluntarily surrendered instead of seeking a last battle was, in some ways, a victory even greater than Trafalgar. Yet there was on the British side a feeling of incompleteness mixed with disgust and incredulity that the Germans had not chosen to fight. Beatty expressed some of this when he said: 'It was a pitiable sight, in fact I should say it was a horrible sight, to see these great ships . . . come in, led by a British light cruiser, with their old antagonists, the battle cruisers, gazing at them.' On the German side, there was nothing but bitterness and shame at their ignominious surrender. It was, wrote Ludwig Freiwald, a sailor on the battleship *Nassau*, 'the most shameful deed in all the history of the sea'.

On the next day, the interned ships were searched for ammunition before being moved up to Scapa Flow in smaller groups during the following week. The destroyers were then moored in pairs off Hoy, while the larger vessels anchored around the small island of Cava. When the warships delayed by repairs eventually joined the force, it consisted of 11 battleships, five battle cruisers, eight light cruisers and 50 destroyers, the fleet flagship *Baden* having also been added to the list in December in place of the unfinished battle cruiser *Mackensen* to make up the number of capital ships specified in the armistice conditions. The wireless equipment on all the interned ships was removed and the guns were put out of order by the confiscation of the breech-blocks. Nor would the Germans be able to make a surprise escape, for very little fuel was allowed on board. These precautions having been taken, the British permitted a steady reduction in crew numbers on these vessels, so that only enough were left for care and maintenance; the rest of the men were shipped back to Germany.

The German fleet was originally guarded by the Battle Cruiser Force but in May 1919 these duties were taken over by Vice-Admiral Fremantle's 1st Battle Squadron: to assist him, armed trawlers and drifters were posted near the anchorages, with instructions to report immediately if the Germans attempted to scuttle the interned ships. The position of these vessels in international law was a rather special one. When the original intention of internment in a neutral harbour fell through, it was too late for the British to change the Armistice conditions. Under these, it would clearly be a breach of the agreement to place armed guards on board each ship, since Reuter's fleet had not been legally surrendered. There was always a danger, therefore, that the Germans might try to scuttle their fleet, even though this would also constitute a violation of the Armistice; Article XXXI stipulated: 'No destruction of ships . . . to be permitted.' However, although contingency plans had been drawn up by the authorities at Scapa Flow — and some of these involved seizing the interned vessels even *before* a peace treaty was signed — the Admiralty was too concerned with the negotiations in Paris to pay any attention to such suggestions.

Disposal problem

While the pride of the German fleet rusted at their anchors at Scapa, Allied politicians and admirals argued over what to do with the warships. It was difficult enough to find a solution for the U-Boats, 176 of which either sailed or were towed into Harwich harbour. While the British and American admiralties, who had regarded these vessels as being in some way 'uncivilised', pressed for their destruction and the complete banning of submarines by all countries, this was opposed by both France and Italy, who, as weaker powers, could appreciate their uses. By March 1919 it had been decided that the U-Boats should be divided among the Allies and then either sunk or broken up, while those under construction in Germany would be destroyed under supervision, since she was not to be allowed such weapons in the future. Even so, the exact disposal of the captured vessels was still under discussion after the Versailles Treaty had been signed. In December 1919 it was decided that the French should be allowed to keep ten U-Boats, all the rest to be broken up within a year.

It was equally difficult for the Allies to decide on the future of the German surface fleet, both at Scapa and in the home ports (the latter included eight dreadnoughts, six pre-dreadnoughts, 14 light cruisers, 54 destroyers and 62 torpedo-boats). Once again, it proved easier to deal with the German side first and to decree that the defeated foe's navy would be restricted to 15,000 personnel and to the six pre-dreadnoughts, six of the light cruisers, 12 destroyers and 12 torpedo-boats. But what of the remaining ships, which constituted the second-largest navy in the world? The Americans wanted them all to be sunk, particularly if the alternative was for them to be distributed to the Allies on the basis

Below: Some of the 50 destroyers moored in pairs in Gutter Sound. Isolation and excess of leisure, no less than dirt and shortage of food, contributed to the demoralisation of the German crews

of war losses, which would mean that they would get very few and the British would obtain the lion's share. While the British shared the Americans' preference, they were prepared to argue for sharing out the ships of the High Seas Fleet among the Allied powers if the Americans persisted in their own vast warship construction programmes. The French and Italians were, as ever, eager to augment their own naval forces with captured vessels. Fortunately for the British, and perhaps for all concerned, the decision was taken out of their hands.

The long months at Scapa had not been happy ones for Admiral von Reuter or his crews. The latter were in a sullen and bitter mood, particularly on board the capital ships. They were cut off from home by the lack of wireless communications and the inadequacy of the postal service. Food, though sufficient, was very poor and the sailors often bartered their decorations and binoculars with the British seamen in return for chocolate and cigarettes. At the same time there was an excess of alcohol in the German vessels, resulting in many cases of drunkenness. The interned crews were not allowed ashore, so they had little recreation or relief from the sheer monotony of their lives. Added to all this was the fact that many of the men had been influenced by the naval mutinies and were no longer amenable to discipline; in any case, most of the officers were too demoralised to enforce the

normal regulations. As a result, the ships were neither polished nor cleaned out, and soon became very shabby and stinking, causing further deterioration in morale. On the anniversary of the battle of Jutland on May 31, red flags as well as the Imperial ensign were hoisted on many ships. Reuter encountered so much trouble with the crew of the *Friedrich der Grosse* that he was allowed to transfer his flag to the light cruiser *Emden*. To his British captors, however, the Admiral was polite and reasonable, and always extremely efficient in carrying out instructions. In these circumstances, the prospects of the Germans taking decisive action and scuttling their vessels appeared to grow less and less.

In the event, the British greatly under-estimated Reuter and his fellow officers. As soon as it became clear from the press reports that the discussions in Paris concerned only the question of whether the German warships should be sunk or retained by the Allies and that there was no chance of them being returned to the Fatherland, plans were begun for scuttling the interned force. As Reuter wrote afterwards, 'It was unthinkable to surrender defenceless ships to the enemy'. Scuttling in these circumstances was expected by his superiors, although it seems very doubtful indeed whether specific instructions about this were sent from Wilhelmshaven. After the event, Reuter claimed full responsibility and initiative, and there is no reason to dispute this.

Ironically, the hoisting of the red flag by the rebel sailors on May 31 gave Reuter the chance to further his plans; for he suggested that the crews' numbers should be cut by about 40% to forestall future troubles. Although the Admiral had earlier insisted that the existing numbers were necessary to look after his warships properly, the British agreed to this request, not recognising until too late the implication that Reuter had decided that he no longer needed to keep his vessels in good running order. On June 17, certain that the German fleet would be seized as soon as the Armistice expired at noon on the 21st, he ordered preparations on all ships for the scuttling, which would begin about two hours before the deadline. Since Reuter was allowed the privilege of communicating with the vessels under him and his suggested action was welcomed by every officer, there were few difficulties of co-ordination and co-operation.

What of the British side? On June 16, Fremantle submitted to Admiral Madden, the new C-in-C, Atlantic Fleet (as the Grand Fleet was now called), a plan for seizing the ships at midnight on the 21st. This action would have been too late in any case, but other factors intervened to change the British schemes. Fremantle was eager to take his 1st Battle Squadron to sea to practise a large-scale tactical exercise, and the weather prospects for this seemed good for June 21, the only drawback being the political uncertainty about the ending of the Armistice. However, on the evening of the 20th he learnt that the deadline had been postponed two days by the Council of Four in Paris, and he therefore had no qualms about postponing his planned action until the evening of the 23rd and taking his ships to sea on the following morning. Though there is still some doubt about whether Fremantle informed Reuter of the extension of the Armistice, this does not alter the German Admiral's responsibility in the matter, since he planned to violate it in any case.

Loyal or dishonourable?
After the 1st Battle Squadron had departed, the only British warships left in the huge anchorage were several destroyers and trawlers. At 1120 hours, Reuter gave the fateful order to scuttle, having prepared for this by an earlier signal at 1000 hours. At once, the sea-cocks and watertight doors were opened, while the small boats were prepared for the evacuation. By noon the *Friedrich der Grosse* and many others were already beginning to list, and all the German warships had broken out the Imperial ensign. Only at this stage did the British realise that something was amiss and at 1220 the message 'German battleship sinking' was flashed to Fremantle, then in the Pentland Firth, some eight miles away. The fleet exercise was swiftly cancelled but the ships of the 1st Battle Squadron, arriving back at 1430 hours, were too late to do anything but watch. It is difficult to see how, even if they had been there, they or anyone else could have prevented the scuttling once the sea-cocks were opened. Certainly, the few small British vessels and launches already in Scapa Flow were helpless, although they did fire at the German fleet in an effort to compel the evacuating crews to go back and save the listing warships. The captain of the battleship *Markgraf* and nine others were killed in the shooting, which added to the picture of utter confusion, with dozens of vessels sinking all over the vast bay.

All five battle cruisers went down, as did ten out of the 11 battleships; only the newly-completed *Baden* failed to sink and was beached in shallow water. Half of the eight light cruisers sank, while the other half were beached. Of the 50 destroyers, four were only partly flooded, 14 were beached, and the remaining 32 sank. Reuter's scuttling operation had been almost completely successful. As Professor Marder notes: 'It was all over by 5 pm: 400,000 tons of metal and machinery worth £70 million had been sent to the bottom of the Flow.'

The immediate British reaction was one of sheer disgust and fury. Fremantle ordered the 1,800 German officers and men to be treated as prisoners of war since they had broken the Armistice; before Reuter was taken away, the British Admiral insisted on publicly scolding him for adding 'one more to the breaches of faith and honour of which Germany has been guilty in this war'. The Admiralty itself considered (and abandoned) the idea of trying Reuter by court-martial, and requested that more ships be taken as compensation from Germany, although the government in Berlin declared that they had not ordered the scuttling and knew nothing about it. On the other hand, Admiral Scheer openly rejoiced that 'the stain of surrender has been wiped from the escutcheon of the German fleet', and the German press was as full of praise for the act as the British newspapers were of scorn.

A short while afterwards, however, the mood of British official circles began to change. After all, they had always wanted to sink the German fleet in any case, and the question of its redistribution was leading to tedious and irritating discussions with the French and the Italians. By June 1919 much of the heat had gone out of the Anglo-American naval rivalry, and the Admiralty felt that it no longer needed to employ the threat of taking over large numbers of German dreadnoughts for the Royal Navy. For these reasons, therefore, the First Sea Lord, Wemyss, privately informed his Deputy: 'I look upon the sinking of the German fleet as a real blessing. It disposes once for all of the thorny question of the distribution of these ships and eases us of an enormous amount of difficulties.' Indeed, the scuttling was so fortuitous for the British that certain members of the French and Italian governments believed that it might have been connived at: the absence of the entire 1st Battle Squadron on that very morning seemed too much of a coincidence to be accidental. Yet the official and private correspondence of those authorities concerned both at London and Scapa Flow reveals no evidence for this assertion. The Admiralty were very quick to refute American and French suggestions that an armed guard should have been placed on the German ships by pointing out that it was precisely the insistence of those two governments that the German fleet should be interned rather than surrendered which had made this precaution impossible.

In an effort to reach a compromise between the American determination to have all the remaining German fleet sunk except those allowed her in the Versailles settlement, and the Franco-Italian desire to obtain some good vessels (or at least the scrap metal), the great powers finally agreed, on December 9, 1919, that the surviving German surface warships were to be distributed according to war losses; but they were then to be broken up within five years, except for some light cruisers and destroyers which France and Italy were to be permitted to incorporate into their own navies. By this decision, Great Britain obtained 70% of the German total, but with one proviso: that the ships scuttled at Scapa Flow be included in her share. This proposal, made by Lloyd George in an effort to avert a deadlock, proved acceptable to all. Of the larger vessels remaining of Reuter's fleet, only the light cruisers *Emden* and *Frankfurt* passed into other navies, the rest becoming the property of the British Admiralty, along with a number of older warships in Germany. The one battleship not scuttled at Scapa, the *Baden,* was subjected to various trials and then sunk in 1921. As for the many vessels lying on the bottom of that vast and gloomy anchorage, a private salvage firm was given the contract to raise them for scrap, a task which was still being carried out at the start of the Second World War. Seven warships (three battleships and four light cruisers) were too deep to be salvaged. They are still there, a hidden and almost forgotten memorial to the dramatic end of the German High Seas Fleet.

Below: June 21, 1919—the end of SMS *Bayern.* Her sister ship, the flagship *Baden,* was the only one of the 16 capital ships not to sink

The end of World War I found Britain still the mightiest maritime power in the world. But during the inter-war years the balance of naval power was conditioned by a series of new considerations.

One was the development of naval aviation. This had begun as early as 1910, and by 1919 both Britain and the United States were busy building aircraft-carriers. Naturally there was much opposition in traditional naval circles to this new weapon. But experiments and exercises by the Americans during the 1920s demonstrated that aircraft were capable of sinking even heavily armoured ships, and that a superior force of surface ships – and even strategic targets ashore – could be neutralised by carrier-launched aircraft.

At the same time, the activity of the military men was matched by that of the politicians. As soon as the Armistice was signed haggling began: first over the disposition of the surrendered German fleet, then over the future of their own – and each other's – navies.

The discussions culminated in the Washington Conference of 1921-22. The five-power Naval Limitations Treaty which resulted was signed by Britain, the United States, France, Italy and Japan, and included rules limiting the displacement of major warships and the size of their main armament as well as restrictions on the number of ships of each class allowed to be built by each nation.

The treaty was due to run until 1936, and one of the main concerns on the American side had been to limit the growth of the Japanese Navy. However, Japan renounced the treaty in 1934 to embark on an ambitious programme of warship building – while on the other side of the world Germany, too, was planning a new navy.

As the German military build-up continued, war games and studies produced the 1938 'Z Plan'. This aimed at producing a powerful and balanced navy by the mid-1940s, and included aircraft-carriers and fast, heavily armed surface ships, as well as a large force of submarines.

War came sooner, however: in 1939 the Z Plan was abandoned and efforts were concentrated on submarine building. In spite of having only a small number of U-boats ready at the start of the war there were several early successes.

By March 1940 U-boats had sunk 222 British ships weighing nearly 750,000 tons, and in the following month the Royal Navy failed to prevent the German landings in Norway, though inflicting great damage on German warships. Then the rapid conquest of the Low Countries and France dealt a double blow: the support of the powerful French Navy was lost, and the U-boats were provided with a vastly increased coastline and many new bases from which to operate. The only hopeful sign was the success of Operation Dynamo in rescuing the BEF.

With more U-boats based closer to their hunting grounds, the struggle in the Atlantic grew more acute. Until May 1941 losses mounted steadily, though from then until November they declined as more escorts became available and air cover was extended. During 1941 the surface raiders became more active, though they dared not attack escorted convoys. The climax was reached with the ill-fated sortie of the *Bismarck*.

In the Mediterranean the Italian Navy had been so completely contained that Germany was forced to intervene, the arrival of the Luftwaffe and U-boats causing a serious setback there. Moreover, the fall of Greece and Crete was accompanied by almost crippling losses of naval forces during the evacuation.

Then, in December, the war took on an entirely new dimension. Japanese carrier-launched aircraft devastated the American battleships at Pearl Harbor, and sank the British battleships *Prince of Wales* and *Repulse*, before spearheading a five-month series of runaway victories in the Pacific.

The end of the victories came with the Battle of the Coral Sea in May 1942. This was a milestone in naval history: for the first time a full-scale engagement was fought by aircraft alone, without the opposing fleets coming within sight of one another. Though the battle was not decisive in itself, it caused the Japanese invasion fleet headed for Port Moresby to turn back, and the losses inflicted left fatal weaknesses for the big one: the Battle of Midway.

On 4 June the full American fleet inflicted a crushing defeat on the Japanese force destined for the island of Midway, sinking all four Japanese carriers present and wiping out, at a stroke, Japan's carrier supremacy.

Meanwhile, the Japanese conquests in the Pacific were mirrored in a renewed German offensive in the Atlantic. And as well as convoys across the ocean, since September 1941 the Allies had to protect Arctic convoys to Russia. These had to follow a dangerous 2000-mile route past Norway, with its Luftwaffe bases, and in early 1942 they attracted the added attentions of the most powerful German surface ships and two flotillas of U-boats. Losses were high, reaching their peak in July when only 10 of the 31 merchant ships of convoy PQ 17 reached their destination.

Convoys to Russia had to be suspended until September while escorts were transferred to the Mediterranean. Desperate battles along the convoy route from Gibraltar to Malta managed – just – to keep the island alive until the siege was finally raised by the Torch landings in North Africa in November.

Shortly afterwards the fate of the German surface fleet was decided. Its failure to win the Battle of Barents Sea in the last week of 1942 led to Hitler's scrapping the battle fleet: now the final stage of the Battle of the Atlantic was at hand.

In March 1943 Atlantic convoy losses reached a peak of 140,000 tons, a rate which would soon have brought disaster. But at the same time numbers of escort carriers became available, and the tide began to turn. Losses in April were half those in March, and in May the U-boats were effectively defeated – 41 being sunk and the remainder withdrawn. Enemy submarines continued to trouble convoys until the end of the war, but they never again came within sight of victory.

In the Pacific, after Midway, it was the Allies who were on the offensive. Fierce sea battles accompanied the landings on Guadalcanal and the other Solomon Islands, though the odds were now always against the Japanese. Both in Europe and the Pacific the emphasis was more and more on amphibious landings in enemy territory.

There was, however, one last great carrier battle in the Pacific. At Leyte Gulf, in October 1944, the Japanese Navy was virtually annihilated. American supremacy in the Pacific was now complete: not only was the Japanese Navy extinct, but her merchant shipping had been almost completely wiped out by American submarines. The final blow came in April 1945 when the *Yamato*, the greatest battleship ever built, was sunk by aircraft on her maiden voyage.

Air power had been decisive throughout the war at sea, and the *Yamato's* sinking was the final demonstration of its absolute effectiveness against undefended surface ships. Battleships were relegated to bombarding shore emplacements or to protecting the aircraft-carriers, which had now become unquestionably the most powerful weapon in the war at sea.

THE WARSHIPS

Technology and the War at Sea, 1939/1945. In the Second World War, air power proved decisively that the days of the dreadnought battleship were numbered. But the war at sea produced many tasks which demanded the development of new techniques, as well as new kinds of warship

It would be no overstatement to say that the Royal Navy through its own fault entered the Second World War at a considerable disadvantage. Almost exactly 20 years elapsed between the ending of the First World War and the start of the Second, and these were the years when the navy should have been absorbing the lessons learned at such fearful cost between 1914 and 1918 and adapting the new navy to take account of them. In fact they were 20 wasted years of largely sterile discussion on largely irrelevant subjects.

The initial mistake, the thread which runs like a rogue's yarn through the whole pattern of interwar naval thought, was the failure to recognise the dominant weapon of the four years of 1914/18. The disappointing result of the fighting at Jutland in 1916 permeated official naval thought during the years between the two wars, resulting in acceptance of the doctrine of the big gun and the battle fleet as the continuing basis of naval supremacy at sea. The unrestricted U-boat campaign of 1917 onwards was never studied, either strategically or tactically. The fact that the submarine and its weapon, the torpedo, had caused infinitely more damage than the gun, and moreover had a profound influence on all tactical movement for gun action, went unrecognised. It is a strange fact, remembering that knife-edge margin by which Britain survived the U-boat attack, that of all the naval exercises carried out between the wars, not a single one was based on defence of trade convoys.

At the outbreak of war, some 180 naval ships were fitted with asdic, the only known method of underwater submarine detection. Of these, 150 were destroyers, 24 were sloops, and six were coastal patrol vessels. A majority of the destroyers were of course required for fleet work and were therefore not available for merchantile convoys. The sloops turned out to be unable to withstand the normal gales experienced in winter in the North Atlantic, leaving the coastal patrol vessels, later classed as corvettes, with such destroyers as could be spared from other duties, as the backbone of Britain's escort forces.

Corvettes – the lightweight escorts

The first essential, therefore, was a crash programme of building, using whatever was readily available for design purposes. The Admiralty choice fell on a whale-catcher design, partly because the design was already in existence and partly because the overall length of 190 feet would make available a number of slips in the smaller shipbuilding firms and thus result in a more rapid rate of building. At the same time a four-cylinder, triple-expansion engine, as fitted in existing whale-catchers, was adopted, simply because patterns for its manufacture were already in existence. This engine gave a speed of 14 or 15 knots, which was well below the 20 knots specified by the naval staff as the minimum required for anti-submarine operations. But in the emergency of the immediate situation, it was the best that could be done.

These ships were Flower class corvettes, and

56 of them were built. They were remarkable little ships with a fantastic ability to keep going in weather in which other ships, such as destroyers, were unable to operate. But they needed crews with strong stomachs, for they rolled excessively in heavy seas and their general habitability was poor. They suffered too from lack of speed – their maximum was some 2 to 3 knots slower than a surfaced U-boat – and lack of size – there was insufficient space on board to accommodate the more sophisticated anti-submarine weapons and equipment as they were developed.

These limitations pointed to the need for a larger type of ship, and the Castle class corvettes, with a waterline length of 252 feet, were designed with improved habitability, better fighting power, and a longer range. Simultaneously, a longer term plan was adopted to produce twin-screw ships with greater speed and better manoeuvrability. These were the River class frigates, with an overall length of 301 feet and a speed of 20 knots, giving a sufficient margin of superiority over a surfaced U-boat. Some 36 of this class were built.

With these frigates well on the way, the Admiralty moved forward to a large degree of prefabrication, a new development for rapid building for the next two classes of frigates, the Loch and the Bay classes, of which 25 and 22 were built respectively. They were built to a slightly modified design giving an increase of 7 feet in waterline length. All frigates had the triple-expansion engine with the exception of two of the Loch class, which were fitted with geared turbines.

With the additional frigates and sloops it was at last possible to introduce support groups of anti-submarine vessels, or a combination of anti-submarine vessels and an escort carrier, in addition to the escort groups whose responsibility was to the convoy direct. It was a simple matter to order a support group to reinforce a convoy on which a U-boat pack was suspected of concentrating, and this reinforcement provided the ability to hunt U-boats to destruction without stripping the convoy of its proper number of escorts. It was a new tactic which paid considerable dividends, and after its introduction the sinking rate of U-boats was eventually more than doubled. The first support groups became active in the Atlantic early in 1943 and were to become an increasing feature of the pattern of anti-submarine warfare as new frigates and sloops became available. One other feature, of course, of the increase in numbers of anti-submarine vessels was that specialist training in the latest techniques, weapons, and tactics could be carried out on the group system and no longer individually as had been the case when the shortage of escorts had been so acute.

Together with the frigates, 25 sloops were built, the Black Swan and modified Black Swan classes. With a very similar hull to the frigates, they carried complete asdic equipment and were fitted with geared turbines and Denny-Brown roll reducers, improving speed and seaworthiness.

Together with ship development went weapon development. The Admiralty had relied on the

asdic (a supersonic underwater reflected beam giving range and bearing), and the depth-charge as adequate anti-submarine weapons with which to counter any U-boat threat such as had been experienced between 1914 and 1918. As late as 1937 the Admiralty had informed the Shipping Defence Advisory Committee that: 'the submarine menace will never be . . . what it was before. We have means of countering a submarine which are very effective and which will normally reduce our losses from that weapon. It will never be . . . a fatal menace again as it was in the last war. We have taken effective steps to prevent that.' Unhappily that statement was being proved far from true almost from the start of the war.

The asdic had certain limitations. Its beam was fixed in elevation, so it had a minimum range, varying according to the depth of the target, as well as a maximum. This meant that when going into the attack, contact with a deep submarine was lost at an early stage of the run-in to drop depth-charges. Its maximum range in normal conditions was around 1,500 yards, but with a ship steaming at speed, or in rough weather, the set's efficiency fell off very rapidly. It could measure range within an accuracy of about 25 yards, and bearing within about 10 degrees, but it could not measure the depth at which the submarine lay beneath the surface.

The depth-charge had hardly been developed since the First World War. To kill a submarine it had to explode within 7 yards. Its method of release was from chutes fitted on the stern of the attacking ship and from throwers on each beam which projected it about 70 yards on either side. The normal attack pattern was five charges. Depth-charges also had a slow rate of sinking to enable the attacking ship to get clear before they exploded. A very early discovery in the war against the U-boats was that the standard depth-charge could not be set to explode deep enough to damage a submarine at the greater depths to which they were now able to dive, and so a new and heavier depth-charge with a setting down to 500 feet was developed.

This doctrine of asdic hunt and depth-charge attack foundered against the U-boat tactic of the surface attack by night. The asdic could not detect a surfaced U-boat, and the night became almost a cloak of invisibility in view of the tiny silhouette presented by a surfaced submarine.

The first necessity was to devise a weapon with which a U-boat could be attacked while still held in the asdic beam of the attacking ship. This obviously meant a forward-firing weapon of sufficient range to avoid the inevitable loss of asdic contact as the attacker closed the submarine before releasing depth-charges. An ahead-throwing weapon had been devised during the First World War but had never been developed in the years between the wars. The idea was revived, and by the end of 1941 escorts were being fitted with the 'Hedgehog', a multi-spigot mortar which threw 24 contact-fused projectiles for a distance of 250 yards ahead of the firing ship. Being contact-fused, no predetermined depth at which the projectile exploded was necessary,

Left: the CAM ship (Catapult Aircraft Merchantman), was the forerunner of the escort carrier. A merchant ship was fitted with a rocket-assisted hydraulic catapult designed to launch a Hurricane fighter to intercept enemy reconnaissance or bomber aircraft. This task completed, the fighter had to be ditched in the sea or flown back to land, as there was no method of its being recovered by the parent ship

and explosion on contact was enough to produce lethal damage. The 'Hedgehog' was a considerable advance over the previous method of attack, as it considerably reduced the time between the start and delivery of the attack, but it suffered from the disadvantages that it was difficult to direct it accurately against a deep submarine, that a projectile had to hit to effect a kill, that it also lacked the cumulative damage that near-misses of the much larger depth-charges, which exploded automatically at their pre-set depths, could inflict.

In April 1943 the Asdic Q Attachment was developed which enabled contact to be kept with a deeply submerged U-boat, and this led in its turn to the development of the Type 147B asdic which measured a submarine's depth below the surface. These asdic sets were being fitted in escorts in the autumn of 1943, and with depth now ascertainable in addition to range and direction, the next step forward was obvious. This was the 'Squid', an ahead-throwing weapon which fired three rapid-sinking, time-fused projectiles. These came into operation in January 1944, and possessed the great advantage over the 'Hedgehog' that the projectiles did not have to hit the submarine before exploding, with the consequent chance of inflicting damage even if they were not within lethal range on explosion.

Two further aspects of the war against the U-boats were the early developments to counter the threat posed by the German long-range Focke-Wulf reconnaissance bombers. Operating from bases in western France, they flew deep into the Atlantic, searching for convoys and homing the U-boats on to them when found. Their areas of operation were far beyond the range of any British fighter. The immediate answer was the development of the CAM ship (catapult-fitted merchant ship), in which a single Hurricane fighter was embarked and catapulted off whenever a German Focke-Wulf was sighted. After the ensuing action, the Hurricane was ditched alongside any convenient ship and the pilot picked up. Those CAM ships came into operation in the early summer of 1941. Mean-

while another development had been conceived —that of converting merchant ships to auxiliary aircraft-carriers to accompany convoys. The first to be so treated was a captured German prize, renamed *Audacity,* which with a flight deck of 400 by 62 feet was able to operate six fighters. In the late autumn of 1941, escorting a convoy to Gibraltar, she not only drove off the Focke-Wulf aircraft but also reported and attacked four U-boats shadowing the convoy.

More than 100 of these ships were eventually built, the majority in the USA, of which 32 were commissioned into the Royal Navy. They played a notable part, both in the anti-submarine rôle and as assault carriers, providing air support to amphibious operations in the European and Pacific theatres.

Yet another type of auxiliary carrier developed was the tanker or grain ship on which a flight deck was erected from which, while still serving as a cargo carrier, a few anti-submarine aircraft could be operated. In all, 19 of these MAC-ships (Merchant Aircraft-Carriers) were completed, and between them spent no less than 4,437 days at sea on convoy escort duty combined with cargo carrying.

Mine warfare was another field which saw considerable material development during the war. It is often said that the German magnetic mine—Hitler's first secret weapon—took Britain by surprise when it was first employed in 1939. In fact, magnetic mines were a British invention first used in 1918, and their capabilities were well known. What was not known was the polarity of the German mines when they were first discovered in British waters, and whether it worked in the vertical or horizontal magnetic field set up by metal-hulled ships. Fortunately, one of these mines fell in the mud off Shoeburyness on November 22, 1939, was recovered, stripped, and evaluated by a team from HMS *Vernon,* and revealed the secret of its polarity. The mine was actuated when subjected to a field of 50 milligauss (one gauss, the unit for measuring the intensity of a magnetic field, is one line of force per square centimetre) and it was a simple

matter to reduce the magnetic field of any ship below 50mg by winding a current-bearing coil round a ship so as to give her less North-Pole down polarity. This method of countering the magnetic mine was known as degaussing. Later, ships could be effectively degaussed by 'wiping', a process in which a single electric cable carrying a heavy current was hauled up a ship's side. Wiping was a simple and quick process which changed a ship's magnetisation, though only for a period of up to six months.

It was one thing to make ships immune from the magnetic mine, but quite another to sweep it, or explode it harmlessly on the bottom. There were various possible methods, all based on the principle of towing electro-magnetics by mine-sweepers, but it was not always easy to ensure that the minesweeper was far enough away at the time of explosion to escape shock and damage. Eventually, a method was found for making buoyant cables, and once this was done, the solution was relatively simple. Minesweepers towed two electric cables on the surface, one of 750 yards, the other 175 yards, and passed an electric current down them. This produced a magnetic field of sufficient strength to explode the mines, and with minesweepers working in pairs, a wide area could be swept without difficulty. This electric sweep was known as the LL sweep.

British offensive and defensive minelaying was, of course, carried out on a large scale throughout the war. Most of the offensive minelaying was by aircraft, mainly in the Baltic and the Heligoland Bight, and almost entirely with magnetic mines. Huge defensive mine barriers of conventional moored mines were laid the length of the east coast of Britain and between the Orkneys and Faroes. Submarine trap minefields were laid on the northern exit route from the U-boats' Norwegian bases, consisting of deep laid fields combined with a surface and air patrol to force the U-boats to dive deep. These trap minefields accounted for three U-boats, while a great many more were sunk or damaged in the Baltic fields of magnetic mines.

THE BATTLE FOR THE ATLANTIC

The outbreak of war found the German navy still in the making but far from unprepared. To the tenuous Allied blockade of the Axis powers came the challenge of the Nazi surface raiders and the deadlier threat of the U-boats

The war plans of the Royal Navy had been taking shape since 1936, when Hitler's march into the Rhineland had set the pattern of his future path of aggression. Even at that time, it was apparent to the British Chiefs-of-Staff that war would come, and in a memorandum to the Cabinet they assumed it would break out in the latter part of 1939.

As a result of the Rhineland occupation a supplementary naval estimate was introduced into the House of Commons in 1936 to build two new battleships, an aircraft-carrier, five cruisers, and a variety of smaller ships, to be followed in 1937 by estimates which included another three battleships, two more aircraft-carriers, seven cruisers, and a big increase in small craft. And when the nation went to war in 1939, the first of these ships was beginning to join the fleet.

The war plans, which were sent out from the Admiralty on January 30, 1939, represented the adoption of a defensive strategy. That this has to be so in the early stages of a war is a well-proved element in the exercise of sea power. The desire to rush into offensive action has so often been the prelude to local disaster that naval planning in the initial stages of a maritime war must always allow time for a sufficient force to be built up and trained for the offensive. Only when that stage has been reached can the true dividends of an offensive strategy be harvested.

The naval plan in 1939, which was based on the assumption that the war would be fought against both Germany and Italy from the start, fell into three broad parts. The first looked to the defence of trade in home waters and the Atlantic. This was fundamental to any national strategy, for supplies are the vital sinews of war. Second came the defence of trade in the Mediterranean and the Indian Ocean. It was obvious that, if Italy became an energetic enemy, her dominating geographical position in the Mediterranean would force all seaborne trade to use the longer route round the Cape of Good Hope, but it was hoped to contain her adequately with a strong fleet in the Mediterranean. The third broad part of the naval plan was the imposition of a blockade on Germany and Italy, and with the actual declaration of war was published the list of contraband liable to seizure at sea, even if carried in neutral ships.

To put the plan into operation, the main strength of the Home Fleet was concentrated in Scotland. Far to the north the cruisers of the Northern Patrol kept watch, waiting to intercept any enemy or neutral ship, whether inward or outward bound. From the Shetlands to the coast of Norway a line of search was mounted, partly by air patrols, partly by submarines. The Home Fleet, less a few units stationed elsewhere, lay at Scapa Flow, more than capable of meeting any surface threat which the enemy could mount at sea. At Rosyth lay the aircraft-carrier *Furious* and her attendant destroyers, while submarine flotillas were based at Dundee and Blyth to carry the naval war into German waters. A cruiser squadron and a destroyer flotilla lay in the Humber, while far to the south a force of battleships, aircraft-carriers, cruisers, and destroyers was based at Portland to hold the southern exit into the Atlantic.

In addition to the Home Fleet, the four

Grand Admiral Raeder (centre), Hitler's naval commander until replaced by Dönitz, plans the course of the Atlantic war Germany's U-boats so nearly won.

home commands—Plymouth, Portsmouth, the Nore, and Rosyth—each had forces of destroyers, anti-submarine vessels, and minesweepers for convoy duties and local defence, under the command of the local commanders-in-chief. In the light of existing naval knowledge in 1939, all this formed a net strong enough and wide enough to catch any enemy ship attempting to force a way out or in.

In the Mediterranean, the agreement was that the French navy would hold the western basin in force. The British Mediterranean Fleet was therefore based on Alexandria, to operate in and dominate the eastern basin. To implement the blockade, the naval plan called for strong forces in the Gibraltar Straits and the Red Sea, where examination anchorages for all merchant ships entering the Mediterranean were set up.

The German war plans were, of course, tailored to a fleet which was basically unready for war. Shortly after coming to power, Hitler had told Admiral Raeder that he would not precipitate a general war until 1944, and it was on this assumption that Raeder had planned German naval expansion. When the war came in 1939, many of the ships which Raeder had hoped would be ready were still building or in the planning stage. Nevertheless, he still had a useful navy. The three pocket-battleships—nominally of 10,000 tons to keep within treaty limitations but secretly built to 13,000 tons—were immediately available. The battle-cruisers *Scharnhorst* and *Gneisenau*, which also exceeded their treaty limits, by 6,000 tons, were formidable opponents, and the big Hipper-class cruisers, some 4,000 tons overweight, were nearly ready. There were 56 U-boats, of which all but ten were operational, and their crews had been well trained, during the years when no U-boats were permitted, under the pretence that they were undergoing anti-submarine exercises.

The German battle instructions were issued to their fleet in May 1939. The plan envisaged a continuous series of operations in the North Sea to create as much nuisance as possible, mainly by attacks on shipping, and thus tying down large British forces to contain them. All the larger ships were due to cruise in the oceans in a heavy and sustained attack on merchant shipping. The U-boats were to operate against trade in the Atlantic and in the approaches to the main British ports. And to counterbalance the delay in the new heavy ships still under construction, a number of merchant ships were to be taken in hand for conversion into fast, heavily armed raiders.

In the German battle instructions, one ominous phrase was inserted: 'fighting methods will never fail to be employed merely because some international regulations are opposed to them.' It was a foreshadowing of the unrestricted submarine and raider warfare which, it had been hoped in Britain, had by now been outlawed for all time as an instrument of naval warfare.

The German navy made its war dispositions in good time. On August 21, 1939, the pocket-battleship *Graf Spee*, using darkness for her passage of the North Sea, slipped into the Atlantic unobserved. Three days later the *Deutschland*, another pocket-battleship, made a similar move, also undetected. Their supply tankers, *Altmark* and *Westerwald*, joined them there, their passages also being unobserved. Between August 19 and 29, 17 of the ocean-going type of U-boat were sent out to their Atlantic war patrol areas while seven of the smaller coastal type were dispatched to lay mines off the Channel ports. Six more were sent out to patrol the central North Sea.

Under clear skies in mid-Atlantic, a U-boat—safe from sudden aerial attack—finishes off its victim in a surface attack in 1943

Bapty & Co Ltd

The initial task of the Royal Navy was to draw a ring round the enemy, denying him the supplies which could only come over the seas. From the south of Norway, across and down the North Sea, and throughout the length of the Mediterranean, Allied sea power held the ring. Allied land and air power filled the Continental gaps. Only to the east, where Russia enjoyed a breathing space through her non-aggression pact with Germany, was a possible supply line left open. One result of this closing of the ring can be judged by the fact that, from the outbreak of war to the end of 1939, the Royal Navy seized 530,000 tons of supplies destined for Germany.

It was outside this ring, however, that the problems accumulated. Within hours of the declaration of war the Donaldson liner *Athenia* was attacked by U-30 200 miles west of Hebrides, and was sunk with a loss of 112 lives. It is true that the captain of U-30 exceeded his instructions in sinking this ship, but her loss was taken in the British Admiralty as evidence that unrestricted submarine warfare was already in force. The provisional arrangements in the war plan for the defence of ocean trade, which was to have been by the patrol of focal points and the evasive routing of merchant ships, was abandoned, and it was decided to adopt the full convoy system as soon as it could be introduced.

It was at this stage that the Royal Navy began to feel acutely the pre-war lateness of the naval rebuilding programme. Such destroyers and other ships as were available as convoy escorts lacked the endurance to take them far out into the Atlantic, and until the new ships came along, a 'limit of convoy' had to be drawn at about 300 miles to the west. After that point, the ships in convoy dispersed and proceeded independently. Incoming convoys were escorted across the Atlantic by an anti-raider escort, usually an armed merchant cruiser, and then were picked up by the escort forces at the limit of convoy and escorted into British ports. Later, as the new ships became available, the convoy limit was pushed farther out into the Atlantic, but it was not until mid-1941 that the Royal Navy was able to provide an anti-submarine escort all the way across the Atlantic.

But even with these limitations, the shipping loss figures were fairly encouraging. Up to the end of 1939, U-boats had sunk 114

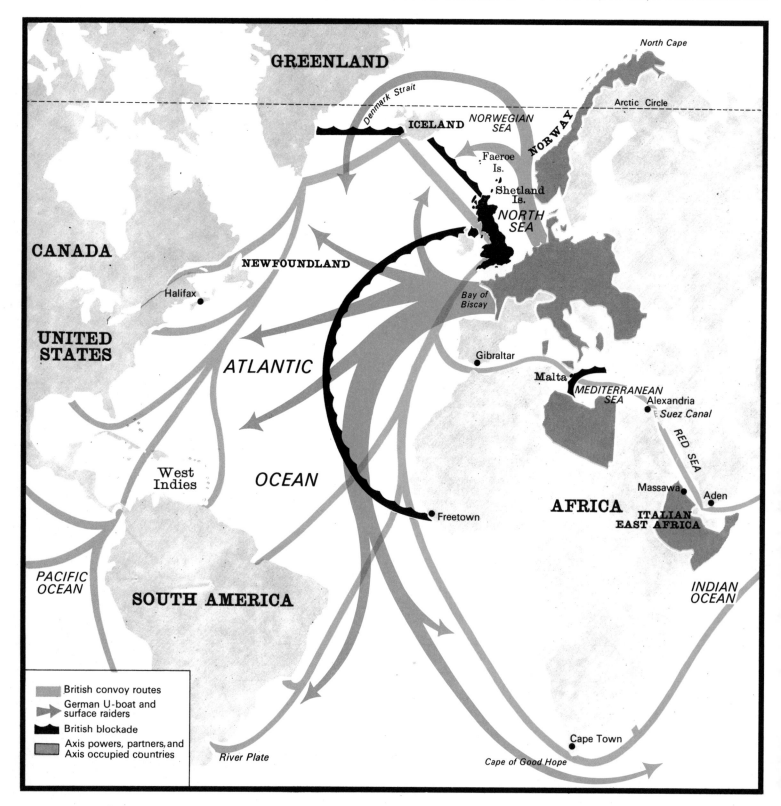

British convoy routes

German U-boat and surface raiders

British blockade

Axis powers, partners, and Axis occupied countries

ships with a tonnage of 421,156, but nine U-boats had paid the price. Considering the attenuated strength of the escort forces, these figures were satisfactory. But that these results were ephemeral in the overall picture was always present in the British Admiralty's mind. It was known that Germany was embarking on a very substantial programme of U-boat construction, and that, by 1941 at latest, the number of operational submarines would be doubled or trebled, and that this number would be progressively increased as the war lengthened. There was no blinking the fact that,

FOCKE-WULF Fw 200 CONDOR
Based on a pre-war design for a commercial transport, the Condor established an excellent reputation in *Luftwaffe* service as a long-range anti-shipping bomber, operating to deadly effect primarily over the North Atlantic. **Gross weight:** 50,045 lb **Span:** 107 ft 9½ in **Length:** 76 ft 11½ in **Engine:** 4 × 1,200 hp BMW Bramo 323 R-2 **Armament:** 2 × 7·9-mm, 3 × 13-mm, 1 × 20-mm machine-guns **Crew:** 7 **Speed:** 224 mph at 15,750 ft **Ceiling:** 19,000 ft **Range:** 2,210 miles **Bomb load:** 4,620 lb

once the U-boat fleet was at full strength, merchant ship losses would be grievous.

In the meantime, an attempt to take the offensive against the U-boat led to disaster. Two hunting groups were formed, each consisting of an aircraft-carrier and four destroyers, to operate against U-boats in the western approaches. On September 14 the *Ark Royal* was narrowly missed by torpedoes from U-39. The escorting destroyers counterattacked, sank the U-boat, and captured her crew. But it had been a narrow shave.

BRISTOL BEAUFORT Mk 11
The RAF's standard Coastal Command torpedo-bomber from 1940 to 1943, when it saw service over the North Sea, English Channel, the Atlantic, Mediterranean and North Africa. **Gross weight:** 21,050 lb **Span:** 57 ft 10 in **Length:** 44 ft 7 in **Engine:** 2 × 1,200 hp Twin Wasp **Armament:** 4 × ·303 machine-guns **Crew:** 4 **Speed:** 268 mph **Ceiling:** 25,000 ft **Range:** 1,054 miles **Bomb load:** 1 × 1,605 lb torpedo or 1,500 lb bomb load

E-BOAT
A serious threat to Allied shipping in the inshore waters of the North Sea, the Channel and the Western Approaches, the German E-boats were larger, more seaworthy, more heavily armed and more reliable mechanically than their British counterparts the MTBs. **Displacement:** 92¼ tons **Armament:** one 37-mm AA, one 20-mm AA; two 21-inch torpedoes

Three days later the second hunting group was in action. The aircraft-carrier *Courageous* was sighted by U-29, which torpedoed and sank her with a loss of 519 lives, and lived to tell the tale. At that stage of the war aircraft-carriers were particularly valuable ships, since those ordered in 1936 and 1937 were not expected to be operational until 1941 at earliest, and the British Admiralty quickly decided that it was asking for trouble to risk them on that type of warfare. The *Ark Royal* was quickly withdrawn to take her proper place again with the Home Fleet.

With the horizon clear, crew members sun themselves on the deck of a U-boat

Inside the Admiralty an organisation was growing to co-ordinate the war against the U-boat. Before the war an operational intelligence centre had been set up to deal with all intelligence received of an operational nature, to deduce its value, and to pass it out to the fleet.

On the submarine side a 'tracking room' was established into which came every piece of U-boat intelligence. Reports from agents in enemy countries, giving details of arrivals and departures, U-boat sightings by ships and aircraft, U-boat attacks, and, most prolific source of all, wireless bearings of every message transmitted at sea by a U-boat—all were channelled into the intelligence centre. The tracking room was connected by teleprinters to every wireless direction-finding station in the country, and within minutes of a U-boat using her wireless the bearings were coming in. By plotting the bearings on a chart, the U-boat's position was established.

Alongside the submarine tracking room was the 'trade plot', which showed the position, course, and speed of every convoy and independent ship at sea. By putting these two plots together, the position of any U-boat could be seen in relation to any convoy, and evasive action taken by signalling to the convoy to alter course if it were heading into danger of attack. Both the tracking room and the trade plot were manned day and night, and, as the war developed, a high degree of expertise in forecasting the movement of U-boats was built up. Indeed, so great became the efficiency of the tracking room that by 1943 more U-boats were being sunk at sea than ships sunk by U-boats.

Mine warfare

U-boats, however, by no means constituted the only danger to merchant ships. As early as the first week of war, some ships were being sunk or damaged by mines of a new type, quickly identified as 'magnetic influence' type, for which the British had no minesweeping countermeasure. It was not until November 23 that a German aircraft presented them with the answer. It dropped its mine in the mudflats off Shoeburyness, and at great personal risk it was dismantled by Lieutenant-Commander J. G. D. Ouvry, and revealed its polarity.

With that knowledge it became possible to develop a magnetic sweep which would explode the mines harmlessly and also to provide ships with a 'degaussing mantle' which enabled them to pass over the mines without actuating their firing gear. But by the end of November the magnetic mine had cost the British 46 ships of 180,000 tons, as well as a destroyer sunk and several warships damaged. The total loss by mines up to the end of 1939 was 79 merchant ships totalling 262,697 tons.

Another source of loss, and one much more difficult to counter, was the armed surface raider. It has been mentioned above that the Germans sent two pocket-battleships into the Atlantic, together with their supply tankers, before the outbreak of war. The first hint that they were at sea came to the Admiralty in the form of ships sunk or missing in waters far beyond those where the U-boats lurked. Gradually the picture was built up as more losses were reported, and the reaction of the Admiralty was to form hunting groups to cover the North and South Atlantic Oceans and the Indian Ocean. In addition, battleships and cruisers were sent across the Atlantic to Halifax to act as

A Sea Hurricane about to be launched from a Catapult Armed Merchantman (CAM). With the acute shortage of Royal Navy convoy escort vessels, the CAM ship was vital in Atlantic convoy protection. Unfortunately, each mission for one of these planes meant the loss of the plane as well as a ducking for the pilot who ditched beside his 'mother' ship

SHIPPING LOSSES TO DECEMBER 1940

Shipping sunk by:

U-BOATS 2,606,000 tons

MINES 772,000 tons

BOMBERS 583,000 tons

SURFACE RAIDERS 514,000 tons

E-BOATS 48,000 tons

■ = 50,000 tons

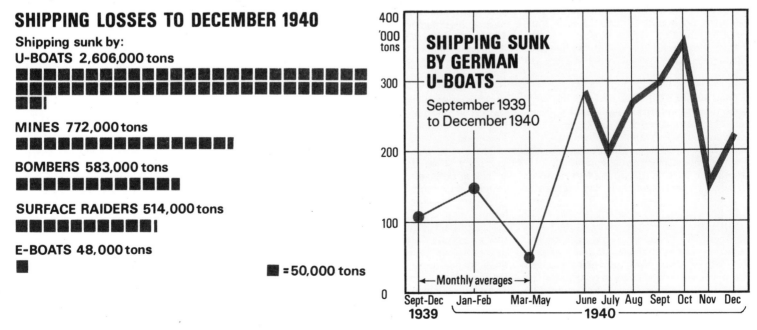

SHIPPING SUNK BY GERMAN U-BOATS

September 1939 to December 1940

400 '000 tons

300

200

100

0

←— Monthly averages —→

Sept-Dec **1939** | Jan-Feb | Mar-May | June | July | Aug | Sept | Oct | Nov | Dec
1940

raider escorts to successive convoys sailing to Britain.

The first success, and one that enormously boosted British war morale, was the destruction of the pocket-battleship *Graf Spee* in the estuary of the River Plate. She had been tracked down by the positions of the ships she had sunk, and a brilliant piece of deduction by Commodore Henry Harwood had led to his hunting group being in position to intercept her as she moved towards the South American coast in search of other victims. She had sunk nine ships of some 50,000 tons before she was brought to action, a poor result in comparison with her overwhelming strength and fire-power. The cruise of the *Deutschland* was even less productive. She sank two ships in the North Atlantic before being called home.

The *Deutschland's* efforts in the Atlantic were followed in November by a more ambitious venture on the part of Admiral Raeder, who sent out the battle-cruisers *Scharnhorst* and *Gneisenau* on a combined cruise into the North Atlantic, with the object of dislocating the British patrol lines. It was a preliminary operation to give the two big ships some experience before letting them loose on the main trade routes. They sailed from Germany on November 21, but on the evening of the 23rd, just as they were breaking out into the Atlantic between the Faeroe Islands and Iceland, they were sighted and engaged by the armed merchant cruiser *Rawalpindi*. She, of course, was no match for a battle-cruiser, and was quickly sunk by the *Scharnhorst,* but not before she had sent out two wireless sighting reports.

Admiral Forbes, the Commander-in-Chief, at once sailed from Scapa Flow with the Home Fleet, and HMS *Newcastle,* the next ship to the *Rawalpindi* in the patrol line, closed the position and sighted the two battle-cruisers, but lost them again in a heavy rainstorm. Admiral Marschall, who commanded the two German ships, broke away at high speed and abandoned the operation, returning to Germany. The Home Fleet had little chance of catching the two battle-cruisers, for the distance was too great.

This whole operation raised some doubts in the British Admiralty's mind as to the degree of severity with which these German raiding ventures were to be carried out. It seemed inexplicable that, on sighting the *Newcastle,* these ships should not turn on her and send her to the bottom. Her 6-inch guns were no match for the 11-inch guns carried by the two battle-cruisers, and the fact that they turned back and ran for home hardly made sense in real naval warfare. At the time it was believed by the Admiralty and by Admiral Forbes that the *Rawalpindi* had been sunk by the *Deutschland,* but even this would not explain the sudden disengagement. She also carried 11-inch guns. This was an aspect of German naval warfare that was to recur throughout the war at sea, and one which caused constant surprise.

One other part of the initial German war plan went amiss in the early days. This was the design to employ forces in the North Sea to disrupt British shipping and tie down a sizable portion of the British fleet. On December 12 a force of five destroyers, covered by three cruisers, sailed to lay a minefield off the Northumberland coast. They were sighted on their return by the submarine *Salmon,* which torpedoed the cruisers *Leipzig* and *Nürnberg,* damaging them both. Two days later, as this force

approached the Danish coast, it was again attacked, this time by the submarine *Ursula.* The *Leipzig* escaped the torpedoes, but one of her escorting destroyers was hit and sunk.

But the Royal Navy, too, was having its troubles. The biggest blow occurred early in the morning of October 14 when U-47, commanded by Lieutenant Prien, penetrated the defences of Scapa Flow and torpedoed and sank the battleship *Royal Oak.* The loss of the battleship herself was relatively unimportant in the context of the strengths of the opposing navies, but what was of concern was the realisation that the main operational base of the Royal Navy was vulnerable to submarine attack. Until its defences could be made secure by the use of more blockships in the entrances, the Home Fleet was forced to use Loch Ewe on the western coast of Scotland as an anchorage, even though it, too, was open to submarine attack. Indeed, only six weeks later, HMS *Nelson,* the fleet flagship, was damaged by a mine as she was entering Loch Ewe.

A balance sheet drawn up at the end of 1939 would have shown figures favourable to the Royal Navy. The main doubt in the mind of the British Admiralty before the war had begun was whether the threat to British trade poised by surface raiders could be held, and particularly were the three pocket-battleships held in dread. And here there was already a favourable balance, with only 15 British, Allied, and neutral merchant ships sunk and one of the three pocket-battleships lying on the sea bed in Montevideo Roads. The toll by the U-boats had not been unduly heavy: 114 ships of 421,000 tons had been sunk with a loss to the enemy of nine U-boats. Casualties from mines (79 ships of 262,000 tons) were severe, but with the discovery of the polarity of the German magnetic mine, it was believed that the back of this particular problem had been broken. On the debit side could be placed the loss of the *Royal Oak* and *Courageous,* one armed merchant cruiser, three destroyers, and one submarine. Taken as a whole, the picture was reasonably encouraging.

Yet in the longer view there was still much to worry the Admiralty in London. It had been believed before the war – and still was, since no evidence had come in to the contrary – that the British 'asdic' submarine detector, as fitted in all anti-submarine vessels, was a sufficient guarantee against any repetition of such merchant ship losses as had been experienced between 1914 and 1918, particularly when allied to the modern depth-charge, with its multiple depth settings. But evidence was already accumulating within the Admiralty of the size of the German U-boat building programme, and there were those who foresaw a time, judged at around a couple of years, when the defence could well be in danger of being swamped by sheer weight of numbers.

There was one other aspect of the submarine war which caused some uneasiness: a lack of sufficiently 'long-legged' escorts to provide merchant ship convoy for the whole length of passage. As matters stood at the beginning of 1940, there was, on the transatlantic passage alone, a gap of some 1,700 miles across which merchant ships were beyond the range of surface escort. It was an even longer gap on some of the other main trade routes.

As events turned out during the first six months of 1940, these early doubts became real enough. The campaign in Norway in

The bases of the Home Fleet; as in the First World War, the Scapa Flow anchorage was the main base. However, after the *Royal Oak* was sunk at anchor by U-47 in October 1939 it became apparent that the defences were incomplete. Submarine nets were then placed across the entrance. The bulk of the British battle fleet waited here to counter any German attempt to break out into the North Atlantic.

April and May of 1940 and the evacuation of the British Expeditionary Force from the Channel ports in May and early June of the same year are well-known episodes from the history of the war, but a brief reference to them here is necessary to assess their influence on the overall picture of trade defence. During the Norwegian campaign ten destroyers and sloops were sunk and another 14 damaged. The evacuation of the BEF added six more destroyers and sloops sunk and a further 20 damaged.

This was a serious drain of those ships which, by their nature, were the best escorts for the defence of trade – but an even more serious gap in possible escort vessels was caused by the obvious corollary of the fall of France. The Germans were now poised on the Channel coast, and talk of invasion was in the air. This inevitably meant that many naval ships, and particularly destroyers, were tied up to watch for any enemy movement across the Channel, and this duty, which lasted for four months until the danger of invasion began to fade, inevitably led to further and serious shortages in the forces available for merchant ship escort.

Bad as this was, there was worse to follow. In the last months of 1939 the enemy had attempted, though with little success, to organise attacks on convoys by groups of U-boats instead of by single boats. On a convoy being sighted and reported, U-boat headquarters would call in adjacent boats to

▽ Lookouts on the *Scheer*   △ *Admiral Scheer* in action   ▽ An 11-inch shell from the *Scheer* misses *Jervis Bay*

▽ Sunk by the *Scheer*: a refrigerated freighter

press home the attack. From this beginning, it was not difficult to develop a more efficient method of the group attack. The U-boats were organised into operational 'wolf-packs', and when a convoy's course was reasonably well identified, the nearest pack was ordered to the vicinity by the U-boat headquarters. When the convoy was sighted, the U-boat concerned 'homed' the rest of the pack to the convoy by directional wireless signals. No attack developed until the whole pack had arrived.

With this tactic there was added the surface attack by night. A surfaced submarine presents only a tiny silhouette and is difficult to see even in the best conditions of visibility. They are also able to use their diesel engines on the surface and so are much faster than when submerged—indeed, their surface speed exceeded that of most British escort vessels. There was, therefore, very little hope of catching them even if they were sighted during the attack. Even more disastrous from the British point of view was the fact that a U-boat on the surface was virtually immune from discovery by 'asdic' detection.

This completely reversed the confidence with which, before the war, the Admiralty had contemplated an enemy attack on seaborne trade. The 'asdic' and the depth-charge were the twin foundations on which the whole theory of anti-submarine warfare had been firmly based, and these new German tactics completely outmanoeuvred them. The fitting of radar sets in escort vessels was the immediate and obvious answer, since radar would indicate the presence of a surfaced U-boat, but as yet there were no sets available, and another year was to elapse before enough became available to equip the escort fleet.

In the meantime, another duty lay before the Royal Navy. Almost as the evacuation of

Carelessness could easily lead a convoy into the jaws of a U-boat wolf-pack

the BEF from Dunkirk and the Channel ports was taking place, other British troops were being landed in France in an attempt to form a line on which the advancing Germans could be successfully held. But in the rapidly crumbling situation ashore, any hope of stopping the German advance was slim indeed. It became even slimmer when it became apparent that the defeatist element in the French government was strongly in favour of negotiating with the Germans for an armistice.

The decision to bring home the remaining British troops in France, many of them landed only a few days earlier, was taken on June 15, using the ports of Cherbourg, St Malo, Brest, St Nazaire, and La Pallice. In the few days during which this operation was carried out, another 136,963 British troops were brought safely home, as well as some 38,500 Allies, of whom the majority were Polish.

The whole operation was carried out with only one loss, but that was a grievous one. Among other ships sent to carry troops home from St Nazaire was the liner *Lancastria*. She was lying out in the anchorage and had already taken more than 5,300 soldiers on board when she was hit during a heavy German air raid. Although she took some little time to sink, more than 3,000 of those on board lost their lives—mainly because, in the urgency of evacuation, there were insufficient lifebelts in the ship for all the extra men she was carrying.

With this final evacuation of British forces from France, coupled with the armistice which the French government signed with Germany, a completely new problem faced the Admiralty. The situation on which the original war plans had been drawn had now been shattered beyond recognition.

Taking stock, the Royal Navy had to face a situation in which the whole of the western coast of Europe, from the North Cape in Norway to the Spanish frontier in the Bay of Biscay, lay in the hands of the enemy. With the Norwegian ports and bases in his hands, Hitler could now command the eastern North Sea right up to the Arctic Circle. This gave him a wide corridor through which to pass his U-boats, his armed merchant raiders, and his blockade runners in the Atlantic. With similar facilities in the Bay

PRINZ EUGEN
She was the third German heavy cruiser to be built in defiance of the Versailles naval restrictions on the German navy, following the *Hipper* and the *Blücher*.
Displacement: 13,900 tons
Max speed: 32 knots
Armament: eight 8-inch; 12 4·1-inch AA, 12 37-mm AA, eight (later 28) 20-mm AA; 12 21-inch torpedo-tubes; three aircraft. (Complement: 1,600)

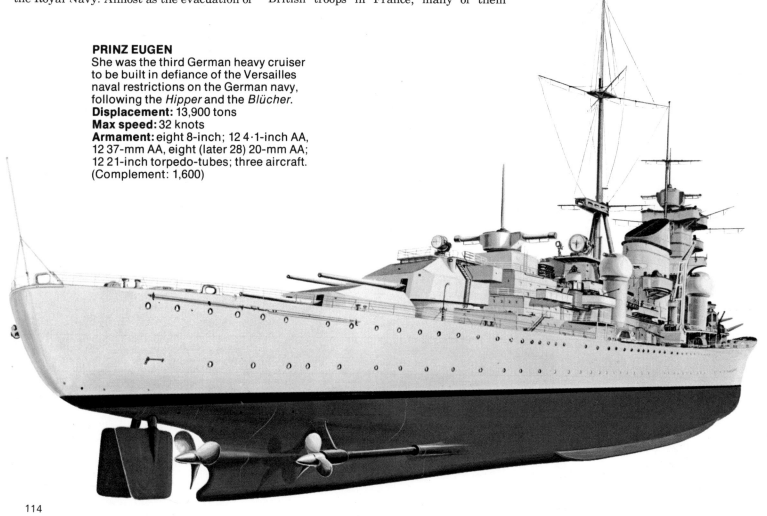

of Biscay, U-boats could reach farther out into the Atlantic, and raiders and blockade runners could penetrate deep into ocean waters before they reached areas where British ships could seize them. This made the British Admiralty's task infinitely more difficult, for a ship is easily concealed in the immensity of the oceans.

A yet more potent threat to the nation's seaborne trade lay in German occupation of the airfields of western France, from which long-range Focke-Wulf 'Condor' aircraft could search the Atlantic for British convoys and report their positions to the waiting U-boats.

This particular problem was solved in a typically extempore fashion. A few merchant ships were fitted with catapults which could launch a Hurricane fighter, and one of these accompanied the more important convoys as they sailed within range of the Condors. When one of them was sighted, the Hurricane was catapulted into flight, shot down or drove off the intruder, and then ditched itself alongside a merchant ship so that the pilot could be picked up.

These catapult-armed-merchant ships or CAM-ships, as they were known, gave way in time to the MAC-ship (merchant-aircraft-carrier), in which a full flight deck was built over the top of a merchant ship, usually a tanker because of her length. The MAC-ships could carry up to about six fighters, which of course could land on again after operations and did not have to

ditch alongside. And as time went on, the MAC-ships were replaced by auxiliary (or 'Woolworth') carriers, which embodied merchant ship hulls converted into full aircraft-carriers.

Strangulation of trade
While the battle of the skies was being fought by the Royal Air Force against German bombers and fighters intent on hammering Britain into submission, another battle was being fought in the coastal waters around Britain. Hitler's plan to defeat Britain lay not so much in invasion across the Channel, which was in fact to be his last resort if all else failed, but in the strangulation of trade.

In the wake of the advancing German armies came his motor torpedo-boats, known as E-boats, pushing their bases westward until they reached Cherbourg during the second half of June 1940. Their targets were the coastal convoys, combined with offensive minelaying before the ports of Britain. Heavy air attacks on convoys and ports also took their toll of ships. Although all these were hit-and-run attacks, they tied down a large number of British naval vessels, and it was to take some months of hard and incessant skirmishing before the enemy was held and the coastal trade could pass in comparative security.

Another naval task was the defence against seaborne invasion, which everyone in Britain expected during the summer and autumn of 1940. But this was nothing new; and the Royal Navy swung into its traditional defence, tried and proved through centuries of experience. It was based on the close watch of the invasion forces by flotilla vessels: in the old days by sloops, cutters, and gun-vessels; in 1940 by destroyers, motor torpedo-boats, and gunboats. Behind

them, in the east and west coast ports, lay the immediate stiffening of the defence by ships of greater power: in the old days by frigates; in 1940 by cruisers. And behind them again lay the final safeguard of all—the immense strength of the battle fleet, which would be called south to action when the forces of invasion actually sailed.

Here, in 1940, across the waters of the English Channel stood the army of Hitler, as before it had stood the armies of Napoleon, of Louis XIV, of Philip II of Spain. Between them all and their dreams of conquest had stood the British navy. Between Hitler and his dreams it still stood. As the days and the weeks passed, as the invasion barges and the transports which had been taken from the inland waterways with so much dislocation of local trade still lay stationary at their moorings in the Channel ports, the Lords of the Admiralty could echo the words of the Earl of St Vincent, a First Lord of 150 years ago, that 'being a military question they must hesitate to express an opinion about invasion as such'. All they knew was that an invasion 'could not come by sea'.

In all the major fighting which had fallen to the Royal Navy so far—in the Norwegian campaign and in the evacuation from Dunkirk—one unmistakable new lesson had emerged: that ships at sea could not operate in waters dominated by enemy air power. The major naval weapon against the Axis powers—for Italy had joined the conflict on the fall of France—was still the blockade, and to keep this weapon in operation the ring of sea power around Europe still needed to be held. Now, however, it had to be drawn beyond the range of aircraft using the newly won airfields of Norway, Denmark, Holland, Belgium, and France. Britain, outflanked now to the south and east,

GNEISENAU
With her sister-ship *Scharnhorst,* the *Gneisenau* represented a new phase of battle-cruiser design when the two ships were launched in 1936.
Displacement: 32,000 tons
Max speed: 31½ knots
Armament: nine 11-inch, 12 5·9-inch; 14 4·1-inch AA, 16 37-mm AA, 10 (later 38) 20-mm AA guns; six 21-inch torpedo-tubes; four aircraft. (Complement: 1,800)

had to guard well the north and west if she were not to be herself defeated. So, to the north, British sea power stretched out to Iceland and across the Denmark Straits to the coast of Greenland. In the west it reached from Northern Ireland out into the Atlantic, sweeping down in a wide arc to the south, to Gibraltar and Freetown. To complete the circle, the Mediterranean Fleet held the eastern waters of the Mediterranean from Malta to the western coast of Greece.

Within this tenuous circle were held the Axis powers. This was the barrier through which they had to break if they were to reach the raw materials of the rest of the world. It could not as yet be held strongly enough to prevent the surface raiders slipping through, nor could it ever stop the U-boats from reaching the outer oceans. But it could, and did, effectively stifle almost the whole of that seaborne trade without which the two dictators could not win their war.

This was a barrier which had to be held at all costs, for if final victory were to be won, the barrier had to serve a dual purpose. There was more to it than stopping the seaborne trade of Germany and Italy; while containing them in isolation, it had also to safeguard the slow build-up of British power and resources against the day when the national strategy could turn from the defensive to the offensive.

Behind its strength had to come the huge imports of oil, steel, tanks, guns, aircraft, and food without which the only future for Britain was defeat. And behind its strength, too, had to come the men, from the Dominions and colonies and, later, from the United States, who would add their strength to the armies which, one day, would carry the war back into Europe. And behind its strength must sail all those troops, weapons, and stores to hold the other vital theatres of war in the Middle East and, a year later, the Far East.

The task, in those summer months of 1940, appeared stupendous—and it was aggravated both by the loss of ships during the operations in Norway and at Dunkirk and by those which were now tied up in the anti-invasion duties. Where, in 1939, it had been possible to provide an average of two escort vessels for each convoy that sailed, now, in the summer of 1940, the average escort strength was down to 1·8 per convoy. The U-boats, now beginning to use French and

Norwegian bases, were saving 1,000 miles or more on their passage to their patrol areas, and so were able to operate considerably farther out into the Atlantic, and well beyond the limit to which convoys could be escorted.

Two gleams of light shone fitfully into this dark prospect. The first was produced by the occupation by British troops of the Faeroe Islands and Iceland. Both were dependencies of Denmark, and on the invasion of that country by Germany in April 1940 had been quickly taken over by Britain to deny them to Hitler.

Iceland was notably well placed to act as a base on the Atlantic convoy routes, a base from which escorts could operate to lengthen substantially the limit of convoy both from Britain and from the Canadian ports. There was no question of using it at once, for it takes time to develop the essential facilities of a naval base, but it would unquestionably pay substantial dividends in the future.

The other gleam of light came from the negotiations between Churchill and Roosevelt over the release by the United States of 50 over-age destroyers in exchange for the lease of bases in Newfoundland and the West Indies. These destroyers, of the old 'flush deck and four-pipe' class, were hurriedly overhauled and re-equipped in US bases and taken into the British and Canadian navies. There they served to augment the already over-stretched escort force, at least temporarily until the new construction escort vessels began to join the fleet.

Return of the U-boats

The first six months of 1940 had been a relatively quiet time in the Atlantic on the U-boat front, due partly to the wild weather of January, in which U-boats found it very difficult to operate, and partly to the large-scale withdrawal of U-boats from the Atlantic to take part in the Norwegian campaign. But by June 1940 they were back on the Atlantic trade routes, not in any great strength as yet, as the building programme was only just beginning to bear fruit, but with a steadily increasing monthly total.

From their new Biscay bases, even the small 500-ton U-boats could now operate in areas as much as 600 miles out into the

Atlantic, well beyond the limit of surface anti-submarine escort from Britain. There was little opposition to them out there, and the incoming and outgoing merchant ships were sitting ducks to their torpedoes. Closer in, they chose as their targets ships which—because of their speed—sailed independent of convoys, or ships which straggled from the convoys. These, too, were sitting ducks.

During September the U-boat command introduced the first serious wolf-pack attacks against British convoys. Two successive Atlantic convoys, SC-2 and HX-72, were attacked by a pack of ten U-boats north-west of Iceland, and 16 ships were sunk out of them. A month later an even more savage wolf-pack attack was launched. Again the victims were two successive Atlantic convoys, SC-7 and HX-79, and a wolf-pack of eight U-boats, attacking them on four successive nights, sank 32 ships.

It was not unduly difficult to discover the answers to this form of attack. One of them, as mentioned above, was the fitting of radar in the escorts. Another was to discover a method of turning night into day more efficiently than by starshell from the escorts' guns. This was eventually provided by the scientists with the invention of 'Snowflake', a flare which lit up a large area of the ocean at once. But, like radar, this answer also lay in the future.

Another answer was the provision of air escort of convoys. This was a powerful deterrent to the U-boat, for aircraft ranging over the convoy area forced the shadowing U-boat to submerge and thus lose touch. And when fitted with ASV (airborne radar), escorting aircraft had an even wider range of effectiveness, for their sets could detect a surfaced U-boat in thick weather, and at a greater range, where the human eye would fail. But here again, at this stage of the battle, the necessary numbers of long-range aircraft did not exist in Coastal Command, and the protection from attack which they could provide was not available.

Yet another source of protection was deduced from the habits of the shadowing U-boat. In order to 'home' the remainder of the pack on to the convoy, the shadowing U-boat had to make a succession of wireless signals. While these might not be heard by the shore wireless direction-finding stations, because they were made on low power, they

German **Type IXB** U-boat. These ocean-going boats were developed from the UEII Type of the First World War, with more endurance than the Type VII series. They proved less than suitable for the Western Approaches and were used instead in distant waters. Nonetheless, their average of tonnage sunk was as high as any other group of U-boats. Their main drawback was that they took too long to build, and only 14 were ever finished. **Displacement:** 1,051 tons (surfaced) **Armament:** Six 21-inch torpedo-tubes; 22 torpedoes carried; one 37-mm gun; one 20-mm gun **Speed:** 18¼ knots (surfaced) 7¼ knots (submerged)

would normally appear as strong signals on board the escorts. If these ships, therefore, carried a direction-finding receiver, they could run down the bearing of the shadowing U-boat and expect to find her at the other end. This aid to U-boat destruction was, again, only embryonic in 1940, but it was from this date that steps were taken to produce suitable ship-borne direction-finding receivers. They eventually came into the escort fleet in July 1941.

All that remained, therefore, was to strive to extend the range of surface escort farther out into the Atlantic, and to try to divert the convoys, by evasive routing, clear of those areas where the U-boat packs were thought to be lurking. This was the task of the U-boat tracking room in the Admiralty, using every piece of intelligence information that came in. The most prolific source of this intelligence was found to be the wireless bearings taken from shore stations of every signal made by the U-boats at sea.

Actual sighting reports made by the U-boats were quickly recognised as such from the form of the message itself, and convoys could be immediately warned that they were in danger. Sometimes a drastic alteration of course away from the U-boat would shake the shadower off. But although some of the best brains in the Navy were concentrated in the tracking room, the volume of intelligence coming in was not sufficient to enable them to do much more than grope in the dark. Later, as the raw material of intelligence improved both in quantity and quality, the tracking room was to achieve some spectacular successes. But that time was not yet.

Merchant ship sinkings
The losses of merchant ships caused by the U-boats through 1940 tell their own story. The two months of January and February had seen the loss of 85 ships totalling 290,000 tons. During March, April, and May, the U-boats had been largely withdrawn from the Atlantic to play their part in the Norwegian campaign, and during those three months only 43 ships of an aggregate of 140,000 tons were lost. But in June the U-boats were coming back and, moreover, beginning to operate farther afield in the Atlantic, and beyond the reach of the convoy escorts. June saw the loss to the U-boats rise to a figure of 58 ships with a total

tonnage of 284,000. And the figures for the remainder of the year were equally grievous.

Losses such as these were beyond the replacement capacity of the British building yards, and although there was still as yet plenty of 'fat' in the total of pre-war tonnage afloat under the British flag, these figures clearly showed the writing on the wall. A fair amount of merchant ship tonnage—particularly Norwegian and Dutch—had accrued to Britain with the German invasion of the western European countries in April and May, but even that could not allow anyone to contemplate the loss figure with anything but a feeling of apprehension. And as yet the peak of U-boat strength had not been even approached.

U-boats in profusion
It was known in the British Admiralty that several hundred new U-boats were on order, and the existing operational strength was but a shadow of what was inevitably to come. Before the war, in his book on submarine warfare, Admiral Dönitz had put forward the estimate that 300 operational U-boats would be required to win a war against Britain. That meant a total force of some 900 submarines, to allow for losses, training, rest periods for crews, refits, and so on. This book had, of course, been read by many British naval officers, and none doubted the German capacity to build up to this figure. Moreover, the declaration by Hitler on August 17 of a total blockade of the British Isles, giving warning that neutral shipping would be sunk at sight, gave an added indication that the U-boat campaign was to be the means by which Germany expected to win her victory.

The loss to the enemy during 1940 was 22 U-boats, although the Admiralty at the time only knew of 16 confirmed cases; the remaining six were sunk by accident or unknown causes. But in view of the German building programme, this was not a satisfactory exchange rate. Taken over the whole year, it meant that for each U-boat lost, very nearly 100,000 tons of Allied shipping were sent to the bottom. Great Britain and her allies would need to do much better than that if the Atlantic battle, on which the outcome of the war depended, was to be won.

There was one great hope. During the year the limit of escorts had been pushed farther out into the Atlantic. As soon as the Iceland

base became operational, an even larger step outwards could be made. And with the new construction of escort vessels now beginning to come forward, the time was not far distant when convoy could be established right across the Atlantic from coast to coast. Convoys, the Royal Navy knew, had beaten the U-boat in 1917 and 1918. The Admiralty in London hoped, and expected, that they would do so again.

If U-boats had been the only cause of merchant ship losses, the problem of containment would not have been too great a

1939 **September 3:** The SS *Athenia* is torpedoed off north-west Ireland.
September 4: The RAF raids warships in Heligoland Bight.
October 14: HMS *Royal Oak* is torpedoed in Scapa Flow by U-47.
November 18: New German magnetic mines are sown from the air.
November 23: The armed merchant cruiser *Rawalpindi* is sunk by the *Scharnhorst* and *Gneisenau* south-east of Iceland.
December 13: Battle of the River Plate.
December 14: The RAF raids warships in Schillig Roads.

1940 **January:** The British begin to use protective 'de-gaussing' of ships to meet the threat of the magnetic mine.
February 15: Germany announces that all British merchant ships will be treated as warships.
March 1: Germany announces 750,000 BRT sunk by U-boats, 63,000 BRT sunk by surface ships, 36,000 BRT sunk by Luftwaffe, and 281,000 BRT sunk by mines.
March 19: The RAF bombs German installations at Hörnum.
May 11: Churchill gives Bomber Command authority to attack Germany.
May 15: The RAF raids the Ruhr.
June 18: The RAF raids Hamburg and Bremen.
August 24: Central London is bombed for the first time.
August 25: First RAF raid on Berlin.
September 3: The Anglo-American 'Lend-Lease' agreement is signed. Fifty US destroyers are traded for certain British bases in the West Indies and Newfoundland.
October 29: Allied weekly tonnage losses: 88,000.
November 5: The German pocket-battleship *Admiral Scheer* attacks an Atlantic convoy, sinking the *Jervis Bay*.
November 7: The RAF raids the Krupp munition works, Essen.
December 18/19: The RAF raids Mannheim.

task. But at the same time there were serious losses from other causes. German aircraft, operating mainly against the East Coast and English Channel coastal convoys, sank, during 1940, 192 ships of 580,000 tons. Mines throughout the year accounted for 201 ships of 510,000 tons, while the German E-boats claimed a further 23 ships of 48,000 tons. Although the great majority of these were comparatively small ships engaged in coastal trade, and thus more easily and quickly replaced by new construction, the total tonnage added to the overall loss was in excess of 1,000,000.

Return of the raiders

One other cause of loss gave an even greater degree of anxiety and apprehension to the Admiralty: the losses caused by armed merchant raiders—fast and heavily armed merchant ships sent out from Germany to operate individually in the distant oceans. The difficulty was to find them. It had been appreciated, when the raider hunting groups had been formed at the beginning of the war to deal with the pocket-battleships, that this was a most uneconomic use of ships. These groups had steamed many hundreds of thousands of miles, mostly to no avail, for by the time a hunting group could arrive in the vicinity of the last sinking report, the raider herself was by then many hundreds of miles away. And what was, perhaps, even worse than the actual merchant ship sinkings which the raiders achieved was the dislocation and disorganisation which their presence caused to the normal flow of seaborne trade.

What the Germans called the 'first wave' of the armed merchant raiders put to sea during the first half of 1940. The first out was the *Atlantis,* which left Germany on March 31. She was followed by the *Orion* (April 6), and the *Widder* (May 5). Two more, the *Thor* and *Pinguin,* broke through the Atlantic defences, such as they were, in June, and a sixth (the *Komet*), assisted by the Russians, made the Arctic passage to the north of Siberia to the Pacific in July and August. To prolong their periods of activity, a number of supply ships were also sent out, with which they could rendezvous when required.

Only on two occasions—and each time it was the same raider—was any contact made with them by a British warship. On July 28 the armed merchant cruiser *Alcantara* encountered the *Thor* in the West Indies, off Trinidad. The British ship was outsteamed, outgunned, and outfought by the enemy, and as the *Alcantara* limped into port with serious damage, the *Thor* moved down into the South Atlantic to repair her damage and be replenished from a convenient supply ship.

A little over four months later, off the coast of South America, the *Thor* ran into another armed merchant cruiser, the *Carnarvon Castle.* The story was the same, and while the British ship was seriously damaged, the enemy suffered no injury and, after the action, made off into the blue. These two encounters were, in fact, the nearest the Royal Navy ever came during 1940 to sinking one of these elusive and dangerous ships. The damage they caused was widespread and serious. During the year, in the North and South Atlantic, Indian, and Pacific Oceans, these six ships sank 54 ships of an aggregate of 367,000 tons, but in addition they caused a considerable upheaval in the pattern of British seaborne trade through the delays in sailings and rerouting of merchant ships in the vicinity of their attacks. Some, too, were fitted as minelayers in addition to their usual gun and torpedo armament, and the minefields they laid were another cause of loss and delay.

It was not to be expected that the limited success of the first cruises of the *Deutschland* and *Graf Spee,* and the abortive attempt of the *Scharnhorst* and *Gneisenau* to break out in November 1939, would deter the enemy from further attacks on trade by warship raiders. In September 1940 the cruiser *Hipper* made an attempt to reach the Atlantic, but trouble in her engine-room caused her to abandon her planned sortie, and return home.

The next warship to make the attempt was the pocket-battleship *Scheer.* She left Germany on October 27, was not sighted by any British air patrols as she made her way up the Norwegian coast, and reached the Atlantic through the Denmark Straits undetected. On November 5 she sank a British merchant ship, which unfortunately failed to send a wireless report of the attack. Had she done so, it would have been possible to reroute a homeward-bound convoy from Halifax, which was steaming towards the position where the *Scheer's* attack had been made.

The convoy was HX-84, escorted by HMS *Jervis Bay,* an armed merchant cruiser which carried six 6-inch guns mounted on her upper deck. On the evening of November 5, only a few hours after the *Scheer's* earlier attack, the *Jervis Bay* sighted the pocket-battleship approaching the convoy at high speed from the northward. The result, even before the first gun was fired, was a foregone conclusion, for the armed merchant cruiser was not only outgunned, but also outranged by some 10,000 yards.

To save as many of the ships in the convoy as possible, Captain Fegen of the *Jervis Bay* ordered them to scatter to the south under cover of smoke. This they did, using the smoke-making apparatus with which they were all fitted, while Captain Fegen took the *Jervis Bay* into action with her huge adversary to provide as much time as possible for the ships in the convoy to get away. The *Scheer,* naturally, was undamaged during the action—the shells of the *Jervis Bay* could not even reach her—but the delay caused by Captain Fegen's defiance of the raider gave the convoy the chance it needed. By the time the *Jervis Bay* was sunk, the convoy was so scattered that the *Scheer* was unable to find more than five ships to sink, and one more to damage. The remainder escaped. For his gallantry and self-sacrifice on this occasion, Captain Fegen was awarded a posthumous Victoria Cross.

The epic of the *Jervis Bay* gave rise to another epic of skill and endurance, one which has few parallels in nautical history. The ship damaged by the *Scheer* after the sinking of the *Jervis Bay* was the tanker *San Demetrio.* She was hit and set on fire, and abandoned by her crew.

On the following day, some 18 hours after the attack, a handful of her crew, in an open boat under the command of her second officer, sighted her, still alight. They rowed alongside and climbed on board. Her decks were still hot from the fire on board, but they managed to rig some hoses and gradually got the fire under control. After working for several hours on the engines, they succeeded in getting one of them to function, and the ship began her long, slow journey

Depth-charges

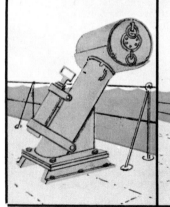

Depth-charge mounted on a 'carrier' ready to be fired out in a wide arc from the ship's side, to port or starboard

The detonator hurls the depth-charge away from the ship; the 'carrier' drops away from the charge and is abandoned

A charge is dropped over a ship's stern from a chute where another charge is in place, ready to follow in a close pattern

Underwater explosions have a tremendous effect, due to the concentrated shock-waves. A near-miss could crack a U-boat's hull

A hunting escort-ship could fire wide or close patterns of charges, as the 'asdic' groped for the elusive 'ping' of a U-boat

Fairey Albacore
Overshadowed by the Swordfish for which the Albacore was planned as a replacement, this rugged biplane proved a useful anti-submarine aircraft

Span: 50 ft *Length:* 39 ft 9½ in *Engine:* Bristol Taurus II, 1065 hp *Armament:* 1 Vickers mg; 2 Vickers 'K' mg *Max Speed:* 161 mph at 4000 ft *Ceiling:* 20,700 ft *Range:* 930 miles *Bomb load:* 1 × 18-in torpedo or 2000 lb bombs

to Britain. Without charts beyond a school atlas found on board, with no other navigational aid, and averaging a little less than 5 knots, these few men succeeded in bringing the *San Demetrio* home together with the greater part of her valuable cargo of oil.

After her attack on HX-84 the *Scheer* steamed south, away from the area in which she had so recently operated. She replenished her oil and ammunition from a supply ship and, after operating off the Azores, moved into the South Atlantic. Here she captured a British merchant ship loaded with foodstuffs, and deliberately allowed her to broadcast a raider report before sending a prize crew on board. The reason for this was to draw attention to her position in the South Atlantic and thus attract to the area any British hunting forces which might be engaged in anti-raider operations. This was to leave the coast clear in the north, where the cruiser *Hipper* was trying to make her second attempt to break out into the Atlantic.

The *Hipper* sailed from Germany on November 30, like the *Scheer* evaded the North Sea air patrols, and successfully broke through the Denmark Straits into the North Atlantic on December 7. She spent a few days in the North Atlantic searching for

convoys to attack, but found none, as her captain did not realise that convoys were still at that date taking the northerly route across the Atlantic. As a result of her lack of success she proceeded south to investigate the Sierra Leone route, and in the evening of December 24 gained touch with a convoy. She shadowed it throughout the night, hoping for fat pickings on the following day.

The convoy she was shadowing was, in fact, a troop convoy bound for the Middle East. These were always heavily guarded when at sea. As the *Hipper* approached on Christmas Day to attack, she was disconcerted to find it escorted by an aircraft-carrier and three cruisers. They had no difficulty in driving her off, but unfortunately lost sight of her in the low visibility. The *Hipper* was, in fact, slightly damaged during the exchange of gunfire. She decided to cut short her raiding cruise, and two days later arrived at Brest, on the French Biscay coast.

Next came the turn of the *Scharnhorst* and *Gneisenau,* acting as a squadron. Both had been fairly extensively damaged during the Norwegian campaign, and this was to be their first action since those days, having spent the intervening seven months in dockyard hands. Their effort was abortive. The *Gneisenau* was damaged in heavy seas while steaming up the coast of Norway, and both ships thereupon reversed their course and returned to Kiel.

This 'second wave' of the warship raiders

accounted for the loss of 17 ships of 97,000 tons, bringing the total losses of the year from all causes up to the formidable total of 1,059 ships of 3,991,641 tons. Of these, nearly 60% had been sunk by U-boats, the majority of them on the vital North Atlantic trade route.

It is necessary for a moment to leave the Atlantic and take a quick look at the last link of the circle of sea power drawn around the Axis nations. When Italy joined Germany in hostilities during the last days of the fighting ashore in Europe, the naval position in the Red Sea at once gave some cause for alarm. Here, based on Massawa, the Italians had a force of nine destroyers, eight submarines, and an armed merchant raider.

The Red Sea was an essential link with British forces operating in the Middle East, and it was essential to hold this sea area if Germany and Italy were to be effectively denied access to the trade of the outside world and if British forces were to receive the replenishment in men, weapons, and stores they would need to conduct active operations.

As it turned out, the Italian naval threat never materialised. Three of the submarines were sunk and another captured intact within the first month of Italy joining the war; the destroyers took no action to attempt to harass British convoys in the Red Sea; and the spasmodic efforts of Italian aircraft to interfere with British shipping were un-

Magnetic mine

Lowered by parachute, the magnetic mine also had a contact fuse: if it hit a solid surface it was meant to explode like a bomb

As the mine sank, the rear parachute attachment was released: freed from the parachute, the mine would then rest on the sea bed

As a ship approached, the weak magnetic field set up would finally detonate the mine by closing the circuit with the magnetic needle

In shallow water, the explosion, directly below the ship's hull, was devastating. These mines caused heavy tonnage losses

1. 'Chute case (two halves)
2. Folded 'chute 3. Needle
4. Case join 5. Detonator
6. High explosive (approx 650 lb) 7. Anti-roll horns

Chris Harrison

availing. The Red Sea route remained firmly in British hands, and the circle of sea power remained unbroken.

The end of 1940 saw the situation at sea more or less in a state of balance. The Allies had been defeated on the land, both in Norway and France, but the sea defence still held, even if stretched thin in some places. Against the enemy occupation of naval bases in Norway and France, with all that

they meant in extending the range of operations of the U-boats, Britain had occupied Iceland and was equipping a naval and air base there which, in the end, would prove decisive to the ultimate outcome of the U-boat war. Against the rapid build-up in numbers of the U-boat fleet, which was to rise at one period to over 360 operational boats, there was the certainty that, during 1941, end-to-end Atlantic convoy of merchant ships would be achieved, and the task of the U-boats would be made much more difficult and dangerous.

Only in one aspect of convoy warfare was there some distress. It had been apparent even in the First World War that submarines hesitated to attack convoys which had air as well as surface escort, even though at that time there was no airborne weapon capable of sinking a submarine. The same hesitation was being experienced in 1940.

But air escort of convoys at sea called for aircraft of long range and endurance – the same aircraft particularly in demand for the bombing offensive on Germany. RAF Coastal Command, which under naval direction provided the convoy air escort, was starved of long-range aircraft, and the convoys suffered severe losses as a result. This was a problem which was not solved until 1943, by which time the navy had acquired enough auxiliary aircraft-carriers to operate their own aircraft on the convoy routes. Later still, American production of long-range aircraft filled the gap, and released the aircraft-carriers for other duties.

As the year ended, there were hopeful signs in a situation which still remained dark from the British military defeats on the Continent. Although now thrust far out into the Atlantic, the sea defence of the nation still held, and behind it the blockade of Germany and Italy was virtually intact. This was still the fundamental weapon which, if it could be maintained, would in the end lead to victory. The great danger which now faced Britain was no longer invasion from the Continent – the chance of that had gone (if it ever really existed) – but defeat in the war against the U-boats.

The whole future of the war now hung upon that groping battle being fought in the vastness of the oceans. It was to be a race between the German U-boat building programme and the time when it would be possible to bring into operation a fully integrated system of end-to-end surface and air escort of convoys. Once that was in operation, the defeat of the U-boats was certain, although there was a long and painful road still to travel.

German 'Milch Cow' Type XIV
To extend the range of the Type VII U-boats the German navy built ten submarine tankers in 1941. With a fatter and shorter hull than the Type IX boats, and less power, they could carry sufficient fuel to keep four or five U-boats at sea for twice as long as usual, and they also carried four spare torpedoes in external stowage. They were made top priority targets for Allied ships and all ten were sunk. *Displacement:* 1,688 tons (surfaced) *Armament:* Two 37-mm AA guns; one 20-mm AA gun; no torpedo-tubes

German Type VII (*U236*)

The Type VII U-boat was the standard
design for the U-boat in the Second World
War. It was developed from the Finnish
Vetehinen design before the expiry of the
Versailles Treaty, and many improvements
were effected as a result of war experience.
U236 was one of the Type VIIC, the third
version, and she came into service in
January 1943. She was scuttled in 1945
after suffering damage by air attack.
Displacement: 769 tons (surfaced)
Armament: Five 21-in torpedo-tubes; 14
torpedoes carried; plus a variety of light
AA guns *Speed:* 17 knots (surfaced)
7½ knots (submerged)

BATTLE OF THE RIVER PLATE

Due to restrictions of the Treaty of Versailles, Germany had been forbidden to build ships of over 10,000 tons—which ruled out battleships. So it became necessary to evolve a new kind of ship which, though restricted in tonnage, would have guns superior to those of a heavy cruiser and armour thick enough to resist high-calibre shells of up to 8 inches. The result was the pocket-battleship 'Graf Spee', launched at Wilhelmshaven on New Year's Day, 1936

On August 23, 1939, an armoured cruiser slipped out of the German port of Wilhelmshaven, headed north around the Faroe Isles, turned south to pass Iceland and cruised out into the grey expanses of the Atlantic Ocean. This was the beginning of an odyssey of daring and destruction which was to end four months later in what has come to be called the Battle of the River Plate.

The cruiser was the *Admiral Graf Spee*—a powerful, fast, heavily-armed and heavily-armoured vessel mounting as main armament six 11-inch and eight 5.9-inch and 4.1-inch guns and protected by up to 5½ inches of armour. The term 'pocket-battleship' admirably suited this dangerous, 12,100-ton surface raider, destined to cause widespread confusion and destruction among vulnerable merchant shipping during its short but effective life.

Restrictions imposed on German naval construction between the world wars had ensured that Hitler would be denied in 1939 the support of a mighty High Seas Fleet of the sort which Germany had in 1914. Nevertheless the combination of raiders such as *Graf Spee* and her menacing submarine fleet, still made Germany a formidable naval adversary for the overstretched British Navy at the outbreak of war.

When Britain declared war on Germany on September 3, 1939, *Graf Spee* was already in position to begin ranging the South Atlantic. Her presence posed a serious threat to the trade routes around South America and the Cape of Good Hope.

But although the first directive from the German High Command was clear enough— 'The German Navy will conduct mercantile warfare having England as its principal target'—Hitler hesitated. Hopes of containing the war, after the defeat of Poland, by some form of agreement with the Western Allies, deterred him for a few weeks from unleashing the *Graf Spee* on British shipping.

But on September 26 the order was given and *Graf Spee* began to hunt for its prey. Four days later it made its first killing when it stopped and sank the British merchant vessel *Clement*. With the loss of the *Clement* confirmed, the British Admiralty concluded that a German surface raider was loose and began to build up and deploy available forces to hunt her down.

Graf Spee's commanding officer, Captain Langsdorff, was, however, several steps ahead of his pursuers and he was to remain so until the fateful encounter of the River Plate between Uruguay and Argentina, which led to the destruction of his ship and his own death.

After sinking *Clement*, Langsdorff headed next for the Cape of Good Hope and, in a bid to confuse hostile ships, disguised the *Graf Spee* by painting his turret mast to resemble Allied warships. This simple trick enabled him to approach and capture three more ships before making for a rendezvous with his auxiliary ship, the *Altmark,* on October 14. But powerful forces were now gathering to threaten *Graf Spee*—an aircraft carrier, two battleships, cruisers and destroyers—as the British Navy concentrated its power in the South Atlantic against the German raider.

On October 23 Langsdorff had a narrow escape when his ship passed a fast-moving, blacked-out vessel in darkness—later believed to have been the aircraft carrier *Furious*. So on October 28, after a further rendezvous with *Altmark*, *Graf Spee* headed for the Indian Ocean reaching an area north-east of Lourenço Marques on November 14.

Langsdorff's intention was to cause maximum chaos and alarm among merchant traffic in this area before returning to hunt the South Atlantic. But pickings were thin so he headed back around the Cape of Good Hope to strike at traffic making for the River Plate.

On December 6, after capturing two more merchant ships and sinking one, he made a further rendezvous with his supply ship to take on oil and transfer prisoners. The next day *Graf Spee* intercepted and sank the British ship *Streonshall*, capturing in the process valuable information on merchant

ships' assembly points in the area of the River Plate. Langsdorff made his fateful decision to hunt in this area on December 7. Six days later the tops of two masts were sighted to starboard. This was Langsdorff's first glimpse of the British naval force of three cruisers which was to bring about his destruction. It signalled the beginning of the Battle of the River Plate.

The force which Langsdorff faced was part of the British South America division, under Commodore Harwood, consisting of the *Ajax*, *Achilles* and *Exeter*. Ten days earlier, Harwood, by a combination of naval intuition, careful deduction, accurate plotting and sheer guesswork, had come to a crucial conclusion. This was that by December 12 the German raider could be off Rio; by December 13 she could be in the area of the River Plate by December 14 off the Falkland Islands. But which? Harwood guessed that the temptation of the rich pickings in the crowded sea routes of the River Plate would be too much for Langsdorff. So he waited. Early on December 13 his inspired guess proved accurate.

From the first contact Langsdorff decided that the ships in his sights were protecting a convoy. Rich prizes were in prospect. So he decided on all-out attack. Harwood, meanwhile, had seen the black smoke pouring from the *Graf Spee* as her engines developed full power. Thinking that he was looking at a merchant ship in trouble, Harwood sent the *Exeter* to investigate.

The two ships approached each other at 0614, closing at almost 50 miles per hour. Two minutes later the *Achilles* signalled *Ajax:* 'I think it is a pocket-battleship' and then 'Enemy in sight bearing 322 degrees'.

The *Graf Spee* opened fire at once on the *Exeter*. A shell burst amidships, killing the starboard torpedo tube crew, damaging communications and starting fires. Shortly afterwards an 11-inch shell from the German ship's eighth salvo hit *Exeter*'s 'B' turret ripping off the front, killing eight men and putting it out of action. Only the Captain and two other officers remained alive in the section.

In the meantime the *Ajax* and *Achilles*, on *Graf Spee*'s port bow, were firing, but their salvoes were dropping short. Langsdorff now turned his massive 11-inch guns away from the *Exeter* and on to the *Ajax* and *Achilles*. *Ajax* was immediately struck and the two ships turned away.

Exeter was by now so badly damaged that the Commodore ordered her to break off the action. Meanwhile *Ajax* and *Achilles* had taken up positions in a bid to close with the German ship. By 0700 the *Graf Spee* was heading to the north-west at 24 knots and making smoke to hide her from her assailants. This marked the close of the first phase of the battle.

The second phase began with a bold gamble by Commodore Harwood. He decided to try to close right in with the German ship and bring all the guns of *Ajax* and *Achilles* to bear. After rapid and accurate exchanges of fire between the three ships, interrupted by manoeuvring to avoid each others' torpedo salvoes, he decided to withdraw. He wrote in his official report: 'I therefore decided to break off the day action and try to close in again after dark.' Then, at 0830, two and a half hours after the *Graf Spee* was first sighted, *Exeter*, *Ajax* and *Achilles* began to shadow the pocket-battleship at a range of 15 miles. Thus the second phase of the battle ended. *Ajax* and *Achilles* had escaped with surprisingly little damage. On board the *Graf Spee*, however, the situation was developing much more dramatically.

Langsdorff had toured his ship and inspected the damage. This, after such a fierce and concentrated action, was comparatively insignificant. *Graf Spee* had been struck by some 17 shells and two guns among the secondary armament had been put out of action. The main guns were intact, however, and there was no significant damage to the engines. None of the nine holes that the British attackers had caused posed any serious danger. Casualties were 37 dead and 57 wounded out of a total crew of 1,100.

Langsdorff, however, had come to his decision: *Graf Spee* was no longer sufficiently seaworthy and he must run for port. His navigating officer advised Montevideo, Uruguay's capital.

Harwood, meanwhile, was broadcasting warnings to all merchant ships in the area, but the time had come for him to try to assess the *Graf Spee*'s precise intentions. The German ship seemed to be heading for the River Plate, but how badly damaged was she and might she make a feint and dash for the open sea in the darkness? The questions never arose. Just after midnight the Graf Spee entered Montevideo Harbour. Repairs were started, supplies were taken on board and wounded crew members were transferred.

On December 16, amid intense British and German diplomatic and intelligence activity in Montevideo, Langsdorff telegraphed the German Admiralty stating that escape from Montevideo was impossible and requesting orders as to whether he should scuttle the ship in the shallow waters of the estuary or be interned. Hitler and his naval advisers replied that escape should be attempted but otherwise Langsdorff should try to destroy *Graf Spee* completely.

On the afternoon of December 17, Langsdorff made his preparations and at 1815 the *Graf Spee* weighed anchor and headed out of Montevideo Harbour. Harwood's cruisers waited for the kill. But they were cheated. At 2045, watched by thousands of people gathering around the harbour, *Graf Spee* was rent by a series of devastating explosions. Langsdorff had scuttled his ship and the Battle of the River Plate was over.

Churchill records that Langsdorff was broken-hearted at the loss of his ship, despite the fact that he had received full authority from the German government for his action. On the night of December 19, after writing a letter taking full responsibility for scuttling the *Graf Spee*, Langsdorff shot himself.

Langsdorff's last words

From the reasonable, logical point of view which took account only of figures on paper, the *Graf Spee,* with her unique combination of remarkable speed plus devastating fire-power, should never have been caught. Wars, however, are fought by men, whose behaviour is often illogical, sometimes inspired, and rarely completely predictable—and Captain Langsdorff of the *Graf Spee* was no exception. Few men have been spoken of so highly by all who came into contact with him—his own crew and his prisoners alike—and perhaps the qualities which made him so pleasant and chivalrous a person also made him fatally gullible. A meaner man, a more suspicious mind, might have seen through the trap which was so elaborately constructed for him once he had taken his great ship into the neutral waters of Montevideo Harbour. Certainly he was thoroughly and efficiently tricked there by the British—and if the spectacular end of his ship caused exultation in Allied hearts, his own tragic end in Buenos Aires was mourned by all. He was a gallant sailor in the tradition of Admiral von Spee after whom his ship had been named.

Communication between Captain Langsdorff and the German Naval Command, December 16:
Langsdorff: *Strategic position off Montevideo. Besides the cruisers and destroyers, Ark Royal and Renown. Close blockade at night; escape into open sea and break-through to home waters hopeless . . . Request decision on whether the ship should be scuttled in spite of insufficient depth in the estuary of the Plate, or whether internment is to be preferred.*
Reply: *Attempt by all means to extend the time in neutral waters . . . Fight your way through to Buenos Aires if possible. No internment in Uruguay. Attempt effective destruction if ship is scuttled.*

On December 20 Langsdorff committed suicide, leaving this letter to the German minister:
Your Excellency,

After a long struggle I reached the grave decision to scuttle the pocket-battleship Admiral Graf Spee, in order to prevent her from falling into enemy hands. I am still convinced that under the circumstances this decision was the only one left, once I had taken my ship into the trap of Montevideo. For with the ammunition remaining, any attempt to fight my way back to open and deep water was bound to fail. And yet only in deep water could I have scuttled the ship, after having used the remaining ammunition, thus avoiding her falling to the enemy.

Sooner than expose my ship to the danger that after a brave fight she would fall partly or completely into enemy hands, I decided not to fight but to destroy the equipment and then scuttle the ship. It was clear to me that this decision might be consciously or unwittingly misconstrued by persons ignorant of my motives, as being attributable entirely or partly to personal considerations. Therefore I decided from the beginning to bear the consequences involved in this decision. For a Captain with a sense of honour, it goes without saying that his personal fate cannot be separated from that of his ship.

I postponed my intention as long as I still bore responsibility for decisions concerning the welfare of the crew under my command. After today's decision of the Argentine government, I can do no more for my ship's company. Neither will I be able to take an active part in the present struggle of my country. I can now only prove by my death that the fighting services of the Third Reich are ready to die for the honour of the flag.

I alone bear the responsibility for scuttling the pocket-battleship Admiral Graf Spee. I am happy to pay with my life for any possible reflection on the honour of the flag. I shall face my fate with firm faith in the cause and the future of the nation and of my Führer.

I am writing this letter to Your Excellency in the quiet of the evening, after calm deliberation, in order that you may be able to inform my superior officers, and to counter public rumours if this should become necessary.

For four days the *Graf Spee* burned

HMS *Exeter*

HMS *Ajax*

HMNZS *Achilles*

	Armament	Speed	Broadside Range
Graf Spee	six 11-inch guns/ eight 5.9-inch guns/ six 3.5-inch AA guns	26 knots	30,000 yards
HMS *Exeter*	six 8-inch guns/ four 4-inch AA guns	31.25 knots	27,000 yards
HMS *Ajax*	eight 6-inch guns/ eight 4-inch AA guns	31.25 knots	25,000 yards
HMNZS *Achilles*	eight 6-inch guns/ eight 4-inch AA guns	31.25 knots	25,000 yards

German troops land in Norway
– in the background the *Blücher*

The last battle of the *Glowworm* —
chased by the *Hipper* through her
smoke screen, she turned on her
stronger adversary, suicidally ramming
the German (left and below)

The *Altmark*'s prisoners after their release

The *Altmark* — aground after her action with the *Cossack*

HITLER STRIKES NORTH

Two things brought war to Scandinavia: Norway's geographical position, involving her coastline inevitably in the strategy of the North Sea, and Sweden's iron ore.

The British Isles, lying like a gigantic breakwater across the western exits of the North Sea, bar the German ports in the south-eastern angle of that sea from the Atlantic. A navy weaker than the British one might be effective against Britain's sensitive sea communications if its ships could reach the wide areas of the Atlantic—but from German ports they could do so only at the risk of being brought to battle. In the First World War individual German surface raiders had sometimes been highly successful, but with no refuge open to them they were in the end rounded up and sunk, while the High Seas Fleet lay inactive for four years, slowly disintegrating into mutiny. Submarine warfare was more effective, but submarines had had to face either the heavily guarded Straits of Dover or the long haul around the Shetlands.

In 1929 Vice-Admiral Wegener published his book, *Die See Strategie des Weltkrieges* ('The Sea Strategy of the World War'), describing this situation and claiming that Germany should have solved her dilemma by seizing bases in Norway. The blockade line between the Shetlands and Norway would then have been turned and, suggested Wegener, 'the fresh ocean winds would have blown away the deadly miasma of the hunger blockade'. Although Admiral Raeder, Commander-in-Chief of the new German navy, sharply dissented, the book commanded great interest among his rising officers.

In 1939 Germany imported about 10,000,000 tons of iron ore from Sweden; of this about 1,000,000 tons came from central Sweden and the remainder from Gällivare in the far north. From Gällivare ore railways run to the Swedish port of Luleå on the Baltic, and to Narvik on the western coast of northern Norway. Narvik is the better port and, being ice-free, the only one for winter shipments from January to April. In peacetime more ore went to Germany through Narvik than through Luleå, but with a little capital expenditure Luleå could have been made capable of shipping the full 9,000,000 tons during the eight months it was open. So long as Norway was neutral and the Allies respected her neutrality, German warships and blockade runners could use the many narrow channels between the islands to reach the Norwegian Sea to try for the Atlantic, and German ore ships might come and go from Narvik safe from any blockade.

Most of this was, of course, realised in Berlin, Oslo, and London in September 1939, but the British Home Fleet at Scapa Flow seemed to dominate the North Sea, and Raeder believed that on balance Norwegian neutrality offered greater advantages to Germany than would the seizure of Norwegian bases. The Norwegians believed that the Germans could not invade them in the face of British sea power, and that the British would not; while the British Chiefs-of-Staff—even as late as March 1940, as the Germans mounted their invasion—held that a German invasion of Norway's western seaboard was impracticable.

Churchill continues to press for action

To Churchill and other active and warlike minds, however, it was clear that the war could not be won by inaction. Britain was much inferior to Germany on land and in the air. Could not some way be found to exploit her great superiority at sea—some method more dramatic and immediate in effect than the slow and doubtful process of blockade? On September 12, 1939, Churchill signed an Admiralty minute ordering the preparation of specially protected ships to enter the Baltic, a project subsequently dropped; on September 19 he informed the Cabinet of the need to stop Norwegian shipments of Swedish iron ore; and on September 29 he proposed that the Leads should be mined, if the ore traffic, temporarily stopped at the outbreak of war, started again. The Cabinet refused to take action in breach of Norwegian neutrality, but Churchill continued to press for it.

In Berlin, as the Polish war drew to an end, Raeder and the naval staff discussed the conduct of the war against Britain and the problem of Scandinavia. When the army staff was consulted, it supported Raeder, saying that land forces to seize and hold Norway were not available. However, on October 10, 1939, Raeder passed to Hitler warnings he had received from Admiral Canaris, Head of the OKW (Armed Forces High Command) Intelligence Bureau, of British interest in Norway. That day Hitler issued his directive for an early offensive in the west; at the time, he was not much interested in Norway, so there the matter rested.

On November 30, 1939, Russia attacked Finland. To the admiration of the world, Finland was at first successful in holding off her powerful assailant, and moral pressure to assist her increased. Norway and Sweden had deep sympathy for Finland but, for fear of Germany, dared not implicate themselves in any Allied attempt to assist her. Yet the only practicable route for Britain or France to send forces to Finland was via the far north of Norway and Sweden—which in turn offered them the temptation to secure Narvik and Luleå and stop the ore traffic to Germany.

Hoping that general benevolence towards Finland might turn into active, or at least passive, co-operation by Norway and Sweden, and underestimating the strength and violence of the German threat to these countries, the Allies planned to move forces through Narvik and Luleå and to send others via Trondheim to guard central Sweden against German attack. In January 1940 this project was dropped in the face of firm refusal from Norway and Sweden to co-operate. In March it re-appeared in an even weaker and more ramshackle form, designed to test Norwegian reaction by a tentative landing in Narvik, to be followed, if accepted, by an advance to Luleå and by landing weak forces at Trondheim, Bergen, and Stavanger. On March 13, while the Cabinet still hesitated on the brink of decision, news arrived that the Finns had sued for peace. On Chamberlain's order, the forces were then dispersed in case Hitler heard of them and used them as excuse to invade Norway.

Although in Germany there was also a great deal of sympathy for the Finns, Hitler, having made his pact with Stalin, preferred to postpone his settling day. Raeder warned him that the Allies might use the pretext of aid to Finland to gain control of Swedish ore shipments; then, on December 11, Raeder was instrumental in bringing to Hitler Major Vidkun Quisling.

Quisling, soon to become the namesake of all Nazi-indoctrinated traitors, was a well-meaning but unbalanced individual who had for a short time been Minister of Defence in Norway. Later, giving way to his fear of Communist penetration and aggression, he had turned towards National Socialism and Germany but, until Raeder sent him to Hitler, had failed to excite interest in Berlin. Now he told Hitler that the British had suborned the Norwegian government, but that he controlled an indigenous National Socialist Party that could, with German aid, seize power. His charges and his claims were imaginary, and it is doubtful if even Hitler really believed them, but his appearance in Berlin turned Hitler's attention to Norway, and on December 14 the Führer ordered the OKW to make a preliminary study of the problem of invasion—a study which, as tension grew, developed into an operational plan.

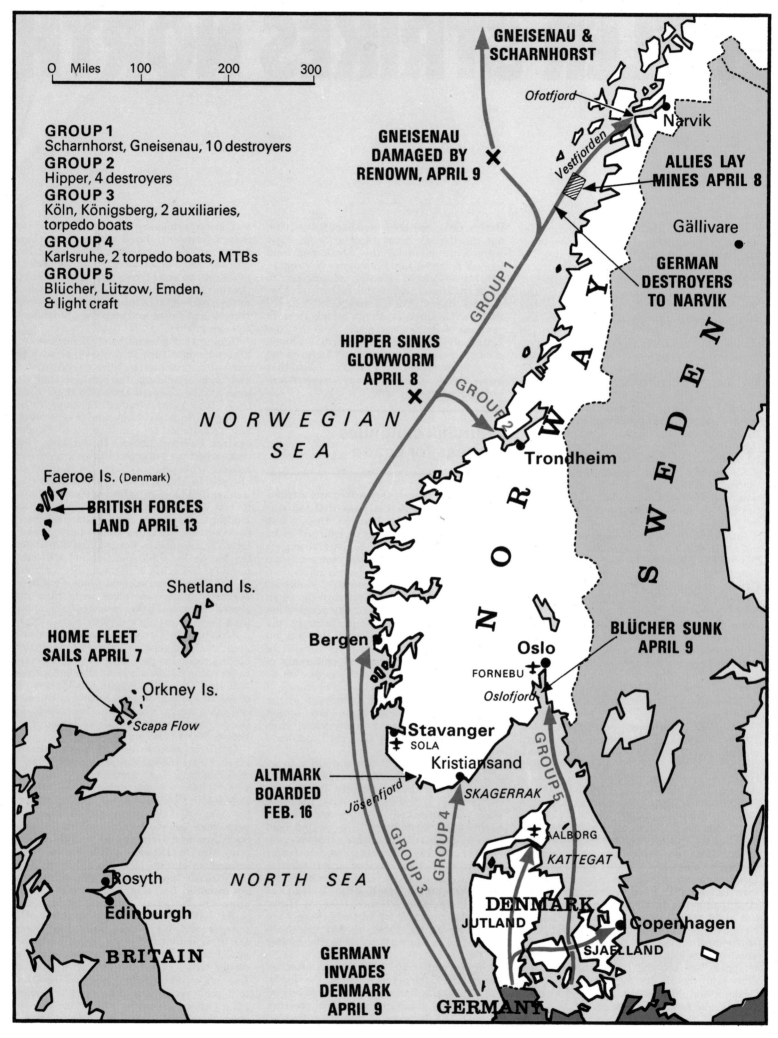

GNEISENAU &
SCHARNHORST

Ofotfjord

Narvik

GNEISENAU
DAMAGED BY
RENOWN, APRIL 9

Vestfjorden

ALLIES LAY
MINES APRIL 8

Gällivare

GERMAN
DESTROYERS
TO NARVIK

GROUP 1
Scharnhorst, Gneisenau, 10 destroyers
GROUP 2
Hipper, 4 destroyers
GROUP 3
Köln, Königsberg, 2 auxiliaries,
torpedo boats
GROUP 4
Karlsruhe, 2 torpedo boats, MTBs
GROUP 5
Blücher, Lützow, Emden,
& light craft

GROUP 1

HIPPER SINKS
GLOWWORM
APRIL 8

GROUP 2

N O R W E G I A N
S E A

Trondheim

Faeroe Is. (Denmark)

BRITISH FORCES
LAND APRIL 13

N
O
R
W
A
Y

S
W
E
D
E
N

Shetland Is.

HOME FLEET
SAILS APRIL 7

Orkney Is.

Scapa Flow

Bergen

Oslo

FORNEBU

Oslofjord

BLÜCHER SUNK
APRIL 9

Stavanger
SOLA

ALTMARK
BOARDED
FEB. 16

Kristiansand

Jösenfjord

SKAGERRAK

GROUP 3

GROUP 4

GROUP 5

AALBORG

KATTEGAT

Rosyth

N O R T H   S E A

Edinburgh

BRITAIN

GERMANY
INVADES
DENMARK
APRIL 9

DENMARK

JUTLAND

SJAELLAND

Copenhagen

GERMANY

Left: **The German assault on Denmark and Norway. Denmark was occupied and the Germans had captured all Norway's main cities, ports and airfields by the evening of April 9, ostensibly to protect them from Anglo-French invasion**

In February 1940 the *Altmark*, a supply ship for the pocket-battleship *Graf Spee,* which had been scuttled in the River Plate, was returning to Germany through the Leads with a large number of British seamen, prisoners taken from ships sunk by the *Graf Spee.* As a naval auxiliary she claimed freedom from search when challenged by the Norwegians off Trondheim and, later, off Bergen. Allowed after some delay to proceed unsearched, she was intercepted on February 16 near Jösenfjord on the southern coast of Norway by the British cruiser *Arethusa* and the 4th Destroyer Flotilla under Captain Vian. Two small Norwegian warships escorting her insisted that the British must not interfere with her while she was in neutral waters, and the *Altmark* took refuge in Jösenfjord.

Three hours later Vian, acting on direct orders from Churchill at the Admiralty,

The *Altmark's* prisoners are set free

approached the *Altmark* to board her, having first offered the Norwegians the option of escorting her back to Bergen for further searching. By then it was dark. As the destroyer *Cossack,* with Vian aboard, came alongside her much larger opponent, the *Altmark* attempted to ram her, but went aground in the fjord. British seamen leapt on board the *Altmark* and seized her bridge at pistol point. Others went for the prisoners and were fired upon by German guards, who then fled across the ice. Eight Germans were shot or drowned and 299 British prisoners transferred to the *Cossack.* The *Altmark* was left to extricate herself from the ice and continue her voyage to Germany.

The legality of this affair could be—and was—argued differently by the three nations concerned. In Britain it was hailed as a feat of arms, and the boarding party's shout to the prisoners—'The Navy's here!'—became famous. In Norway, government and citizens alike were angry and dismayed by what they regarded as a flagrant breach of neutrality, although other neutrals saw the incident as a mild turning of the tables on a power which had shown little respect for humanity or law. In Germany there was a great outcry in press and radio. Hitler was furious, and in the opinion of his associates, the incident ended his hesitation over whether to invade Norway.

On February 19 Hitler ordered planning for *Weserübung* ('Exercise Weser'), the code name for the invasion of Norway, to be speeded up. Two days later a corps commander, General von Falkenhorst, and his staff were put in charge of the operation. Germany's need for airfields close to Norway and to the sea crossings from Germany sealed Denmark's fate, for Falkenhorst modified the plan to include the occupation of Denmark and the forcible seizure of the Aalborg airfields at the northern end of the Jutland peninsula. On March 1 Hitler issued his

A Norwegian ski patrol

formal directive for the invasions, overriding heated objections from the army and air staffs, and insisting that all preparations should be pushed ahead energetically.

Norway, similar in area to the British Isles, had in 1940 a population of about 3,000,000. Land communications, although improving slowly, were limited, most of the main ones fanning out from Oslo. The older seaborne communications were circumferential, by the Leads and the fjords running inland from them, and much of the population centred about the coastal cities.

In *Weserübung Nord,* the occupation of Norway, the Germans planned to seize Oslo, the coastal cities, and Narvik in the far north by *coups de main,* and then thrust out from Oslo to link up by land, finally establishing air and land communication with Narvik. The *coups* at Narvik, Trondheim, Bergen, and Kristiansand would be made initially by troops carried in warships, that at Stavanger by parachute assault and air landing at the vital Sola airfield. Oslo, the linchpin of the plan, would be taken by assault from both sea and air. In the hope that the Norwegians would submit to the inevitable, German forces were ordered not to fire unless first fired upon but, if resisted, to carry through the attack with full force. In all, six divisions would be employed in Norway with strong air support. About 10,000 men from three divisions would make the initial *coups.*

In *Weserübung Süd,* the occupation of Denmark, two motorised brigade groups would force the Danish frontier and drive on north up the Jutland peninsula for the Aalborg airfields, which would be seized in advance by a parachute platoon and an air-landed battalion. Other groups would land on the Danish islands, secure the bridges connecting them to the mainland, and drive across Sjælland Island for Copenhagen. At Copenhagen itself, the old battleship *Schleswig-Holstein* would force the harbour entrance and land an infantry battalion, while the Luftwaffe overhead threatened the city and destroyed the aircraft on the military airfield. In all, two divisions and an independent brigade group would be used.

When the Finnish peace was announced, Hitler and Raeder hesitated, then decided to go ahead in spite of it. On April 2 Hitler gave the executive order, setting the invasions for the early hours of April 9. The next day German merchant ships carrying troops and supplies began to leave German

ports unescorted, and early on April 7 the first warships sailed with the troops for the initial landings.

Meanwhile, in London, Churchill had at last persuaded Chamberlain to permit mining the Leads. Warning notes were handed to Norway and Sweden on April 5, the same day that the mining forces sailed. The operations mounted in Britain were, however, very different in scale and intent from *Weserübung.* While the Home Fleet remained in Scapa Flow, eight destroyers were to lay a minefield in Vestfjorden on the approach to Ofotfjord and Narvik. A minelayer escorted by four destroyers was to lay another field in the Leads between Trondheim and Bergen, and two more destroyers were to mark a dummy field near Trondheim. Later, the battle-cruiser *Renown* with a screen of four destroyers was sent to reinforce the Vestfjorden force. Four battalions of the 146th and 148th Infantry Brigades embarked in cruisers at Rosyth, a battalion each of the 24th Guards and the 146th Infantry Brigades embarked in transports in the Clyde; the rest of the 24th Guards Brigade was held in readiness. All troops embarked were to remain in British ports until indications of German action against Norway seemed to justify their dispatch.

Raeder was well aware of the risks he ran in sending his ships to land troops in the west and north, but he counted on the unexpectedness of his attack to take both British and Norwegians off their guard. He insisted, however, that the warships return immediately they had landed the troops, so that they would not be caught when the British fleet appeared off the Norwegian coast.

On April 7 British aircraft found and later bombed, without effect, German warships steaming north in company. Group 1 of this force comprised the battle-cruisers *Gneisenau* and *Scharnhorst,* escorting ten destroyers carrying a regiment of the III Mountain Division to Narvik; Group 2 was the cruiser *Hipper* and four destroyers with two battalions of another regiment of the division, bound for Trondheim. Although the

The Home Fleet sails from Scapa Flow

sighting report reached the Admiralty and Sir Charles Forbes, Commander-in-Chief, Home Fleet, the more detailed and accurate report of the single squadron which found and bombed the German ships was not received until the returning aircraft landed. Then, on the evening of April 7, the Home Fleet sailed from Scapa Flow for the Norwegian coast to intercept the Germans.

On the night of the 7th a gale arose and swept the Norwegian Sea for the whole of the 8th and the early hours of the 9th. Meeting it during the night of the 7th, the German destroyers of Groups 1 and 2, driving on to keep station on the big ships, were damaged and thrown into disorder. On the morning of the 8th one of them sighted an unknown destroyer, which fired two salvoes at her before disappearing into the murk. A little later another German destroyer, the *Bernd von Arnim,* sighted the stranger, which turned to pursue her. It was the British destroyer *Glowworm*—one of the *Renown's* screen—which had parted company in search of a man washed overboard. With troops crowding her mess decks and intent on her main task of landing them, the *Bernd von Arnim* increased speed, trying to shake off her smaller but more seaworthy pursuer. She ran her fo'c's'le under, and had to reduce speed again, while other German destroyers, turning to come to her aid, incurred more damage and lost men overboard. Then the two destroyers, exchanging gunfire in the storm, met the *Hipper* coming back to aid the Germans. For a moment both mistook her for British: then she opened fire, hitting the *Glowworm* with her first salvo.

The *Glowworm* made smoke and appeared to turn away: the *Hipper* followed her into the smoke. But Lieutenant-Commander Roope, in command of the *Glowworm*, had decided to ram, and as the *Hipper* came through the smoke cloud she saw the *Glowworm* at close range on her starboard bow. Now the *Hipper* too decided to ram, fearing torpedoes, but she answered her helm slowly, and the *Glowworm's* bow struck her side, tearing away 120 feet of armour. Then the *Glowworm* passed astern, on fire and sinking. There was an explosion, and she disappeared. The *Hipper* stopped to pick up oil-covered survivors, but Roope, as he was being hauled on board, fell back into the sea exhausted, and was lost. Later, when the story became known in Britain, he was awarded a posthumous Victoria Cross.

Vice-Admiral Sir Max Horton, commanding British submarines, and noted for his intuition of German intentions, had on his own initiative sent all available submarines to lie off German ports and sea routes to Norway. They saw many cargo ships, northward-bound, pass before their periscopes, but because their orders were to torpedo only warships and ships recognisable as troop transports, they had to let them go. Then, on April 8, the Polish submarine *Orzel* torpedoed and sank the *Rio de Janeiro*. A hundred or so survivors picked up by Norwegian fishing boats turned out to be German soldiers who said that they were on their way to save Bergen from the British, thus confirming earlier reports received in London and Oslo of German troop movements and embarkations.

The Home Fleet was late in leaving Scapa Flow, and by now the German Groups 1 and 2 were well to its north. At 0400 hours on the 8th Forbes, with two battleships and several cruisers, was 120 miles south-west of the entrance to Trondheimfjord, with other British cruisers farther south 70 or 80 miles off the coast at Bergen. The *Renown* was about to join the destroyers laying mines in Vestfjorden, 500 miles to the north of Forbes, and the battle-cruiser *Repulse* and the cruiser *Penelope,* sent ahead by Forbes on the *Glowworm's* enemy reports, were between the two.

Of the Germans, Group 1 was now some 200 miles north-east of Forbes, and Group 2 about 100 miles away from him, waiting to enter Trondheimfjord. Farther south Group 3, the light cruisers *Köln* and *Königsberg* with two naval auxiliaries and some torpedo boats, was about to enter the fjords leading to Bergen. Group 4, the light cruiser *Karls-*

Torpedoed on their way to save Bergen from the British

ruhe with torpedo boats bound for Kristiansand, and Group 5, the cruisers *Blücher* and *Emden,* the pocket-battleship *Lützow,* and light craft for Oslo, were off the Danish coast steaming north.

A British flying boat found and reported the *Hipper,* but she happened to be on a westerly course, and Forbes, failing to realise that she was bound for Norway, turned north-west and missed her. Then, at 2000 hours on the 8th, after further reports had reached him, Forbes began to realise the Germans' intentions and turned south, ordering the *Repulse* and *Penelope* to continue north and join the *Renown.* Thus in the early hours of the 9th, as the German ships entered the fjords and approached the cities, the Home Fleet was steaming south about 60 miles off the coast, while in the far north the *Renown* and her destroyers battled with the full force of the gale.

The *Gneisenau* and *Scharnhorst,* having sent their destroyers into Vestfjorden for Narvik, broke north-west. Early that morning they met and were chased by the *Renown.* The *Gneisenau* suffered minor damage before the Germans could shake off their pursuer, but in withdrawing they failed to take the chance to sink the isolated, older, and more lightly armoured British battle-cruiser.

Early in the morning of April 9 the ten weather-beaten German destroyers of Group 1 steamed up Ofotfjord for Narvik. Off the port they sighted, between snow squalls, the 40-year-old Norwegian coastal defence vessel *Eidsvoll,* which fired a warning shot. Commodore Bonte, in the *Wilhelm Heidekamp,* with General Dietl commanding the III Mountain Division, lowered a boat and sent an officer to the Norwegian ship. He explained to Captain Willoch of the *Eidsvoll* that the Germans came as friends to protect the Norwegians from the British, and demanded that the *Eidsvoll's* guns and engines should be put out of action. Willoch refused, and as the German boat returned to the destroyer he began to train his guns on the Germans. A moment later the explosion of three German torpedoes ripped his ship apart. Eight of the crew of 182 were saved.

Three other German destroyers had already crossed the fjord to Bjerkvik on the north shore for their soldiers to seize the nearby Norwegian army depot. Now Bonte took three others into Narvik. As the soldiers jumped ashore on the quay, the *Eidsvoll's* sister ship, the *Norge,* opened fire. Although the harbour was full of merchant ships and icing hampered the Germans in directing their torpedo tubes, soon two torpedoes struck the *Norge* and she capsized and sank. Half her crew was saved from the icy waters of the fjord.

Dietl was soon ashore, demanding to see the garrison commander. Confused, and half expecting the strangers to be British, the

The Germans land at Narvik

Norwegian soldiers had not fired. Colonel Sundlo, the garrison commander, warned Dietl that he would resist and would open fire in half an hour. Dietl pleaded with him to avoid what he claimed would be utterly useless bloodshed, and the old colonel lost his nerve and surrendered the port. (Though Sundlo was later charged with having be-

trayed the port to the enemy, a post-war court-martial exonerated him.) Then Dietl and Bonte, their small force isolated in the northern snows and short of heavy weapons and ammunition, had to prepare to meet the superior Allied forces they knew would be approaching.

Off Trondheim the *Hipper* exchanged shots with the batteries guarding the narrow fjord entrance, as she led her destroyers past them at 25 knots and then landed her troops at the defenceless city. At Bergen the defence batteries were slow to open fire and suffered from misfires and jams, but they did manage to damage the *Königsberg* and the naval auxiliary *Bremse* before German soldiers landed and took the city. At Stavanger the air assault on Sola went through with hardly a hitch, and soon the city was in German hands. At Kristiansand the batteries were at first effective in holding off the German ships approaching in a sea fog, but they then mistook the returning Germans for French, and the Germans took the city.

So far as Denmark was concerned, the country had fallen with hardly a shot, and German aircraft began to operate from the Aalborg airfields. In Copenhagen the King ordered resistance to cease, and his country to pass quietly under the German yoke.

Ironically, it was the vital Oslo attack, reinforced by assault from both sea and air, that came nearest to failure. In the morning twilight of the 9th the new German heavy cruiser *Blücher,* carrying Vice-Admiral Kummetz and General Engelbrecht of the 169th Infantry Division with 1,000 of his soldiers, was sunk in the Drøbak Narrows, two-thirds of the way up Oslofjord, by the guns and torpedoes of Oscarsborg fortress, and the ships following her forced to turn back to the lower fjord. Meanwhile the air assault ran into fog, the formation carrying the paratroopers turned back, and the airlift was recalled to land at Aalborg. One troop-carrying formation, however, disregarded the recall and landed at Fornebu, the Oslo airport, and although some of its aircraft were destroyed by Norwegian fire, the remaining troops seized the airfield. The recalled aircraft then refuelled at Aalborg and came on to Oslo, while others were diverted there from Stavanger. By the afternoon the airlift was back on schedule, and the Germans marched into the city.

1939
October 10: Admiral Raeder reports to Hitler on the strategic importance of Norway.
December 14: Hitler orders the OKW to make a preliminary study of the invasion of Norway.

1940
February 16: HMS *Cossack* rescues British prisoners from the German supply-ship *Altmark.*
March 1: Hitler issues his formal directive for Weserübung – the invasion of Norway and occupation of Denmark.
March 28: Allied War Council decides to mine Norwegian waters and occupy bases in Norway.
April 7: Allied force sails for Norway.
April 9: Weserübung begins. German troops occupy Denmark and invade Norway.
April 15: British troops land in Norway near Narvik.
April 30: German forces advancing from Oslo link up with Trondheim force.
May 28: Narvik is captured by British and Norwegian forces.
June 3: Evacuation of Narvik begins.
June 10: Last Norwegian forces surrender.

OPERATION DYNAMO

Operation Dynamo—the attempt to evacuate the Allied troops besieged at Dunkirk (below)—could have been one of the worst disasters in military history. Trapped within a tiny perimeter and exhausted by the Blitzkrieg, the BEF appeared to be at the mercy of the Luftwaffe which, Göring claimed, could annihilate them without help from the army. But Göring had not reckoned on the nullifying effect of the sand on his bombs, or on the brilliant direction of Admiral Ramsay—or on the gallant and unstinting efforts of the civilians who helped to rescue over 330,000 troops in nine days

△ Queues of British and French troops waiting to be rescued   ▽ Part of the varied armada that rescued the trapped BEF from Dunkirk.

'Operation Dynamo' was based on the assumption that three ports would be available but the fall of Boulogne, followed on 26th May by the collapse of British resistance in Calais left only Dunkirk. Yet the defence of Calais termed by Guderian 'heroic, worthy of the highest praise' gave Lord Gort time in which to elaborate his plans for the evacuation. The Allies' predicament grew steadily worse. On 25th May the Belgians expended their last reserves and their front broke. On the following day Hitler rescinded the halt order in view of Bock's slow advance in Belgium and the movement of transports off the coast, authorizing the resumption of Rundstedt's advance by 'armoured groups and infantry divisions in the direction of Dunkirk'. However, for technical reasons sixteen hours were to pass before the armoured units were ready to move forward and assail the town. By 28th May the Allies had organized a tighter perimeter defence around Dunkirk stretching from Nieuport along the canals through Fumes and Bergues to Gravelines. Repeatedly assaulted by German tanks and without the support of the Belgian army which had capitulated the same day, the perimeter shrank. South-west of Lille, however, the Germans encountered spirited resistance from the French 1st Army which detained seven of their divisions from 29th May to 1st June thus preventing their participation in the assault on the Dunkirk pocket. The exhausted and bewildered Allies often fragmented into separate battalions or separate companies retreated steadily along congested roads into the perimeter and by midnight on the 29th the greater part of the BEF and nearly half of the French 1st Army lay behind the canal line, by which time the naval measures for evacuation had begun to demonstrate their effectiveness.

At 1857 on 26th May the Admiralty launched Operation Dynamo. Besides an inspiring example of gallantry and self-sacrifice it was to display what Hitler had always held to be one of Great Britain's greatest strengths — the genius for improvisation.

The first day of the evacuation, 27th May, proved disappointing. Only 7,669 troops were brought out by a motley assortment of destroyers, passenger ferry steamers, paddle steamers, self-propelled barges, and Dutch *schuits* which Vice-Admiral Ramsay had collected. But after the loss of Boulogne and Calais only Dunkirk with its adjacent beaches remained in Allied hands. For the intrepid rescuers, entering the harbour, when not impossible, was a hazardous task. Not only had they to contend with fire from shore batteries and ferocious air attack but they had to negotiate the many wrecks that lay between them and the blazing town.

It became clear that the hungry, exhausted troops would have to be embarked from the sandy beaches on either side of the town, but as yet Ramsay had few small craft capable of embarking men in shallow water. He signalled urgently for more. The next day, 28th May, utilizing the beaches together with the surviving but precarious East Mole of the harbour 17,804 men were embarked for Britain. The losses in craft on that day, however, were very heavy. Ships that left the congested mole unscathed were frequently damaged or sunk by bombing as they steamed down the narrow offshore channel unable to manoeuvre adequately for wrecks, debris, and bobbing corpses.

Despite the fact that 47,310 men were snatched from Dunkirk and its neighbouring beaches the following day, as soon as the wind had blown aside the pall of smoke obscuring the harbour and roadstead, the Luftwaffe wreaked fearful havoc with a concentrated bombardment of the mole, sinking three destroyers and twenty-one other vessels.

On 30th May smoother seas, smoke, and low cloud ceiling enabled the rescuers to remove 13,823 men to safety. Although a number of small craft had arrived off Dunkirk on 29th May they were only the vanguard of a volunteer armada of some 400 yachts, lifeboats, dockyard launches, river tugs, cockle boats, pleasure craft, French and Belgian fishing boats, oyster dredgers, and Thames barges which, with small craft called into service by the Royal Navy, ferried 100,000 men from the beaches to the deeper draught vessels from the following day. Moved by the desperate plight of the Allies, the seafaring population of south and south-eastern England had set out in a spontaneous movement for the beaches of Dunkirk where in innumerable acts of heroism they fulfilled a crucial role in the evacuation.

On 31st May despite intense bombing and shelling, 68,014 troops were removed to safety but on the following day a furious artillery bombardment and strafing of the whole length of the beaches together with resolute dive-bombing of shipping out at sea and in the harbour effectively halted daylight operations.

The climax of the evacuation had taken place on 31st May and 1st June when over 132,000 men were landed in England. At dawn on 2nd June only 4,000 men of the BEF remained in the perimeter, shielded by 100,000 French troops. On the nights of 2nd and 3rd June they were evacuated along with 60,000 of the Frenchmen. Dunkirk was still defended stubbornly by the remainder who resisted until the morning of 4th June. When the town fell 40,000 French troops who had fought tenaciously to cover the evacuation of their Allied comrades marched into captivity.

'Let us remember,' wrote Churchill, 'that but for the endurance of the Dunkirk rearguard the

The diagram shows the British and French embarkation points off Dunkirk for the troops driven into the Dunkirk pocket by the German advance. The photo shows part of the Armada which saved the BEF

Some survivors from the *Bourrasque* managed to clamber aboard a nearby ship

Paul Popper

re-creation of an army in Britain for home defence and final victory would have been gravely prejudiced.'

The British with French and Belgian assistance had evacuated 338,226 troops, of whom 139,097 were French, from a small battered port and exposed beaches right under the noses of the Germans. They had extracted every possible advantage from the valuable respite accorded them when the armour was halted, consolidating defensive positions in the west, east, and on the Channel front. Moreover they had fought tenaciously, upholding traditions that had so impressed the Germans in the First World War.

The primary German error was to regard the Dunkirk pocket as a subordinate front. In fact its strategic importance was not recognized until too late largely because it was not clear until almost the last moment how many Allied troops were actually in the pocket.

Moreover, for the nine days of Operation Dynamo, the Luftwaffe, due to adverse weather conditions only succeeded in seriously interfering with it for two-and-a-half days—on 27th May, the afternoon of 29th May, and on 1st June. The Luftwaffe's mission, readily shouldered by the vain, ambitious Göring proved too much for it. If Rundstedt had made a mistake, Göring fatally miscalculated. His aircraft had failed to prevent the Allied evacuation because the necessary conditions for success—good weather, advanced airfields, training in pin-point bombing—were all lacking. Bombers and dive-bombers for the first time suffered heavy losses at the hands of British Spitfires and Hurricanes now operating from their relatively near home bases.

For Germany's military leadership Dunkirk was the first great turning point in the Second World War, for it was during the campaign that Hitler first forced OKH to accept his own military views, by short-circuiting it at a critical juncture of the fighting and transferring a decision of far-reaching importance to a subordinate command whose views happened to coincide with his own. OKH, the actual military instrument of leadership, was in future to be undermined, overruled, and with terrible consequences for the German people, finally abolished altogether.

The grim realities

At Dunkirk instead of winning a battle of annihilation the German army had to content itself with an ordinary victory. Great Britain on the other hand could console itself with the knowledge that almost its entire expeditionary force had been saved. 'In the midst of our defeat,' Churchill later wrote, 'glory came to the Island people, united and unconquerable . . . there was a white glow, overpowering, sublime, which ran through our Island from end to end . . . and the tale of the Dunkirk beaches will shine in whatever records are preserved of our affairs.'

If the British people felt they had won a great victory the grim realities belied their euphoria. The BEF, no longer in any condition to defend the country had suffered 68,111 killed, wounded, and taken prisoner. It had been compelled to abandon 2,472 guns, 90,000 rifles, 63,879 vehicles, 20,548 motorcycles and well over 500,000 tons of stores and ammunition. Of the 243 ships sunk at Dunkirk, out of 860 engaged, six were British destroyers. A further nineteen British destroyers were damaged. In addition the RAF had lost 474 aircraft.

Dunkirk had been a catastrophe alleviated, not by a miracle, but by German miscalculation and Allied tenacity and improvisation. Yet the elation of victory pervaded Britain. A supreme effort had cheated Hitler of his prey and a little self-congratulation seemed appropriate. The British had been the first to confound the German military juggernaut and after Dunkirk they resolved with a wholehearted determination to defeat it.

THE MEDITERRANEAN
SEPTEMBER 1940–MARCH 1941

Britain's bases in the Middle East depended on the free passage of her Mediterranean convoys, so the Axis resolved to cut off the convoy route from Gibraltar to Alexandria. But timely strikes by the Royal Navy and the Fleet Air Arm at Taranto and Genoa shattered all Italian hopes of dominating the Mediterranean—and Mussolini was forced to admit that his proud battle fleet had shunned the decisive fleet action demanded by Axis strategy

The air arm of Force H: *Ark Royal* and her Swordfish

After the fall of France, Britain held the two ends of the Mediterranean with strong forces based at Gibraltar and Alexandria. Italy held the centre, her forces based at Messina and Palermo in Sicily, at Taranto and Naples in southern Italy, and at Benghazi and Tripoli on the North Africa coast. In heavy ships the British fleets had a small advantage; they numbered seven battleships and two aircraft-carriers. The Italians had six battleships, and depended entirely on land-based air forces; but they could deploy 21 cruisers against Britain's eight, 50 destroyers, and as many torpedo-boats, against 37 British destroyers, and over 100 submarines against eight British ones. The Italians also had some 2,000 aircraft in the area, against about 200 British. Finally, any superiority that the British Mediterranean fleets held at any particular time was nullified by the position held by the Italians in the central Mediterranean.

The Sicilian Strait, dividing Europe from Africa and the eastern from the western Mediterranean, is 90 miles wide; but the part of it between Sicily and the island of Pantelleria is shallow and can be made dangerous with mines, and only 30 miles separate Pantelleria from Cape Bon in Tunisia. This narrow channel is easy to patrol with land-based planes, submarines, and destroyers; but this was the only channel of communications between the British eastern and western Mediterranean fleets. The British Admiralty therefore had the choice of concentrating the fleet permanently in the eastern or western Mediterranean, or of dividing it permanently between the two. If it were concentrated in the eastern Mediterranean, then Gibraltar would be abandoned, and the Italian fleet given access to the Atlantic. If it were concentrated in the western Mediterranean, the Suez Canal, the Middle East, and eventually the Red Sea and safe communication with India and Australia would be sacrificed. The division between the east and the west was therefore clearly necessary, and the fact that the British fleet could not be concentrated at will for any particular operation (whereas the Italian fleet could concentrate at will upon either British squadron) was a handicap that had to be accepted.

At this time the eastern squadron, directly commanded by the C-in-C Admiral Sir Andrew Cunningham, was known as the Mediterranean Fleet. It consisted of the battleships *Warspite, Malaya,* and *Ramillies,* the aircraft-carrier *Eagle,* the heavy cruiser *Kent,* the light cruisers *Orion, Sydney, Gloucester, Liverpool,* and *Neptune,* and 20 destroyers.

No flag officer had a higher reputation in the service than Admiral Cunningham. At this time 56 years old, he had in his early days served ashore with the Naval Brigade in the Boer War, and most of his sea service had been aboard destroyers. He had commanded the destroyer *Scorpion* at the Dardanelles, and throughout most of the First World War he had continued in the Mediterranean; in 1918 he was transferred to home waters, where his ship HMS *Termagant* formed part of the Dover Patrol.

Between the wars he had been a captain (D) commanding a destroyer flotilla; and then successively captain of the battleship *Rodney*; Rear-Admiral (D) commanding the destroyers in the Mediterranean; and second-in-command of the Mediterranean Fleet, flying his flag in the *Hood.* He had been appointed to command the Mediter-

ranean Station in June 1939.

The western squadron at Gibraltar, designated 'Force H', received its orders direct from the Admiralty, but as it operated mainly within the Mediterranean a large part of its work came under Admiral Cunningham's general control. The Flag Officer Commanding was Vice-Admiral Sir James Somerville, who had been Cunningham's class-mate as a naval cadet, but whose career had been spent more in big ships. He had, however, succeeded Cunningham as Rear-Admiral (D) in the Mediterranean. He had once been retired from the active list as a suspect case of tuberculosis, but this did not prevent him from fighting a very active war; in fact he came to the Mediterranean fresh from earning great distinction while organising the evacuation from Dunkirk. His command consisted of the battle-cruiser *Renown,* the battleship *Resolution,* the aircraft-carrier *Ark Royal,* the cruisers *Sheffield* and *Enterprise,* and a number of destroyers that varied from time to time, but was sometimes as high as 17.

Besides the responsibilities of defending and supplying the British garrisons in Egypt, Palestine, Cyprus, and Malta, the British Mediterranean Fleet at the end of 1940 had the potential task of maintaining communications with Greece and Turkey in the event of their being attacked by either of the Axis powers. The immediate task consisted of proving to both Greece and Turkey the readiness of Britain to go to their help if they were attacked.

Thus the problems confronting Admiral Cunningham were complex. They were further complicated by the fact that the Egyptian-Libyan frontier and the frontiers of Italian East Africa were the only lines at this time along which the British and Axis ground forces stood face to face. In both areas the Italians held a large numerical superiority; in both they were on the flank of British communications with the east; and in Libya, whereas British supplies and reinforcements had long distances to travel, the Italians could be reinforced across the 90 miles of the Sicilian Channel.

Malta—the key
Here, in fact, lay the importance of the British base at Malta. Already large Italian forces lay almost within striking distance of the Suez Canal, faced by small and ill-organised, though well-trained, British units. The British Middle East Command was busy building these units into an effective striking force, but in June 1940 the question was whether the task could be completed in time to halt an Italian offensive. What *was* certain was that even if an offensive were halted, the quicker communications and nearer bases of the Italians would make it likely that a second or third thrust might succeed.

Only in the sealanes between Italy and Africa could these communications be attacked, and only at Malta could the attacking forces be based. If Malta fell, or even were neutralised, all would fall.

Appropriately, then, a fleet operation planned for the end of August 1940 had a double purpose: to reinforce the Mediterranean Fleet with the modernised battleship *Valiant,* the large aircraft-carrier *Illustrious,* and the anti-aircraft (AA) cruisers *Coventry* and *Calcutta*; and to reinforce and supply Malta. A third purpose—urged by the Prime Minister—to pass merchant ships carrying

tanks right through the Mediterranean to Egypt, was opposed by the Admiralty and the naval commanders. It was eventually dropped owing to lack of support from General Wavell, the C-in-C in the Middle East, on whose support Churchill had been counting. Wavell preferred to have his tanks 12 weeks late via the Cape route than to risk not getting them at all.

Valiant, Illustrious, and the AA cruisers left Gibraltar on August 30, with Force H in support. Several ships in the force had radar and could direct attacks, by fighters, from the two aircraft-carriers, to intercept shadowing enemy aircraft; there were no successful Italian air attacks on the fleet, but several shadowing planes were claimed shot down.

The operation was timed to allow the reinforcements to pass through the Sicilian Channel during the night of September 1/2. Before dusk on September 1 the whole force altered course towards Naples, and after dusk Force H turned back towards Gibraltar; *Valiant, Illustrious,* and the AA cruisers altered course towards the Sicilian Channel, and next morning made their rendezvous with the Mediterranean Fleet south of Malta.

This fleet, comprising the battleships *Warspite* and *Malaya,* the aircraft-carrier *Eagle,* two cruisers, and nine destroyers, had left Alexandria two days before. They were covering a convoy of two merchant ships and a tanker, and a detached squadron of three cruisers and nine destroyers had joined up a little later.

Late the same day the Italian fleet was reported at sea and heading for the convoy, but to the disappointment of the British they turned back, and next morning were reported near Taranto. The strengths on this occasion had been nearly equal: both had two battleships; the Italians were stronger in cruisers and weaker in destroyers, and, of course, had no aircraft-carriers. The British convoy and its escort were attacked by enemy aircraft, and one merchant ship was damaged, but all reached Malta on September 2. The merchant convoy entered Malta harbour, and the Mediterranean Fleet met the reinforcements from the west at the appointed rendezvous south of Malta.

On the return journey to Alexandria the Mediterranean Fleet passed north of Crete, taking the opportunity of attacking targets in the Italian Dodecanese Islands with bombs and gunfire. Four carrier-based Swordfish torpedo-bombers were shot down by Italian fighters in a raid on Rhodes; of a flotilla of Italian motor torpedo-boats (MTBs), one was sunk by the gunfire of the British ships as a counterattack was beaten off; and a convoy of British merchant ships trading with Greece and Turkey, which had collected from ports in the Aegean, was escorted to Alexandria.

The most noticeable thing about this series of operations was its intricacy, caused by the shortage of destroyers making it necessary to dove-tail together several different purposes.

On September 13, after four days' air and artillery preparation, the Italian advance into Egypt at last began. For some time Mussolini had been pressing Marshal Graziani, the new Italian commander in Libya, to undertake the advance; but as often happens, the soldier found his task far harder than his political master expected. In four days Graziani occupied the British advanced positions at Sollum and Sidi

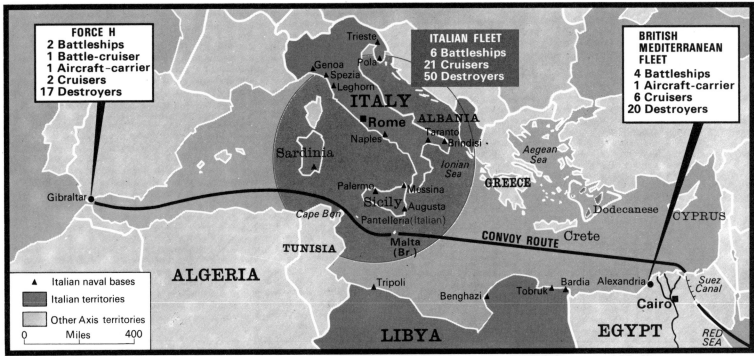

△ June 1940: the Italian battle fleet was slightly outnumbered, but Italian bases dominated the central Mediterranean

FORCE H
2 Battleships
1 Battle-cruiser
1 Aircraft-carrier
2 Cruisers
17 Destroyers

ITALIAN FLEET
6 Battleships
21 Cruisers
50 Destroyers

BRITISH MEDITERRANEAN FLEET
4 Battleships
1 Aircraft-carrier
6 Cruisers
20 Destroyers

▲ Italian naval bases
■ Italian territories
□ Other Axis territories

Admiral Cunningham, the British C-in-C	Admiral Iachino, the Italian C-in-C	Raid on Taranto, November 11, 1940

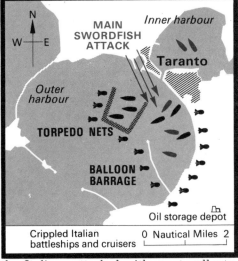

Crippled Italian battleships and cruisers

Barrani—an advance of 60 miles on a narrow front close to the coast—and as the British forces opposing him were far too weak to think of profiting by the narrowness of this penetration, the gain was held. So far, so good; but despite the time taken in the preparation for this quite rapid advance, Graziani found himself unable to continue without a pause for further reorganisation of his communications.

This limited success, however, was not without its effect on the general position in the Mediterranean. Italian fighters could now operate over Marsa Matrûh, whereas the nearest British fighter bases were not even within range of Sidi Barrani.

Further army and air force reinforcements for the Malta garrison were ready at Alexandria by September 25, but they could not be sailed for a few days; the British and Free French attempt on Dakar had begun on September 23, and for the moment there was even a chance of war between Britain and France. Clearly this was not the time to leave French naval units alone in Alexandria harbour. However, by September 29 the Dakar attack had been called off, so Admiral Cunningham then took his fleet out of harbour, leaving two battleships to keep a wary but friendly eye on the French. The rest of the fleet, battleships *Warspite* and

Valiant and aircraft-carrier *Illustrious*, the cruiser squadron, and 11 destroyers, with 1,200 soldiers and some air force reinforcements on board, proceeded towards Malta.

Between Crete and Malta, Cunningham received reports of an Italian fleet of four or five battleships, 11 cruisers, and 25 destroyers, about 100 miles to the north-west. It was steaming directly away from the British force, so Cunningham decided—'after some thought', as he wrote—that it would be safe to press on to Malta and land his troops. The Italians showed no signs of aggressiveness, and the British had no thought of trying to bring so greatly superior a fleet to battle, so both fleets reached port, in Taranto and Malta, next day, and the British troops were disembarked. The British fleet returned immediately to Alexandria.

About a week later, on October 8, Cunningham was out of Alexandria again, this time to convoy four supply ships to Malta—he had his full battleship strength this time. Owing to bad visibility and heavy weather the Italian fleet stayed in port; but on the way home the light cruiser *Ajax* encountered a flotilla of torpedo-boats (the Italians rated destroyers of under 1,000 tons as torpedo-boats) and engaged them at ranges of 4,000 yards and less. In sharp contrast to the conduct of the Italian fleet of a few days before,

the Italians attacked with great gallantry in the moonlight; two of the torpedo-boats were destroyed, and a destroyer which supported them, the flotilla-leader *Artigliere*, was damaged.

Another destroyer took *Artigliere* in tow, and together they tried to make harbour on the south Italian coast; but next morning a Sunderland flying-boat from Malta spotted them, and called up the heavy cruiser *York*. When *York* came in sight the would-be rescuer had to drop the tow and retire. *Artigliere* surrendered, and after her crew had gone overboard *York* sank her with gunfire. The Italians' bravery on this occasion was not entirely unrewarded. They had pressed home their attack on *Ajax* to a point where they could inflict damage and casualties on her with their guns.

Early in November one further infantry battalion could be spared from the beleaguered fortress of Britain for the defence of the equally hard-pressed island of Malta. As it was considered too dangerous to send troopships through the western Mediterranean, this battalion and some artillery reinforcements for the island—in all over 2,000 men—were embarked on the battleship *Barham*, the cruisers *Berwick* and *Glasgow*, and six destroyers. These ships, except for three of the destroyers, were

further reinforcements for Cunningham's fleet. On November 10 the warships that were carrying troops ran into Malta to disembark them, and escorted out again a convoy of empty supply ships.

Meanwhile, the Mediterranean Fleet had also been escorting a supply convoy to Malta, and this arrived on the same day. The fleet and the reinforcements made their rendezvous east of Malta at dawn on November 11; from there the supply ships started for Alexandria with a destroyer escort, and the main force moved north-east to carry out a plan dear to the Admiral's heart. Even before the war a certain Captain Lyster of the Fleet Air Arm had been studying the possibility of an air attack on the Italian fleet in harbour at Taranto. Lyster was now Cunningham's Rear-Admiral (aircraft-carriers), and for the last three months his studies had been carried on with more and more confidence.

Now all was ready. Air reconnaissance planes from Malta had taken photographs from which the net, boom, and balloon defences of Taranto could be charted in detail. Moreover, the latest air reconnaissance photos, which reached Cunningham and Lyster by air on the afternoon of November 11, showed that five of the six Italian battleships then in commission were berthed in the harbour, and at noon on the same day the standing British patrol over Taranto reported the sixth entering. 'All the pheasants had gone home to roost,' wrote Cunningham with satisfaction.

Cunningham had a liking for symbolic dates. The attack had originally been planned for October 21 – Trafalgar Day – and when it had had to be postponed, owing to a fire in *Illustrious,* he ordered that it should be made on Armistice Day – a day that was suitable in other ways. It fitted in with other operations, and there was a suitable moon.

The fleet took station off the Ionian Isles, and after dusk *Illustrious,* with her destroyer screen, parted company and made for her flying-off position, about 170 miles south-east of the target. By 2100 hours the first wave of 12 Swordfish was in formation and on course for Taranto, led by Lieutenant-Commander K. Williamson. Six Swordfish carried torpedoes. The other six carried bombs, and two of these carried parachute flares as well.

The first flight arrived over their target just before 2300 hours. The two planes with the flares began their vital task of circling the south and east sides of the Grand Harbour, dropping their flares at regular intervals. This done, they bombed the oil storage depot, which was on the same side of the harbour, to occupy the attention of the searchlight batteries. The other four bombers made diversionary attacks on cruisers and merchant shipping in the inner harbour, while the torpedo-planes made a circuit to the west in order to approach the harbour from the west and north.

The leading sub-flight of three planes flew in directly from the west, diving down through the barrage to a height of 30 feet before releasing their torpedoes. Commander Williamson's own plane, the first, crashed in the harbour, but not before it had released its torpedo, which hit the southernmost battleship, the *Conte di Cavour,* on her port side forward. Another plane's torpedo hit the brand-new battleship *Littorio* on her port side. The second sub-flight flew on a parallel course further to the north, and rounded the northern end of the balloon

◁ **Italian cruiser in line ahead**

barrage. One of its torpedoes hit the *Littorio* for the second time, on her starboard side, but the other torpedoes missed or failed to explode. The Swordfish of the first wave then started on their return flight.

At midnight the second wave, led by Lieutenant-Commander J. W. Hale, arrived over the target. It consisted of nine planes—five with torpedoes and four with bombs—of which two dropped flares. Precisely the same tactics were followed, with almost precisely the same degree of success; one more torpedo-hit was scored on the *Littorio* and one on the *Caio Duilio,* and this second wave, like the first, lost one plane shot down. By 0300 hours on November 12 all the aircraft but the two shot down were safely back aboard *Illustrious,* and at dawn the fleet was once more concentrated.

Considering that only five torpedoes had found their marks—considering, indeed, that the attack was mounted by a squadron that carried only 11 torpedoes—the damage suffered by the Italian fleet in this attack was enormous. Of the three battleships that had been hit, one, the *Conte di Cavour,* which Lieutenant-Commander Williamson had hit as he was crashing, was never brought back into service, and the two others were out of action for a vital six months. The attack on Taranto, therefore, had effects far out of proportion to the forces employed. The British battleships *Ramillies* and *Malaya* were no longer needed in the Mediterranean, and could be transferred to equally vital duties in the Atlantic, where the German navy was beginning to recover from its losses at Narvik.

The Italian battle fleet was forced to withdraw from Taranto for some time, taking refuge in ports on the west coast of Italy—Naples, La Spezia and Genoa—where it felt itself safer, but where it was farther from its vital areas of operation.

In Britain, this first unquestionable victory since the fall of France sent a wave of triumph and optimism through the country, like the one that had saluted the victory of the River Plate a year before. In Italy the effect of the news, muffled by censorship, was harder to discern; but the effect on the minds of the Italian naval commanders was traceable in later events. After Taranto, an Italian admiral encountering a force that included an aircraft-carrier felt himself—not without reason—to be fighting at a disadvantage, even if he was superior in all other types of ship.

All these advantages were gained for the loss of two aircraft and one life, for of the four airmen lost, three were picked up by the Italians and taken prisoner.

However, not all the air operations over the Mediterranean at this time proved so successful for the British. A week later an attempt was made to reinforce Malta with planes flown off the aircraft-carrier *Argus,* and this unhappily turned out a costly failure: of 12 Hurricanes and their two Skua guides, only four Hurricanes and one Skua arrived. The reasons for this misfortune are unknown. The range was long, especially for rather inexperienced pilots—it took a lot of knowledge to get the best possible range out of a Hurricane—but this does not account for the Skua. Perhaps the Skua pilot got lost, crashed, or was even shot down. The Hurricanes depending on him would then have had little chance of finding their airfield.

Another composite naval operation had been planned for the end of November. The battleship *Ramillies* and the cruisers *Newcastle* and the newly-arrived *Berwick* were to be detached from the British Mediterranean fleet and to join the forces in the north Atlantic. They could be spared from the Mediterranean because of the temporary weakness of the Italian fleet after Taranto. Naturally, the opportunity was taken to pass reinforcements to Malta and Egypt, supplies to Malta from both east and west, and empty merchant ships out of Malta.

Force H left Gibraltar on November 25, and all went well until the heavy ships from the east, having delivered their convoy at Malta and passed through the Sicilian Channel, made their rendezvous with Force H south of Sardinia. At almost the same moment, contact was made with an Italian fleet. The forces present were, on the Italian side, two battleships—*Vittorio Veneto* and *Giulio Cesare*—seven 8-inch-gun cruisers, and 16 destroyers; on the British side one battleship (*Ramillies*), one battle-cruiser (*Renown*), one 8-inch and five 6-inch cruisers (of which one was detached to guard the convoy), ten destroyers, and the aircraft-carrier *Ark Royal*.

When the Italian Admiral Campioni first steamed down to the attack he believed that he had only to deal with one battleship, two light cruisers, and four destroyers from Force H—and he meant to take full advantage of his superiority. But just as the fleets came in sight of each other, and fire was opened between the cruisers—*Renown* and *Ramillies* joining in at long range—he learned not only of the reinforcements from the east, but also of the unexpected presence of *Ark Royal*. With the memory of Taranto fresh in his mind—and with the knowledge that he had two of the only three serviceable Italian battleships under his command, and that these were now exposed to the attack of the carrier-based aircraft—Campioni order-

△ **Italian heavy cruiser in action off Cape Spartivento**

Alfredo Zennaro

139

Sunk at Taranto: the battleship *Littorio*

Taranto harbour after the attack

Alfredo Zennaro

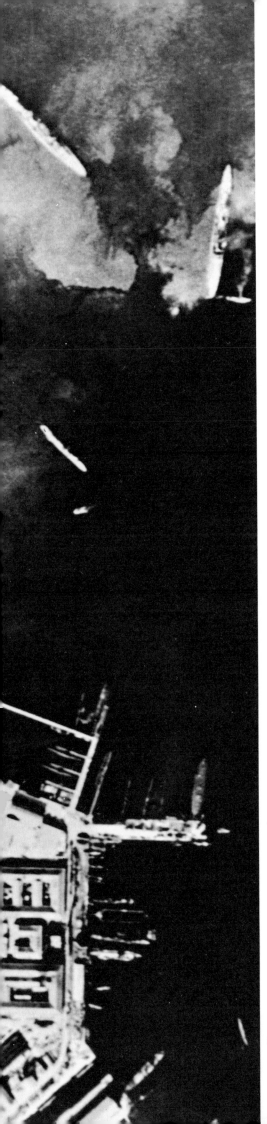

ed his cruisers to break off the action. They retired at high speed, after inflicting damage on one British cruiser.

Two air attacks were made on the Italian fleet, but no hits were scored. The British cruisers pursued the Italians until they found themselves within range of their battleships, when they retired in the hope of drawing them in turn within range of the British battleships; but finding they were not pursued they again steered towards the Italian fleet. This feint had not stopped its withdrawal, and in a few minutes it was out of range.

This ended the action, except for the second of the British air attacks mentioned above, and three attacks made by the Italian land-based bombers. As Admiral Somerville, the British commander, could see little hope of bringing the Italian fleet to battle within gun range before they reached their Sardinian bases, he ordered his force to proceed eastward, and at dusk his merchant ships, two cruisers carrying troops, and a destroyer escort, were detached to rendezvous with the British Mediterranean fleet, and later to enter Malta harbour.

Even before they had received Somerville's report on the action, the British Admiralty ordered an enquiry into the circumstances in which he had broken off the action. The court of enquiry found that Somerville had been entirely in the right; but the Admiralty decided that he had been 'over-influenced by anxiety for the safety of his convoy'. This was plainly an attempt to convince the Prime Minister that his policy of passing supplies through the western Mediterranean was an unwise one, since it was hampering the offensive power of the British fleets.

On December 21 the battleship *Malaya* was transferred from the Mediterranean Fleet to Force H, since one of the results of Taranto was the transfer of Italian battleships to west coast Italian ports. At the same time empty merchant ships were escorted out of Malta to the west. In the course of this operation the British destroyer *Hyperion* was sunk by a mine.

The great accomplishment at the end of 1940 on the British side was the launching, on December 9, of the first offensive in the Western Desert. The navy played a supporting role in this drama. Light coastal forces bombarded Italian positions near the coast, and supplies, especially water and petrol, were carried to Sollum, the port on the Italian side of the frontier.

On the whole the British had cause to be well satisfied with the position in the Mediterranean at New Year. On land, on sea, and in the air the position was far better than after the fall of France six months earlier. In the desert operations the Italians had lost one-fifth of their air forces, and they had not the industrial capacity to replace losses as Britain could.

A convoy of four merchant ships, one for Malta and three for Greece, sailed from Gibraltar on January 6. As usual Force H escorted them past Sardinia, and the narrows were passed at night, with the extra protection of the cruiser *Bonaventure*, which was equipped with radar, and coming out to join the Mediterranean Fleet. The fleet met them west of Malta; up to this point all had gone well, and one large Italian torpedo-boat had been sunk.

This happy situation did not last long. South-east of Pantelleria the destroyer *Gallant* hit a mine and had to be towed along miles behind the fleet. So near were they to

enemy sea and air bases that it was out of the question for the whole fleet to conform to the slow pace of a tow, yet some risk had to be taken to try to save *Gallant*. As some empty merchant ships were waiting to be escorted out of Malta, Admiral Cunningham ordered the ships designated as their escort—three cruisers, including *Bonaventure*—to escort *Gallant* there. The two forces were already some miles apart when the Luftwaffe, long expected to intervene in the Mediterranean, chose the moment to launch their first attack. They were lucky. A strong force of German dive-bombers unexpectedly came 'out of the sun', on to the main body of Cunningham's fleet, now deprived of the invaluable protection of *Bonaventure's* radar.

Illustrious's fighters had been drawn down almost to sea-level by the first wave low-level attack by Italian torpedo-planes, so when they arrived overhead the Stukas could concentrate the main weight of their attack upon the aircraft-carrier—the most important ship, along with the *Ark Royal,* in the Mediterranean—and she was hit by six 1,000-pound bombs, the German pilots pressing home their attack with great bravery and skill. *Warspite* was hit by one bomb, but little damaged, and *Valiant* suffered three casualties (including one killed) by splinters from a near-miss. About nine hours later *Illustrious* struggled into Malta harbour under her own power, and next morning *Gallant* and her escort arrived.

Next day the dive-bombers attacked two cruisers—*Gloucester* and *Southampton*—escorting the three ships from the western Mediterranean bound for Greece. *Gloucester* was only lightly hit, but *Southampton* was set on fire, and as the damage made it impossible to flood the magazines she had to be abandoned and sunk. Every merchant ship in all the convoys arrived safely but the naval losses had been heavy.

Despite continuing strong German air attacks intended to finish her off, *Illustrious* was patched up in Malta and struggled back to Alexandria; but she obviously had to return to a fully equipped dockyard before she could be made fit for further action.

Besides the Luftwaffe, other German units were on their way to the central Mediterranean. Within days of the last battle of Wavell's offensive in Cyrenaica, the first of the German units that were to make up the Afrika Korps were landing at Tripoli, and Lieutenant-General Rommel, who was to command them, had arrived on February 12. The convoys carrying their transport and supplies suffered some losses due to the British 'U' class submarines, *Usk, Upholder,* and others of their class, now beginning to replace the larger ones that had been operating from Malta. These small submarines were far better suited to operating in the narrow, clear Mediterranean waters.

The same month, February, saw a notable exploit by Force H. On February 6 the battle-cruiser *Renown*, the battleship *Malaya*, the cruiser *Sheffield*, and supporting destroyers sailed from Gibraltar to bombard Genoa at close range; and *Ark Royal* accompanied them to fly off her bombers for attacks on the naval base at La Spezia and factories at Leghorn. The attacks took place at first light on February 8. The Italian battleship *Caio Duilio*, which was in dry dock at Genoa, was not spotted by the air reconnaissance, and so escaped further damage, but nearly 300 15-inch high explosive shells, and many smaller ones, plastered the port and dockyard, doing severe damage. After an attack lasting half an hour the squadron withdrew, joined *Ark Royal,* and returned to Gibraltar; the Italian ships which had put to sea to intercept the withdrawal failed to find the British due to poor air reconnaissance.

Perhaps more surprisingly there was no air attack on Force H as it withdrew. Undoubtedly there was a serious lack of liaison between the Italian naval and air force commands; the French Admiral de Belot, writing after the war, and drawing largely on Italian sources, noted that: 'With every failure the rivalry between *Superaero* and *Supermarina* increased in bitterness, preventing the establishment of a rational and efficient organisation.' Britain, on the other hand, had good reason to be thankful for the good relations between her three Commanders-in-Chief in Egypt.

The raid on Genoa, and its full effects, could not be concealed from the Italian people as the damage inflicted by the Taranto attack had been. The ineffectiveness of the naval reaction particularly infuriated them—the more so as they were never told that their navy had put to sea at that time. In Britain, the news was of course welcomed—by none more than by Churchill.

The German dive-bombers continued to be the most effective opponents the British navy had in the Mediterranean. On February 23 and 24, the monitor *Terror* and the destroyer *Dainty,* of the Inshore Squadron (which had done such effective work in supporting the land offensive in Cyrenaica) were bombed and sunk off Tobruk—a loss partly offset by the torpedoing, on the 25th, of the Italian cruiser *Armando Diaz,* sunk by the British submarine *Upright.* On March 6, German aircraft—probably operating from the Dodecanese—dropped magnetic and acoustic mines in the Suez Canal, and for three weeks nothing could pass through it. This was especially serious, because, for a good deal of the time, the aircraft-carrier *Formidable*—which had come out round the Cape to replace *Illustrious*—was held up at the south end of the Canal, and could not join the fleet.

Until *Formidable* reached Alexandria no more convoys to Malta could be sailed, and by the time one did get through, the situation on the island was very serious. However, a convoy of four supply ships at last reached Malta harbour on March 23, and relieved the shortages there for the moment.

On February 8, with the capture of El Agheila, the British advance along the North African coast had reached its high-water mark. Aid to Greece now received the highest priority for the British commanders in the Mediterranean, and it so happened that at this time the Greeks were at last convinced that the Germans intended to come to the aid of the Italians against them. They now reversed their earlier decision to refuse the help of British land forces, and requested that all possible assistance should be given. Accordingly, as troops became available with the end of the Cyrenaican offensive, General Wavell concentrated them in Egypt, where they would be ready to embark for Greece. Even now the decision to send infantry and field artillery was not final, but depended on the possibility of intervention being effective. The Foreign Secretary, Anthony Eden, and the Chief of the Imperial General Staff, Sir John Dill, were sent to the Middle East to decide whether this was possible, and with the land and air commanders-in-chief they flew to Athens for talks with the Greeks.

Their report to the Prime Minister was that there was a sufficiently good chance that British support could be effective, and that the attempt should be made, though Dill, at least, had his misgivings.

Although it soon became plain that the commitment of the Greek army to the campaign against the Italians would prevent them from bearing the share they had hoped to bear against the Germans, the local British commanders and Sir John Dill continued to believe that there was a chance of successful resistance, and the convoys that were to transfer the British Expeditionary Force to Greece began to sail on March 5.

When the Germans learned of this they were by no means pleased that British troop convoys seemed to be able to sail as they would through the 'Italian lake'. According to Luftwaffe claims, two of the available British battleships were disabled on March 16; presumably they claimed that they had been bombed in harbour.

This was quite untrue, but on March 19 a strongly worded dispatch from the German to the Italian naval staff was forwarded by the German naval liaison officer, in effect demanding that the Italians make some effort, with their greatly superior forces, to interrupt the flow of British reinforcements to Greece.

On March 26, the Italians launched the first of a very successful series of attacks on British warships in harbour with what were described as 'naval assault machines' *(Mezzi Navali d'Assalto).* A motor-boat loaded with explosives was directed at the cruiser HMS *York*—at this time the only 8-inch gun cruiser in the eastern Mediterranean—while she was anchored off the north coast of Crete in Suda Bay. The explosion blew a hole in her hull and *York's* engine-room was flooded so that she had steam neither to move nor to operate her gun-turrets; she was run ashore and was later destroyed on the beach by bombing during the Battle of Crete.

But under German pressure, Italian naval operations were not to be limited to those by small vessels. As they did not accept German reassurances about the balance of forces, however, and as they had no intention of being caught by the British Mediterranean fleet if they could help it, the Italians first of all increased the number of their air reconnaissance sorties.

Back in Alexandria, Admiral Cunningham noticed this and began to suspect that something was afoot. On March 27, he received a sighting report from a Malta-based reconnaissance Sunderland that three Italian cruisers and a destroyer were at sea, steaming towards Crete—and he also had reason to believe that Italian battleships were at sea. He issued signals to detached elements of his command, ordered steam raised aboard the main fleet, and sailed from Alexandria after dark. The fleet was on its way to Cape Matapan, scene of a decisive British victory.

January 1941: at sea, about 100 miles off Malta, the Luftwaffe strikes at *Illustrious*

1940 November 11: The Fleet Air Arm attacks the Italian fleet in Taranto harbour.
November 27: The Italian fleet breaks off an action with British Mediterranean fleet off Cape Spartivento.

1941 January: The Luftwaffe attacks British shipping in the Mediterranean for the first time.
February 8: Genoa is bombarded by British battleships of Force H.
March 6: The Luftwaffe blocks the Suez Canal for three weeks with acoustic and magnetic mines.
March 26: The first Italian attack using 'naval assault machines' cripples the British cruiser *York.*
March 27: An RAF Sunderland sights the Italian fleet at sea.
March 28: The Battle of Matapan is fought off the coast of Greece.

THE LAST HOURS OF THE BISMARCK

After the sinking of HMS *Hood* and the withdrawal of HMS *Prince of Wales,* the atmosphere aboard the *Bismarck* was jubilant. The successful defence against the aircraft from the *Victorious,* and the shaking-off of the shadowing cruisers, further increased this feeling. Admiral Lütjens, however, felt that this exaggerated air of victory should be moderated, and as it was his birthday that Sunday, he addressed the crew shortly before midday, May 25. In precise language he thanked the crew for their good wishes, and then proceeded to speak his mind. He praised the crew's magnificent discipline and fulfilment of duty which had already accomplished so much, but said the worst still stood before them—for the whole of the British fleet had now been commanded to sink the killer of the *Hood.* Now it was 'win or die'—but before the *Bismarck* went down she would meet and send many of the enemy before her.

The Admiral wished with these words to rid the crew of their over-exuberance and bring them into a more realistic frame of mind; but in fact he overdid it, and there was a feeling of depression among the crew which spread through all ranks from the highest to the lowest. But the idea must not be rejected that the Admiral, with deep insight into the political situation in Ger-many, more or less knew that the end of Germany was certain, and that the life of the *Bismarck* would be even shorter. The atmosphere on the *Bismarck* therefore remained tense.

For the next 30 hours the *Bismarck* sailed at full speed towards the French coast, without the Royal Navy being aware of her position or intentions; but at 1030 hours on Monday morning the *Bismarck* sighted a British flying-boat in a cloudless patch of sky and opened fire. The flying-boat vanished into cloud cover, but the *Bismarck*—which might have escaped recognition because of her second funnel and knowledge of British recognition signals—had given away her identity by shooting at the aircraft.

It was now obvious that the enemy would bring attack-planes against the *Bismarck,* and these planes could only come from the *Ark Royal,* which was stationed at Gibraltar. The day passed in anxious calculation of *Ark Royal*'s probable position—and then at last the air-raid warning came at 2045 hours. The *Ark Royal*'s planes made two strikes with their torpedoes, diving down on us from all angles out of low cloud. One torpedo which hit amidships caused no damage, but the second affected the rudders disastrously, jamming the port-side rudder at a 15-degree angle. Immediately, the *Bismarck* became no longer manoeuvrable.

The torpedo-hit on the rudder shook the ship so badly that even in my zone of action in the turbine-room, the deck-plates were thrown into the air, and the hull vibrated violently. Shortly after the blow, water flooded through the port-side gangways into the turbine-room, and clouds of gas and smoke filled the room until the forced ventilation cleared it.

The stern compartments of the ship were now flooding, but the men who had been stationed there could still be saved, and soon the carpenters and repair-crew came through, making their way aft.

All possibilities were now being considered to restore the ship's manoeuvrability—even if only temporarily. The Commander, Captain Lindemann, considered reports from Chief Engineer Lehmann, who was in continual contact with the repair and rescue teams. There was much gesticulation, and at one point the Chief Engineer stepped out of the circle, walked away, turned about, and made a sign of complete refusal. What this was about I am not certain, but eventually it was found possible to connect the hand rudder. But the old rudder would not budge, and to attempt to cut it away with underwater saws was quite impossible because of the heavy swell.

1. Into action: *Bismarck* fires a salvo at the *Hood*

2. A 15-inch shell-burst (on right) from the *Hood* misses *Bismarck*

3. *Hood* explodes under *Bismarck*'s fifth salvo

4. Shells burst near the vanished *Hood* as *Prince of Wales* retires

Imperial War Museum

BISMARCK was the strongest battleship of her time. Her main armament was conventional, but she displaced over 50,000 tons as opposed to *Hood*'s 44,000 tons—and over 40% of *Bismarck*'s displacement was her armour. Yet despite this enormous advantage in protection, *Bismarck* still was capable of a speed of 29 knots. And in comparison with other new battleships of her period, *Bismarck* had formidable secondary and tertiary armaments. Launched in 1939. **Displacement:** 50,000 tons. **Speed:** 29 knots. **Armament:** eight 15-inch, 12 5·9-inch, 16 4·1-inch AA, 16 20-mm AA guns. Two Arado 196 aircraft. **Complement:** 2,200

15-inch main armament

Twin 37-mm
(two each side)

20-mm

5.9-inch secondary armament
(three each side)

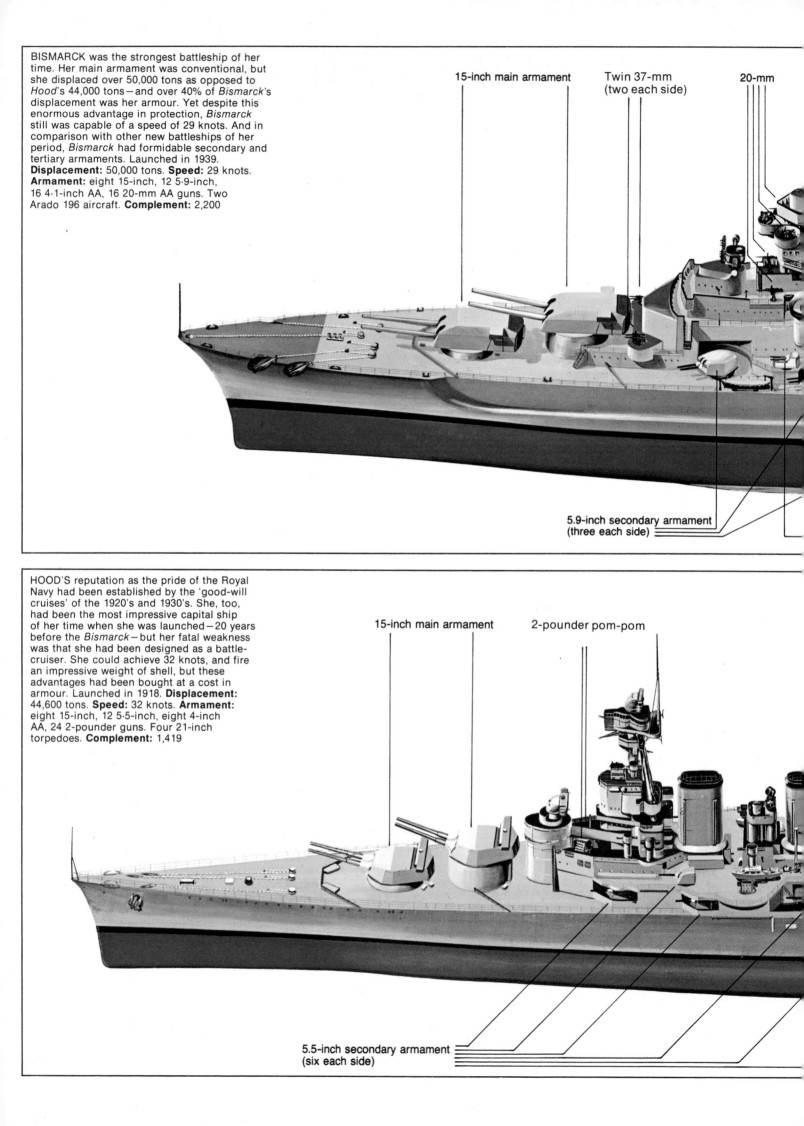

HOOD'S reputation as the pride of the Royal Navy had been established by the 'good-will cruises' of the 1920's and 1930's. She, too, had been the most impressive capital ship of her time when she was launched—20 years before the *Bismarck*—but her fatal weakness was that she had been designed as a battle-cruiser. She could achieve 32 knots, and fire an impressive weight of shell, but these advantages had been bought at a cost in armour. Launched in 1918. **Displacement:** 44,600 tons. **Speed:** 32 knots. **Armament:** eight 15-inch, 12 5·5-inch, eight 4-inch AA, 24 2-pounder guns. Four 21-inch torpedoes. **Complement:** 1,419

15-inch main armament

2-pounder pom-pom

5.5-inch secondary armament
(six each side)

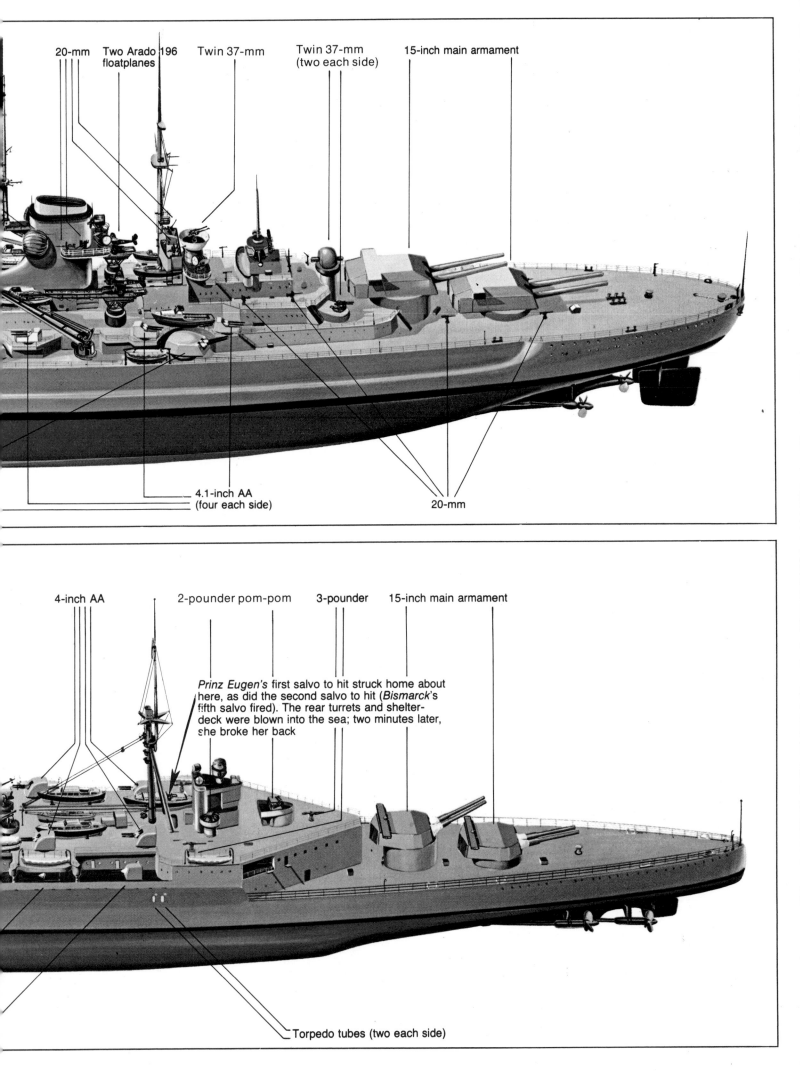

20-mm   Two Arado 196 floatplanes   Twin 37-mm   Twin 37-mm (two each side)   15-inch main armament

4.1-inch AA (four each side)

20-mm

4-inch AA   2-pounder pom-pom   3-pounder   15-inch main armament

Prinz Eugen's first salvo to hit struck home about here, as did the second salvo to hit (*Bismarck's* fifth salvo fired). The rear turrets and shelter-deck were blown into the sea; two minutes later, she broke her back

Torpedo tubes (two each side)

Despite all attempts to steer with the propellers, the ship could no longer be kept on a south-easterly course; it was therefore necessary to turn head-on to the sea—towards the north-west—at a slow speed, and into the face of the enemy.

One cannot help wondering whether everything humanly possible was really done in order to try and save the *Bismarck* on this critical night. The ship had gone to sea well constructed and it is possible that the damaged rudder might have been blown out of the stern of the ship without damage to the propellers. But this risk was not attempted—nor was there any attempt to improvise a sea-anchor to stabilise the course. With three propellers capable of driving *Bismarck* at 28 knots, it is difficult to accept that there was no alternative but to head straight for the enemy at a slow speed.

During the night the British destroyers appeared once more, coming in close to deliver their torpedoes again and again, but the *Bismarck*'s gunnery was so effective that none of them was able to score a hit. But around 0845 hours a strongly united attack opened, and the last fight of the *Bismarck* began. Two minutes later, *Bismarck* replied, and her third volley straddled the *Rodney*, but this accuracy could not be maintained: because of the continual battle against the sea, and attack now from three sides, the *Bismarck*'s fire was soon to deteriorate. Shortly after the battle commenced a shell hit the combat mast, and the fire-control post in the fore-mast broke away. At 0902 hours both forward heavy-gun turrets were put out of action. A further hit wrecked the forward control-post, the rear control-post was wrecked soon after—and that was the end of the fighting instruments. For some time the rear turrets fired singly, but by about 1000 hours all the guns were silent.

Gradually the noise of combat became more irregular until it sank, to become nothing more than a series of sporadic crashes; even the control bells from the bridge stopped ringing. All three turbine-rooms were filled with smoke from the boiler-room; fortunately no shells had yet come through the plating protecting the engine-room or the electric generators (though the electric plant on the port side had been hit on the Saturday morning by a shell from the *Prince of Wales*).

Somewhere about 1015 hours, I received an order over the telephone from the Chief Engineer: 'Prepare the ship for sinking.' That was the last order I received on the *Bismarck*. Soon after that, all transmission of orders collapsed.Eventually I left with the turbines still moving slowly in compliance with the Engineer's orders.

The lower decks were brilliantly lit up; a *peaceful* mood prevailed, such as that on a Sunday afternoon in port—the silence broken only by the explosion of our own demolition-charges below. I myself saw the result of the battle on the battery-deck. There was no electric light, only the red glow from numerous fires; smoke fumes billowed everywhere; crushed doors and hatches littered the decks, and men were running here and there, apparently aimlessly: it seemed highly unlikely that one would survive.

Cadet officers and more than 100 petty officers and men were collecting between the rear turrets, but amidships there was a smoke-screen which prevented us from seeing what was happening forward; only the combat mast stood out from the dense black smoke. The flag was still waving from the rear mast, and the barrels of the rear turrets stood out starkly against the sky; one barrel had been split by a tremendous explosion. Only occasionally did I see dead or wounded comrades.

Meanwhile the ship sank deeper, and we knew that it would eventually capsize. After a triple *'Sieg heil!'*, I ordered 'abandon ship'.

Hardly were we free of the ship when it keeled over to port, rolling the deck-rail under and bringing the bilge-keel out of the water. A pause—then the *Bismarck* turned keel-up, and we could see that its hull had not been damaged by torpedoes. Then, slowly, the bows rose in the air, and, stern first, *Bismarck* slid down to the bottom.

From the original complement of almost 2,400 men, 115 men of the *Bismarck* survived; of the officers only two out of 100 were saved.

End of a Leviathan

1941

May 18: *Bismarck* and *Prinz Eugen* sail from Gdynia for Operation *Rheinübung*, Raeder's attempt to concentrate a German naval force against the Allied Atlantic convoys.
May 20: *Bismarck* and *Prinz Eugen* are sighted in the Skagerrak. The British Admiralty is alerted.
May 21/22: *Bismarck* and *Prinz Eugen* reach Kors Fjord near Bergen, Norway. They sail at dusk in thick weather. RAF reconnaissance meanwhile has identified the German ships; the British fleet is alerted; *Hood* and *Prince of Wales* sail to cover the Denmark Strait.
May 22: Foul weather prevents the British from pinpointing the German ships; at 2000 hours the British C-in-C finally learns that *Bismarck* and *Prinz Eugen* have escaped, and he puts to sea from Scapa Flow.
May 23: *Bismarck* and *Prinz Eugen* enter Denmark Strait at noon; as night falls they encounter the British cruisers *Norfolk* and *Suffolk*, who shadow the German ships and report their position to *Hood* and *Prince of Wales*.
May 24: *Hood* and *Prince of Wales* encounter *Bismarck* and *Prinz Eugen* at a range of 17 miles; after an engagement of eight minutes *Hood* blows up; *Prince of Wales*, out-gunned, retires. The German Admiral Lütjens decides to proceed independently of *Prinz Eugen* and heads south in *Bismarck*.
May 24/25: British Swordfish aircraft from *Victorious* attack the *Bismarck* but fail to damage her.
May 25: *Bismarck* heads for France; the British hunting-forces lose contact. The British C-in-C guesses that *Bismarck* will turn in her tracks so he heads away from *Bismarck*'s actual position. British Admiralty assumes that *Bismarck* is making for France; at 1810 hours the British C-in-C turns towards France but *Bismarck* has a lead of 110 miles.
May 26: RAF Catalina sights *Bismarck* and alerts the British pursuers. A Swordfish strike from *Ark Royal* nearly sinks HMS *Sheffield* in error. A second strike locates *Bismarck* and a torpedo hit wrecks her steering-gear. During the night of May 26/27, Captain Vian's British destroyers keep in contact with *Bismarck*.
May 27: British battleships *Rodney* and *King George V* close in on the crippled *Bismarck*; hopelessly out-gunned, the German battleship is pounded into a wreck and finished off with torpedoes from the cruiser *Dorsetshire*. At 1040 hours *Bismarck* finally sinks.
June 1: Captain Brinckmann in *Prinz Eugen*, having refused to carry out independent commerce-raiding as ordered by Lütjens, arrives in Brest.

The long-standing partnership of Force H: (top to bottom) *Sheffield, Ark Royal,* and *Renown*

THE STRUGGLE FOR CRETE

Crete was conquered by the German supremacy in the air, a supremacy which was a terrible threat to the British naval forces operating in support of the garrison. Despite the battering received from the Stukas, the British Mediterranean Fleet stood by the retreating land forces to provide their evacuation—but at a heavy cost

△ Stuka's view of a stricken target in Suda Bay

1941 May 15: The Germans begin intensive bombing of Crete.
May 19: The British withdraw their last fighters from Crete, thus assuring the Luftwaffe of air control.
May 20: The German airborne attack on Crete begins. Admiral Cunningham begins to send British naval sweeps north of Crete by night.
May 20/21: British destroyers bombard Scarpanto airfield to the north-east of Crete. Stukas sink British destroyer *Juno*. Admiral Glennie scatters the light German invasion fleet from Mílos.
May 22: German bombers attack Admiral King's force, damaging British battleships *Warspite* and *Valiant*, and sinking the destroyer *Greyhound* and cruisers *Gloucester* and *Fiji*.
May 23: British 5th Destroyer Flotilla bombards the German troops in control of Máleme airfield. Stukas sink British destroyers *Kelly* and *Kashmir*.
May 24: British minelayer *Abdiel* and destroyers supply British land forces at Suda Bay.
May 25: British battleships *Queen Elizabeth*, *Barham*, and the aircraft-carrier *Formidable* sail from Alexandria with eight destroyers.
May 26: Stukas surprise and damage the *Formidable*.
May 27: German bombers damage the *Barham*. Admiral Cunningham prepares the British naval forces for the evacuation of Freyberg's troops.
May 28/29: Admiral Rawlings embarks 4,000 men from Heráklion. German bombers cause the loss of British destroyers *Hereward* and *Imperial,* and damage the cruisers *Dido* and *Orion*. Captain Arliss lands supplies at Sfakia and embarks 700 men.
May 29: Admiral King embarks 6,000 men from Sfakia. German bomber damages British cruiser *Perth*.
May 30: Captain Arliss embarks 1,500 more troops from Sfakia.
May 31/June 1: Admiral King embarks 4,000 men from Sfakia, leaving 5,000 on the beaches. Cruiser *Calcutta* bombed and sunk.

The battle of Crete was to the Royal Navy the culmination of a period of continuing strain and heavy losses. At the turn of the year, the Italian fleet, crippled at Taranto in November 1940, had seemed willing enough to leave the British unchallenged in the Mediterranean, while the high-level bombing and torpedo attacks of the Regia Aeronautica had been more of a nuisance to the British fleet than a threat to its strength. Then the Germans had come to the rescue of their allies, and all had been changed.

First, X Fliegerkorps had appeared in Sicily. In the previous year, its Ju-88 and He-111 aircraft had been rather ineffective against warships off Norway. The Ju-87, the Stuka dive-bomber—intended primarily for the close support of the army—had proved far more formidable. Tenth Fliegerkorps now included a large force of Stukas, and its skilful and determined pilots were ready to press home their attacks.

The Mediterranean Fleet met them on January 10 and 11, 1941, as it escorted a convoy to Malta. The German pilots hit the aircraft-carrier *Illustrious* six times with heavy bombs, and only her armoured flight-deck saved her to limp into the Grand Harbour for temporary repairs, after which she left for more extensive repairs in America. The cruiser *Southampton* was sunk, and the *Gloucester* damaged. Admiral Sir Andrew Cunningham, Commander-in-Chief of the Mediterranean Fleet, reported to London that a serious situation had developed off Malta, and called for a greater degree of air support.

Next had come the German threat to Greece and the decision to send there a British and Commonwealth expeditionary force. The convoys from Egypt had started to run on March 5, and ran every three days for three weeks. Urged on by the Germans, the Italian fleet came out to attack, only to find Cunningham and the Mediterranean Fleet ready for them, and to return to harbour after losing three large cruisers in the night action off Cape Matapan on March 28. The British suffered no losses, but two days earlier the cruiser *York* had been attacked by Italian 'naval assault machines' in Suda Bay, where she was eventually lost.

In February, Rommel and the Afrika Korps had arrived in Tripoli. Their counteroffensive against the weakened British desert army opened on March 24. On April 3, they entered Benghazi, and on April 12 they reached the Egyptian frontier at Sollum, having besieged Tobruk. The emergency to the British army demanded intensive effort by the inshore forces of the Royal Navy, and the Luftwaffe took its toll of them. Malta became the base for destroyers, submarines, and aircraft attacking Rommel's convoys on the Tripoli run and drew upon itself heavy air attack from Sicily.

The intensive activity called for logistic support and for fighter reinforcements, and, with Cyrenaica in German hands, convoys had to be fought through to Malta and fighters ferried there by aircraft-carrier. Force H from Gibraltar and the Mediterranean Fleet from Alexandria co-operated in the task, and on April 21 the battleships of the latter bombarded Benghazi harbour.

On April 7 the Germans had crossed the Bulgarian frontier to invade Greece, and in the next three weeks had forced the withdrawal of the British and Commonwealth force. The evacuation took place between April 24 and April 29. Six cruisers, 19 des-

STUKA VERSUS SEA POWER

In the fighting for Crete, the Ju-87 Stuka, which had suffered a severe mauling in the Battle of Britain, won new laurels as a destroyer of enemy shipping. Once again, the superiority of the air arm over enemy shipping was plainly demonstrated: Stukas of the 'Immelmann' *Stukageschwader* (dive-bomber wing) caused tremendous damage to the Mediterranean Fleet: not even the faster destroyers were safe from their attack. Specifications of the Ju-87 B-1: **Max speed:** 217 mph. **Armament:** two fixed 7·9-mm machine-guns firing forward, and one movable 7·9-mm machine-gun mounted in the rear cockpit. **Max bomb-load:** one 1,110-lb bomb and four 110-lb bombs

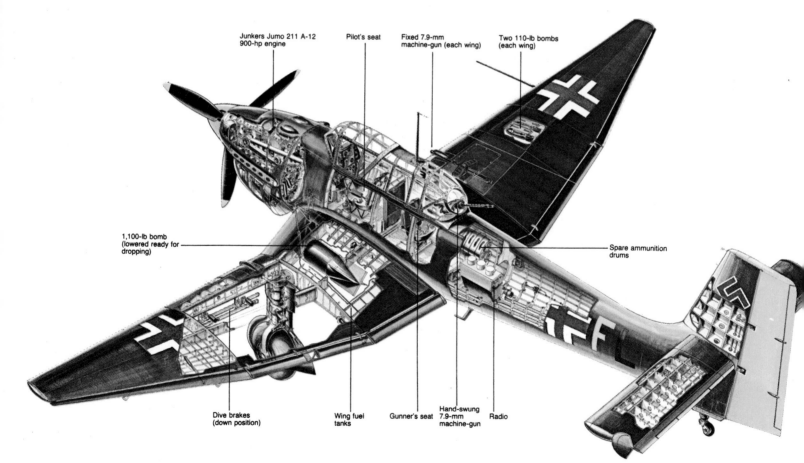

Junkers Jumo 211 A-12 900-hp engine

Pilot's seat

Fixed 7·9-mm machine-gun (each wing)

Two 110-lb bombs (each wing)

1,100-lb bomb (lowered ready for dropping)

Spare ammunition drums

Dive brakes (down position)

Wing fuel tanks

Gunner's seat

Hand-swung 7·9-mm machine-gun

Radio

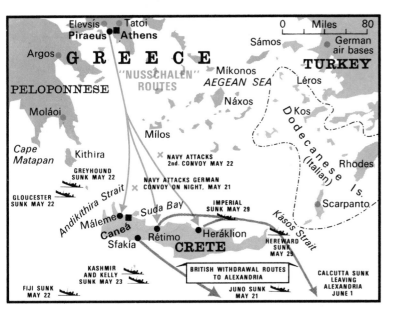

The map shows German air bases, Nusschalen routes, naval attacks, and ship sinkings around Crete and the Aegean Sea.

Map labels include: Elevsís, Tatoí, Piraeus, Athens, Argos, GREECE, Sámos, German air bases, TURKEY, "NUSSCHALEN" ROUTES, Míkonos, AEGEAN SEA, Léros, PELOPONNESE, Náxos, Kos, Molóoi, Dodecanese (Italian) Is., Mílos, Rhodes, Cape Matapan, Kithira, NAVY ATTACKS 2nd CONVOY MAY 22, GREYHOUND SUNK MAY 22, NAVY ATTACKS GERMAN CONVOY ON NIGHT, MAY 21, Scarpanto, GLOUCESTER SUNK MAY 22, Andikíthira Strait, Suda Bay, IMPERIAL SUNK MAY 29, Kásos Strait, Máleme, Caneá, Rétimo, Heráklion, HEREWARD SUNK MAY 29, Sfakia, CRETE, KASHMIR AND KELLY SUNK MAY 23, BRITISH WITHDRAWAL ROUTES TO ALEXANDRIA, CALCUTTA SUNK LEAVING ALEXANDRIA JUNE 1, FIJI SUNK MAY 22, JUNO SUNK MAY 21

◁ The battle for Crete inflicted grievous losses on the Mediterranean Fleet: the British squadrons smashed the German seaborne reinforcements for Crete, but in the process suffered intense attacks from the Luftwaffe

troyers, numerous smaller naval craft, transports, and merchant ships embarked over 50,000 men; and under the attacks of the Luftwaffe four transports and two destroyers were lost. On May 4 the Mediterranean Fleet reassembled in Alexandria; then, after a short period of rest and refit, sailed for Malta to re-supply the island and to bring through the vital 'Tiger convoy' carrying tanks for the 8th Army, which Force H was escorting from Gibraltar.

On May 13 Cunningham informed the British Admiralty that since April 20 his fleet had expended between one-third and one-half of its anti-aircraft ammunition; and that remaining stocks of 5·25- and 4·5-inch shells were down to three-quarters of the amount required to fill the magazines. With Crete in mind and without fighter cover, he looked forward to the future with great anxiety.

Crete—the liability

When, in October 1940, the Italians invaded Greece, the British welcomed the Greek invitation to occupy Crete, where they hoped to establish an advanced fleet base at Suda Bay, and airfields along the coast. In May 1941, with Suda Bay and the landing strips at Máleme, Rétimo, and Heráklion open to Luftwaffe attacks from Greece, and with no adequate fighter defence, Crete was a liability. Ships entering Suda Bay were at the mercy of air attack; and after fighting gallantly against hopeless odds, the last fighters were withdrawn from the island on May 19. In the Mediterranean Fleet, the *Formidable* had replaced the *Illustrious,* but in operations off Benghazi and Malta her aircraft had been reduced to a mere four serviceable machines. So, at sea off Crete, it was to be a straight fight between the guns of the British fleet and the Luftwaffe.

Cunningham realised that the main German attack would be airborne. The task of the fleet, therefore, could only be to prevent any accompanying seaborne invasion, to cover supply and reinforcement of the garrison, to bombard in its support—and, if the worst came to the worst, to evacuate the island. Thus the fleet had to be risked in what could only be a secondary role in the defence of Crete.

Cunningham could not, however, ignore the possibility that the Italian fleet would come out to escort a seaborne attack on the island. When the bombing of Crete began in earnest in mid-May, his battleships took station west of the island, and light forces swept northward at night, watching for invasion.

After reliefs for refuelling, the dawn of May 20 found Rear-Admiral Rawlings with the battleships *Warspite* and *Valiant,* one cruiser, and ten destroyers, 100 miles west of the island. Rear-Admiral Glennie, with the cruisers *Dido* and *Orion,* was, after a night sweep, withdrawing through the Andikíthira Strait to join Rawlings. Rear-Admiral King, with the cruisers *Naiad* and *Perth,* and four destroyers, was withdrawing to the east through Kásos Strait; and Captain Rowley with the cruisers *Gloucester* and *Fiji* was coming north from Alexandria. Cunningham himself, with his widespread responsibilities, had decided to control events from Alexandria.

Under General Löhr, Luftflotte IV had been pushing forward its preparations for the attack on Crete since May 15: improvising airfields, stocking fuel and bombs, assembling troops. Road and rail communications in Greece were poor, and had been damaged in the recent fighting; and much of the heavy supply came by sea. Airfields were inadequate, and flying was much hampered by dust. Available airfields had to be shared between XI Fliegerkorps—the transport force—and VIII Fliegerkorps, comprising the fighters, bombers, and reconnaissance aircraft.

The responsibilities of General von Richthofen, commanding VIII Fliegerkorps, were:
● To cover the mounting of the attack, and sea movements in the Aegean necessary for it;
● To destroy British air forces in Crete and to silence the ground defences while the attack went in;
● To support the troops landed, by bombing and machine-gunning;
● To destroy enemy shipping off the island and to cover the sea movement of troops and heavy weapons planned to support the attack.

As one would expect, the short-range Stukas and single-engined fighters were based forward, in the Peloponnese and the nearby islands, with the bombers and twin-engined fighters farther back. Intensive bombing of Crete started on May 15, and reached its peak on the 20th, covering first the air landing on Máleme and Caneá, then shifting east to cover the afternoon landings at Rétimo and Heráklion.

That night British cruisers and destroyers swept north of Crete, finding no signs of German sea movement, although they had a brush with Italian motor-boats. Three British destroyers bombarded Scarpanto airfield, and the next morning Stukas sank the destroyer *Juno.*

A German convoy of 25 motor/sailer caiques, carrying a mountain battalion and heavy-weapon groups—2,300 men in all—from Piraeus, was due to land west of Máleme on the afternoon of May 21. A second light convoy—38 caiques with 4,000 men—was to reach Heráklion on the 22nd. German accounts refer to this 'cockleshell invasion' as the *Nusschalen* ('nut-shells') and the *Mückenflotilla* ('midge flotilla'). A heavy convoy of steamers with artillery and a few tanks was to wait at Piraeus until ordered forward. At dawn on May 21, when the first convoy was well on its way to Máleme, it was recalled to Mílos on overnight reports of British naval forces north of Crete. In the afternoon it was ordered to sea again. Thus it approached Crete not, as intended, by daylight—when the Luftwaffe could protect it—but at night, when British ships swept the waters it must traverse.

Overwhelmed by the British

At 2330 hours that night, the convoy was intercepted by Admiral Glennie with *Dido, Orion, Ajax,* and four destroyers. As the alarm was given and the mountain soldiers stumbled on deck, they saw their frail craft caught in the beams of British searchlights and heard the first salvoes. A caique loaded with ammunition blew up, others began to burn, and yet another was rammed and sliced in two. The Italian torpedo-boat *Lupo,* their only escort, faced the overwhelming odds gallantly, and in seeking to protect her charges was hit 18 times. After two-and-a-half hours the British ships turned south, believing that they had destroyed the convoy and drowned about 4,000 men—but in fact the *Lupo* and nearly two-thirds of the caiques remained afloat, and picked up survivors before returning to Mílos. After air-sea rescue operations had been carried out, the German loss was only 297 men drowned.

Next morning Admiral King—with *Naiad, Perth, Carlisle, Calcutta,* and four destroyers—was ordered to sweep to the north.

◁ This sequence of the *Gloucester* sinking was taken by a Luftwaffe pilot. *(Above)* Dead in the water and listing to port, note the smoke from her internal fires *(centre)*. *(Below)* The end of the *Gloucester*

He found a couple of surviving ships from the first convoy, which he sank; and then, at about 1000 hours, and 25 miles south of Mílos, he sighted the second convoy. A group of Ju-88s from Elevsís saw far below them the helpless caiques turn north at their best speed of 5 or 6 knots, while south of them the Italian torpedo-boat *Sagittario* zig-zagged at high speed, making smoke; beyond her steamed the British cruisers and destroyers in chase, guns firing. The Ju-88 group turned to attack, and as the first attack began their shallow dives the flak came streaming up at them.

On this same day King had already been under air attack for three hours, and with ammunition seriously depleted and the *Carlisle's* speed down to 20 knots, he decided to turn south. Stukas, Ju-88s, and Do-17s continued to engage his ships for the next three-and-a-half hours, during which the *Naiad* was seriously damaged and the *Carlisle's* captain was killed.

Luftwaffe reconnaissance aircraft had found Admiral Rawlings' ships on May 21. On the 22nd, with the critical first two days on Crete over, the urgency of supporting the German paratroops was less, and VIII Fliegerkorps eagerly took up the challenge, long awaited by the German airmen. In the fine weather of an early summer forenoon in the Mediterranean, dive-bombers and bombers had attacked the British cruiser forces. Glennie and Rowley had joined Rawlings some 20 to 30 miles west of Kíthira, and now Rawlings turned east to support King as he came south under air attack. They met in the Kíthira Channel early in the afternoon, and almost at once the *Warspite* was hit by a heavy bomb, putting out of action her starboard 6- and 4-inch batteries.

This was the opportunity for which the Luftwaffe had been waiting. Refuelling and bombing-up after their earlier attacks, and now reinforced by two fresh groups transferred from X Fliegerkorps, the German aircraft converged on the British fleet. Stukas, bombers, and fighters — with no British fighters to consider — made rough and ready formations as aircraft became ready and returned to the attack. At first the concentrated fire of the British ships held them off, but, 30 minutes after the *Warspite* was hit, two bombs struck the destroyer *Greyhound* and sank her. King ordered Rowley back to pick up survivors, and then, realising that *Gloucester* and *Fiji* were very short of anti-aircraft ammunition, ordered them to rejoin the main fleet, and turned back to meet them. The move came too late. As she came in sight, the *Gloucester* was hit, flames spread along her deck, she lost way, and drifted in a circle. At 1600 hours there was an internal explosion and she sank. The *Fiji*, now isolated and under continuous air attack, had to keep going, throwing overboard her life-saving floats as she passed the *Gloucester's* survivors. A little later the *Valiant* was hit and damaged.

The *Fiji* and her two attendant destroyers had missed the main fleet, and now steamed south. At 1845 hours, a lone Me-109 at the limit of its range found her and dropped a single bomb. It exploded close alongside, and with singular good fortune succeeded in crippling the cruiser's engines. Half an hour later a few other aircraft appeared, called up by the lone Messerschmitt — a bomb exploded above a boiler room, and at 2015 hours the *Fiji* turned over and sank.

That night Cunningham, due to a mistaken report that the battleships had expended all their light anti-aircraft ammunition, recalled them to Alexandria. The 5th Destroyer Flotilla, however, had arrived during the afternoon from Malta — Captain Lord Louis Mountbatten in the *Kelly,* with the *Kashmir, Kipling, Kelvin,* and *Jackal.* Now it was their turn to sweep north of Crete. They sank two caiques carrying Germans and bombarded Máleme airfield, which was now in German hands. Next morning a formation of 24 Stukas found the *Kelly* and *Kashmir* south of the island and sank them. Under heavy air attack, the *Kipling* rescued 279 survivors.

The nightly sweeps to the north of Crete continued. Destroyers and the fast minelayer *Abdiel* landed forces and ammunition for the troops around Suda Bay and a destroyer evacuated the King of Greece from the island. Under pressure from London, Cunningham embarked a battalion in the converted merchant ship *Glenroy*, but she was damaged and set on fire by bombs and forced to turn back on the morning of the 26th.

At last a dozen serviceable Fulmar fighters had been mustered for the *Formidable*, and escorted by the *Queen Elizabeth*, the *Barham*, and eight destroyers, she left Alexandria on May 25.

Triumph for the Stukas

At dawn next morning four Fulmars and four Albacores, flown off 100 miles away, attacked Scarpanto airfield, destroying or damaging grounded aircraft and shooting others down; but at 1325 hours, 25 Stukas appeared from the south, two bombs hit the *Formidable's* flight-deck, and she had to return to Alexandria severely damaged.

The II Group from *Stukageschwader* (Dive-Bomber Wing) 'Immelmann' of X Fliegerkorps had been an early arrival in Sicily, and on January 10 they had attacked and severely damaged the *Illustrious*. Later, the group had gone to Africa to support Rommel. On May 26 it was patrolling northwards from the African coast, hoping to catch British ships returning from Crete. It was this group that found the *Formidable,* and as she turned into wind with her fighters starting up on deck, the Stukas screamed down to hit and damage her as they had the *Illustrious*. The next day aircraft hit and damaged the *Barham*.

On May 26 Freyberg reported that the situation in Crete was hopeless, and at 1500 hours on May 27, after approval had been received from London, the decision to evacuate was taken. Now the battered ships and their exhausted crews had to expose themselves again to the Luftwaffe, this time to rescue their comrades of the British, Australian, and New Zealand armies. Cunningham needed no persuasion to take the risk, but warned Wavell that the moment might come when loss of life among troops embarked would force him to end the evacuation. All embarkation would be by night, as far as possible between midnight and 0300 hours, which would allow the ships about three hours' start before full daylight. The troops from Heráklion would be embarked in one lift direct; the remainder would withdraw across the mountains to embark at Sfakía on the south coast.

Rawlings, with the *Orion, Ajax, Dido,* and six destroyers, was given the task of taking off the Heráklion garrison. At 1700 hours on May 28 the Luftwaffe found them about 90 miles south of the Kásos Strait, and attacked until dark. The *Ajax* was damaged and returned to Alexandria, and the destroyer *Imperial* was 'near-missed', without apparent damage. Between 2330 and 0320 hours, some 4,000 were taken off from Heráklion, and the force started back. Half an hour later the *Imperial's* steering failed. Rawlings ordered the *Hotspur* to take off her troops and crew and to sink her, and as she steamed south at full speed after doing so—with 900 troops

on board, 50 miles from Scarpanto, and dawn breaking—the *Hotspur's* position was desperate.

Rather than desert the *Hotspur,* however, Rawlings had waited; now he had to face the Stukas. They appeared at 0600 hours. At 0625 the *Hereward* was hit and her speed reduced, so she had to be left, and was last seen making for the Cretan coast; the Stukas sank her, but Italian motor-boats rescued most of the men on board.

Hits and near-misses reduced the speed of the squadron to 25 knots, then to 21. First the *Dido* was hit, then—repeatedly—the *Orion,* and the bombs bursting in the crowded ships did terrible damage. Stuka attacks ended about 1045 hours; but later high bombers appeared, though their bombs failed to hit the ships. Cunningham saw the ships entering Alexandria that evening, guns awry or broken off, decks crowded with troops, the mess decks reduced to shambles. Of the 4,000 men embarked, 800 had been killed, wounded or, like the survivors from the *Hereward,* were prisoners. Meanwhile Captain Arliss with four destroyers had landed ammunition and supplies at Sfakía and had taken off 700 men without loss.

Long-range fighters from Egypt had attempted to cover Rawlings's withdrawal, but missed his ships owing to his reduced speed. During the rest of the evacuation they gave useful cover to ships returning from Sfakía, which were moreover far less exposed to air attack. On the night of May 29 King took the *Phoebe, Perth, Glengyle, Calcutta, Coventry,* and three destroyers to Sfakía and brought out 6,000 men; but the *Perth* was damaged by a Ju-88 on the way back. On May 30 two of Arliss's four destroyers were damaged, but the other two took off another 1,500 men, and then Wavell asked for a final effort to bring off 3,000 on the night of the 31st. King was sent with the *Phoebe, Abdiel,* and three destroyers. They embarked 4,000 men, but then at 0300 hours on June 1 they were forced to sail from Sfakía, leaving another 5,000 on the beach—and the *Calcutta,* coming out from Alexandria to meet them, was bombed and sunk.

Early on June 1 Major Garrett of the Royal Marines found a derelict landing-craft from the *Glengyle* on Sfakía beach. With 137 volunteers on board he sailed for the African coast. He beached 19 miles west of Sidi Barrani at 0230 on June 9, having had to sail his cumbersome craft most of the way using blankets for sails. Another landing-craft reached Sidi Barrani about the same time with 50 men, and a third arrived next day with 37. In all, some 600 men escaped from Crete and made their way back to Egypt or Syria in the next few months, in Greek fishing-boats or in submarines sent to pick them up.

It was as he risked his battered ships in the evacuation that Cunningham was heard to say: 'It takes the Navy three years to build a ship. It would take three hundred to re-build a tradition.' His total losses off Crete were: three cruisers and six destroyers sunk; three battleships, one aircraft-carrier, six cruisers, and seven destroyers damaged; in the fleet, 1,828 killed and 183 wounded. Cunningham had realised the risks he was forced to run. As shown by the messages Cunningham received, Churchill and the Chiefs-of-Staff were less realistic. Before the year was out, Japanese aircraft off Singapore would ram home the lesson Cunningham drew from Crete: the proper way to fight aircraft is in the air, and if shore-based fighters cannot cover the fleet, it must carry its own fighters with it.

NAVAL BALANCE BEFORE PEARL HARBOR

THE JAPANESE SIDE

When Japan struck at Pearl Harbor in December 1941, she had built up the third strongest navy in the world. In many ways it was similar to the German navy—young, self-assured, and inspired by an aggressive tradition dating back to the destruction of the Russian fleet at Tsushima in 1905. In the Pacific, the Japanese had a slight numerical advantage over the American navy, although its battle fleet was approaching obsolescence—all Japanese battleships in commission in December 1941 had been laid down or designed in the First World War. Her carrier forces were well trained and equipped, and her naval strategy fully appreciated the role of the aircraft-carrier in modern war. All six fleet carriers were used in the attack on Pearl Harbor; and the *Zuiho*, supporting the southern offensive, was joined by the *Ryujo*, and the *Hosho*, two of the smaller carriers (not shown here). Admiral Yamamoto, the C-in-C, predicted that Japan could win a rapid series of victories with such a naval strength, but that in the long run Japan's industrial capacity would prove insufficient against that of the Allies. With her limited reserves, Japan did not have the cruiser strength necessary to hold a widely-extended naval perimeter

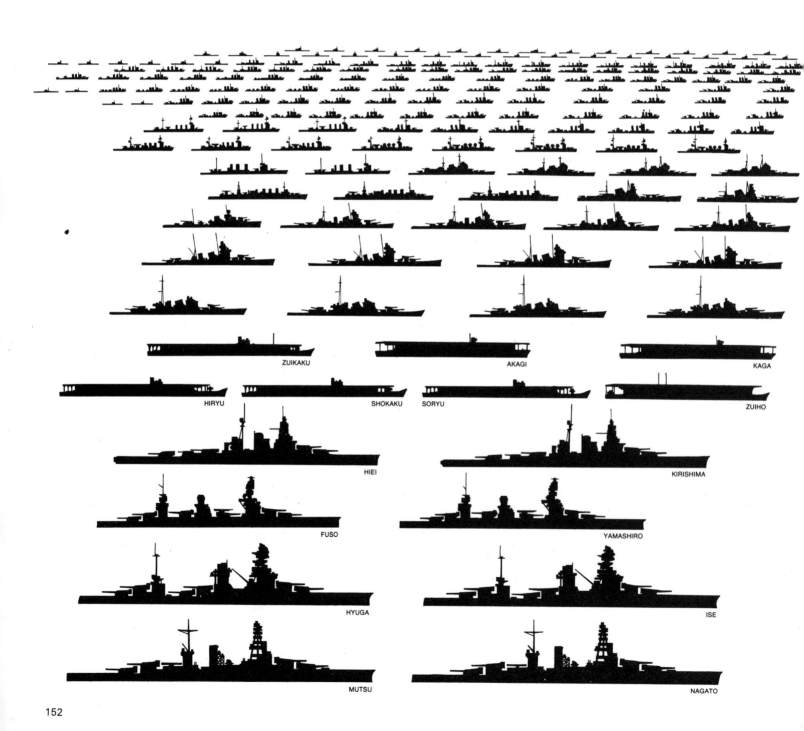

ZUIKAKU

AKAGI

KAGA

HIRYU

SHOKAKU

SORYU

ZUIHO

HIEI

KIRISHIMA

FUSO

YAMASHIRO

HYUGA

ISE

MUTSU

NAGATO

THE AMERICAN SIDE

Pearl Harbor caught the American navy at a time of transition; although the second strongest in the world, it suffered from the need to maintain two virtually independent fleets in the Pacific and Atlantic. In May 1940, the decision had been made to build up a 'Two-Ocean Navy' which would be superior to any potential aggressor on either side of the continent; and 1,325,000 tons of warship construction was ordered. But in December 1941 none of these new ships were ready, and the US Pacific Fleet was not only slightly smaller than the Japanese, but similarly verging on obsolescence—all nine battleships in Pearl Harbor had been designed or built before the First World War. Thus the Japanese gamble on a quick strike to eliminate the US capital ships in the Pacific was a reasonable one— but its effect could never hope to be permanent. American naval strategy had grasped the value of the aircraft-carrier as well as the Japanese had, and a new class of carrier was under construction. And in fact the US carrier strength in the Pacific in 1941/42, although taxed to its limits, was to claim the credit for halting the run of Japanese victories

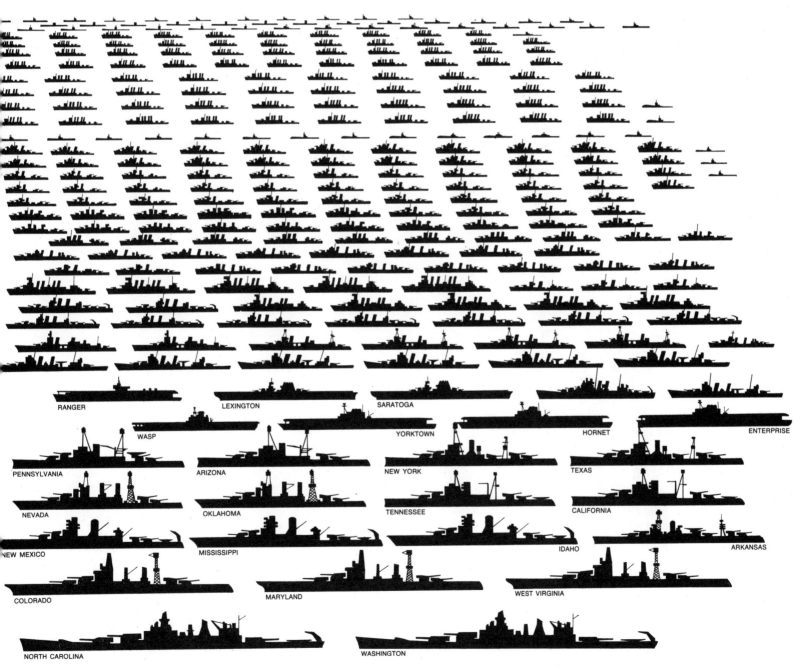

RANGER

LEXINGTON

SARATOGA

WASP

YORKTOWN

HORNET

ENTERPRISE

PENNSYLVANIA

ARIZONA

NEW YORK

TEXAS

NEVADA

OKLAHOMA

TENNESSEE

CALIFORNIA

NEW MEXICO

MISSISSIPPI

IDAHO

ARKANSAS

COLORADO

MARYLAND

WEST VIRGINIA

NORTH CAROLINA

WASHINGTON

Inside the map:

1st ATTACK   2nd ATTACK

PACIFIC OCEAN

50 HIGH-LEVEL BOMBERS
70 TORPEDO-BOMBERS
51 DIVE-BOMBERS
43 FIGHTERS
36 FIGHTERS
80 DIVE-BOMBERS
54 HIGH-LEVEL BOMBERS

O A H U

WHEELER
KANEOHE
Pearl Harbor
EWA
HICKHAM
Honolulu

+ US Airbases

PEARL HARBOR: A BLOW FOR EMPIRE

For years before Pearl Harbor, Japan's military and political leaders had been flexing their Imperial muscles on the mainland of China in an attempt to win territory both along the coast and inland in the productive wastes of Manchuria.

In contemplating an extension of this Imperial war in Asia, those same Japanese leaders had one idea fixed firmly in their minds: that a war involving the United States was quite feasible in the short run, but should that war last more than a year then America's enormous industrial capacity would inevitably become the decisive factor.

Japan's initial war strategy was, as a result, quite simply to direct all her military and naval might southwards against the productive, oil-rich states of South-East Asia — Thailand, Malaya, the Philippines and the Dutch East Indies. Subsequently put into practice and known to historians as the 'Oriental Blitzkrieg', this strategy was intended to rapidly establish a Japanese Empire and a sound industrial base in South-East Asia — an Empire so costly of American lives to eliminate that any negotiated peace settlement would leave it essentially intact.

This strategy was, however, to be dramatically modified before it was ever put into action. Aware that the 'Oriental Blitzkrieg' would, anyhow, bring the United States into the war, Admiral Yamamoto — C-in-C of the Japanese Fleet — reasoned that if war with the USA was inevitable, then it should be provoked to Japan's best advantage.

1st ATTACK BY TORPEDO-BOMBERS

PEARL HARBOR

Pearl City

SOLACE

CURTISS

NEVADA

RALEIGH

ARIZONA   VESTAL

UTAH

Ford
Island

TENNESSEE   WEST VIRGINIA

MARYLAND

CALIFORNIA

OKLAHOMA

HONOLULU   ST LOUIS

OGLALA   HELENA

SHAW

PENNSYLVANIA

CASSIN   DOWNES

The way to do this, he insisted, was to strike a direct blow against America's greatest military asset in the Pacific—her Fleet, whose home base was Pearl Harbor.

As a result—and after Yamamoto's ideas had only weeks before overcome the opposition of the Japanese army and navy Establishment—the morning of November 26th, 1941, saw six Fleet carriers, two battleships, three cruisers and numerous other warships and supply ships of Admiral

L to R: *West Virginia, Tennessee* and *Arizona* after the attack

US Navy

Pearl Harbor—December 7, 1941. *Above:* **Rescue of survivors from blazing** *West Virginia. Inset opposite:* **Japanese attack paths.** *Inset above:* **Disposition of the American Fleet at anchor**

Nagumo's Fast Carrier Strike Force slip anchor from their staging-post off the Kurile Islands to the north of Japan and, observing strict radio silence, head off 3,000 miles east across the Pacific. Their destination was to be the launch-point for a massive air-strike planned to deal 'a devastating blow against the sea power of the nation standing between Japan and the glorious destiny mapped out by her leaders.'

Meanwhile, despite their knowledge of Japanese diplomatic codes, their monitoring of naval radio communications and the certainty that Japan was, indeed, about to open hostilities against the USA, no one on the American side had any idea of the movement of the Fast Carrier Strike Force . . . nor, on that sunny, early morning of December 7th, 1941, had any particular alert been ordered to protect the warships riding placidly at their Hawaiian moorings around Ford Island, Pearl Harbor.

. . . Pearl Harbor was under air attack.

Since 0615 hours the first wave of Japanese aircraft had been winging their way southwards led by Commander Mitsuo Fuchida, the air group commander, in the leading high-level bomber. A pair of trainee radar operators at the mobile station at Opana, practising with the equipment beyond the normal closing-down hour of 0700 hours, saw them appear on the screen at a range of 137 miles and plotted their approach just as a matter of interest: they were told by the information centre, to which they reported, that the contact could be disregarded as it was probably a flight of Fortresses due to arrive that morning from the mainland.

Fuchida led his swarm of aircraft down the western coast of Oahu, watched with idle curiosity by the many service and civilian families living along the shore, who took them for the air groups returning from the *Lexington* and *Enterprise*. By 0750 hours Fuchida could see across the central plain of the island to Pearl Harbor, its waters glinting in the early sunshine of a peaceful Sunday morning, and through binoculars he was able to count the seven capital ships moored two by two in 'Battleship Row' on the eastern side of Ford Island.

Surprise was complete: he gave the order to attack.

From endlessly repeated practice and meticulous study of maps and models of Oahu and Pearl Harbor, every Japanese pilot knew exactly what he had to do. While the squadrons of dive-bombers split up into sections which were to swoop simultaneously on the several army, navy, and marine airfields, the high-level bombers settled on to their pre-arranged approach course, bomb aimers adjusting their sights, and the torpedo-bombers began the long downward slant to their torpedo launching positions abreast the battleships. A few minutes before 0800 hours, to the scream of vertically plummeting planes, bombs began to burst among the aircraft drawn up, wing-tip to wing-tip in parade-ground perfection on the various airfields. Simultaneously the duty watch aboard the ships in 'Battleship Row', preparing for the eight o'clock ceremony of hoisting the colours, saw the torpedo-bombers dip low to launch their tor-

Sunk at Pearl Harbor, the USS **California. Length:** 624 feet. *Beam:* 97·5 feet. **Draught:** 32 feet. **Displacement:** 32,600 tons. **Speed:** 21·5 knots. **Armour:** *Belt:* 14 inches; *Conning tower:* 16 inches; **Armament:** 1 x 14-inch and 12 x 5-inch guns. **Launched:** 1921

Ford Island and 'Battleship Row' under Japanese attack. Note Japanese aircraft and explosions on far side of Ford Island

US Navy

pedoes and watched, horror-stricken, the thin pencil line of the tracks heading for their helpless, immobile hulls. Not an American gun had yet opened fire. Not an American fighter plane had taken off.

Moored together in the harbour, five of the battleships—*West Virginia, Arizona, Nevada, Oklahoma,* and *California*—were rent open by torpedo hits in the first few minutes; only the *Maryland* and *Tennessee,* occupying inside berths, and the flagship *Pennsylvania* which was in dry dock, escaped torpedo damage. Other ships torpedoed were the old target battleship *Utah,* and the light cruisers *Raleigh* and *Helena.*

Nevertheless, although to the shudder and shock of underwater explosions was soon added the rising whine of dive-bombers and the shriek and shattering detonation of bombs from them and from the high-flying bombers, the American crews, for the most

part, went into action with speed and efficiency, shooting down several of their attackers. Damage-control parties worked manfully to minimise the consequences of flooded compartments, counter-flooding to keep the foundering ships on an even keel, restoring electric and water power and communications, fighting the fires.

Meanwhile, however, high up above the smoke and confusion, hardly able at first to credit the total absence of any fighter opposition, and little inconvenienced by the sparse gunfire directed at them, Fuchida's high-level bombers were calmly selecting their targets and aiming with cool precision. An armour-piercing bomb sliced through the five inches of armour of a turret in the *Tennessee* to burst inside it; another plunged down through the several decks to explode in the forward magazine of the *Arizona,* which blew up. Both the *Maryland* and the *California* were hit with devastating effect.

When a lull occurred at 0825 hours, as the first wave of Japanese aircraft retired, almost every US aircraft at the air bases was damaged or destroyed, the *West Virginia* was sinking and on fire, the *Arizona* had settled on the bottom with more than a

thousand of her crew fatally trapped below. The *Oklahoma* had capsized and settled on the bottom with her keel above water; the *Tennessee,* with a turret destroyed by an armour-piercing bomb, was badly on fire; and the *California* had received damage that was eventually to sink her, in spite of all efforts of her crew. Elsewhere, all that was visible of the *Utah* was her upturned keel. The *Raleigh,* deep in the water from flooding and counter-flooding, was being kept upright only by her mooring wires.

While all this had been taking place, at least one Japanese midget submarine succeeded in penetrating the harbour, passing through the gate in the boom defences which had been carelessly left open after the entry of two minesweepers at 0458 hours. During a lull in the air attacks this submarine was sighted just as it was firing a torpedo at the seaplane tender *Curtiss.* The torpedo missed and exploded harmlessly against the shore, as did a second one. The submarine was attacked by the destroyer *Monaghan* and sunk by depth charges. Of the other three midgets launched from their parent submarines, two were lost without trace; the third, after running on a reef and being fired at by the destroyer *Helm,* was finally beached and her crew taken prisoner. The parent submarines and the 11 other large boats of the Advanced Expeditionary Force achieved nothing.

The second wave of Japanese aircraft—54 bombers, 80 dive-bombers, and 36 fighters, led by Lieutenant Commander Shimazaki of the aircraft-carrier *Zuikaku*—had taken off an hour after the first wave. They were met by a more effective defence and thus achieved much less. In the breathing space between the two attacks, ammunition supply for the US anti-aircraft guns had been replenished, gun crews reorganised, and reinforced; and a number of the Japanese dive-bombers were shot down. Nevertheless, they succeeded in damaging the *Pennsylvania,* wrecking two destroyers which were sharing the dry-dock with her, blowing up another destroyer in the floating dock, and forcing the *Nevada*—feeling her way towards the harbour entrance through the billowing clouds of black smoke from burning ships—to beach herself. Meanwhile the high-level bombers were able to make undisturbed practice and wreak further damage on the

already shattered and burning US ships.

At 1000 hours it was suddenly all over. The rumble of retreating aircraft engines died away leaving a strange silence except for the crackle of burning ships, the hissing of water hoses and the desperate shouts of men fighting the fires. For the loss of only nine fighters, 15 dive-bombers, and five torpedo-bombers out of the 384 planes engaged, the Japanese navy had succeeded in putting out of action the entire battleship force of the US Pacific Fleet.

To the anxious Nagumo the success seemed so miraculously complete, and the price paid so small, that when Fuchida and other air squadron commanders urged him to mount a second attack, he felt it would be tempting fate to comply. Against their advice, he gave orders for his force to steer away to the north-west to rendezvous with his replenishment aircraft-carriers, and thence set a course for Japan.

This was a bad mistake—but Nagumo, who was no airman, was not alone at that time in a lack of appreciation of the fact that the massive gun armaments of majestic battleships were no longer the most effective means of exercising sea power. In the vast spaces of the Pacific, only the aircraft-carrier had the long arms with which to feel for and strike at an enemy fleet—and a rich reward would have awaited a second sortie by his exultant airmen. Not only was the *Enterprise* approaching Pearl Harbor from her mission to Wake, and could hardly have survived a massed aerial attack, but the repair facilities of Pearl Harbor and the huge oil-tank farm, its tanks brimming with fuel, still lay intact and now virtually defenceless. Without them the naval base would have been useless for many months to come, forcing what remained of the US Pacific Fleet to retire to its nearest base on the American west coast, out of range of the coming area of operations in the Pacific.

Thus Yamamoto's daring and well-planned attack failed to reap the fullest possible harvest—though undoubtedly the blow it delivered to the United States navy was heavy indeed. But it had one effect even more decisive than that on sea power, for it brought the American people, united, into the war.

Perhaps only such a shock as that delivered at Pearl Harbor could have achieved such a result.

THE BATTLE OF

Above and below: Near misses burst alongside the *Shokaku* as it frantically zig-zags to avoid US bombs. **Above, centre and right:** The loss of the *Lexington*. Listing and on fire from leaking fuel, the carrier is abandoned by its crew after several violent explosions. **Below, centre and right:** The *Lexington*'s crew is picked up

The outstanding success of the 'Oriental Blitzkrieg' in the first months of the Pacific War left Japan in a commanding strategic position. With the conquest of Burma, Malaya, the Dutch East Indies and the Philippines, the defensible perimeter in the Pacific and Southern Asia that her initial war plans called for had been achieved.

By the early spring of 1942, then, Japan's military planners were faced with choosing between the various conflicting possibilities open to them in their conduct of the second phase of the Pacific War.

First, there was the proposal from the Army for an offensive against the powerful Allied base of Port Moresby in Papua, continuing through the Solomons, New Hebrides, New Caledonia, Fiji and Samoa—an offensive that would effectively isolate Australia and put her out of the war.

Second, the Naval General Staff advocated either an advance against India and Ceylon or a direct thrust at Australia.

Third, Admiral Yamamoto—forever aware of the economic might of the United States and the counter-offensive capacity of her carriers still loose within the Pacific defence perimeter

—urged a thrust against Midway and the Aleutian Islands to precipitate a decisive battle with what remained of the US Pacific Fleet.

As a result—in a fatal combination of all but the Indian option — the occupation of Port Moresby was scheduled for the beginning of May, to be followed early in June by operations against Midway and the Western Aleutians. The Port Moresby operation—which would not only leave Australia isolated, but also put the Japanese in control of the Coral Sea area—was planned along simple premises, but its detailed operation involved a tactical complexity and separation of forces that was to prove disastrous.

In overall command of the Japanese force heading for the Coral Sea at the end of April, 1942, was Vice-Admiral Inouye. Under him the main elements of the Japanese force of three carriers, 180 aircraft and six cruisers were split into the Port Moresby Invasion Group, a Covering Group commanded by Rear-Admiral Goto and including the light carrier *Shoho*, and a Striking Force under Vice-Admiral Takagi including Rear-Admiral Hara's carriers *Shokaku* and *Zuikahu* of the

THE CORAL SEA

The small map shows the Japanese strategy behind their outflanking move against New Guinea. Operations hinged on the vital bastion of Port Moresby; and Admiral Nimitz knew that the Japanese were planning yet another amphibious operation. The Japanese invasion-group, with the carrier *Shoho* and a cruiser force, was to head straight for Moresby around the tail of New Guinea. The carrier striking-force was to cruise into the Coral Sea past the Solomon Islands and ward off any US carrier opposition. The US Navy countermoves *(large map, overleaf)* resulted in the first of the war's great carrier actions—one which lasted three days. In terms of enemy ships destroyed, the Japanese had the higher score; but they were forced to content themselves with occupying Tulagi and Florida islands in the Solomons. Their attempt to seize Port Moresby had been a definite failure—their first major setback of the war, and a major portent of what was to follow at Midway.

V Carrier Division charged with the task of repelling any US forces that might attempt to interfere.

But interference was just the thing that Admiral Chester W. Nimitz, C-in-C US Pacific Fleet, and General MacArthur, C-in-C SW Pacific Area, had in mind. Unlike the Japanese, who had divided their ships assigned to the operation into six separate forces, Admiral Nimitz boldly concentrated every ship available to meet the Japanese in the Coral Sea, where —because the Americans had cracked the Japanese naval code—he knew he could expect an attack on Port Moresby on or after May 3.

Nimitz's force of two carriers, 121 aircraft and seven cruisers comprised the *Yorktown* task force under the command of Rear-Admiral Fletcher, the *Lexington* task force commanded by Rear-Admiral Fitch, and a force under Rear-Admiral Grace (RN) comprising the Australian heavy cruisers *Australia* and *Hobart* and the American heavy cruiser *Chicago* and destroyer *Perkins*. Called Task Force 17, the fleet was under overall command of Rear-Admiral Fletcher.

By May 3, 1942, the Allied force had assembled in the Coral Sea area. There, on hearing reports of Japanese landings at Tulagi in the Lower Solomons, Fletcher took the *Yorktown* force north to launch an attack on the 4th. Dauntlesses and Devastators from the carrier took off at 0630 hours and, in a brief action later known as the 'Battle' of Tulagi, despatched an enemy destroyer, three minesweepers and various smaller craft for the loss of three planes.

The following two days, though, were anti-climactic for the Americans who had already tasted blood. Instead of the long-awaited combat, the days were spent refuelling and jockeying for position as reports came in of the movement of the enemy forces into the Coral Sea area, suitably advertised by a bombing attack on Port Moresby on the 5th.

On the evening of the 6th, as news reached the Japanese force of the surrender of the last Allied resistance on Corregidor in the Philippines the Port Moresby Invasion Group was beginning the run up to its objective, covered on its left flank by Rear-Admiral Goto on board the carrier *Shoho*. Further out to sea, Vice-Admiral Takagi's Strike Force was cruising, preparing to move in and support the Invasion Group.

The next day the battle began in earnest. Accepting Hara's recommendation that a thorough search to the south should be made before he moved to provide cover for the Port Moresby Invasion Group, Takagi accordingly launched reconnaissance aircraft at 0600 hours. As Hara later admitted: 'It did not prove to be a fortunate decision.' At 0736 one of the aircraft reported sighting an aircraft-carrier and a cruiser at the eastern edge of the search sector, and Hara, accepting this evaluation, closed distance and ordered an all-out bombing and torpedo attack. In fact, the vessels which had been sighted were the luckless *Neosho* and *Sims*.

After a single Japanese aircraft had attacked at 0900 hours, 15 high-level bombers appeared half an hour later, but failed to hit their targets. At 1038 the *Sims,* by swinging hard to starboard, avoided nine bombs dropped simultaneously by ten aircraft attacking horizontally. However, about noon, a further attack by 36 dive-bombers sealed the fate of the destroyer. Three 500-pound bombs hit the *Sims*, of which two exploded in her engine room. The ship buckled and sank stern first within a few minutes, with the loss of 379 lives.

Meanwhile, 20 dive-bombers had turned their attention to *Neosho*, scoring seven direct hits and causing blazing gasoline to flow along her decks. Although some hands took the order to 'make preparations to abandon ship and stand by' as a signal to jump over the side, the *Neosho* was in fact to drift in a westerly direction until May 11, when 123 men were taken off by the destroyer *Henley* and the oiler was scuttled. But the sacrifice of these two ships was not

in vain, for if Hara's planes had not been drawn off in this way, the Japanese might have found and attacked Fletcher on the 7th, while he was busy dealing with the *Shoho*.

Fortune indeed smiled on Fletcher that day. At 0645, when a little over 120 miles south of Rossel Island, he ordered Crace's support group to push ahead on a north-westerly course to attack the Port Moresby Invasion Group, while the rest of Task Force 17 turned north. Apparently Fletcher, who expected an air duel with Takagi's aircraft-carriers, wished to prevent the invasion regardless of his own fate but, by detaching Crace, was in fact weakening his own anti-aircraft screen while depriving part of his force of the protection of carrier air cover.

The consequences of this move might have been fatal but, instead, the Japanese were to make another vital error by concentrating their land-based air groups on Crace rather than Fletcher's aircraft-carriers. A Japanese seaplane spotted the support group at 0810, and at 1358, when the ships of Crace's force were south and a little west of Jomard Passage, 11 single-engined bombers launched an unsuccessful attack. Soon afterwards, 12 Sallys (land-based naval bombers) came in low, dropping eight torpedoes. These were

avoided by violent manoeuvres, and five of the bombers were shot down. Then 19 high-flying bombers attacked from 15,000 to 20,000 feet, the ships dodging the bombs as they had the torpedoes.

Before the day was out, Crace had survived another attack, this time from American B-26s which mistook his vessels for Japanese. By midnight he had reached a point 120 miles south of the New Guinea tail, later turning back south on hearing that the Port Moresby Invasion Group had retired.

While Takagi's aircraft were dealing with *Neosho* and *Sims*, the *Shoho*, of Goto's Covering Group, had turned south-east into the wind to launch four reconnaissance aircraft and to send up other aircraft to protect the invasion force 30 miles to the south-west. By 0830 Goto knew exactly where Fletcher was, and ordered *Shoho* to prepare for an attack. Other aircraft had meanwhile spotted Crace's ships to the west. The result of these reports was to make Inouye anxious for the security of the Invasion Group, and at 0900 he ordered it to turn away instead of entering Jomard Passage, thus keeping it out of harm's way until Fletcher and Crace had been dealt with. In fact, this was the nearest the transports got to their goal.

Fletcher had launched a search mission early on the 7th, and at 0815 one of *York-town's* reconnaissance aircraft reported 'two carriers and four heavy cruisers' about 225 miles to the north-west, on the other side of the Louisiades. Assuming that this was Takagi's Striking Force, Fletcher launched a total of 93 aircraft between 0926 and 1030, leaving 47 for combat patrol. By this time Task Force 17 had re-entered the cold front,

Douglas TBD-1 Devastator. The backbone of the US Navy's carrier torpedo forces at the outbreak of the Pacific War, the Devastator was already obsolete. With its light armament and slow approach speed, it was easy prey for Japanese Zeros. **Max speed:** 225 mph. **Max range:** 985 miles. **Armament:** 1×·3-inch and 1×·5-inch machine-guns plus 1×1000-lb bomb or 1×21-inch torpedo

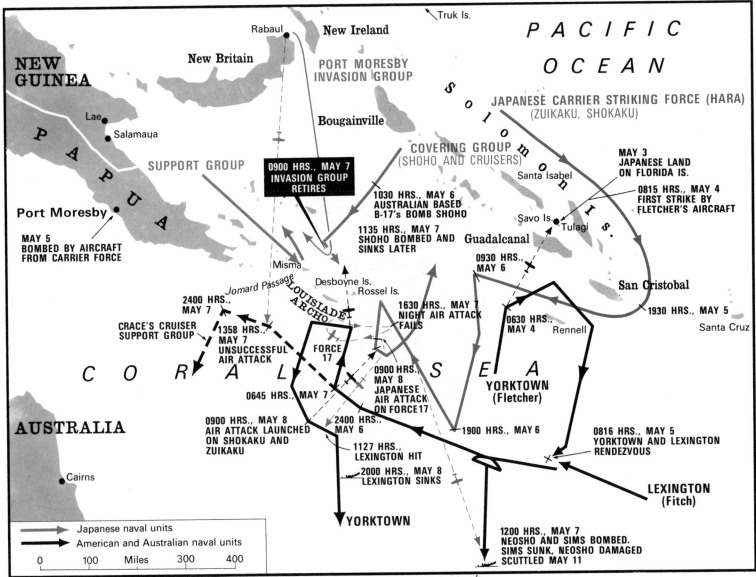

Coral Sea: the progress of the battle

Map labels:

- Truk Is.
- PACIFIC OCEAN
- New Ireland
- Rabaul
- New Britain
- PORT MORESBY INVASION GROUP
- NEW GUINEA
- Lae
- Salamaua
- PAPUA
- SUPPORT GROUP
- Bougainville
- JAPANESE CARRIER STRIKING FORCE (HARA) (ZUIKAKU, SHOKAKU)
- COVERING GROUP (SHOHO AND CRUISERS)
- Santa Isabel
- 0900 HRS., MAY 7 INVASION GROUP RETIRES
- MAY 3 JAPANESE LAND ON FLORIDA IS.
- 0815 HRS., MAY 4 FIRST STRIKE BY FLETCHER'S AIRCRAFT
- Port Moresby
- 1030 HRS., MAY 6 AUSTRALIAN BASED B-17's BOMB SHOHO
- Savo Is.
- Tulagi
- MAY 5 BOMBED BY AIRCRAFT FROM CARRIER FORCE
- 1135 HRS., MAY 7 SHOHO BOMBED AND SINKS LATER
- Guadalcanal
- 0930 HRS., MAY 6
- San Cristobal
- Misma
- Jomard Passage
- Desboyne Is.
- Rossel Is.
- 1630 HRS., MAY 7 NIGHT AIR ATTACK FAILS
- 0630 HRS., MAY 4
- Rennell
- 1930 HRS., MAY 5
- Santa Cruz
- 2400 HRS., MAY 7
- LOUISIADE ARCHO.
- CRACE'S CRUISER SUPPORT GROUP
- 1358 HRS., MAY 7 UNSUCCESSFUL AIR ATTACK
- FORCE 17
- CORAL
- SEA
- YORKTOWN (Fletcher)
- 0645 HRS., MAY 7
- 0900 HRS., MAY 8 JAPANESE AIR ATTACK ON FORCE 17
- 1900 HRS., MAY 6
- 0816 HRS., MAY 5 YORKTOWN AND LEXINGTON RENDEZVOUS
- AUSTRALIA
- 0900 HRS., MAY 8 AIR ATTACK LAUNCHED ON SHOKAKU AND ZUIKAKU
- 2400 HRS., MAY 6
- 1127 HRS., LEXINGTON HIT
- LEXINGTON (Fitch)
- Cairns
- 2000 HRS., MAY 8 LEXINGTON SINKS
- YORKTOWN
- 1200 HRS., MAY 7 NEOSHO AND SIMS BOMBED. SIMS SUNK, NEOSHO DAMAGED SCUTTLED MAY 11

Legend:
- Japanese naval units
- American and Australian naval units
- 0 100 Miles 300 400

while Goto's force lay in bright sunlight near the reported position of the 'two carriers'. However, no sooner had *Yorktown*'s attack group become airborne than her scouts returned, and it immediately became obvious that the 'two carriers and four heavy cruisers' should have read 'two heavy cruisers and two destroyers'—the error being due to the improper arrangement of the pilot's coding pad. Actually the vessels seen were two light cruisers and two gunboats of Marushige's Support Group. Fletcher, now knowing that he had sent a major strike against a minor target, courageously allowed the strike to proceed, thinking that with the invasion force nearby there must be some profitable targets in the vicinity.

The attack group from *Lexington*, well ahead of the *Yorktown* aircraft, was nearing Misima Island in the Louisiades shortly after 1100, when Lieutenant-Commander Hamilton, leading one of *Lexington*'s Dauntless squadrons, spotted an aircraft-carrier, two or three cruisers, and some destroyers, about 25 miles to the starboard. This was the *Shoho* with the rest of Goto's Covering

Group. As the *Shoho* was only 35 miles south-east of the original target location, it was a simple matter to re-direct the attack groups over the carrier. The first attack, led by Commander W. B. Ault, succeeded only in blowing five aircraft over the *Shoho*'s side, but he was closely followed by Hamilton's ten Dauntlesses at 1110, the *Lexington*'s torpedo squadron at 1117, and the *Yorktown*'s attack group at 1125. Under

such a concentrated attack, the *Shoho* stood little chance: soon she was on fire and dead in the water—and, smothered by 13 bomb and seven torpedo hits, she sank soon after 1135.

Only six American aircraft were lost in the attack off Misima. Back on the American aircraft-carriers, listeners in the radio rooms heard the jubilant report from Lieutenant-Commander Dixon, leading *Lexington*'s other Dauntless squadron: 'Scratch one flat-top! Dixon to carrier, scratch one flat-top!'

With the air groups safely landed again, Fletcher decided to call off any further strikes

against Goto, as he now knew, from intercepted radio messages, that his own position was known to Takagi—although he had not yet located the other Japanese aircraft-carriers himself. The worsening weather dissuaded him from further searches, and he thus set a westerly course during the night of May 7/8, thinking that the Japanese invasion force would come through the Jomard Passage the next morning. He did not yet know of Inouye's timid decision to recall the transports.

May 7 had been a day of serious blunders from the Japanese viewpoint, but Takagi and Hara were determined to try once more to destroy the American aircraft-carriers before the next day. Selecting the 27 pilots best qualified in night operations, Hara launched a strike from the *Shokaku* and *Zuikaku* just before 1630, with orders to attack Fletcher. Although the Japanese aircraft passed close to Task Force 17, they failed to locate owing

Below: A Japanese reconnaissance seaplane casts off from its parent warship

to the foul weather and poor visibility. The American combat air-patrol, vectored out by radar to intercept, shot down nine of Hara's precious aircraft. An hour later, some of the returning Japanese laid a course for home right over the American carriers, which they mistook for their own. At 1900 three Japanese aircraft were spotted on *Yorktown*'s starboard beam, blinking in Morse code on Aldis lamps. Though recognised, they managed to escape. Twenty minutes later, three more attempted to join the *Yorktown*'s landing circle, and one was shot down. Hara was to lose 11 more aircraft which 'splashed' when attempting night landings on his aircraft-carriers. Only six of the original 27 got back safely.

With the day's operations virtually at an end, the commanders on both sides now toyed with the idea of a surface night action. At 1930 the *Lexington*'s radar showed what appeared to be a Japanese landing circle 30 miles to the east, but Fletcher did not receive the report until 2200, by which time he knew it might be impossible to locate Takagi's new position (at that moment the Japanese carriers were actually 95 miles to the east of Task Force 17). Fletcher rejected the idea of detaching a cruiser/destroyer force for a night attack, as the last-quarter moon would not afford much light, and he urgently needed all the anti-aircraft protection he could get for the next day's operations. In his

own words: 'The best plan seemed to be to keep our force concentrated and prepare for a battle with enemy carriers next morning.'

Inouye, meanwhile, had ordered Goto's cruisers to rendezvous east of Rossel Island and make an attack on the Allied force, though he did not specify whether the target was to be Fletcher or Crace. By midnight he had reconsidered the plan, ordered the invasion to be postponed for two days, and split Got's cruisers up between the invasion transports and Takagi's force. Takagi, too, on receiving his pilot's reports that the American carriers were 50-60 miles away, considered a night action, but his air crews were tired — and he was in any case forestalled by a call for protection from the transports, which it was his basic mission to protect, and which had now lost the cover of the *Shoho*. Thus the main action was delayed yet again, although both sides expected a decision on the 8th. Everything now depended on locating the enemy as early as possible in the morning.

In the event, reconnaissance aircraft of both sides, launched a little before dawn, located the opposing aircraft-carrier force almost simultaneously, between 0815 and 0838. Fitch, now in tactical command of the American aircraft-carrier operations, had 121 aircraft available, while Hara, his opposite number, had 122. The Japanese had more combat experience and better torpedoes, while the Americans were stronger in bomber aircraft. Thus the two sides began the first ever 'carrier-versus-carrier' battle roughly on equal terms, although by moving south during the night, Fletcher had run out of the bad weather and lay under clear skies, while the Japanese remained under the shelter of clouds and squalls.

The first sighting of the Japanese carriers had been at 0815, by one of *Lexington*'s scouts, the pilot reporting that Takagi was 175 miles to the north-east of Fletcher's position. Later, at 0930, Lieutenant-Commander Dixon sighted the Japanese Striking Force steaming due south in a position 25 miles north-east of the original contact, but about 45 miles north of Takagi's expected position at 0900 as predicted on the strength of that contact.

The discrepancy was to cause trouble for *Lexington*'s attack group, which by this time was airborne. Fitch had begun launching his strike between 0900 and 0925, the *Yorktown* group of 24 bombers with two fighters, and nine torpedo-bombers with four fighters, departing ten minutes before the *Lexington* aircraft. The dive-bombers spotted the Japanese first, at 1030, and took cloud cover to await the arrival of the Devastators. While *Shokaku* was engaged in launching further combat patrols, *Zuikaku* disappeared into a rain squall. The attack, which began at 1057, thus fell only on the *Shokaku*. Although the *Yorktown*'s pilots co-ordinated their attack well, only moderate success was achieved. The slow American torpedoes were either avoided or failed to explode, and only two bomb hits were scored on the *Shokaku*, one damaging the flight-deck well forward on the starboard bow and setting fire to fuel, while the other destroyed a repair compartment aft. The *Shokaku*, now burning, could still recover aircraft, but could no longer launch any.

Of the *Lexington* group, ten minutes behind, the 22 dive-bombers failed to locate the target, leaving only 11 Devastators and four reconnaissance-bombers for the attack. Once again the torpedoes were ineffective, but the bombers scored a third hit on the Japanese aircraft-carrier. Although 108 of the vessel's crew had been killed, she had not been holed below the waterline, and her fires were soon brought under control. Most of her aircraft were transferred to the *Zuikaku* before Takagi detached *Shokaku* at 1300, with orders to proceed to Truk. Although in poor shape, she was not 'settling fast', as the American pilots had reported.

Captain Sherman, in the *Lexington*, had

Aichi D3A2 'Val'. This rugged carrier-borne dive-bomber sank more Allied fighting ships than any other Axis aircraft type. **Max speed:** 267 mph at 9845 feet. **Max range:** 840 miles. **Armament:** 3×7·7-mm machine-guns, 1×550-lb bomb plus 2×132-lb bombs

Doolittle's Raid on Tokyo—great dividends from a small investment

Some of Col Doolittle's B-25 bombers on the *Hornet*'s flight-deck before the attack on Tokyo. ▽ A B-25 takes off: flying off these big bombers from a carrier was a considerable feat. **Inset:** Doolittle (front row, third from right) in China with his crew after the raid

estimated that the Japanese attack on Task Force 17 would begin at about 1100, basing his deduction on Japanese radio traffic. In fact, the *Yorktown* and *Lexington* were to come under attack in the interval between the strikes of their respective air groups on the Japanese aircraft-carriers. The Japanese had begun launching at about the same time as the Americans, but their attack group of 18 torpedo-bombers, 33 bombers, and 18 fighters was larger, better balanced, and more accurately directed to the target. Although the American radar picked them up 70 miles away, Fitch had far too few fighters to intercept successfully, and was forced to rely mainly on his AA gunners for protection.

At 1118 hours the battle 'busted out', as one American sailor described it. The *Yorktown*, with a smaller turning circle than the *Lexington*, successfully avoided eight torpedoes launched on her port quarter. Five minutes later she came under dive-bomber attack but, skilfully handled by Captain Buckmaster, escaped unscathed until 1127, when she received her only hit—from an 800-pound bomb which penetrated to the fourth deck, but did not impair flight operations. During this time, the evasive manoeuvres gradually drew the American aircraft-carriers apart and, although the screening vessels divided fairly evenly between them, the breaking of their defensive circle contributed to Japanese success.

Above: **A Japanese photograph of the Coral Sea action, showing the heavy cruisers of Fletcher's force taking action to evade a Japanese air attack**

The *Lexington*, larger than the *Yorktown*, had a turning circle of 1,500 to 2,000 yards in diameter, compared with the 1,000-yard tactical diameter of her consort. Moreover, she had the misfortune to suffer an 'anvil' attack from the Japanese torpedo-bombers, which came in on both bows at 1118 to launch their missiles at altitudes of about 50 to 200 feet, and about half a mile from the 'Lady Lex'. Despite valiant manoeuvres by Sherman, she received one torpedo hit on the port side forward at 1120, quickly followed by a second opposite the bridge. At the same time a dive-bombing attack commenced from 17,000 feet, the *Lexington* receiving two hits from small bombs. One exploded in a ready-ammunition box on the port side, while the other hit the smokestack structure. To add to the din of battle, the ship's siren jammed as a result of an explosion and shrieked weirdly throughout most of the attack.

Some 19 minutes later, the aircraft-carrier battle was, to all intents and purposes, at an end. At this point, honours were more or less equal – but for the Americans the real tragedy was still to come. At first it appeared that the doughty *Lexington* had survived to fight another day. A list of 7 degrees caused by the torpedo hits was corrected by shifting oil ballast, while her engines remained unharmed. To her returning pilots she did not appear to be seriously damaged, and the recovery of the air group went ahead. At about 1240 hours, Commander H. R. 'Pop' Healy, the damage control officer, reported to Captain Sherman: 'We've got the torpedo damage temporarily shored up, the fires out, and soon will have the ship back on an even keel. But I would suggest, sir, that if you have to take any more torpedoes, you take 'em on the starboard side.'

Minutes later, at 1247, a tremendous internal explosion, caused by the ignition of fuel vapours by a motor generator which had been left running, shook the whole ship. Although the *Lexington* continued landing her planes, a series of further violent explosions seriously disrupted internal communications. Yet another major detonation occurred at 1445, and the fires soon passed beyond control. Despite the fact that the

destroyer *Morris* came alongside to help fight the blaze, while *Yorktown* recovered all aircraft still airborne, the need for evacuation became increasingly apparent.

At 1630 hours the *Lexington* had come to a dead stop, and all hands prepared to abandon ship. At 1710 Fitch called to Sherman to 'get the men off', the *Minneapolis*, *Hammann*, *Morris*, and *Anderson* assisting with the rescue operations. Evacuation was orderly – even the ship's dog being rescued – and Sherman was the last to leave the aircraft-carrier, sliding down a line over the stern. At 1956 the destroyer *Phelps* was ordered to deliver the 'coup de grace' with five torpedoes, and the *Lexington* sank at 2000, a final explosion occurring as she slipped beneath the waves.

The Battle of the Coral Sea was now over. The Japanese pilots had reported sinking both American aircraft-carriers, and Hara's acceptance of this evaluation influenced Takagi's decision to detach the *Shokaku* for repairs, as well as Inouye's order that the Striking Force should be withdrawn. Even though he thought that both American aircraft-carriers had been destroyed, the cautious Inouye still deemed it necessary to postpone the invasion, apparently because he felt unable to protect the landing units against Allied land-based aircraft. Yamamoto did not agree with this decision and, at 2400 hours, countermanded the order, detailing Takagi to locate and annihilate the remaining American ships. But, by the time Takagi made his search to the south and east, Fletcher had gone.

Tactically, the battle had been a victory for the Japanese. Although they had lost 43 aircraft on May 8 (as against 33 lost by the Americans), and Hara had been left with only nine operational aircraft after the *Zuikaku* had proved unable to take on all *Shokaku*'s aircraft, their air strikes had achieved greater results. The sinking of the *Lexington*, *Neosho*, and *Sims* far outweighed the loss of the *Shoho*.

Strategically, however, Coral Sea was an American victory: the whole object of the Japanese operation – the capture of Port Moresby – had been thwarted. Despite the

occupation of Tulagi, later won back by the US Marines at a heavy price, the Japanese had gained very little of their initial objectives. Moreover, the damage to the *Shokaku*, and the need to re-form the battered air groups of the *Zuikaku*, was to keep both these carriers out of the Midway battle, where they might have been decisive.

Though the Coral Sea engagement was full of errors by the commanders on both sides, the Americans did take its lessons to heart. The ratio of fighters to bombers and torpedo-bombers was increased, and improvements were made in the organisation of attacks in the weeks that remained before the next great naval clash. But the really significant feature of the Coral Sea battle was that it opened a new chapter in the annals of naval warfare: it was the first ever 'carrier-against-carrier' action in which all losses were inflicted by air action, and no ship on either side made visual surface contact with the enemy.

The stage for Midway was now set.

1942 May 1: Task Force 17 is formed under Rear-Admiral Fletcher to operate in the Coral Sea. *Japanese take Mandalay.*
May 2: Fletcher *(Yorktown)* leaves Rear-Admiral Fitch *(Lexington)* refuelling, and heads west to search for the Japanese.
May 3: 1100 hours: Following the successful Japanese attack on Tulagi, Rear-Admiral Goto *(Shoho)* moves to cover the Port Moresby Invasion Force.
1900 hours: Fletcher receives news of Tulagi landings and moves north. *Neosho, Russell* detached to rendezvous with Fitch.
May 4: Following an air-strike against Tulagi, Fletcher returns south.
May 5: Fletcher rejoins Fitch, and spends the day refuelling. The Japanese Striking Force under Vice-Admiral Takagi *(Shokaku and Zuikaku)* enters Coral Sea.
May 6: Fletcher re-forms his forces and sends *Neosho* and *Sims* south to the next refuelling rendezvous. *Corregidor surrenders: the whole of the Philippines is now in Japanese hands.*
May 7: 0600 hours: Japanese reconnaissance aircraft discover *Neosho* and *Sims*.
0645 hours: Fletcher detaches Cruiser Support Group under Rear-Admiral Crace (RN) to attack Japanese Port Moresby Invasion Group.
0810 hours: Crace sighted by Japanese aircraft.
0815 hours: American aircraft sight 'two carriers and four heavy cruisers'.
0830 hours: Fletcher sighted by *Shoho*.
0900 hours: Japanese attack *Sims* and *Neosho*. Inouye orders invasion fleet to turn away.
0926-1030 hours: Fletcher launches strike.
1100 hours: *Shoho* sighted.
1135 hours: *Shoho* sunk.
1358 hours: Crace attacked by land-based aircraft.
1630 hours: Hara launches air-strike which fails to locate the Americans.
2400 hours: Invasion of Port Moresby is postponed.
May 8: 0815 hours: American aircraft locate *Shokaku* and *Zuikaku*. Japanese locate *Lexington* and *Saratoga*.
0900-0925 hours: Both sides launch strikes.
1030 hours: *Shokaku* attacked and disabled.
1118 hours: *Yorktown* and *Lexington* attacked.
1120 hours: *Lexington* hit by torpedo, but continues to receive aircraft.
1247 hours: Major explosion on *Lexington*.
1300 hours: Takagi sends *Shokaku* to Truk.
1710 hours: *Lexington* abandoned.
1956 hours: *Lexington* sunk by torpedo.
2400 hours: Yamamoto orders Takagi to locate and destroy American forces, but these have withdrawn out of range.

THE BATTLE OF MIDWAY

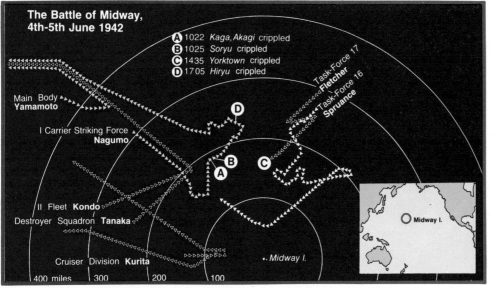

The Battle of Midway,
4th-5th June 1942

- Ⓐ 1022 *Kaga, Akagi* crippled
- Ⓑ 1025 *Soryu* crippled
- Ⓒ 1435 *Yorktown* crippled
- Ⓓ 1705 *Hiryu* crippled

Task-Force 17
Fletcher
Task-Force 16
Spruance

Main Body
Yamamoto

I Carrier Striking Force
Nagumo

II Fleet **Kondo**

Destroyer Squadron **Tanaka**

Cruiser Division **Kurita**

400 miles   300   200   100   •. *Midway I.*

Ⓞ Midway I.

Above: The *Yorktown*, listing and doomed

Above: Midway, the course of the battle. Below: *Yorktown* struck by a torpedo

...TURNING POINT OF WW2

Japan's naval strategists had long prepared for a 'decisive fleet action' with the Americans in the Pacific. At Midway in early June, 1942, they hoped to destroy the surviving vessels of the US Pacific Fleet in just such an encounter.

Admiral Yamamoto, C-in-C of the Japanese Combined Fleet, was rightly convinced that a threat to Midway Island —the westernmost outpost of the Hawaiian island chain— would compel the weaker enemy fleet to challenge overwhelming Japanese forces . . . under whose guns and bombs, he imagined, it could not hope to survive.

At the Battle of the Coral Sea the month before, though, there had been several important indications that should have suggested to Yamamoto that his confidence at the outcome of a fleet action in the Pacific was perhaps misplaced.

Although roughly equal shipping losses had been sustained —the Americans had lost the carrier *Lexington* and 81 aircraft, the Japanese the carrier *Shoho* and 105 aircraft—every advantage had actually fallen with the Americans. Not only had the Japanese attack on Port Moresby been countermand-

ed, but the carriers *Shokaku* and *Zuikaku* had also been withdrawn from service as a result of the action.

Most importantly, though, the US carrier force in the Pacific had lived to fight another day . . . despite all the efforts of a clearly superior enemy force. This had only been made possible because the Japanese tactics of dividing their ships into small, relatively ineffective units operating separately within an overall operational plan had proved indecisive in practice despite their foolproof appearance on paper.

Arrogant and over-confident, unaware of the lessons to be learned from Coral Sea, Japan's naval planners were now about to fall into the same tactical trap once again. The Battle of Midway—when seven Japanese battleships, six carriers, 13 cruisers, 50 destroyers and 325 aircraft lined up against Admiral Nimitz's three carriers, eight cruisers, 14 destroyers and 348 land- and sea-based aircraft—was to prove one of the truly decisive battles of history . . . the turning-point of the Second World War, and the beginning of the end for the ill-starred fortunes of the Rising Sun.

Below: Devastators prepare to leave the *Enterprise*. Only four returned, but the *Yorktown* and *Hornet*'s losses were even heavier

Imperial War Museum

L to R: Spruance, Task Force 17, evaded the trap. Nimitz, who foresaw the enemy moves. Yamamoto, whose plan was too complex. Kondo, of the Support Group. Fletcher, who lost his flagship, *Yorktown*. Nagumo, whose vacillation proved to be fatal

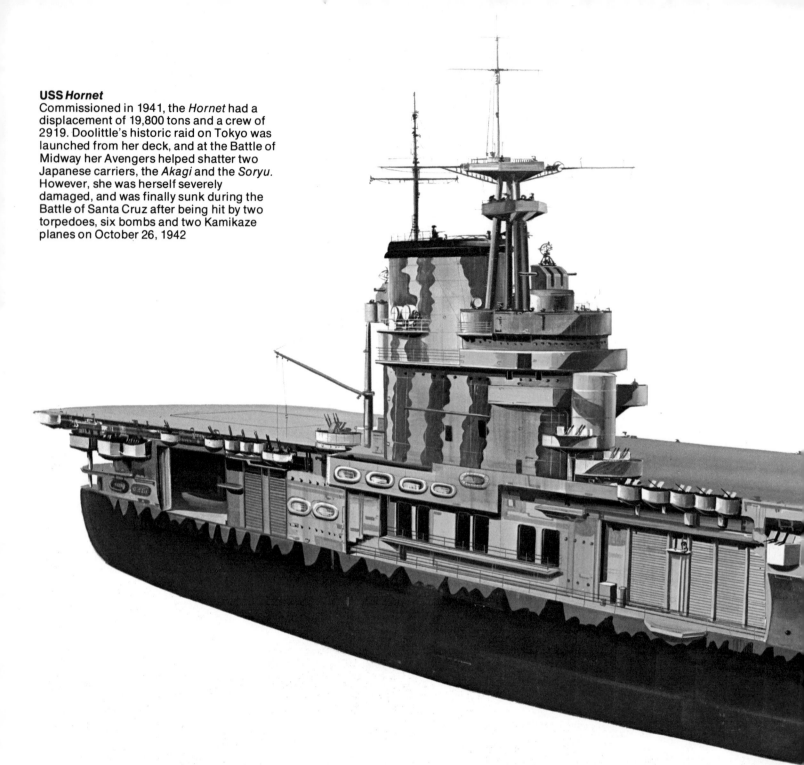

USS _Hornet_
Commissioned in 1941, the _Hornet_ had a displacement of 19,800 tons and a crew of 2919. Doolittle's historic raid on Tokyo was launched from her deck, and at the Battle of Midway her Avengers helped shatter two Japanese carriers, the _Akagi_ and the _Soryu_. However, she was herself severely damaged, and was finally sunk during the Battle of Santa Cruz after being hit by two torpedoes, six bombs and two Kamikaze planes on October 26, 1942

Pearl Harbor was a scene of intense activity during the last week of May 1942: a feeling of great impending events pervaded the atmosphere. On the 26th the aircraft-carriers _Enterprise_ and _Hornet_ of Task Force (TF) 16 had steamed in and moored, to set about in haste the various operations of refuelling and replenishing after a vain race across the Pacific to try to go to the aid of Rear-Admiral Frank Fletcher's Task Force 17 in the Battle of the Coral Sea. On the next day the surviving carriers of TF 17, the _Yorktown_'s blackened sides and twisted decks providing visible signs of the damage sustained in the battle, berthed in the dry dock of the naval base where an army of workmen swarmed aboard to begin repairs.

Under normal circumstances, weeks of work lay ahead of them, but now word had reached the dockyard that emergency repairs in the utmost haste were required. Work was to go on, night and day, without ceasing, until the ship was at least temporarily battle-worthy. For at the headquarters of the C-in-C Pacific, Admiral Chester Nimitz,

it was known from patient analysis and deciphering of enemy signals that the Japanese fleet was moving out to throw down a challenge which, in spite of local American inferiority, had to be accepted.

So on May 28, Task Force 16 sailed again, the _Enterprise_ flying the flag of Rear-Admiral Raymond Spruance, and vanished into the wide wastes of the Pacific. Six cruisers and nine destroyers formed its screen; two replenishment tankers accompanied it. The following day the dockyard gave Nimitz the scarcely credible news that the _Yorktown_ was once again battle-worthy. Early on the 30th she, too, left harbour and, having gathered in her air groups, headed north-westward to rendezvous with Task Force 16 at 'Point Luck', 350 miles north-east of the island of Midway. Forming the remainder of Task Force 17 were two cruisers and five destroyers.

The main objective of the Japanese was the assault and occupation of the little atoll of Midway, 1,100 miles west-north-west of Oahu, and forming the western extremity of

the Hawaiian island chain. Together with the occupation of the Aleutian Islands, the capture of Midway would extend Japan's eastern sea frontier so that sufficient warning might be obtained of any threatened naval air attack on the homeland—Pearl Harbor in reverse. The plan had been given added impetus on April 18 by the raid on Tokyo mounted by Colonel Doolittle's army bombers taking off from the _Hornet_.

Doubts on the wisdom of the Japanese plan had been voiced in various quarters; but Yamamoto, the dynamic C-in-C of the Combined Fleet, had fiercely advocated it for reasons of his own. He had always been certain that only by destroying the American fleet could Japan gain the breathing space required to consolidate her conquests and negotiate satisfactory peace terms—a belief which had inspired the attack on Pearl Harbor. Yamamoto rightly believed that an attack on Midway was a challenge that Nimitz could not ignore. It would bring the US Pacific Fleet out where Yamamoto, in overwhelming strength, would be waiting to bring it at last to a final, decisive action.

The Japanese plan was an intricate one, as their naval strategic plans customarily were, calling for exact timing for a junction at the crucial moment of several disparate forces; and it involved—also typically—the offering of a decoy or diversion to lure the enemy into dividing his force or expending his strength on a minor objective.

Between May 25/27, Northern Force would sail from Ominato, at the northern tip of Honshu, for the attack on the Aleutians. The II Carrier Striking Force, under Rear-Admiral Kakuta—comprising the small aircraft-carriers *Ryujo* and *Junyo*, two cruisers, and three destroyers—would be the first to sail, its task being to deliver a surprise air attack on Dutch Harbor on June 3. This, it was expected, might induce Nimitz to send at least part of his fleet racing north, in which case it would find waiting to intercept it a Guard Force, of four battleships, two cruisers, and 12 destroyers.

Kakuta's force would be followed two days later by the remainder of the Aleutians force—two small transport units with cruiser and destroyer escorts for the invasion of Attu and Kiska on June 5. Meanwhile, from Hashirajima Anchorage in the Inland Sea, the four big aircraft-carriers of Vice-

Yamamoto's battle-squadron

In support of the Transport Group, four heavy cruisers under Vice-Admiral Kurita would also sail from Guam. Finally, three powerful forces would sail in company from the Inland Sea during May 28:

• The Main Body, comprising Yamamoto's splendid new flagship *Yamato*, the biggest battleship in the world, mounting nine 18-inch guns, the 16-inch battleships *Nagato* and *Mutsu*, with attendant destroyers;

• The Main Support Force for the Midway invasion force—two battleships, four heavy cruisers, and attendant destroyers—under Vice-Admiral Kondo;

• The Guard Force (mentioned above).

Parting company with Yamamoto's force after getting to sea, Kondo was to head for a supporting position to the south-west of Midway, while the Guard Force would proceed to station itself near the route from Pearl Harbor to the Aleutians. Yamamoto himself, with the Main Body, was to take up a central position from which he could proceed to annihilate whatever enemy force Nimitz sent out. To ensure that the dispatch of any such American force should not go

had passed in favour of the aircraft-carrier which could deliver its blows at a range 30 times greater than that of the biggest guns. The role of the battleship was now as close escort to the vulnerable aircraft-carriers, supplying the defensive anti-aircraft gunpower the latter lacked. Nagumo's force was supported only by two battleships and three cruisers. Had Yamamoto's Main Body kept company with it, the events that were to follow might have been different.

Far more fatal to Yamamoto's plan, however, was his assumption that it was shrouded from the enemy, and that only when news reached Nimitz that Midway was being assaulted would the Pacific Fleet leave Pearl Harbor. Thus long before the scheduled flying-boat reconnaissance—which in the event failed to take place because French Frigate Shoal was found to be in American hands—and before the scouting submarines had reached their stations, Spruance and Fletcher, all unknown to the Japanese, were beyond the patrol lines and poised waiting for the enemy's approach. Details of this approach as well as the broad lines of Yamamoto's plan were known to Nimitz. Beyond sending a small force of five cruisers and ten destroyers to the Aleutians to harass

Admiral Nagumo's I Carrier Striking Force —*Akagi, Kaga, Hiryu*, and *Soryu*—would sail for the vicinity of Midway. There, at dawn on the 4th, their bombers and fighters would take off for the softening-up bombardment of the island prior to the assault landing two days later by troops carried in the Transport Group.

The original plan had called for the inclusion of the *Zuikaku* and *Shokaku* in Nagumo's force. But, like the *Yorktown*, the *Shokaku* had suffered damage in the Coral Sea battle and could not be repaired in time to take part in the Midway operation, while both carriers had lost so many

undetected, Pearl Harbor was to be reconnoitred between May 31 and June 3 by two Japanese flying-boats via French Frigate Shoal (500 miles north-west of Hawaii), where a submarine was to deliver them petrol. As a further precaution, two cordons of submarines were to be stationed to the north-west and west of Hawaii by June 2, with a third cordon farther north towards the Aleutians.

Yamamoto's plan was ingenious, if over-intricate: but it had two fatal defects. For all his enthusiasm for naval aviation, he had not yet appreciated that the day of the monstrous capital ship as the queen of battles

the invasion force, he concentrated all his available force—TF 16 and 17—in the area.

He had also a squadron of battleships under his command, to be sure; but he had no illusions that, with their insufficient speed to keep up with the aircraft-carriers, their great guns could play any useful part in the events to follow. They were therefore relegated to defensive duties on the American west coast.

For the next few days the Japanese Combined Fleet advanced eastwards according to schedule in its wide-spread, multi-pronged formation. Everywhere a buoyant feeling of confidence showed itself, generated

by the memories of the unbroken succession of Japanese victories since the beginning of the war. In the I Carrier Striking Force, so recently returned home after its meteoric career of destruction—from Pearl Harbor, through the East Indies, and on to Ceylon without the loss of a ship—the 'Victory Disease' as it was subsequently to be called by the Japanese themselves, was particularly prevalent. Only the admiral—or so Nagumo was subsequently to say—felt doubts of the quality of the many replacements who had come to make up the wastage in experienced aircrews inevitable even in victorious operations.

Spruance and Fletcher had meanwhile made rendezvous during June 2, and Fletcher had assumed command of the two task forces, though they continued to manoeuvre as separate units. The sea was calm under a blue sky split up by towering cumulus clouds. The scouting aircraft, flown off during the following day in perfect visibility, sighted nothing, and Fletcher was able to feel confident that the approaching enemy was all unaware of his presence to the north-east of Midway. Indeed, neither Yamamoto nor Nagumo, pressing forward blindly through rain and fog, gave serious thought to such an apparently remote possibility.

Far to the north on June 3, dawn broke grey and misty over Kikuta's two aircraft-carriers from which, soon after 0300 hours, the first of two strike waves took off to wreak destruction among the installations and fuel tanks of Dutch Harbor. A further attack was delivered the following day, and during the next few days American and Japanese forces sought each other vainly among the swirling fogs, while the virtually unprotected Kiska and Attu were occupied by the Japanese. But as Nimitz refused to let any of his forces be drawn into the skirmish, this part of Yamamoto's plan failed to have much impact on the great drama being enacted farther south.

Setting the scene

The opening scenes of this drama were enacted early on June 3 when a scouting Catalina flying boat some 700 miles west of Midway sighted a large body of ships, steaming in two long lines with a numerous screen in arrowhead formation, which was taken to be the Japanese main fleet. The sighting report brought nine army B-17 bombers from Midway, which delivered

Mitsubishi A6M2 Zero fighter first saw service in 1940 over China. During the period of runaway Japanese victories in the Pacific this model performed outstandingly. **Max speed:** 331 mph at 16,000 feet. **Max range:** 1160 miles. **Armament:** 2×20-mm cannon; 2×7·7-mm machine-guns

three high-level bombing attacks and claimed to have hit two battleships or heavy cruisers and two transports. But the enemy was in reality the Midway Occupation Force of transports and tankers, and no hits were scored on them until four amphibious Catalinas from Midway discovered them again in bright moonlight in the early hours of June 4 and succeeded in torpedoing a tanker. Damage was slight, however, and the tanker remained in formation.

More than 800 miles away to the east, Fletcher intercepted the reports of these encounters but from his detailed knowledge of the enemy's plan was able to identify the Occupation Force. Nagumo's carriers, he knew, were much closer, some 400 miles to the west of him, approaching their flying-off position from the north-west. During the night, therefore, Task Forces 16 and 17 steamed south-west for a position 200 miles

Brewster F2A Buffalo fighter. Small and underpowered this aircraft was long outclassed by 1942. Nonetheless, it performed heroically at Midway. **Max speed:** 313 mph at 13,500 feet. **Max range:** 650 miles. **Armament:** 2×·5-inch machine-guns

north of Midway which would place them at dawn within scouting range of the unsuspecting enemy. The scene was now set for what was to be one of the great decisive battles of history.

Deadly game of hide-and-seek
The last hour of darkness before sunrise on June 4 saw the familiar activity in both the carrier forces of ranging-up aircraft on the flight-deck for dawn operations. Aboard the *Yorktown*, whose turn it was to mount the first scouting flight of the day, there were Dauntless scout dive-bombers, ten of which were launched at 0430 hours for a search to a depth of 100 miles between west and east through north, a precaution against being taken by surprise while waiting for news from the scouting flying boats from Midway.

Reconnaissance aircraft were dispatched at the same moment from Nagumo's force. One each from the *Akagi* and *Kaga*, and two seaplanes each from the cruisers *Tone* and *Chikuma* were to search to a depth of 300 miles to the east and south. The seaplane carried in the battleship *Haruna,* being of an older type, was restricted to 150 miles. The main activity in Nagumo's carriers, however, was the preparation of the striking force to attack Midway – 36 'Kate' torpedo-bombers each carrying a 1,770-pound bomb, 36 'Val' dive-bombers each with a single 550-pound bomb, and 36 Zero fighters as escort. Led by Lieutenant Joichi Tomonaga, this formidable force also took off at 0430.

By 0445 all these aircraft were on their way – with one notable exception. In the cruiser *Tone,* one of the catapults had given trouble, and it was not until 0500 that her second seaplane got away. This apparently minor dislocation of the schedule was to have vital consequences. Meanwhile, the carrier lifts were already hoisting up on deck an equally powerful second wave; but under the bellies of the 'Kates' were slung torpedoes, for these aircraft were to be ready to attack any enemy naval force which might be discovered by the scouts.

The lull in proceedings which followed the dawn fly-off from both carrier forces was broken with dramatic suddenness. At 0520, aboard Nagumo's flagship *Akagi,* the alarm was sounded. An enemy flying boat on reconnaissance had been sighted. Zeros roared off the deck in pursuit. A deadly game of hide-and-seek among the clouds developed, but the American naval fliers evaded their hunters. At 0534 Fletcher's radio office received the message 'Enemy carriers in sight', followed by another reporting many enemy aircraft heading for Midway; finally, at 0603, details were received of the position and composition of Nagumo's force, 200

miles west-south-west of the *Yorktown.* The time for action had arrived.

The *Yorktown*'s scouting aircraft were at once recalled and while she waited to gather them in, Fletcher ordered Spruance to proceed with his Task Force 16 'south-westerly and attack enemy carriers when definitely located'. *Enterprise* and *Hornet* with their screening cruisers and destroyers turned away, increasing to 25 knots, while hooters blared for 'General Quarters' and aircrews manned their planes to warm-up ready for take-off. Meanwhile, 240 miles to the south, Midway was preparing to meet the impending attack.

Radar had picked up the approaching aerial swarm at 0553 and seven minutes later every available aircraft on the island had taken off. Bombers and flying-boats were ordered to keep clear, but Marine Corps fighters in two groups clawed their way upwards, and at 0616 swooped in to the attack. But of the 26 planes, all but six were obsolescent Brewster Buffaloes, hopelessly outclassed by the highly manoeuvrable Zeros. Though they took their toll of Japanese bombers, they were in turn overwhelmed, 17 being shot down and seven others damaged beyond repair. The survivors of the Japanese squadrons pressed on to drop their bombs on power-plants, seaplane hangars, and oil tanks.

At the same time as the Marine fighters, ten torpedo-bombers had also taken off from Midway – six of the new Grumman Avengers (which were soon to supersede the unsatisfactory Devastator torpedo-bombers in American aircraft-carriers) and four Army Marauders. At 0710 they located and attacked the Japanese carriers; but with no fighter protection against the many Zeros sent up against them, half of them were shot down before they could reach a launching position. Those which broke through, armed with the slow and unreliable torpedoes which had earned Japanese contempt in the Coral Sea battle, failed to score any hits; greeted with a storm of gunfire, only one Avenger and two Marauders escaped to crash-land on Midway.

Unsuccessful as these attacks were, they had important consequences. From over Midway, Lieutenant Tomonaga, surveying the result of his attack, at 0700 signalled that a further strike was necessary to knock out the island's defences. The torpedo attacks seemed to Nagumo to bear this out, and, as no inkling of any enemy surface forces in the vicinity had yet come to him, he made the first of a train of fatal decisions. At 0715 he ordered the second wave of aircraft to stand by to attack Midway. The 'Kate' bombers, concentrated in the *Akagi* and *Kaga,* had to be struck down into the hangars to have

their torpedoes replaced by bombs. Ground crews swarmed round to move them one by one to the lifts which took them below where mechanics set feverishly to work to make the exchange. It could not be a quick operation, however, and it had not been half completed when, at 0728, came a message which threw Nagumo into an agony of indecision.

The reconnaissance seaplane from the *Tone* – the one which had been launched 30 minutes behind schedule – was fated to be the one in whose search sector the American fleet was to be found; and now it sent back the signal – 'Have sighted ten ships, apparently enemy, bearing 010 degrees, 240 miles away from Midway: Course 150 degrees, speed more than 20 knots.' For the next quarter of an hour Nagumo waited with mounting impatience for a further signal giving the composition of the enemy force.

Only if it included carriers was it any immediate menace at its range of 200 miles – but in that case it was vital to get a strike launched against it at once. At 0745 Nagumo ordered the re-arming of the 'Kates' to be suspended and all aircraft to prepare for an attack on ships, and two minutes later he signalled to the search plane: 'Ascertain ship types and maintain contact.' The response was a signal of 0758 reporting only a change of the enemy's course; but 12 minutes later came the report: 'Enemy ships are five cruisers and five destroyers.'

Nagumo's hopes crushed
This message was received with heartfelt relief by Nagumo and his staff; for at this moment his force came under attack first by 16 Marine Corps dive-bombers from Midway, followed by 15 Flying Fortresses, bombing from 20,000 feet, and finally 11 Marine Corps Vindicator scout-bombers. Every available Zero was sent aloft to deal with them, and not a single hit was scored by the bombers. But now, should Nagumo decide to launch an air strike, it would lack escort

Below: The doomed Japanese carrier *Akagi* evades US bombs at Midway

US Air Force

171

fighters until the Zeros had been recovered, refuelled, and re-armed. While the air attacks were in progress, further alarms occupied the attention of the battleship and cruiser screen when the US submarine *Nautilus*—one of 12 covering Midway—fired a torpedo at a battleship at 0825. But neither this nor the massive depth-charge attacks in retaliation were effective; and in the midst of the noise and confusion of the air attacks—at 0820—Nagumo received the message he dreaded to hear: 'Enemy force accompanied by what appears to be a carrier.'

The luckless Japanese admiral's dilemma, however, had been disastrously resolved for him by the return of the survivors of Tomonaga's Midway strike at 0830. With some damaged and all short of fuel, their recovery was urgent; and rejecting the advice of his subordinate carrier squadron commander—Rear-Admiral Yamaguchi, in the *Hiryu*—to launch his strike force, Nagumo issued the order to strike below all aircraft on deck and land the returning aircraft. By the time this was completed, it was 0918.

Refuelling, re-arming, and ranging-up a striking-force in all four carriers began at once, the force consisting of 36 'Val' dive-bombers and 54 'Kates', now again armed with torpedoes, with an escort of as many Zeros as could be spared from defensive patrol over the carriers. Thus it was at a carrier force's most vulnerable moment that—from his screening ships to the south—Nagumo received the report of an approaching swarm of aircraft. The earlier catapult defect in the *Tone*; the inefficient scouting of its aircraft's crew; Nagumo's own vacillation (perhaps induced· by the confusion caused by the otherwise ineffective air attacks from Midway); but above all the fatal assumption that the Midway attack would be over long before any enemy aircraft-carriers could arrive in the area—all had combined to plunge Nagumo into a catastrophic situation. The pride and vainglory of the victorious carrier force had just one more hour to run.

When Task Force 16 had turned to the south-west, leaving the *Yorktown* to recover her reconnaissance aircraft, Nagumo's carriers were still too far away for Spruance's aircraft to reach him and return; and if the Japanese continued to steer towards Midway, it would be nearly 0900 before Spruance could launch his strike. When calculations showed that Nagumo would probably be occupied recovering his aircraft at about that time, however, Spruance had decided to accept the consequences of an earlier launching in order to catch him off balance. Every serviceable aircraft in his two carriers, with the exception of the fighters required for defensive patrol, was to be included, involving a double launching, taking a full hour to complete, during which the first aircraft off would have to orbit and wait, eating up precious fuel.

It was just 0702 when the first of the 67 Dauntless dive-bombers, 29 Devastator torpedo-bombers, and 20 Wildcat fighters, which formed Task Force 16's striking force, flew off. The torpedo squadrons had not yet taken the air when the sight of the *Tone*'s float plane, circling warily on the horizon, told Spruance that he could not afford to wait for his striking force to form up before dispatching them. The *Enterprise*'s dive-bombers led by Lieutenant-Commander Mc-Clusky, which had been the first to take off, were ordered to lead on without waiting for the torpedo-bombers or for the fighter escort whose primary task must be to protect the slow, lumbering Devastators. At 0752, McClusky took departure, steering to intercept Nagumo's force which was assumed to be steering south-east towards Midway. The remainder of the air groups followed at intervals, the dive-bombers and fighters up at 19,000 feet, the torpedo-bombers skimming low over the sea.

This distance between them, in which layers of broken cloud made maintenance of contact difficult, had calamitous consequences. The fighters from the *Enterprise*, led by Lieutenant Gray, took station above but did not make contact with Lieutenant-Commander Waldron's torpedo squadron from the *Hornet*, leaving the *Enterprise*'s torpedo squadron, led by Lieutenant-Commander Lindsey, unescorted. *Hornet*'s fighters never achieved contact with Waldron, and flew instead in company with their dive-bombers. Thus Task Force 16's air strike advanced in four separate, independent groups—McClusky's dive-bombers, the *Hornet*'s dive-bombers and fighters, and the two torpedo squadrons.

All steered initially for the estimated position of Nagumo, assuming he had maintained his south-easterly course for Midway. In fact, at 0918, having recovered Tomonaga's Midway striking force, he had altered course to north-east to close the distance between him and the enemy while his projected strike was being ranged up on deck. When the four air groups from TF 16 found nothing at the expected point of interception, therefore, they had various courses of action to choose between. The *Hornet*'s dive-bombers decided to search south-easterly where, of course, they found nothing. As fuel ran low, some of the bombers returned to the carrier, others made for Midway to refuel. The fighters were not so lucky: one by one they were forced to ditch as their engines spluttered and died.

The two torpedo squadrons, on the other hand, low down over the water, sighted smoke on the northern horizon and, turning towards it, were rewarded with the sight of the Japanese carriers shortly after 0930. Though bereft of fighter protection, both promptly headed in to the attack. Neither Waldron nor Lindsey had any doubts of the suicidal nature of the task ahead of them. The former, in his last message to his squadron had written: 'My greatest hope is that we encounter a favourable tactical situation, but if we don't, and the worst comes to the worst, I want each of us to do his utmost to destroy our enemies. If there is only one plane left to make a final run in, I want that man to go in and get a hit. May God be with us all.'

His hopes for a favourable tactical situation were doomed. Fifty or more Zeros concentrated on his formation long before they reached a launching position. High overhead, Lieutenant Gray, leading the *Enterprise*'s fighter squadron, waited for a call for help as arranged with Lindsey, thinking that Waldron's planes were the torpedo squadron from his own ship—a call which never came. From the cruisers and destroyers of the screen came a withering fire. One by one the torpedo-bombers were shot down. A few managed to get their torpedoes away before crashing, but none hit

the enemy. Only one of the pilots, Ensign George H. Gay, survived the massacre, clinging to a rubber seat cushion which floated away from his smashed aircraft, until dusk when he could inflate his life-raft without attracting strafing Zeros.

Five minutes later it was the turn of Lindsey's 14 Devastators from the *Enterprise*. Purely by chance, as he was making his attack on the starboard side of the *Kaga*, the torpedo squadron from the *Yorktown* came sweeping in from the other side, aiming to attack the *Soryu*, and drawing off some of the fighter opposition.

The *Yorktown*'s strike group of 17 dive-bombers led by Lieutenant-Commander Maxwell F. Leslie, with 12 torpedo-bombers of Lieutenant-Commander Lance E. Massey's squadron and an escort of six Wildcats, had taken departure from their carrier an hour and a quarter after the strike groups of Task Force 16. A more accurate assessment of probabilities by Leslie, however, had brought the whole of this force simultaneously over the enemy to deliver

the co-ordinated, massed attack which alone could hope to swamp and break through the defences. In addition, at this same moment, McClusky's dive-bombers also arrived overhead. McClusky, after reaching the expected point of interception, had continued for a time on his south-westerly course and had then made a cast to the north-west. There he had sighted a destroyer steering north-east at high speed. This was the *Arashi*, which had been left behind to depth-charge the *Nautilus*. Turning to follow her, McClusky was led straight to his objective.

The simultaneous attack by the two torpedo squadrons brought no result of itself. Scores of Zeros swarmed about them, brushing aside the puny force of six Wildcats. The massacre of the clumsy Devastators was re-enacted. Lindsey and ten others of his force were shot down. Of Massey's squadron, only two survived. The few torpedoes launched were easily evaded.

The sacrifice of the torpedo-bombers had not been in vain, nevertheless. For, while every Japanese fighter plane was milling about low over the water, enjoying the easy prey offered to them there, high overhead there were gathering, all unseen and unmolested, the dive-bombers—McClusky's 18, and Leslie's 17. And now, like hawks swooping to their prey, they came plummeting down out of the sky.

Vought-Sikorsky SB2U-1 Vindicator. Known as 'Vibrators' by their Marine crews, the SB2 was one of the US Navy's first monoplane types. Some were still in service at Midway. **Max speed:** 257 mph at 11,000 feet. **Max range:** 700 miles. **Armament:** 5 machine-guns and 1500-lb bombload

In the four Japanese carriers the refuelling and re-arming of the strike force had been almost completed. The decks were crowded with aircraft ranged for take-off. Nagumo had given the order to launch and ships were turning into wind. Aboard the *Akagi*, all eyes were directed downwards at the flight-deck.

Suddenly, over the rumbling roar of engines, the high-pitched rising scream of dive-bombers was heard. Even as faces swivelled upwards at the sound, the black dots which were 1,000-pound bombs were seen leaving three 'Hell-Divers' as they pulled out from their near-vertical dive. Fascinated eyes watched the bombs grow in size as they fell inexorably towards that most vulnerable of targets, a full deck load of armed and fuelled aircraft. One bomb struck the *Akagi* squarely amidships, opposite the bridge and just behind the aircraft lift, plunged down into the hangar and there exploded, detonating stored torpedoes, tearing up the flight deck, and destroying the lift. A second exploded in the midst of the 'Kates' on the after part of the deck, starting a tremendous conflagration to add to that in the hangar. In a matter of seconds Nagumo's proud flagship had been reduced to a blazing shambles. From time to time she was further shaken by internal explosions as the flames touched off petrol tanks, bombs, and torpedoes. Within a few minutes Captain Aoki knew that the damage and fires were beyond control. He persuaded the reluctant Nagumo that it was necessary to transfer his flag to a ship with radio communication intact. Admiral and staff picked their way through the flames to reach the forecastle whence they lowered themselves down ropes to a boat which took them to the light cruiser *Nagara* of the screen.

Carnage in the Japanese carriers

Only three dive-bombers from the *Enterprise* had attacked the flagship. The remainder of the air group, 34 dive-bombers, all concentrated on the *Kaga*. Of four bombs which scored direct hits, the first burst just forward of the superstructure, blowing up a petrol truck which stood there, and the sheet of flame which swept the bridge killed everyone on it, including the captain. The other three bombs falling among the massed aircraft on the flight deck set the ship ablaze and started the same fatal train of fires and explosions as in the *Akagi*. Within a few minutes, the situation was so beyond control that the senior surviving officer ordered the transfer of the Emperor's portrait to an attendant destroyer – the custom obligatory when a ship was known to be doomed, and conducted with strict naval ceremony. The *Kaga* was to survive for several hours, nevertheless.

Simultaneously, with the *Akagi* and *Kaga*, the *Soryu* had also been reeling under a devastating attack. Leslie of the *Yorktown* was leading veterans of the Coral Sea battle, probably the most battle-experienced aviators in the American navy at that time. With deadly efficiency they dived in three waves in quick succession from the starboard bow, the starboard quarter, and the port quarter, released their bombs and climbed away without a single casualty. Out of the shower of 1,000-pound bombs, three hit. The first penetrated to the hangar deck and the explosion lifted the steel platform of the lift, folding it back against the bridge. The others landed among the massed aircraft, causing the whole ship to be engulfed in flames. It took Captain Ryusaku Yanaginoto only 20 minutes to decide to order 'Abandon Ship' to save his crew from being burnt alive, though the *Soryu*, like her sisters, was to survive for some hours yet.

Thus, in five brief, searing minutes, half of Japan's entire fleet carrier force, her naval *corps d'élite*, had been shattered. For the time being the *Hiryu*, some miles away, remained untouched. She was to avenge her sisters in some measure before the day was over; but before going on to tell of her part in the battle let us follow the remainder to their deaths in the blue Pacific waters.

On board the *Akagi*, though the bomb damage was confined at first to her flight and hangar decks and her machinery spaces remained intact, the fires fed by aviation petrol from aircraft and from fuel lines were beyond the capacity of the Japanese crew to master. They fought them for seven hours

Imperial War Museum

Above: The major US casualty at Midway, the *Yorktown*, lies dead in the water.

but by 1715 Captain Aoki had decided there was no hope of saving his ship. The Emperor's portrait was transferred to a destroyer and the ship was abandoned. Permission was asked of the C-in-C to hasten her end but it was not until nearly dawn on the following day – when Yamamoto at last fully understood the fullness of the Japanese defeat – that he gave his approval and the *Akagi* was sent to the bottom by torpedoes from a destroyer.

Petrol-fed fires similarly swept the *Kaga* and defeated all efforts to save her. Lying stopped and burning she became the target for three torpedoes from the *Nautilus* which, after her earlier adventure, had surfaced and chased after the Japanese carriers. Even the stationary target, however, was too much for the unreliable torpedoes with which the Americans were at that time equipped. Of three fired, two missed, and the third struck but failed to explode. At 1640 orders were given to abandon the *Kaga*, and at 1925 two great explosions tore her asunder and sent her to the bottom.

The *Soryu*'s story was a similar one, of intermittent internal explosions from within the great mass of flame and smoke which she had become. When Captain Yanaginoto gave the order 'Abandon Ship', he determined to immolate himself, dying in the flames or going down with her. A party of his men returning on board with the intention of persuading him or, if necessary, of forcing him to save himself, fell back

abashed at the heroic, determined figure of their captain, standing sword in hand, facing forward, awaiting his end. They left him to his chosen fate. As they did so they heard him singing the Japanese national anthem. Yanaginoto's resolution held fast till 1913 hours when at last the *Soryu* and the bodies of 718 of her crew slid beneath the surface.

Much had taken place in the meantime before Nagumo's three aircraft-carriers suffered their death throes. The first survivors of the American strike groups to land back on their ships made it clear that one Japanese carrier had not yet been located. This was the *Hiryu* which, at the time of the attack, had become separated from the remainder. Admiral Fletcher therefore launched a ten-plane search from the *Yorktown*, and sent up a defensive patrol of a dozen Wildcats. It was none too soon. At a few minutes before noon, the *Yorktown*'s radar gave the warning of enemy planes coming in from the west.

These were the *Hiryu*'s attack group of 18 dive-bombers and six fighters, led by Lieutenant Michio Kobayashi, a veteran leader who had taken part in every operation of the Nagumo force. As soon as they had flown off, a further strike of ten torpedo-bombers and six Zeros, to be led by the redoubtable Tomonago, was ranged up. Kobayashi's force had followed some of the *Yorktown*'s attack planes back and now concentrated on Fletcher's flagship. Wildcats – for once outnumbering the escorting

Below: A crippling collision with another heavy cruiser, US bombs and engine-room

US Navy

It was later sunk by an enemy submarine

Zeros—broke through to get at the 'Vals', shooting down ten of them, including the leader. Of the eight which remained, two were knocked down by anti-aircraft fire from the cruiser screen.

The six survivors, however, showed that they had lost none of their skill as they screamed down on the carrier. One 'Val' broke up under anti-aircraft fire, but its bomb sped on to burst on the flight-deck, killing many men, and starting a hangar fire below. A second bomb plunged through the side of the funnel and burst inside, starting more fires. With three boiler up-takes smashed and the furnaces of five or six boilers extinguished, the carrier's speed fell away until, 20 minutes later, she came to a stop. A third bomb penetrated to the fourth deck where for a time a fire threatened the forward petrol tanks and magazines.

His flagship immobilised, her radio and radar knocked out, Admiral Fletcher transferred his flag to the cruiser *Astoria*, and ordered the *Portland* to take the aircraft-carrier in tow. The damage-control organization worked wonders, however. Before the towline had been passed, the *Yorktown* was under way again and working up to 20 knots, and the refuelling of the fighters was in progress. Prospects seemed bright. Then a cruiser's radar picked up Tomonaga's air group, 40 miles away and coming in fast. There was just time to launch eight of the refuelling Wildcats to join the four already in the air, but they were unable to get

explosions sank the *Mikuma* at Midway

through the screen of fighters to get at the 'Kates'—though they shot down three of the 'Zeros'. A tremendous screen of bursting shells spread itself in front of the attackers, while the cruisers raised a barrage of splashes with their main armament, a wall of water columns through which it seemed impossible that the skimming 'Kates' could fly.

Yorktown fatally damaged

Five 'Kates' were shot down, but the remainder, coming in from four different angles, displayed all their deadly skill, boring doggedly in to drop their torpedoes at the point-blank range of 500 yards. It was impossible for the carrier to avoid them all. Two hit on her port side, tearing open the double-bottom fuel tanks and causing flooding which soon had her listing at 26 degrees. All power was lost, so that counter-flooding was impossible. It seemed that the *Yorktown* was about to capsize. At 1500, Captain Buckmaster ordered 'Abandon Ship'.

Meanwhile, however, the dive-bombers from Spruance's Task Force 16, operating some 60 miles to the north-east of the *Yorktown*, had wreaked vengeance on the *Hiryu*. Twenty-four Dauntlesses, of which ten had been transferred from the *Yorktown*, arrived overhead undetected soon after the few survivors of *Hiryu*'s attack had been recovered. The aircraft carrier circled and swerved to avoid the bombs from the plummeting dive-bombers, but in vain. Four of them hit, one of which blew the forward lift bodily on to the bridge. The others started the inevitable fires and explosions, and the same prolonged death agonies as the *Hiryu*'s sisters were still suffering. By 2123 she had come to a stop. Desperate efforts to subdue the flames went on through the night; but at 0230 the following morning she was abandoned to be torpedoed by her attendant destroyers.

When the night of June 4 closed over the four smoking Japanese carriers and over the crippled *Yorktown*, the battle of Midway was, in the main, over. Neither of the opposing commanders yet knew it, however, and manoeuvres and skirmishes were to continue for two more days. The Japanese commanders, except Nagumo, were slow to realise that the shattering of their four fleet carriers signified defeat and the end of the Midway operation. Admiral Kondo, with his two fast battleships, four heavy cruisers, and the light carrier *Zuiho* had set off to the help of Nagumo at midday on June 4, and soon afterwards Yamamoto was signalling to all his scattered forces to concentrate and attack the enemy. He himself, with the main body of his fleet, was coming up fast from the west bringing the 18-inch guns of the giant *Yamato* and the 16-inch ones of the *Nagato* and *Mutsu* to throw in their weight. Still underestimating his opponent, he was dreaming of a night encounter in which his immensely powerful fleet would overwhelm the American task force and avenge the losses of the previous day. The great 'fleet action' with battleships in stately line hurling huge shells at each other was still his hope and aim.

Such a concept had been forcibly removed from American naval strategy by the shambles of Pearl Harbor. Raymond Spruance, one of the greatest admirals to come to the fore during the war, was not to be lured within range of Yamamoto's battleships, above all at night, when his carriers, at this

time untrained for night-flying, would be at a tremendous disadvantage. At sunset he turned away eastwards, aiming to take up a position on the following day from which he could either 'follow up retreating enemy forces or break up a landing attack on Midway'.

The Japanese C-in-C refused to credit the completeness of the disaster that had overtaken his fleet and the Midway plan until early on June 5 when, at 0255, he ordered a general retirement. Thus, when Spruance, after prudently steering eastwards to keep his distance from the still overwhelmingly superior Japanese surface fleet, and reversing course at midnight so as to be within supporting distance of Midway at daylight, sent a strike of 58 dive-bombers from his two ships during the afternoon of the 5th to seek out Yamamoto's Main Body, his airmen encountered nothing but a lone destroyer sent to search for the *Hiryu*.

Two final incidents remain to be briefly recounted. When Yamamoto ordered his general retirement, the squadron of four heavy cruisers of Admiral Kurita's Support Force, the *Kumano, Suzuya, Mikuma,* and *Mogami*, was to the westward of Midway, steering through the night to deliver a bombardment at dawn. They now swung round to reverse course full in view of the American submarine *Tambor*. As they steadied on their retirement course, from the flagship the *Tambor* was sighted in the moonlight ahead. The signal for an emergency turn to port was flashed down the line but was not taken in by the rear ship, *Mogami*. Failing to turn with the remainder she collided with the *Mikuma*, suffering serious damage which reduced her speed to 12 knots. Leaving the *Mikuma* and two destroyers to escort the cripple, Kurita hurried on with the remainder.

News of this attractive target soon reached Midway. Twelve army Flying Fortresses took off but were unable to locate it; but 12 Marine Corps dive-bombers sighted the long oil slick being trailed by the *Mikuma*, followed it up—and at 0805 dived to the attack. Their bombs failed to achieve direct hits, but the plane of Captain Richard E. Fleming crashed on the after turret of the *Mikuma*. Petrol fumes were sucked down into the cruiser's starboard engine-room and exploded, killing the whole engine-room crew.

The two cruisers nevertheless continued to limp slowly away, until the following day when Spruance, having abandoned hope of delivering another blow on Yamamoto's Main Fleet, was able to direct his dive-bombers on to them. The *Mikuma* was smothered and sunk, but the *Mogami* miraculously survived, heavily damaged, to reach the Japanese base at Truk.

While these events were taking place, far to the east the abandoned *Yorktown* had drifted crewless through the night of June 4/5. She was still afloat at noon the next day and it became clear she had been prematurely abandoned. A · salvage party boarded her and she was taken in tow. Hopes of getting her to port were high until the Japanese submarine *I-168*, sent by Yamamoto for the purpose, found her, penetrated her anti-submarine screen, and put two torpedoes into her. At 0600 on June 7 the *Yorktown* sank at last.

At sundown on the previous day Spruance had turned his force back eastwards to meet his supply tankers. That the Battle of Midway was over was finally clear to all.

THE FIRST ARCTIC CONVOYS

On hearing of the urgency of Russia's need for equipment and supplies, Churchill had told Stalin that he intended to run 'a continuous cycle of convoys' around the north of Norway to Archangel and Murmansk. Although at first the Germans were slow to intervene from their bases in northern Norway, the difficulties were immense: the British had to combat not only the Arctic weather conditions and the permanent threat of an air or U-boat attack, but also the possibility that powerful German ships might break out and attack

Germany's seizure of Norway in April 1940 —although prompted mainly by a desire to forestall the Allies who, it was rightly believed, were about to carry out a similar coup—had given the German navy a considerable strategic advantage in the war at sea by facilitating its access to the Atlantic. The full extent of the gain, however, did not become apparent until Hitler launched his attack on Russia on June 22, 1941. Then the ports and anchorages on the north and west coasts of the country, and the airfields which had been constructed in the northern part of it, enabled the Germans to dominate the approaches to the northern Russian ports of Murmansk and Archangel—which afforded the most direct means of supplying European Russia at that time.

The area between Iceland and Norway in the approaches to the Barents Sea is notorious for foul weather. It is swept by a never-ending succession of gales which in winter take the form of snow-laden blizzards, and it is noted also for the frequency of fog caused by a mingling of the warm water of the Gulf Stream which flows northward through the area, with cold water from the polar regions. This occurrence also produces unusual variations in the thermal layers of the sea and is a serious handicap to the use of sound-ranging apparatus (sonar) for the detection of submarines.

Another factor which had an important bearing on operations in Arctic waters was the seasonal movement of the southern edge of the polar ice pack, which sometimes approached to within 80 miles of the North Cape, and which even at its most northerly limit did not permit ships to keep outside striking distance from the German airfields, even when proceeding to Archangel, 450 miles to the east of Murmansk. This latter port was only a few minutes flying time from Petsamo and Kirkenes, so ships approaching it or at anchor there were liable to air attack at all times. The alternating periods of complete darkness and perpetual daylight during winter and summer respectively, which are a feature of high latitudes, also had a considerable influence on the events about to be described. The complete darkness added greatly to the difficulties of navigation without lights in bad weather, while the perpetual daylight made it easy for the enemy to locate and attack the convoys 'all round the clock'.

Admiral Sir John Tovey, on whom responsibility for running the Arctic convoys now devolved, had under his command in September 1941 the two new battleships HMS *King George V* and *Prince of Wales* (the former was his flagship), the carriers HMS *Furious* and *Victorious,* three 8-inch-gun and three 6-inch-gun cruisers, and some 20 destroyers. Constant demands, however, were made on his fleet to provide ships for such duties as escorting troop convoys destined for the Middle East via the Cape, reinforcing Malta, or searching for enemy supply ships in the Atlantic. Although his fleet included two carriers, the *Furious* was 22 years old when the war began, and neither she nor the *Victorious* was equipped with modern aircraft capable of engaging with success those which the enemy was able to operate from his shore airfields in Norway. This was a serious weakness which was to have a profound effect on the operations of the Arctic convoys.

There were three forms of attack to which these convoys were exposed – surface ship, submarine, and air. Pre-eminent in the first category was the *Tirpitz,* a sister ship of the *Bismarck.* The submarine threat, while most severe in the Atlantic, was, of course, an unknown quantity in the waters around Norway, and so was the threat from the air.

This problem put a severe strain on the all-too-few reconnaissance aircraft of Coastal Command, which were primarily responsible for detecting the movements of the German ships.

On September 28, the first of the PQ series of convoys, consisting of ten merchant ships, sailed from Iceland bound for Archangel (when returning in the reverse direction these convoys were designated QP). There was still an acute shortage of anti-submarine escorts even for the Atlantic convoys, and in the early stage of the Arctic convoys all that could be provided as close escort was a force of two destroyers, a minesweeper, and two trawlers. A cruiser also went right through to Russia with each convoy to provide defence against air and surface attack by light forces, while a second cruiser patrolled west of Bear Island ready to give support if needed. Five British minesweepers, based on the Kola Inlet, were used to reinforce the convoy escort as it approached the Murman coast, and from time to time a few Russian destroyers also came out to assist the convoy on the last leg of its voyage. These, with their powerful anti-aircraft armament, were a most welcome addition when air attacks on the convoys began to increase in their intensity.

But it was lack of air cover, both for fighter protection and for anti-submarine patrols, that was to prove the weak spot in the defence of the convoys when the long Arctic night gave way to perpetual daylight. Coastal Command, operating from bases in Iceland and the Shetlands, could only give cover to the convoys for the first 150 miles of their long voyage and, despite repeated requests, the Russians provided very little help with this problem. Besides the close escort referred to above, whenever a convoy was on passage a covering force of heavy ships put to sea and cruised in a position to intercept the *Tirpitz* or the *Scheer,* should either or both of them venture out.

However, in mid-November 1941 Raeder decided that steps must be taken to interfere with the movement of the convoys, and in addition to transferring the five large destroyers to northern Norway, as already mentioned, he ordered Admiral Dönitz, chief of the U-boat arm, to increase the number of these vessels in Norwegian waters so that three would be on constant patrol in the waters through which the convoys had to pass. But so ineffective did these measures prove, that by the end of the year 53 loaded ships had made the voyage in seven convoys without loss, and 34 had returned – the remaining 19 having been delayed in unloading. In all, some 750 tanks, 800 fighters, 1,400 vehicles, and more than 100,000 tons of stores had been sent to Russia since she had been invaded, and although this represented only a fraction of the Red Army's needs, it amounted to a real sacrifice on the part of Britain.

Then, on December 7, 1941, Japan's savage attack on the United States fleet in Pearl Harbor opened the flood gates of American war production, and the problem was soon to become one of how to transport to Russia all the equipment now becoming

available. The last convoy to reach Archangel before the ice closed in that year arrived on December 12 – and from then until June 1942 only Murmansk could be used for unloading supplies. Admiral Golovko, Commander-in-Chief of the Russian Northern Fleet, wrote in his diary on December 10: 'Matters are evidently moving in favour of Murmansk becoming the reception port for the convoys'. And although he referred to having raised the problems which this would create in August and September, no notice appears to have been taken of his representations in Moscow. A fortnight later he recorded: 'The signs are that the cargo vessels will sail to Murmansk. Now there is no end to our troubles.' In fact seven ships reached the port on December 20 to find that – despite the Russian admiral's contention that 'the quays and cranes are adequate for unloading' – this was far from being the case where heavy lifts like tanks were concerned, and a crane ship had to be sent out from England to help deal with them.

Admiral Tovey concluded from the build-up of German strength in the area that action by enemy surface ships to interfere with the convoys would not long be delayed. His assumption proved correct: on March 6 Hitler gave approval for the *Tirpitz,* accompanied by three destroyers, to be sailed to intercept PQ-12, a convoy of 16 ships which had been located the previous day by a reconnaissance aircraft.

The narrow escape of the battleship, however, led Raeder to press with renewed vigour for a strengthening of the air forces in northern Norway, and this time he was successful – the last convoy to reach Murmansk unscathed was in fact PQ-12 which, although not known at the time, had nar-

rowly missed destruction at the hands of the *Tirpitz.* From then on German opposition to the movements of the convoys steadily increased, and it was clear to the Admiralty that even if stronger escorts were provided, increasing losses must be expected, because at the time there was no satisfactory way of dealing with the threat from the air.

This premonition proved correct: during the next three convoy operations, two cruisers were lost together with 15 merchantmen. German destroyers, U-boats, and aircraft all contributed to these losses, but a significant fact was that the aircraft, besides being partially responsible for the loss of one cruiser, accounted for seven of the 15 merchant ship casualties. The First Sea Lord, Admiral of the Fleet Sir Dudley Pound, supported Admiral Tovey's view that unless some means could be found of neutralising the enemy airfields, very serious and heavy losses might be expected, and he recommended that the sailing of the convoys be suspended until the period of perpetual daylight ended in September.

But although he shared the Chiefs-of-Staff's misgivings, Churchill decided that the convoys must continue. Thus PQ-16, of 35 ships, and QP-12 of 15 ships, sailed from Iceland and Murmansk respectively on May 21. The homeward convoy was lucky and got through unscathed, but the outward one was subjected to the full fury of sustained attack by U-boats and some 260 enemy aircraft, which now included squadrons of torpedo-bombers. Six ships were lost during the battle, which raged unceasingly for five days and nights, though by now the distinction was not apparent in those northern latitudes. It was under these gloomy auspices that convoy PQ-17 set sail.

An AA crew mans the guns on one of the escorting destroyers as the convoy nears Archangel.

TEN GOT THROUGH

Churchill had promised the Russians 'three convoys every two months with either 35 or 25 ships in each convoy', but the number of vessels loaded and waiting was by now so great that there was strong pressure on the Admiralty to take as many ships as possible, and they therefore agreed to 35 ships being sailed in the next convoy, designated PQ-17. Admiral Tovey would have preferred that the convoy sail in two sections, and it was during a telephone conversation with the First Sea Lord, Admiral Sir Dudley Pound, over this point that he learned that it was Pound's intention to order the convoy to scatter should it be attacked in the Barents Sea by a powerful German force—especially if it included the battleship *Tirpitz*.

The stage was thus set when on June 27, 1942, Convoy PQ-17 in charge of Commodore J. C. K. Dowding RNR set sail from the port of Reykjavik in Iceland where it had been assembled. One ship grounded on leaving harbour and another was damaged by ice in the Denmark Strait, so the convoy which shaped course for Archangel comprised 33 ships plus a tanker. As close escort it had six destroyers, two AA ships, four corvettes, three minesweepers, four trawlers, and two submarines, which it was hoped might discourage enemy ships.

Enemy reconnaissance aircraft first located PQ-17 at noon on July 1, and the U-boats placed to intercept it were soon on its trail, but were prevented from attacking by the close escort. However, from now on the convoy was under constant observation. The cruisers some 40 miles to the north of the convoy were not seen, which was what Admiral Hamilton intended, as he

wanted to keep the enemy guessing as to the strength of the cover. On the following day the convoy ran into fog which lasted for 24 hours and under cover of which it was able to alter course to the eastward towards Bear Island without being observed by the shadowing aircraft—but the U-boats still followed it tenaciously.

The Admiralty learned on July 3 that the *Tirpitz* and *Hipper* had left their usual anchorage in a fiord near Trondheim, and although it seemed likely that the movement was connected with that of PQ-17, this could not be confirmed.

Negative intelligence—which is all the Admiralty had to work on, since no further reports of the movements of the enemy ships had been received—is always difficult to evaluate. As the First Sea Lord, the Vice-Chief of the Naval Staff, and some half

The need to convince the Russians that Britain was still determined to send them support at all costs meant that Convoy PQ-17 *had* to sail—even though it was known that the operation would be strategically unsound. For, by June 1942, the Germans had assembled a powerful force of surface ships in northern and central Norway and had strengthened the Luftwaffe: they were determined to destroy the next Arctic convoy with an all-out attack

dozen senior officers concerned with the operation of the Arctic convoys gathered in Admiral Pound's office in the Admiralty on the evening of July 4, and pored over the charts spread out in front of them, all they knew was that time was fast running out, and that a decision whether or not to countermand the existing instructions to the convoy and the forces escorting it could not be further delayed. The German ships might be anywhere within an area bounded by the circumference of a circle marking their estimated furthest-on position at any given time, and this showed that it was possible for them to reach the convoy any time from now on.

At about 2200 hours on July 4 as Admiral Hamilton with his four cruisers, in accordance with the last orders he had received, was keeping company with the convoy as it steamed steadily eastward, a message from the Admiralty prefixed 'Most Immediate' was brought to him. It read: 'Cruiser force withdraw to the westward at high speed.' And it was followed by another message a few minutes later: 'Immediate—Owing to threat from surface ships the convoy is to disperse and proceed to Russian ports.' The word 'disperse' was corrected in a subsequent message to 'scatter'.

The captains of the heavily-laden merchant ships who saw the main strength of their escort fast disappearing over the western horizon but who knew nothing of the reasons which had prompted the surprising message they had just received from their Commodore, nevertheless obeyed the order to 'scatter' with the precision of a well-drilled fleet. In order to separate as quickly as possible from each other, they

had to steer for a prescribed time on widely diverging courses before resuming the easterly course which would take them to their destination. The enemy was quick to notice this change in formation—and the advantage offered to their aircraft which no longer had to face the concentrated fire of a compact body of ships and could now press home their attacks and make sure of hitting. Similarly the U-boats, now that the destroyers had gone, could afford to surface and make use of their higher surface speed to chase after ships reported by aircraft. A disaster unparalleled in the history of convoy operations was about to take place.

The first victim, the *Empire Byron*, was sunk by a U-boat early on July 5 and just to the north of her four more ships sank after a joint attack by dive-bombers and U-boats.

Soon afterwards the *Pankraft,* proceeding on her own, was similarly attacked and went down. Just after midday a U-boat overtook Commodore Dowding's ship, the *River Afton,* and sank her, together with another ship in her vicinity. And in the late afternoon, two ships which had sought cover in a bank of fog emerged and were set on immediately by aircraft. Although they fought back fiercely and successfully dodged several sticks of bombs aimed at them they finally succumbed to the weight of the attack and were sunk by a U-boat after the crews had abandoned ship. The minesweeper *Salamander* had collected a small group round her consisting of a tanker, a cargo ship, and a rescue ship, when they were attacked by aircraft and both the tanker and the rescue ship were sunk, to bring the total for the first 24 hours to 12. With the three ships previously sunk, this loss represented almost half the convoy.

But the end was not yet. All the next day the onslaught continued, and the U-boats, correctly suspecting that surviving ships might be heading for the west coast of Novaya Zemlya, hurried eastward. During the next 48 hours they came across four such ships which were steaming south towards the White Sea and sank them, while

aircraft scouring the Barents Sea found another ship and sent her to the bottom.

The two AA ships, with a group composed of some corvettes, minesweepers, and two of the merchant ships, managed to reach the Matochkin Straits which separate the two halves of Novaya Zemlya. There they were joined by the minesweeper *Salamander,* three more merchant ships, and the rescue ship *Zamalek.* Last to arrive was the corvette *Lotus* with Commodore Dowding and other survivors from the *River Afton* whom she had valiantly turned back to rescue. Quickly realising their dangerous and exposed position, a small convoy was formed and headed south for the White Sea.

Although at first shielded by fog, during which one ship lost touch and returned to the anchorage, when only 60 miles off the Russian coast they were subjected to four hours of high-level bombing during which two more merchant ships were lost, while urgent appeals for Russian fighter cover went unanswered. Thus with only two out of the 33 ships with which he had started the voyage, Commodore Dowding reached Archangel on July 10. There he found two more ships which had miraculously escaped destruction, and with one more still off the coast of Novaya Zemlya, the fate of

which was unknown, it looked as if only five ships had survived the assault. He did not know that the trawler *Ayrshire,* with a fine display of initiative, had shepherded another three ships towards the ice barrier, which they had penetrated to a depth of 20 miles, and after waiting two days for the enemy's fury to spend itself, she had escorted them to the coast of Novaya Zemlya. Here they were found by Commodore Dowding, who had set out again on a search for any possible further survivors from his decimated convoy. He also found another ship aground which was subsequently salvaged, the CAM ship *Empire Tide* with over 240 survivors from sunken ships on board, and the Russian tanker which had been torpedoed before the convoy had scattered. All were brought safely to port. The final count, therefore, was 23 ships lost, and with them 430 tanks, 210 aircraft, 3,350 vehicles, and nearly 100,000 tons of cargo.

That the scattering of the convoy was at best premature and at worst a mistake is now generally agreed.

It was a case of political expedience insisting on the carrying out of an operation which, before it even began, was known to be strategically unsound.

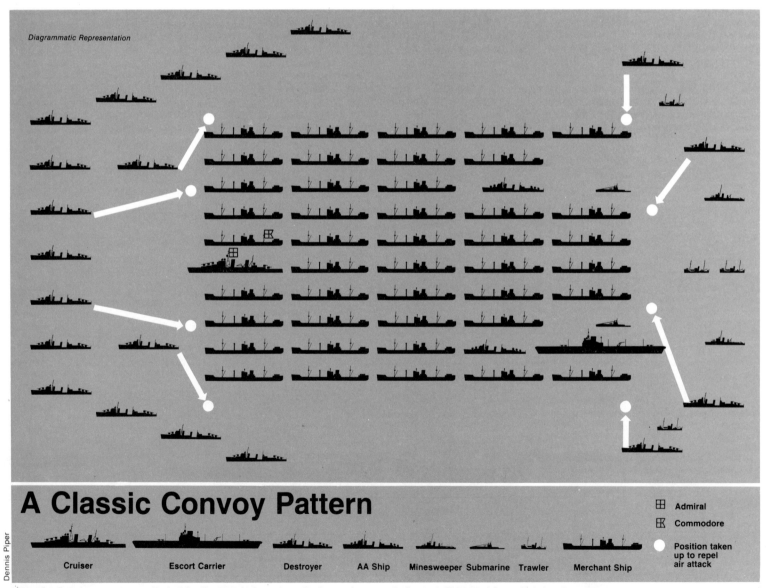

Diagrammatic Representation

A Classic Convoy Pattern

Dennis Piper

| Cruiser | Escort Carrier | Destroyer | AA Ship | Minesweeper | Submarine | Trawler | Merchant Ship |

⊞ Admiral

⊞ Commodore

○ Position taken up to repel air attack

How the Russian convoys sailed: this diagram is based on the formation of one of the classic convoys to Archangel. The 'fighting destroyer escort' is shown deployed around the convoy in its defensive position. The line-abreast cruising order of the convoy itself was intended to throw the greatest weight of AA fire against enemy air attack. When the Luftwaffe appeared, the inner screen would move to the positions indicated. The need for a fighting formation was rammed home by the PQ-17 disaster, and it was first used by PQ-18. This convoy lost 13 out of its 40 ships to enemy attacks, but the experiment had succeeded: the attacks failed to split up the convoy to suffer the fate of PQ-17. The German pilots could not launch an effective attack against the columns of merchantmen because of the widespread escort screen plus fighters

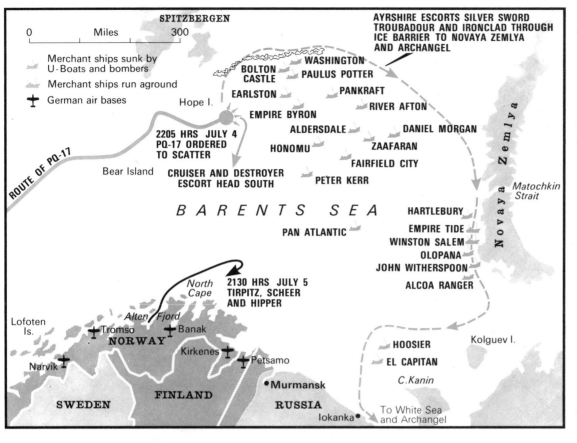

SPITZBERGEN

0 — Miles — 300

Merchant ships sunk by U-Boats and bombers
Merchant ships run aground
✝ German air bases

AYRSHIRE ESCORTS SILVER SWORD TROUBADOUR AND IRONCLAD THROUGH ICE BARRIER TO NOVAYA ZEMLYA AND ARCHANGEL

Hope I.

BOLTON CASTLE
WASHINGTON
EARLSTON
PAULUS POTTER
PANKRAFT
EMPIRE BYRON
RIVER AFTON
ALDERSDALE
DANIEL MORGAN
HONOMU
ZAAFARAN
FAIRFIELD CITY
PETER KERR

ROUTE OF PQ-17

2205 HRS JULY 4 PQ-17 ORDERED TO SCATTER

Bear Island

CRUISER AND DESTROYER ESCORT HEAD SOUTH

BARENTS SEA

PAN ATLANTIC

HARTLEBURY
EMPIRE TIDE
WINSTON SALEM
OLOPANA
JOHN WITHERSPOON
ALCOA RANGER

Novaya Zemlya

Matochkin Strait

North Cape
Alten Fjord

2130 HRS JULY 5 TIRPITZ, SCHEER AND HIPPER

Lofoten Is.

✝ Tromsö
✝ Banak
NORWAY
Kirkenes ✝
✝ Petsamo

Narvik ✝

SWEDEN
FINLAND

RUSSIA

• Murmansk

HOOSIER
EL CAPITAN
C. Kanin

Kolguev I.

Iokanka •

To White Sea and Archangel

◁ PQ-17 was the most disastrous of the Russian convoys: out of the 33 ships which had left Iceland, 23 were lost—and the abortive sortie of the *Tirpitz* had never gone anywhere near the ill-fated convoy. The Allied hope that the German heavy ships would be tempted within the reach of the Home Fleet's battleships also came to nothing. And when the U-boat commanders realised that the convoy had broken formation and headed east, they concentrated in the waters between Novaya Zemlya, Spitzbergen, and the White Sea—with deadly effect

▽ Soviet destroyers move out into the White Sea to escort the remnants of PQ-17 into Archangel

1941 September 28: The first Allied convoy to Russia, consisting of ten merchant ships, sails from Iceland bound for Archangel.
October 2: German Operation 'Typhoon'— the final attack on Moscow—begins.
October 6: Churchill promises Stalin to send a convoy to Russia every ten days.
December 5: Russian counterattack to drive Germans back from Moscow begins.
December 31: By the end of the year, 53 loaded ships in seven convoys have made the run to Russia without loss. In all, some 750 tanks, 800 fighters, 1,400 vehicles, and more than 100,000 tons of miscellaneous stores have been sent to Russia since the German invasion.
1942 January 14: The German battleship *Tirpitz* moves from the Baltic to Trondheim, Norway, as Germany begins to build up strength along the Arctic Convoy routes.
March 6: The *Tirpitz* sails to intercept Convoy PQ-12, but is driven off by torpedo-bombers from the carrier *Victorious*.
June: The Admiralty learns that Germany is planning an all-out attack on the next convoy to northern Russia.
June 27: Convoy PQ-17, consisting of 33 ships, sets sail for Archangel from Iceland, with a close escort of six destroyers, two AA ships, four corvettes, three mine-sweepers, four trawlers, and two submarines.
July 1: German scout planes sight Convoy PQ-17, and U-boats begin to trail it.
July 4: Convoy PQ-17 is attacked by German dive- and torpedo-bombers which sink two merchantmen and damage two others. The Admiralty then orders the convoy to scatter immediately.
July 5: U-boats and Luftwaffe dive-bombers now press home the attack on the dispersed convoy. In the first 24 hours of the assault, 12 merchantmen are sent to the bottom.
July 10: Commodore Dowding reaches Archangel with only two out of the 33 ships that began the voyage. In the next few days, he recovers several more of his ships: his final count is 23 ships lost—and with them 430 tanks, 210 aircraft, 3,350 vehicles, and nearly 100,000 tons of cargo.

Imperial War Museum

181

On Italy's declaration of war on 10th June 1940, Mussolini with typical flamboyance called for 'an offensive at all points in the Mediterranean and outside'. Within hours, Italian aircraft dropped their first loads of bombs on Malta.

In the wider context of the Mediterranean war, both sides were evenly matched in surface vessels. But Italy had a huge advantage in submarines and aircraft, and the British suffered from the disadvantage of having to cover both the Suez Canal (with the Mediterranean Fleet under Admiral Sir Andrew Cunningham) and Gibraltar (with Force H under Vice-Admiral Sir James Somerville).

They were helped by the timidity of the Italian naval leaders, who held to the need to maintain 'a fleet in being'. This meant attacking only when circumstances were clearly favourable. They were never, it seemed, favourable enough, and this uncertainty led to Italy's failure to seize the initiative even in 1940 when her fleet could have taken Malta and won control of the Mediterranean.

▽ Seen from *Victorious* during 'Pedestal': *Indomitable* launches an Albacore, with *Eagle* bringing up the rear of the line

MALTA: THE SIEGE IS RAISED

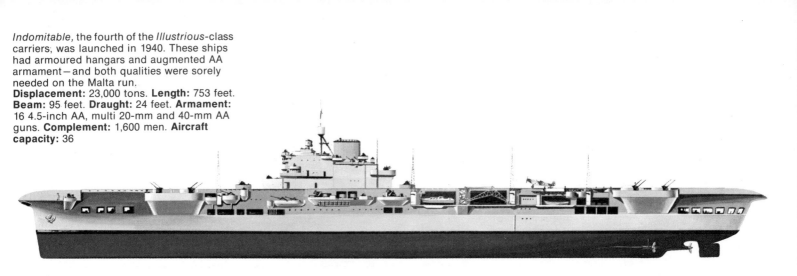

Indomitable, the fourth of the *Illustrious*-class carriers, was launched in 1940. These ships had armoured hangars and augmented AA armament—and both qualities were sorely needed on the Malta run.
Displacement: 23,000 tons. **Length:** 753 feet. **Beam:** 95 feet. **Draught:** 24 feet. **Armament:** 16 4.5-inch AA, multi 20-mm and 40-mm AA guns. **Complement:** 1,600 men. **Aircraft capacity:** 36

With the Italians unwilling to engage, it was clear that air-power was going to be the decisive factor, and its importance was brought home dramatically to the Italians by two actions—in Taranto and off Cape Matapan—before the Allied withdrawal from Crete in April 1941 focused Axis attention finally on Malta.

In October 1940 three Glen Martin Maryland reconnaissance planes arrived in Malta. They allowed Cunningham to keep a close watch on the Italian fleet and gave him a chance to put into action a plan he had long dreamed of: an attack on the Italian fleet in harbour.

All six Italian battleships were together in Taranto as the British approached on the night of 11th November. Italian reconnaissance reports had been so confused that the Italian commander, Campioni, remained in harbour, vainly waiting for information. In a very short space of time, the twenty-one swordfish torpedo-bombers, dipping and weaving to avoid the hawsers of barrage balloons and the storm of tracer shells, reduced Italy's serviceable battleships to two, the *Vittorio Veneto* (the strongest) and the *Cesare,* for the loss of two aircraft. After Taranto, the mere presence of a carrier was enough to make an Italian naval commander nervous of any engagement.

Four months later, on the night of 27th-28th March, the Italian navy, under German pressure, set out to break the British convoy route to Greece. Iachino, who had replaced Campioni after Taranto, expected Luftwaffe support. None came. Instead, he was taken by surprise by aircraft from the carrier *Formidable.* The cruiser *Pola* was damaged, and two other cruisers returning to help her were picked up on British radar and sunk within five minutes. The crew of the *Pola,* meanwhile, having abandoned ship, found she was not sinking after all, climbed back on board and set about warming themselves—with alcohol. When the British boarded, the Italians were in no state to offer any resistance. They were taken prisoner and the *Pola* too was sunk.

By this time the Germans had already seen the need for full-scale support in the Mediterranean. By January, about 100 bombers and 25 fighters of X Fliegerkorps had arrived in Sicily from Norway to bring the Axis forces there up to 150 bombers and 100 fighters. The Germans signalled their arrival dramatically on 10th January with a devastating dive-bomber attack on the carrier *Illustrious.*

The *Illustrious* limped into Malta, and over the next fortnight the Germans launched what are still known as the 'Illustrious raids' to knock out the carrier and the airfields. The exhausted ground crews on Malta were only able to put some ten fighters in the air at any one time against perhaps eighty German aircraft, but the *Illustrious* was hit only once. She made her way out on the 23rd bound for America for repairs.

Malta itself now stood in immediate peril of subjection by the Luftwaffe. From February to May 1941 only thirteen ships reached the island, bringing some 100,000 tons of supplies.

The second half of 1941 saw an immense improvement in the Allied position. The Axis forces in North Africa needed some 50,000 tons of supplies a month, but in September they lost a quarter en route and in November a staggering sixty per cent. The speed of Auchinleck's successful Crusader offensive in November was due largely to Malta's domination of the Mediterranean.

Submarines too operated with enormous success. One was particularly effective, *HMS Upholder,* captained by a lanky, black-bearded Scot, M.D.Wanklyn. *Upholder* sank 94,000 tons of Axis shipping, for which Wanklyn won the VC and two DSO's, before he was killed in 1942.

Malta's real test was still to come, however, and the end of 1941 saw the pendulum swing once more against the Allies. In November, the carrier *Ark Royal* was torpedoed. In December, Force K, a four-vessel reinforcement from Force H, ran on to a mine-field off Malta and was almost totally destroyed.

On 23rd March, two freighters, *Talabot* and *Pampas,* the survivors of a four-vessel convoy, came steaming through bomb splashes to a delirious welcome from Malta's inhabitants

thronging the harbour walls. Kesselring, however, had assured Hitler he would 'wipe Malta off the map' and he directed over 300 bombers to destroy the two freighters. In three days of ceaseless attack, they succeeded. Only 5,000 of the 20,000 tons which had left Alexandria with the convoy was unloaded before the *Talabot* and *Pampas* were sunk in harbour.

The idea of reinforcement seemed hopeless, and Malta was slowly starving. A soldier on active service was supposed to get 4,000 calories a day; in Malta the average was now half that, with a bread ration of ten ounces. Communal—or 'Victory'—kitchens were set up in which goat stew became the staple diet.

It was in recognition of the island's spirit of endurance and defiance that on 15th April a simple message arrived for the governor of Malta: 'To honour her brave People I award the George Cross to the Island Fortress of Malta to bear witness to a Heroism and Devotion that will long be famous in History. George R.I.'

The pendulum began to swing finally against the Axis on 9th May when sixty Spitfires landed from the carriers *Wasp* and *Eagle.* The next day, just when Kesselring was reporting the neutralization of Malta, his raiders were met by a superior force for the first time in months.

But there had to be aid from outside. In June a massive double operation from both ends of

A Swordfish turns into its landing approach on HMS *Ark Royal*

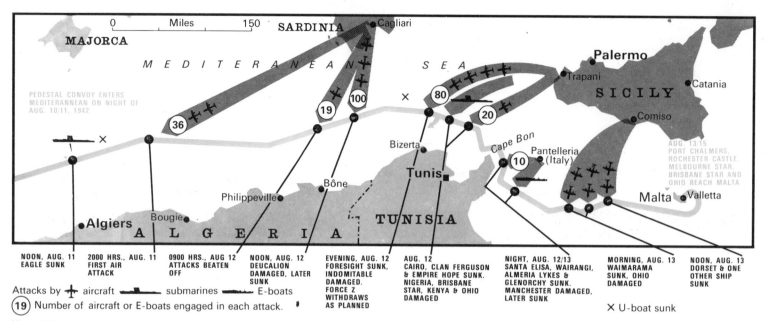

SARDINIA · Cagliari

MAJORCA

0   Miles   150

M E D I T E R R A N E A N   S E A

Palermo

PEDESTAL CONVOY ENTERS
MEDITERANNEAN ON NIGHT OF
AUG. 10/11, 1942

Trapani

SICILY

· Catania

(36)

(19)   (100)

×   (80)

(20)

· Comiso

Bizerta

Cape Bon

Pantelleria
(Italy)

AUG. 13/15
PORT CHALMERS,
ROCHESTER CASTLE,
MELBOURNE STAR,
BRISBANE STAR AND
OHIO REACH MALTA

(10)

Tunis

Bône

Malta · Valletta

Philippeville

· Bougie

Algiers

A L G E R I A

T U N I S I A

NOON, AUG. 11
EAGLE SUNK

2000 HRS., AUG. 11
FIRST AIR
ATTACK

0900 HRS., AUG 12
ATTACKS BEATEN
OFF

NOON, AUG. 12
DEUCALION
DAMAGED, LATER
SUNK

EVENING, AUG. 12
FORESIGHT SUNK,
INDOMITABLE
DAMAGED.
FORCE Z
WITHDRAWS
AS PLANNED

AUG. 12
CAIRO, CLAN FERGUSON
& EMPIRE HOPE SUNK.
NIGERIA, BRISBANE
STAR, KENYA & OHIO
DAMAGED

NIGHT, AUG. 12/13
SANTA ELISA, WAIRANGI,
ALMERIA LYKES &
GLENORCHY SUNK.
MANCHESTER DAMAGED,
LATER SUNK

MORNING, AUG. 13
WAIMARAMA
SUNK, OHIO
DAMAGED

NOON, AUG. 13
DORSET & ONE
OTHER SHIP
SUNK

Attacks by ✈ aircraft ▬ submarines ▬ E-boats
(19) Number of aircraft or E-boats engaged in each attack.   × U-boat sunk

None of the other Malta convoys was quite like 'Pedestal'. This convoy made the Malta run when Rommel was on the doorstep of Alexandria and the Axis was supreme in the Mediterranean—and all available Axis strike resources were massed to exterminate the convoy. U-boats stalked the ships from their first entry into the Mediterranean; the Luftwaffe would attack up to three times a day; torpedo-boats struck at the survivors which struggled through the Sicilian narrows; and the might of the Italian battle fleet posed a constant menace. Fourteen fast merchantmen set out from Gibraltar; only five of them, battered, scorched, or sinking, got through to unload their vital cargoes in the Grand Harbour. But their determination meant that Malta could hold out through the desperate summer of 1942

Pedestal—one of the most sensational naval operations of the war

▽ The carrier *Eagle* was 'Pedestal's' first
casualty: torpedoed by U-73 on August 11,
she capsized and sank within minutes

▽ Near-misses alongside one of the fast
merchantmen. Three days after entering
the Mediterranean, half of 'Pedestal's'
14 merchantmen had been sunk

New Lease of Life for Malta

1942 August 10/11: Pedestal convoy – 13 merchantmen and the tanker *Ohio* – leave Gibraltar for Malta.
August 11: U-73 sinks the carrier *Eagle*; the first air attacks from Sardinia are beaten off.
August 12: The carrier *Indomitable* is disabled south of Sardinia. Heavy submarine and air attacks throw the convoy into confusion.
August 12/13: The convoy rounds Cape Bon; a torpedo-boat attack sinks four merchantmen.
August 13: The convoy is reduced to three ships, with two damaged and separated from the convoy.
August 14: The three ships reach Malta.
August 15: *Ohio* reaches Malta; the vital oil cargo means that Malta can hold out until December.
October 23: Montgomery begins the Alamein offensive.
November 7/8: The Allies land in Algeria.
November 13: 8th Army enters Tobruk.
November 17: The Stoneage convoy leaves Alexandria for Malta.
November 19/20: Stoneage arrives in Malta, unmolested.
December 5: Portcullis convoy arrives in Malta, whose supplies can now last until March/May 1943.

the Mediterranean set out to end Malta's permanent fuel and food crisis. Five freighters and a tanker were to come from the west (Operation Harpoon) and eleven freighters from the east (Operation Vigorous). Its tragic results showed how hopeless was the task of running convoys with inadequate air cover.

The convoy from the east was an utter failure. Movement and counter-movement in 'Bomb Alley' between Crete and Africa took their toll of ammunition, and the whole convoy had to turn about and return to base, with the loss of several freighters and warships. But the Italian admiral, da Zara, misjudged the path of the western convoy and two freighters escaped the devastating Axis air attacks to deliver their 15,000 tons of supplies to Malta. Without them, Malta would undoubtedly have fallen. Of the seventeen supply ships loaded for Malta, covered by eighty-two warships, just two had got through and six had been lost.

But by July, the siege was nearing its end. Fighters shot down sixty-five Axis aircraft for the loss of only thirty-six Spitfires. The submarines returned, and seven Axis supply ships en route to North Africa were sunk. By 10th August, Operation Pedestal was ready: fifty-nine warships were to escort fourteen merchant ships from Gibraltar to Malta. Lying in wait for the convoy were twenty-one Axis submarines and some 800 aircraft.

The first blow was the torpedoing of the carrier *Eagle,* which sank within eight minutes taking 200 of her crew with her. The heavy ships turned back as planned on the 12th, and immediately a night of chaos began. Axis MTBs

surged to within fifty yards of their prey, sweeping decks with automatic fire, while Allied vessels steamed in all directions to avoid torpedoes as best they could. By morning on the 13th there were just seven merchantmen left. One of them was the tanker *Ohio,* lying dead in the water with her vital 11,000 tons of fuel, awaiting a tow over the last ninety miles to Valletta. The following day two more freighters were sunk, but four of the scattered fleet arrived in Malta. The Italian navy, deprived of air cover by the German demand that fighters should accompany the Luftwaffe bombers, was deterred from any attacks by a massive display of air strength from Malta.

It took forty-eight hours to tow the sinking *Ohio* to Grand Harbour, and having discharged her cargo she lay immovable in the harbour until she was expended as an RAF gunnery target in 1946.

Stocktaking after Pedestal showed that Malta could hold out until December, at a pinch. But even with the Allied victories of October and November in North Africa, there was no sign of relief, and discussion started on how the island's surrender was to be made known. It was not until 17th November that the last convoy, code-named Stoneage, sailed from Port Said. It entered Malta on the night of 19th–20th November without interference, and the siege was finally over.

The balance of power had passed to the Allies, now pouring troops into the western Mediterranean following the Torch landings, and Malta was free to back the Allied invasion of Sicily in July 1943.

▽ The air attack that disabled the carrier *Indomitable*: her flight-deck was wrecked by bombs, and her aircraft were forced to land on *Victorious*

▽ *Victorious* provided extra air cover for 'Pedestal' – but within 48 hours of leaving Gibraltar she was the only British carrier left in action

BATTLE OF BARENTS SEA

End of the German battle fleet, December 1942/January 1943

In the last days of 1942, the heavy German warships *Hipper* and *Lützow* steamed out of their Norwegian base with the aim of sending Convoy JW-51B to the bottom. The ensuing action with the convoy's escort, though seldom publicised, resulted in such a complete and humiliating failure for the German navy that an infuriated Hitler ordered the scrapping of his entire battle fleet

△ HMS *Onslow*, leader of the flotilla of six destroyers which escorted Convoy JW-51B
▽ *Admiral Hipper*, flagship of the German battle squadron which attempted to destroy the convoy

By the spring of 1942, the small British Commando raids on the European coast had so alarmed Hitler that he looked for a deeper significance behind them. He guessed that the Allies would counter-attack soon, and as early as January 12, 1942, he was convinced that an Allied invasion of Norway was imminent, telling Raeder, Keitel, and Jodl that Sweden was on the point of joining the Allies. Then, he declared, the attack on Norway would become a pincer movement: Britain would attack by sea while the Swedes and the Russians attacked by land, allowing the Western Allies and the USSR to join forces.

Hitler considered that to counter such a threat would be comparatively simple: he was determined not to move troops from the Russian front, so the Luftwaffe and Kriegsmarine must defend Norway by attacking the Allied forces off the coast. For this purpose, *Scharnhorst*, *Gneisenau*, and *Prinz Eugen* were to move north from Brest. 'If the surprise break-out through the Channel is impossible,' he told Raeder, 'it would be best to pay off the ships and use the guns and crews for reinforcements in Norway.' By January 22, 1942, he had convinced himself that Norway was 'the zone of destiny in this war'—but Raeder disagreed: he thought that the Allied counterattack would be in North Africa.

But it was these preparations against a supposed Allied landing in Norway that enabled the Germans to make a massive attack on Convoy PQ-17 in June, and with the concentration of the heavy ships in northern waters Raeder decided that the fuel situation had improved enough to use the big ships against Convoy PQ-18. Yet—and this was a vital factor in what was to come—the pocket-battleship *Admiral Scheer*, the heavy cruiser *Hipper*, and the cruiser *Köln* did not sail out from Altenfjord. At the last minute, Hitler had warned Raeder that the ships were vitally important for the defence of Norway: he 'must not accept any undue risks'. Not unnaturally, Raeder had cancelled the plan and left it to the Luftwaffe and U-boats to deal with this particular convoy, which lost 13 of its 40 ships.

From PQ-18 in September until the completion of the North African landings in November, when the Home Fleet was strengthened once more, no Allied convoys were sailed to Russia. After the break for Operation Torch, the Russian convoys began again in December 1942 with plans to sail 30 ships in two operations: a 15-ship convoy on the 18th and another of the same size on the 22nd. The designation of the outward-bound convoys was changed from PQ to JW—beginning at 51—so the first half was called JW-51A, and the second JW-51B. At the same time, the homeward-bound convoys were redesignated RA instead of QP; and the first of them—RA-51—was timed to sail from Murmansk on December 30, its escorts being those that arrived there with JW-51A.

Admiral Tovey, C-in-C Home Fleet, decided that in addition to the 'fighting destroyer escort' sailing with the convoys, a separate force of two cruisers—called 'Force R'—would also cover the convoys; but that, because of the danger from U-boats, it would not approach nearer than 50 miles to the convoy unless a surface attack developed. JW-51A sailed as planned and arrived safely, covered by the 6-inch-gun cruisers *Sheffield* and *Jamaica* under the command of Rear-Admiral R. L. Burnett, a veteran of the summer convoy battles.

Although JW-51A was not attacked, the German Naval Staff had drawn up a detailed plan—Operation *Regenbogen* ('Rainbow')—which provided for the pocket-battleship *Lützow* and the heavy cruiser *Hipper*, with an escort of six destroyers, to sail from Altenfjord to attack some unspecified Arctic convoy. Only the choice of convoy remained.

Convoy JW-51B sailed from Scotland on December 22, comprising 14 merchantmen. Some idea of the amount of aid sent to Russia is given by this small convoy's cargo: 202 tanks, 2,046 vehicles, 87 fighters, 33 bombers, 11,500 tons of fuel oil, 12,650 tons of aviation spirit, and 54,321 tons of miscellaneous supplies. Three small destroyers, a minesweeper, two corvettes, and two trawlers escorted it to a position just east of Iceland, where the three destroyers handed over to six larger 'fleet' destroyers.

The 'fleet' destroyers were commanded by Captain R. Sherbrooke in the *Onslow*, who had been Captain (D) of the 17th Destroyer Flotilla (D-17) for only four weeks. The rest of his flotilla comprised the *Oribi*, *Obedient*, *Obdurate*, *Orwell*, and *Achates*. Sherbrooke planned that at the first sign of a surface attack all destroyers except for *Achates* would leave their position around the convoy and join the *Onslow* on the threatened side; the convoy would turn away from that direction, and *Achates* would lay a smoke-screen. The remaining escorts—the minesweeper *Bramble*, corvettes *Hyderabad* and *Rhododendron*, and trawlers *Northern Gem* and *Vizalma*, would re-form on the convoy.

By December 28, JW-51B was well to the north of the latitude of the North Cape when it ran into a gale, and was driven far to the

Two of the destroyers which escorted the *Lützow* and *Hipper* move out of Altenfjord: they too failed to press home their attacks adequately

south of its intended route. In heavy seas, blinding snow squalls, and with ice forming thick on every ship, the *Oribi* lost contact because of gyro-compass failure and eventually steamed on alone to Russia, while the trawler *Vizalma* and a merchant ship also lost the convoy and, while trying to catch up, actually overtook and passed it. On the 29th, the minesweeper *Bramble* was sent off to make a radar search for the missing ships, and was never seen again by British eyes.

By Wednesday, December 30, the convoy had turned east—and Altenfjord was less than 200 miles away. During the morning, the British Admiralty signalled a warning to Captain Sherbrooke that there was a lot of activity by German radio stations along the Norwegian coast—a tantalising piece of information, which could mean many things. Since the Germans had not attacked JW-51A, had they guessed that a large convoy was being sailed in two sections and planned a major attack on the second half, JW-51B? Or had Force R been sighted? Or was the increased radio traffic unconnected with JW-51B? Sherbrooke could only ensure that the ice covering the ships and their armament was cleared as fast as possible.

'Immediate readiness for attack'

In fact the Germans were preparing a heavy attack: earlier in the day U-354, commanded by Leutnant Herschleb, had sighted the convoy and reported its course and speed. Later she shadowed for nearly eight hours until she was spotted by the *Obdurate*, which tried to ram her.

The chain of command for the German navy in the north ran from the Naval Staff in Berlin (through the Operations Division) to Admiral Carls at Group North in Kiel; to Admiral Kluber, the Flag Officer, Northern Waters, at Narvik; and then—for Operation Rainbow—to Admiral Kummetz, Flag Officer, Cruisers *(B de K)* in the *Hipper* at Altenfjord. As soon as U-354's signal was received, Carls signalled Kluber (who had gone to Altenfjord): *B de K with six destroyers immediate readiness for Rainbow.* The preliminary order to Kummetz contained a significant phrase: *Procedure on meeting the enemy: avoid a superior force, otherwise destroy according to tactical situation.* The phrase seems of no consequence, but it was only to be the first of several cautionary and morale-destroying signals which Kummetz was to receive.

On the same day—December 30—Hitler held a conference at Wolfschanze about a clash between Raeder and Göring over the command of transport ships in the Mediterranean. This had led to Kesselring, the C-in-C South, threatening to arrest any admiral who disobeyed his orders. Such a quarrel was frequent between the services, but earlier Raeder, Admiral Krancke (the navy's representative at OKW HQ), and several staff officers had decided that 'It can be rightly assumed that the Führer had no previous knowledge' of the affair. Krancke was given the task of discussing it with Hitler on December 30; but he immediately found that Göring had also flown in unexpectedly for the conference and had given his version first.

Krancke explained the navy's views; Hitler listened in silence, but then started off an angry monologue—not about the Mediterranean shipping problem, but about the superiority of the British navy, 'which is able to sail through the Mediterranean without paying attention to the Italian navy and the Axis air force'. Krancke, reporting later the violence of Hitler's voice, quoted him as saying: 'Our own navy is but a copy of the British—and a poor one at that. The warships are not in operational readiness; they are lying idle in the fjords, utterly useless like so much old iron.'

When eventually Hitler stopped, someone then reported that there was no British convoy traffic to Murmansk, whereupon Krancke said that he had just received a signal from the Operations Division, which reported U-354's sighting of JW-51B and adding: *Vice-Admiral Krancke* [is to] *inform Führer that C-in-C Navy approves in principle the operational use of* Hipper, Lützow, *and destroyers. Execution is in accordance with the decision of Group North depending on the existing information that the escort with the convoy is not in fact superior.*

Hitler was at once interested, and in the meantime detailed orders were sent by Admiral Carls to Kluber for Kummetz. They contained the following: *There is to be no time wasted in rescuing enemy crews. It would be of value only to take a few captains and other prisoners with a view to interrogation. The rescue of enemy survivors by enemy forces is not desirable.* The implication of the last sentence should not be missed, since there was only one way to prevent it.

Later on December 30, the *Hipper* and destroyers *Friedrich Eckholdt, Richard Beitzen,* and *Z-29,* and the *Lützow* (commanded by Kapitän Stange), with destroyers *Theodor Riedel, Z-30,* and *Z-31,* sailed from Altenfjord. Kummetz's plan was simple and potentially

Hitler thought that Norway would be the scene of an Allied invasion: here, units of the High Seas Fleet gather in northern waters

effective. The two groups would separate during the night so that the *Lützow* would be 75 miles south of the *Hipper* at 0800 hours next morning, when the two heavy ships would turn eastward to search along the convoy's track, each ship with her three destroyers spread out 15 miles apart and 15 miles ahead. When the convoy was found, the *Hipper* group would attack first from the north, drawing off the escorts and forcing the convoy to turn south towards the approach of the *Lützow.*

But less than an hour after sailing from Altenfjord, Kummetz received a signal from Kluber which said: *Contrary to the operational order regarding contact with the enemy* [you are to] *use caution even against enemy of equal strength because it is undesirable for the cruisers to take any great risks.* Here was the fatal result of the cumulative losses of the German navy: that signal was to have an almost devastating effect on Kummetz's morale. Yet it had only been sent because Raeder, at the last moment, had felt that he must again remind Carls not to take unnecessary risks. Carls had sent a cautionary signal to Kluber at Altenfjord who, in turn, cleared his own yardarm with the signal to Kummetz—who did not know that it originated only because of Hitler's frequently expressed fears for the big ships.

'An enemy of equal strength' could mean anything; there are no tables equating destroyers to cruisers, or cruisers to pocket-battleships. An enemy of equal strength to a heavy cruiser could—in darkness and snow storms—mean three radar-equipped destroyers. In daylight, it could mean six. Much depended on the characters of individual commanding officers—as the Battle of the River Plate had proved, when Langsdorff in the pocket-battleship *Graf Spee* fled from Harwood's three cruisers.

Hitler always failed to realise that a gun, torpedo, or ship is only a piece of apparatus used by men, with or without skill and courage. Different characters, training, and aptitudes always count more in the end than speed or fire-power; and war at sea—more often than most affairs—can be a case of 'nothing venture, nothing gain'. The *Hipper* might have been sunk because she struck a mine off Altenfjord, or she might have been torpedoed by a British submarine lying in wait—but a mine or a submarine could not be regarded as 'an enemy of equal strength'.

Later that evening at Wolfschanze, Krancke told Hitler that the ships had sailed 'and would probably locate the convoy in the early hours of the morning'. He later wrote that 'The Führer emphasised that he wished to have all reports immediately, since—as I well knew—he could not sleep a wink when ships were operating.' In fact, Kummetz's plan and estimate of the convoy's position worked well; next morning—New Year's Eve—he noted in his war diary, '0718: Bearing 060° two silhouettes', and then '0725: signalled to *Eckholdt: Bearing 092° several silhouettes. Investigate.'*

Thus the stage was set for the Battle of the Barents Sea.

By this time, JW-51B was steering east, but had been driven well to the south of the planned route by the gale and was far behind its time schedule. Unknown to Captain Sherbrooke, the minesweeper *Bramble* was about 15 miles to the north-east, while the trawler *Vizalma* was shepherding her merchantman 40 miles to the north and steaming at 11 knots. The two cruisers *Sheffield* and *Jamaica* were getting into position to steam across the convoy's wake 50 miles astern and then turn eastwards to follow it. Both Burnett and Sherbrooke guessed that New Year's Eve would be the critical day, and both had been warned in the early hours that radio monitoring stations had detected a German destroyer off North Cape, a U-boat ahead of the convoy, and another to the south.

The battle begins

A signal three days earlier saying that Russian aircraft might meet the convoy had been misunderstood by the corvette *Hyderabad*, ahead of the convoy, to refer to destroyers; and when one of her lookouts reported at 0830 hours on New Year's Eve that there were two destroyers bearing due south on the convoy's starboard beam, it was assumed that they were Russian—and Sherbrooke was not warned. Fortunately, the *Obdurate* sighted and reported them as they passed astern of the convoy a few minutes later, and Sherbrooke told her to investigate. Signalling by lamp takes time, and it was not until 0915 that *Obdurate* could reach a position where—having by now sighted *three* destroyers—she made her challenge. There was no reply, but had they been Russians this would not have been unusual—and then one of the German ships revealed her nationality by opening fire, the gun flashes being seen by Sherbrooke, several miles away at the head of the convoy.

All the British ships went to action stations, and at once began to move to the positions ordered by Sherbrooke before the convoy sailed. *Onslow, Obdurate, Obedient,* and *Orwell* steamed for the rear of the convoy, *Achates* got into position to lay smoke, and an 'enemy report' was transmitted on Fleet waves. Then, as Sherbrooke in *Onslow* left the port side of the convoy, he sighted a large black shape among the snow squalls which was certainly larger than a destroyer, and was heading straight for the convoy. Immediately, he ordered *Onslow* to steer straight for it instead of waiting for his other destroyers. The shape was the *Hipper,* approaching from the north, and the three destroyers astern of the convoy were her escort which had been searching ahead, and which had for some time been shadowing the Allied ships.

At first Kummetz had not been at all sure that he had sighted the convoy. 'Probably our own destroyers are in wrong position,' he noted. 'I have the *Hipper* turned towards silhouettes in order to diminish our own silhouette'—and more than ten minutes were to pass before, at 0753, the convoy had been positively identified. Kummetz then wrote: 'Everything depends on making full use of this opportunity. Only speed of action can solve the problem of the danger of torpedo attacks from destroyers, which have to be considered in the light of my directive not to take any serious risks....'

At 0800—while Sherbrooke was still unaware that he was being shadowed—Kummetz had increased speed to 20 knots to catch up with the convoy for an attack at first light, and he was still doing this at 0830 when the *Obdurate* sighted the destroyers. At 0915, as one of them opened fire, Kummetz was far from happy, noting: 'Visibility very poor. Everything seems hazy. Cannot make out whether I am dealing with friend or foe. A total of ten ships now in sight, some of which look like destroyers. It cannot be said for certain whether our shadowing destroyers are not among them...'

But as soon as he saw the *Achates* begin to lay a smoke-screen, Kummetz gave permission to open fire on her, and the *Hipper* turned to bring all her 8-inch guns to bear. She had fired several broadsides when suddenly the *Onslow* was seen approaching, followed, in fact, by the *Orwell,* although *Hipper* did not sight her at first.

Although Sherbrooke had previously told his commanding officers that German surface ships would probably be scared of torpedo attacks by destroyers, he also knew that it was extremely unlikely that the British ships would ever get close enough to score hits. But he guessed the threat would be enough—and he was proved right. The *Hipper*'s log records: '0944: a destroyer [*Onslow*] approached from the south-east and then put her helm hard over. She had fired torpedoes.' She had not, but to complete the illusion one of the *Hipper*'s lookouts reported seeing one approaching. The German heavy cruiser swung away, turning her stern to the *Onslow* and presenting a smaller target. This also took her away from the convoy, which was what Sherbrooke had intended, and both British destroyers turned away, keeping between the convoy and the enemy, their torpedoes still in the tubes. As the *Hipper* turned, she opened fire on the *Onslow,* using radar.

Although he had been temporarily driven off, Kummetz was nevertheless full of admiration for Sherbrooke's destroyers, which 'conducted themselves very skilfully. They placed themselves in such a position between the *Hipper* and the convoy that it was impossible to get near the ships.... Their relative position forced the *Hipper* to run the risk of a torpedo attack while trying to use her guns on the convoy.' But for all that, the range from the convoy to the *Hipper* was at times down to 6 miles.

At 0957 the *Hipper* again headed for the convoy and opened fire on the *Onslow* and the *Orwell.* Her eight 8-inch guns fired a broadside weighing more than 2,000 pounds, and her 4·1-inch guns another 200 pounds. At that time the *Onslow,* the only destroyer in the flotilla armed with 4·7-inch guns (the others had First World War vintage 4-inch), had two of her four guns frozen up and was firing a 96-pound reply; the *Orwell,* with all four guns firing, 124 pounds. And, of course, the *Hipper* knew that the destroyers' shells could not hurt her.

After three minutes on the new course for his second attempt, Kummetz turned away again, to swing back four minutes later and close on the *Onslow* and *Orwell,* keeping up a high rate of fire which the destroyers managed to avoid by weaving, although still steering eastwards to shield the convoy. Yet again Kummetz turned away, much to the relief and surprise of the two British destroyers.

Sherbrooke then received a radio message from Force R—*Am approaching you on a course of 170*—and, realising that this put Force R to the north, whereas it should have been to the south, began to wonder if the *Hipper* was not luring him round to the north-east while another German force slipped in to attack the convoy from the south. He therefore ordered the *Obedient* and the *Obdurate*—which were still trying to catch him up—to rejoin the convoy.

Kummetz began his fourth approach at 1013, again bringing all his 8-inch, and 4·1-inch armament to bear on the *Onslow* and *Orwell,* and his own three destroyers following astern also opened fire. Both British destroyers dodged salvo after salvo until—at 1019

△ *Lützow:* her 11-inch guns played no part in the battle because her captain vacillated when the convoy was at his mercy

Admiral Kummetz: his fear of a torpedo attack allowed the RN destroyers to hold off the *Hipper* until Force R arrived

—the fifth shell in one of the *Hipper*'s salvos hit the *Onslow* abaft the bridge, ripped open the funnel, blew open the boiler side casing doors, lifted the safety-valve so that high-pressure steam shrieked out, cut radio aerials, and wrecked the radar office. One of the thousands of splinters ricocheted down from a gunnery radar aerial and hit Sherbrooke in the face, smashing his left cheekbone, his nose, and the left side of his forehead, and leaving him with his left eye hanging down his cheek. For the time being, no one else on the bridge knew he had been hit: he continued giving orders without a change in his voice. Eventually another officer, finding himself covered in blood and thinking he was himself hit, looked round to see that Sherbrooke had been badly wounded.

Hipper cripples the Onslow

A few moments later, two more of the *Hipper*'s 8-inch shells burst on the foredeck, wrecking both guns and starting fires which soon set cordite charges ablaze. Sherbrooke ordered the ship to be turned to starboard, speed cut to reduce the effect of the wind on the flames, and a smoke-screen to be laid. The *Hipper* then turned her attention to the *Orwell*, which had held to her course, and as her commanding officer was deciding whether to make a solo torpedo attack on *Hipper*—which would have meant certain destruction for *Orwell*—or to cover the stricken *Onslow*, the *Hipper* swung away yet again, to vanish in the obscurity of a snow squall. In the *Onslow*—apart from heavy damage to the ship—40 men had been killed or wounded in less than two minutes. Command of the escort was passed to *Obedient,* and Sherbrooke, finally agreeing to have his wounded dressed (he was subsequently awarded the Victoria Cross), ordered the *Onslow* to fall back on the convoy and home Force R by radio.

Imperial War Museum

△ HMS *Jamaica*: with HMS *Sheffield* she formed the covering Force R whose arrival completed the rout of the German squadron

After having dealt the *Onslow* a crippling blow without realising it, and having missed the opportunity of knocking out the *Orwell*—the only other ship between him and the convoy—Kummetz took the *Hipper* away at 31 knots to the east-north-east, hoping that the convoy would soon steam into the arms of the approaching *Lützow*. A ship sighted on the port side proved to be the missing minesweeper *Bramble,* which Kummetz sank before turning towards the convoy again. As he did so he noted: 'I was aware that with the decreasing visibility I was taking a risk. But I was hoping, after maintaining a heavy fire on the destroyers, to find one or more gaps in the defence through which I could attack the merchant ships.'

The *Lützow* had in the meantime come up from the south, sighted silhouettes at 0922 hours, received the *Hipper*'s signal that she was in action, and for the next 50 minutes steamed slowly north-east to intercept the convoy. Soon the pocket-battleship was steaming across its course, and her log noted: 'Several targets sighted through snow squalls.' The nearest was 3 miles away, the farthest 7 miles; the *Lützow*'s guns had a range of 15 miles. Her log then added—despite the reference to 'targets'—'No identification possible.'

At 1050 hours, the *Lützow*'s log recorded: 'Impossible at first to ascertain whether dealing with friend or foe because of the poor light and the smoke and mist on the horizon. To avoid observation from *Lützow* being obscured by the snow squalls and smoke drifting south, I [Kapitän Stange] decided to proceed at slow speed in the vicinity of the convoy, clear of the snow squalls, in order to take advantage of opportunities for attack as visibility improved.'

But Stange had missed his chance: the prize for which Operation Rainbow had been planned was between 2 and 3 miles away. As he passed across the convoy's bows, there was no British escort

Imperial War Museum

Captain Sherbrooke: his gallant handling, even when severely wounded, of the destroyer flotilla won him the VC

whatsoever nearby—yet not one of the *Lützow*'s six 11-inch guns, eight 5·9-inch guns, six 4·1-inch guns, or eight torpedo tubes was fired. Ironically, Admiral Kummetz's plan had worked perfectly: the *Hipper* had drawn off the main escorts, and the comparatively unprotected convoy had run straight towards the *Lützow*. The pocket-battleship then steamed ahead of the convoy, parallel with its course, but Stange wrote: 'Seeing no possibility of approaching the convoy from the east owing to the persistent lack of visibility, I decided to turn west to bring under my fire the enemy engaged with the *Hipper* to the north.' Ten minutes later, destroyers were sighted on the port bow, but Stange increased speed to 24 knots, explaining that 'the intended engagement of these vessels is abandoned due to darkness and extremely poor light.'

At 1106 the *Hipper* made her fifth foray against the convoy, opening a heavy fire on the already badly damaged *Achates*, which was still faithfully laying a smoke-screen, although badly holed forward and with her speed down to 15 knots. Almost at once the *Achates'* bridge was destroyed by an 8-inch shell, leaving a young lieutenant in command of the ship, which was then hit by two more 8-inch shells and began to sink.

The *Hipper* then turned as if to steer across the wake of the convoy, and the *Obedient*, *Orwell*, and *Obdurate* promptly attacked. The *Hipper* fired back but turned away because—once again—Kummetz was afraid of torpedo attacks. At 1136 hours, he signalled to the *Lützow*: *In action with escorting forces. No cruiser with convoy.* Only a few moments later, 24 6-inch shells burst round the *Hipper*: the *Jamaica* and *Sheffield* had arrived, and had achieved such complete surprise that the German cruiser still had her guns trained in the opposite direction.

At 0830 that morning, when the *Obdurate* had first sighted the three German destroyers, Admiral Burnett's Force R had been steaming north-west, in a good position, he thought, to intercept any attackers from astern, who would be silhouetted against the lighter southern horizon. But because the convoy had been driven so far south by the gale, he was some 60 miles to the north of it. At 0858 hours, the *Sheffield*'s radar picked up two echoes, one larger than the other, 7½ miles ahead, to the north-west and steering eastwards. They could have been stragglers from the convoy, or—more likely—enemy surface ships; and Burnett increased speed and tracked them by radar.

Force R tips the scale

They were in fact the trawler *Vizalma* and her merchantman. Then, at 0932, the reflection of gun flashes—from the German destroyer firing at the *Obdurate*—was seen to the southward. This put Burnett in a perplexing situation—a large and a small ship to the north, and gunfire to the south. Where was the convoy he was charged with protecting? The recent gale meant stragglers, and the gunfire might be from a detached escort. But at 0946 he saw the reflection of what was obviously heavy gunfire to the south—the *Hipper*, opening fire on the *Achates*. A few minutes later, Sherbrooke's 'enemy report' revealed that the convoy was far to the south of its estimated position, and Burnett 'increased speed to 25 knots and steamed towards the sight of the guns'. They were 40 or 50 miles away—between one and one-and-a-half hours' steaming.

For nearly an hour the British cruisers steamed south, the men on their bridges almost frozen stiff by the biting wind, until at 1030 hours *Sheffield*'s radar picked up a large ship 10 miles ahead—the *Hipper*—and a few minutes later a second—the *Lützow*—15 miles on the port bow. Burnett decided to attack, and both cruisers fired broadsides at a range of 8 miles. A shell from *Sheffield*'s fifth, and one each from *Jamaica*'s fourth and fifth salvos hit the *Hipper*. Her log recorded: '1133: *Hipper* hit on starboard side. . . . Number Three boiler gradually filled with oil and water and had to be shut off. . . . Maximum speed reduced to 23 knots. 1137: *Hipper* received two hits on port side. Fire broke out in the aircraft hangar. . . .'

The *Hipper* turned into a smoke-screen being laid by her own destroyers, and one of them—the *Friedrich Eckholdt*—followed by the *Richard Beitzen*, mistook the *Sheffield* for the *Hipper* and steered straight for her. The *Sheffield* hit her with seven salvos and left her smothered in smoke and flame, and sinking fast. The *Jamaica* engaged the *Beitzen*, which managed to escape.

The battle was now virtually over. The *Hipper*, the *Lützow*, and the five German destroyers fled back towards Altenfjord with Force R following long enough to make sure that they did not turn back. The convoy re-formed, but the battered *Achates* finally sank. The Battle of the Barents Sea, as it was subsequently called, was later described by Admiral Tovey, the C-in-C Home Fleet, as 'one of the finest examples in either of the two world wars of how to handle cruisers and destroyers in action with heavier forces'.

1942 Operation Regenbogen fails

December 22: Convoy JW-51B sails from Scotland for Murmansk, escorted by Captain Sherbrooke's six destroyers and the shadowing cruiser escort of Force R.

December 28: The convoy is blown far south of its intended track by a violent gale.

December 30: The convoy is sighted by U-354; German Admiral Kummetz is ordered to take *Hipper*, *Lützow*, and six destroyers and sink the convoy (Operation 'Rainbow'). Kummetz plans to attack with *Hipper* to the north and *Lützow* to the south.

December 31: 0915 hours: *Hipper*'s attendant destroyers sight the British destroyers and open fire, but Sherbrooke keeps his force between *Hipper* and the convoy.

0944 hours: Two of Sherbrooke's destroyers simulate torpedo attacks and cause the *Hipper* to turn away from the convoy.

1019 hours: On the fourth attempt to get at the convoy, *Hipper* cripples the *Onslow* but wastes the chance to dispose of the last destroyer in her way (*Orwell*).

1050 hours: *Lützow* has closed on the convoy from the south: Kummetz's plan has worked perfectly and all escorts have been drawn off from the convoy, but *Lützow* misses her chance and does not attack.

1106 hours: *Hipper* turns against the convoy for the fifth time but again turns away for fear of torpedoes.

1133 hours: The cruisers *Sheffield* and *Jamaica* of Force R arrive on the scene and open fire on *Hipper*, who retires. *Sheffield* sinks the German destroyer *Eckholdt*.

1137 hours: Kummetz breaks off the action and runs for Altenfjord: 'Rainbow' has been a complete failure, but the battered destroyer *Achates* sinks from damage from *Hipper*'s shells.

Admiral Raeder, who commanded the Kriegsmarine during its rapid pre-war build-up, and was now sacked by Hitler when he protested against the death sentence on the High Seas Fleet

Admiral Dönitz, C-in-C U-boats, who succeeded Raeder as leader of the Kriegsmarine. Although he persuaded Hitler to reverse his decision, the surface fleet never played an important role again

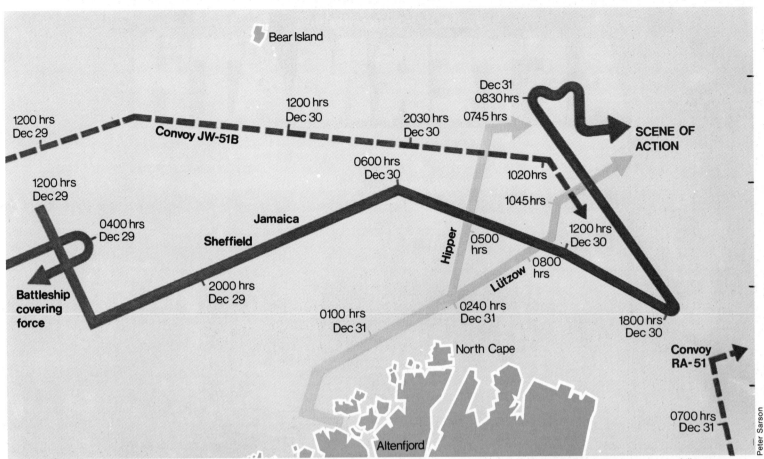

Bear Island

1200 hrs
Dec 29

Convoy JW-51B

1200 hrs
Dec 30

2030 hrs
Dec 30

Dec 31
0830 hrs

0745 hrs

SCENE OF
ACTION

1200 hrs
Dec 29

0400 hrs
Dec 29

0600 hrs
Dec 30

1020 hrs

1045 hrs

Jamaica

Sheffield

Hipper

0500
hrs

1200 hrs
Dec 30

2000 hrs
Dec 29

Lützow

0800
hrs

Battleship
covering
force

0100 hrs
Dec 31

0240 hrs
Dec 31

1800 hrs
Dec 30

Convoy
RA-51

North Cape

0700 hrs
Dec 31

Altenfjord

Peter Sarson

△ It was intended that *Hipper* would attack first from the north to draw off the escorts and turn the ships south towards *Lützow*.
But the plan failed because gales forced Convoy JW-51B to the south, *Hipper* was fought off — and *Lützow* hesitated until too late

The Kriegsmarine surface fleet in northern waters: the attack on Convoy JW-51B was its last attempt to justify its existence

AFTERMATH

Twilight of the Kriegsmarine

Hitler's fury at this latest failure was inflamed by the time-lag before an accurate report arrived from Altenfjord—especially as a Reuter statement had preceded it by almost 24 hours. At 1700 hours on January 1, 1943, Hitler summoned Krancke and again asked for news. According to Krancke, Hitler then 'walked up and down the room in great excitement. He said that it was an unheard-of impudence not to inform him; that such behaviour and the entire action showed that the ships were utterly useless; that they were nothing but a breeding-ground for revolution, idly lying about and lacking any desire to get into action. This meant the passing of the High Seas Fleet, he said, adding that it was now his irrevocable decision to do away with these useless ships. He would put the good personnel, the good weapons, and the armour-plating to better use.' Admiral Raeder was to be informed immediately.

Thus Hitler disposed of his surface fleet—the battleship *Tirpitz*, the two pocket-battleships *Lützow* and *Admiral Scheer*, the old battleships *Schleswig-Holstein* and *Schlesien*, the battle-cruisers *Scharnhorst* and *Gneisenau*, the heavy cruisers *Hipper* and *Prinz Eugen*, and the light cruisers *Leipzig*, *Köln*, *Nurnberg*, and *Emden*. From now on, the navy would have no ship larger than a destroyer. Raeder, in a well-reasoned memorandum, argued in vain the role of the Kriegsmarine in German strategy. His staff even produced a list of the men, material, and guns which would become available as a result of carrying out the order. They are of interest—particularly since Hitler ignored them completely.

Scrapping the fleet would make available only 300 officers and 8,500 ratings—about 1·4% of the total naval personnel—and 125,800 tons of steel from the scrapped ships—only one-twentieth of Germany's monthly requirements. The guns would make 15 coastal batteries, but a large part of the saving in yard facilities and workshops would be used up in mounting the guns, the first battery of which could be ready in a year and the last in 27 months. Scrapping the ships would require 7,000 men in five large shipyards, but the effect on the submarine programme would be slight: if all the steel yielded by the scrapping was used for submarine construction, seven more could be built monthly—provided that 13,000/14,000 specialised workers could be allocated to the task. Of the 300 officers made available, only about 50 would be of use for submarines, the rest being too old or otherwise unsuitable.

Raeder's memorandum pointed out that it was 'an irrevocable act', and concluded: 'I believe that the small gain in personnel and material which may be accomplished by paying off the fleet cannot outweigh the grave political and naval consequences that will result. I am firmly convinced that with the nucleus fleet [the smaller ships that would remain] the German navy is no longer capable of carrying out the task assigned to it in the Greater German War for Freedom.' Hitler's reaction to the memorandum was typical of his lack of understanding, and the Naval Staff soon heard that he had made several comments 'which were more or less sarcastic [and] dealt with minor questions only'. Raeder also composed an unusually outspoken letter to Hitler in which he said: 'The paying-off of the large surface vessels will be a victory gained by our enemies without any effort on their part . . . It will be viewed by the Allies as a sign of weakness and a lack of comprehension of the supreme importance of naval warfare in the final stages of the war.'

When Raeder eventually managed to see Hitler to try to make him change his mind, he was treated to an hour and a half's monologue on the role played by the Prussian and German navies since they came into existence, including the scuttling of the High Seas Fleet at Scapa Flow in 1919. 'The navy has always been careful to consider the number of their own ships and men as compared with the enemy before entering an engagement. The army does not follow this principle. As a soldier, the Führer demands that, once forces have been committed to action, the battle be fought to a decision.' Raeder did not point out that it was Hitler's own policy of not allowing the big ships to take risks that had led to the recent abortive Operation Rainbow, and at the end of the conference he spoke to Hitler in private and resigned as Commander-in-Chief. Hitler finally agreed, and chose Admiral Dönitz, one of the most junior in the navy and C-in-C U-boats, as Raeder's successor.

Although he was Germany's leading exponent of U-boat warfare, within three weeks of taking up his new appointment Dönitz—who had for years spread the gospel that the naval war could be won entirely by his U-boats—was arguing with Hitler to be allowed to keep the battleship *Tirpitz* and the battle-cruiser *Scharnhorst*. The next time the *Scharnhorst* sailed, on Christmas Day, 1943, it was to attack convoy JW-55B. In the convoy's escort were the *Onslow* and the *Orwell* and among the three cruisers covering the convoy under the command of Admiral Burnett was the *Sheffield* while the *Jamaica* was with the battleship *Duke of York,* flying the flag of Admiral Sir Bruce Fraser. Admiral Burnett's cruisers found the *Scharnhorst*; Sir Bruce's force sank her. The rest of the German capital ships were sunk at their moorings, or captured at the end of the war. Thus perished the navy which, under the capricious leadership of Hitler, had been in existence for 13 years, and was to have been a major factor in building the 'Thousand-Year Reich'.

BATTLE FOR THE ATLANTIC: THE SECOND PHASE

By the beginning of 1941 the difficulties and complexities of the Battle of the Atlantic were really starting to make themselves felt. The severe merchant ship losses in 1940 – 2,186,158 tons were sunk by the U-boats alone – had in part been met by wartime redeployment of peacetime shipping, but from 1941 on there was no hope of meeting further losses by this means. By this time merchant shipping had been stretched to its limit, and future losses could be made good only by new construction.

There were several factors which were to single out 1941 and 1942 as the years of special peril in that swaying, groping battle against the U-boats. The most immediate of them was the rapid build-up in numbers of the U-boats themselves, for the increased building programme put in hand by Germany at the outbreak of war was, by 1941, beginning to take effect. From the beginning of 1941 to the middle of 1943, the rate of building far exceeded the rate of loss, so that each succeeding month saw more and more U-boats in the Atlantic.

There were other factors in this battle which also came to the aid of the U-boats. An important one was the length of time a convoy took to cross the Atlantic. Allowing for diversions, weather, and other delays, the average time of passage of an Atlantic convoy throughout the whole of the war was just over 15 days; convoys to and from Freetown took four days longer. These long passages in effect presented the U-boats with more targets as the merchant ships made their laborious voyages across the ocean.

Another important factor was the short sea endurance of British escort vessels. At the outbreak of war, escort for convoys could only be provided up to a distance of about 500 miles from the British coast; beyond that the merchant ships were on their own. The occupation of Iceland after the disastrous land campaign of 1940 provided the opportunity of increasing the range of escort by the provision of a refuelling base on the island, but it was not until April 1941 that the first base there was fully in commission. Simultaneously, the Canadian navy de-

veloped bases in Newfoundland and eastern Canada, and by the use of these bases the range of surface escort was pushed even farther out into the Atlantic. By April 1941 it was as far as 35°W, a little more than half-way; two months later the first convoy with end-to-end surface anti-submarine escort sailed across the Atlantic. But because of the shortage of escort vessels, the average strength of escort was, in 1941, no more than two ships per convoy. It was not until the new long-range escorts, laid down just before the war, began to join the fleet that the strength of escort could be increased, in 1942 and 1943, to more adequate numbers.

As important as the surface escorts were those of the air, for of all the enemies of the U-boat the one most feared was the aircraft. Their range of vision and speed of attack were both vastly superior to those of the surface escorts, and an aircraft circling a convoy would force every U-boat within attacking range to submerge, thus condemning them to their low underwater speed and a much reduced range of vision. But here again, as with the surface escorts, the problem was range and endurance. As yet there were no aircraft in Coastal Command with a range or endurance long enough to cover Atlantic convoys for more than a short period of their passage, even using Iceland and Newfoundland as additional bases. To try to fill the gaps with carrier-borne aircraft was out of the question, for the few aircraft-carriers in the fleet were all required for other operational duties. Perhaps even more important, in 1941 efficient airborne radar by which aircraft could locate U-boats on the surface was as yet still in the future, as was an efficient airborne weapon which could kill a submarine.

The odds, then, were still strongly in favour of the U-boat, and they remained in its favour throughout 1941 and 1942. These were the years of building up the Allied anti-submarine escort forces, both surface and air, in numbers, in training, in tactical doctrine, and in the provision of scientific aids to locate U-boats — a long and tedious road to travel, made longer and harder by the rapid increase in numbers of the U-boats and by the development of their pack tactics of attack.

Early in 1941 the first step along this road was taken by the removal of the headquarters of the Western Approaches command from Plymouth to Liverpool, and by the appointment of a commander-in-chief whose sole responsibility was to conduct the campaign against the U-boats. Into this new headquarters was integrated the headquarters of 15 Group, Coastal Command, so that both surface and air escort could be co-ordinated from one operations room. Duplicates of the U-boat and trade plots in the British Admiralty were set up in the Western Approaches operations room, and the two connected with direct telephone and teleprinter links between Whitehall and Liverpool.

Admiral Sir Percy Noble was appointed as Commander-in-Chief Western Approaches in February 1941. He was, perhaps, the first to appreciate that the key to victory in this campaign lay just as much in the training of the officers and men as in the number of available escorts. Anti-submarine training establishments were set up at Dunoon and Campbeltown, experimental work was carried out at Fairlie, and a sea training organisation was based at Tobermory. To this last establishment went all new escort vessels as they completed their acceptance trials. For a month they were engaged in arduous sea exercises designed to harden crews, who were largely new recruits, to accustom them to normal Atlantic weather conditions, and to give them a reasonably intimate knowledge of their own ship and her capabilities.

Specialist training followed the sea training, so that by the time the new ship became fully operational her complement had not only been toughened by the Tobermory training but had also acquired the necessary professional and technological skills. All this, however, took time, and it was not until mid-1943 that the total overall training could be considered adequate. Until that time, the operational need in the Atlantic for all and every escort had to take precedence.

Another decision by Admiral Noble was to organise all the escorts into groups. By allocating eight escort ships to a group, the C-in-C could count on an effective strength of five or six escorts for each group, leaving a margin for refits of ships, leave periods,

After the first 'Happy Time' of the U-boats, Allied losses fell off —but not for long

training, and other contingencies. The great value of the group system was that each escort captain quickly became familiar both with the other escorts in the group and with the group commander's methods.

It is in this reorganisation of the escort forces, and the emphasis on proper anti-submarine training, that the seeds of ultimate victory in the Atlantic were sown. Yet if it was one important thing to recognise the correct road to travel in search of victory, Britain's actual journey along that road was a vastly more difficult business. The priorities in naval building in 1940 and 1941 had to be balanced between the needs of the operational fleet for aircraft-carriers, cruisers, destroyers, and landing-craft of various shapes and sizes, and of the anti-submarine fleet for frigates, sloops, and corvettes for purely escort purposes. There could obviously be no absolute priority for escort vessels, and so there was no possibility of keeping even level with the rate of U-boat building in Germany, let alone overtaking it. Two and a half bitter years were to pass before the escort groups finally established their superiority in this vast campaign.

The tribulations of 1941, when Britain was still in the throes of reorganising her anti-submarine forces, were magnified by the establishment of German long-range bomber squadrons on the coasts of France and Norway. These consisted mainly of Focke-Wulf Condors able to operate up to 800 miles into the Atlantic. Their mission was two-fold. Primarily their task was to locate British convoys so that the U-boats could be directed to them, but a secondary role was to sink merchant ships proceeding independently or straggling from their convoys. And in their secondary role alone they came a very close second to the U-boats. While, in January 1941, U-boats sank 21 ships of 126,782 tons, the long-range bombers accounted for 20 of 78,517 tons. The figures for February were similar: 39 ships of 196,783 tons to the U-boats, 27 ships of 89,305 to the bombers.

The answer to the Focke-Wulf bombers came in many ways. One was to route the independently sailed merchant ships far to the north, beyond the range of the bombers based in Norway and France, and to bring in convoys along a narrow route patrolled by long-range fighters. Another was to press ahead with the mounting of anti-aircraft guns in the merchant ships themselves, manned by gun-crews of seamen and marines. A third was to fit catapults in the old seaplane-carrier *Pegasus* and use her, with naval fighters embarked, as an anti-aircraft escort for convoys.

A development of the *Pegasus* idea was to fit catapults in selected merchant ships and embark a Hurricane fighter, which could then be catapulted off whenever an enemy aircraft was sighted. On completion of its mission, the Hurricane was ditched alongside a friendly ship and the pilot rescued. It was through means such as these, and also through the reluctance of the Luftwaffe to work in harmony with the Kriegsmarine, that the attack of the long-range bombers on shipping was eventually beaten.

With the gradual extension of convoy across the Atlantic, the reign of the German U-boat 'aces' came to an end. These were the men who had distinguished themselves in the Atlantic battle by the actual tonnage of merchant shipping they personally had sunk. In the first 18 months of warfare, while the convoy system was still being built up and the ocean still carried a large proportion of independently routed merchant ships, the number of easy targets had presented many opportunities to skilled commanders to amass a considerable tonnage to their personal credit.

The U-boat commanders themselves referred to the first year and a half of the war as 'the happy time'. By February 1941 the three greatest of the U-boat 'aces' were Gunther Prien, who had sunk the *Royal Oak* in Scapa Flow and claimed over 150,000 tons of merchant shipping, and Joachim Schepke and Otto Kretschmer, both of whom claimed over 200,000 tons of Allied shipping sunk. All three of them had been decorated by Hitler with the Knight's Cross with Oakleaves for their outstanding success, and all three were men from whom other U-boat commanders drew their inspiration. But by March all three had been eliminated from the battle. Prien, in U-47, was sunk on March 7 by the corvettes *Arbutus* and *Camellia* and the destroyer *Wolverine*; Schepke, in U-100, was sunk on March 17 by the *Walker* and *Vanoc*; and on the same night these same destroyers sank U-99, taking Kretschmer prisoner as he escaped

from his sinking U-boat. It was a heavy blow for Germany, for these three had been widely recognised in Germany as the cream of the U-boat commanders.

March 1941 saw the virtual end of the independent U-boat attack. As more and more merchant ships were brought into the convoy organisation, and as the range of convoy was extended farther across the Atlantic, the day of the individual U-boat was over. The British adoption and extension of convoy forced the U-boat command to work out new tactics, and it was from this situation that the pack attack at night was developed.

There was nothing basically new in this. A rudimentary form of pack attack had been evolved during the last year of the First World War, but had not been very successful because wireless signals, necessary for control of the pack, were still, relatively speaking, in their infancy. Tentative pack tactics had appeared in the Atlantic in 1940, but had not been developed because the individual U-boat operating in a fixed area was still finding sufficient targets to make its presence there well worth while. Those days, however, were now over for good, although in early 1942 the U-boats experienced another brief 'happy time'. This followed

the entry of the United States into the war, when a small number of U-boats concentrated on the eastern American seaboard and took a heavy toll of the unescorted shipping there. Six months later, when this shipping, too, was organised into convoys, these U-boats withdrew abruptly.

In the organisation of the pack attack, the U-boat command relied on one U-boat of the pack shadowing a convoy during daylight and homing in the remainder by directional wireless as night approached. All attacks were then made on the surface during the hours of darkness, when the tiny superstructure of the U-boat was well-nigh invisible to the defenders. With her high surface speed and her virtual invisibility, the advantages of night attack to the U-boat were considerable.

Yet the whole system had in it one element of weakness. The shadowing U-boat was forced to make a series of wireless signals reporting the convoy's position, speed, and alterations of course. These signals were invariably picked up by Allied directional-finding stations, and the bearings, when plotted in the British Admiralty's U-boat tracking room, revealed the position of the shadower.

For the Germans, the Battle of the Atlantic had two purposes and two phases. At first the Germans were trying to strangle Britain's lifelines across the Atlantic, but by 1942 the U-boats were fighting to prevent the establishment of an Allied invasion-force in Britain. Both phases were governed by the 'Black Gap' in mid-Atlantic, where Allied escorts could not protect the vital convoys. The occupation of Iceland in 1940 had been the first step towards closing the gap, but no positive counterattack could hurt the U-boats until long-range frigates and escort-carriers could shepherd the convoys all the way across. In the spring of 1943, with the Torch landings safely over, the attack on the U-boats began in earnest. The diagram below shows how the gap was closed, and depicts the major Atlantic convoy routes and U-boat bases

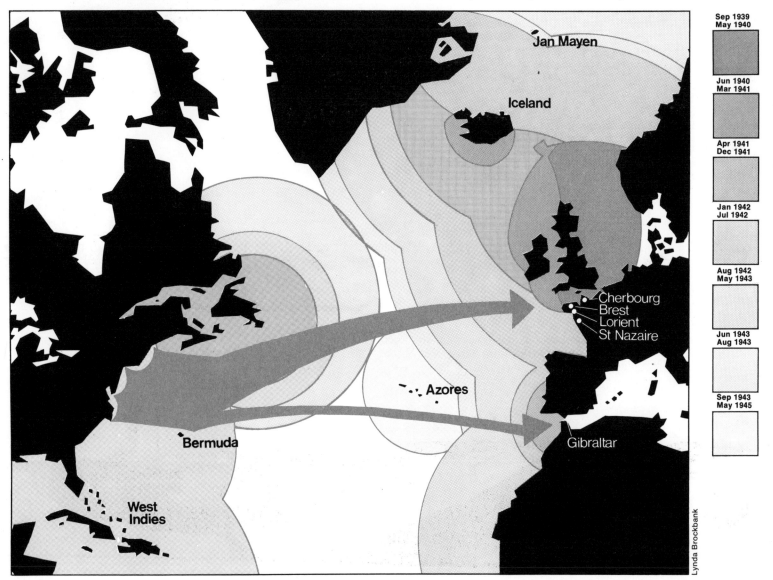

Jan Mayen

Iceland

Cherbourg
Brest
Lorient
St Nazaire

Azores

Bermuda

Gibraltar

West Indies

Sep 1939
May 1940

Jun 1940
Mar 1941

Apr 1941
Dec 1941

Jan 1942
Jul 1942

Aug 1942
May 1943

Jun 1943
Aug 1943

Sep 1943
May 1945

Lynda Brockbank

'The Battle of the Atlantic was the dominating factor all through the war. Never for one moment could we forget that everything elsewhere depended on its outcome' Churchill

For the Allies, the Battle of the Atlantic was not only a race to develop new and more advanced equipment than the enemy, but it was also a struggle to build even the basic minimum of aircraft and ships to provide an adequate escort for all convoys. Before the war, the escort programme and Coastal Command had been the 'Cinderellas' of the defence budget, and the chronic shortage of ships and aircraft was not something which could be rectified at once, when all other branches of the services were crying out for new equipment. It was not until the middle of 1942 that a massive building programme—much of which was undertaken in Canada—meant that the ships to provide a shore-to-shore escort became available in adequate numbers, and the RAF began to receive aircraft specially designed for the anti-submarine patrol role—instead of having to make do with old equipment which lacked the necessary range and duration. But once the escort forces had received the vital ships and aircraft, equipped with the new anti-submarine weapons, the 'happy time' of the U-boats was quickly ended

HMS *Starling:* an escort sloop of the modified *Black Swan* class. This class, the first of which were laid down before the outbreak of war, proved to be a most efficient escort design, combining good AA and anti-submarine armament with adequate speed and seaworthiness. **Displacement:** 1,350 tons. **Dimensions:** $299\frac{1}{2} \times 38\frac{1}{2} \times 8\frac{3}{4}$ feet. **Speed:** 20 knots. **Armament:** Six 4-inch and 12 20-mm anti-aircraft guns. **Complement:** 192

HMS *Clematis:* a corvette of the *Flower* class. This class was ordered before the war as part of the massive rearmament programme, and the design was based on the whale catcher. The ships proved to be too small to fulfill the ocean escort role adequately, in spite of being excellent seaboats. **Displacement:** 925 tons. **Dimensions:** $205 \times 33 \times 11\frac{1}{2}$ feet. **Armament:** One 4-inch gun, one multiple pom-pom. **Complement:** 85

HMS *Towey:* a frigate of the *River* class. This was the first of the new ocean escort classes, larger and faster than the corvettes and designed for mass production. The subsequent *Loch* and *Bay* classes were developments of this design. **Displacement:** 1,370 tons. **Dimensions:** $301\frac{1}{4} \times 36\frac{1}{2} \times 9$ feet. **Speed:** 20 knots. **Armament:** Two 4-inch guns, ten 20-mm anti-aircraft guns. **Complement:** 140

HMS *Biter:* one of the escort carriers which were brought into service to bridge the 'mid-Atlantic gap' in land-based air cover. They were built on merchant ship hulls and had wooden flight-decks. **Displacement:** 8,200 tons. **Dimensions:** $492\frac{1}{4} \times 66\frac{1}{4} \times 23\frac{1}{4}$ feet. **Speed:** $16\frac{1}{2}$ knots. **Armament:** Three 4-inch and 15 20-mm anti-aircraft guns, 15 aircraft. **Complement:** 555

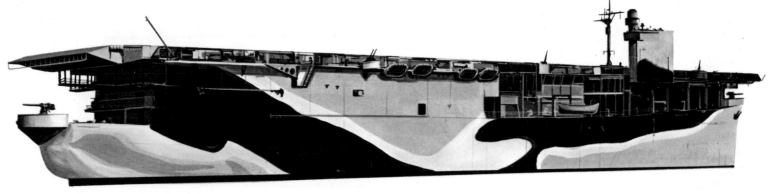

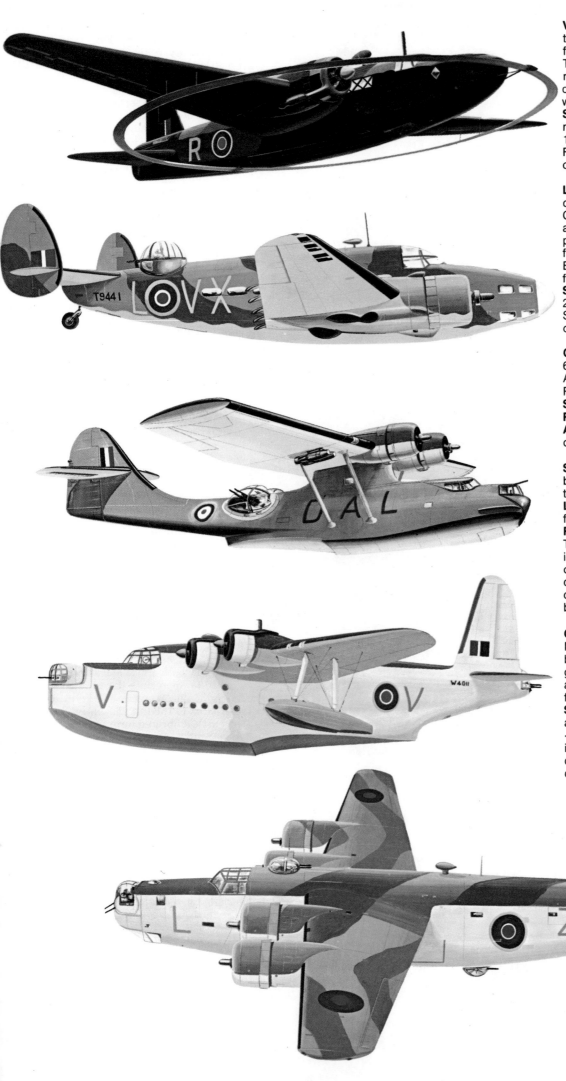

Vickers Wellington Mark I: One of the older designs which was modified for use by Coastal Command. This aircraft is fitted with the magnetic ring which was used to destroy magnetic mines in shallow waters. **Length:** 64 feet 7 inches. **Span:** 86 feet. **Speed:** 265 mph maximum. **Range:** 3,200 miles at 180 mph. **Crew:** Five. **Armament:** Four ·303-inch MG. Up to 6,000 lb of bombs

Lockheed Hudson: An American design which was in service with Coastal Command as a training aircraft before the war, and was pressed—very successfully—into front-line service for much of the Battle of the Atlantic. **Length:** 44 feet 2½ inches: **Span:** 65 feet. **Speed:** 292 mph maximum. **Range:** 2,160 miles at 254 mph. **Armament:** Seven ·303-inch MG. Four 500-lb depth charges. **Crew:** Four

Consolidated PBY Catalina: Over 650 of this tough and dependable American design were used by the RAF. **Length:** 65 feet 1¼ inches. **Span:** 104 feet. **Speed:** 185 mph. **Range:** 3,750 miles at 130 mph. **Armament:** Six ·303-inch MG, four depth charges. **Crew:** Up to eight

Short Sunderland: Over 700 were built of this military development of the pre-war 'C' class flying boats. **Length:** 85 feet 4 inches. **Span:** 112 feet 9½ inches. **Speed:** 212 mph. **Range:** 2,980 miles. **Armament:** Two ·50-inch and up to 12 ·303-inch machine-guns. Up to 2,000 lb of bombs or depth charges were carried internally and wound out on racks through panels just below the wing roots

Consolidated B-24 Liberator: Maritime patrol version of the bomber which was built in far greater numbers than any other US aircraft. **Speed:** 300 mph at 30,000 feet. **Length:** 67 feet 2 inches. **Span:** 110 feet. **Range:** 2,100 miles at 215 mph. **Armament:** Up to 14 ·50-inch MG, 5,000 lb of bombs internally—up to 12,800 lb could be carried on wing racks for short distances. **Crew:** 12

Left: A U-boat tackles heavy weather in the Bay of Biscay. *Right:* A lookout keeps watch from a surfaced U-boat. In this condition U-boats were very vulnerable to air attack

△ Concrete shelters for U-boats were built all along the coast of occupied Europe
▽ A returning U-boat crew is congratulated by the flotilla commander

Yet even with this essential knowledge, there was still a very long road to travel before victory could come to the Allies in the Atlantic. There were, in the years 1941 and 1942, shortages in almost every aspect of the war against the U-boats—shortage of escort vessels, shortage of training time, shortage of adequate weapons, shortage of the technological advances required to deal with the modern German U-boat and her new tactics. But of all the shortages, the most chronic was that of long-range and long-endurance aircraft. It had already become apparent that the convoy which had both air and surface escort to protect it was virtually immune from attack. The problem was to devise a method whereby aircraft could always be on hand throughout the whole of a convoy's Atlantic passage.

To close the mid-Atlantic gap, which was as yet far beyond the range of any shore-based aircraft yet developed, the Admiralty in 1941 placed orders in America for a number of small escort carriers (virtually a Liberty ship hull fitted with a flying deck and hangar space). Yet even with American production methods it would be over a year before they could be expected to become operational. In the meantime, Coastal Command had to rely on a single squadron of very long-range Liberator aircraft which, originally composed of 20 aircraft, was very quickly reduced to a strength of ten by wastage and allotment to Ferry Command and BOAC. All attempts to increase the number, and to obtain long-range Lancaster bombers for the Atlantic battle, failed. The convoys and surface escorts were left to battle it out against the U-boats, handicapped as they were by the lack of one of the most powerful agents for success. Such air escort as did exist (700 miles from Northern Ireland and Western Scotland, 400 miles from Iceland, and 700 miles from Canadian bases) not only left a large gap in mid-Atlantic completely beyond reach of shore-based air escort, but was of itself spasmodic and in any case limited to daylight hours.

The Battle of the Oceans
It is difficult, over so immense a stage as the seas which both divide and join the Commonwealth, to appreciate the vast extent of the Battle of the Atlantic. The term itself is a restriction of the full encounter, for in effect the battle embraced far more than the North and South Atlantic oceans themselves. U-boats and armed raiders operated in the Indian Ocean, across which ran the main sea routes to India, Australia, and New Zealand, as important to global strategy as was the Atlantic. And for a long time the Arctic Ocean was the only available highway for supplies to Russia after the start of her great campaign, though later an alternative route was opened through the Persian Gulf. All of them called for protection from U-boat and raider attack, and what has come to be known as the Battle of the Atlantic was, more truly, a battle of the oceans.

In terms of voyages, this vast encounter ran into several hundreds of thousands of miles steamed each week; in terms of ships it could mean as many as 1,000 at sea on any one day throughout the whole of the war, all of them to be protected against attack by an enemy who could operate virtually unseen and unheard. This was the true yardstick against which the battle must be measured, an immense and ceaseless conflict waged over millions of square miles of ocean.

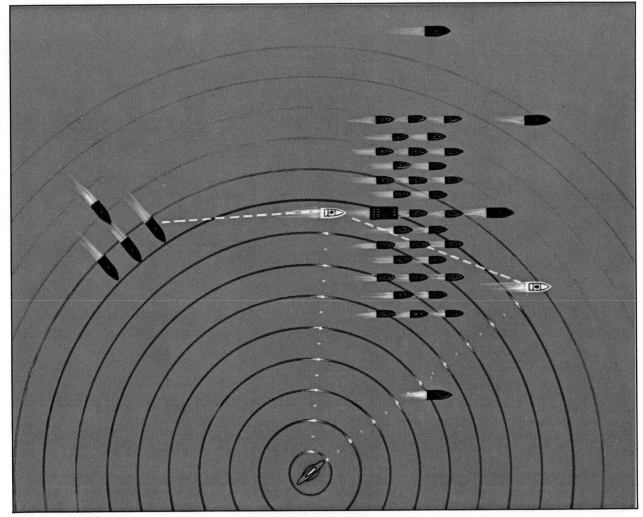

The Huff-Duff, or High Frequency Direction Finder, was developed to locate attacking submarines and destroy them without any prior warning of detection. The device was installed in two of the escort ships, which, by taking a cross-bearing on a U-boat's radio signals, pinpointed its position. This was then transmitted to the 'Hunter Killer' group which could close within Asdic range and destroy the U-boat. This device enabled U-boats to be located at far greater distances, and destroyed or driven off before they could get within range of the convoy

One other aspect of this battle needs to be mentioned. As early as 1941 the Chiefs-of-Staff were already laying their plans to move from the defensive to the offensive. All realised that when this time came, it would call for a vast Allied army based in Britain, with a huge logistic backing, poised for the assault on Europe which alone could lead to complete victory. Most of this great army, and most of its logistic backing, could only come from across the Atlantic, men and materials from the United States and Canada. Security of the Atlantic was vital for this vast movement, and only a clear-cut victory over the U-boats could guarantee such security. This Atlantic battle was the one vital cog in the whole machinery of the war, for failure there would inevitably bring defeat to the whole Allied cause. It was the one and only key which could unlock the door to final victory.

The merchant ship losses in 1941 were grievous. U-boats alone sank 432 ships of 2,171,754 tons, while aircraft claimed another 371 ships of 1,017,422 tons. Merchant and warship raiders added during the year to the total by 84 ships of 428,350 tons, while a further 111 ships of 230,842 tons were lost in enemy minefields laid around the British coasts. From all causes, the final loss for the year was 1,299 ships totalling 4,328,558 tons – an overall loss well beyond Allied building capacity to replace.

These figures give an accurate idea of the severity of the battle, but they were far surpassed by the figures for the following year. The U-boats alone exceeded the total losses for 1941 by very nearly 2,000,000 tons (6,226,215 tons), and the overall loss for the year was 7,790,697 tons, represented by 1,664 ships.

'The U-boat attack of 1942,' wrote Churchill, 'was our worst evil.' Indeed, in no other theatre of the war, save perhaps in the Pacific, was the outlook quite so black. And again it was the same story, the inability of the Allies, in the face of all their maritime commitments, to produce escort vessels and long-range aircraft fast enough to hold the U-boat growth. German ship production facilities were concentrated almost entirely on U-boats to the exclusion of almost every other type of vessel, and the speed with which they were produced can be measured by the steady increase in operational boats. Excluding those used for training and other purposes, the numbers of U-boats available for operations at sea rose from 91 in January 1942 to 196 in October of the same year, to 212 as the year came to its close, and to a peak of 240 in April 1943. And although during 1942 a total of 87 U-boats were sunk, including those lost through accidents in German home waters, the steady production of new boats far outweighed losses.

The entry of the United States into the war brought to the U-boat captains their second 'happy time'. For six months the US relied on sea and air patrols as the means of countering U-boat attacks, in spite of all British experience that convoy was the only method of holding in check the mounting ship losses. Admiral Dönitz, commander-in-chief of the U-boat area, sent five U-boats into the area on the declaration of war against the United States, increasing the number by stages to a total of 21. By June 1942, when the Americans eventually put all their ships into convoy, these U-boats had sunk no less than 505 vessels. This holocaust moved even Dönitz into song. 'Our submarines,' he exulted, 'are operating close inshore along the coast of the United States of America, so that bathers and sometimes entire coastal cities are witnesses to that drama of war, whose visual climaxes are constituted by the red glorioles of blazing tankers.'

Dönitz and the German High Command had calculated that if an average of 800,000 tons of Allied shipping could be sunk each month, an Axis victory was certain. The overall rate of loss throughout 1942 was fractionally below 650,000 tons a month; but optimistic reports on estimated tonnage sunk made by the individual U-boat commanders led Dönitz to believe that his objective of 800,000 tons monthly was being achieved. Yet even 650,000 tons a month was a crippling rate for the Allies, far beyond their capacity for replacement, and it is true enough that, throughout these grim months of 1942, defeat in the Atlantic, and hence in the war as a whole, was a possibility that haunted the thoughts of all the war leaders.

Just as serious as the loss of essential imports which this rate of sinking made inevitable was the unforeseen cutback in the rate of building up forces in Britain for the assault on Europe, without which there could be no final victory over Germany. This build-up of forces had been given the code-word 'Bolero', and the plans hammered out by the Chiefs-of-Staff of Britain and the United States had called for a strength of five divisions of Canadian and United States troops in Britain by the end of 1942. As the year ended, 'Bolero' was so far in arrears that less than one division had arrived, and the overall plan was falling more and more into arrears. The whole future course of the war, every hope, every plan, hung in the balance poised over the Atlantic.

Normal gun principle—
expensive and requiring
special steel

The ideal complement to Asdic, Hedgehog (in action, above) fired a pattern of 24 32-lb bombs. Their contact fuses made the identification of 'kills' easy

Spigot principle—
steel rod takes the
place of the shell;
projectile replaces
barrel

THE NEW TECHNIQUES

The Hedgehog
The original Hedgehog was refined, and by the end of the war was a very elaborate weapon. This was the US Navy's version, but in essence it is the same spigot mortar firing a cluster of contact-fused bombs ahead of the ship

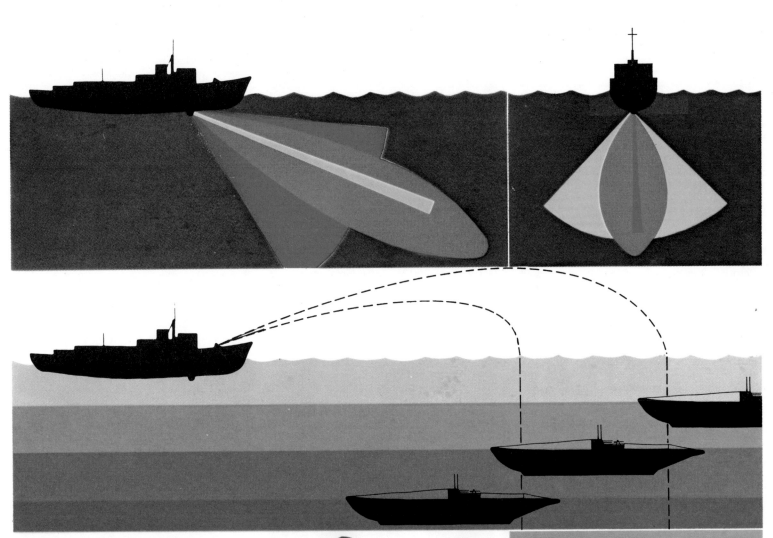

With new techniques and better tools, now, for the first time in the Atlantic, Britain had the upper hand

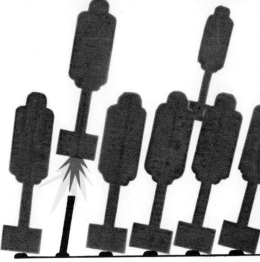

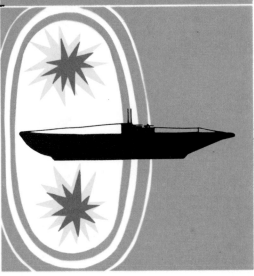

Asdic (top) consisted of a transmitter/receiver which sent out sound impulses, and picked up the echo if an impulse struck an object. By noting the time between transmission and return of the 'ping' the range of the object could be worked out. In its developed form, Asdic used three impulses: one diffused over a wide area (orange) to locate a U-boat, and two others—narrow vertical (pink) and horizontal (green)—to fix its position more accurately. But Asdic had its drawbacks: the receiver picked up echoes from fish, tidal disturbances, and changes in water temperature, and as long as depth charges had to be dropped astern, the Asdic would lose contact with the U-boat as it passed underneath during the last stages of the run in.

To overcome this, **Hedgehog** and **Squid** were developed. Both threw their bombs ahead of the ship in a pattern designed to straddle a U-boat (above). The charges dropped and exploded at different speeds and depths so as to give maximum coverage of an area. The main difference between the weapons was that Hedgehog (▷ top) fired a pattern of 24 bombs which would explode on contact, while Squid (▷ bottom) fired three bombs intended to explode around a U-boat and crack its hull with concussion. The advantage of Hedgehog was that the Asdic contact would not be disturbed unless there was a hit, but with the Squid it was often possible for a near miss to force a U-boat to the surface

Chris Harrison

During 1942, however, the anti-submarine frigates, ordered in 1939 and 1940, began to come forward from the builders' yards. These were ships which had the speed and endurance so vital in the Atlantic battle. One of the great problems of convoy escort had been the danger of allowing the existing escorts to hunt U-boats to their final destruction, more often than not a long and exacting operation. Their prime duty had always been to protect the merchant ships; but a convoy could not stand still in mid-Atlantic while its escorts were engaged in hunting and destroying. A great number of U-boats, located by radar and asdic, lived to fight again simply because the convoy escorts could not spare the time to hunt them to destruction. The merchant ships always had to come first.

The commissioning of the anti-submarine frigates, however, provided an answer to this problem. The growth in overall force represented by these frigates enabled Admiral Noble to build up support groups of ships, which could be directed to join the defences of any convoy threatened by a pack attack. While the normal escort group could continue with the convoy, providing the necessary close defence, the support group could engage in prolonged hunting operations, holding a detected U-boat with its asdics while the attacks were made. The first support group, under the command of Commander F. J. Walker, was at sea by the third week of September, 1942, but other events were to delay the full implementation of this new contribution to the Atlantic battle.

Almost simultaneously with the arrival of the frigates came the new ahead-throwing anti-submarine weapons; first the 'Hedgehog', a multi-barrelled mortar which threw 24 charges ahead of the attacking ship; and then the 'Squid', which threw a pattern of three full-sized depth-charges. The old method of attack, by dropping depth-charges over the ship's stern, had suffered from the great drawback that asdic contact with the U-boat was lost during the run-in, and the final stages of any attack had to be made by guesswork. The new weapons enabled asdic contact to be held throughout the attack and right up to the moment of depth-charge explosion, resulting in a far greater degree of accuracy.

By the late summer of 1942 the first of the new, small escort carriers, which had been ordered from the United States the previous year, was commissioned for service. She was the *Avenger,* and by the end of the year six more were serving in the fleet. These aircraft-carriers were to provide the final answer to the U-boat threat, their aircraft filling the Atlantic gaps which were still beyond the range of shore-based aircraft. It was in these gaps—in mid-Atlantic, off the north coast of Brazil, and around the hump of Africa—that the U-boats concentrated and continued to find convoys unprotected by air escort. Pack attacks on convoys in these areas were made in such strength as to swamp the surface escorts, and provided a rich harvest for the U-boats.

The stage, then, was set by the late autumn of 1942 to turn to the offensive in the Atlantic. With support groups to augment the surface escorts of threatened convoys, with carrier-borne aircraft to provide the essential air escort across the Atlantic gaps, with the new weapons of attack which enabled the full benefit of asdic contact to be held to the last moment, the prospects of success looked bright. And to Liverpool, in November 1942, came Admiral Sir Max Horton as com-

mander-in-chief. He was a submarine officer of great distinction, and thus brought to his task an intimate knowledge of submarine warfare in all its aspects. He inherited from Admiral Noble an organisation in which most of the essential groundwork had already been done and a command whose forces were growing almost daily as the new ships ordered in 1940 and 1941 reached completion.

One other aspect of this Atlantic battle needs a mention. A part of the difficulties which beset the Allies in 1942, resulting in such heavy losses of shipping, had been caused by the withdrawal from Atlantic duties of the United States escort forces in June of that year. These vessels were needed partly for the Pacific war and partly to escort troop and logistic convoys for the projected assault on North Africa in November 1942.

By the end of the year the division of escort forces in the Atlantic was: Britain providing 50%, Canada 48%, and the United States 2%. Early in 1943, at a convoy conference held in Washington, the United States declared that she would have to withdraw completely from all trade convoy protection in the Atlantic. It was a decision which came at an awkward moment, with the battle at its height and the British and Canadian forces stretched to their uttermost. The American decision, though it represented but a small part of the burden, had to be absorbed equally between Britain and Canada.

As the escort forces were poised, in the late autumn of 1942, to turn to the offensive against the U-boats, a new blow struck the

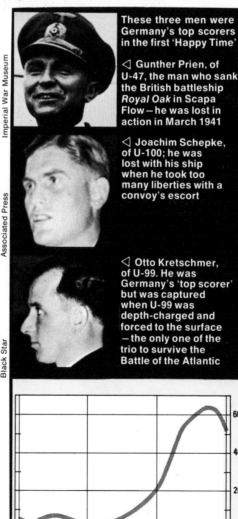

These three men were Germany's top scorers in the first 'Happy Time'

◁ Gunther Prien, of U-47, the man who sank the British battleship *Royal Oak* in Scapa Flow—he was lost in action in March 1941

◁ Joachim Schepke, of U-100; he was lost with his ship when he took too many liberties with a convoy's escort

◁ Otto Kretschmer, of U-99. He was Germany's 'top scorer' but was captured when U-99 was depth-charged and forced to the surface —the only one of the trio to survive the Battle of the Atlantic

Imperial War Museum

Associated Press

Black Star

Western Approaches command. Operation 'Torch', the invasion of French North Africa, was mounted in November, and both the escort carriers and the newly formed support groups were detached from the Atlantic convoy routes to provide protection for the troop convoys in which this expeditionary force was transported. This campaign was to last until May 1943, and until the end of March the Atlantic escort forces had to continue the battle still with no air cover over the three 'gaps', and still with no support groups to supplement the escort groups in the battles around the convoys.

As the year turned, the rate of loss in the Atlantic showed little change from the figures of 1942. Wild weather in the Atlantic during January produced difficulties for the U-boats in their operations, and the loss during the month was 203,000 tons. In February it rose to 359,000 tons; by March it was back to the high average rate of 1942, 627,000 tons of shipping being sunk in that month. It was during this month that the American decision to withdraw completely from the Atlantic was announced at the conference in Washington.

It was, in fact, while this conference was in session that one of the biggest and most disastrous convoy battles of the whole war was fought out in the Atlantic. Two convoys had been sailed from Halifax to Britain, one fast convoy of 25 ships and one slow one of 52. The fast convoy was sighted by a U-boat early in its passage, and before long a pack of eight U-boats was in contact. Over the next three days and nights they sank 12 merchant ships. Some hundred or so miles ahead, the slow convoy was also sighted and reported, and a pack of 12 U-boats concentrated against it. As the two convoys closed up, the two packs merged into one, swamping the defence and causing heavy loss. Out of these two convoys alone 21 ships of 141,000 tons were sunk.

What made this particular convoy battle even harder to bear was that only one U-boat was sunk by the escort forces. It was without question a serious defeat, remarkable even in a period in which there were few gleams of light to encourage the Allies in their desperate struggle.

Climax of the battle

Few could doubt, in March 1943, that the Atlantic battle had reached its climax, and that out of the operations of the next three or four months one side or the other must slide down into defeat. Admiral Dönitz was making his supreme effort, and out of an operational strength of 240 U-boats he concentrated no fewer than 112 in the North Atlantic. Flushed by success, and highly trained, the U-boat commanders were able, by the very nature of submarine warfare, to dictate the conditions in which they fought the battle. Almost without exception the U-boat packs were concentrated in those areas beyond the reach of air escort, and it was here that they reaped almost the whole of their grim harvest.

To the Atlantic, at the end of March, came the escort carriers, released at last from their duties with the Torch convoys. With them, too, came the support groups, so that at long last there existed in the Atlantic the possibility of hunting detected U-boats to their final destruction. And almost simultaneously, two other events made notable contributions to the battle. Using his authority as commander-in-chief of the US forces, President Roosevelt took a hand in the dis-

Hitting back at the U-boats

△ A depth-charge is hurled from an American Coast-Guard cutter in the early stages of a battle with a U-boat (eventually destroyed). ▽ Illustration of the supreme power of the Atlantic air patrols: strafing, bombing, and surface-charge attacks on U-boats in mid-Atlantic

tribution of the very long-range Liberator aircraft being delivered from America. By the end of March, 20 of them were in operation in the North Atlantic; by mid-April the number had grown to 41. It was still far too few to cover the essential needs, but it was at least an earnest promise of better things to come.

The other great contribution came from the scientists. They designed a very short-wave radar set which could reflect from much smaller objects at sea and against which the German radar search receiver, as fitted in the U-boats, was of no avail. These centimetric radars were fitted to many of the surface escorts around the end of 1942 and beginning of 1943, and they led to many more contacts with attacking U-boats, with the added advantage that the U-boats had now no knowledge that they had been detected. The new radar was also being fitted in aircraft, but other priorities in the RAF made it slow to arrive in Coastal Command.

Early in May another considerable convoy battle was fought, providing the first real opportunity of testing the value of the support group and continuous air escort in anti-submarine warfare. An outward bound convoy was delayed and to some extent scattered by a violent storm south of Greenland, an area which was known to contain a heavy concentration of U-boats. A pack of 12 U-boats concentrated around the convoy. This was the type of situation for which the support groups were formed, and two groups were ordered out from St John's, Nova Scotia, as the convoy approached the area. They were somewhat delayed by the storm which had scattered the convoy, and before they could arrive the U-boats had sunk five ships during night attacks, following this with four more sunk during the following day. One of the convoy's escorts, the corvette *Pink*, attacked and sank U-192.

The two support groups joined the convoy that evening, and for the first time U-boats came up against the full application of the new countermeasures. As the convoy was collected and re-formed after its battering in the storm, the U-boats renewed their attacks, but each one was detected and driven off before damage could be done to the merchant ships. HMS *Loosestrife* detected, chased, and sank U-638; the destroyer *Vidette* held U-125 with her asdic and sent her to the bottom with a hit from her Hedgehog, the *Oribi* rammed and sank U-531, and the sloop *Pelican* detected and held U-438 with her asdic and hunted her to final destruction. Aircraft operating over the convoy accounted for two more, U-710 being destroyed by a Coastal Command aircraft and U-630 by an aircraft of the Royal Canadian Air Force. But the cup of bitterness was not yet full for the U-boats, for U-659 and U-439 collided in the darkness and both were lost.

This was a severe defeat for the U-boats, but one defeat in a campaign does not necessarily mean victory for the other side. Yet the fate of the convoys which followed was to prove that this was, in fact, no flash in the pan. The next fast convoy lost three ships, but the cost to the enemy was three U-boats sunk. The slow convoy which made its passage at the same time had two ships sunk, while two U-boats were sunk by the escorts and others from the attacking pack were seriously damaged. Of the next pair of convoys, the result was even more dramatic. The slow convoy reached Britain with all its merchant ships in company, but in its path lay the sunken hulls of U-954, U-258,

U-209, U-273, and U-381. The fast convoy also arrived without loss, with U-752 joining her sisters on the bed of the Atlantic.

Perhaps more impressive still were the overall figures from April to July. In April, when the new and integrated system of surface and air escort was only just getting into its stride, the U-boats sank 245,000 tons of shipping and lost 15 of their number in the process. In May they sank 165,000 tons at a cost to themselves of 40 U-boats. In June the figures were 18,000 tons and 17 U-boats; and in July, 123,000 tons and 37 U-boats.

Nor was this the whole of the Atlantic story, for Coastal Command was conducting a separate offensive over the main U-boat transit areas to and from the Atlantic. Using the new centimetric radar, depth-charges set to explode at a shallow depth, and searchlights to illuminate U-boats detected at night, they sank a further 13 U-boats during April and May, taking full advantage of a tactical mistake made by Admiral Dönitz, who ordered his U-boats to proceed to and from their operational areas on the surface, and fight it out against attacking aircraft. Against the new weapons, they had small chance of success.

Against losses such as these it was hardly surprising that morale in the U-boats cracked. It was a staggering reversal of the trend of the battle in the Atlantic, and even more so in the realisation that it took no more than five weeks from the time the full offensive was mounted to drive the U-boats, at the very height of their power and success, to search for less hazardous waters in which to operate. For nearly three months after the decisive May battles, the Atlantic was empty of U-boats, and even when they did return, though never again in the same numbers, it was very noticeable that the individual U-boat commanders had lost their will to attack.

On the purely analytical plane, one could attribute this victory in the Atlantic battle to the influence of the support groups in anti-submarine warfare, to the provision of continuous air escort over the convoys, to the centimetric radar and the other new weapons provided by the scientists and technologists. A considerable element in the victory must go, too, to the expertise in the interpretation of U-boat Intelligence developed in the Submarine Tracking Room in the British Admiralty. Their handling of all forms of Intelligence, and in particular the directional bearings of U-boat wireless signals, enabled them to predict with considerable accuracy the build-up of U-boat concentrations in the Atlantic and to divert convoys from the main danger areas.

But the real victory went much deeper than this. It lay just as much in the skill and endurance of the men who manned the escort vessels and the merchant ships, in their refusal to acknowledge defeat in the dark years of 1941 and 1942, in their courage which fortified them to return again and again to that vast battlefield where the odds were weighted so heavily against them. Over the centuries there have been, in British naval history, victories which shine like jewels across the years: none can shine more brightly than that achieved in this long, bitter, groping battle fought across the oceans.

In the concept of overall strategy in the European theatre, the winning of the Battle of the Atlantic was always recognised as the essential prerequisite of ultimate victory. When the German armies overran most of

Europe in 1940 and 1941, it was British sea power, fortified by the navies of the Dominions and of such allies as had ships to contribute, that alone stood between the Axis and the domination of the world. Sea power, with its flexibility and natural resilience, held the ring around Germany and Italy, denying to the enemy the riches of the world which lay across the oceans. The U-boat campaign was the chosen, indeed the only, weapon of the Axis to break the ring. How nearly it succeeded can be read in the figures of Allied shipping losses in 1941, 1942, and the first three months of 1943. But with the clear-cut victory which emerged in May 1943, not only was the ring still unbroken, but now it could contract, closing in every day until even the coastal waters of Germany became too dangerous for her shipping to use.

With the Atlantic battle won, an endless stream of convoys, securely guarded and virtually immune from loss, crossed the Atlantic, bringing to Britain the troops, the guns, the tanks, the supplies needed to launch in 1944 the direct attack on German-held Europe. With the road now open, the whole future course of the European campaign lay clear and inevitable. To Britain, to North Africa, to Russia, to Malta, an endless stream of men, weapons, and supplies came and gathered against the day of the final assaults. All were carried by sea, and their safe arrival at their destinations proclaimed the planned offensive. The victories which lay so surely in the future, in which the armies and the air forces of the Allies were to shatter the resistance of the enemy, were all made possible by the full opening of the sea routes across the world.

So history repeated itself, for in all war experience it is the winning of the maritime war which precedes the land victory. By mid-1943 the maritime war had been won and the main task of the navies of the Allies had been accomplished; now it was the task of the armies and the air forces to go in and win the final victory.

Winning the maritime war

1941 February: Admiral Sir Percy Noble appointed C-in-C Western Approaches.
March: The leading German U-boat aces — Prien, Schepke, and Kretschmer — are eliminated.
April: The Allied refuelling base in Iceland begins operation.
June: First Allied convoy with end-to-end surface escort crosses the Atlantic.
December: The United States enters the war: a second 'happy time' for the U-boats begins.

1942 June: US escort forces are withdrawn from Atlantic duties.
September: The first British support group begins operation.
November: Admiral Sir Max Horton takes over as C-in-C Western Approaches.

1943 March: In a running battle with the escorts of convoys HX-229 and SC-122, U-boat packs sink 21 ships for the loss of only one submarine. But at the end of the month the escort carriers and support groups return from the Torch operation.
April: U-boats sink 245,000 tons of shipping for the loss of 15 submarines.
May: During attacks on five convoys, 20 U-boats are sunk. During the whole month 165,000 tons of shipping are sunk — for the loss of 40 U-boats.
June: The U-boat toll mounts: for only 18,000 tons sunk, 17 U-boats are destroyed. For the first time, the balance favours the Allies.

This flotsam of war tells its own tale of another merchantman that failed to get through

THE LIFE AND DEATH OF THE TIRPITZ

Germany and Norway, 1939/November 1944

April 1, 1939 (April Fool's Day): the birth of a great hope, as *Tirpitz* takes to the water at Wilhelmshaven

Central Press

To the 20th century there was nothing new in the naval concept of 'a fleet in being' — by which one means the existence of a naval force, smaller than its adversary and therefore unwilling to engage in full fleet combat, but strong enough to cause concern to the superior naval power, lest it emerge to disrupt the sea routes or catch and overwhelm part of that power's naval forces. In fact, the strategy is as old as civilised man's reasoning itself, and many examples of it can be seen long before the time of Captain Mahan and Admiral Tirpitz, both of whom refined the doctrine. Yet it is arguable whether the policy had been so deliberately, systematically, and successfully operated before January 15, 1942, when the German battleship *Tirpitz* entered Norwegian waters, where she was to remain for some 34 months.

With Germany engaging her forces against Russia in the East, and the British and Americans in the West, Norway was the ideal position from which a 'fleet in being' policy could be pursued. German naval forces based in the many fjords along her coastline could threaten either the Atlantic, or the Arctic, convoy routes, and the advantages, both of position and of the choice of when and where to strike, greatly counterbalanced the Royal Navy's superiority in numbers.

The *Tirpitz* was the ideal vessel to pose

such a threat, for at the time of her launching she and her sister-ship *Bismarck* were the most powerful warships in the world. With a deep-water displacement of over 42,000 tons (her builders had flouted all naval limitation treaties) she carried a crew of some 2,500 men, and an armament of eight 15-inch guns, 12 5·9-inch guns, plus dozens of smaller 37-mm and 20-mm guns. Her armour plate, 12 inches thick at the sides and at least 8 inches thick on deck, made her the most heavily protected warship of that time — and, despite her vast size, she could make a top speed of nearly 30 knots.

All this meant that she completely out-classed the older British battleships and battle-cruisers, and even the new *King George V* class were not so well armoured nor so fast, although they fired a heavier broadside and had the advantage of radar control. The *Bismarck*'s war cruise had given the British a nasty indication of the striking power and defensive strength of such battleships, with the result that the Admiralty had decided that only a Home Fleet which included at least 2 *King George V* class ships and an aircraft-carrier could be an adequate match for them.

The battleship *Tirpitz* was launched at Wilhelmshaven in the presence of Hitler and Raeder on April 1, 1939, by Frau von

Hassell — the daughter of the admiral who had striven so hard to construct a rival to the Royal Navy before the First World War, and whose name this vessel commemorated. Only at this point was its name revealed publicly, and the significance of the choice was not lost upon German and foreign observers alike: once again, the supremacy of the Royal Navy was being challenged. Only later was it also noticed that it had been launched on April Fool's Day.

The vessel was completed by the end of February 1941 and began trials in the Baltic in the following month, much to the anxiety of the British Admiralty. Luckily for the Royal Navy, the *Tirpitz* was unable to partake in the *Bismarck* operation, for one can imagine what a threat to Britain's position those two ships, acting in concert, would have been. By the end of 1941, however, the shortage of fuel oil necessary for long ocean voyages, plus the effect of the *Bismarck*'s end upon Hitler's mind, ruled out the prospect of an Atlantic sortie for the *Tirpitz*. Moreover, as the Führer's intuition told him that Norway was the crucial area on the western flank of his dominions, it became necessary to deter a British invasion there. The *Tirpitz* therefore left for Trondheim with a destroyer screen on the night of January 14/15, 1942, going by way of the

Tirpitz had perhaps the most inglorious and tragic career of any warship in the Second World War. She never saw action with an Allied convoy or battle fleet: her activities were limited to scurrying from one Norwegian fjord to another and making furtive excursions which ended as soon as any danger approached. She was the last heavy warship left to the German navy by 1944; but for the British, she was too great a threat to be ignored. At long last, after 34 months in Norwegian waters, the 'Lone Queen of the North' followed the *Graf Spee*, the *Bismarck*, and the *Scharnhorst* to her doom

A sad end for a great ship: bottom-up in Tromsöfjord, with nearly 1,000 crewmen trapped in her hull

Imperial War Museum

Kiel Canal to avoid being spotted by Swedish coastwatchers—for the German Naval Command suspected that the early detection of the *Bismarck* had been due to the sighting of that ship in the Kattegat.

This move provoked the British into flying constant reconnaissance flights over Norway, and Churchill into writing that: 'the destruction, or even the crippling, of this ship is the greatest event at sea at the present time. No other target is comparable to it. The entire naval situation throughout the world would be altered [by its destruction].' Consequently, on the night of January 28/29, 1942, the first of the many bombing attacks against the *Tirpitz* was carried out by RAF Halifaxes and Stirlings, but without success. Meanwhile, increased German air and naval activity indicated the employment of the battleship against either the Atlantic or the Arctic convoys—the latter, in fact, for the Germans were just beginning to appreciate their significance to the Russian war effort. The target was to be the outward and homeward convoys PQ-12 and QP-8, which left Iceland and Kola Inlet respectively on March 1.

Five days later, the *Tirpitz*, flying the flag of Vice-Admiral Ciliax, left Trondheim with three destroyers, but they were quickly spotted by the British submarine *Seawolf*, and the alarming news passed on to Admiral Tovey, C-in-C Home Fleet. Taking no chances, Tovey was already at sea with the battleships *King George V, Duke of York*, the battle-cruiser *Renown*, the aircraft-carrier *Victorious*, plus one heavy cruiser and 12 destroyers. On the following day, March 7, bad weather and low visibility prevented aerial reconnaissance by either side—so the Home Fleet did not know that at one time it was within 90 miles of its prey, while Ciliax was not only unaware of the presence of a powerful British battle fleet nearby, but also did not realise that at one stage he came within a few miles of both the outward and homeward convoys. The distress signals of a Russian merchantman sunk by the German destroyers gave Admiral Tovey a small clue, but sweeps by his main squadron and by a detached destroyer force found nothing, for the *Tirpitz* was by this time some 150 miles to the north of the Home Fleet.

At last, on the morning of the 9th, the *Tirpitz* was sighted by search planes, and the *Victorious* flew off a strike of 12 Albacore torpedo-bombers, which soon found the German battleship. British hopes were high of repeating the success they had scored against the *Bismarck*, but this time no hits were scored, for the attacks were launched from astern. The Albacores' speed of approach on to target was not fast at any time, and now they were trying to catch a fast-moving ship, which thus easily and almost contemptuously dodged their torpedoes. By that evening, the *Tirpitz* was safe in Narvik, and a few days later ran the gauntlet of British submarine and destroyer patrols to return to Trondheim.

Though inconclusive, both sides were worried by the results of this foray. Raeder and Hitler, probably realising the narrow escape of the *Tirpitz*, decided that the German heavy ships would not be used again unless the Luftwaffe gave support, and unless the exact strength and position of the enemy, and especially his carriers, was known beforehand—a proviso guaranteed to cramp any future offensive operations. Moreover, as this unsuccessful strike against the Russian convoys had used up 8,000 tons of precious fuel oil, the *Tirpitz* was virtually immobilised. The British, however, did not know this and were very anxious at the vulnerability of the route to Murmansk, which the *Tirpitz* now appeared to dominate, and at the possibility of an Atlantic foray—both threats necessitating the retention of many units in the Home Fleet, desperately needed elsewhere.

The fear of the *Tirpitz* getting loose in the Atlantic prompted one of the most daring raids of the Second World War, the attack upon the heavily-defended French port and industrial centre of St Nazaire, for if the *Tirpitz* had broken into the Atlantic, it was most likely that she would return to a base on the west coast of France—and the only place there in which she could be docked was the great 'Normandie' dock at St Nazaire. If this dock were put out of action, any major damage sustained by the *Tirpitz* in an Atlantic sally could only be repaired in a German port—and the unlikelihood of the Royal Navy allowing her to return to home waters would be sufficient to deter the German navy even from planning such a sortie.

The overall purpose of the raid was a complete success, and aerial reconnaissance soon showed that the gates of the lock were utterly demolished, and that docking the *Tirpitz* there would be impossible. Ten months after the raid, the dock was still out of action. Crippling the battleship itself, however, was still the chief priority, and three days after the St Nazaire exploit 33 bombers attacked the *Tirpitz* while it lay near Trondheim, but neither this raid, nor two more strikes on April 28 and 29, scored any hits, for bad weather and an efficient electrically-operated smoke-screen shrouded the target in the fjord.

The most powerful—and tragic—demonstration of the influence of this giant battleship came in the summer of 1942, when the mere threat of its being at sea was the direct cause of the dispersal and near-annihilation of the ill-fated Convoy PQ-17. By the end of June, sufficient fuel had been scraped up by the German Naval Command to allow their major warships based in Norway the chance of a sortie, and thus the *Tirpitz*, the pocket-battleship *Admiral Scheer*, and the heavy cruiser *Hipper* were assembled at Altenfjord on the North Cape. If used with resolution, they had the power to strike a severe blow against the convoys—particularly as the British Admiralty had just decided that the capital ships of the Home Fleet would not proceed further east than Bear Island, a decision forced upon them by the fact that, if they went further east, they would be operating over 1,000 miles from their base without shore-based air support, while Germany's heavy warships enjoyed powerful submarine and air cover, and operated close to their own bases.

The blow came late on July 4, as Convoy PQ-17, edging close to the ice limit, pounded through the Barents Sea. It was then learned that the German ships were no longer in their anchorage, so that First Sea Lord, Admiral Sir Dudley Pound, realising that the Home Fleet was hundreds of miles away and that the cruisers and destroyers escorting the convoy were no match for their opponents, ordered the escort to withdraw westwards while the merchantmen were told to scatter. The latter order gave the German forces an unbelievable chance of easy plunder which they readily seized: of the 33 ships which had left Iceland only 10 eventually reached Russia. Ironically, the *Tirpitz* and the other surface forces played no part in the actual slaughter, for they were recalled late on July 5; their job was done as soon as the convoy scattered.

After this, the *Tirpitz* was sent to Trondheim for a long refit, for although repair facilities there could not match those in Germany, the danger of mines on the way home or bombing attacks by the RAF on German shipyards, were sufficient reason for keeping the battleship in Norway. The two primary motives, as given by Raeder himself, still remained: 'Only by keeping the fleet in Norwegian waters can we hope to meet danger successfully. Besides, it is especially important in view of the whole Axis strategy that the German "fleet in being" tie down the British Home Fleet, especially after the heavy Anglo-American losses in the Mediterranean and the Pacific' — a view with which the Royal Navy glumly concurred.

The two-man torpedo raid

With the *Tirpitz* settled for a while at Trondheim, the British attempted to cripple her by a new method. On October 26, the fishing boat *Arthur,* commanded by the outstanding Norwegian Resistance leader Leif Larson, left the Shetlands and proceeded north-eastwards, carrying six British frogmen and their two mounts — overgrown steerable torpedoes called 'Chariots'. The party survived engine failure and, more miraculously, an examination by the Germans at the head of the fjord — but by a cruel stroke of luck bad weather intervened when they were only 5 miles from their target, and in a violent storm the Chariots, which were towed underwater, broke adrift and were lost. All but one man succeeded in reaching Sweden after they had landed at a nearby fjord — but once again the *Tirpitz* had escaped.

A greater risk to the battleship's future at this time was Hitler himself, who, after powerful German forces had been beaten away from Convoy JW-51B by much smaller escorts on December 31, 1942 (see 'Battle of the Barents Sea', page 186) raged against the German navy and ordered the scrapping of all its heavy surface ships. As a result, Raeder resigned on January 30, 1943, and it took his successor Dönitz weeks to persuade Hitler to repeal an order which would have caused nothing but joy and relief for the Allies. However, the *Tirpitz* was sent to join the battle-cruiser *Scharnhorst* at Altenfjord after her refit was completed in late February, and once again a great threat to the Russian convoys existed. But by this time instructions regarding the use of these

German heavy ships — the chief reason for their timidity — were even more restricted.

September 1943 saw the *Tirpitz* putting its main armament to use for the one and only time in its career, though it hardly was against what could be called worthwhile opposition. The weather station at Spitzbergen provided valuable information regarding ice movements and weather forecasts, and both sides had previously sent small expeditions to occupy it. Now the Norwegians were again in control, transmitting reports to Britain, and the German navy decided to send the *Tirpitz, the Scharnhorst,* and ten destroyers to deal with them. Arriving from Altenfjord on September 8, this overwhelming force systematically destroyed the base and then scuttled back to Norway before the Home Fleet could reach the area. The sortie did little in fact but waste Germany's small fuel stocks, for the weather station was functioning again by September 22.

The Royal Navy's counter to this foray was to attempt yet another attack upon the battleship, this time with midget submarines called X-craft. These vessels, 53 feet long and weighing 30 tons, could dive to 300 ft and make 8 knots while submerged, and their crews, four for each craft, had been experimenting and preparing for the attack for many months. The plan was that six X-craft were to be towed by conventional submarines to the entrance of Altenfjord where they would be cast off, make their way submerged to the targets (the *Tirpitz, the Scharnhorst,* and the *Lützow)* under which they would detach their charges and then withdraw before the time fuses expired.

Between September 11 and 12, the X-craft, towed by parent submarines, left Loch Cairnbawn in north-west Scotland and proceeded to Altenfjord. Two of the craft were lost on the journey northwards, while X-7 became entangled in a mine cable until her commander kicked it away — but on the evening of September 20, the four remaining midgets were detached to make their way up the fjord. Of these, X-5 was destroyed — probably in Kaafjord on the 22nd — and X-10 encountered so many difficulties that she was forced to abandon the attack altogether. This left X-6 (Lieutenant D. Cameron, RNR) and X-7 (Lieutenant B. C. G. Place, RN), both of which were scheduled to attack the *Tirpitz.*

The crews spent September 21 in crossing the minefields, remedying defects, and charging the batteries of the X-craft, and early on the morning of the next day they made for the heavily-defended Kaafjord where their target was lying. Lieutenant Place managed to penetrate the anti-submarine boom only to encounter, first of all, a German motor launch which forced him to submerge; and then anti-torpedo nets surrounding the battleship in which he became entangled for over an hour.

X-6 was not having an easy time of it either, for Lieutenant Cameron found that he could only work his periscope by hand. Despite this impediment, he reached the target by about 0700 hours when, with the compass also failing, the X-craft ran aground — and then broke surface to give the surprised Germans the first inkling that an attack was under way. X-6 submerged again, was forced to the surface by a rock, became entangled in anti-torpedo nets, and attracted grenades and small-arms fire. Incredibly, Lieutenant Cameron then managed to released his charges near the battle-

ship's forward turrets before he ordered the scuttling of his craft. The crew of X-6 was rescued by the *Tirpitz*'s motor boat, which had been sent to investigate the first sighting of the submarine. But aboard the battleship confusion reigned — and it was only after some time that the watertight doors were closed and the guns manned. The commander ordered the crew to prepare to proceed to sea, but at this moment (about 0740 hours) another object was sighted, orders were given for the net gates to be closed again, and the ship swung on her cable away from where the X-6 had sunk.

The other object was, of course, X-7, which Place had by now succeeded in extricating from the nets. In doing so, however, his vessel broke surface 30 yards from the *Tirpitz,* so Place promptly dived again, striking the battleship's side as he did so. He released one charge under the forward turrets, and then proceeded some 200 feet further aft where he released the other charge. Though X-7 was now suffering from compass failure and with the air pressure running low, Place now attempted to escape, only to run the craft into the nets again. He was still entangled there at 0812 when the charges placed under the *Tirpitz* blew up, so damaging his own vessel that constant submerging became impossible. X-7 'porpoised' for a while — being fired at every time it surfaced — before Place ran it alongside a gunnery target on to which he scrambled, but the craft then sank, taking the other three members of the crew down with it. Astonishingly, $2\frac{1}{2}$ hours later, Sub-Lieutenant Aitken popped to the surface using the Davis Escape Apparatus. He had in fact been battling all that time to save the other two of the crew — but had to give up when his oxygen was exhausted.

The mark of the X-craft

The explosion which had seriously damaged X-7 had done the same to the *Tirpitz* — for although the battleship had been slewed as much as her cables would allow, the four charges, each containing 2 tons of amatol, were still near the hull. The first two charges countermined the others so that they exploded simultaneously, lifting the great battleship 6 feet out of the water, throwing the crew about, wrecking the lighting system, jamming doors, and giving the great ship a 5-degree list to port. The most serious damage was to three sets of main turbines, while the port rudder was twisted, two turrets immobilised, and the fire control, radio, and electrical equipment were smashed. Later examination also revealed that many of *Tirpitz*'s hull frames were badly damaged — a blow that prevented her reaching full speed again for the rest of her life.

Only a full refit in a German dockyard could repair such damage, but again the fear that the crippled vessel might be set upon by British aircraft and ships on her journey prevented such a move. Besides, Dönitz adhered as firmly as his predecessor to the 'fleet in being' concept. 'This ship is to be repaired and to remain stationed in northern Norway,' he afterwards told Hitler. 'This course will be followed even if further damage is sustained. Regardless of how much work and manpower may be involved, the repairs must be made. After all, the presence of the *Tirpitz* ties up large enemy forces.' Thus it was that repair ships were sent from Germany to assist the stricken battleship, which would be out of action for at least six months — a result which, in the

△ *Tirpitz* **opens up with her forward 15-inch guns on a training shoot**

△ *Tirpitz* **close inshore, after the X-craft attack, as seen by RAF reconnaissance**
▽ *Tirpitz***'s last hiding-place: Tromsö, where she was finally sunk by RAF bombers**

words of Admiral Fraser, C-in-C Home Fleet, 'considerably altered the strategic situation'. As was fitting both Cameron and Place were awarded the Victoria Cross.

The period of inaction for the *Tirpitz* after this gallant attack was a great boon to the Royal Navy, and by the time the German vessel was working up again (spring 1944) the whole picture of naval balance had changed. *Scharnhorst* had been sunk in the Battle of North Cape by British destroyers and *Lützow* was back in Germany – *Tirpitz*, lying at Altenfjord by herself, now really was the 'Lone Queen of the 'north' as the Norwegians called her. Nevertheless, the British were not satisfied, for they were well aware of Grand Admiral von Tirpitz's own dictum, 'A ship's best characteristic is that provided it can stay afloat and horizontal it is a gun platform!' Only when the battleship was completely destroyed could the heavy warships of the Home Fleet be permanently freed for the Far East – so yet another form of attack was tried out.

Though Altenfjord was beyond the range of the RAF's bombers it could, of course, be attacked by aircraft launched from carriers – the only problem being the lack of available carriers for duty with the Home Fleet. But in the spring of 1944, the fleet carriers *Victorious* and *Furious,* and the escort carriers *Emperor, Searcher, Pursuer,* and *Fencer* were assembled at Scapa Flow and these vessels possessed sufficient aircraft to enable two strikes to be flown, each group comprising 21 Barracudas with 40 fighters as escorts. Throughout March planning for this operation pressed ahead, assisted by frequent reconnaissance flights over the target area, and so late on the afternoon of April 2, in fine weather, the carriers and their escorts under the overall command of Admiral Moore, assembled to the northwest of Altenfjord. The evening and night were spent in preparing the two strikes, the first of which left at 0437 hours on the 3rd, followed nearly an hour later by the second group.

Absolute surprise was gained at Altenfjord, where the Germans were preparing the *Tirpitz* for trials in deeper water; and the last-minute alarm being too late, many of the smokescreen machines and anti-aircraft guns were unmanned. The only warning that most of the crew received was the sound of numerous aircraft engines breaking the stillness of the early morning. Then the fighters struck, raking the decks with fire while above them the Barracuda dive-bombers rained down armour-piercing, semi-armour-piercing, high-explosive, and anti-submarine bombs on to the immobile target. At the end of the strike (which lasted only about one minute) the battleship was on fire in numerous places. Further hits were scored by the second attack group, which, however, arriving on the scene an hour later, encountered heavier AA fire and a more effective smokescreen.

Only four aircraft were lost in the whole operation, but chaos existed aboard the battleship: she had suffered 14 hits and one damaging near miss, while 122 of her crew had been killed and a further 316 injured. The damage was not so grievous as the British believed, however, for the 1,600-pound bombs, the only ones which might deal mortal blows, had been dropped from too low an altitude and failed to penetrate the *Tirpitz*'s main armoured deck. In fact, she was disabled for only three months.

But the Fleet Air Arm, once it had tasted blood, was not content to let its prey escape, and it was moreover sound strategy to keep hitting the enemy once he had been knocked off-balance. On April 28, a force of carriers, again under Admiral Moore, left Scapa Flow to repeat their earlier success, but this time stormy weather forced the abandonment of the mission. A further attempt on May 15 suffered the same fate, and on May 28 a fresh strike was cancelled for the same reason. It seemed as if the fates were unwilling to give the Royal Navy a chance to finish off its opponent, for an attack on July 17 was foiled by the German smoke-screen system and no hits were scored; and on August 22, while the Russian convoy JW-59 was *en route,* the *Tirpitz* escaped unscathed from yet another raid. Admiral Moore decided to persist in the attempt, however, and two days later a force of 77 bombers and fighters struck the battleship – and scored just two hits in an attack which was probably the most frustrating of all. One of the hits was by a 500-pound bomb which failed to penetrate the forward turret; and the other, a 1,600-pound armour-piercing bomb, struck the ship just forward of the bridge, penetrated eight decks, including the main armoured layer, and then failed to explode. Subsequent investigation by the relieved Germans revealed that it had been only half-filled with explosives – and the failure of another strike five days later filled the Fleet Air Arm's cup of bitterness to the brim.

The fact of the matter was that much larger bombs were required. A great deal of luck was also needed, for good weather and the element of surprise were essential, and neither was likely to occur. The solution to the first of these problems was to use RAF instead of Fleet Air Arm aircraft, so on September 11, 1944, Bomber Command sent No. 9 and 617 Squadrons, equipped with Lancasters carrying 12,000-pound armour-piercing bombs, to Yagodnik airfield in North Russia – a necessary detour because the round trip from Scotland to Altenfjord was still too great a distance for them.

Early on September 15, some 28 of these bombers left Yagodnik for Altenfjord, where despite the customary smokescreen, a hit was obtained – and a most spectacular one, for the bomb burst through the battleship's forecastle and peeled back the upper deck rather like the lid of a sardine tin. This was, in fact, the end – for *Tirpitz* was now no longer seaworthy, her maximum speed could only be 8 knots, and Dönitz could see that the only practical function left for this stricken giant was to use it as a floating fortress to help ward off an Allied invasion of Norway. As the extreme northern region was precariously held, the ship was now sent 200 miles further south and anchored by Haakoy island, 3 miles from Tromsö, where a sandbank was built up under her keel to prevent her toppling over if sunk.

The fact which mattered to the British now was that *Tirpitz* was at last within range of bombers based in Scotland, provided certain modifications were made – and an indication of the importance still attached to the *Tirpitz* can be seen from the preparation of these bombers. All dispensable armour plate was taken off, mid-turrets were removed, extra fuel tanks were fitted, and new, more powerful Merlin 24 engines installed in the Lancasters of No. 9 and 617 Squadrons, which, back from Russia, were again selected for the task of finally disposing of the great ship. Once again they were armed with the giant 12,000-pound bombs with armour-piercing noses.

Their first attempt, on October 29, was a failure, for bad visibility intervened and only one near miss was recorded. German reaction to the raid was instant and effective, for they moved up a force of 20 to 30 fighters to the nearby airfield at Bardufoss. As the Lancasters needed fine weather in order to successfully locate and bomb the battleship, they would now be exposed in clear visibility to attacks by the German fighters, while they lacked much armour-plate and their mid-turrets. Now, it seemed, three simultaneous near-miracles were being asked for – no fighters or AA defences: no smoke-screen: and fine weather over northern Norway as winter approached.

At 0300 hours on Sunday, November 12, 1944, some 29 Lancasters, each carrying about 2 tons overweight and ignoring the grim probability that they would be massacred by German fighters, flew from Lossiemouth airfield under the leadership of Wing-Commander J. B. Tait. Reaching the Norwegian coast, they turned inland and proceeded on a roundabout course so as to approach the battleship from the least expected quarter, the landward side – but despite this caution, just after 0800 hours, the crew of the *Tirpitz* received warning of the raid and closed to action stations. On shore the smokescreen machines were manned and eight fighters rose from Bardufoss airfield 20 miles away. The morning was clear and sunny, and the probability of interception was high. Would the British fail again in their attempts to destroy the *Tirpitz*?

As the Lancasters of No. 617 Squadron ('The Dambusters') droned nearer and nearer the target, their crews anxiously scoured the skies for enemy planes. But none appeared – and then, 14,000 feet below them, they spied their quarry, a slim, dark shape anchored close to land, and miraculously free from smoke. Here indeed was the golden opportunity – and the Lancasters, equipped with the new and deadly Mark XIV bombsight and in ideal conditions, took it. The 'blockbuster' bombs seemed to take an age to fall (and already the aircraft of No. 9 Squadron were beginning their runs) but just as, with supreme irony, the smoke screen began to shroud the target, a great plume of smoke gushed up amidships, followed by another one aft. Near misses covered the target with spray, flames and smoke belched out of *Tirpitz*'s stricken hull, and she immediately took on a list of 30 degrees to port, where a 100-foot-long hole had been ripped open. No ship, not even *Tirpitz,* could withstand direct hits by such great bombs.

Aboard the stricken vessel counterflooding

Tirpitz, sister-ship to the *Bismarck,* was given additional AA protection, like most of the later battleships of the Second World War. Her operational career was drastically curtailed by the general shortage of fuel oil: forced to lurk in the shallow waters of Norwegian fjords, she suffered crippling and in the end fatal damage from heavy submarine explosions caused by the X-craft attack, and by RAF 'blockbuster bombs'. *Displacement:* 42,900 tons. *Overall length:* 792 feet. *Max speed:* 30 knots. *Range:* 9,000 miles at 19 knots. *Max armour thickness:* 12½ inches. *Armament:* eight 15-inch, 12 5·9-inch guns; 16 4·1-inch AA, 16 37-mm AA, 58 20-mm AA guns; eight 21-inch torpedo tubes; six aircraft. *Complement:* 2,400

had been ordered to correct the list, but the already slim chances of saving the ship were quickly crushed by another bomb spectacularly obliterating one of her main turrets, while further near misses shook the the ship violently. Her end came very suddenly. The first two direct hits had pierced her vitals and while she listed still further, her after magazines blew up with a tremendous explosion, causing her immediately to roll over. As the last of the Lancasters droned towards the sea, the crews could see the long, black hull glinting above the waters of the fjord through the ever-thickening smoke. The Lone Queen of the North, the ship the British dared not leave alone, was dead.

A sad and inglorious end

How did the German precautions fail? Fine weather was difficult enough to explain in northern Norway in mid-November, but the lack of fighters and of the smokescreen as well proved to be disastrous. The eight fighters which took off from Bardufoss had been, in fact, recalled before they reached Tromsöfjord – for the Germans, bemused by the Lancasters' roundabout approach, believed that the airfield itself was to be the target. Investigation into the failure of the electrically operated smokescreens revealed that not all of them had been in order due to their recent transfer from Altenfjord, and the failure of the plan to prevent Tirpitz capsizing by building a sandbank under her keel was due to the fact that this project had not been fully completed. Furthermore, near misses exploding around the ship excavated huge craters, and caused what existed of the sandbank to disintegrate.

The death toll among the crew was great, for more than 1,000 were trapped when she heeled over so suddenly. Over 80 of these picked their way through the various decks to the upturned bottom of the hull, upon which they knocked furiously, attracting the attention of those outside. A hole was cut in the steel hull through which they escaped, 30 hours after the battleship turned turtle. Other knockings were heard too, but before the unfortunate men could be reached, the waters of the fjord filled their compartments. Almost unbelievingly, the rescue teams heard strains of 'Deutschland über Alles' from them before silence settled upon the hull.

It was a sad and inglorious end – and rather an anticlimax – but this was the path the Tirpitz had long sailed. Not for her the fate of the Bismarck – a brief moment of glory and then a valiant fight against the odds – and she was always unable, apart from the minor affair at Spitzbergen, to use her strength in action because of Hitler's perverse commands. Her destruction was thus piecemeal and her end has an air of tragic inevitability, for though she sank quickly enough when the Lancasters' bombs ripped her apart, she had in reality been wasting away for months before that.

And yet, some success must be accredited to her. She had brilliantly achieved the aim of every 'fleet in being' – that of tying down far greater enemy forces. Intact, she had presented a permanent threat to the Atlantic and Arctic sea-routes of the Allies, and a tremendous annoyance to the Royal Navy, which desperately needed to send the battleships and aircraft-carriers of the Home Fleet to more active theatres, yet dare not while she floated. Little wonder, then, that all possible means were used to destroy her and that her epitaph, if one is to be written, should be – 'She could not be left alone.'

X-Craft: A Midget Submarine

These small submarines were one of the main British 'naval special operations' craft developed for attacks on specialised naval targets in difficult waters. *Range:* 1,200 miles at 4 knots. *Endurance:* 23 hours submerged at 2 knots. *Warhead:* two external, crescent-shaped charges (each 30 feet long, and 5½ tons); limpet mines were also carried. *Crew:* five. *Displacement:* 30 tons. *Diving depth:* 300 feet. *Speed:* 6/8 knots submerged. *Overall length:* 53 feet

CARRIER WARFARE

When war broke out in September 1939, of the protagonists only the British and French had aircraft-carriers in service. France in fact had only the *Béarn,* which had been converted in 1927 from an uncompleted battleship. She saw no action prior to the collapse of France, after which she remained in the West Indies until the liberation.

The British had been the pioneers in the early development of aircraft-carriers, the principal early experiments having been with the fast cruiser *Furious,* where decks for takeoff and landing had been superimposed during the First World War. The outcome of these had been to make it clear that only by giving a ship a single, unobstructed deck over virtually her entire length could ship-borne aircraft operate effectively. Such a deck had been first provided by the *Argus,* converted from an uncompleted passenger liner, completed in 1918 with a full-length flush deck, the boiler smoke and gases being discharged over the stern.

The *Argus* was followed in 1920 by the *Eagle,* converted from a battleship, and the *Hermes,* in 1923, the first vessel to be designed and built as a carrier. Both ships were 'island' as opposed to 'flush-deck' carriers, with their funnel, bridge, and superstructure situated to one side of the otherwise unobstructed deck. All these ships were unsuitably slow (20-25 knots) and could handle less than 20 aircraft. The *Furious,* when she emerged in 1925 in her final form as a flush-deck carrier, had characteristics nearer to the ideal with a speed of 31 knots and accommodation for 36 planes, though 30 was the comfortable limit for operating. Con-

version of the *Courageous* and *Glorious,* originally sisters to the *Furious,* was completed in 1928 and 1930, both of them as island carriers and capable of handling about 36 aircraft.

This early lead over other navies (the US and Japanese navies only commissioned their first small, experimental carriers in 1922), allied to the restrictions imposed by the Washington Treaty, had the unfortunate result that when war began to loom ahead, Britain's carrier force was largely composed of veteran ships of old-fashioned design. The one exception was the *Ark Royal,* the construction of which had been wisely delayed until 1935 so as to take advantage of experience gained in operating the earlier ships. Completed in November 1938, she was able to handle 60 aircraft.

With the expiration of the Washington Treaty, four more fleet carriers of the *Illustrious* class had been laid down in 1937 and two similar ships, the *Implacable* and *Indefatigable* in 1939. Starting with the *Illustrious* in May 1940, the first four were to commission during 1940 and 1941, the last two in 1944. A feature of these six ships and one which contemporary ships of the US and Japanese navies did not possess, was their stoutly armoured flight-deck. Together with armoured sides this made a vast steel box of their hangars. Not only did they thus enjoy a large degree of protection from bomb damage but, with hangars isolated from the rest of the ship, it was possible to make their aviation fuel systems safer.

They carried with them, however, the disadvantage that, for their size, they could handle fewer aircraft. The *Illustrious, For-*

The War at Sea, 1939/1945. The Second World War saw the naval aircraft come into its own as the chief agent of sea power. Of the major belligerent powers, only Italy made no use of aircraft carriers, although Germany had only one the *Graf Zeppelin*. Both in European waters and, more important in the Pacific, the aircraft carrier supplanted the battleship. It's not surprising that great strides were made in the design and construction of both ships and aircraft.

Imperial War Museum

midable, and *Victorious* (which had a single hangar deck) could handle only 36 planes, though this was increased when a deck 'park' was designed forward of the landing area, separated from it by a crash barrier—a system first introduced by the Americans. The *Indomitable* was given an additional half-hangar deck which brought her complement up to 50. By giving them two full-length hangars and dispensing with side armour, the last two ships were enabled to accommodate 72 aircraft under cover.

Opposed first by the German navy and then by the Italian, neither of which had a naval air arm and had to rely upon an independent, shore-based force to provide air support, the quality of British carriers would not have mattered too much if their aircraft had had a performance comparable to contemporary shore-based planes.

The RAF takes charge

Unfortunately, when the independent Royal Air Force was formed in 1918, not only had provision of shore-based air support for the Royal Navy become the responsibility of the new service, but the design and provision of ship-borne aircraft had also been taken out of Admiralty hands. As virtually all naval officers with knowledge of aviation had transferred to the RAF, the Admiralty was forced, thereafter, to rely upon the sister service for technical advice. Inevitably, in a period of disarmament and financial stringency, the new service, struggling for survival, concentrated its energies and its meagre funds on its own requirements.

The result was a quantitative and qualitative starvation of the Royal Navy's air strength. Only exactly enough aircraft for which accommodation was available in the carriers or in catapult-fitted cruisers were provided and they were of designs far behind those of contemporary aircraft elsewhere. The decision taken in 1937 to restore to the Admiralty control of its own air arm—though not the responsibility for design of its aircraft—was too late to restore the situation by the outbreak of war.

Thus the aircraft embarked in British carriers were all, with one exception, biplanes with fixed undercarriages and open cockpits. Combining the roles of bomber, torpedo strike, and reconnaissance was the Swordfish with a cruising speed of less than 100 knots. The carrier-borne fighter was the biplane Sea Gladiator. Some squadrons were equipped, however, with the Royal Navy's only monoplane, the Blackburn Skua, which was designed to fill the incompatible rôles of fighter and dive-bomber. Though it was to have a notable success in the latter rôle, its performance as a fighter was far below requirements.

War experience was soon to show the vital necessity for a high-performance fighter. The dive-bomber, though a deadly weapon in attack on thin-skinned warships and merchantmen, was of limited value to the Royal Navy, which relied on the torpedo to attack the German and Italian armoured ships. The Skua and the Gladiator began to be replaced in May 1940 by the two-seater Fairey Fulmar This design by Marcel Lobelle for a carrier-borne fighter for the Fleet Air Arm was 50 knots slower than a Hurricane and 30 knots slower than the contemporary Italian CR 42 biplane

Far left: The USS *Saratoga,* after receiving seven hits from enemy aircraft, burns furiously. Petrol fires were a perpetual hazard aboard a crippled carrier, even when the main fires had been brought under control
(1) Unlike the *Saratoga,* the USS *Wasp,* hit during the battle for the Solomon Islands, did not survive
(2) The hangar on HMS *Argus.* Carrier-borne aircraft needed a good deal of maintenance, and, of course, repairs
(3) An Anglo/US carrier force moves through the Straits of Messina to the south of France to cover the landings of Operation 'Dragoon'
(4) The USS *Ticonderoga* burning. Her Captain put her into tight turns, making the list spill the burning petrol from the decks
(5) A partially completed Japanese carrier sinking after an Allied attack on the Kure naval base

Imperial War Museum

Imperial War Museum

Imperial War Museum

Brown Bros.

Imperial War Museum

The eyes and wings of the British Fleet

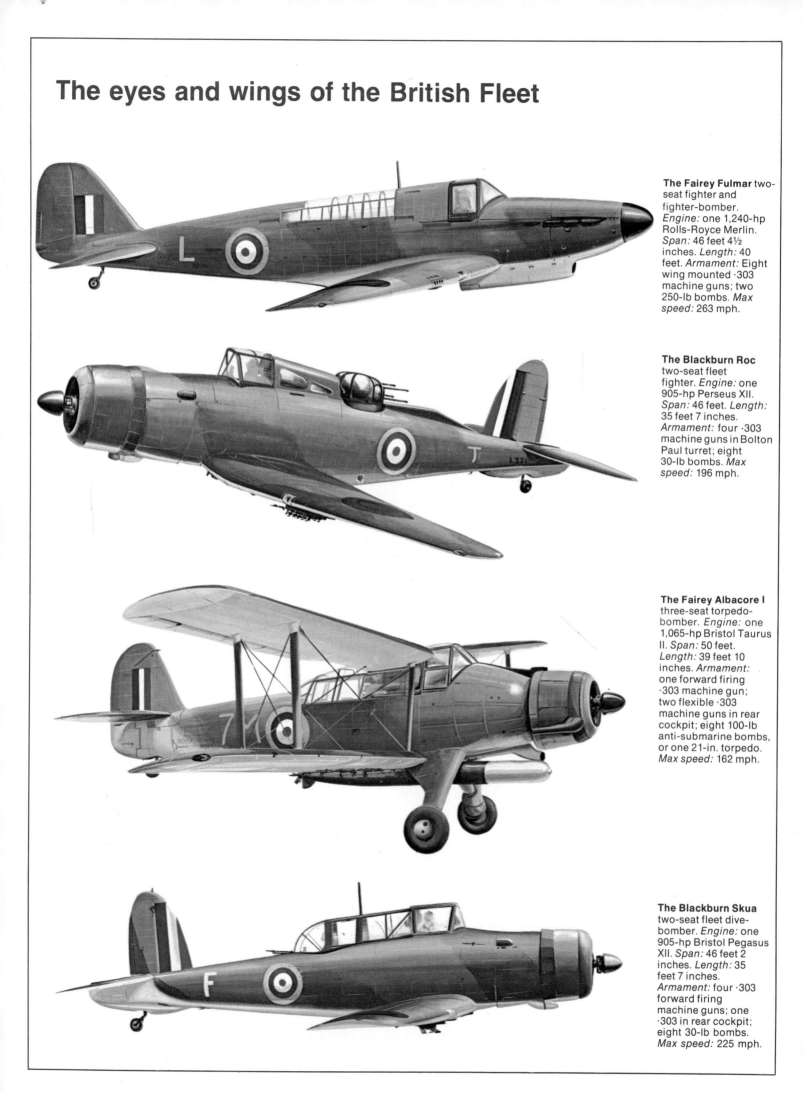

The Fairey Fulmar two-seat fighter and fighter-bomber. *Engine:* one 1,240-hp Rolls-Royce Merlin. *Span:* 46 feet 4½ inches. *Length:* 40 feet. *Armament:* Eight wing mounted ·303 machine guns; two 250-lb bombs. *Max speed:* 263 mph.

The Blackburn Roc two-seat fleet fighter. *Engine:* one 905-hp Perseus XII. *Span:* 46 feet. *Length:* 35 feet 7 inches. *Armament:* four ·303 machine guns in Bolton Paul turret; eight 30-lb bombs. *Max speed:* 196 mph.

The Fairey Albacore I three-seat torpedo-bomber. *Engine:* one 1,065-hp Bristol Taurus II. *Span:* 50 feet. *Length:* 39 feet 10 inches. *Armament:* one forward firing ·303 machine gun; two flexible ·303 machine guns in rear cockpit; eight 100-lb anti-submarine bombs, or one 21-in. torpedo. *Max speed:* 162 mph.

The Blackburn Skua two-seat fleet dive-bomber. *Engine:* one 905-hp Bristol Pegasus XII. *Span:* 46 feet 2 inches. *Length:* 35 feet 7 inches. *Armament:* four ·303 forward firing machine guns; one ·303 in rear cockpit; eight 30-lb bombs. *Max speed:* 225 mph.

fighter, but it was an advance on its predecessors and gave the Fleet Air Arm its first eight-gun fighter.

In the opening month of the war, with no enemy surface fleet at sea, the British carriers *Ark Royal, Courageous,* and *Hermes* were all deployed on anti-submarine patrols in the Western Approaches, a misemployment which resulted in a narrow escape from a U-boat's torpedo by the *Ark Royal* and the loss of the *Courageous* on September 17, 1939. The lesson was taken to heart: the carriers were withdrawn from this task. They next came into action in the Norwegian campaign in the spring of 1940, when it was quickly apparent that they could only operate their Swordfish, Skuas, and Gladiators in the Narvik area, far to the north and out of reach of German Messerschmitt fighters. Besides providing the only means of transporting RAF fighters to the Norwegian airfields, their own fighters gave a good account of themselves in combat with Dornier, Heinkel, and Junkers bombers. When the campaign ended with an Allied withdrawal, however, the *Glorious* allowed herself to be surprised by the battlecruisers *Scharnhorst* and *Gneisenau* and was quickly sunk by their radar-controlled guns.

The British were now left with the *Ark Royal*, backed by the veteran *Furious, Eagle, Hermes,* and *Argus,* the last three able to operate only a handful of aircraft. When the collapse of France and the entry of Italy into the war on the German side added the Mediterranean to the war theatres to be covered, this depleted force had to be parcelled out in single units instead of operating in carrier groups which pre-war exercises had shown to be the ideal. The *Ark Royal* was allocated to the Gibraltar-based Force 'H' where her first employment was in the lamentable operation against the French at Oran, in which Swordfish torpedo planes succeeded in damaging the battleship *Dunkerque*. Swordfish from the *Hermes* similarly damaged the *Richelieu* at Dakar.

Spectacular début in the Mediterranean

The *Eagle,* with a complement of 17 Swordfish and three Gladiators, provided the total air component of the Mediterranean Fleet, which was based at Alexandria until reinforced by the newly commissioned *Illustrious* in August 1940. In the confined waters of the Mediterranean, much of it within range of the Italian air force bases, such a degree of air support was, theoretically, quite inadequate. Fortunately the Italians concentrated their efforts on high-level bombing attacks which, contrary to the beliefs of so many fanatics of the gospel of air power, were to prove largely ineffective against fleets at sea in all theatres of the war.

The British Mediterranean Fleet was thus able to confront the Italian Fleet even in the narrow central basin where, on July 9, 1940, the first fleet action came about in which carrier-borne aircraft took part. Though the *Eagle's* Swordfish proved invaluable in scouting for enemy submarines and locating and shadowing the enemy fleet, in the strike rôle, armed with torpedoes, they confirmed the conclusions of peacetime exercises that only massed attacks stood a good chance of success. The small force of nine planes, twice launched during the battle, failed to achieve anything. That they all returned safely also confirmed that fighter aircraft, which the Italians did not have with their fleet, were the essential defence against air attack rather than guns.

Following this encounter, in which the Italian flagship was damaged by a 15-inch shell from the *Warspite,* the Italians adopted the strategy of maintenance of a 'fleet in being' and remained in harbour. With the arrival of the *Illustrious,* therefore, it was decided to attack them in their base at Taranto. Swordfish could not, of course, face fighters. The attack was, therefore, planned for a moonlit night. Even so, the 11 torpedo planes and ten others armed with bombs and illuminating flares which attacked on the night of November 11, 1940, had to face torpedo nets behind which the Italian battleships lay, an extensive balloon barrage, and a huge concentration of anti-aircraft guns and searchlights.

The result exceeded all expectations. For the loss of two aircraft the battleship *Conte di Cavour* was sunk, the *Caio Duilio* and the *Littorio* were both torpedoed, the former having to be beached and both put out of action for several months. For a while the Mediterranean Fleet operated unopposed to dominate the central basin and cut Axis communications with their North African armies. When the Germans decided, at the end of 1940, to send the Afrika Korps to the aid of their allies, they found this situation intolerable. To rectify it they deployed, on Sicilian airfields, X Fliegerkorps, including 150 dive-bombers which had been given special training in attacking ships.

They did not have to wait long for a worthwhile target. On January 10, 1941, the Mediterranean Fleet was operating in the Sicilian Narrows to cover the passage of a convoy of transports to Alexandria. Junkers 87 and Junkers 88 dive-bombers came out in a swarm to concentrate on the *Illustrious,* making three massed attacks during the afternoon and evening. The carrier's fighters, a handful of the two-seater Fairey Fulmars which had replaced the Skuas, were overwhelmed. The carrier suffered six direct hits, mostly by 1,100-pound armour-piercing bombs. The armoured deck saved her from destruction; but she was heavily damaged and after temporary patching at Malta she sailed for Alexandria and thence to the United States for full repairs. That single carriers could not operate within range of massed, shore-based dive-bombers had been savagely demonstrated. The brief domination of the central basin by the Mediterranean Fleet was at an end.

Nevertheless the *Illustrious* was replaced by the *Formidable* in March and when the Italian fleet was encountered off Cape Matapan on the 28th, the advantage held by a fleet with carrier-borne planes, even the lumbering Swordfish, was demonstrated when a handful of them succeeded first in crippling the battleship *Vittorio Veneto* which barely escaped being brought to close action and destruction as a result, and then the heavy cruiser *Pola*. To rescue the latter the Italian admiral sent back two more cruisers and destroyers which blundered across the path of the oncoming Mediterranean Fleet battleships in the night, to be blown out of the water by the latter's radar-controlled guns.

The *Formidable* soon suffered the same fate as the *Illustrious,* however, during operations in the defence and evacuation of Crete, and in July 1941 she followed her sister to America for repairs. Thereafter the Mediterranean Fleet was bereft of carrier support and its operations much restricted as a result.

The dominant position which carriers had assumed in fleet operations in less restricted waters was at the same time being demonstrated in the Atlantic and in the western Mediterranean. In the Atlantic, the German battleship *Bismarck,* which broke out into the high seas in May 1941, had defied the efforts of the whole British Home Fleet to bring her to book until, at the eleventh hour, Swordfish from the *Ark Royal* had crippled her, leaving her immobilised to be sunk by the guns and torpedoes of the fleet.

Convoys to Malta

It was the *Ark Royal,* too, which enabled a series of vital convoys to be fought through the western Mediterranean from Gibraltar against massive shore-based air opposition to Malta to keep that vital fortress in action, while the older carriers, *Furious* and *Argus* and later the USS *Wasp,* made repeated runs into the central basin to fly off reinforcements of Hurricane fighters to the island. In the end it was a skilfully delivered submarine attack in November 1941 which cut short the *Ark Royal's* notable career and with it the convoy operations for the next seven months, bringing Malta near to capitulation.

Only the island's desperate situation could have led to the attempt in June 1942 to get a convoy through to her with air cover provided by those two veterans *Eagle* and *Argus*. Nevertheless, the 22 fighters they carried, 16 of which were Sea Hurricanes (another carrier adaptation of an early RAF fighter), enabled two out of the six freighters to get through to relieve the fortress in the nick of time.

In a further convoy in August 1942, the last one before the defeat of Rommel re-opened the sea-route from Alexandria, it was possible to include the fleet carriers *Victorious* and *Indomitable* as well as the *Eagle*. The *Eagle* succumbed early in the operation to a U-boat attack, but the 60 Sea Hurricanes of the others successfully beat off a series of massed, co-ordinated attacks by high bombers, dive-bombers, and torpedo planes through two long days of ceaseless fighting. Malta was once again and finally relieved.

In the first two years of the war at sea which we have been considering, the conflict had been between a navy possessing carriers and its own air arm and opponents who relied upon independent air forces for support.

Before we turn to the Pacific where, in December 1941, warfare began in which the carrier would establish itself as the capital ship in place of the battleship, we must record the birth and development of a type of carrier other than that intended to work with the main fleet. This was the escort carrier, at first cheaply converted from mass-produced tankers and grain ships, but later specially built for the purpose.

Escort carriers were conceived with the object of providing air cover to convoys either against attack by long-range bombers or by submarines where shore-based aircraft were unable to do so. The first of these, the British *Audacity,* converted from a captured German merchant ship, brilliantly justified the conception during convoy operations in December 1941 before being herself sunk by a U-boat. In the meantime the United States had also converted their first escort carrier, the *Long Island* which, with a flight-deck and a hangar connected by lift, could handle some 20 aircraft.

A large programme of such ships was now put in hand, six being

A Barracuda overshoots when landing on a carrier after a raid on the *Tirpitz*

US crewmen flag in an aircraft. The 'bats' here indicate 'one wing low'

lent to the British to reinforce five conversions being undertaken by British yards. Although they had been intended primarily for convoy duties, their value in amphibious operations to provide fighter cover until air bases could be established on shore was quickly appreciated: except for the *Avenger* — one of the first lend-Lease ships — which performed very successfully in defence of a convoy to Russia in August 1942, they were therefore all at first allocated to take part in the Allied landings in North Africa in November 1942 in which US and British escort carriers took part.

British escort carriers went on to play a vital role off the beaches at Salerno, while the US ships comprised the air element of assault forces in numerous island assaults in the Pacific. It was not until March 1943 that these ships took up the task in the Atlantic for which they had been designed, the first to operate there being the USS *Bogue,* closely followed by HMS *Biter* and *Archer.* They arrived at the height of the crisis in the Battle of the Atlantic and played a vital part in the decisive defeat of the U-boats in that theatre in May 1943.

Subsequently six US escort carriers operating singly or in pairs with destroyer escorts as Hunter/Killer Groups accounted for 40 German U-boats in the Atlantic, while British escort carriers with convoys to Russia accounted for 17 during 1944 alone.

One further type of small carrier developed for escort duty was the merchant aircraft carrier or MAC-ship. This was either a tanker or a grain ship on which a flight deck, but no hangar or lift, was constructed. Carrying a few Swordfish planes on deck, they continued to carry cargoes of oil or grain and supplied air cover for whatever convoy they joined. They were a most successful concept; but emerging only after the U-boats had been driven from the North Atlantic convoy routes they really saw very little action.

Triumph of the Rising Sun

In December 1941 a totally different kind of sea war began in the Pacific in which each side was equipped with carriers. Because the US and Japanese navies had retained control of their own air arms ever since their inception, their ship-borne aircraft were not only of the most recent design but were expressly designed for carrier operation, rugged and reliable for deck-landing and with the long range necessary for operation in the wide ocean spaces.

Of the two the Japanese had advanced further, since each had commissioned their first small carriers — the *Langley* and the *Hosho* — in 1922. Under the terms of the Washington Naval Treaty, each had next converted, between 1927 and 1928, two uncompleted capital ships which would have otherwise had to be scrapped, the *Saratoga* and *Lexington* for the US navy, *Akagi* and *Kaga* for the Japanese, all of them ships of some 36,000 tons. These were all 'island carriers', though the superstructure in the Japanese ships was comparatively small as it did not incorporate the funnels. Instead, the boiler smoke was exhausted through funnels projecting over the ship's side, a feature of the majority of Japanese carriers. All American carriers except one were to adopt the large island design, the exception being the *Ranger*, mentioned later, which had a small island and three short funnels on the starboard side.

Over the next ten years both navies had steadily built up their carrier strength. The Japanese by 1941 had commissioned four more fleet carriers, *Soryu, Hiryu, Shokaku,* and *Zuikaku,* each of which could operate from 50 to 70 aircraft, and two more light carriers *Ryujo* and *Zuiho,* flush-deck ships handling, like the *Hosho,* some 30 planes. The Americans had followed their first two fleet carriers with the smaller *Ranger* and, when the next two ships, the *Enterprise* and *Yorktown* of 20,000 tons and handling 80 aircraft, brought them to within 14,700 tons of the total permitted by the Washington Treaty, they built the *Wasp* to that size. Finally in September 1939, after expiration of the Treaty, the *Hornet,* similar to the *Yorktown,* was laid down. The *Langley* having been relegated to the status of a seaplane carrier, the Japanese thus had nine carriers and the Americans seven in December 1941, though the USA had laid down 11 of the 27,100-ton *Essex* class.

The Japanese navy, including its carriers, had played an active part in the operations against China which had been in progress since 1937. The quickening influence of war had led to development of carrier planes of outstanding quality. The Nakajima 97 torpedo-bomber (known to the Allies as the 'Kate') and the Aichi 99 ('Val') dive-bomber were at least the equals of the contemporary American Douglas Devastator and Dauntless. In the Mitsubishi O (Zero) they had far the best naval fighter in the world, greatly superior in performance, gun-power, and endurance to the American fighter, the Grumman Wildcat. And flying these planes were experienced veterans of four years of air warfare.

Having used their whole force of six fleet carriers successfully

to neutralise the American Pacific Fleet in the devastating surprise attack on Pearl Harbor on December 7, 1941, the Japanese were able to take advantage of their central position in the theatre of war to employ them *en masse* with maximum effectiveness in a series of surprise attacks on Allied bases in a destructive sweep through the East Indies in support of their invasion forces and then on into the Indian Ocean to Ceylon to neutralise the hastily gathered British Eastern Fleet. Rabaul in the Bismarcks, Amboina in the Dutch East Indies, Darwin at the northern tip of Australia — each in turn was devastated. Colombo and Trincomalee were heavily damaged, the *British* cruisers *Dorsetshire* and *Cornwall* and the carrier *Hermes* all sent to the bottom by dive-bombers.

Vice-Admiral Chuichi Nagumo's Fast Carrier Striking Force returned to Japan in April exultant at their unbroken run of four months of victory. Later they were to regret succumbing to a 'victory disease'. Their task at Pearl Harbor had been only half completed: carriers of the US Pacific Fleet, *Saratoga, Lexington,* and *Enterprise* had been absent on December 7 and so had escaped the holocaust which had wiped out the Pacific battle squadrons. Though the *Saratoga* was removed from the scene in January, damaged by a Japanese submarine's torpedo, the *Yorktown* came to replace her. The *Hornet* was to follow in April.

Even so, ten Japanese carriers (the new light carrier *Shoho,* sister to the *Zuiho,* had joined the fleet in January), backed by a powerful fleet of fast battleships, were opposed by only four US carriers. The Americans were faced with the task of defending a sea frontier stretching from Hawaii to Australia with this meagre force. To the Japanese it seemed impossible that the enemy could risk concentrating it in any one threatened area. They did not know that their naval codes had been broken, betraying in advance to the Americans every move they planned.

Prelude in the Coral Sea

When the Japanese decided, therefore, to launch an expedition in May to expand their conquests further by capturing Port Moresby on the southern coast of Papua, whence they could threaten Australia, they felt confident that the *Shoho,* accompanying the invasion force with the *Shokaku* and *Zuikaku* in distant support, was sufficient air cover against the single enemy carrier in the South Pacific. But the American C-in-C Pacific, Admiral Chester Nimitz, warned by his cryptanalysts, was able to send in good time the *Lexington* Carrier Group to join that of the *Yorktown* in the Coral Sea.

In the battle which followed between May 3 and 8, 1942, defects showed up in the American airborne torpedoes which were to take more than two years to overcome. American striking power was therefore largely confined to the Douglas Dauntless scout dive-bomber. The *Shoho* was sunk and the *Shokaku* severely damaged. In reply the *Lexington* was sunk by a combination of torpedo and bomb hits, tipping the balance of success at first sight in favour of the Japanese. But not only were they forced to abandon their invasion plans: in the course of the battle a great many of their veteran, skilled pilots were lost, pilots for whose replacement the training facilities and suitable manpower were lacking. The *Shokaku's* damage and this lack of trained aviators for the *Zuikaku* were to keep the two ships out of action at a critical moment approaching.

Two weeks before the Coral Sea battle the victory-proud Japanese had been shocked to the core by the sight of American B-25 bombers over Tokyo. They had been flown off the deck of the *Hornet*; this was not realised by the Japanese, however, and the raid clinched the decision to press ahead with their ambitious plan to expand their defensive perimeter eastwards by capturing Midway and occupying the Aleutians.

The whole fleet was to be employed in the expectation that an assault on Midway would bring the US Pacific Fleet out to give battle. Still unaware that his plans were known in advance by the enemy, the Japanese C-in-C widely dispersed his huge force. Two of his carriers, the little *Ryujo* and the *Junyo,* newly converted from a passenger liner to handle 48 aircraft, were sent to raid Dutch Harbor in the Aleutians. The *Zuiho* was retained with her Main Body centred on the battle fleet, which was to occupy a central position ready to move into action whenever and wherever it developed, which was not expected until after Midway had been attacked.

Thus Nagumo's Carrier Force, entrusted with the task of neutralising Midway before the assault landing, comprised, in the absence of the *Zuikaku* and *Shokaku,* only four fleet carriers, *Akagi, Kaga, Soryu,* and *Hiryu.* The Americans, with their foreknowledge of Japanese plans, were able to deploy their full strength, *Yorktown, Enterprise,* and *Hornet,* against the Japanese, reducing the odds to reasonable proportions. A combination of bad scouting by Japanese cruiser-borne reconnaissance float-planes and fatal vacillation by Nagumo, led to his carriers being caught with their decks and hangars thronged with planes, re-fuelling and rearming after their return from attacking Midway, when the American dive-bombers swooped to inflict fatal damage on the *Akagi, Kaga,* and *Soryu* in a matter of minutes.

The *Hiryu,* separated from the others, survived long enough to launch two successful torpedo and bomb strikes against the *Yorktown* before she, too, was overwhelmed by massed dive-bombers from the *Enterprise* and *Hornet.* Though the *Yorktown* was eventually sunk by a Japanese submarine when under tow, the Battle of Midway, which wiped out the previous Japanese carrier superiority, was one of the decisive battles of history.

Midway had also made it clear that so long as carriers were present on either side, fleet actions would no longer be fought at the range of the battleships' guns but at that of the carrier planes. The Japanese battle squadrons, including the monstrous *Yamato,* biggest battleship in the world, were unable to play any part at Midway. From now on the strength of the opposing sides had to be measured by that of their carrier force.

After Midway: a straight fight

Both sides were fairly evenly balanced. Each had four fleet carriers, though those of the Japanese handled fewer aircraft than the Americans — the ex-passenger liners, *Hiyo* and *Junyo,* in particular (commissioned that summer), could handle only about 50 each, the *Shokaku* and *Zuikaku* 72. In comparison, the American *Enterprise* and *Hornet* could handle 80 aircraft, the *Saratoga* some 72, and the *Wasp,* which joined the Pacific Fleet at this time, rather less. The Japanese, however, had also the light carriers *Zuiho* and *Ryujo* operating a score or so of aircraft. The remaining ships which they converted to carriers during 1942 — *Taiyo, Unyo,* and *Chuyo* from passenger liners and *Ryuho* from a submarine tender — were too slow or lacked the equipment to form part of the fighting fleet and were confined to training and transport duties.

Each side had a large programme of carrier construction under way. But the Japanese only initiated theirs after Midway and it would not start to bear fruit until the end of 1943, whereas the Americans had had 11 ships of the *Essex* class, capable of handling more than 100 aircraft each, under construction since 1940, the first of which would be commissioned at the end of 1942, and nine fast, light carriers of the *Independence* class (35 aircraft) being converted from cruiser hulls, the first of which was to join the fleet at the beginning of 1943.

In the meantime, however, each side had to make do with what it had in the naval battles for Guadalcanal, a struggle which did not end in Allied victory until February 1943. In the course of these battles the American carriers played, firstly, a vital part in providing fighter cover to the occupation force until the US Marine fighters could be firmly established on Henderson Field on Guadalcanal, and subsequently in opposing naval forces either bombarding the airfield or covering the transport of Japanese troop reinforcements to the island.

In the Battle of the Eastern Solomons at the end of August a long-range duel between the opposing carriers was again fought, as at Midway: the *Saratoga* and *Enterprise* against the *Zuikaku, Shokaku,* and the *Ryujo.* The *Ryujo* was sunk by dive-bombers from the *Saratoga*: the *Enterprise* was heavily damaged, a result which might have been considered a 'draw' but for the casualties, amounting almost to annihilation, suffered by the Japanese strike planes.

The balance of carrier strength now tipped sharply in favour of the Japanese through American lack of appreciation of the submarine threat. Operating over long periods in the same stretch of the Coral Sea, the *Saratoga* was torpedoed and put out of action for three months on August 31, 1942; the *Wasp* was torpedoed and sunk, and the battleship *North Carolina* damaged two weeks later. The *Enterprise,* incompletely repaired, was hurried south from Pearl Harbor in time to join the lone *Hornet* and take part in the next carrier battle, that of the Santa Cruz Islands on October 26, in which the *Hornet* was sunk, the *Shokaku* and the *Zuiho* heavily damaged.

The British lend a hand

Reduced to the single, partially effective *Enterprise,* the Americans appealed to the British for help, resulting in the dispatch of the *Victorious.* It took some time to re-equip her with American aircraft — no British carrier planes of that date could have matched the Japanese. By the time she was operational, the *Saratoga* had also been repaired and the two ships operated together in the South Pacific for some months, allowing the *Enterprise* to return home for full repairs.

But for the time being the Japanese carriers had shot their bolt. Their air groups had been deployed on island bases in the Bismarcks to take part in the fight for Papua and against the American advance up the island chain, operations for which carriers were unsuited. They suffered steady attrition until November 1943 when they were re-embarked and returned to Japan to rehabilitate and rest.

Japanese naval air power, indeed, was in rapid decline. Though two new carriers, the *Chiyoda* and *Chitose,* converted from seaplane tenders, were about to join the fleet, the air crews for them and for the other carriers were for the most part unfledged, inexperienced aviators. Replacements for casualties would be of even lower calibre. Not until March 1944 would another new fleet carrier be completed. This was the *Taiho,* in whose design the lessons of Midway had been taken into account by giving her an armoured flight deck and side armour in a similar way to British carriers which, with her large island enclosing a vertical funnel, she closely resembled. Like the British carriers, however, she thereby sacrificed some of her aircraft complement, which was only 53.

The Americans, in comparison, had an apparently inexhaustible supply of suitable manpower and a flourishing training organisation through which flowed the pilots for the new carriers following each other in rapid succession from the shipyards. By the summer of 1944, six fleet and five light fleet carriers had been formed into a task force with each of its task groups screened by fast battleships and cruisers as well as destroyers. The carriers were equipped with new aircraft which, for the first time, had performances better than those of their opponents — the Grumman Hellcat fighter and the Avenger torpedo plane.

Showdown in the Marianas

In addition there was a steadily growing force of escort carriers. These would give air support to the amphibious expeditions with which it was now decided to cut the Japanese perimeter defences by occupying Japanese-held island groups along it.

Tarawa and Makin in the Gilberts were taken in November 1942, the Marshalls at the end of January 1944, while the carrier task force ranged far and wide delivering devastating attacks on Japanese bases, forcing the Japanese fleet back until it finally had to base itself on Singapore. When in June the Marianas Islands were attacked, however, the Japanese were forced to come forward and challenge the Pacific Fleet in defence of these vital links in their communications between Japan and their conquered territories in the south.

In the Battle of the Philippine Sea which followed, the American commander, Admiral Spruance, stood on the defensive and met the massed Japanese carrier strikes with the full force of Hellcat fighters from seven fleet and eight light carriers — some 300 planes. The slaughter that followed, exultantly called 'The Great Marianas Turkey Shoot' by the American airmen, spelt the end of Japanese ship-borne air power. In the course of the battle the *Shokaku* and *Taiho* were both torpedoed and sunk by American submarines, the *Hiyo* by Avengers from the American carriers, the *Zuikaku* and *Chiyoda* heavily damaged.

But all this was of little consequence compared to the holocaust of Japanese airmen. Never again could sufficient crews to man even the carriers which survived the battle be trained to fly from their decks. When next the carriers sortied — during the Battle of Leyte in October 1944 — it was to offer themselves as a sacrificial lure, in which they succeeded admirably and were sunk in the process.

Reduced now to throwing untrained airmen into battle, the Japanese sought to ensure their hitting the target by diving suicidally on to it. These kamikazes, attacking at first singly, but later in massed attacks *(kikusui),* comprised the most deadly form of attack yet experienced. Joined in March 1945 by the British Pacific Fleet, some of whose carriers had been re-equipped with American aircraft while others operated the Seafire fighter, an adaptation of the Spitfire, and Firefly fighter-bombers, this huge Allied force pounded the Japanese shore installations in support of the amphibious assaults moving ever closer to the sacred soil of their homeland.

Casualties among Allied ships were heavy; they included kamikaze hits on four British carriers whose armoured decks saved them from disablement and enabled them to continue in action. American ships similarly hit usually required dockyard repair. By their nature the kamikazes were a wasting asset, however. By the end of June the Japanese effort had almost exhausted itself and when the atomic explosions over Hiroshima and Nagasaki ended the war, Allied carrier planes were ranging over the length and breadth of the land, meeting little opposition from their Japanese counterparts.

GUADALCANAL: THE SEA BATTLES

The struggle of the Marines on Guadalcanal was accompanied by an equally bloody campaign at sea to intercept the 'Tokyo Express' and secure control of the approaches. In one disastrous action alone—the Battle of Savo Island—the Allied naval force was shattered; at the Battle of Santa Cruz on October 23/24 the large carriers on both sides were temporarily eliminated; and in a series of battles in November, Japanese ships scored notable victories over American cruisers and destroyers. In the end both sides lost 24 warships of roughly equal tonnage off Guadalcanal—but the Americans were able to accept such attrition far more easily than the Japanese . . .

A Japanese dive-bomber swoops on USS *Hornet* while a torpedo plane circles— Battle of Santa Cruz

1. SAVO ISLAND — August 8/9, 1942

A Japanese cruiser force under Vice-Admiral Mikawa advances down 'The Slot' to attack the American transports unloading off Guadalcanal. An Allied cruiser force under Rear-Admiral Crutchley RN, divided into three squadrons, patrols the approaches around Savo Island. 0100 hours: The Japanese cruisers slip past the destroyers *Blue* and *Ralph Talbot*. 0138 hours: The cruisers *Canberra* and *Chicago* are sighted and disabled with accurate gunfire. When the *Vincennes*, *Quincy*, and *Astoria* intervene they too are disabled. The Japanese then retire damaging the *Ralph Talbot* as they go.

2. EASTERN SOLOMONS — August 23, 1942

An attempt to run supplies to the Japanese troops on Guadalcanal is supported by the aircraft-carriers *Shokaku*, *Zuikaku*, and *Ryujo*. Vice-Admiral Fletcher's Task Force 61, patrolling to the east of the Solomon Islands, sights the Japanese fleet. The Japanese reverse course, and avoid the American strike aircraft.
August 24: *Ryujo*, sailing ahead of the main Japanese fleet, is sighted by an American flying boat. An armed reconnaissance is flown off from *Enterprise*, and followed, at 1345 hours, by a strike force from *Saratoga*. *Ryujo* launches her aircraft to attack Henderson Field. Just as the American strike flies off, another reconnaissance aircraft sights *Shokaku* and *Zuikaku*, who have launched a massive striking force. An attempt to divert the US aircraft to the new target fails, but the *Ryujo* is sunk. *Enterprise* is hit three times by dive-bombers, but is able to continue recovering her aircraft.

3. CAPE ESPERANCE — October 11/12, 1942

American supply convoy sails for Guadalcanal. It is escorted by a cruiser squadron commanded by Rear-Admiral Scott, which is also to ambush any Japanese forces moving down the Slot.
October 11/12: A Japanese convoy, covered by Rear-Admiral Goto's cruiser squadron, moves down the Slot. Scott receives information of its approach, and steers to intercept it. 2325 hours: The cruiser *Helena*'s radar detects the Japanese at a range of 14 miles but she fails to inform Scott. At 2333 hours he decides to reverse course, but in the confusion the cohesion of his force is broken. Scott then learns of the enemy's approach. The destroyer *Duncan* attacks independently, and the *Helena* opens fire, followed by the other cruisers. An order to cease fire does not take effect until the *Aoba* and *Furutaka* have been severely damaged. The Japanese turn and retreat, and during the pursuit they damage the *Boise* and lose the destroyer *Fubuki*.

4. SANTA CRUZ — October 24/26, 1942

The Japanese Combined Fleet moves to the north of Guadalcanal, ready to fly aircraft in to Henderson Field as soon as it is captured.
October 24: US Task Force 16 (*Enterprise*) rejoins Task Force 17 (*Hornet*), and is ordered to sweep in a wide circle around the Santa Cruz Islands to intercept any Japanese forces approaching Guadalcanal.
October 25: At noon an American flying boat sights two Japanese aircraft-carriers, but an American strike fails to make contact.

Grumman TBF-1 Avenger. With the defensive and strike capabilities of a twin-engined aircraft, the Avenger had the handling of a carrier aircraft and could carry bombs, depth charges or torpedoes. **Max speed:** 259 mph at 11,200 feet. **Max range:** 1000 miles loaded. **Armament:** 2×5-inch, 1×3-inch and 1×·5-inch machine-guns; 1×22-inch torpedo or 2000-lb bombload

October 26: The Japanese fleet is again sighted and the *Enterprise* launches 16 dive-bombers to make an armed reconnaissance. At 0658 hours the Japanese aircraft-carriers (*Shokaku*, *Zuikaku*, and *Zuiho*) launch a first striking force. As a second force is being ranged up, two of the *Enterprise*'s dive-bombers attack *Zuiho* and put her out of action. 0730/0815 hours: *Enterprise* and *Hornet* launch three small strike forces. 0822 hours: *Shokaku* and *Zuikaku* launch their second strike. The main Japanese attack falls on *Hornet*, which is struck by two torpedoes and six bombs. Meanwhile *Shokaku* is seriously damaged by American dive-bombers. The second Japanese strike concentrates on the *Enterprise*: her forward lift is put permanently out of action, but her speed and manoeuvrability are unaffected. A third Japanese strike fails to achieve any results. The American forces then withdraw. *Hornet* is sunk by the Japanese when they find her burning hulk.

Below: Santa Cruz. A Japanese Kate makes a torpedo run on the *South Dakota*

Below: Santa Cruz. The Japanese cruiser *Chikuma* evades an American attack

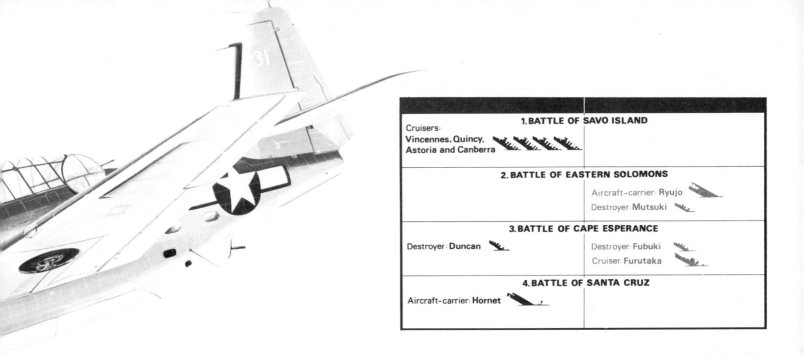

1. BATTLE OF SAVO ISLAND	
Cruisers: Vincennes, Quincy, Astoria and Canberra	
2. BATTLE OF EASTERN SOLOMONS	
	Aircraft-carrier: Ryujo
	Destroyer: Mutsuki
3. BATTLE OF CAPE ESPERANCE	
Destroyer: Duncan	Destroyer: Fubuki
	Cruiser: Furutaka
4. BATTLE OF SANTA CRUZ	
Aircraft-carrier: Hornet	

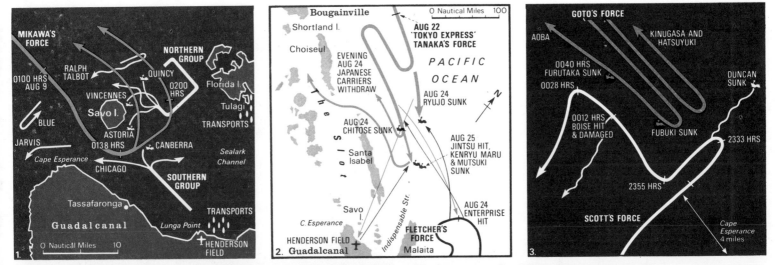

Map 1:

MIKAWA'S FORCE

0100 HRS AUG 9

RALPH TALBOT

NORTHERN GROUP

QUINCY

0200 HRS

Florida I.

VINCENNES

Savo I.

Tulagi

TRANSPORTS

BLUE

ASTORIA

0138 HRS

CANCERRA

Sealark Channel

JARVIS

Cape Esperance

CHICAGO

SOUTHERN GROUP

Tassafaronga

Guadalcanal

Lunga Point

TRANSPORTS

0 Nautical Miles 10

HENDERSON FIELD

1.

Map 2:

Bougainville

0 Nautical Miles 100

Shortland I.

AUG 22 'TOKYO EXPRESS' TANAKA'S FORCE

Choiseul

EVENING AUG 24 JAPANESE CARRIERS WITHDRAW

PACIFIC OCEAN

AUG 24 RYUJO SUNK

AUG 24 CHITOSE SUNK

AUG 25 JINTSU HIT, KENRYU MARU & MUTSUKI SUNK

Santa Isabel

AUG 24 ENTERPRISE HIT

Savo I.

C. Esperance

FLETCHER'S FORCE

HENDERSON FIELD

2. Guadalcanal

Malaita

Map 3:

GOTO'S FORCE

AOBA

KINUGASA AND HATSUYUKI

0040 HRS FURUTAKA SUNK

0028 HRS

DUNCAN SUNK

0012 HRS BOISE HIT & DAMAGED

FUBUKI SUNK

2333 HRS

2355 HRS

SCOTT'S FORCE

Cape Esperance 4 miles

3.

Below: The end of the US carrier *Wasp*, torpedoed by the Japanese submarine *I-19* while escorting a transport convoy

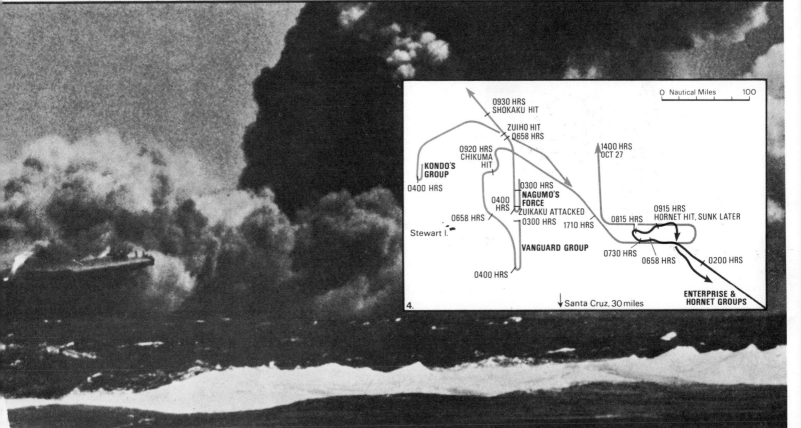

Map 4:

0 Nautical Miles 100

0930 HRS SHOKAKU HIT

ZUIHO HIT 0658 HRS

0920 HRS CHIKUMA HIT

1400 HRS OCT 27

KONDO'S GROUP

0300 HRS NAGUMO'S FORCE

0400 HRS

0400 HRS ZUIKAKU ATTACKED

0915 HRS HORNET HIT, SUNK LATER

0658 HRS

0300 HRS

0815 HRS

1710 HRS

Stewart I.

VANGUARD GROUP

0730 HRS

0658 HRS

0200 HRS

0400 HRS

ENTERPRISE & HORNET GROUPS

↓ Santa Cruz, 30 miles

4.

CRUISERS: KEY WARSHIPS IN TH

When the battle for Guadalcanal began in August 1942, the sea approaches to that vitally important island were dominated during the daylight hours by air power. And since two-thirds of the Japanese carrier fleet had been shattered at the Battle of Midway, and the Americans held the only air base in the Solomon Islands, air power was largely in American hands. No Japanese surface forces dared operate by day in those waters, but as darkness fell, the surface forces of both sides—particularly the cruisers and destroyers—moved in and clashed in savage combat in the narrow straits between the islands. In these skirmishes the Japanese showed themselves initially the masters. The Americans had radar, but the Japanese crews were trained to the highest pitch of night-fighting efficiency, and they had the superb 'Long Lance' torpedo—better than any torpedo in the American armoury. But the Americans had enormous reserves of ships and men to throw into the fight, whereas the Japanese ships and their crack crews, exhausted by battle after battle, were irreplaceable

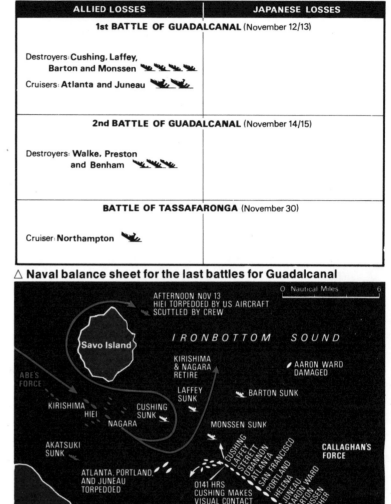

ALLIED LOSSES	JAPANESE LOSSES
1st BATTLE OF GUADALCANAL (November 12/13)	
Destroyers: Cushing, Laffey, Barton and Monssen	
Cruisers: Atlanta and Juneau	
2nd BATTLE OF GUADALCANAL (November 14/15)	
Destroyers: Walke, Preston and Benham	
BATTLE OF TASSAFARONGA (November 30)	
Cruiser: Northampton	

△ **Naval balance sheet for the last battles for Guadalcanal**

O Nautical Miles 6

AFTERNOON NOV 13
HIEI TORPEDOED BY US AIRCRAFT
SCUTTLED BY CREW

Savo Island

IRONBOTTOM SOUND

ABE'S FORCE

KIRISHIMA & NAGARA RETIRE

AARON WARD DAMAGED

LAFFEY SUNK

BARTON SUNK

KIRISHIMA

HIEI   CUSHING SUNK

NAGARA

MONSSEN SUNK

AKATSUKI SUNK

CUSHING
LAFFEY
STERETT
O'BANNON
ATLANTA
SAN FRANCISCO
PORTLAND
HELENA
JUNEAU
AARON WARD
BARTON
MONSSEN
FLETCHER

CALLAGHAN'S FORCE

ATLANTA, PORTLAND, AND JUNEAU TORPEDOED

0141 HRS CUSHING MAKES VISUAL CONTACT

Guadalcanal

0124 HRS NOV 13
HELENA'S RADAR
LOCATES JAPANESE

△ **'1st Guadalcanal', November 12/13. Callaghan's line of destroyers and cruisers was surprised by the Japanese, who smashed four destroyers and threw the US force into confusion — but *Hiei* was lost after US air attacks the following afternoon**

GUADALCANAL BATTLES

USS BOISE

Boise belonged to the *Brooklyn* class of light cruisers, which had been started in the mid-1930s. In this class, the hull design placed the seaplane catapult in the stern, and the main armament was mounted in triple turrets. *Boise* received heavy damage in the Battle of Cape Esperance on October 9, where she was part of Admiral Scott's squadron. **Length:** 608½ feet (overall). **Beam:** 61¾ feet. **Draught:** 19½ feet. **Max speed:** 34 knots. **Range:** 14,500 miles at 15 knots. **Armament:** 15 6-inch, eight 5-inch, four 3-pounder; multiple 20-mm AA guns. Four aircraft. **Complement:** 868

CHOKAI (far left)

Chokai belonged to the *Takao* class, which was launched in 1927/28, and which represented the 'second generation' of Japan's 10,000-ton cruisers. Main distinguishing features were the massive bridge structure and the high elevation of the main battery (up to 70° for AA use). *Chokai* was Admiral Mikawa's flagship in the Battle of Savo Island on the night of August 8/9, 1942. **Length:** 650 feet (overall). **Beam:** 62½ feet. **Draught:** 16⅔ feet. **Max speed:** 33 knots. **Range:** 14,000 miles at 15 knots. **Armament:** ten 8-inch guns, four 4·7-inch guns; eight 24-inch torpedo tubes. **Complement:** 692

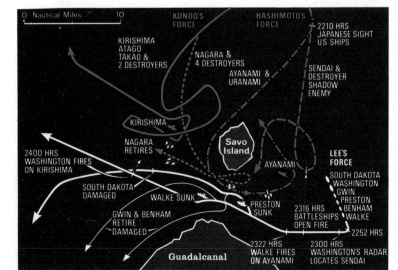

△ '2nd Guadalcanal', November 14/15. Again the Japanese were able to exploit their mastery of night combat; but the superior gun-power of the US battleships recouped the initial losses and sank the battleship *Kirishima*

BATTLESHIPS CLASH AT GUADALCANAL

The later naval battles off Guadalcanal saw the first direct clashes between battleships of the American and Japanese fleets — clashes that were disastrous for the Japanese battle fleet. In two successive battles, the Japanese lost first the *Hiei* and then the *Kirishima*; serious damage was caused to the USS *South Dakota*, but neither of the two American battleships in the actions was lost. Ship for ship, the Americans had all the advantages: superior manoeuvrability, superior hitting-power, and vastly superior protection; against these advantages, the Japanese superiority in speed proved of little value. But in the crews the story was different: the Japanese crews were the product of long training and were able to get the very best out of their ships. The Americans had only just managed to produce another Pacific battle fleet out of new crews and new ships

South Dakota and *Washington* represented the first two classes of the US Navy's new fast battleships; they featured shorter length to improve manoeuvrability, a massive armour-belt, and 16-inch guns.
Specifications for *South Dakota*. *Length:* 680 feet. *Beam:* 108 feet. *Draught:* 29 feet. *Speed:* 28 knots. *Max armour belt thickness:* 18 inches. *Armament:* nine 16-inch, 16 5-inch, 56 40-mm. AA. Three aircraft. *Complement:* 2,500

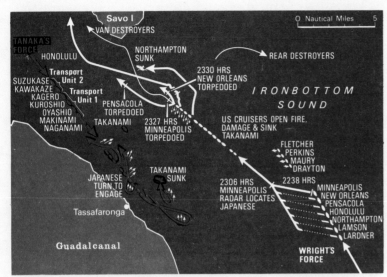

△ 'Battle of Tassafaronga', November 30. This was the last major clash before the Japanese pulled out of Guadalcanal. Tanaka repeated all the successful Japanese tactics, sinking one US cruiser and crippling four others which were towed back to Tulagi for repairs

Kirishima and her sister-ship **Hiei** were both *Kongo*-class battleships. These ships had been classed as battle-cruisers when completed during the First World War, but were reclassed as fast battleships during the 1930s.
Specifications for *Kirishima*. *Length:* 730 feet. *Beam:* 101 feet. *Draught:* 32 feet. *Speed:* 30 knots. *Max armour belt thickness:* 8 inches. *Armament:* eight 14-inch, 14 6-inch, eight 5-inch AA, 20 25-mm AA. Three aircraft. *Complement:* 1,437

When the US armada—the greatest yet seen in the Pacific theatre—descended on Leyte Gulf in the southern Philippines, the Japanese were ready. Their navy had been ordered to combat any invasion with a desperate plan—Operation *Sho* (Victory). The last surviving battleships and carriers of the Imperial Japanese Navy were to stake all for victory, and they duly steamed out to do battle when the news of the invasion came. The result was the Battle of Leyte Gulf, a mighty three-day struggle which resulted in the virtual annihilation of the Japanese fleet

BATTLE OF LEYTE

Philippine Islands, October/December 1944

Right: MacArthur returns to the Philippines
Below: US rocket bombardment before the Leyte landings

Leyte Gulf: the rival fleets

The Japanese were gambling on the surprise arrival of their imposing battleship force, including the huge *Yamato* and *Musashi*. Ozawa's carriers, starved of planes, were to be the bait

Halsey's 3rd Fleet had the bulk of the US strike carriers; Kinkaid's 7th Fleet had the lighter force of escort carriers, backed by a stronger battleship force than Halsey's

American
Right: Halsey, C-in-C US 3rd Fleet: he commanded the main US carrier and strike forces in the action
Far right: Kinkaid, C-in-C US 7th Fleet: he had the task of guarding the invasion fleet in Leyte Gulf
Bottom right: Oldendorf, Kinkaid's subordinate, whose battle squadron smashed the Japanese attempt to break into Leyte Gulf through Surigao Strait
Bottom far right: Sprague, commander of the 7th Fleet's small escort carrier force which narrowly escaped annihilation off Samar

Japanese
Top left: Kurita, the commander of the main Japanese battle squadron, whose premature retreat off Samar cost him a great victory over an inferior force
Bottom left: Ozawa, the cool, gallant commander of the decoy carrier force which drew Halsey's 3rd Fleet away from Leyte Gulf

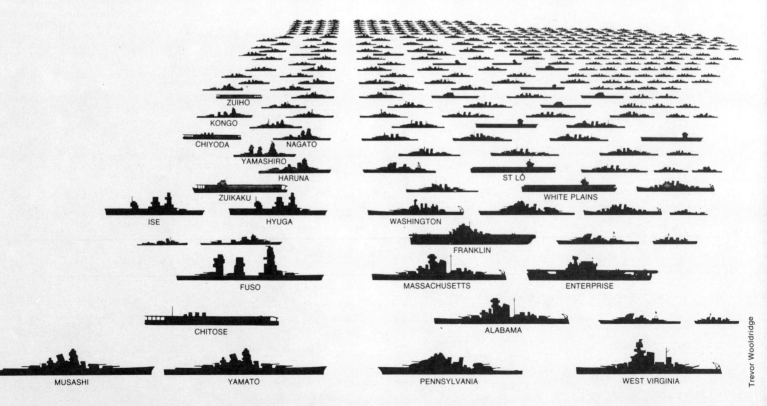

ZUIHO
KONGO
CHIYODA · NAGATO
YAMASHIRO
HARUNA
ZUIKAKU
ISE · HYUGA
FUSO
CHITOSE
MUSASHI · YAMATO

ST LÔ
WHITE PLAINS
WASHINGTON
FRANKLIN
MASSACHUSETTS · ENTERPRISE
ALABAMA
PENNSYLVANIA · WEST VIRGINIA

Trevor Wooldridge

When the sun rose over Leyte Gulf in the central Philippines on the morning of October 20, 1944, it disclosed the largest and mightiest fleet of amphibious assault vessels and warships yet assembled in the Pacific. Over 700 transports, combat ships, and service and support craft were concentrated in the waters east of Leyte Island, or guarding the entrance to the gulf. Further east and north, four powerful task groups of carriers and battleships provided distant cover in the Philippine Sea. Scores of aircraft maintained a constant vigil overhead, while many more prepared to support the assault that morning of four American divisions against the shore of Leyte. The presence of this huge armada signalled the fulfilment of General MacArthur's pledge to return to the Philippines.

The island of Leyte in the central Philippines is some 115 miles long but only 45 miles wide at its broadest and barely 15 at its narrow waist. Its eastern shore, washed by Leyte Gulf, boasts some of the finest landing beaches in the Pacific. Most of the island is mountainous save for the flat, marshy Leyte Valley in the northeast and, in the west, the Ormoc Valley, a narrow corridor running north from the port of Ormoc.

For the seizure of Leyte, General MacArthur had under his command the 200,000 men of General Krueger's 6th Army, Lieutenant-General George C. Kenney's Far East Air Forces, with over 2,500 combat aircraft, and Vice-Admiral Thomas C. Kinkaid's 7th Fleet — often called 'MacArthur's Navy' — which included more than 100 combat vessels, over five times as many transports, supply vessels, landing ships, and other support craft, and 500 planes. In a supporting role, but not under MacArthur's control, was Halsey's 3rd Fleet, one of the largest and most powerful naval striking forces ever assembled, containing nearly 100 of the most modern warships and over 1,000 aircraft.

Kinkaid was responsible for carrying the 6th Army to Leyte and putting it ashore. Halsey meanwhile would cover the landings with pre-invasion airstrikes on the Philippines, Formosa, and the Ryukyus. Close air support for the landings would come from Kinkaid's escort carriers, but only for the first few days. By the end of this period, General Krueger would have captured the east Leyte airfields and Kenney could move in his fighters and light bombers to take over the air-support mission from the navy. The 6th Army could then proceed with the business of occupying Leyte, and MacArthur could use the island as a base from which to move on to other conquests.

The Leyte invasion represented a significant departure from previous MacArthur operations in that it was to be attempted beyond the range of land-based air cover. If carrier protection was lost before Kenney could bring his planes in, then the entire operation might be jeopardised. Naval support was therefore extremely important. Yet Halsey, who was still operating under Nimitz, had as his primary mission not the protection of the beachhead but, if the opportunity arose or could 'be created', the destruction of the Japanese fleet. This left Halsey with the option of withdrawing his support of the invasion whenever he wished. MacArthur could neither prevent this nor could he ever be certain for just how long he could rely on Halsey's presence.

There was still, to be sure, the 7th Fleet. But Kinkaid's small escort carriers could boast only a fraction of the planes that Halsey had. Furthermore, without Halsey, Kinkaid would be hard put to defend himself and the beach-head against a major Japanese fleet effort while at the same time providing Krueger with close air support.

American success, therefore, might well rest on just how soon General Kenney could establish his air units on Leyte. And here the weather entered the picture. From September until early spring, eastern Leyte is subject to frequent heavy rains and, for much of this time, to typhoons. The ground, naturally soft and marshy in many areas, becomes almost completely saturated. Constructing airfields on the spongy Leyte soil under these conditions would be extremely difficult, and without adequate airfields there would be no place for Kenney to put his planes.

MacArthur's staff was well aware of these problems. But the only way to avoid them was to postpone the Leyte invasion, either until bases could be seized on Mindanao or until the weather cleared. And this would mean passing up the opportunity to hit the Japanese while they were weak and off-balance. Better instead to take some risk in order to win a swift and important victory. Besides, Halsey's September raids had shown that the Japanese were in no shape to put up much of a fight. A bold stroke might capture Leyte before the Japanese could even respond to the invasion.

The lack of resistance to Halsey's raids had been in part the result of Japanese weakness. But it had also been based on Japanese determination to husband their main strength for use against a major American offensive. The Japanese, indeed, had developed an elaborate and, as it turned out, dangerously complicated scheme of manoeuvre by which they hoped to throw massive sea, air, and land forces into a 'decisive battle' to crush the Americans.

The Japanese plans — code-named *Sho* ('Victory') — were aimed at defending important territories from the Kuriles to the Philippines. An American invasion — but only one which was clearly a major operation — would be met by a combined air and sea attack launched just as the enemy landings were getting under way. It would be an all-out effort to destroy transports and covering warships in a single blow at the last possible moment. The sadly reduced strength of Japanese carrier airpower, however, meant that the carriers could contribute little to this attack. So they were, instead, to be used as a decoy force to draw off American carriers and expose the rest of the invasion force to Japanese land-based air assaults and naval firepower. Any of the invaders who survived to carry out a landing would be dealt with by the Japanese army.

Timing and close co-ordination were essential features of the *Sho* plans. But unfortunately for the Japanese, their confused and divided command structure denied them the central control so vital to their hopes. This was particularly true for *Sho*-1, the defence of the Philippines. In those important islands there was no single command to integrate land, air, and sea operations. Ground warfare was the responsibility of the XIV Area Army, whose newly appointed commander, General Tomoyuki Yamashita, did not, in fact, reach the Philippines until early October. Under Yamashita, and charged with the defence of the central and southern Philippines, was Lieutenant-General Sosaku Suzuki's XXXV Army. But Yamashita had no control over the Philippine-based IV Air Army of Lieutenant-General Kyoji Tominaga.

Both Yamashita and Tominaga reported on an equal basis to Field-Marshal Count Hisaichi Terauchi who, as Southern Army commander, was responsible for the area from the Philippines through the Indies to Burma. Among his many other duties, then, was the task of co-ordinating army, air, and ground activities in the Philippines.

Naval forces operated completely independent of any of these commands. Practically all Japanese naval units belonged to Admiral Soemu Toyoda's Combined Fleet. The main combat elements, each operating separately and responsible directly to Toyoda, were: Vice-Admiral Takeo Kurita's I Striking Force, battleships, cruisers, and destroyers, based at Lingga Roads, across from Singapore, where they were assured a ready supply of fuel; Vice-Admiral Jisaburo Ozawa's Main Body, a carrier force located in the Inland Sea; and Vice-Admiral Kiyohide Shima's II Striking Force, a few cruisers and destroyers, also in northern waters. Major naval air units in the Philippines and elsewhere were linked to the other fleet elements and, for that matter, to each other only through Toyoda.

The Combined Fleet commander thus had the herculean responsibility of co-ordinating all Japanese naval elements assigned to *Sho*, even as Marshal Terauchi had the same broad task for major army units. But neither Toyoda nor Terauchi were required to have much to do with each other. And Imperial General Headquarters, which theoretically linked the two commanders in Tokyo, did little to achieve this end. Instead of being a joint overall headquarters, it was in fact two separate commands, with independent army and navy sections split by animosities too strong to permit any close co-operation or integration of operations. From top to bottom, then, co-ordinating execution of *Sho* would be extremely difficult, if not impossible.

Overwhelming display of airpower

Clear evidence of this was provided by events in mid-October. To soften the Japanese for the coming Leyte assault, on October 10 Halsey's carriers began a sustained attack against Japanese bases from the Ryukyus to the northern Philippines. In an unprecedented and overwhelming display of sea-borne airpower, Halsey sent as many as 1,000 planes at a time into action, smothering the Japanese defences, destroying ground installations, and driving Japanese aircraft from the sky. To Admiral Toyoda, the weight of these blows indicated the imminence of a major American invasion. After some confusion, he directed naval air units to execute operations under both *Sho*-1, the defence of the Philippines, and *Sho*-2, the defence of Formosa and the Ryukyus.

The result of this premature commitment of Japanese naval air strength was the involvement of practically all of Toyoda's planes in a fruitless effort to halt a non-existent invasion. General Tominaga, meanwhile, did practically nothing in response to Halsey's blows and, for that matter, was probably unaware of Toyoda's unilateral issuing of the 'Sho-execute' orders. Thanks to this restraint, he suffered few losses.

But Toyoda's forces were severely battered. In less than a week of action, over 600 Japanese naval aircraft were destroyed.

Japanese naval air strength on Formosa and in the Philippines was badly crippled and even the small body of planes assigned to Admiral Ozawa's carriers had been committed to the fight and dissipated. American losses were not quite 100 planes.

To add insult to injury, Japanese aircrews had been making ridiculous and completely unfounded claims of success against the US 3rd Fleet. Radio Tokyo announced that as many as 19 American carriers had been sunk, along with a great number of battleships, cruisers, and destroyers. The Emperor issued a special rescript, and mass celebrations were held throughout Japan.

Toyoda too was completely fooled. When Halsey decided to use two damaged cruisers—the only ships in his entire fleet to be hurt at all—as a lure to trap the Japanese fleet, Toyoda rose to the bait. Convinced that he had victory in his grasp, he committed additional air power to the attack and simultaneously directed Admiral Shima's II Striking Force to pursue the supposedly crippled Halsey and mop up. 'Needless to say,' wrote one Japanese commander later, 'all this pursuit business ended in fiasco.' More Japanese planes were lost and Shima barely escaped destruction when Toyoda, finally realising something of the truth, directed the II Striking Force to withdraw.

Toyoda's blunder was a serious blow to Japanese chances of successfully executing the *Sho* plan. Without the hundreds of naval aircraft now lost, it would be impossible to carry out the all-important air phase of the plan. There were still about 300 navy planes on Formosa, some 150 more planes of the IV Air Army widely scattered throughout the Philippines, and perhaps 100 carrier aircraft, flown by inexperienced and ill-trained pilots, gathering again with Admiral Ozawa. But the best planes and pilots were gone.

The strength of Japanese naval surface forces was somewhat more reassuring. Yet without adequate air power, even Admiral Kurita's powerful battleship force at Lingga Roads would have a difficult time when he sortied to meet the Americans. And in the face of uncontested American air operations, General Yamashita would be equally hard pressed to redeploy his forces to meet the expected landings. He had, altogether, some 300,000 troops in the Philippines. But only a third of these were in the southern Philippines, while Leyte was defended by but 20,000 men.

The first landings in the American return to the Philippines took place on October 17 and 18 on three small islands guarding the eastern approaches to Leyte Gulf. Ranger and infantry elements swept the islands with little difficulty, destroyed Japanese radio installations, and set up navigation lights to guide the Leyte invasion convoy. Minesweepers and underwater demolition teams checked and cleared the approaches on the 18th and 19th and

warships and planes of the 7th Fleet began a heavy pre-invasion bombardment of beaches and inland installations on the morning of the 19th. To this activity came almost no Japanese response.

The Japanese were experiencing their usual co-ordination difficulties. Admiral Toyoda had the fastest reaction. When the first alert reached him on the 17th, he ordered his main combat elements to sea and, on the 18th, directed an all-out attack on the invasion force in Leyte Gulf. The other Japanese were more sceptical. Bad weather limited initial observation of the Leyte Gulf area and, unlike Toyoda, they were still under the impression that heavy 3rd Fleet losses the previous week would delay a major American operation for some time. Any American shipping in Leyte Gulf was probably the crippled remnant of Halsey's armada.

By noon of the 18th, however, the Southern and IV Air Army commanders, Field-Marshal Terauchi and General Tominaga, were convinced that the invasion had come. Their recommendations and those of Toyoda convinced their respective superiors in Tokyo. Just after 1700 hours, after reporting their decision to the Emperor, the army and navy sections of Imperial General Headquarters issued separate orders activating *Sho*-1.

The Combined Fleet was already moving to the attack. At noon on the 20th, Kurita's powerful I Striking Force reached Brunei Bay, Borneo. From here, Kurita would lead the bulk of it through the central Philippines and San Bernardino Strait to the Philippine Sea and then rush south to attack Admiral Kinkaid's invasion force in Leyte Gulf. For this purpose, Kurita had five battleships—including the 64,000-ton behemoths *Musashi* and *Yamato*—12 cruisers, and 15 destroyers. A smaller and slower force under Vice-Admiral Shoji Nishimura—two old battleships, a cruiser, and four destroyers—would take a southern route and enter Leyte Gulf through Surigao Strait. Kurita and Nishimura would, hopefully, arrive simultaneously at dawn of the 25th, three days later than called for by the *Sho* plan, but the earliest they could make it. Admiral Shima's II Striking Force of three cruisers and four destroyers, now in Formosan waters, would follow Nishimura (see maps).

There was, however, no plan to co-ordinate their movements. Meanwhile, Admiral Ozawa's Main Body would move south from the Inland Sea. It included four carriers, two battleships partially converted to carry aircraft, three cruisers, and eight destroyers. Yet with barely 100 planes aboard and pilots so poor that many could not even make a carrier landing, the force had no real offensive capability. Its mission was to decoy Halsey's covering fleet away from Leyte and, if possible, engage and destroy it.

The difficulty and danger of the whole complicated manoeuvre against Leyte Gulf was greatly increased by the fact that the earlier Japanese air losses now deprived the fleet of precious air cover.

234

Far left: US bombs burst around the battleship *Yamashiro,* Nishimura's flagship
Top left: US carrier *Princeton,* abandoned and blazing beyond hope of recovery
Bottom left: The mighty 18-inch-gun battleship *Yamato* under air attack

Right: US battleship *West Virginia,* firing a broadside in the night battle of Surigao Strait

Whatever Japanese planes were available would concentrate on the invasion force and beach-head. There were no air elements left to protect Kurita, Nishimura, and Shima against air and submarine attacks during their long voyage to Leyte Gulf.

Kurita's mighty flotilla left Brunei on the morning of the 22nd. Nishimura, following a shorter course, sailed that afternoon. A few minutes after midnight, two American submarines patrolling west of Palawan spotted Kurita and radioed a contact report. They attacked him just after dawn of the 23rd. Their torpedoes sank two heavy cruisers, and so badly damaged a third that it had to return to Brunei, taking two destroyers with it as a screen. In manoeuvring, however, one of the submarines grounded on a reef and had to be blown up by its escaping crew. But Kurita's 32 warships had been reduced by five, and his approach route was now evident to the Americans. He continued to advance, nevertheless, and on the morning of the 24th entered the Sibuyan Sea and came into range of Halsey's planes.

Halsey had spent the 23rd deploying his carrier forces to launch airstrikes against both Kurita and Nishimura, who had also been detected. But it was Japanese air power that drew first blood. Early on the 24th, from bases on Luzon, nearly 200 navy planes set out to attack the nearest American carrier group. Detected by radar as they approached, they met skilful and determined opposition from American fighters. In an hour's engagement, nearly half the Japanese planes were downed and the rest driven off. Only a few of the defenders were lost. Not a ship had come under attack.

Just after 0930 hours, however, a lone Japanese dive-bomber emerged from a low cloud, made a shallow approach on its target, and dropped a 550-pound bomb through the flight deck of the light carrier *Princeton.* The bomb exploded within the ship, setting off other explosions, and sending flaming gasoline throughout the *Princeton*'s interior.

For a few hours it seemed as if the holocaust might be contained. But in mid-afternoon a huge blast rent the carrier, shattering her stern and sending great deadly fragments of steel into the firefighters and across the loaded deck of the cruiser *Birmingham,* which had drawn in close to assist. The *Birmingham,* her topsides strewn with the dead and mutilated, was forced to pull clear, and all efforts to save the *Princeton* were abandoned. Late in the day, American torpedoes sank the blazing ship, the first fast carrier to be lost in two years. But this, and the damaging of the *Birmingham,* was all the Japanese had accomplished. The *Sho* mission of the naval air units—to sink any American warships that might block the approach of the Japanese fleet—had failed.

Nor had General Tominaga's IV Air Army done any better in attacking 7th Fleet units in Leyte Gulf that day. Nearly all of Tom-inaga's planes struck repeatedly at the landing area throughout the 24th. So frequent were these attacks that aircraft from the escort carriers had to suspend ground-support missions in order to defend the anchorage. But few of the American ships were hit, and Tominaga lost nearly 70 planes to US fighters and AA fire.

Admiral Halsey, on the other hand, had been exacting a heavy revenge. A single strike that morning inflicted light damage on a battleship and cruiser in Nishimura's force. Then the entire weight of the 3rd Fleet carrier planes was thrown against Kurita. Beginning about 0900 and lasting till mid-afternoon, five separate attacks hit his ships as they doggedly made their way through the narrow, reef-filled waters of the Sibuyan Sea. At a cost of only 18 aircraft out of well over 250 sorties, Halsey's bombers and torpedo planes sank the mighty *Musashi*—although it took 19 torpedoes and 17 bombs to do it—and sent a crippled heavy cruiser limping back to Brunei. Other Japanese warships also sustained damage, particularly to their exposed communications and fire-control equipment.

Kurita, moreover, was badly shaken by the fury of the assaults. 'We had expected air attacks,' said his chief-of-staff later, 'but this day's were almost enough to discourage us.' Finally, at 1530, after several false submarine alarms, and in anticipation of continued air attacks in the narrow waters of San Bernardino Strait that lay just ahead, Kurita decided to reverse course temporarily. An hour and three-quarters later, when he felt that no more American airstrikes could be launched that day, he turned again and resumed his original course. A little later he received an order from Admiral Toyoda: 'All forces will dash to the attack, trusting in divine assistance!' Kurita replied that he would 'break into Leyte Gulf and fight to the last man'.

Meanwhile, Admiral Ozawa's decoy force had finally attracted Halsey's attention. That morning he had sent his planes in an unsuccessful strike at Halsey's northernmost carrier group. About half were shot down and the rest, since their pilots were incapable of making carrier landings, continued on to Luzon. Then, in the afternoon, Halsey's search planes found Ozawa, giving the 3rd Fleet commander the final 'pieces of the puzzle', as he put it.

For Halsey, Ozawa was the main threat and thus his primary target. The Nishimura and Shima forces seemed to constitute no real danger, certainly nothing that could not be handled by Kinkaid's more numerous and heavier units. Kurita's armada was obviously stronger, but it appeared to have suffered considerable damage—Halsey, like Toyoda earlier, was at the mercy of exaggerated reports by his pilots—and Kurita's vacillations before San Bernardino Strait raised doubts about whether or not he would continue to advance. Even if he did, he could only hit and run, and Kinkaid could probably take care of both Kurita and Nishimura/Shima.

In any event, Ozawa's force contained most of Japan's carriers and, as far as Halsey had any way of knowing, a full complement of aircraft. It seemed to be the strongest and the most dangerous of the Japanese forces approaching Leyte Gulf. To wait for it near Leyte would leave the initiative with the Japanese and allow them to shuttle planes back and forth between their carriers and Luzon, with Halsey's ships in the middle. His best course, he reasoned, was to go after Ozawa with sufficient force to destroy him completely. He would thus wipe out the major threat to the Leyte invasion and achieve his primary mission: 'the destruction of a major portion of the enemy fleet'.

Shortly before 2000 hours on the 24th, Halsey ordered the entire 3rd Fleet north after Ozawa. Assuming that Kinkaid was keeping San Bernardino Strait under aerial observation and that the 7th Fleet commander would notice and be able to handle any attempt of Kurita's to break through, Halsey left not even a single destroyer to watch the strait. Ozawa had thus succeeded in opening the way for Kurita's attack. The Japanese plan, for all its weaknesses, seemed to be working.

While these events were taking place, Admiral Nishimura had been steaming toward Surigao Strait. Kurita's hesitancy before San Bernardino Strait now denied Nishimura the support he would have received had both Japanese elements attempted to penetrate Leyte Gulf simultaneously. Nishimura's smaller force would have to make the effort unaided. To make matters worse, Admiral Kinkaid was well aware of Nishimura's—and, by now, Shima's—approach, and he had sent the entire 7th Fleet Bombardment and Fire Support Group under Rear-Admiral Jesse B. Oldendorf to intercept and destroy the Japanese warships.

Oldendorf positioned his six battleships—most of them survivors of the Pearl Harbor attack—in a line across the northern end of Surigao Strait. Eight cruisers extended the flanks of this battle line, while 21 destroyers took their place on and ahead of both flanks. And at the southern entrance to the strait, 39 motor torpedo-boats deployed to make the first contact. Nishimura and Shima would have to run a gauntlet of torpedoes from the PT boats and destroyers and then come under the punishing weight of heavy shellfire from the battleships and cruisers that crossed the 'T' of their advance. It was a beautiful example of a classical naval tactic.

And it worked almost perfectly. Nishimura reached the entrance to Surigao Strait about an hour before midnight on October 24. He brushed aside the PT attacks with little difficulty and turned into the strait itself around 0200 hours on the 25th. Then, an hour later, the first of three separate but well coordinated destroyer torpedo attacks hit him. Performing their traditional role flawlessly, the American destroyers blew one Japanese battleship in two, damaged another, and sank two destroyers. The American cruisers and battleships then finished the job, sending Nishimura and most of his ships to the bottom. A damaged cruiser and destroyer, *Mogami* and *Shigure,* fled south. In the confusion, the American shelling also heavily damaged the destroyer *Grant* before Admiral Oldendorf could give the order to cease fire.

No sooner had Nishimura been disposed of, than Shima's force arrived. Unaware of the fate of Nishimura, Shima took a PT's torpedo in one of his cruisers, exchanged signals but little information with *Shigure,* and then suffered the ignominy of a careless collision between his flagship and *Mogami*. By 0500 hours, he was convinced that only complete destruction lay ahead: soon the surviving Japanese ships were in full retreat. Not all escaped, however, for American planes continued to harry them and exacted further losses. Of the two battleships, four cruisers, and eight destroyers that entered Surigao Strait with Nishimura and Shima, only a single cruiser and five destroyers were still afloat two weeks later.

At about 0530 hours on October 25, Admiral Kurita received word from Shima of the Japanese defeat in Surigao Strait. By this time, Kurita had passed through San Bernardino Strait and was speeding down the east coast of Samar towards Leyte Gulf. His passage was undetected, thanks to the fact that poor communications and misunderstood messages had left both Halsey and Kinkaid unaware that neither of them was guarding the vital strait.

An hour or so later, at daybreak, Kurita suddenly came upon what he believed to be a 'gigantic enemy task force', including many large carriers, cruisers, and destroyers, and perhaps even a battleship or two. Throughout the engagement that followed, he was never aware that the only force standing between him and Leyte Gulf consisted of half a dozen slow and tiny escort carriers, three destroyers, and four puny destroyer escorts. These ships, commanded by Rear-Admiral Clifton F. Sprague, were the northernmost of three similar task units operating under Kinkaid in support

Samar: 'We were saved by the definite partiality of Almighty God' Sprague

△ Japanese shells straddle the US carrier *Gambier Bay*

△ Scene aboard another US carrier at the height of the chase
▽ An Avenger is prepared for take-off aboard the *Kitkun Bay*

Cape Engaño: 'I turned my back on the opportunity I had dreamed of since my days as a cadet' Halsey

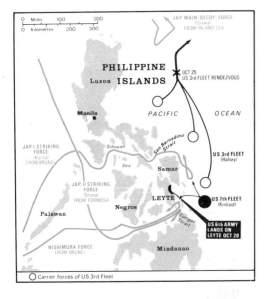

This map shows the triple Japanese threat to the US landings in Leyte Gulf, with the dispositions of the two US fleets. Of the four Japanese admirals only Ozawa played his role correctly; but his success in drawing off Halsey's 3rd Fleet was wasted by Kurita's premature retreat and the defeat of the Nishimura/Shima force

US Navy

△ Japanese carrier *Zuiho,* completely open to attack
▽ One of Ozawa's carriers dodges US bombs

US Navy

of the Leyte landings.

Kurita was momentarily confused by the sudden encounter, but Sprague wasted no time. He ordered his planes aloft and called back those out on missions, headed for the cover of a nearby rain squall, and sent out a frantic plain-language radio call for help. A moment later Kurita's powerful flotilla attacked, sweeping down on the fleeing American vessels and discharging a murderous barrage of fire. To Sprague it seemed improbable that any of his command 'could survive another five minutes'.

What followed was an incredible series of events. The American ships used smoke, rain squalls, and excellent seamanship to dodge and evade their pursuers. Sprague sent his destroyers and destroyer escorts in repeated and remarkably courageous attacks on the heavier Japanese vessels, while overhead the American planes, unopposed in the air, made strike after strike at the increasingly frustrated Japanese. These counterblows caused great confusion in Kurita's units. They forced the Japanese to take evasive action, split their formations, crippled three cruisers, and all but destroyed Kurita's control of his forces.

But Sprague's men paid heavily for their boldness. Despite remarkably poor Japanese marksmanship, the volume and weight of fire was too much to allow the exposed American vessels to remain unscathed. By about 0900 hours, one of the fleeing escort carriers had been sunk along with three of the gallant destroyers and destroyer escorts. A similar fate for the rest of Sprague's command seemed imminent.

At this moment, what Sprague later referred to as 'the definite partiality of Almighty God' took a hand. Kurita—confused about the situation, believing that he had done as much damage as he could to a powerful and swift American battle force which was now outrunning him, anticipating continued airstrikes, and still determined to reach Leyte Gulf—broke off the action. He ordered his scattered warships to fall back and reorganise. 'I could not believe my eyes,' Sprague was to recall. 'It took a whole series of reports from circling planes to convince me.'

But the agony of his small force was not yet over. Two hours after Kurita gave up his pursuit, Sprague's vessels came under a new and no less fearsome type of attack. That morning Japanese suicide planes had carried out the first organised *Kamikaze* strike of the war against some of the other 7th Fleet escort carriers. Now it was Sprague's turn. Nine of these macabre craft swept in low over the water to avoid the American radar, climbed swiftly at close range, and then hurled themselves down on their surprised targets. American gunners destroyed some of them, but several scored hits on the vulnerable escort carriers, sinking one and badly damaging others. A second *Kamikaze* attack, 20 minutes later, sank no ships but inflicted heavy damage and casualties.

Kurita, meanwhile, was headed back toward San Bernardino Strait. After briefly resuming his advance on Leyte Gulf, he had finally concluded that the game was no longer worth the candle. Not only did he believe that he would be faced with a mighty combination of aroused American naval and air power, but—and this was the decisive factor in his reasoning—he felt that by now most of the American transports in Leyte Gulf had unloaded and withdrawn. He had, he thought, already destroyed a large American carrier unit. To risk his country's last major naval striking force for the sake of a few empty cargo vessels seemed ridiculous. It was about 1230 hours when he gave the order to turn north. Leyte Gulf was then but 45 miles away.

Far to the north, Halsey had finally come to grips with Ozawa. From early morning of the 25th until late afternoon, 3rd Fleet carrier pilots under the tactical direction of Vice-Admiral Marc A. Mitscher pounded away at the all but defenceless Japanese decoy force. By the end of the day, of his original 17 ships, Ozawa had lost all four carriers, a cruiser, and two destroyers. That the destruction was not greater was the direct consequence of Halsey's attention being diverted sharply elsewhere.

Beginning shortly after 0800 hours, Halsey had received from Admiral Kinkaid a series of increasingly desperate reports on Sprague's situation accompanied by sharp pleas for aid. He continued to chase Ozawa, nevertheless, in the firm belief that the Japanese carriers still represented the major threat and primary target. But at 1000 hours he received a sharp message from Admiral Nimitz, who had been monitoring Kinkaid's communications from his headquarters at Pearl Harbor. Nimitz's message, a query rather than an order, finally caused Halsey to change his mind. Just before 1100, he directed most of the 3rd Fleet to turn south after Kurita, leaving Mitscher with a carrier striking force to finish off Ozawa from the air. 'At that moment,' Halsey was to write, 'Ozawa was exactly 42 miles from the muzzles of my 16-inch guns. . . . I turned my back on the opportunity I had dreamed of since my days as a cadet.'

Leyte Gulf: the Four-Stage Epic

Phase One: Battle of Sibuyan Sea. Kurita, Shima, and Nishimura *(orange tracks)* head for Leyte Gulf. US air strikes sink battleship *Musashi* in Kurita's force and damage others. Nishimura is also attacked. Land-based Japanese attacks from Luzon airfields sink carrier *Princeton* in US 3rd Fleet. Halsey, locating the southerly approach of Ozawa's force, concentrates 3rd Fleet and sets off to engage Ozawa, leaving 7th Fleet to cover Leyte Gulf; Kurita and Nishimura continue toward San Bernadino and Surigao Straits

Phase Two: Battle of Surigao Strait. Without Shima's support, Nishimura heads directly into Surigao Strait in line-ahead. US destroyers on both sides of the strait savage the Japanese line with torpedoes, sinking battleship *Fuso*. Oldendorf deploys his US cruisers and battleships across the mouth of the strait, crossing the Japanese 'T'; and a heavy barrage of gunfire halts and repulses the Japanese remnants. Nishimura goes down in *Yamashiro*; Shima arrives too late to be of any assistance and his ships play no further part

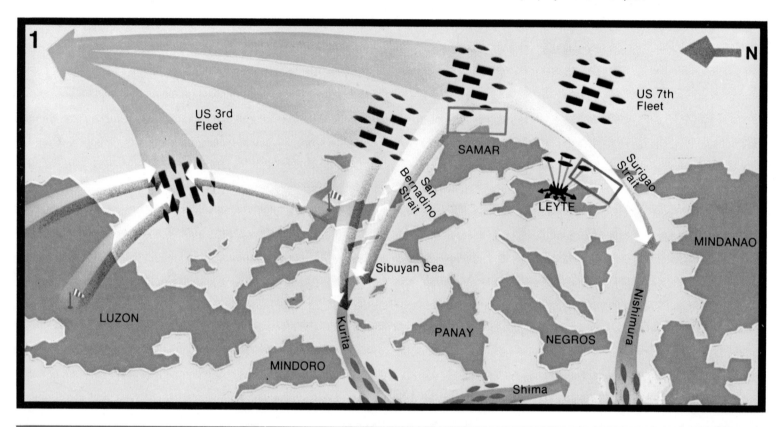

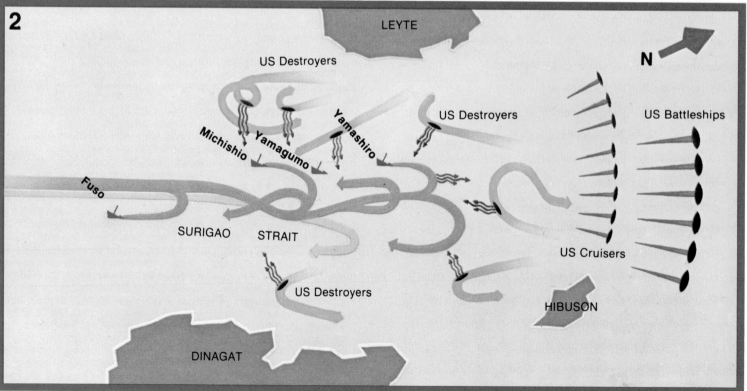

Phase Three: Battle off Samar. Kurita's force emerges from San Bernadino Strait and swings south toward Leyte Gulf, surprising Sprague's small carrier force which turns and runs south. Japanese cruisers *(orange track at top)* steadily overhaul the fleeing US carriers and Sprague is only saved from annihilation by Kurita's retreat, pursued by repeated US air strikes. But Sprague's ships still have to cope with long-range *Kamikaze* attacks *(diagonal white track)* which sink the carrier *St Lô* and damage several other 7th Fleet vessels

Phase Four: Battle of Cape Engaño. Halsey and Mitscher, with an overwhelming superiority, head north to finish off Ozawa's carrier force. Ozawa's ships are defenceless against the US carrier attacks and he loses three carriers to repeated strikes. Halsey is forced to head back toward Samar due to the crisis caused by Kurita's arrival there, but he is too late to engage Kurita. Mitscher launches further air strikes against the remnants of Ozawa's force, but his planes only succeed in sinking a light cruiser as Ozawa retires north

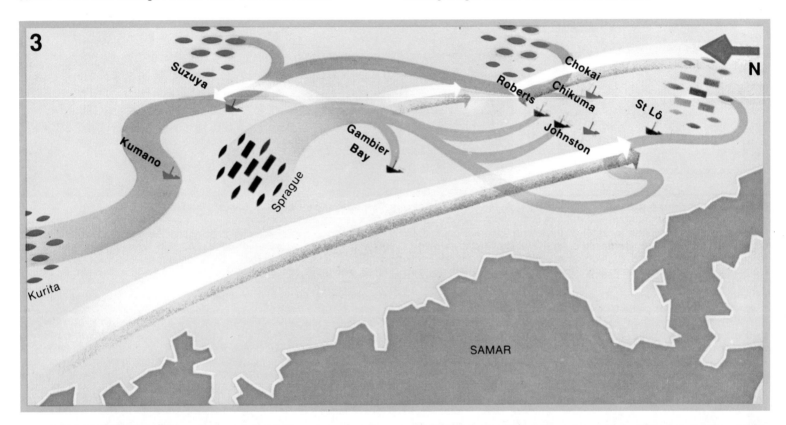

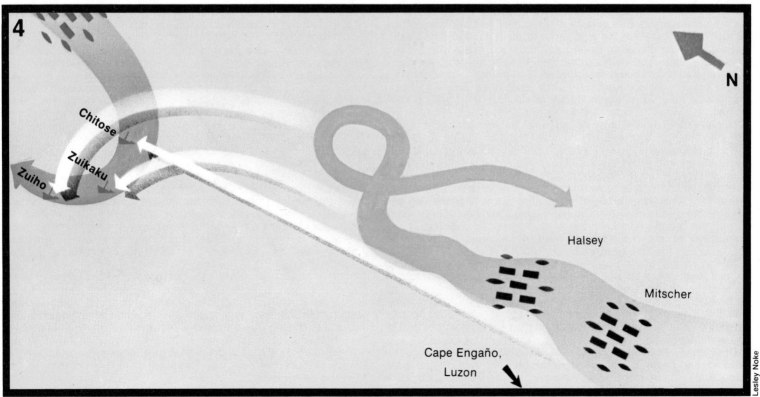

Lesley Noke

Leyte: end of the land battle

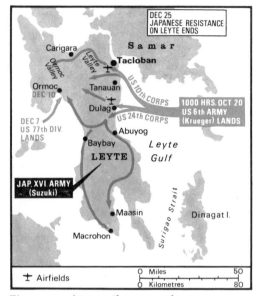

The campaign on the ground

A 155-mm 'Long Tom' bombards the Carigara sector in northern Leyte

But it was now too late to catch Kurita, who escaped practically unscathed through San Bernardino Strait. All that Halsey's mighty force of battleships and cruisers was able to overtake and sink was a single Japanese destroyer. The huge armada had covered a total distance of 600 miles in a futile race north and then south, without actually engaging either Ozawa or Kurita.

While the Battle of Leyte Gulf ended in the destruction of a major portion of the Combined Fleet and the removal of the primary threat to the Leyte beach-head, it also served to nurture a growing body of criticisms, recriminations, and second-guessing. Yet out of the welter of confusion and argument that surround the battle, certain conclusions suggest themselves.

First, given what he knew, Halsey was justified in going after Ozawa. Had the Japanese carriers been loaded with planes—as he had every reason to believe—he would have been foolhardy to ignore them. Nevertheless, he should have left at least a destroyer patrol to watch San Bernardino Strait. Second, if the decision to go after the carriers was correct, then Halsey was probably wrong to turn south just when he was about to make the kill. And finally, even if Halsey's chase north had permitted Kurita to fight his way into Leyte Gulf—and this is debatable, in light of the presence of Admiral Oldendorf's battle line and the planes from Kinkaid's escort carriers—it is doubtful if Kurita could have done significant damage or held up American operations ashore more than a week or two.

The American naval victory had secured MacArthur's communications and supply line and the seaward flank of the 6th Army. By the end of October, Krueger's troops had completely occupied the Leyte Valley and all of the airfields in the east-central part of the island. But now the invaders encountered a more difficult foe than even the Japanese, an enemy that increasingly frustrated the American effort. This was the weather: continuous drenching rain and high winds that soaked men and supplies, blew over shelters, and turned the ground into a morass of mud and giant puddles. Thirty-five inches of rain in the first 40 days of the campaign proved far too much for the low, poorly drained ground to absorb.

The worst that MacArthur's staff had feared came to pass when it proved impossible to put the newly captured airstrips into any reasonable shape. One field, at Tacloban, was operational. The strip at Dulag was able to handle a few planes by the end of November. But it was not until December that a new field could be built on more solid ground at Tanauan, in time to support the end of the campaign.

Until then, however, only a few American fighters could be advanced to Leyte, and these were too busy fighting off Japanese airstrikes—staged from dryer bases in the central and northern Philippines—to do much in the way of supporting the infantry.

Nor could General Kenney's bombers be moved forward to the primitive, muddy Leyte fields. So the bulk of support missions had to be flown from Kinkaid's battered escort carriers and Halsey's tired and overworked larger ships. It was late November before direct-support missions could take off from Leyte airstrips, and no more than a dozen strikes were made from these fields before the end of the year.

With the weather as their ally, the Japanese, who by now had determined to make an all-out defence of Leyte, were able to bring in enough additional troops through the western port of Ormoc to prolong the struggle for many weeks. Before the battle was over, more than 45,000 Japanese reinforcements reached General Suzuki's embattled XXXV Army, despite the valiant and at times extremely successful efforts of American aircrews to knock out the Japanese convoys. Japanese air strength in the central Philippines also increased somewhat as both army and navy planes staged forward to the area. These aircraft harried the American airstrips, struck at the beach-head, and launched *Kamikaze* attacks in growing numbers at American shipping.

The Japanese never really won air control over Leyte itself, but they kept the Americans from achieving it until the campaign was just about over. They could not, however, prevent a 6th Army ground build-up, as General Krueger brought in additional divisions to strengthen his own forces, nearly doubling his combat elements by mid-December.

During November, a bitter struggle took place on the ground. The American 10th Corps secured north-eastern Leyte but ran into stubborn Japanese defences along the steep ridges and rough, rocky hills that blocked the northern entrance to the Ormoc Valley. The 24th Corps cleared the southern portion of the island. It had little luck, however, in its attempt to penetrate the mountain barrier in central Leyte. Elements of the 7th Division finally pushed overland along an unguarded trail that crossed the island's narrow waist. But as these units turned north toward Ormoc in the middle of the month they were halted and thrown back by an aggressive Japanese defence of a series of spiny ridgelines running inland from Ormoc Bay.

In all of these operations, Krueger was seriously hampered by the continued tropical downpour which blinded men and inundated supply areas, turned roads into streams of slippery mud, frustrated construction efforts, and made a quagmire of the island. The Japanese, shielded by the central mountains from the full force of the north-east monsoons, were hampered only slightly less. Yet they were operating on shorter lines and, since this sort of weather always favours the defence, they had more to gain than to lose from the heavy rains.

Still, the XXXV Army was gradually being squeezed in a tightening

A surprise Japanese air raid smashes a Liberty Ship

US infantrymen close in on a Japanese machine-gun nest

vice between the northern Ormoc Valley and the ridges south of Ormoc. From Manila, therefore, Yamashita ordered Suzuki to make a major effort to recapture the Leyte airfields and regain the initiative on the island. General Tominaga agreed to help with a paratroop drop on the airstrips and all available army and navy planes were also to be thrown into the offensive.

The operation began in late November with a series of heavy but largely unsuccessful airstrikes. A small Japanese raiding party attempted to crash-land four transports on the airfields, but one plane was shot down and the others missed their mark and came down in Leyte Gulf or on the beach, where they did no damage. A larger airdrop—planned in brigade strength but actually carried out by barely 350 men—took place with somewhat more success on the night of December 5. The paratroops succeeded in occupying Buri airstrip and destroying supplies and installations there, but superior American forces wiped them out within a few days.

Suzuki's ground offensive, meanwhile, had been delayed by rough terrain, the poor condition of the Japanese units, and the swift reaction of the Americans. Of two divisions assigned to seize the airfields, only about two infantry battalions were able to advance far enough to make a disorganised and confused attack. Like the paratroops, they caused little real damage.

Ironically enough, the targets of the Japanese offensive, including the one airstrip temporarily occupied, had been all but abandoned by the end of November. American engineer officers had concluded that rain, poor drainage, and unstable soil conditions made the muddy strips all but unredeemable. The Japanese assault thus achieved almost nothing, except to throw a fright into some of the rear-echelon 6th Army troops. Yamashita failed completely to disrupt American air operations or to delay appreciably Krueger's advance. Indeed, by dissipating Suzuki's strength, he helped to ensure continued American success.

The final American offensive on Leyte began on December 5 with a drive by the 10th Corps into the northern Ormoc Valley, and simultaneous attacks by the 24th Corps in central and south-western Leyte. Two days later, the 77th Division landed virtually unopposed just below Ormoc. Despite Japanese attempts to disrupt the landing from the air, the division pushed into the city against increasing resistance and finally secured it on the 10th. The commitment of Japanese troops to the abortive attack on the airfields had made it difficult for General Suzuki to shift forces to meet this new threat.

Further north, the American 10th Corps' drive had less initial success, since most of XXXV Army remained dug into the rough terrain across the top of the Ormoc Valley. Still, the increased American pressure here tied down Suzuki's units, easing the going for the 24th Corps and 77th Division. American success in the

south now denied the Japanese their main supply port on Leyte, cut off many XXXV Army troops still operating inland, and compressed the remainder of the troops in the narrow corridor of the Ormoc Valley. American artillery and aircraft pounded the trapped Japanese.

The battle for Leyte was all but over. General Krueger continued to tighten the vice on the stubborn, courageous, but all but helpless defenders. Pressed from three sides, Suzuki was slowly forced out of the Ormoc Valley and into final positions in the rugged wilderness of western Leyte. On December 19, he learned from General Yamashita that he would receive no more reinforcements or other aid. By now there was little left of the XXXV Army but scattered elements, harried from position to position by the overwhelming American pressure. Of the more than 65,000 Japanese troops that had fought on Leyte, no more than 15,000 were left.

Final messages from Yamashita reached Suzuki on the 25th. These directed him to evacuate those troops that he could to other islands in the central Philippines, and then bid the XXXV Army commander a sad farewell. On the same day, General MacArthur announced the end of organised resistance on Leyte. The grim and dangerous business of mopping up continued for several months, however. Suzuki himself, with part of his staff, did not leave the island until late March 1945. Three weeks later he was dead, the victim of an American airstrike.

The Leyte campaign in all its phases—air, sea, and land—cost the United States approximately 5,000 dead and 14,000 wounded and a relatively light toll in planes and warships. It had taken longer than planned, less because of Japanese resistance than as a result of the fierce opposition of the elements. The bad weather and unsuitable soil conditions on the island also prevented Leyte from becoming the major base that American strategists had hoped to make of it. Yet the accomplishments at Leyte far outweighed the costs and disappointments of the victory.

The Japanese defeat at Leyte, the failure of the *Sho* plan, was a heavy blow to Japan's fortunes. In the abortive attempt to hold the island, a major portion of Japanese airpower, the bulk of the Japanese fleet, and an important segment of the Japanese army were all destroyed. Japan's air force was reduced to the terrifying but indecisive strategy of *Kamikaze* attacks, the fleet was no longer capable of significant offensive action, and the army was isolated on hundreds of Pacific islands without hope of support or rescue. Finally, the American return to the Philippines cut the Japanese supply line to the resources of the Indies and denied the home islands the means to wage effective warfare.

'Our defeat at Leyte,' said Admiral Mitsumasa Yonai, the Navy Minister, 'was tantamount to the loss of the Philippines. And when you took the Philippines, that was the end of our resources.'

SUBMARINES IN THE PACIFIC

Japanese *I70*

The lack of numerical sequence makes Japanese submarine classes hard to follow; *I70*'s sisters were renumbered *I168–169* and *I171–172*. They were big ocean-going submarines with a range of 14,000 miles on the surface. *I70* was sunk by carrier aircraft only three days after the attack on Pearl Harbor. *Displacement:* 1,785 tons (surfaced) *Armament:* Six 21-in torpedo-tubes; 14 torpedoes carried; one 3·9-in AA gun; one 13-mm machine-gun *Speed:* 23 knots (surfaced) 8¼ knots (submerged)

American *Drum* (SS228)

The *Gato* Class was the standard wartime design for the USN, and proved a superb weapon for the Pacific. As the war progressed the AA armament was increased, because American submarines operated on the surface for much of the time. The *Drum* is preserved at Mobile, Alabama. *Displacement:* 1,526 tons (surfaced) *Armament:* Ten 21-in torpedo tubes (6 forward, 4 aft); 24 torpedoes carried; one 3-in gun; two 5 and two ·3 machine-guns *Speed:* 20¼ knots (surfaced) 8¾ knots (submerged)

American submarines were designed for the vast expanses of the Pacific, emphasising high surface endurance, habitability and good torpedo capacity, and were ruthlessly standardised. Operating in three-unit wolf pack-style groups—with such fanciful names as 'Ed's Eradicators' and 'Ben's Busters'—they sank, in conjunction with submarine- and aircraft-laid mines, more than four million tons of Japanese shipping The Japanese, on the other hand, built an unduly large number of big cruiser types; the 1940 Additional Programme sought to rectify this, but of 80 *K6* type 1,100-tonners ordered only 18 were built, and all but one sunk. Among the few Japanese successes were the torpedoing of the carriers *Wasp* south of the Solomons and the crippled *Yorktown* at Midway, but American superiority under water was almost absolute.

American *S25 (SS130)*

The 'S' Class was the last design produced for the USN in the First World War, and in 1941 a few units were stationed in the Far East. They proved to have too little endurance for the Pacific, and so they were withdrawn. *S25* was lent to the Royal Navy for training, and then became the Polish *Jastrzab*. She was sunk in error by friendly ships in 1942

YEOMEN OF THE PACIFIC WAR

While the battle fleets fought their occasional and critical actions, the smaller craft of the US and Japanese navies were waging their own continual and equally vital battle: the unglamorous struggle to control the Pacific sealanes. If Japan's naval empire were to survive, these must be held; but her leaders failed to realise that the navy had to be well and continuously supplied with submarines, escort craft, and light ships capable of fighting off the US challenge. Long before the Japanese battle fleet fought its last desperate actions, the Japanese navy was doomed, for its smaller ships were too few, and US forces, particularly submarines, were sinking merchant ships, particularly those carrying vital oil, without any opposition

US *Fletcher* Class Destroyer: The most numerous class of US destroyers used during the war (over 170 were built). One of two basic designs laid down for mass-production at the beginning of the war. *Displacement:* 2,050 tons. *Dimensions:* 376½×39½×17¾. *Speed:* 37 knots. *Armament:* Five 5-inch and 10 40- and 20-mm AA guns, 10 21-inch torpedo-tubes. *Crew:* 300

US T Class Fleet Submarine: The class which stabilised US fleet submarine design, and enabled America to launch a massive building programme. *Displacement:* 1,475 tons (surfaced), 2,370 tons (submerged). *Dimensions:* 307¼×27¼×13¾. *Speed:* 20.8 knots (surfaced), 8.7 knots (submerged). *Armament:* Ten 21-inch torpedo-tubes. *Crew:* 85

Japanese Type KD 7 Fleet Submarine: A fleet design ordered in 1937, this class was able to remain at sea for 75 days. Some were modified in 1942 to act as transport submarines, carrying a 46-foot landing craft. *Displacement:* 1,833 tons (surfaced), 2,602 tons (submerged). *Dimensions:* 346× 27×15 feet. *Speed:* 23 knots (surfaced), 8 knots (submerged). *Armament:* One 4.7-inch and two 25-mm guns, six 21-inch torpedo-tubes. *Crew:* 80

Japanese *Kagero* Class Destroyer: The ultimate in Japanese destroyers: the design of this class, ordered in 1937 and 1939, was so successful that only minor changes were made for later types. *Displacement:* 2,033 tons. *Dimensions:* 388×35½×12⅓. *Speed:* 35½ knots. *Armament:* Six 5-inch, four 25-mm, and two 13-mm guns, eight 24-mm torpedo-tubes. *Crew:* 240

US Elco Type PT Boat: One of the two main US-built MTB types (the other was by Higgins). Proved particularly useful fighting in confined waters around island groups. *Displacement:* 38 tons. *Dimensions:* 80×20¾×5. *Speed:* 40 knots. *Armament:* One 20-mm AA gun, four .5-inch MG, eight depth-charges, two 21-inch torpedo-tubes. *Crew:* 14

Japanese Type T14 MTB: All Japanese MTB designs were based on the Thorneycroft CMB-type boats. By the latter part of the war, most were inoperative due to faulty engines or lack of fuel. *Displacement:* 15 tons. *Dimensions:* 49¼×12×2 feet. *Speed:* 33 knots. *Armament:* One 25-mm gun, two 18-inch torpedo tubes, two depth-charges. *Crew:* seven or eight

DEATH OF A BEHEMOTH

Battle for Okinawa, April 7, 1945

The *Yamato,* the greatest battleship ever built, had also the shortest active career of any capital ship in the Second World War. Intended originally to be the first of a 'super' battle fleet, she was the foundation of Japanese naval hopes of defeating the Americans at sea. She was believed to be absolutely superior in guns, speed, and armour to any other capital ship, as indeed she was—but without air cover these great assets were of no avail. The pointless loss of this ship in a 'special' attack on the Okinawa landings, and the story of her sinking, emphasise the straits to which the Japanese navy was reduced

National Archives

Before the lapsing of the naval limitation treaties in the 1930s, the Japanese Naval General Staff, discussing its armament policy, reached the conclusion that Japan should construct super-power warships and abandon the number ratio principle of international naval power-limitation. In October 1934 it requested the Naval Department to work out a plan of a 'super-battleship', having big guns of 18-inch calibre and a speed of more than 30 knots. At the end of March 1937, three months after the naval treaties had lost effect, the final detailed plan was completed. The ship's keel was laid down at the Kure Naval Arsenal on November 4, 1937. This was the *Yamato,* which entered service on December 16, 1941, eight days after the outbreak of the Pacific War. Although *Yamato*'s maximum speed was inferior to the original request of 30 knots, 27·46 knots was attained at the official trial. The *Yamato,* with its mighty guns and high speed, was intended to outrange American battleships. The main guns' projectile of 3,000 pounds could not only pierce the thickest armour of the US battleships, but could also cause severe damage underwater. The maximum range was 41,400 yards, several thousand yards longer than that of a 16-inch gun.

To be effective it was absolutely necessary to keep the *Yamato* a complete secret to prevent the US navy from building similar giant ships, although it had been calculated that ships of such size would not be able to pass through the Panama Canal. The number of people, therefore, allowed to know of the *Yamato*'s size and strength was strictly limited. The fact that experts from all fields were excluded from the project resulted in some defects, particularly in the areas of anti-aircraft armament and underwater protection.

Due to many confrontations with the US fleet after hostilities began, the AA fire-power was greatly reinforced in the spring of 1944, and was further increased at the end of that year. Before these augmentations, the *San-shiki* shells of the main guns had been added for anti-aircraft use. These specially-designed shells contained about 6,000 rounds of 25-mm bullets which could produce a conical zone of fire 400 yards across and 1,000 yards long. But their terrible blast and thick smoke badly hampered the simultaneous firing of the newly installed AA guns, which had no shields. The effective range of the *San-shiki* shell was about 30,000 yards.

Yamato's underwater protection was strength-ened to some extent when the damage caused by a torpedo hit from an American submarine on December 25, 1943, west of Truk atoll, was repaired. After the Leyte battle, more improvements were planned, but never executed.

In any event, so far as an artillery duel with battleships was concerned, *Yamato*'s firepower and armour were believed absolutely superior to those of all other battleships. Among the high-ranking officers who knew *Yamato*'s superiority, there were several who were probably a little optimistic about war with the USA. For although there were three more sister ships under construction at the beginning of the war— only one, *Musashi,* was ever completed, and she was sunk in the Battle of Leyte Gulf by US air strikes.

At the beginning of 1945, the Naval General Staff concluded that the Allied forces would surely occupy Okinawa in order to facilitate the proposed invasion of Japan. As a result, it insisted on fighting a decisive battle there. If it were successful, it might delay the American attack and might even prevent the Soviet Union from entering the war against Japan. Besides, some leading officers of the High Command faintly hoped that such a battle would bring the hostilities to an end altogether.

The Army General Staff, however, due to a series of bitter failures on isolated islands, disapproved of the navy's plan, and was instead preparing for the final decisive battle to be fought in Japan. Thus, during the Philippine operation, the army removed a crack division to Formosa, leaving only two and a half divisions on Okinawa. This resulted in a change of the defensive plan of Lieutenant-General Ushijima, commander of the garrison at Okinawa. Abandoning the principle of destroying the invaders at the beginning of its landing, he adopted instead a plan for endurance by holding the main positions in the southern rugged area of Okinawa. Later the army attempted to send back one battalion from Formosa to Okinawa, but by this time it was too late to transport it.

The navy faced the difficulty of preparing the fighting forces for this decisive battle on Okinawa. During the Philippine operation, the Combined Fleet suffered heavy losses of both warships and aircraft. It also was forced to limit its training operations due to the lack of oil. For the Okinawa operation, first priority was to be given to secur-ing air domination. Under the circumstances, the Naval High Command had no alternative but to prepare the land-based air force as a main fighting power. Thus, the naval air force was reorganised with all units available, including those assigned to aircraft-carriers and the training school squadrons.

Okinawa overture: the kamikazes prepare
The Japanese total was roughly 2,100 aircraft. Many pilots were unskilled, especially half of the III Air Force and most of the X Air Force. The only assignment for unskilled pilots was the 'special' attack which was first adopted during the Philippine operation. If the X Air Force continued training its pilots, by the end of April its strength would increase to about 1,900 planes: 700 aircraft for combat, and 1,200 training aircraft for suicide attacks.

So, to delay the Allied invasion of Okinawa, 24 long-range bombers were sent at dusk on March 11 to make a special attack on the US aircraft-carriers at Ulithi atoll. Due to engine failure and other setbacks, only 15 reached their destination, and obtained no marked results.

The American task force, leaving Ulithi atoll a few days after the kamikaze attack, made air raids on March 18 and 19 on the air bases and warships in western Japan. The V Air Force made counter-attacks, including special suicide attacks, on the American fleet every day from March 18 to 21, with estimated results of three or four carriers sunk or heavily damaged. But the air force itself also suffered severe losses. As a result, the Army Staff decided to place the VI Air Army (about 750 aircraft on Kyushu and the Ryukyu Islands) under the command of the Combined Fleet and to make the VIII Air Division (Formosa) co-operate with them.

Every day, from March 23 on, the Allied forces made heavy air raids with carrier aircraft and violent bombardments with ten battleships and others in the Okinawa area. On March 25, they carried out landings on the Kerama Islands west of Okinawa, capturing more than 300 special attack boats hidden there to attack American troopships.

At this point Admiral Toyoda, Commander-in-Chief of the Combined Fleet, ordered that *Ten* (meaning 'Heaven') No. 1 Operation be put into action, and placed the III and X Air Fleets under

The *Yamato*'s cruise

Yamato's actual course in her last mission compares poorly with her intended course. Supposed to make a suicidal attack on the Okinawa beaches, Yamato was attacked by American aircraft while still 270 miles from her objective. US air superiority was overwhelming and, despite her massive anti-aircraft armament, Yamato was sunk without ever striking a decisive blow

The San-shiki anti-aircraft projectile was developed to protect Japan's all-important capital ships from attack by formations of low-flying aircraft. Fired from the main armament, it had a time fuse in the nose, fused to explode in front of an approaching formation of aircraft. The shell was packed with tiers of incendiary-filled shot, resting on a base of explosive. The time fuse detonated a central column of explosive, and as the flash passed down the column it ignited in turn each tier. As the flash reached the base of the shell it ignited a charge of explosive which broke the shell casing and scattered the incendiary shot in a 'shotgun' effect, mowing down the opposing aircraft. This development came too late to save the Japanese fleet, however, and never took a significant toll of American aircraft

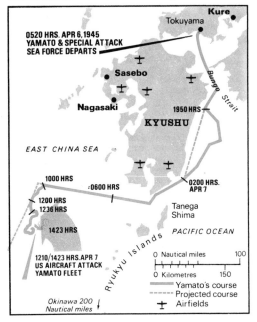

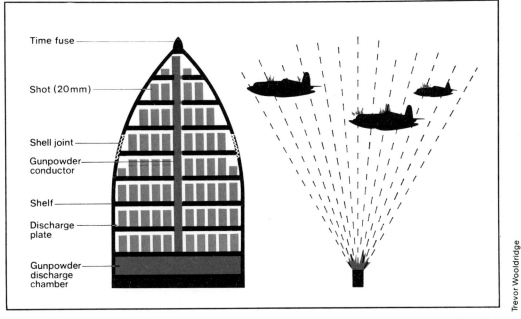

Trevor Wooldridge

the command of Vice-Admiral Ugaki, commander of the V Air Fleet. The Vice-Admiral ordered both fleets to move at once to the Kyushu area. This movement was completed on March 31.

Therefore, when the American carrier groups again attacked the Kyushu area on March 28 and 29, the Japanese naval air forces were not in a position to counterattack. Upon receiving a report that a large American transport group was entering the anchorage between the Kerama Islands, Admiral Toyoda ordered the VI Air Army to strike them immediately; but this order was not executed because of a delay in the air army's preparations. From March 30 on, sporadic air attacks were carried out by both naval and army air forces against the American carrier groups and transport ships. Meanwhile, on the morning of April 1, the Americans started landing on the western coast of central Okinawa and before noon had captured, without serious resistance, the north (Yontan) and middle (Kadena) airfields. Thereafter, the US landing force smoothly expanded its position.

This situation deeply depressed the Japanese navy, which had been using both airfields for air raids. So, on April 3, after consulting the General Staff and the V Air Force Headquarters, the Combined Fleet Command strongly requested the Okinawa defensive force to strike back at least to prevent the enemy from using the airfields. In return, the Okinawa defensive force command demanded that the Combined Fleet first of all destroy Allied battleships and aircraft-carriers, explaining that one battleship had a firepower equivalent to that of seven field divisions.

At this the C-in-C of the Combined Fleet, deciding to make a united front using all forces in order to boost the garrison's counteroffensive, on April 4 ordered the naval air forces and the VI Air Army to attack the invading forces with all their strength. He also ordered the organisation of a Special Sea Attack Force made up of the *Yamato* and a torpedo squadron to attack the enemy's ships off the western coast of Okinawa.

As the only sea force for the Okinawa operation, the *Yamato* and the II Torpedo Squadron of the II Fleet were assigned the name of 'I Mobile Force', with task force classification, and were put under the command of Vice-Admiral Seiichi Ito, previously Vice-Chief of the Naval Staff, then commander of the II Fleet. The aircraft from

the II Fleet's six aircraft-carriers were transferred to the land-based air force. The aircraft-carriers, as well as other warships, were used as local anti-aircraft guards around the military ports.

At first, the task of the I Mobile Force for the Okinawa operation was to lure Allied aircraft-carriers by its sortie into the attacking area of the land-based air forces. On the morning of March 29, the I Mobile Force started to move out in an attempt of the above plan, but gave up mid-way because of Allied air raids that day on southern Kyushu.

On April 4, Vice-Admiral Ito organised the Special Sea Attack Force, which included most of the I Mobile Force, and ordered it to be ready to move. The assigned vessels were the *Yamato* with an escort of the light cruiser *Yahagi*, and eight destroyers which belonged to the II Torpedo Squadron.

The fleet order dated 1500 hours, April 5, ordered the Special Sea Attack Force to put to sea through the Bungo Straits at dawn on April 7 and speed along the Ryukyu Islands into the Okinawa berth before the following dawn to destroy all Allied ships there. But Vice-Admiral Ito, with permission, changed the operational schedule as follows: to leave the Bungo Straits after dark on April 6, and, during the day of April 7, keep away from the Allied carrier groups expected to be east of Okinawa, and dash into the Okinawa berth before dawn of April 8 (see map).

For lack of oil, although destroyer tanks were nearly full, the *Yamato* and the *Yahagi* were supplied with only half-tank capacity. 'Special attack' meant suicide attack.

'The most tragic and heroic attack ...'

On April 5, Admiral Toyoda, Commander-in-Chief of the Combined Fleet, sent an address of instructions to all fleets:

'. . . The fate of our Empire depends upon this one action. I order the Special Sea Attack Force to carry out on Okinawa the most tragic and heroic attack of the war. We shall concentrate our Imperial naval forces on this action and give full play to the brilliant tradition of the Imperial Navy's Sea Force and make its glory remembered forever.'

In the afternoon of April 6, prior to sailing, Vice-Admiral Kusaka, Chief-of-Staff of the Combined Fleet, went aboard the *Yamato* ac-

companied by his staff to announce the High Command's plan and say farewell to the leaders of the fleet. The staff said that all crew, after firing all projectiles, should land and join the defensive forces of Okinawa. And the Chief-of-Staff prayed for them in hopes that their courage in this suicide attack would inspire the entire Japanese nation to fight to the end.

The Special Sea Attack Force, leaving its Tokuyama anchorage in the western region of the Inland Sea, set sail at 1520 hours under a protective guard against Allied submarines of two seaplanes and six destroyers. This sailing was watched by a B-29. By 1830 hours the Japanese seaplanes found two Allied submarines near the exit of the Bungo Straits and one off the eastern coast of Kyushu. As a result, the *Yamato* force, immediately after getting out of the protective gateway of the channel, assumed a protective formation at 1950 hours and, at 22 knots, took a roundabout course with zigzag movements to evade Allied submarines. From 2020 hours on, the fleet's radars, direction-finders, and hydrophones detected signs of Allied submarines in pursuit. At 2130 an emergency Allied report was intercepted concerning the sortie of the Special Sea Attack Force.

Around midnight, the Combined Fleet Command announced that several enemy vessels, including aircraft-carriers, had been sunk during the big raids made that day by the air force.

The *Yamato* fleet entered the projected course at 0200 hours on April 7, and seemed likely to succeed in shaking off Allied submarines. At 0600 hours—sunrise—the fleet made a ring formation around the *Yamato,* above which one or two seaplanes flew in search of submarines. The C-in-C did not issue any order concerning air protection against enemy aircraft. Even the Chief-of-Staff, Kusaka, who was then at the V Air Force Headquarters, did not wish to send fighters for fear of disturbing the air raid operations against US carriers. So the V Air Force commander, on his own initiative, sent ten fighters twice between 0630 and 1000 hours to destroy the enemy's reconnaissance aircraft—if nothing else.

The sky was heavily overcast; the ceiling was between 3,000 and 3,500 feet, and was often as low as several hundred feet. Except for squalls in certain places, the visibility, once below the clouds, was fairly good. Thus there were con-

247

End of an Era

The period of naval history that began with the Dreadnoughts ended with the sinking of *Yamato*. Although many powers retained battleships for years afterwards, the Second World War had amply demonstrated their fatal vulnerability to air attack, and a great 'fleet action' was clearly a thing of the past. Nevertheless the Second World War produced some of the fastest and most heavily armed ships that have ever been built. Here we show four of the most famous of these; and, as a contrast to these leviathans, one of their smallest assailants, a Japanese suicide boat

Yamato (above and right): *Displacement:* 64,170 tons. *Dimensions:* 863 × 127 × 35 feet. *Protection:* Main belt armour 16 in., deck 7¾ in., turrets 20-25 in. *Armament:* 9 18-inch, 12 6.1-inch, 12 5-inch AA, 24 25-mm AA, 4 13-mm guns, plus 6 aircraft. *Crew:* 3,332. *Speed:* 27 knots

Shinyo (suicide craft): About 6,000 of these had been manufactured by the end of the war. They carried one man and a massive charge of TNT in the bows, which detonated on impact. *Length:* 18 feet. *Speed:* 30 knots

Right: The chart shows the comparative armour strengths of the major capital ships of the war. The Axis ships—*Yamato* and *Bismarck*— are noticeably better armoured than their Allied counterparts, *Missouri* and *King George V*

venient conditions for the Allied reconnaissance and attack aircraft, but extremely unfavourable ones for the fleet and interceptors.

The night search aircraft of the Japanese Naval Air Force found nothing on the eastern sea of Okinawa, but the morning scout aircraft discovered at 0810 hours a carrier group slowly sailing south, about 70 nautical miles to the east of Okinawa. Then, around 0900 hours, another three groups, aircraft-carriers included, were spotted to the south, and the V Air Force commander ordered the air forces to launch strikes on them.

At 0730 hours, the *Yamato* fleet sighted far away toward the east two small aircraft flying north and, at 1014 hours, soon after turning south, it sighted far to the west two flying boats and fired its main guns at them. But the flying boats disappeared behind a cloud. So the fleet often changed its heading and speed to deceive them and jammed their communications. At 1114 hours, eight US fighters were sighted; some 30 minutes later, another group of ten was noticed circling around the fleet. Assuming that strikes would follow, Admiral Ito informed both commands of the Combined Fleet and the V Air Force of the situation.

It was not until noon that the fleet received the warning of 1045 hours issued by the Kikaigashima Lookout reporting some 250 carrier aircraft heading in a north-westerly direction. The lookout's next alarm of 1130 hours, reporting another big formation flying north, also reached the fleet only after much delay.

At 1210 hours, the destroyer *Asashimo*, which was out of sight far behind the fleet due to engine trouble, reported that she was in action with enemy planes, and at 1221 hours she sent her

last message, reporting more than 30 aircraft seen to the east.

Long before noon, warship radar equipment had already detected signs of approaching aircraft formations. At 1232 hours, formations of some 150 aircraft broke through the clouds and were sighted about 13 miles away by the fleet. Here was the chance for the *Yamato*'s *San-shiki* shells to prove their worth. But the clouds made it difficult to continue ranging and aiming, and the radar was not accurate enough to direct firing through the clouds, and the weather was still bad. As the first group of US formations was launching its attack on the fleet, the fleet's speed was increased to 24 knots at 1234 hours, and the *Yamato*'s machine-guns opened up. The American aircrew, with no threat of Japanese fighters, could devote all their attention to attacking the fleet in turn, using the clouds as screens against the Japanese gunnery. At first, fighters and bombers dived to smother the AA guns with machine-gun fire and bombs; then torpedo planes followed. The 18-inch big guns had to refrain from firing so as not to hamper the shooting from smaller guns. Under these circumstances, all ships had taken evasive action independently, which severely hampered accurate gunnery.

The fleet was ordered to maximum battle speed at 1241 hours, when the *Yamato* was successively struck by two bombs which hit near the aft secondary gun turret, heavily damaging the machine-guns thereabouts. A few minutes later, one torpedo blew a big hole in the port bow, and *Yamato* began to take on water. At about the same time, the *Yahagi* was hit on the starboard stern by a torpedo which halted the engine. Another torpedo, followed by a bomb, left the cruiser dead in the water. Meanwhile the des-

troyer *Hamakaze* had been sunk by a torpedo and a bomb.

Minutes before 1300 hours, during a lull, Vice-Admiral Ito ordered the fleet to turn toward Okinawa. Rear-Admiral Komura, commander of the Torpedo Squadron, tried to shift his flag to a destroyer, but was interrupted by the appearance of fresh formations of some 100 planes from three directions (east, south-east, and west).

At 1300 hours, a bomb heavily damaged the destroyer *Suzutsuki*. The *Yamato*, saturated with bombs and torpedoes, received, along with many near-miss bombs, two torpedoes around her port beam which severed her radio communications. So the Fleet Commander sent his report through a destroyer to the Combined Fleet Command, advising it to change the operation date in the light of the increasing damage. A second wave of attacks dealt a fatal blow to the destroyer *Kasumi*.

The change of the flagship of the Torpedo Squadron was begun all over again, but was further hindered by a third raid of about 150 aircraft, including many torpedo aircraft, intended to finish off the big ships. At 1333 hours some 20 torpedo planes attacked the *Yamato*'s port side, which already had a greatly weakened firepower. The results were three hits scored on the mid-portside, which increased the list to port beyond the ballasting capacity of the starboard tanks, and at the same time jammed the secondary rudder hard to port. To recover the level quickly, there was no choice but to flood both starboard engine and boiler rooms. In several minutes, the rudder was returned to centre line, but remained immovable, thus severely limiting the ship's manoeuvrability. The *Yamato*'s speed was greatly reduced due to this flooding and in-

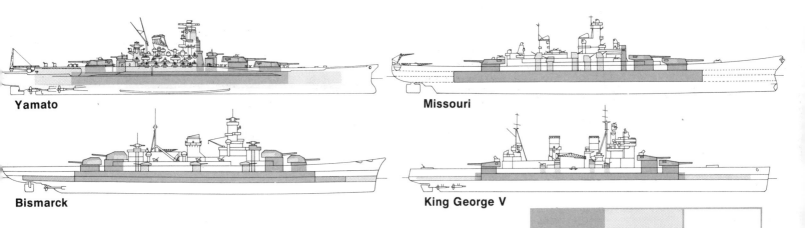

Yamato

Missouri

Bismarck

King George V

| 12-14 | 9-10 | 7-8 | 5-6 | 3-4 |

inches

creased draught. After receiving direct hits by seven torpedoes and twelve bombs, the motionless *Yahagi* sank. Meanwhile the *Yamato* could not escape repeated strikes and, by 1402 hours, had been hit in her amidships by three bombs, two of which severely damaged the smaller guns on the port side. Minutes later, a torpedo struck her on the starboard side, and then, five minutes later, two more hit the port side. These made the ship's port list gradually increase, the sharp inclination making most of the machine-guns impossible to fire. The *Yamato*'s speed was now reduced to about 7 knots.

At about 1417 hours, the tenth torpedo, which was the ninth to hit the port side, dealt the ship the decisive blow. Captain Ariga, commanding the *Yamato,* reported to Admiral Ito that there was no means left to help the ship. On hearing this, Admiral Ito directed his staff to transfer to a destroyer; he himself went down to be confined in his room under the bridge.

Captain Ariga, at his own request, was bound to the pedestal of the compass. He ordered all hands on deck. Meanwhile the ship's list continued to increase until the projectiles in the lockers rolled down, leading to an explosion which hurled a huge pillar of flames and smoke into the sky. The super-battleship sank within seconds, disappearing at 1423 hours. Ten torpedoes, six bombs, innumerable bullets and near-miss bombs—these had led the *Yamato* to her death. Of a total crew of 3,332 only 269 were saved.

The American aircraft wisely concentrated their attacks chiefly on the port side of the ship, causing it to list and putting many guns out of action. For the *Yamato*, it was regrettable that her firing power was greatly restricted by clouds and squalls. This was particularly true of the *San-*

shiki shells which, contrary to great expectations, were never fired during the air strikes.

The American aircraft withdrew about 1425 hours, after having witnessed the *Yamato*'s death and strafed the survivors afloat. A total of 386 aircraft (180 fighters, 75 bombers, and 131 torpedo planes) belonging to Vice-Admiral M. A. Mitscher's High Speed Carrier Force took part in this action.

No fighters were sent to protect the *Yamato* fleet against air strikes. The V Air Force Command, although well informed of the air raids, was busy attacking the American carrier force. Here also was a matter for regret: if the night search planes had succeeded in finding the American forces and had been allowed to attack them before they launched their formations against the *Yamato* fleet, the Japanese situation might have been better.

Admiral Toyoda, upon receiving the report of the *Yamato*'s death, issued the cancellation order of the Okinawa operation. He sent the following message to the Combined Fleet: 'The self-sacrificing and brave fighting of the I Mobile Force made a great contribution to the Air Force's raids against the enemy task force.'

In fact, the sortie of the Special Sea Attack Force made the air force's assaults easier by attracting the American carrier groups nearer. The results of the air assaults were judged at two aircraft carriers sunk and two more damaged.

Of the Japanese fleet, only four destroyers (one badly damaged) under the command of Rear-Admiral Komura returned the next day to the naval port of Sasebo. Total Japanese losses were one super-battleship, one cruiser, and four destroyers, two of which were heavily damaged and sunk *en route* to Sasebo by Japanese ships to avoid being sunk by US aircraft on the follow-

ing day. As to the fleet's direct battle results, the Torpedo Squadron counted 19 Allied planes shot down. The *Yamato* reported only three downed and 20 damaged, saying that it was hard to destroy the fire-proofed enemy aircraft. The American record says that ten US aircraft were lost.

The *Yamato* action was the last battle of the Imperial Japanese Navy's warships. There was much criticism of the operation and many objections made at the time and later concerning a Special Sea Attack Operation without air cover.

A total of 386 aircraft belonging to Vice-Admiral M.A. Mitscher's (below) High Speed Carrier Force took part in the destruction of the *Yamato*

Imperial War Museum

BEHIND THE ALLIED VICTORY

Even in the early days of the Pacific war, when the Japanese had the numerical advantage, they tended to split their forces and thus fall prey to the compact and well-deployed American task forces. But the American victory in the Pacific was due as much to her transports and replenishment craft as to the main arm of her sea power, her mighty aircraft-carriers. It was also due to the spectacular losses inflicted by US submarines and surface raiders on Japanese transports, replenishment craft, and merchant shipping in general. Here we show two typical support ships—a transport and an oiler—an *Essex* class carrier, a chart showing the Allied success against Japanese tonnage, and a plan view of a typical task group. It was these elements which helped to give the Americans the upper hand in the Pacific

A typical US task group, protected by a screen of destroyers and an inner ring of cruisers, contained at its heart its main striking force: the aircraft of the carriers, and the guns of the battleships

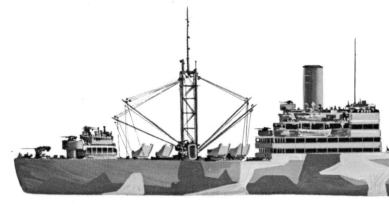

Type C2-5-B1 Attack Cargo Ship. The attack cargo ship, essential for amphibious operations, could carry troops, their inshore landing craft, plus follow-up supplies, ammunition, spare parts, and so on. For operations in the Pacific, the US Navy had some 95 to 100 of these craft. *Length (overall):* 459 feet. *Beam:* 63 feet. *Armament:* one 5-inch gun, and eight 40-mm AA guns. *Crew (plus troops):* 404. *Displacement:* 6,556 tons

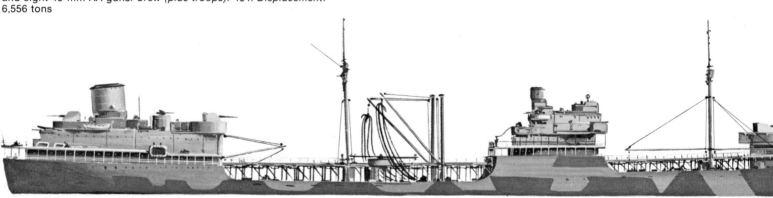

US Fleet Oiler T3-S2-A1. The huge distances involved in the Pacific war made some method of refuelling the fleet at sea indispensable. It also meant that the oiler, full, became an extremely important ship, and a much-prized target for submarine captains. *Length (overall):* 553 feet. *Beam:* 75 feet. *Armament:* four 5-inch guns, eight 40-mm guns. *Crew:* 304. *Displacement:* 7,356 tons

The *Essex* class (the *Wasp* is shown here) became the standard US fleet carrier of the war and made up the core of the fast carrier forces. It introduced the outboard elevator on the port side. *Length:* 820 feet (waterline), 872 (overall). *Max Beam:* 147 feet. *Max Speed:* 32 knots. *Armament:* 12 5-inch guns, 44 to 68 40-mm AA guns, and 100 aircraft. *Crew:* 3,500. *Displacement:* 27,100 tons

Trevor Wooldridge

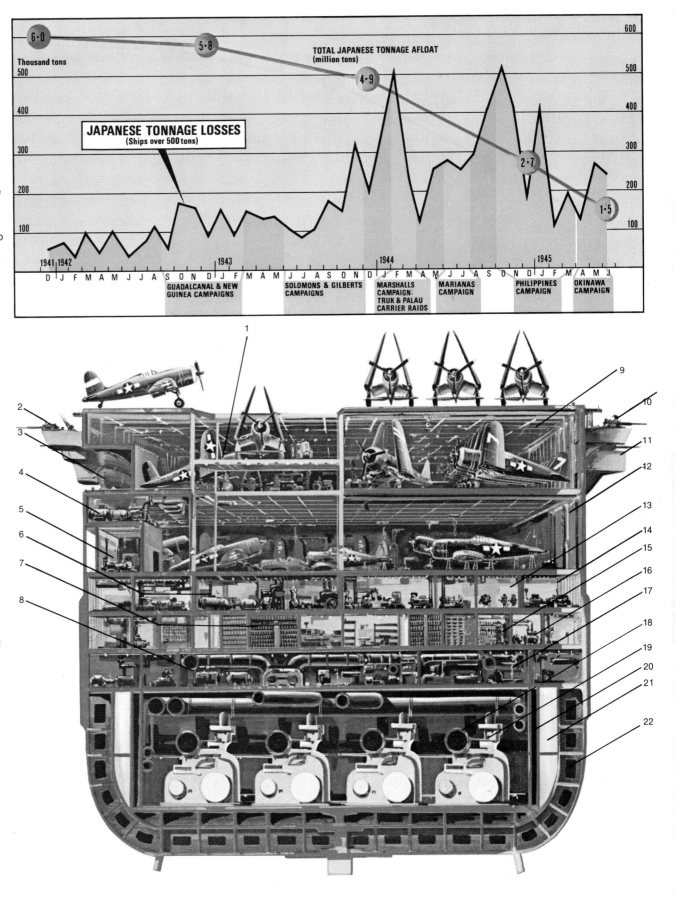

The Diminishing Asset: At the outbreak of war the Japanese had afloat some 6,000,000 tons of shipping, but by 1945 this had declined to 1,500,000 tons. With much Japanese shipping devoted to the hopeless task of maintaining their isolated island garrisons, the rate of sinkings by the Allies rose sharply to coincide with each major campaign. The result was a crescendo of destruction at a time when the Japanese could least afford it

Thousand tons

JAPANESE TONNAGE LOSSES
(Ships over 500 tons)

TOTAL JAPANESE TONNAGE AFLOAT
(million tons)

6·0   5·8   4·9   2·7   1·5

1941 1942   1943   1944   1945
D J F M A M J J A S O N D J F M A M J J A S O N D J F M A M J J A S O N D J F M A M J J A S O N D J F M A M J

GUADALCANAL & NEW GUINEA CAMPAIGNS

SOLOMONS & GILBERTS CAMPAIGNS

MARSHALLS CAMPAIGN: TRUK & PALAU CARRIER RAIDS

MARIANAS CAMPAIGN

PHILIPPINES CAMPAIGN

OKINAWA CAMPAIGN

This cross-section view of an *Essex* class carrier, taken from the lift looking aft, shows many of the features of the improved design of this class. Two of them are the reinforced armour at and below the waterline, and the oil storage tanks well isolated from vulnerable spots

1. Lift
2. 20- & 40-mm AA guns
3. Two stacked lifeboats
4. Fan motors
5. Airframe workshop
6. Workshop deck & lift machinery
7. Ammo & aircraft stores
8. Air-conditioning plants
9. Main hangar (aft)
10. AA guns
11. AA guns
12. Servicing hangar
13. Aero engine stores
14. Engine servicing shop
15. Port ammunition stores
16. Emergency lighting plant
17. Engine-cooling motor
18. Steam pipes to turbines
19. Turbines
20. Fireproof coffer-dam
21. Aviation spirit tank
22. Oil fuel tanks

INDEX

Index compiled by Jack Haigh
Page references in *italics* indicate illustrations

A

Abdiel (British minelayer), Jutland 1916, 87, 151
Aboukir (British armoured cruiser), sunk by *U-9* 1914, *34–38*
Abruzzi, Duke of the, 70, 72
Achates (British destroyer), sunk Barents Sea 1942, *187–92*
Achilles (New Zealand cruiser), River Plate 1939, *122–25*
Admiral Graf Spee (German pocket-battleship), 106, 112, 118, scuttled Montevideo harbour 1939, *122–25*, 129, 189
Admiral Hipper (German cruiser), 118, 119, *126*, 128, 129, 130, 178, Barents Sea 1942, *186–94*, 209
Admiral Scheer (German pocket-battleship), *113*, 118, 119, 177, 187, 209
Admiral Spaun (Austrian light cruiser), 70
Admiralty 'tracking room', 110, 117, 197, 206
aeroplane illustrations
 Aichi 'Val', *162–63*
 Blackburn Roc, *218*
 Blackburn Skua, *218*
 Brewster Buffalo, *170*
 Bristol Beaufort, *109*
 Consolidated Catalina, *199*
 Consolidated Liberator, *199*
 Douglas Devastator, *160–61*
 Fairey Albacore, *119*, *218*
 Fairey Fulmar, *218*
 Focke-Wulf, *109*
 Grumman Avenger, *224–25*
 Lockheed Hudson, *199*
 Mitsubishi Zero, *170–71*
 Short Sunderland, *199*
 Stuka, *148*
 Vickers Wellington, *199*
 Vought-Sikorsky Vindicator, *172–73*
Agincourt (British battleship), 8, Jutland 1916, *74–75*
Aircraft—carrier warfare *see* Carrier Warfare
Aitkin, Sub-Lieutenant R., 210
Ajax (British light cruiser), River Plate 1939, *122–25*, 137, 149, 151
Akagi (Japanese aircraft-carrier), sunk Midway 1942, *168–74*, 221, 222
Alcantara (British armed merchant cruiser), 118
Alighieri (Italian battleship), 8
Altmark (German supply tanker), 106, 122, *126*, 128, 129
Amalfi (Italian armoured cruiser), torpedoed 1915, 72
Amethyst (British light cruiser), 72
Amphion (British light cruiser), 20
Anderson (American destroyer), Coral Sea 1942, 165
Aoki, Captain, 174
Arashi (Japanese destroyer), Midway 1942, 173
Arbutus (British corvette), 197
Archer (British escort carrier), 221
Arctic Convoys, 176–81, 186–92
Ardent (British destroyer), sunk Jutland 1916, 87
Arethusa (British light cruiser), Heligoland 1914, *20–27*; Dogger Bank 1915, *63–67*, 129
Argus (British aircraft-carrier), 139, 214, *217*, 219
Ariadne (German light cruiser), sunk Heligoland 1914, *26*, 27
Ariga, Captain, 249
Arizona (American battleship), sunk Pearl Harbor 1941, *155*, 157
Ark Royal (British aircraft-carrier), 109, 136, 139, 141, 142, 143; torpedoed 1941, *183*, 214, 219
Armando Diaz (Italian cruiser), sunk by *Upright* 1941, 142
armed merchant raiders *29*, 30, 118
Artigliere (Italian destroyer), sunk by *York* 1940, 137
Asashimo (Japanese destroyer), 248
Asdic
 early application, 104, 105
 limitations, 104, 203
 new developments, 105, 201, 202, 203
Asi (Japanese battleship), 9
Astoria (American cruiser), Midway 1942, 175
Athenia (liner), sunk by *U-30*, 1939, 108
Atlantic, battle for, *106–121*, *195–207*
Atlantis (German armed merchant raider), 118
Attack (British destroyer), Dogger Bank 1915, 66
Audacious (British battleship), sunk by mine 1914, 10
Audacity (British escort carrier) 105, 219
Ault, Commander W. B., 162
Aurora (British light cruiser), Dogger Bank 1915, *63–67*
Australia (Australian heavy cruiser), 8, Coral Sea 1942, 159
Avenger (British escort carrier), 204, 221
Ayrshire (British trawler), 180

B

B2 'Q' ship, British, *29*
Bacchante (British cruiser), 35
Baden (German battleship), 96, 98, 100, 101
Baden (German supply ship), sunk Port Pleasant 1914, 60
Barents Sea, battle of, *186–93*; Aftermath, 194
Barham (British battleship), Jutland 1916, *76–87*, 137, 151
Battenburg, Prince Louis Alexander, biographical details *18*
battles
 Barents Sea, *186–193*
 Coral Sea, *158–165*
 Coronel, *45–51*
 Dogger Bank, *62–67*
 Falkland Islands, *52–61*
 Guadalcanal, *223–229*
 Heligoland, *20–27*
 Jutland, *74–87*
 Leyte Gulf, *230–241*
 Midway, *166–175*
 Okinawa, *246–249*
Bayern (German battleship), 9, *96*, *100*
Béarn (French aircraft-carrier), 214
Beatty, Admiral Sir David, biographical details *18*, 62–67, 74–87, 95, *96*, 98
Bernd von Arnim (German destroyer), 129, 130
Berwick (British cruiser), 137, 139
Birmingham (British light cruiser), sinks *U-15* 1914, 22; Dogger Bank 1915, 62–67
Bismarck (German battleship), sinking of, *143–46*, 208, 219, *249*
Bisson (French destroyer), 70
Biter (British escort carrier), *198*, 221
Blackburn Roc, fleet fighter plane, 215, *218*
Blackburn Skua, dive-bomber, 215, *218*
Black Prince (British armoured cruiser), sunk Jutland 1916, 87
Black Swan sloops, 104
blockade
 Adriatic blockade, 68–73
 Allied strategy, 15–16, 28–33
 economic blockade policy, 91
 effects on Germany, 89–94
 see also Carrier Warfare, Convoys and Submarines
Blücher (German armoured cruiser), 8, 10, 17, sunk Dogger Bank 1915, *62–67*, 74
Blücher (2) (German heavy cruiser), *126*, 128, sunk off Norway 1940, 130
Bogue (American escort carrier), 221
Boise (American light cruiser), *227*
Bonaventure (British cruiser), 141
Boy-Ed, Captain, 41, 44
Bradford, Vice-Admiral E. E., 64
Bramble (British minesweeper), sunk Barents Sea 1942, 187–91
Bremse (German naval auxiliary), 130
Brewster Buffalo fighter, 170
Briggs, Admiral Sir John, 10
Bristol Beaufort torpedo-bomber, *109*
Bristol (British light cruiser), Falklands 1914, 52–61
Broke (British destroyer), Jutland 1916, 87
Buckmaster, Captain, 164, 175
Burnett, Admiral R. L., 187, 189
Busche, Lt-Cdr. Johann, 54

C

Caio Duilio (Italian battleship), 139, 141, 219
Calcutta (British cruiser), 136, 149; sunk Crete 1941, 151
California (American battleship), sunk Pearl Harbor 1941, *156*, 157
Camellia (British corvette), 197
Cameron, Lieutenant D., 210–11
Campbell, Rear-Admiral H., 35, 38
Campioni, Admiral A., 139, 183
CAM ships, 105, *111*, 115
Canada (British battleship), 8
Canopus (British battleship), 47, 51, 52, 54
Cape Esperance, battle of, *224*, *225*
Cardiff (British light cruiser), 97, 98
Carlisle (British cruiser), 149, 150
Carnarvon (British armoured cruiser), Falklands 1914, 52–61
Carnarvon Castle (British armed merchant cruiser), 118
carrier warfare
 American construction, 221, 222
 early development, 13, 214, 215
 Japanese growth, 221
 Malta convoys, 219
 Mediterranean operations, 136–38
 Midway lessons, 221–22
 types of planes, *109*, *119*, *148*, *160–61*, *162–63*, *170–71*, *172–73*, *199*, *218*
Catapult Aircraft Merchantmen (CAM ship), 105, *111*, 115
Chicago (American heavy cruiser), Coral Sea 1942, 159
Chikuma (Japanese cruiser), Midway 1942, 224
Chitose (Japanese aircraft-carrier), 222
Chiyoda (Japanese aircraft-carrier), 222
Chokai (Japanese cruiser), *226*, 227
Christian, Rear-Admiral A., 35, 36, 38
Churchill, Sir Winston, 12, 26, 35, 36, 38, 62, 64, 127, 133, 134, 178, 209
Ciliax, Vice-Admiral O., 209
Clematis (British corvette), *198*
Consolidated PBY Catalina, *199*, Consolidated B-24 Liberator, *199*
Contest (British destroyer), Jutland 1916, 87
Conti di Cavour (Italian battleship), damaged Taranto 1940, 138, 139, 219
convoys
 air escort, 116, 120
 Arctic convoys, 176–81, 186–92
 classic convoy pattern, 180
 JW-51B convoy, 186–94
 Mediterranean operations, 136–38, 182–85
 Operation 'Pedestal', 183–85
 PQ-17 convoy, 177–81, 187, 209–10
 success of convoy system, 89, 204–6
 see also Atlantic, battle for, Blockade, and Submarines
Coral Sea, battle of, *158–65*
Cornwall (British armoured cruiser), Falklands 1914, 52–61, sunk 1942, 221
Coronel, battle of, *45–51*
Courageous (British aircraft-carrier), sunk by *U-29* 1939, 109, 112, 214, 219
Coventry (British cruiser), 136, 151
Crace, Rear-Admiral, J. C., 159–65
Cradock, Rear-Admiral Sir Christopher, 41, 47–51
Cressy (British armoured cruiser), sunk by *U-9* 1914, *34–38*
Crete, battle for, 147–51
Cunningham, Admiral Sir Andrew, 136, *137*, 147, 182

D

Dainty (British destroyer), 142
Danzig (German light cruiser), 27
Dartmouth (British light cruiser), 72
Defence (British armoured cruiser), 41, sunk Jutland 1916, *76–87*
'Degaussing' protection against magnetic mines, 105, 110
Depth charges, 92, *94*, *118*
Derfflinger (German battle-cruiser), 8, Dogger Bank 1915, 62–67; Jutland 1916, 75–87, 96
Deutschland (German pocket-battleship), 106, 112, 118
Dido (British cruiser), 149, 151
Director system of gunnery, 10
Dixon, Lt-Cdr. R. E., 162, 163
dockyard facilities, 1914, 9, 12–13
Dogger Bank, battle of, *62–67*
Dönitz, Grand Admiral Karl, 91, 117, 177, *192*, 194, 201, 204, 206, 212
Doolittle, Colonel J. H., *164*, 168
Dorsetshire (British cruiser), 146; sunk 1942, 221
Douglas Devastator, *160–61*
Dowding, Commodore J. C. K., 178, 180
Dreadnought (British battleship), *12*
Dresden (German light cruiser), 39, *41*, 44; Coronel 1914, *47–51*; Falklands 1914, 56–61, 96
Drummond, Captain John, 36, 38
Dublin (British light cruiser), 72; damaged at Jutland 1916, 87
Duke of York (British battleship), 209
Dunkirk, evacuation (Operation Dynamo), 131–34

E

Eagle (British aircraft-carrier), 136, 183; torpedoed by *U-73* 1942, *184*, 185, 214, 219
East Asiatic Squadron, Germany, 39, 45
Eastern Solomons, battle of, *224*, *225*
Eidsvoll (Norwegian coastal defence vessel), sunk 1940, 130
Elbing (German light cruiser), sunk Jutland 1916, 80–87
Elco Type PT Boat (American), *245*
Emden (German cruiser), 39, 41, sunk by *Sydney* 1914, *42–43*; chart of voyage in Indian Ocean, 44, 46
Emden (2) (German light cruiser), 96, 99, 101, 128, 130
'E' motor torpedo boats, *109*, 115
Empire Tide (British CAM ship), 180
Enterprise (American aircraft-carrier), 156, 157; Midway 1942, *167–75*, 221, 222
Enterprise (British cruiser), 136
Erin (British battleship), 8; Jutland 1916, *74–75*
escort carrier protection against submarines, 200, 204
'E' type submarines, British: *E4*, Heligoland 1914, *23*; *E6*, 21; *E8*, 21
Euryalus (British cruiser), 35, 36, 70
Evan-Thomas, Rear-Admiral H., 86
Exeter (British cruiser), River Plate 1939, *122–25*
explosive sweep device, *94*

F

Fairey Albacore biplane, *119*; Albacore 1 torpedo-bomber, *218*
Fairey Fulmar fighter-bomber, *218*
Falkenhorst, General von, 129
Falkland Islands, battle of, *52–61*
Fearless (British light cruiser), Heligoland 1914, *22–25*
Fegen, Captain E. S. F., 118
Fiji (British cruiser), 149; sunk Crete 1941, 150
Firedrake (British destroyer), 63
Fisher, Lord, 13, 60, 62, 64
Fitch, Rear-Admiral A. W., 159–65
'Fleet in being' concept, 83, 208, 213
Fleming, Captain R. E., 175
Fletcher Class Destroyer (American), *244*
Fletcher, Rear-Admiral F., 159–65, *167–75*
Flower Class corvettes, 104
Focke-Wulf aircraft, 105, *109*, 115, 196
Forbes, Admiral Sir C., 112, 129, 130
Force 'H', Gibraltar, 136, 141, 147
Formidable (British aircraft-carrier), 149, 151, 183, 214–15, 219
Fortune (British destroyer), sunk Jutland 1916, 87
Fox, Captain C. H., 20
Frankfurt (German light cruiser), 96, 101
Frauenlob (German light cruiser), damaged Heligoland 1914, 23, *27*; sunk Jutland 1916, 87
Fremantle, Vice-Admiral S., 98, 99, 100
Friedrich der Grosse (German battleship), 14; Jutland 1916, *75–87*, 96, 97, 99, 100
Friedrich Eckholdt (German destroyer), sunk Barents Sea 1942, 188–92
Friewald, Seaman Ludwig, 98
Fuchida, Commander Mitsuo, 156, 157
Furious (British aircraft-carrier), 106, 122, 176, 214, 219
Fuso (Japanese battleship), sunk Leyte Gulf 1944, 238

G

Galatea (British light cruiser), Jutland 1916, 76–87
Gallant (British destroyer), 141
Gambier Bay (American aircraft-carrier), *236*
Gardenia (British sloop), *29*
Gay, Ensign George H., 173
Geddes, Sir Eric, 89
George Cross awarded to Malta, 183
Giulio Cesare (Italian battleship), 139
Giuseppe Garibaldi (Italian cruiser), sunk by submarine 1915, *68–69*, 72
Glasgow (British light cruiser), Coronel 1914, *46–51*; Falklands 1914, 52–61, 137

Glengyle (British criuser), 151
Glennie, Rear-Admiral I. G., 149
Glorious (British aircraft-carrier), 214; sunk 1940, 219
Glossop, Captain John, *41–43*
Gloucester (British light cruiser), 136, 141, 147, 149; sunk Crete 1941, *150*
Glowworm (British destroyer), *126*, 128, 129; sunk by *Hipper*, 130
Gneisenau (German armoured cruiser), 39; Coronel 1914, *46–51*; sunk Falklands 1914, *54–61*
Gneisenau (2) (German battle-cruiser), 106, 112, *115*, 118, 119, 128, 129, 130, 187, 219
Goeben (German battle-cruiser), 39, 40
Goodenough, Commodore W. E. E., 23, 24, 62, 63, 80, 86
Goodheart, Lt-Cdr. F. H. H., 21
Good Hope (British armoured cruiser), sunk Coronel 1914 *46–51*
Goto, Rear-Admiral A., 158–65
Graf Spee *see* Admiral Graf Spee
Graf Zeppelin (German aircraft-carrier), 215
Grant (American destroyer), 236
Graudenz (German light cruiser), Dogger Bank 1915, 62
Gray, Lieutenant J. S., 172, 173
Greyhound (British destroyer), sunk Crete 1941, 150
Grumman Avenger, *224–25*
Guadalcanal sea battles, *223–229*

H

Halsey, Admiral W. F., *232–40*
Hamakaze (Japanese destroyer), sunk Okinawa 1945, 248
Hamburg (British light cruiser), 21
Hamilton, Lt-Cdr. W. L., 162
Hammann (American destroyer), Coral Sea 1942, 165
Hara, Rear-Admiral C., 158–65
Harvey, Major F. J. W., 86
Haruna (Japanese battleship), Midway 1942, 171
Haun, Captain, 59
Harwood, Commodore Henry, 122–23
Healy, Commander H. R., 165
'Hedgehog' mortars, 104, *202, 203*, 204
Hela (German light cruiser), 27
Helena (British light cruiser), damaged Pearl Harbor 1941, 157
Heligoland, battle of, 20–27
Helm (American destroyer), Pearl Harbor 1941, 157
Henley (American destroyer), Coral Sea 1942, 160
Henry, Prince Albert William, biographical details, *19*
Hereward (British destroyer), sunk Crete 1941, 151
Hermes (British aircraft-carrier), converted from cruiser in 1913, 13
Hermes (2) (British aircraft-carrier), 214, 219; sunk 1942, 221
Hersing, korvettenkapitän, 70
Hiei (Japanese battleship), sunk Guadalcanal 1942, 226, 228, *229*
High Seas Fleet, scuttled at Scapa Flow 1919, 95–101
Hipper, Admiral Franz von, biographical details, *19*, 62, 74, 96
Hipper see Admiral Hipper
Hitler, Adolf, 106, 122, 127, 129, 187, 189, 194, 209, 210
Hiryu (Japanese aircraft-carrier), sunk Midway 1942, 169–75, 221
Hiyo (Japanese aircraft-carrier), sunk Philippines 1944, 222
Hobart (Australian heavy cruiser), Coral Sea 1942, 159
Hogue (British armoured cruiser), Heligoland 1914, 27; sunk by *U-9* 1914, *34–38*
Hood (British battle-cruiser), sunk by *Bismarck* 1941, *143–46*
Hornet (American aircraft-carrier) *164*, damaged Midway 1942, *167–75*; sunk Santa Cruz 1942, *223*
Horton, Vice-Admiral Sir Max, 130, 204, 206
Hosho (Japanese aircraft-carrier), 221
Hotspur (British destroyer), 151
Huff-Duff, or High Frequency Direction Finder, 201
Hyderabad (British corvette), Barents Sea 1942, 187, 189
Hyperion (British destroyer), sunk by mine 1940, 141

I

I-19 (Japanese submarine), torpedoes *Wasp* 1942, 225
I-168 (Japanese submarine), torpedoes *Yorktown*, Midway 1942, 175
Iachino, Admiral A., *137*
Illustrious (British aircraft-carrier), 136, 137, 139, 141, 147, 183, 214, 219
Imperial (British destroyer), sunk Crete 1941, 151
Implacable (British aircraft-carrier). 214
Indefatigable (British aircraft-carrier), 214
Indefatigable (British battle-cruiser), sunk Jutland 1916, 80, 86
Indomitable (British battle-cruiser), Dogger Bank 1915, 62–67
Indomitable (2) (British aircraft-carrier), *182, 183, 185*, 215, 219
Inflexible (British battle-cruiser), Falklands 1914, *52–61*
Inouye, Vice-Admiral S., *158–65*
Invincible (British battle-cruiser), 25; Falklands 1914, *52–61*; sunk Jutland 1916, 76–87
Iron Duke (British battleship), 35; Jutland 1916, *75–87*
Ito, Vice-Admiral Seiichi, 247, 248, 249

J

Jackal (British destroyer), 150
Jamaica (British cruiser), Barents Sea 1942, *187–94*
Jastrzab (Polish submarine), sunk 1942, *242–43*
Jellicoe, Admiral Sir John, 9, 10, 12, 13, 16; biographical details *18*, 22, 63, 74–87, 89
Jervis Bay (British armed merchant cruiser), *113*; sunk by *Admiral Scheer* 1940, 118
Jules Ferry (French armoured cruiser), 70
Juno (British destroyer), sunk Crete 1941, 149
Junyo (Japanese aircraft-carrier), 169, 221, 222
Jutland, battle of, *74–87*
JW-51B Convoy, *186–94*

K

Kaga (Japanese aircraft-carrier), sunk Midway 1942, 169–74, 221, 222
Kagero Class Destroyer (Japanese), *245*
Kaiser (German battleship), 14, 96
Kaiserin (German battleship), 14, 96
Kakuta, Rear-Admiral K., 169
Kamikaze attacks, 222, 237, 239, 241, 246
Karlsruhe (German light cruiser), 39, 40, *41*, 128, 130
Kashmir (British destroyer), 150; sunk Crete 1941, 151
Kasumi (Japanese destroyer), sunk Okinawa 1945, 248
Kelly (British destroyer), 150; sunk Crete 1941, 151
Kelvin (British destroyer), 150
Kenney, General G. C., 233
Kent (British armoured cruiser), Falklands 1914, 52–61, 136
Keyes, Vice-Admiral Sir Roger, 22, 23, 35, 63, 66
Kincaid, Vice-Admiral T. C., *232–40*
King George V (British battleship), 176, 209, *249*
King, Rear-Admiral E., 149
Kipling (British destroyer), 150, 151
Kirishima (Japanese battleship), sunk Guadalcanal 1942, 227, 228, *229*
Kitkun Bay (American aircraft-carrier), 236
Kobayashi, Lieutenant Michio, 174
Kohler, Captain, 41
Kolberg (German light cruiser), Heligoland 1914, 27; Dogger Bank 1915, 62–67
Köln (German light cruiser), sunk Heligoland 1914, *26*, 27
Köln (2) (German light cruiser), 128, 130, 187
Komet (German armed merchant raider), 118
Komura, Rear-Admiral, 249
Kondo, Vice-Admiral N., *167*, 169, 175
König (German battleship), Jutland 1916, *76–87*, 96, *97*
König Albert (German battleship), 14, 96

Königin Luise (German auxiliary minelayer), 20, *21*
Königsberg (German cruiser), *39–40, 41*; sunk 1914, 44
Königsberg (2) (German light cruiser), 96, 128, 130
Kretschmer, Otto, 197, 204
Kronprinz Wilhelm (German armed liner), 40, 41, 44
Krueger, Lt-Gen. W., 233, 240, 241
Kumano (Japanese heavy cruiser), 175
Kummetz, Vice-Admiral O., 130, *188–92*
Kurita, Vice-Admiral T., 169, 175, *232–40*
Kusaka, Vice-Admiral, 247

L

L52 (British submarine), *32–33*
Laertes (British destroyer), Heligoland 1914, 25
Lancastria (British liner), sunk off St. Nazaire 1940, 114
Lance (British destroyer), fired first British shot in WW1, 20
Landrail (British destroyer), 20
Langley (American seaplane-carrier), 221
Langsdorff, Captain Hans, 122–24, 189
Lapeyrère, Admiral Boué de, 70, 72, *73*
Larson, Leif, 210
Laurel (British destroyer), Heligoland 1914, 24–25
Leipzig (German light cruiser), 39, Coronel 1914, *46–51*; sunk Falklands 1914, 54–61
Leipzig (2) (German cruiser), 112
Leon Gambetta (French armoured cruiser), sunk by *U-5*, 1915, 70
Leslie, Lt-Cdr. M. F., 173
Lexington (American aircraft-carrier), 156; sunk Coral Sea 1942, *158–65*, 167, 221
Leyte Gulf, battle of, *230–241*
Liberty (British destroyer), Heligoland 1914, 25
Lindsey, Lt-Cdr. E. E., 172, 173
'line of battle' naval tactics, 16
Lion (British battle-cruiser), Heligoland 1914, 25–27; Dogger Bank 1915, 62–67; Jutland 1916, *76–87*
Littorio (Italian battleship), sunk Taranto 1940, 138, 139, *140*, 219
Liverpool (British light cruiser), 136
Lockheed Hudson aircraft, *199*
London (British battleship), 72
Long Island (American escort carrier), 219
Looff, Captain, 40, 44
Loosestrife (British corvette), sinks *U-638* 1943, 206
Lowestoft (British light cruiser), 36; Dogger Bank 1915, 62
Luce, Captain John, 46, 47, 51, 53, 59
Lupo (Italian torpedo boat), 149
Lurcher (British destroyer), Heligoland 1914, 22, *26*, 63
Lusitania (British liner), sunk by *U-20* 1915, 29–30
Lutjens, Admiral G., 143
Lützow (German battleship), sunk Jutland 1916, *75–87*
Lützow (2) (German pocket-battleship), 128, 130; Barents Sea 1942, *186–94*
Lyster, Rear-Admiral A. L., 138

M

MacArthur, General D., 159, *231*, 233, 241
McClusky, Lt-Cdr. C. W., 172, 173
Maass, Konteradmiral L., 27
Macedonia (British armed merchantman), Falklands 1914, 52, 60
Mackensen (German battle-cruiser), 97, 98
Maerker, Captain, 54, 59
Magdeburg (German light cruiser), ciphers recovered from by Russia, 26, 62
magnetic mines, 92, 105, 110, 112, *119*
magnetic sweep device, 105, 110
Mainz (German light cruiser), sunk Heligoland 1914, 24–25
Malaya (British battleship), damaged at Jutland 1916, 80, 81, 86, 136, 139, 141
Malta, convoys to, 136–37, 139, 182–85, 219; George Cross awarded, 183
Marlborough (British battleship), damaged 1916, 76–87
Maryland (American battleship), damaged at Pearl Harbor 1941, 157
Massey, Lt-Cdr. L. E., 173
Mediterranean operations, 68–73, 91, 135–42
Medusa (Italian submarine), torpedoed 1915, 72

merchant aircraft-carriers (MAC ships), 105, 115, 221
Meteor (British destroyer), damaged at Dogger Bank 1915, 66
Meurer, Rear-Admiral H., 96
midget submarine attack on *Tirpitz*, 210–11, *213*
Midway, battle of, *166–75*
Mikuma (Japanese heavy cruiser), sunk Midway 1942, 175
mines
  anti-mine devices, 105, 110
  blockade barrage, 89–92
  degaussing mantle, 105, 110
  electric sweep device, 105, 110
  magnetic mines, 92, 105, 110, 112, *119*
Minneapolis (American cruiser), Coral Sea 1942, 165
Missouri (American battleship), *249*
Mitscher, Vice-Admiral M. A., 237, 239, 249
Mitsubishi Zero fighter, *170–71*
Mogami (Japanese heavy cruiser), damaged at Midway 1942, 175; damaged Leyte Gulf 1944, 236
Moltke (German battle-cruiser), 27; Dogger Bank 1915, 62–67; Jutland 1916, 75–87, 96
Monaghan (American destroyer), Pearl Harbor 1941, 157
Monmouth (British armed cruiser), sunk Coronel 1914, 46–51
Moore, Rear-Admiral Sir H., 62, 66, 67
Morris (American destroyer), Coral Sea 1942, 165
Mountbatten, Lord Louis, 36, 150
Möwe (German armed merchant raider), *29*, 30
Müller, Captain Karl von, 41, *42*, 43
Musashi (Japanese battleship), sunk Leyte Gulf 1944, 232, 234, 235, 238, 246
Mutsu (Japanese battleship), Midway 1942, 169, 175

N

Nagato (Japanese battleship), Midway 1942, 169, 175
Nagumo, Vice-Admiral Chuichi, 155, 157, 167–75, 222
Naiad (British cruiser), 149
Nassau (German battleship), Jutland 1916, 87, 98
Nautilus (American submarine), Midway 1942, 172, 173, 174
Naval power, comparisons of strength: 1914/18, 8–9; 1939/45, 152–53
Nelson (British battleship), 112
Neosho (American tanker), sunk Coral Sea 1942, 160
Neptune (British light cruiser), 136
Nestor (British destroyer), sunk Jutland 1916, 86
Nevada (American battleship), damaged Pearl Harbor 1941, 157
Newcastle (British cruiser), 112, 139
New Zealand (British battle-cruiser), Heligoland 1914, 25–27; Dogger Bank 1915, 62–67; Jutland 1916, 80
Nimitz, Admiral Chester W., 159–65, 167–75, 221, 233
Nishimura, Vice-Admiral S., 234–38
Noble, Sir Percy, 196, 204, 206
Nomad (British destroyer), sunk Jutland 1916, 86
Norge (Norwegian coastal defence vessel), sunk 1940, 130
North Carolina (American battleship), 222
Northern Gem (British trawler), Barents Sea 1942, 187
Nottingham (British light cruiser), Dogger Bank 1915, 62
Nürnberg (German light cruiser), 39; Coronel 1914, *46–51*; sunk Falklands 1914, 54–61
Nürnberg (2) (German light cruiser), 112

O

Obdurate (British destroyer), Barents Sea 1942, *187–94*
Obedient (British destroyer), Barents Sea 1942, 187
Ohio (tanker), operation 'Pedestal', 1942 184, 185
Okinawa, battle for, *246–249*
Oklahoma (American battleship), sunk Pearl Harbor 1941, 157
Oldendorf, Rear-Admiral J. B., *232–40*
Oliver, Vice-Admiral H., 63, 64
Onslow (British destroyer), Barents Sea 1942, *186–94*

Operation 'Pedestal', *182–185*
Oribi (British destroyer), Barents Sea 1942, 187; sinks *U-531* 1943, 206
Orion (British light cruiser), 136, 149, 151
Orion (German armed merchant raider), 118
Orwell (British destroyer), Barents Sea 1942, 187–91
Orzell (Polish submarine), sinks *Rio de Janeiro* 1940, 130
Ostfriesland (German battleship), damaged at Jutland 1916, 87
Otranto (British armed merchant cruiser), 47, 51
Ouvry, Lt-Cdr. J., 110
Ozawa, Vice-Admiral J., *232–40*

P

Pearl Harbor 1941, *154–57*
'Pedestal' Operation, *182–185*
Pegasus (British light cruiser), sunk by *Königsberg* 1914, 40
Pelican (British sloop), sinks *U-438* 1943, 206
Pelly, Captain, H. B., 65, 67
Penelope (British cruiser), 130
Pennsylvania (American battleship), damaged at Pearl Harbor 1941, 157
Perkins (American destroyer), Coral Sea 1942, 159
Perth (British cruiser), 149, 151
Phelps (American destroyer), Coral Sea 1942, 165
Phoebe (British cruiser), 151
Pierse, Admiral Sir Richard, 70, *73*
Pinguin (German armed merchant raider), 118
Pink (British corvette), sinks *U-192* 1943, 206
Place, Lieutenant B. C. G., 210–11
Pohl, Admiral, 16, 40, 41
Pola (Italian cruiser), sunk 1941, 183, 219
Polyanthus (British sloop), *29*
Pommern (German battleship), sunk Jutland 1916, 82, 87
Portland (American heavy cruiser), Midway 1942, 175
Pound, Admiral Sir Dudley, 177, 178
PQ-17 Convoy, *177–81*, 187, 209, 210
Prien, Lieutenant G., 112, 197, 204
Prince of Wales (British battleship), 72, *143*, 146, 176
Princess Royal (British battle-cruiser), Heligoland 1914, 25–27; Dogger Bank 1915, 62–67; Jutland 1916, 80
Princeton (American aircraft-carrier), sunk Leyte Gulf 1944, *234*, 235, 238
Prinz Eitel Friedrich (German armed liner), 44
Prinz Eugen (German heavy cruiser), *114*, 145, 146, 187
Prinzregent Luitpold (German battleship), *14*, 96

Q

'Q' ship decoy vessels, *29*, 91
Queen (British battleship), 72
Queen Elizabeth (British battleship), 95, 98, 151
Queen Mary (British battle-cruiser), Heligoland 1914, 25–27; sunk Jutland 1916, 80, 82, 86
Quinet (French heavy cruiser), 8
Quisling, Major Vidkun, 127

R

R12 (British submarine), *32*
radar, use of against U-boats, 114, 116
Raeder, Grand Admiral E., *106*, 112, 127, 129, 177, 187, *192*, 194, 209, 210
Raleigh (American light cruiser), damaged at Pearl Harbor 1941, 157
Ramillies (British battleship), 136, 139
Ranger (American aircraft-carrier), 221
Rawalpindi (British armed merchant cruiser), sunk by *Scharnhorst* and *Gneisenau* 1939, 112
Rawlings, Rear-Admiral H. B., 149, 150, 151
Renown (British battle-cruiser), 128, 130, 136, 139, 141, 209
Repulse (British battle-cruiser), 130
Resolution (British battleship), 136
Reuter, Admiral Ludwig von, 97, 99, 100
Rheinland (German battleship), *11*
Rhododendron (British corvette), Barents Sea 1942, 187
Richard Beitzen (German destroyer), Barents Sea 1942, 188–92
Richtungsweiser system of gunnery, 10
Rio de Janeiro (German troop transport), sunk by *Orzell* 1940, 130
river class frigates, 104
River Afton (British destroyer), sunk 1942, 180
River Plate, battle of, *122–25*
Rodney (British battleship), 146
Rommel, Field Marshal E., 141
Roope, Lt-Cdr., 130
Rostock (German light cruiser), Dogger Bank 1915, 62–67; sunk Jutland 1916, 87
Rousseau (French heavy cruiser), 8
Royal Oak (British battleship), sunk by *U-47*, Scapa Flow 1939, 112, 197, 204
Rurik (Russian armoured cruiser), 8, *17*
Ryujo (Japanese aircraft-carrier), 169; sunk Eastern Solomons 1942, 221, 222

S

St. Lô (American aircraft-carrier), sunk Leyte Gulf 1944, 239
St. Nazaire raid, 209
St. Petersburgh (British steamer), 20
Salmon (British submarine), 112
San Demetrio (tanker , damaged by *Admiral Scheer* 1940, 118–19
San-shiki anti-aircraft projectile, *247*, 249
Santa Cruz, battle of, 223, *224*, *225*
Santa Isabel (German supply ship), sunk Port Pleasant 1914, 60
Sapphire (British light cruiser), 72
Saratoga (American aircraft-carrier), *216–17*, 221, 222
Savoia, Admiral H.R.H. Luigi di, Duke of the Abruzzi, 70, 72
Savo Island, battle of, 223, *224*, *225*
Scapa Flow, scuttling of German High Seas Fleet 1919, *95–101*
Scharnhorst (German armoured cruiser), 39; Coronel 1914, *46–51*; sunk Falklands 1914, 54–61
Scharnhorst (2) (German battle-cruiser), 106, 112, 118, 119, 128, 129, 130, 187, 210, 219
Scheer, Admiral Reinhard, *14*, 16; biographical details, *19*, 74–87, 92, 96, 100
Scheer see Admiral Scheer
Schleswig-Holstein (German battleship), 129
Schönberg, Captain von, 51
Scott, Admiral Sir Percy, 10
Sea Gladiator biplane, 215
Sea Hurricane fighter plane, *111*
Seawolf (British submarine), 209
Seydlitz (German battle-cruiser), *26*, 27; Dogger Bank 1915, 62–67; Jutland 1916, 74–87, 96
Seydlitz (German supply ship), 60
Shark (British destroyer), sunk Jutland 1916, 76, 86
Sheffield (British cruiser), 136, 141; Barents Sea 1942, *187–94*
Sherbrooke, Captain R., *187–92*
Sherman, Captain F. C., 163, 165
Shigure (Japanese destroyer), 236
Shima, Vice-Admiral Kiyohide, 233–38
Shimazaki, Lt-Cdr., 157
Shinyo (Japanese suicide craft), *248*
Shoho (Japanese aircraft-carrier), sunk Coral Sea 1942, 158–65, 167, 221
Shokaku (Japanese aircraft-carrier), damaged Coral Sea 1942, *158–65*, 167, 221, 222
Short Sunderland flying boat, *199*
Sims (American destroyer), sunk Coral Sea 1942, 160
Solomon Islands, battle of the, *223–229*
Somerville, Vice-Admiral Sir James, 136, 141, 182
Soryu (Japanese aircraft-carrier), sunk Midway 1942, 168–74, 221, 222
Southampton (British light cruiser), Dogger Bank 1915, 62–67; damaged at Jutland 1916, 87, 141; sunk in Mediterranean 1941, 147
South Dakota (American battleship), *224*, *228*
Sparrowhawk (British destroyer), sunk Jutland, 87
Spee, Vice-Admiral M. von, *39*, 40, 41, *46–51*, *52–61*
Spitfire (British destroyer), damaged at Jutland 1916, 87
Sprague, Rear-Admiral Clifton F., *232*, 236–39
Spruance, Admiral Raymond A., *167–75*, 222
'Squid' depth charge projector, *203*, 204
Stange, Kapitän R., 188, 191, 192
Starling (British escort sloop), *198*
Stettin (German light cruiser), Heligoland 1914, *22*, 23, 27
Stoddart, Admiral, 41
Stralsund (German light cruiser), Heligoland 1914, 22, 27; Dogger Bank 1915, 62
Strassburg (German light cruiser), Heligoland 1914, 22, 24, 27
Stuka dive bomber, *148*
Stumpf, Seaman Richard, 95, 96
Sturdee, Vice-Admiral Sir F. D., 35, 36, 44, *52–61*
submarines
  Asdic underwater detection, 104, 105, 201, 202, 203
  convoy system success, 89, 204–6
  defensive and offensive methods, 29, 89–92, 94, 104–5, 192, *202*, *203*, 204
  escort carrier protection, 200, 204, 206
  illustrations of types of submarines: American *242–43*, *244–45*; British *32*, *33*; German, *30–31*, *32–33*, *37*, *116–17*, *120–21*; Japanese, *242–43*, *244*
  mine warfare, 10, 89–92, 105
  radar introduced, 114, 116
  'wolf pack' operations, 114, 116
  see also Atlantic, battle for; blockade; convoys; and U-boats
support ships: attack cargo ship, *250*; fleet oiler, *250*
Suzuki, Lt-Gen. Sosaku, 233, 240, 241
Suzutsuki (Japanese destroyer), 248
Suzuya (Japanese heavy cruiser), 175
Swiftsure (British cruiser), 70
Sydney (Australian cruiser), sinks *Emden* 1914, *41–44*, 136

T

T14 MTB-type boat (Japanese), *245*
Taiho (Japanese aircraft-carrier), sunk Philippines 1944, 222
Tait, Wing Commander J. B., 212
Takagi, Vice-Admiral T., 158–65
Talbot, Lt-Cdr. C. P., 21
Taranto, attack on Italian fleet, 135, *138–41*, 183, 219
Tassafaronga, battle of, 226, *229*
Tennessee (American battleship), damaged at Pearl Harbor 1941, *155*, 157
Tennyson-d'Eyncourt, Sir E., 9
Terauchi, Field Marshal Count H., 233
Terror (British monitor), sunk off Tobruk 1941, 142
Theodor Riedel (German destroyer), 188
Thor (German armed merchant raider), 118
Thursby, Rear-Admiral Cecil, 72
Ticonderoga (American aircraft-carrier), *217*
Tiger (British battle-cruiser), 8; Dogger Bank 1915, 62–67; Jutland 1916, 76–87
Tipperary (British destroyer), sunk Jutland 1916, 87
Tirpitz (German battleship), 177, 178, 181; sinking of, *208–13*
Tirpitz, Grand Admiral Alfred von, biographical details, *19*, 39, 40, 70, 211
Tominaga, Lt-Gen. Kyoji, 233, 235, 241
Tomonaga, Lieutenant J., 171, 172, 174, 175
Tone (Japanese cruiser), Midway 1942, 171, 172
Tovey, Admiral Sir John, 176, 177, 178, 187, 192, 209
Towey (British frigate), *198*
Toyoda, Admiral Soemu, 233, 234, 235, 246, 247, 249
Trapp, Lieutenant Ritter von, 70
Triumph (British cruiser), sunk by *U-21* 1915, *72–73*
Tsingtao, German base in China, 9, 39, 46
Turbine (Italian destroyer), sunk 1915, 72
Turbulent (British destroyer), sunk Jutland 1916, 87
Tyrwhitt, Admiral Sir R., 22, *23*, 35, 36, 63, 65, 66, 96

U

U-boats
  U-5 sinks *Leon Gambetta* 1915, 70
  U-9 successes in 1914, *34–38*
  U-13 accidental loss 1914, 22
  U-15 rammed by *Birmingham* 1914, 22
  U-29 sinks *Courageous* 1939, 109
  U-30 sinks *Athenia* 1939, 108
  U-31 lost in North Sea 1915, *30–31*
  U-39 sunk by destroyers 1939, 109
  U-47 sinks *Royal Oak* 1939, 112; sunk by corvettes 1941, 197, 204
  U-99 and *U-100* sunk by *Walker* and *Vanoc* 1941, 197, 204
  U-125 sunk by *Vidette* 1943, 206
  U-192 sunk by *Pink* 1943, 206
  U-438 sunk by *Pelican* 1943, 206
  U-439 and *U-659* collide and sink 1943, 206
  U-531 rammed and sunk by *Oribi* 1943, 206
  U-638 sunk by *Loosestrife* 1943, 206
  see also submarines
Ugaki, Vice-Admiral M., 247
Undaunted (British light cruiser), Dogger Bank, 1915, 63
uniforms, naval: Austrian *73*, British *55*, German *55*, Italian *73*
unrestricted submarine warfare, 89, 104, 106, 108
Upholder (British submarine), 141, 183
Upright (British submarine), sinks *Armando Diaz* 1941, 142
Ursula (British submarine), 112
Ushijima, Lt-Gen. Mitsuru, 246
Usk (British submarine), 141
Utah (American battleship), sunk Pearl Harbor 1941, 157

V

V187 (German destroyer), sunk by *E4*, Heligoland 1914, 23
Valiant (British battleship), Jutland 1916, 80, 136, 137, 141, 149, 150
Vanoc (British destroyer), 197
Vian, Captain P., 129
Vickers Wellington aircraft, *199*
Victorious (British aircraft-carrier), 143, 176, 182, *185*, 209, 215, 219, 222
Vidette (British destroyer), sinks *U-125* 1943, 206
Vindicator monoplane, Vought-Sikorsky, *173*
Vittorio Veneto (Italian battleship), 139, 183, 219
Vizalma (British trawler), Barents Sea 1942, 187–92
Von der Tann (German battle-cruiser), 10, 27; Jutland 1916, 75–87
Vought-Sikorsky Vindicator monoplane, *173*

W

Waldron, Lt-Cdr. J. C., 172, 173
Walker (British destroyer), 197
Wanklyn, Captain M. D., 183
Warrior (British armoured cruiser), sunk Jutland 1916, 82, 86
Warspite (British battleship), Jutland 1916, 76–86, 136, 137, 141, 149, 150
Washington (American battleship), *228*
Wasp (American aircraft-carrier), 183, *217*, 221, 222; sunk by *I-19* 1942, *224–25*, 243, *250–51*
Weddigen, Leutnant Otto, *36–38*
Westerwald (German supply tanker), 106
West Virginia (American battleship), sunk Pearl Harbor 1941, *155*, 157, *235*
Widder (German armed merchant raider), 118
Wiesbaden (German cruiser), sunk Jutland 1916, *76*, 86
Wilhelm Heidekamp (German destroyer), 130
Williamson, Lt-Cdr. K., 138
Wilson, Sir Arthur K., 62, 63, 64
Wolverine (British destroyer), 197

XYZ

X-craft: midget submarine attack on *Tirpitz*, 210–211, *213*
Yahagi (Japanese light cruiser), 247, 248
Yamaguchi, Rear-Admiral T., 172
Yamamoto, Admiral, 154, 158–65, *166–75*
Yamashiro (Japanese battleship), sunk Leyte Gulf 1941, *234–35*, 238
Yamashita, General Tomoyuki, 233, 241
Yamato (Japanese battleship), Midway 1942, 169, 175, 222, 232, *234*, 235; sunk Okinawa, 1945, 246–49
Yanaginoto, Captain Ryusaku, 174
Yarmouth (British cruiser), 41
Yonai, Admiral Mitsumasa, 241
York (British heavy cruiser), 137; destroyed Crete 1941, 142
Yorktown (American aircraft-carrier), Coral Sea 1942, 159–65; sunk Midway 1942, 166–75, 221, 222, 243
zeppelins, 13, 83
Zero fighter (Mitsubishi), *170–71*
Zhemchug (Russian light cruiser), 41
zig-zag submarine evasion technique, *94*
Zuiho (Japanese aircraft-carrier), 175, 221, 222, *237*
Zuikaku (Japanese aircraft-carrier), 157; damaged Coral Sea 1942, 158–67, 221–2